THE YALE EDITION

OF

HORACE WALPOLE'S

CORRESPONDENCE

EDITED BY W. S. LEWIS

VOLUME THIRTY-SEVEN

HORACE WALPOLE'S
CORRESPONDENCE

WITH

HENRY SEYMOUR CONWAY
LADY AILESBURY
LORD AND LADY HERTFORD
MRS HARRIS

I

EDITED BY W. S. LEWIS
LARS E. TROIDE
EDWINE M. MARTZ
AND
ROBERT A. SMITH

NEW HAVEN
YALE UNIVERSITY PRESS
LONDON · OXFORD UNIVERSITY PRESS

1974

ADVISORY COMMITTEE

TABLE OF CONTENTS

VOLUME I

LIST OF ILLUSTRATIONS

VOLUMES I, II, AND III

Grateful acknowledgment is made to the Duke of Argyll, the Marquess of Hertford, the Marquess of Cholmondeley, the Wallace Collection, London, R. E. Hutchison, Keeper of the Scottish National Portrait Gallery, the Hunterian Collection of the University of Glasgow, and the Trustees of the New York Public Library for permission to reproduce the drawings, paintings, or prints in their possession.

INTRODUCTION

We come now to Walpole's first cousin and closest friend, Henry Seymour Conway, and to Conway's elder brother, Lord Hertford. We postponed the publication of these correspondences in the hope that their lacunæ might be filled, and we have been rewarded by the discovery in Colombo, Ceylon, of 194 letters to Walpole from Conway and from his wife, Lady Ailesbury (as well as one from his sister, Mrs Harris); most of them are here printed for the first time. Large gaps remain, especially in the correspondence with Lord and Lady Hertford, but we cannot delay publication longer. The summary of the 687 letters in these three volumes (of which 362 are now printed for the first time) is given *post* at p. xxi.

Walpole's devotion to Conway and Lady Ailesbury, touched upon in our volume 36 where he makes peace between them and the Duchess of Gloucester, comes out even more strongly in the present volumes. After counselling Conway on 20 July 1744 not to marry the much too frivolous Lady Caroline Fitzroy he offers him half his fortune. He then adds, 'If I ever felt much for anything, which I know may be questioned, it was certainly for my mother. I look on you as my nearest relation by her, and think I can never do enough to show my gratitude and affection to her. For these reasons, don't deny me what I have set my heart on—the making your fortune easy to you.[1] Fourteen years later in the dedication of his *Fugitive Pieces in Verse and Prose,* he wrote, 'I only desire, if I should be remembered for these idlenesses, that it may be known at the same time that you did not dislike them; and [which will do me still more honour] that our FRIENDSHIP was as great as our AFFINITY.' Walpole added a note for our benefit on AFFINITY in his copy of the book (now wsl): 'they were first cousins; their mothers Catherine Lady Walpole and Charlotte Lady Conway, being own sisters.'

The letters first published in this correspondence amplify and modify the accepted public image of Conway as a fearless soldier and perceptive statesman who saw that it was impossible to sub-

1. *Post* i. 170.

jugate the American colonies. The *Dictionary of National Biography* says: 'He was by no means so remarkable a man as Walpole makes him out. His personal advantages were great; he was singularly handsome, his voice was sweet, and his manner, though reserved, was gracious. No man of his time was so generally liked. While he was a man of fashion his tastes were cultivated and his habits respectable. In a period marked by political intrigue and corruption he was conspicuous for integrity and a delicate sense of honour. His talents were not brilliant: he lacked decision and insight, and he was easily swayed both by his emotions and his friends. He had not the ability either to form or carry out a plan for himself, and he unconsciously allowed Walpole to use him as a means of gratifying his spite and caprices. . . . Of his personal courage there is no doubt; he was a better soldier than he was a general, a better general than a statesman.' In this correspondence we find the heroic soldier, general, secretary of state and leader of the House of Commons but also a gardener, littérateur, and man about town capable of persiflage, Latin tags, and French grace notes. A letter from Hannah More (now WSL) that has recently come to light speaks of 'the brilliant society of Field Marshal Conway's house, especially of his and my attached and accomplished friend, Lord Orford.'[2] The new letters emphasize Conway's dependence on Walpole, such as one from the army in Holland that ends, 'Adieu, dear Horry, do write to me again in pity for I shall be miserably dull soon.'[3] The salutations, 'Dear Horry' and 'Dear Harry,' were dropped as time went on, but Conway continued to seek Walpole's opinion on political questions and respected his advice whether he took it or not.

It is fitting to add here that Conway's rôle in carrying out the repeal of the Stamp Act was acknowledged in this country, where the villages of Conway, New Hampshire, and Conway, Massachusetts, were named in his honour. James Otis and Samuel Adams requested his portrait for Faneuil Hall in Boston, and in Philadelphia his health was drunk at the American Philosophical Society along with the healths of Chatham, Burke, and the Duke of Richmond, as Mr Whitfield Bell has kindly informed me.

The fraternal friendship of the cousins underwent a severe trial in 1765. The year before, Walpole demonstrated his passionate loyalty when Conway was turned out of the King's Bedchamber and

2. Hannah More to Sir Alexander Johnston 18 Nov. 1818.
3. Conway to HW 1 Sept. 1748 NS, *post* i. 291.

dismissed from his regiment because he had voted against general warrants and the Grenville Administration, offering him £6000 and altering his will to give Conway 'almost my whole fortune unless his regiment should be restored to him.' After Walpole's friends came into power in July 1765, he wrote in his memoirs (in his rough draft completed 2 July 1769), 'I did hope that on the change some considerable employment would be offered to me, which my vanity would have been gratified in refusing,' but when the new administration dispensed its favours, Conway, who was one of the secretaries of state, gave him a report from which Walpole perceived that 'my name had not been so much as mentioned . . . What could excuse this neglect in Mr Conway? For him I had sacrificed everything; for him I had been oppressed, injured, and calumniated. The foundation of his own fortune, and almost every step of his fortune, he owed solely to me. . . . Such failure of friendship, or to call it by its truer name, such insensibility, could not but shock a heart at once so tender and so proud as mine.'[4] Conway, while ready to ask favours for his brother and brother-in-law, neither of whom had supported him during his time of persecution, would ask nothing for Walpole. Walpole came down with the gout, and, as soon as he could, escaped to Paris, where he stayed eight months. Conway protested, and 'called my retreat desertion of my friends.'[5] Walpole on his return continued his outward intimacy with Conway, but with inner reservations, as shown by this passage in the memoirs, and by a later one, dated 1771 in the rough draft: 'Conway, cold as the Duke, loved to be flattered more than to flatter.'[6]

This justifiable resentment was gradually modified. Walpole softened what he had written in 1769 by inserting two sentences beginning 'But it is justice to him to say . . .' With this revision he let the passage stand in his 'fair copy' of the memoirs, intended for posterity, which he was revising up to 1785. His memorandum of 1790, endorsed in 1796, decreed that Chest A containing the memoirs should be kept sealed until long after his death; another memorandum forbade publication; nevertheless, his annotations to the memoirs presuppose eventual publication. Conway's nephew, Lord Hugh Seymour, was charged with the delivery of the chest.

Outwardly, Walpole's confidence in Conway was restored. In his

4. Rough draft for *Mem. Geo. III* ii. 149–50. See *post* iii. 529–32 (Appendix 7).
5. *Mem. Geo. III* ii. 151.
6. OSSORY iii. 242.

will he made Conway the executor of his estate, leaving him the residue of it. 'As there never was a more sincere attachment than mine,' Walpole wrote him in 1782, 'so it is the most reasonable one too, for I always think for you more than myself.'[7] A characteristic of Walpole's that has not received due emphasis is that he was a forgiving friend.

Walpole's devotion to Lady Ailesbury never lessened. She was the daughter of the fourth Duke of Argyll and was married, unwillingly, at the age of eighteen to the third Earl of Ailesbury, by whom she had one daughter who became the Duchess of Richmond. A few months after Ailesbury's death in 1747 she married Conway, keeping her title, and lived happily ever after. She could speak to Walpole, she wrote him, more freely upon some occasions than to anybody else and she showed her affection for him by embroidering fire-screens for Strawberry Hill[8] and giving to its China Closet fine pieces of Sèvres (Walpole's favourite china) and Delft. He expressed his admiration of her worsted-work pictures in the fourth volume of his *Anecdotes of Painting*, p. 67, where he called her 'a very great mistress of the art' of needlework who surpassed several good pictures she copied. 'As some of these masterly performances have appeared in our public exhibitions, I venture to appeal to that public, whether justice or partiality dictated this encomium.' There is an unflattering picture of her in the correspondence of one of the Duke of Richmond's sisters. Lady Caroline Fox complains of Lady Ailesbury's 'cold, reserved disposition' as shown in a letter to her daughter, the Duchess of Richmond: 'Such a want of frankness and openness.' Lady Caroline marvels 'how Conway and she ever could produce a child [Mrs Damer] with such icy dispositions, but to speak seriously, I do think there is in mother and daughter as much insensibility and want of that sort of cordial unreserved affection in their nature which I can't describe.'[9] A more favourable picture of her is given by another Lennox sister, Lady Louisa Conolly, who calls one of Lady Ailesbury's letters 'so natural and affectionate,' and who forgives her 'many frippery ways, for being a noble friend.'[10] This noble friend is

7. 17 Sept. 1782, *post* iii. 392. I am indebted to my colleagues for their help with this difficult passage in Walpole's friendship with Conway. WSL.

8. Lady Ailesbury to Walpole 16 Sept. 1757, *post* I. 505.

9. *Correspondence of Emily Duchess of Leinster*, ed. Brian Fitzgerald, Dublin, 1949, i. 181–2.

10. Ibid. iii. 86, 94.

the woman we see in Walpole's letters and whom he remembered in his will.

The one child she and Conway had, Anne Seymour Conway, was Walpole's favourite in the next generation. Her husband, the Hon. John Damer, shot himself at the age of thirty-two, after supper 'with four common women, a blind fiddler and no other man.'[11] Thereafter Mrs Damer lived alone, becoming a talented sculptor whose sitters included George III and Nelson. She was lampooned for her lesbianism, an allegation sustained by her unpublished journals now in the Lewis Walpole Library. Walpole made her his executrix, left her the life use of Strawberry Hill and, as Conway had died, the remainder of his estate. At the end of his life she wrote Mary Berry, 'When I think of *what* his dinners are, and *how* he eats them, I wonder he and his cat are not sick together every day for their dessert.'[12] One of Walpole's missing correspondences that we would most like to read is that with Mrs Damer, but we shall never see it because she burned it.

All but seven of the 180 letters from Lord Hertford are printed here for the first time from the originals, 178 of which are in the British Museum. Hertford succeeded his father in 1732 (at the age of twelve) as Lord Conway, was created Viscount Beauchamp and Earl of Hertford in 1750 and Marquess of Hertford in 1793; he was a Knight of the Garter, ambassador to Paris, Lord Lieutenant of Ireland, Master of the Horse, and Lord Chamberlain of the Household. Caricatures mocked his large family, piety, great wealth, and parsimony. The *Complete Peerage* quotes the *Royal Register's* summary of him: 'A man of a known and established character for niggardly avarice, who during his residence at Paris practised all the narrow principles of his beggarly economy to the increase of his own fortune, but at the expense of his country's honour,' which was perhaps rather too strong because Lord Charlemont says in his memoirs that 'the love of money only excepted, his character was negatively good.'

Of the 39 printed letters from Walpole to Hertford, the present whereabouts of only four are known. The 35 that have disappeared were all written in the eighteen-month period from 1763 to 1765 when Hertford was ambassador in Paris. They were first published

11. MANN viii. 234.
12. *Berry Papers,* ed. Lewis Melville, 1914, p. 159.

in Vol. IX of Lord Orford's *Works*, 1825. John Wilson Croker in his preface to them wrote, 'It appears from some circumstances connected with the letters themselves, that Mr Walpole wrote them in the intention and hope that they might be preserved; and although they are enlivened by his characteristic vivacity, and are not deficient in the lighter matters with which he was in the habit of amusing all his correspondents, they are, on the whole, written in a more careful style, and are employed on more important subjects than any others which have yet come to light.' It is likely that Walpole selected them himself for future publication, but what became of the originals and the scores of others never published we shall probably never know. Walpole begins his letters, 'My dear Lord,' Hertford, 'My dear Horry,' and they continue so to the end. One reads Hertford's letters with an increasing dislike of him that culminates in an incredible episode in 1774: Hertford refused to see Walpole who had called at his house in the evening to urge him to find a seat for Conway in Parliament, in the event that the Duke of Grafton, to whose aunt Hertford was married, failed to return him for Thetford. (See Appendix 10.) Hertford's rudeness was particularly painful because Walpole had believed he was second only to Conway in Hertford's affections (*post* 17 September 1767). That he never recovered entirely is suggested in his letter to Conway of 13 June 1793, written in the mistaken belief that Hertford had become Lord Chamberlain: 'If what you heard of your brother proves true, I rather think it deplorable! How can love of money, or the still vainer of all vanities, ambition of wearing a high but most insignificant office . . . tempt a very old man, who loves his ease and his own way, to stoop to wait like a footman behind a chair, for hours, and in a Court whence he had been cast ignominiously?' Hertford's letter to George III (which we give in Appendix 11) jeers at Walpole's concern over his stewardship for his nephew Orford's affairs, and heightens the picture of a faithless friend.

Walpole kept on with him in part, I think, because of his strong family feeling and in part because of his deep affection for Lady Hertford. Their intimacy may be gauged by her long letter to him of 25 September 1775 in which she asked him to bring back from Paris the newest patterns of lace for men's ruffles, 'twelve pair of embroidered shoes not made up, without gold or silver,' and 'twelve roots for cleaning the teeth and twelve yards of broad and twelve yards of narrow white *gros grain* ribbon,' a great deal of trouble for which she apologized charmingly. She also made numerous gifts to Strawberry Hill. We give in Appendix 12 Walpole's moving 'character' of her in the *London Courant* after her death. Of her thirteen children his favourite was the eldest, Lord Beauchamp, who succeeded his father as 2d Marquess of Hertford. While Beauchamp was at Christ Church, Walpole wrote 'a poem on the destruction of the French navy, as an exercise' for him ('Short Notes' Gray i. 35), and Beauchamp continued to bring visitors to Strawberry Hill as long as its creator lived.

Among Walpole's other correspondences in the Conway connection the one with the Duke of Richmond must have been extensive, judging from the three letters that we have. We feel Walpole's respect and affection for him even through the elegant formality of the Dedication of the fourth volume of his *Anecdotes of Painting* printed at Strawberry Hill in 1771. 'The publications of my press have been appropriated to gratitude and friendship, not to flattery. Your Grace's singular encouragement of arts . . . entitles you to this address; and allow me to say, my Lord, it is a proof of your judgment and taste, that in your countenance of talents there is but one instance of partiality—I mean, your favour to, my Lord, your Grace's most faithful and obedient humble servant, Horace Walpole.' Walpole embellished his own copy of this volume (now in the Lewis Walpole Library) with a print of the Duke opposite the Dedication page, and above the Dedication itself he pasted a print of a lion ducally crowned holding the Richmond arms.

Our last volume showed Walpole as the benevolent uncle: these show him as the faithful friend.

With the death of Bernhard Knollenberg in July 1973 the Advisory Committee lost one of its most active and devoted members. From 1938, when he became Librarian of Yale, until he died he read the proofs of each correspondence, including the present ones. He helped us with the eagerness and zeal that marked all he did, and our long journey has been eased by his knowledge and his company.

W. S. L.

MANUSCRIPTS AND EDITORIAL METHOD

In these three volumes are 687 letters, 501 of which are printed from the manuscripts (or from photostats or copies of them). Of these 362 are new and eleven others are printed in full for the first time. In the following summary the new letters are indicated in parenthesis.

	To	*From*
Conway	183 (3)	189 (117)
Hertford	39 (1)	180 (173)
Lady Ailesbury	20	20 (14)
Lady Hertford	0	30 (30)
Lord Beauchamp	3 (2)	10 (10)
Henrietta Seymour Conway	0	9 (9)
Mrs Harris	0	1 (1)
Lord Henry Seymour	0	2 (2)
Lord Hugh Seymour	1	0
	246 (6)	441 (356)

Two hundred sixty-one of these letters are in the Lewis Walpole Library at Farmington; 195 of them, mostly from Conway to Walpole, were acquired in 1955 from Mr James T. Rutnam of Colombo, Ceylon. According to a notice in *Fraser's Magazine*, March 1850, xli. 272, the manuscripts passed on Walpole's death to Mrs Damer, his legatee and executrix, who on 3 May 1797 wrote to Lord Beauchamp (at that time Lord Hertford): 'With regard to the Conway papers, which are innumerable, my uncle Lord Fred. Campbell by the assistance of Kergate has with great attention been endeavouring to separate them from many others, both in Berkeley Square and at Strawberry Hill' (MS now WSL).

On Mrs Damer's death (in 1828) the manuscripts passed to her cousin (Lady Ailesbury's niece) Louisa Campbell, wife of Sir Alexander Johnston, former chief justice of Ceylon. Sir Alexander later intended to have the Conway letters to Walpole edited with a life of Conway by Charles Ollier (1788–1859), the publisher of Shelley and Keats who had edited two volumes of the Bentley edition of Walpole's letters in 1840.[1] Forty-six letters from Conway and one from Lady Ailesbury were printed in *Fraser's Magazine*. In 1852 21 additional letters from Conway to Walpole appeared for the first time in the *Memoirs of the Marquis of Rockingham,* edited by the 6th Earl of Albemarle, who states in a footnote (Vol. I, p. 225), that they were sent to him by Sir Denis Le Marchant, the editor of Walpole's *Memoirs of the Reign of King George the Third* (1845). These 21 letters had presumably been lent or given by Sir Alexander Johnston to Le Marchant. Lord Albemarle may have still had them in 1880 when he gave permission to Capt. Edward Salusbury to reprint them in *Colburn's United Service Magazine* (see Pt I for that year, p. 167), though Capt. Salusbury evidently reprinted them from the *Rockingham Memoirs,* not from the manuscripts.

Some seventy years later the manuscripts of the Conway letters turned up in Ceylon. We do not know when or how they got there. They were discovered about 1950 among the Alexander Johnston manuscripts and papers in the Colombo Museum, the Ceylon Government Archives in Newara Eliya, and the private libraries of Sir Paul E. Peiris and Mr James T. Rutnam. The latter subsequently kindly allowed photostatic copies to be made of Conway's and Lady Ailesbury's letters for this edition, and in 1955 the letters themselves came to the Lewis Walpole Library.

Of the remaining letters in the present correspondence now at Farmington, 27 (including 18 from Walpole to Lady Ailesbury) were bequeathed by Mrs Damer to her Twickenham neighbour Sir Wathen Waller, 1st Bt, in 1828, from whom they descended to Sir Wathen A. Waller, 5th Bt; the subsequent history of each one is given in the headnote to it. Twenty-four new letters, all from Walpole to Conway, passed into the possession of the 6th Earl Waldegrave and were acquired by Mr Lewis from the present earl in 1948. Selected by Mary Berry 'to be published in addition to the former collection [in *Works,* Vol. V, 1798]'[2] and extensively 'edited' by her, they first appeared in the Bentley edition, 1840. Nine letters (six

---

1. Charles Ollier to P. F. Johnson 19 Oct. 1849 (typescript kindly supplied by Mr Rutnam). Ollier described the letters as being 'in two red morocco covers, fashioned like book-bindings, and forming a couple of bulky volumes.'

2. Mary Berry's label on the brown paper packet into which she had placed the letters.

from Conway to Walpole) were sold by George Edward, 7th Earl Waldegrave, to Richard Bentley in 1843, and were acquired by Mr Lewis from the estate of Bentley's grandson in 1937. Six more letters now at Farmington came from other miscellaneous sources specified in the headnotes to them.

The majority of the letters not at Farmington are in the British Museum Additional Manuscripts 23218-19 (178 from Hertford); they were bequeathed to the Government in 1857 by John Wilson Croker.[3] Five letters to Conway, formerly in the possession of Miss Berry, are now in the Pierpont Morgan Library (for the intervening history see the headnote to 31 October 1741 OS). One letter apiece belongs to the estate of the late Sir John Murray (to Conway 6 March 1746 OS), the Royal Archives at Windsor Castle (to Hertford 5 April 1778), the Scottish Record Office (to Lady Ailesbury 29 December 1759), the estate of the late Earl Bathurst (to Hugh Seymour-Conway 13 January 1792), the estate of the late Mrs Robert Vernon (an extract of a letter to Conway in Walpole's letter to Lady Ossory 1 October 1782), and Anthony Powys-Lybbe, Esq. (to Lady Ailesbury 3 October 1773).

Of letters printed from previous editions or other printed sources, 150 are from *Works,* Vol. V, ed. Mary Berry, 1798 (149 to Conway, one from), and 35 from *Works,* Vol. IX, ed. John Wilson Croker, 1825 (all to Hertford). Nearly a third of the letters to Conway in *Works* were written in the sixties, the period of Conway's greatest political ascendancy; the letters to Hertford are all from the period of his Paris embassy (1763–5); the manuscripts of them have disappeared. The 17 letters from Walpole to Lady Ailesbury printed in *Works,* Vol. V, were among the manuscripts bequeathed by Mrs Damer to Sir Wathen Waller, as mentioned above. It is not clear why of all the letters Conway must have written to Walpole, only a handful after 1759 remain. Perhaps some of them found their way into the untraced collection of Conway letters made by Charles Knight in the nineteenth century with the intention of publishing a memoir of him; more likely, they were destroyed by Mrs Damer, who as Walpole's executrix took it on herself to burn what she pleased.

The editorial method for this instalment has been that described in earlier volumes: modernizing the spelling (except in proper names),

3. See the *Nineteenth Report of the Deputy Keeper of the Public Records* [22 March 1858], 1858, pp. 17–18.

retaining Walpole's punctuation but not that of his correspondents, and using square brackets for editorial emendation and angular ones for restoration of a mutilated text. In biographical notes we assume the use of the *Dictionary of National Biography,* the *Complete Peerage,* and the *Complete Baronetage;* for members of Parliament we further assume the use of Romney Sedgwick's and Namier and Brooke's histories (full citations given in the cue-title list). All English books are assumed to be published in London and all French books in Paris, unless otherwise stated. Miss Berry's deletions in Walpole's letters to Conway in *Works* have been silently restored where the name was probably written out in full in the manuscript; an exception is 'Lady A.' (Ailesbury), a form Walpole and Conway habitually used. Some of the notes in *Works* that are attributed by us to Walpole may have been made by Mary Berry, since it appears by the letters she edited to Lady Ailesbury that she was not consistent in initialling her own notes with an 'E.'

Finally, it should be noted that Walpole placed his sign-manual, a cross-crosslet, on certain of his letters to Conway and to Lady Ailesbury to show Miss Berry which he wished printed. We have indicated them in the headings of the letters so marked. Walpole put his sign-manual on eight of his letters to Lady Ailesbury, seven of which Miss Berry included in *Works;* he marked 11 of the 34 extant manuscripts of letters to Conway, none of which was included in *Works,* though ten of them were set aside by Miss Berry for later publication. We may assume that most, if not all, of the Conway letters printed in *Works* (of which none of the manuscripts survive) were selected by Walpole.

W. S. L.
L. E. T.

ACKNOWLEDGMENTS

We wish to acknowledge our indebtedness to Mr James T. Rutnam of Colombo, Ceylon, for providing photostatic copies of 195 letters, mostly from Conway, for use in this edition; in 1955 the manuscripts themselves were turned over to Farmington. We are grateful to the British Museum for permission to reproduce the letters from Lord and Lady Hertford among the Additional Manuscripts; and also to the Pierpont Morgan Library, the Royal Archives at Windsor Castle, the Scottish Record Office, Anthony Powys-Lybbe, Esq., the late Earl Bathurst, the late Sir John Murray, and the late Mrs Robert Vernon for permission to print letters in their possession. We also wish to thank the Duke of Devonshire and the Public Record Office, London, for allowing us to quote from Conway manuscripts owned by them.

The late Charles H. Bennett made the initial annotation of the correspondence with Lord Hertford. The late Bernhard Knollenberg made important additions to footnotes in a careful reading of the proof. Mr John Brooke and Professor George B. Cooper also read the proof and made valuable suggestions. Dr Warren H. Smith as usual read the typescript and the proof at every stage and made significant contributions. Dr Francis Di Stefano allowed us to use his photostatic copies of letters from Conway to the Duke of Devonshire.

We are indebted to Mr David Mandel, Miss Barbara Stoops, and Mrs Bryan Wolf for verifying the references in the notes. The typescripts of the text and the notes were made over the years by Mr Joseph Ambash, Mr Basil V. Igwe, Mr Edward Michewicz, Mr Leigh Miller, Mr Michael Mullin, Mr Jeffrey Sammons, Mr Henry M. Steady, and Mrs Bryan Wolf—some of whom were our assistants under the Yale bursary program.

For helpful information incorporated in specific footnotes we wish to thank Mr Howard Colvin, the Hon. David Erskine, Mr John Fleming, Professor Robert Halsband, Mr John Harris, and Mr W. R. Sergeant. For information concerning the family portraits at Ragley Hall we are indebted to Sir Francis Watson of the Wallace Collection.

W. S L.

CUE-TITLES AND ABBREVIATIONS

Army Lists . . . [Great Britain, War Office], *A List of the General and Field Officers as they Rank in the Army*, 1740–1841.

Bedford Corr. . . John Russell, Duke of Bedford, *Correspondence of John Fourth Duke of Bedford*, ed. Lord John Russell, 1842–6, 3 vols.

BERRY . . . *The Yale Edition of Horace Walpole's Correspondence: The Correspondence with Mary and Agnes Berry*, New Haven, 1944, 2 vols.

Bibl. Nat. Cat. . . *Catalogue générale des livres imprimés de la Bibliothèque nationale*, 1897– .

BM Add. MSS . . Additional Manuscripts, British Museum.

BM Cat. . . . Catalogue of Printed Books in the British Museum.

'Book of Materials' . Three manuscript volumes, the first two entitled by Walpole 'Book of Materials,' the third entitled 'Miscellany,' begun in 1759, 1771 and 1786 respectively; now in the possession of W. S. Lewis.

Chatham Corr. . . William Pitt, Earl of Chatham, *Correspondence*, ed. W. S. Taylor and J. H. Pringle, 1838–40, 4 vols.

Chatsworth MSS . . Devonshire MSS, first series, at Chatsworth, Derbyshire.

CHATTERTON . . *The Yale Edition of Horace Walpole's Correspondence: The Correspondence with Thomas Chatterton . . .* , New Haven, 1951.

CHUTE . . . *The Yale Edition of Horace Walpole's Correspondence: The Correspondence with John Chute . . .* , New Haven, 1973.

Cobbett, *Parl. Hist.*　.　*The Parliamentary History of England,* ed. William Cobbett and John Wright, 1806–20, 36 vols.

Coke, *Journals*　.　.　*The Letters and Journals of Lady Mary Coke,* ed. James A. Home, Edinburgh, 1889–96, 4 vols.

Coke, 'MS Journals'　.　Photostats of unpublished journals (1775–91) of Lady Mary Coke in the possession of Lord Home.

COLE .　.　.　.　*The Yale Edition of Horace Walpole's Correspondence: The Correspondence with the Rev. William Cole,* New Haven, 1937, 2 vols.

Collins, *Peerage,* 1812 .　Arthur Collins, *The Peerage of England,* ed. Sir Samuel Egerton Brydges, 1812, 9 vols.

Country Seats　.　.　'Horace Walpole's Journals of Visits to Country Seats, etc.,' ed. Paget Toynbee, in *Walpole Society 1927–1928,* Vol. XVI, 1928.

Cunningham　.　.　*The Letters of Horace Walpole, Earl of Orford,* ed. Peter Cunningham, 1857–9, 9 vols.

DAB　.　.　.　.　*Dictionary of American Biography,* ed. Allen Johnson and Dumas Malone, 1943, 22 vols.

Daily Adv. .　.　.　*The Daily Advertiser,* 1731–95. Film in the Yale University Library from the file in the Library of Congress.

DALRYMPLE .　.　.　*The Yale Edition of Horace Walpole's Correspondence: The Correspondence with Sir David Dalrymple . . . ,* New Haven, 1951.

Debrett's Peerage .　.　*Debrett's Peerage, Baronetage, Knightage, and Companionage,* ed. Arthur G. M. Hesilrige, London.

'Des. of SH,' *Works* ii. .　Horace Walpole, 'A Description of the Villa of Mr Horace Walpole at Strawberry Hill near Twickenham,' in Vol. II of *The Works of Horatio Walpole, Earl of Orford,* 1798, 5 vols.

DNB　.　.　.　.　*Dictionary of National Biography,* ed. Leslie Stephen and Sidney Lee, reissue, 1908–9, 22 vols.

DU DEFFAND . . *The Yale Edition of Horace Walpole's Correspondence: The Correspondence with Mme du Deffand,* New Haven, 1939, 6 vols.

FAMILY . . . *The Yale Edition of Horace Walpole's Correspondence: The Correspondence with the Walpole Family,* New Haven, 1973.

F. O. . . . Foreign Office, Film in the Yale University Library from the MSS in the Foreign Office, London. The class numbers are followed by volume numbers in arabic numerals.

Foster, *Alumni Oxon.* . Joseph Foster, *Alumni Oxonienses: The Members of the University of Oxford, 1500–1714,* Oxford and London, 1891–2, 4 vols; *1715–1886,* London, 1887–8, 4 vols.

Gazette de Leyde . . *Journal politique, publié à Leyde* . . . [ca 1680–].

GEC . . . George Edward Cokayne, *The Complete Peerage,* revised by Vicary Gibbs *et al.,* 1910–59, 13 vols.

GEC, *Baronetage* . . George Edward Cokayne, *The Complete Baronetage,* Exeter, 1900–9, 6 vols.

Genealog. hist. Nachrichten 1st ser. . Michael Ranfft, *Genealogisch-historische Nachrichten von den allerneuesten Begebenheiten, welche sich an den europäischen Höfen zutragen* . . . , Leipzig, 1739–52, Parts 1–145 in 12 vols.

Genealog. hist. Nachrichten 2d ser. . Idem, *Neue genealogisch-historische Nachrichten* . . . , Leipzig, 1750–63, Parts 1–160 in 13 vols.

Genealog. hist. Nachrichten 3d ser. . Idem, *Fortgesetzte neue genealogisch-historische Nachrichten* . . . , Leipzig, 1762–77, Parts 1–168 in 14 vols.

Geo. III's *Corr.,* ed. Fortescue . . *The Correspondence of King George the Third from 1760 to December 1783* . . . , ed. Sir John Fortescue, London, 1927–8, 6 vols.

GM . . . . *The Gentleman's Magazine.*

GRAY . . . .   *The Yale Edition of Horace Walpole's Correspondence: The Correspondence with Thomas Gray, Richard West, and Thomas Ashton,* New Haven, 1948, 2 vols.

Grenville Papers . .   *The Grenville Papers, being the Correspondence of Richard Grenville, Earl Temple, K.G., and the Right Hon. George Grenville, their Friends and Contemporaries,* ed. William James Smith, 1852–3, 4 vols.

Hardwicke Corr. . .   Philip C. Yorke, *The Life and Correspondence of Philip Yorke, Earl of Hardwicke,* Cambridge, 1913, 3 vols.

Hazen, *Bibl. of HW* .   Allen T. Hazen, *A Bibliography of Horace Walpole,* New Haven, 1948.

Hazen, *Cat. of HW's Lib.* . . .   Allen T. Hazen, *A Catalogue of Horace Walpole's Library,* New Haven, 1969, 3 vols.

Hazen, *SH Bibl.* . .   Allen T. Hazen, *A Bibliography of the Strawberry Hill Press,* New Haven, 1942.

Hist. MSS Comm. .   Historical Manuscripts Commission.

HW . . . .   Horace Walpole.

HW's 'Journal . . . 1769 [and 1770, 1771]'   'Journal of the most remarkable events of the reign of King George the Third, from the beginning of the year 1769, being a supplement to the memoires of Mr Horace Walpole, carried on by himself,' 148 pp., in HW's hand; now in the possession of W. S. Lewis. '1770' starts at p. 30; '1771' at p. 90. A preliminary draft for the end of *Mem. Geo. III.*

Isenburg, *Stammtafeln* .   Wilhelm Karl, Prinz von Isenburg, *Stammtafeln zur Geschichte der europaeischen Staaten,* Berlin, 1936, 2 vols.

Journals of the House of Commons . .   [Great Britain, Parliament, House of Commons], *Journals of the House of Commons . . . Reprinted by Order of the House of Commons,* 1803, 51 vols.

Journals of the House of Lords . . .   [Great Britain, Parliament, House of Lords], *Journals of the House of Lords,* [ca 1777]–1891, 123 vols.

La Chenaye-Desbois	François-Alexandre Aubert de la Chenaye-Desbois and — Badier, *Dictionnaire de la noblesse,* 3d edn, 1863–76, 19 vols.
Last Journals	Horace Walpole, *The Last Journals of Horace Walpole during the Reign of George III from 1771–1783,* ed. A. Francis Steuart, 1910, 2 vols.
Leinster Corr.	*Correspondence of Emily, Duchess of Leinster,* ed. Brian Fitzgerald, Dublin, 1949–57, 3 vols.
London Stage	*The London Stage 1660–1800 . . . ,* Pt I: 1660–1700, ed. W. Van Lennep, Carbondale, Illinois, 1965; Pt II: 1700–1729, ed. E. L. Avery, 1960; Pt III: 1729–1747, ed. A. H. Scouten, 1961; Pt IV: 1747–1776, ed. G. W. Stone, Jr, 1962; Pt V: 1776–1800, ed. C. B. Hogan, 1968.
MANN	*The Yale Edition of Horace Walpole's Correspondence: The Correspondence with Sir Horace Mann,* New Haven, 1954–71, 11 vols.
MASON	*The Yale Edition of Horace Walpole's Correspondence: The Correspondence with William Mason,* New Haven, 1955, 2 vols.
'Mem. 1783–91'	Horace Walpole's manuscript journal 1783–1791 in the possession of W. S. Lewis.
Mem. Geo. II	Horace Walpole, *Memoirs of the Reign of King George the Second,* 2d edn, ed. Henry R. V. Fox, Lord Holland, 1847, 3 vols.
Mem. Geo. III	Horace Walpole, *Memoirs of the Reign of King George the Third,* ed. G. F. Russell Barker, 1894, 4 vols.
MONTAGU	*The Yale Edition of Horace Walpole's Correspondence: The Correspondence with George Montagu,* New Haven, 1941, 2 vols.
MORE	*The Yale Edition of Horace Walpole's Correspondence: The Correspondence with Hannah More . . . ,* New Haven, 1961.
MS Commonplace Book of Verses	Horace Walpole, 'A Common Place Book of Verses, Stories, Characters, Letters, &c. &c. with some Particular Memoirs of a Certain Parcel of People' [1740], MS in the possession of W. S. Lewis.

MS Poems . . . Horace Walpole, 'Poems and Other Pieces by Horace Walpole, Youngest Son of Sir Robert Walpole, Earl of Orford,' MS in the possession of W. S. Lewis.

MS Political Papers . Horace Walpole, 'Political Papers Written by Horace Walpole son to Sir Robert Walpole Earl of Orford,' MS in the possession of W. S. Lewis.

Namier and Brooke . Sir Lewis Namier and John Brooke, *The History of Parliament: The House of Commons 1754–1790*, London, 1964, 3 vols.

NBG . . . . *Nouvelle biographie générale,* ed. Jean-Chrétien-Ferdinand Hoefer, 1852–66, 46 vols.

OED . . . . *A New English Dictionary on Historical Principles*, ed. Sir James A. H. Murray *et al.*, Oxford, 1888–1928, 10 vols.

Oesterr. Erbfolge-Krieg . *Oesterreichischer Erbfolge-Krieg 1740–1748 nach den Feld-Acten und anderen authentischen Quellen bearbeitet in der kriegsgeschichtlichen Abtheilung des K. und k. Kriegs-Archivs*, Vienna, 1896–1914, 9 vols.

OSSORY . . . *The Yale Edition of Horace Walpole's Correspondence: The Correspondence with the Countess of Upper Ossory*, New Haven, 1965, 3 vols.

'Paris Journals' . . Horace Walpole, 'Paris Journals,' in *The Yale Edition of Horace Walpole's Correspondence: The Correspondence with Mme du Deffand*, New Haven, 1939, v. 255–417.

Public Adv. . . *Public Advertiser.*

Royal Calendar . . *The Royal Kalendar; or Complete and Correct Annual Register for England, Scotland, Ireland, and America . . . ,* London, [1767–1813].

Sandwich Papers . . *The Private Papers of John, Earl of Sandwich, First Lord of the Admiralty 1771–1782*, ed. G. R. Barnes and J. H. Owen, 1932–8, 4 vols (Publications of the Navy Records Society, Vols 69, 71, 75, 78).

Scots Peerage	. .	*The Scots Peerage,* ed. Sir James Balfour Paul, Edinburgh, 1904–14, 9 vols.
Sedgwick	. . .	Romney Sedgwick, *The History of Parliament: The House of Commons 1715–1754,* London, 1970, 2 vols.
SELWYN	. . .	*The Yale Edition of Horace Walpole's Correspondence: The Correspondence with George Selwyn . . . ,* New Haven, 1961.
SH	. . . .	Strawberry Hill.
sold SH	. . .	*A Catalogue of the Classic Contents of Strawberry Hill Collected by Horace Walpole,* 25 April – 21 May 1842. The roman and arabic numerals which follow each entry indicate the day and lot number in the sale.
S.P.	. . . .	State Papers. Film in the Yale University Library from the MSS in the Public Record Office in London. The class numbers (78 or 105) are followed by the volume numbers in arabic numerals.
taf.	. . . .	table (*tafel* in German sources).
Thieme and Becker	.	Ulrich Thieme and Felix Becker, *Allgemeines Lexikon der bildenden Künstler von der Antike bis zur Gegenwart,* Leipzig, 1907–50, 37 vols.
Toynbee	. . .	*The Letters of Horace Walpole,* ed. Mrs Paget Toynbee, Oxford, 1903–5, 16 vols.
Toynbee, *Supp.*	. .	*Supplement to the Letters of Horace Walpole,* ed. Paget Toynbee, Oxford, 1918–25, 3 vols.
Venn, *Alumni Cantab.*	*Alumni Cantabrigienses,* Part I to 1751, compiled by John Venn and J. A. Venn, Cambridge, 1922–7, 4 vols; Part II 1752–1900, ed. J. A. Venn, Cambridge, 1940–54, 6 vols.
Vict. Co. Hist.	. .	*The Victoria History of the Counties of England* [with name of county].
W.O.	. . . .	War Office.
Works	. . .	*The Works of Horatio Walpole, Earl of Orford,* 1798, 5 vols.
Wright	. . .	*The Letters of Horace Walpole, Earl of Orford,* ed. John Wright, 1840, 6 vols.
WSL	. . . .	W. S. Lewis.

LIST OF LETTERS

Letters to Walpole are printed in italics; missing letters are indicated by an asterisk after the date; new letters are marked with a dagger (†), and those printed in full for the first time with a double dagger (‡). The arrangement is in actual chronological order, allowing for the difference of eleven days between dates here marked OS (old style) and those labelled NS (new style).

LETTERS BETWEEN WALPOLE AND LADY AILESBURY

		YALE	TOYNBEE	CUNNINGHAM
1751	ca 1 Nov. OS*	i. 315		
	3 Nov. OS†	i. 316		
1752	*ca 15 Feb. OS†*	i. 325		
	ca 18 May OS*	i. 335		
	9 June OS†	i. 337		
	Dec. [?1752]†	i. 351		
1753	*ca 25 March†*	i. 351		
	Oct. (2 letters, 1 possibly to Conway)*	i. 369		
1755	*ca 9 May†*	i. 395		
	ca 20 Dec.*	i. 424		
1756	*31 Jan.*	i. 433		
	15 June†	i. 465		
	21 Oct.†	i. 476		
1757	*3 June†*	i. 484		
	7 July†	i. 492		
	ca 14 Sept.*	i. 504		
	16 Sept.†	i. 504		
	2 Oct.†	i. 509		
	ca 5 Oct.*	i. 510		
	6 Oct.†	i. 510		
	7 Oct.*	i. 511		
	7 Oct.†	i. 511		
1758	*?24 or ?31 ?March [?1758]†*	i. 525		
1759	29 Dec.	ii. 40	iv. 336–8	

		YALE	TOYNBEE	CUNNINGHAM
1760	23 Aug.	ii. 70	iv. 417–19 Supp. ii. 117	iii. 334–4 incomplete
	ca 17 Oct. [?1760]*	ii. 78		
	ca 19 Oct. [?1760]*	ii. 78		
1761	ca 25 May*	ii. 85		
	13 June	ii. 87	v. 65–8 Supp. ii. 119	iii. 405–7 incomplete
	ca 9 July*	ii. 92		
	ca 10 July*	ii. 92		
	ca 19 July*	ii. 99		
	20 July	ii. 99	v. 80–3 Supp. ii. 120	iii. 416–18 incomplete
	ca 9 Sept.*	ii. 118		
	ca 21 Sept.*	ii. 119		
	27 Sept.	ii. 124	v. 117–21 Supp. ii. 122–3	iii. 441–4 incomplete
	10 Oct.	ii. 130	v. 130–3 Supp. ii. 123	iii. 451–2 incomplete
	28 Nov.	ii. 142	v. 145–7 Supp. ii. 123–4	iii. 462–4 incomplete
1762	ca March*	ii. 150		
	15 March	ii. 153	v. 184–5 Supp. ii. 125	iii. 492–3 incomplete
	31 July	ii. 163	v. 221–2	iv. 5
	30 Aug.*	ii. 171		
1765	ca 20 Sept.*	iii. 10		
	ca 13 Oct.*	iii. 21		
	ca 11 Nov.*	iii. 28		
	ca 23 Nov.*	iii. 29		
	ca Dec.*	iii. 33		
	ca 17 Dec.*	iii. 38		
1766	ca 31 Jan.*	iii. 51		
	ca 17 Feb.*	iii. 53		
	ca 28 March*	iii. 58		
	ca 31 March*	iii. 58		
1767	13 Sept.*	iii. 89		
1769	9 Sept.*	iii. 117		
1772	ca 27 Dec.*	iii. 166		
	29 Dec.	iii. 166	viii. 221–3 Supp. ii. 142–3	v. 420–1 incomplete misdated

		YALE	TOYNBEE	CUNNINGHAM
1773	3 Oct.	iii. 173		
1774	27 Sept.*	iii. 188		
	ca 20 Oct.*	iii. 199		
	*ca 20 Oct.**	iii. 199		
	*ca 1 Nov.**	iii. 205		
	7 Nov.	iii. 206	ix. 81–4	v. 141–3
			Supp. ii. 144–6	incomplete
	ca 15 Nov.*	iii. 216		
	23 Nov.	iii. 216	Supp. iii. 237–41	
	13 Dec.*	iii. 225		
	*ca 25 Dec.**	iii. 229		
1775	17 Aug.	iii. 253	ix. 234–5	vi. 242–3
			Supp. ii. 147	
	20 Aug.	iii. 255	ix. 236–7	vi. 244
			Supp. ii. 147	
	ca 19 Sept.*	iii. 263		
	12 Dec.	iii. 272	ix. 294	vi. 290–1
			Supp. ii. 148	incomplete
1776	*22 Aug.*	iii. 282	Supp. ii. 151–2	
1778	*June**	iii. 298		
	25 June	iii. 299	x. 267–8	vii. 83–4
			Supp. ii. 158–9	incomplete
1779	*ca 8 July**	iii. 331		
	10 July	iii. 331	x. 446–8	vii. 225–7
			Supp. ii. 160–1	incomplete
	*ca 21 July**	iii. 334		
	23 July	iii. 335	x. 453–5	vii. 239–41
	before 14 Oct.*	iii. 340		
	28 Oct.	iii. 341	Supp. i. 276–8	
1781	*15 Jan.**	iii. 362		
	21 Jan.	iii. 364		vii. 502–3
1784	8 June	iii. 413	xiii. 158–9	viii. 480–1
			Supp. ii. 166	incomplete
				misdated
1793	*? Sept.*	iii. 499	Supp. iii. 307–8	
	30 Sept. or 1 Oct.*	iii. 507		

LETTERS BETWEEN WALPOLE AND LORD BEAUCHAMP

1760	Feb.*	ii. 42		
	3 March†	ii. 43		

LETTERS BETWEEN WALPOLE AND HENRIETTA SEYMOUR CONWAY

LETTERS BETWEEN WALPOLE AND HENRY SEYMOUR CONWAY

		YALE	TOYNBEE	CUNNINGHAM
	ca 3 Feb. OS*	i. 6		
	8 Feb. OS†	i. 6		
	ca 12 Feb. OS*	i. 10		
	15 Feb. OS†	i. 10		
	ca 19 Feb. OS*	i. 12		
	26 Feb. OS†	i. 12		
	ca 5 March OS*	i. 13		
	ca 8 March OS†	i. 13		
	March*	i. 15		
	22 March OS†	i. 15		
	ca 2 April OS*	i. 18		
	7 April OS†	i. 18		
	ca 30 April OS*	i. 20		
	?5 ?May [?1737]†	i. 20		
	ca 7 May OS*	i. 22		
	10 May OS†	i. 23		
	mid-May*	i. 24		
	ca 20–4 May OS†	i. 24		
	31 May OS†	i. 26		
	11 June OS†	i. 27		
	June (several)*	i. 28		
	23 June OS†	i. 29		
	late June*	i. 30		
	2 July OS†	i. 30		
	late Aug. *	i. 32		
	10 Sept. OS†	i. 33		
	ca 28 Sept. OS†	i. 35		
	early Nov.*	i. 36		
	ca 20 Nov. OS†	i. 36		
1739	ca 8 March OS*	i. 38		
	24 March NS†	i. 38		
	ca 8 Nov. NS*	i. 42		
	18 Nov. NS†	i. 43		
1740	*ca 25 Feb. NS†*	i. 45		
	6 March NS	i. 48	i. 53	i. 38–9
	6 March OS†	i. 49		
	ca 15 March NS*	i. 52		
	24 March OS†	i. 52		
	23 April NS	i. 56	i. 59–61	i. 45–6
	ca 15–20 May NS*	i. 58		
	14 May OS†	i. 59		
	9 June OS‡	i. 63		

		YALE	TOYNBEE	CUNNINGHAM
	21 Aug. NS†	i. 143		
	11 Sept. NS†	i. 145		
	Sept.*	i. 147		
	25 Sept. NS†	i. 147		
	25 Oct. NS	.. i. 149		
1744	*3 June NS*†	i. 152		
	ca 1 June OS*	i. 155		
	1 July NS†	i. 155		
	6 July NS†	i. 158		
	29 June OS	i. 161	ii. 29–32	i. 307–9
	18 July NS†	i. 165		
	20 July OS	i. 168	ii. 35–8	i. 312–14
	5 Aug. NS	i. 171		
	ca 6 Aug. OS*	i. 174		
	2 Sept. NS	i. 175		
	ca 13 Sept. OS*	1. 177		
	7 Oct. NS†	i. 178		
	6 Oct. OS	i. 180	ii. 50–2	i. 324–5
	19 Oct. NS†	i. 182		
	28 Oct. NS†	i. 184		
	31 Oct. NS†	i. 186		
1745	*18 April OS*	i. 187		
	ca 22 April OS*	i. 190		
	14 May NS	i. 190		
	ca 4 May OS*	i. 193		
	26 May NS	i. 193		
	27 May OS	i. 195	ii. 101–3	i. 363–5
	21 June NS	i. 197		
	1 July OS	i. 200	ii. 108–11	i. 369–71
	10 Aug. NS†	i. 203		
	7 Aug. OS*	i. 205		
	30 Aug. NS†	i. 206		
	25 Oct. NS†	i. 208		
	30 Nov. OS	i. 210		
	ca 6–9 Dec. OS*	i. 212		
	13 Dec. OS	i. 213		
1746	*7 Feb. OS*†	i. 216		
	Feb. OS*	i. 219		
	19 Feb. OS†	i. 220		
	ca 27 Feb. OS*	i. 222		
	*ca 27 Feb. OS**	i. 222		

		YALE	TOYNBEE	CUNNINGHAM
	3 March OS†	i. 223		
	4 March OS*	i. 225		
	6 March OS†	i. 225		
	19 March OS	i. 227		
	ca 20 March OS*	i. 231		
	ca 28 March OS*	i. 231		
	30 March OS	i. 231		
	6 April OS	i. 233		
	ca 10 April OS*	i. 237		
	18 April OS	i. 238		
	ca 25 April OS*	i. 241		
	7 May OS	i. 242		
	ca 9 May OS*	i. 247		
	21 May OS†	i. 248		
	12 Aug. OS†	i. 250		
	Aug. OS*	i. 254		
	23 Aug. OS*	i. 254		
	29 Aug. OS†	i. 254		
	ca 15 Sept. OS*	i. 255		
	24 Sept. OS†	i. 256		
	3 Oct. OS	i. 258	ii. 243–4	ii. 59–60
	18 Oct. OS†	i. 259		
	24 Oct. OS	i. 260	ii. 246–8	ii. 61–3
	5 Nov. OS†	i. 263		
1747	*15 April NS†*	i. 264		
	16 April OS	i. 266	ii. 271–3	ii. 80–1
	8 June OS	i. 269	ii. 279–81	ii. 86–8
	12 June NS†	i. 272		
	9 July NS†	i. 273		
	ca 2 July OS*	i. 275		
	14 Aug. NS†	i. 275		
	5 Oct. NS†	i. 277		
1748	*29 April NS†*	i. 281		
	May*	i. 284		
	24 June NS†	i. 284		
	27 June OS	i. 287	ii. 316–18	ii. 114–15
	1 Sept. NS†	i. 290		
	29 Aug. OS	i. 292	ii. 333–6	ii. 124–6
	9 Oct. NS†	i. 295		
	6 Oct. OS	i. 296	ii. 344–5	ii. 131–2
1749	*14 Sept. OS†*	i. 298		

		YALE	TOYNBEE	CUNNINGHAM
1750	28 June OS	i. 300		
	July*	i. 302		
	17 July OS	i. 302		
	Oct. (2)*	i. 304		
	29 Oct. OS	i. 304		
1751	14 July NS‡	i. 307		
	4 Sept. NS	i. 310		
	26 Sept. NS	i. 313		
	3 Dec. NS†	i. 317		
	12 Dec. OS*	i. 321		
1752	23 Jan. NS‡	i. 322		
	?March [?1752]†	i. 328		
	ca 30 April OS†	i. 329		
	2 May OS†	i. 330		
	5 May OS	i. 332	iii. 88–90	ii. 282–3
	22 May OS‡	i. 335		
	23 June OS	i. 339	iii. 99–102	ii. 289–90
	14 July OS	i. 342		
	ca 20 Aug. OS (2)*	i. 344		
	23 Aug. OS†	i. 344		
	27 Aug. OS*	i. 346		
	4 Oct.†	i. 346		
	8 Nov.	i. 347	iii. 130–1	ii. 311–12
	16 Nov.†	i. 349		
1753	5 May	i. 352	iii. 154–7	ii. 330–2
	8 May	i. 355		
	19 May	i. 357		
	24 May	i. 361	iii. 160–3	ii. 334–6
	24 June‡	i. 366		
	26 June*	i. 367		
	28 June†	i. 367		
	26 July†	i. 369		
	23 Oct.†	i. 370		
	18 Dec.†	i. 372		
1754	?1754–8†	i. 374		
	April*	i. 374		
	15 May†	i. 375		
	3 July†	i. 377		
	6 July	i. 378	iii. 247	ii. 393
	7 July†	i. 379		
	ca 20 July*	i. 380		

		YALE	TOYNBEE	CUNNINGHAM
	?23 July†	i. 380		
	30 July†	i. 381		
	4 Aug.†	i. 382		
	6 Aug.	i. 383	iii. 251	ii. 396
	9 Aug. [?1754]†	i. 384		
	20 Oct.†	i. 385		
	24 Oct.	i. 387	iii. 255–7	ii. 399–400
	29 Dec.†	i. 389		
1755	ca 1 Jan.*	i. 390		
	9 Jan.†	i. 391		
	8 May	i. 392		
	May–June*	i. 397		
	18 June‡	i. 397		
	16 Sept.	i. 403		
	23 Sept.	i. 405	iii. 345–7	ii. 467–9
	ca 30 Sept.*	i. 408		
	7 Oct.	i. 409		
	15 Nov.	i. 413	iii. 365–8	ii. 483–5
	27 Nov.	i. 418		
	6 Dec.*	i. 420		
	11 Dec.	i. 421		
1756	5 Jan.†	i. 425		
	22 Jan.	i. 428	iii. 385–7	ii. 498–9 incomplete
	24 Jan.	i. 431	iii. 388–90	ii. 499–501
	12 Feb.	i. 436	iii. 395–8	ii. 505–7
	20 Feb.	i. 440		
	4 March	i. 443	iii. 402–5	ii. 510–12
	6 March	i. 448		
	25 March	i. 451	iii. 407–9	iii. 2–4
	5 April	i. 455		
	16 April	i. 457	iii. 412–14	iii. 4–6
	29 April	i. 461		
	before 29 June*	i. 466		
	29 June†	i. 467		
	ca 3 July*	i. 469		
	6 July†	i. 470		
	ca 22 July*	i. 471		
	25 July†	i. 472		
	2 Sept.	i. 473	iii. 451–2	iii. 101 incomplete misdated

		YALE	TOYNBEE	CUNNINGHAM
	12 Sept.†	i. 475		
	24 Oct.†	i. 478		
	28 Oct.†	i. 479		
1757	ca 26 May*	i. 482		
	29 May†	i. 483		
	ca 7 June*	i. 485		
	9 June†	i. 485		
	ca 11 June*	i. 486		
	12 June†	i. 487		
	16 June	i. 488		
	5 July	i. 490		
	4 Aug.†	i. 493		
	11 Aug.	i. 495		
	14 Aug.	i. 496	iv. 83–4	iii. 95–6
	29 Aug.	i. 499		
	ca 31 Aug.*	i. 501		
	3 Sept.	i. 501		
	7 Sept.	i. 503		
	26 Sept.	i. 506		
	30 Sept.	i. 507		
	ca 7 Oct.*	i. 512		
	7 Oct.	i. 512		
	8 Oct.	i. 513	iv. 100–1	iii. 108–9
	10 Oct.	i. 514		
	11 Oct.*	i. 516		
	13 Oct.	i. 516	iv. 104–6	iii. 112–13
	13 Oct.	i. 519		
	24 Nov.	i. 520		
	ca 25 Nov.	i. 522	iv. 113	
1758	*?16 or ?23 ? March*†	i. 523		
	ca 10 May [to Conway?]*	i. 526		
	ca 26 May*	i. 526		
	28 May‡	i. 526		
	4 June	i. 528	iv. 139–41	iii. 137–9
	ca 7 June*	i. 532		
	ca 9 June*	i. 532		
	11 June‡	i. 532		
	16 June	i. 535	iv. 145–6	iii. 141–2
	16 June	i. 538		
	ca 1 July*	i. 539		
	4 July (first time, this draft)	i. 539		

		YALE	TOYNBEE	CUNNINGHAM
	8 July	i. 543	iv. 154–6	iii. 148–9
	20 July	i. 546		
	21 July	i. 548	iv. 163–6	iii. 154–6
	27 July†	i. 552		
	1 Aug.†	i. 553		
	11 Aug. (2)†	i. 557, 559		
	27 Aug.†	i. 559		
	2 Sept.	i. 562	iv. 182–3	iii. 166–7
	17 Sept.†	i. 564		
	19 Sept.	i. 568	iv. 189–92	iii. 172–4
	28 Sept.†	i. 573		
	15 Oct.†	i. 576		
	17 Oct.	i. 579	iv. 201–5	iii. 181–4
	10 Dec.	i. 583		
1759	19 Jan.	ii. 1	iv. 229–30	iii. 200–1
	21 Jan.	ii. 3		
	28 Jan.	ii. 3	iv. 232–3	iii. 203–4
	28 Jan.	ii. 9		
	3 May†	ii. 12		
	ca 14 June*	ii. 13		
	17 June†	ii. 13		
	14 Aug.	ii. 20	iv. 293–5	iii. 245–6
	13 Sept.	ii. 27	iv. 303–4	iii. 251–2
	after ca 17 Sept.*	ii. 28		
	11 Oct.	ii. 30	Supp. ii. 112–14	
	14 Oct.‡	ii. 34	iv. 306–8 incomplete	iii. 253–4 incomplete
	*ca 16 Oct.**	ii. 36		
	18 Oct.	ii. 37	iv. 310–12	iii. 255–7
1760	?5 May	ii. 48	v. 27–8	iii. 378–9
	21 June	ii. 55	iv. 400–2	iii. 320–2
	*ca 25 June**	ii. 58		
	28 June	ii. 59	iv. 402–5	iii. 322–3
	*ca 4 Aug.**	ii. 65		
	7 Aug.	ii. 65	iv. 414–15	iii. 331–2
	?8 ?Sept. [?1760]	ii. 72	xv. 442 undated	iii. 343
	ca 17 Sept.*	ii. 73		
	19 Sept.	ii. 74	iv. 428–9	iii. 342–3
1761	*ca 1 April**	ii. 82		
	10 April	ii. 82	v. 48–50	iii. 393–4

		YALE	TOYNBEE	CUNNINGHAM
	ca 1 July*	ii. 91		
	8 July*	ii. 92		
	14 July	ii. 93	v. 76–9	iii. 412–14
	17 July*	ii. 98		
	23 July	ii. 105	v. 90–1	iii. 423–4
	5 Aug.	ii. 109	v. 93–7	iii. 425–7
	9 Sept.	ii. 115	v. 103–8	iii. 431–3
	25 Sept.	ii. 119	v. 114–17	iii. 439–41
	ca 6 Oct.*	ii. 129		
	12 Oct.	ii. 135	v. 133–5	iii. 453–4
	ca 12 Oct.*	ii. 137		
	26 Oct.	ii. 139	v. 137–9	iii. 456–8
	ca 26 Nov.*	ii. 141		
1762	ca Aug.*	ii. 165		
	26 Aug.*	ii. 171		
	9 Sept.	ii. 172	v. 242–5	iv. 19–21
	28 Sept.	ii. 178	v. 251–4	iv. 27–9
	4 Oct.	ii. 182	v. 261–2	iv. 34–5
	ca 17 Oct.*	ii. 185		
	29 Oct.	ii. 185	v. 265–70	iv. 38–40
1763	19 Feb.*	ii. 191		
	28 Feb.	ii. 191	v. 288–90	iv. 55–7
	1 May	ii. 196	v. 316–18	iv. 73–5
	6 May	ii. 200	v. 320–2	iv. 77–8
	21 May	ii. 203	v. 331–4	iv. 85–7
	28 May	ii. 206	v. 334–5	iv. 87–8
	Aug.*	ii. 207		
	9 Aug.	ii. 207	v. 357–8	iv. 102–3
1764	19 April	ii. 375	vi. 53	iv. 223–4
	21 April	ii. 380	vi. 59–61	iv. 227–8
	ca 23 April*	ii. 382		
	24 April	ii. 383	vi. 61	iv. 231
	5 June	ii. 395	vi. 77–9	iv. 245–6
	2 July	ii. 405	vi. 86–8	
	ca Aug.*	ii. 414		
	1 Sept.	ii. 437	vi. 119–20	iv. 273–4
	5 Oct.	ii. 445	vi. 126–8	iv. 278–9
	13 Oct.	ii. 449	vi. 129–30	iv. 280
	ca 27 Oct.*	ii. 452		
	29 Oct.	ii. 452	vi. 132–4	iv. 282–3
1765	3 July	iii. 3	vi. 260–1	iv. 379–80

		YALE	TOYNBEE	CUNNINGHAM
	27 Aug.*	iii. 6		
	11 Sept.	iii. 7	vi. 291–3	iv. 401–3
	ca 18 Sept.*	iii. 10		
	ca 22 Sept.*	iii. 10		
	2 Oct.	iii. 11	vi. 311–16 misdated	iv. 415–19 misdated
	ca 3 Oct.*	iii. 17		
	ca 24 Oct.*	iii. 21		
	28 Oct.	iii. 22	vi. 334–6	iv. 427–8
	ca 6 Nov.*	iii. 28		
	*ca 20 Nov.**	iii. 29		
	*ca 22 Nov.**	iii. 29		
	ca 23 Nov.*	iii. 29		
	ca 29 Nov.*	iii. 29		
	29 Nov.	iii. 30	vi. 361–4	iv. 443–5
	5 Dec.	iii. 33	vi. 371–3	iv. 450–1
	ca 20 Dec.*	iii. 38		
1766	*ca Jan.* (2)*	iii. 41		
	before 12 Jan.*	iii. 41		
	12 Jan.	iii. 42	vi. 395–7	iv. 462–4
	ca 14 Feb.*	iii. 53		
	ca 17 Feb.*	iii. 53		
	ca 24 Feb.*	iii. 53		
	ca 6 March*	iii. 53		
	ca 14 March*	iii. 58		
	ca 21 March*	iii. 58		
	6 April	iii. 60	vi. 448–50	iv. 483–4
	8 April	iii. 63	vi. 451–3	iv. 494–6
	2 Oct.	iii. 76	vii. 45–6	v. 13–14
	18 Oct.	iii. 78	vii. 52–3	v. 18–19
1767	ca 2 May*	iii. 82		
	9 Aug.†	iii. 83		
	21 Aug.*	iii. 86		
	ca 23 Aug.*	iii. 86		
	ca Sept. (2)	iii. 86		
	6 Sept.*	iii. 87		
	9 Sept.	iii. 87	vii. 129–31	v. 62–3 incomplete
	16 Sept.*	iii. 91		
	21 Sept.*	iii. 98		
	30 Sept.*	iii. 98		

		YALE	TOYNBEE	CUNNINGHAM
1768	*June**	iii. 98		
	16 June	iii. 98	vii. 96–9	v. 106–8
	ca 7 Aug.*	iii. 103		
	9 Aug.	iii. 103	vii. 210–12	v. 115–17
	ca 23 Aug.*	iii. 107		
	25 Aug.	iii. 107	vii. 225–7	v. 124–5
1769	7 July	iii. 115	vii. 293–4	v. 175–6
	Nov.*	iii. 118		
	14 Nov.	iii. 119	vii. 331–3	v. 202–3
1770	12 Jan.*	iii. 121		
	22 Jan.†	iii. 121		
	ca 23 Jan.*	iii. 122		
	24 Jan.*	iii. 123		
	24 Jan.†	iii. 123		
	20 March†	iii. 125		
	July*	iii. 126		
	12 July	iii. 127	vii. 396–7	v. 249–50
	25 Dec.	iii. 133	vii. 429–30	v. 272–3
	29 Dec.	iii. 134	vii. 430–2	v. 273–4
1771	*June**	iii. 137		
	17 June	iii. 138	viii. 42–3	v. 303–4
	30 July	iii. 143	viii. 61–4	v. 317–20
	Aug.*	iii. 148		
	11 Aug.	iii. 148	viii. 70–1	v. 325–6
	ca 14 Aug.*	iii. 149		
	7 Sept.	iii. 150	viii. 78–9	v. 329–30
1772	7 Jan.	iii. 152	viii. 134–5	v. 367–8
	ca 20 June*	iii. 156		
	22 June	iii. 156	viii. 175–7	v. 393–5
1773	30 Aug.	iii. 172	viii. 322–3	v. 494–5
1774	23 June	iii. 175	ix. 13–14	vi. 94–5
	July*	iii. 177		
	18 Aug.	iii. 178	ix. 33–4	vi. 108–9
	ca 21 Aug.*	iii. 181		
	7 Sept.	iii. 181	ix. 40–2	vi. 113–14
	ca 12–13 Sept.*	iii. 184		
	27 Sept.	iii. 185	ix. 54–7	vi. 123–5
	28 Sept.	iii. 188	ix. 57–61	vi. 125–8
	3 Oct.*	iii. 194		
	6 Oct.*	iii. 195		
	16 Oct.	iii. 195	ix. 69–73	vi. 133–5

		YALE	TOYNBEE	CUNNINGHAM
	23 Oct.*	iii. 199		
	29 Oct.	iii. 200	ix. 78–81	vi. 138–41
	ca 4 Nov.	iii. 205		
	ca 8 Nov.*	iii. 209		
	12 Nov.	iii. 210	ix. 89–95	vi. 146–9
	ca 19 Nov.*	iii. 216		
	ca 22 Nov.*	iii. 216		
	27 Nov.	iii. 220	ix. 102–6	vi. 154–7
	15 Dec.	iii. 225	ix. 106–7	vi. 158–9
	ca 20 Dec. (several)*	iii. 228		
	23 Dec.*	iii. 228		
	25 Dec.*	iii. 229		
	26 Dec.	iii. 229	ix. 110–13	vi. 159–61
	31 Dec.	iii. 235	ix. 115–18	vi. 162–4
1775	Jan.*	iii. 238		
	15 Jan. (also to Lady Ailesbury)	iii. 239	ix. 132–7	vi. 169–74
	19 Jan.*	iii. 245		
	22 Jan.	iii. 245	ix. 150–2	vi. 180–2
	9 July	iii. 249	ix. 215–16	vi. 226–7
	9 Aug.	iii. 251	ix. 230–1	vi. 239–40
	ca 29 Aug.*	iii. 256		
	8 Sept.	iii. 257	ix. 248–50	vi. 253–5
	6 Oct.	iii. 269	ix. 262–5	vi. 264–6
1776	ca 28 June*	iii. 275		
	30 June	iii. 275	ix. 383–6	vi. 352–4 misdated
	ca 16 July*	iii. 278		
	15 or 16 Aug.*	iii. 282		
	ca 29 Oct.*	iii. 287		
	31 Oct.	iii. 288	ix. 429–31	vi. 386–8
1777	ca 3–10 July (several)*	iii. 291		
	10 July	iii. 291	x. 79–80	vi. 456
	16 Sept.	iii. 293	x. 107–9	vi. 478–9
	Oct.*	iii. 294		
	5 Oct.	iii. 295	x. 125–7	vi. 491–3
1778	8 July	iii. 301	x. 276–8	vii. 91–2
	18 July	iii. 306	x. 285–7	vii. 98–9
	ca 19 Aug.*	iii. 309		
	21 Aug.	iii. 309	x. 298–300	vii. 108–9
	23 Oct.	iii. 316	x. 337–8	vii. 143–4

		YALE	TOYNBEE	CUNNINGHAM
1779	*Jan.**	iii. 316		
	9 Jan.	iii. 317	x. 361–2	vii. 163–4
	22 May	iii. 320	x. 412–13	vii. 201–2
	5 June	iii. 323	x. 419–22	vii. 206–8
	16 June	iii. 328	x. 422–5	vii. 208–10
	3 July*	iii. 331		
	13 Sept.	iii. 338	xi. 22–3	vii. 248–9
1780	*3 June†*	iii. 348		
1781	2 Jan.*	iii. 352		
	3 Jan.	iii. 352	xi. 357–9	vii. 487–8
	ca 1 May*	iii. 367		
	*3 May**	iii. 367		
	6 May	iii. 368	xi. 440–2	vii. 38–9
	*ca 10 May**	iii. 371		
	*ca 17 May**	iii. 371		
	26 May*	iii. 371		
	28 May	iii. 372	xii. 1–4	viii. 45–7
	3 June	iii. 378	xii. 4–7	viii. 47–50
	*ca 14 Sept.**	iii. 384		
	16 Sept.	iii. 384	xii. 53–5	viii. 81–2
	18 Nov.	iii. 386	xii. 96–7	viii. 111–12
1782	*Feb.* (cover only)†	iii. 388		
	20 Aug.	iii. 390	xii. 315–16	viii. 268
	*ca 14 Sept.**	iii. 391		
	16 Sept.*	iii. 391		
	17 Sept.	iii. 391	xii. 333–4	viii. 279–80
	ca 30 Sept.	iii. 393		
1783	30 May*	iii. 401		
	*31 May**	iii. 402		
	1 June*	iii. 402		
	27 July	iii. 402	xiii. 28–30	viii. 401–2 misdated
	15 Aug.	iii. 405	xiii. 43–4	viii. 398–9
1784	*ca 2 May**	iii. 407		
	5 May	iii. 407	xiii. 148–51	viii. 473–5
	*ca 18 May**	iii. 411		
	21 May	iii. 411	xiii. 152–4	viii. 476–7
	*ca June**	iii. 413		
	*ca 23 June**	iii. 415		
	25 June	iii. 415	xiii. 161–3	viii. 483–4
	30 June	iii. 417	xiii. 163–5	viii. 484–5

		YALE	TOYNBEE	CUNNINGHAM
	14 Aug.	iii. 420	xiii. 177–8	viii. 495
	16 Oct.	iii. 423	xiii. 198–200	viii. 511–12
	28 Nov.	iii. 428	xiii. 220–2	viii. 527–8
1785	ca 4 Oct.*	iii. 434		
	6 Oct.	iii. 434	xiii. 335–8	ix. 23–5
1786	18 June	iii. 440	xiii. 386–8	ix. 54–5
	29 Oct.	iii. 444	xiii. 414–16	ix. 71–3
1787	17 June	iii. 447	xiv. 7–8	ix. 100
	24 June†	iii. 448		
	20 July†	iii. 453		
	ca 26 Oct.*	iii. 458		
	ca 27 Oct.*	iii. 458		
	11 Nov.	iii. 459	xiv. 31–3	ix. 118–19
1789	26 May†	iii. 464		
	15 July	iii. 467	xiv. 158–9	ix. 192–3
	ca 1 Sept.*	iii. 469		
	5 Sept.	iii. 469	xiv. 205–7	ix. 217–18
1790	25 June	iii. 472	xiv. 252–3	ix. 244–5
	ca 5 July*	iii. 475		
	7 July	iii. 475	xiv. 254–6	ix. 246–7 misdated
	ca 1 Aug.*	iii. 478		
	9 Aug.	iii. 478	xiv. 281–2	ix. 249–50
	23 Dec.	iii. 480	Supp. iii. 301–4	
1791	ca 25 Sept.*	iii. 484		
	27 Sept.	iii. 485	xv. 66–9	ix. 349–51
1792	7 Aug. (cover only)†	iii. 491		
	ca 15 Aug.*	iii. 491		
	ca 16 Aug.*	iii. 491		
	31 Aug.	iii. 491	xv. 133–6	ix. 385–7
1793	ca 6 June*	iii. 495		
	13 June	iii. 495	xv. 188–90	ix. 407–8
	17 July	iii. 497	xv. 190–1	ix. 408–9
	ca 20 Sept.*	iii. 501		
	22 Sept.	iii. 501	Supp. ii. 64–8	
	ca 6 Oct.*	iii. 507		
1794	Jan.*	iii. 507		
	10 Jan.	iii. 508	xv. 280–1	ix. 431–2
1795	2 July	iii. 510	xv. 347	ix. 456–7
	7 July	iii. 511	xv. 347–8	ix. 457–8

LETTERS BETWEEN WALPOLE AND MRS HARRIS

		YALE	TOYNBEE	CUNNINGHAM
1754	Sept.*	i. 384		
	30 Sept.†	i. 385		

LETTERS BETWEEN WALPOLE AND LADY HERTFORD

1757	*?7 ?March*†*	i. 482		
1760	*28 June†*	ii. 61		
	22 Oct.†	ii. 78		
	?15 Dec.†	ii. 81		
1762	ca 12 Aug.*	ii. 167		
	14 Aug.†	ii. 167		
1764	ca 10 Dec.*	ii. 479		
	18 Dec.†	ii. 479		
1765	7 Jan.*	ii. 486		
	ca 26 Oct.*	iii. 22		
	ca 5 Nov.*	iii. 28		
	16 Dec.†	iii. 36		
1766	ca 4 Jan.*	iii. 41		
	20 Jan.†	iii. 47		
	2 April†	iii. 58		
	ca 10 April*	iii. 67		
	25 May†	iii. 72		
	11 June†	iii. 74		
	8 Oct.†	iii. 77		
1769	*10 Sept.†*	iii. 117		
1770	*4 Aug.†*	iii. 130		
	Sept.*	iii. 131		
	8 Sept.†	iii. 131		
1771	ca 24 Aug.*	iii. 149		
	ca 28 Aug.*	iii. 150		
1772	*11 Feb.†*	iii. 153		
	12 Feb.†	iii. 154		
	31 July†	iii. 159		
	?8 Oct.†	iii. 162		
	29 Oct.*	iii. 164		
	30 Oct.†	iii. 165		
	16 Nov.†	iii. 166		
1774	2 Oct.*	iii. 194		

		YALE	TOYNBEE	CUNNINGHAM
	2 Oct.*	iii. 194		
1775	ca 26 Aug.*	iii. 256		
	8 Sept.†	iii. 260		
	ca 10 Sept.*	iii. 263		
	ca 19 Sept.*	iii. 263		
	25 Sept.†	iii. 264		
1776	ca 10 Feb.*	iii. 274		
	?10 Feb.†	iii. 274		
	24 Aug.†	iii. 284		
	24 Aug.*	iii. 285		
	24 Aug. bis†	iii. 285		
	2 Sept.†	iii. 286		
	ca 3 Oct.*	iii. 286		
	3 Oct.†	iii. 287		
1780	7 ?Dec. [?1780]†	iii. 351		

LETTERS BETWEEN WALPOLE AND LORD HERTFORD

1737	ca 3 Feb. OS*	i. 6		
	late June OS*	i. 30		
1741	ca 15 Sept. OS*	i. 106		
1755	ca 29 Aug.*	i. 401		
	1 Sept.†	i. 402		
1756	? April [?1756]*	i. 464		
	?April [?1756]†	i. 464		
	ca 15–20 Oct. (2)*	i. 478		
	15 Nov.	i. 480	Supp. ii. 96	
1758	16 June*	i. 537		
1759	14 July†	ii. 15		
	ca 16 July*	ii. 17		
	18 July†	ii. 17		
	26 July*	ii. 18		
	3 Aug.†	ii. 18		
	7 Aug.†	ii. 19		
	Aug.*	ii. 25		
	1 Sept.†	ii. 25		
	ca 23 Sept.*	ii. 28		
	27 Sept.†	ii. 29		
1760	5 June†	ii. 53		
	June*	ii. 54		
	21 June†	ii. 54		
	ca 25 June*	ii. 58		
	19 July†	ii. 62		

		YALE	TOYNBEE	CUNNINGHAM
	ca 22 July*	ii. 63		
	24 July †	ii. 63		
	10 Aug.†	ii. 67		
	12 Aug.†	ii. 68		
	14 Aug.†	ii. 69		
	25 Sept.†	ii. 75		
	10 Oct.*	ii. 76		
	11 Oct.†	ii. 76		
	1 Nov.†	ii. 79		
	Dec.*	ii. 80		
	13 Dec.†	ii. 80		
1761	?12 June†	ii. 86		
	1 July†	ii. 91		
	ca 9 July*	ii. 92		
	11 July†	ii. 92		
	17 July†	ii. 98		
	20 July†	ii. 104		
	ca 23 July*	ii. 107		
	1 Aug.†	ii. 107		
	15 Aug.†	ii. 113		
	31 Aug.†	ii. 114		
	3 Sept.†	ii. 115		
	10 Sept.†	ii. 118		
	10 Oct.†	ii. 134		
	Oct.*	ii. 138		
	24 Oct.†	ii. 138		
	ca 8 Dec.*	ii. 145		
	10 Dec.†	ii. 145		
	ca 12 Dec.*	ii. 146		
	14 Dec.†	ii. 147		
1762	20 May†	ii. 156		
	30 June†	ii. 161		
	30 June*	ii. 162		
	29 July†	ii. 162		
	ca 4 Aug.*	ii. 165		
	7 Aug.†	ii. 166		
	18 Aug.†	ii. 169		
	19 Aug.*	ii. 171		
	4 Sept.*	ii. 171		
	10 Sept.†	ii. 176		
	21 Sept.†	ii. 177		
	13 Oct.†	ii. 184		

		YALE	TOYNBEE	CUNNINGHAM
	ca 28 Oct.*	ii. 185		
	30 Oct.†	ii. 190		
1763	*9 April*†	ii. 194		
	20 Aug.†	ii. 209		
	27 Aug.†	ii. 210		
	30 Aug.†	ii. 210		
	15 Oct.†	ii. 211		
	18 Oct.	ii. 213	v. 380–2	iv. 120–2
	28 Oct.†	ii. 216		
	ca 11 Nov.*	ii. 219		
	11 Nov.†	ii. 220		
	17 Nov.	ii. 223	v. 384–91	iv. 123–30
	19 Nov.†	ii. 236		
	25 Nov.	ii. 239	v. 397–401	iv. 135–8
	30 Nov.†	ii. 244		
	2 Dec.	ii. 246	v. 401–4	iv. 139–41
	7 Dec.†	ii. 252		
	9 Dec.	ii. 253	v. 406–10	iv. 142–7
	16 Dec.†	ii. 260		
	16 Dec.	ii. 262	v. 415–18	iv. 149–52
	21 Dec.†	ii. 267		
	28 Dec.†	ii. 270		
	29 Dec.	ii. 272	v. 418–22	iv. 152–6
1764	*6 Jan.*†	ii. 278		
	ca 13–20 Jan (1 or 2 letters)*	ii. 282		
	22 Jan.	ii. 282	v. 437–46	iv. 166–74
	23 Jan.†	ii. 297		
	29 Jan.†	ii. 304		
	6 Feb.	ii. 306	v. 449–54	iv. 178–82
	13 Feb.†	ii. 313		
	15 Feb.	ii. 315	vi. 1–12	iv. 182–92
	18 Feb.†	ii. 328		
	24 Feb.	ii. 332	vi. 20–3	iv. 197–200
	25 Feb.†	ii. 336		
	2 March*	ii. 338		
	8 March†	ii. 338		
	11 March	ii. 340	vi. 25–8	iv. 201–4
	18 March	ii. 345	vi. 31–4	iv. 207–9
	22 March†	ii. 350		
	25 March†	ii. 352		

		YALE	TOYNBEE	CUNNINGHAM
	27 March	ii. 354	vi. 34–9	iv. 209–13
	5 April†	ii. 359		
	5 April	ii. 361	vi. 41–5	iv. 215–18
	12 April	ii. 366	vi. 48–52	iv. 220–3
	15 April†	ii. 372		
	16 April†	ii. 374		
	20 April	ii. 376	vi. 53–6	iv. 221–6
	30 April†	ii. 384		
	ca 11 May*	ii. 388		
	17 May†	ii. 388		
	27 May	ii. 390	vi. 65–8	iv. 236–8
	6 June†	ii. 397		
	8 June	ii. 399	vi. 79–82	iv. 247–9
	22 June†	ii. 403		
	ca July (2)*	ii. 405		
	4 July†	ii. 408		
	17 July†	ii. 409		
	28 July†	ii. 411		
	3 Aug.	ii. 414	vi. 95–103	iv. 256–63
	21 Aug.†	ii. 424		
	27 Aug.	ii. 428	vi. 110–17	iv. 265–71
	20 Sept.†	ii. 439		
	1 Oct.*	ii. 441		
	5 Oct.	ii. 442	vi. 124–6	iv. 276–7
	12 Oct.†	ii. 447		
	ca 13 Oct.*	ii. 448		
	21 Oct.†	ii. 450		
	23 Oct.*	ii. 452		
	1 Nov.	ii. 454	vi. 135–9	iv. 283–7
	9 Nov.	ii. 460	vi. 140–4	iv. 287–90
	10 Nov.†	ii. 464		
	25 Nov.	ii. 466	vi. 148–52	iv. 293–7
	3 Dec.	ii. 471	vi. 152–6	iv. 297–301
	7 Dec.†	ii. 477		
	ca 18 Dec.*	ii. 479		
	20 Dec.†	ii. 483		
	28 Dec.†	ii. 485		
1765	10 Jan.	ii. 486	vi. 165–8	iv. 307–10
	18 Jan.†	ii. 491		
	20 Jan.	ii. 493	vi. 172–6	iv. 313–16
	27 Jan.	ii. 498	vi. 176–81	iv. 316–20

		YALE	TOYNBEE	CUNNINGHAM
	ca 24 Feb.*	iii. 53		
	10 March	iii. 54	Supp. i. 126–9	
	10 May†	iii. 67		
	21 May†	iii. 70		
1767	ca ? July†	iii. 83		
	ca 20 Aug.†	iii. 85		
	ca 23 Aug.*	iii. 86		
	6 Sept.*	iii. 86		
	9 Sept.*	iii. 87		
	14 Sept.†	iii. 90		
	17 Sept.†	iii. 92		
	21 Sept.*	iii. 97		
	27 Sept.*	iii. 98		
1768	27 Oct.†	iii. 112		
	ca 14 Nov.	iii. 113		
1769	20 Feb.	iii. 113		
	13 April†	iii. 114		
	30 June†	iii. 114		
	15 July†	iii. 116		
	ca 2 Sept.*	iii. 117		
	28 Sept.*	iii. 118		
1770	8 March†	iii. 124		
	23 July†	iii. 129		
	25 July†	iii. 129		
	7 Aug.	iii. 130		
	15 Nov.†	iii. 132		
1771	18 Feb.	iii. 137		
	ca 14 July*	iii. 140		
	ca 17 July*	iii. 140		
	ca 23 July†	iii. 141		
	ca 31 July*	iii. 147		
1772	27 Aug.†	iii. 160		
	ca 17 Sept. (2)*	iii. 161		
	?late Sept.*	iii. 161		
	Oct.*	iii. 161		
	10 Oct.†	iii. 162		
	22 Oct.†	iii. 164		
1773	1 May	iii. 169		
	26 May†	iii. 170		
	21 June†	iii. 171		
1774	27 Sept.*	iii. 188		

		YALE	TOYNBEE	CUNNINGHAM
	1 Oct.†	iii. 192		
	1 Oct.†	iii. 193		
	*2 Oct.**	iii. 193		
1775	*30 Sept.*†	iii. 268		
1776	*19 Jan.*†	iii. 273		
	15 July†	iii. 278		
	ca 18 July*	iii. 278		
	20 July†	iii. 279		
	?3 Aug.†	iii. 280		
	15 Aug.†	iii. 281		
	31 Oct.†	iii. 290		
1778	ca 27 March*	iii. 297		
	ca 27 March*	iii. 297		
	5 April	iii. 297		
	July*	iii. 300		
	ca 8 July*	iii. 301		
	8 July†	iii. 303		
	10 July†	iii. 305		
	?19 July†	iii. 308		
	ca 27 Aug.*	iii. 312		
	29 Aug.†	iii. 312		
	ca 4 Sept.*	iii. 312		
	6 Sept.†	iii. 313		
	ca Oct.*	iii. 314		
	2 Oct.†	iii. 314		
	10 Oct.†	iii. 315		
1779	*8 May*†	iii. 319		
	ca 31 July*	iii. 337		
	2 Aug.†	iii. 337		
	3 Sept.†	iii. 338		
	ca 26 Oct.*	iii. 340		
	27 Oct.†	iii. 340		
	30 Oct.†	iii. 343		
	?Nov. or ?Dec. [?1779]†	iii. 344		
	25 Dec.†	iii. 344		
1780	*3 Jan.*†	iii. 345		
	4 Jan.†	iii. 346		
	13 June†	iii. 349		
1781	*8 Jan.*†	iii. 357		
	9 Jan.†	iii. 358		
	11 Jan.†	iii. 359		
	14 Jan.†	iii. 361		

LETTERS BETWEEN WALPOLE AND LORD HENRY SEYMOUR

LETTER TO LORD HUGH SEYMOUR

From CONWAY, Tuesday 25 January 1737 OS

Printed for the first time from the MS now WSL, formerly Rutnam. The day and month are supplied by the mention in the postscript that 'this day' is the Conversion of St Paul; 1737 was the only year in which HW was at Cambridge in late January (below, n. 6). The reference to the forthcoming masquerade and Conway's usual practice of writing to HW on Tuesdays are also consistent with 1737 but not with any other year.

In dating the correspondence of 1737 we have taken into consideration the fact that the post left London for the provinces on Tuesdays, Thursdays, and Saturdays and arrived from them on Mondays, Wednesdays, and Fridays (GRAY i. 56, headnote).

At this time HW was at King's College, Cambridge, Conway was living in London while waiting for a commission, and Lord Conway was on the grand tour.

Address: To Horatio Walpole Esquire at King's College Cambridge.

Postmark: <25 J> A.

Dear Horry,

YOU'LL excuse me, I hope, if I am a little dull tonight; I am just emerged out of Rapin[1] and so bepuzzled with sieges and battles and treaties that I am become a very soldier with respect to writing, and am within an ace of scribbling intolerable nonsense with more intolerable spelin' from one corner of the paper to the other.

I could surprise you with an account of certain phenomena which have appeared here lately, I mean the return of two *stellæ crinitæ*[2] with fiery tails and dark heads long before the supposed time of their revolution, but however as they have always been reckoned propitious to some certain sublunary bodies, and, I believe, not pernicious to any, we have nothing to fear from their influence; to strip myself of my allegory my Lady Vene[3] and Lady Pen. Chol-

1. The English translation, published 1725–31, of Paul de Rapin-Thoyras (1661–1725), *Histoire d'Angleterre,* The Hague, 1724 and later editions. It had become the standard English history.

2. Comets.

3. I.e., Vane: Frances Hawes (ca 1716–88), m. 1 (1732) Lord William Hamilton; m. 2 (1735) William Holles Vane (1714–89), 2d Vct Vane; the 'lady of quality' whose memoirs were included in Smollett's *Peregrine Pickle,* 1751. She had eloped with one of the Shirleys; Vane advertised for her in the newspapers at the end of Jan. 1737 (GEC xii pt ii. 215, n. *a*). The MS might be read 'Vere' but there was no Lady Vere in 1737, and Lady Vere Beauclerk and Lady Vere Bertie can both be rejected as possibilities.

mondely[4] are both returned or upon the point of returning after their several elopements, and their good men stand with open arms to receive them.

My resolution of going to the masquerade[5] incog. which was but in embryo last time I saw you[6] is now come to perfection, and in pursuance to it I have borrowed a sachée,[7] and I will take care not to want anything that will help to disguise and adorn me, and now, my dear Horry, this is one of the many times in which I find myself in want of your good company, that you might employ to my improvement and instruction those female airs and coquetries which you have so often practised for my diversion. I have squandered away since this design was formed a considerable sum of money in going in quest of the Duchess of Manchester,[8] no public place has been unfrequented by me; but in vain; I have not yet seen her, and am now no less at a loss to know how to act my part, than I was at first to procure a dress. I am resolved, if there is a good comedy acted tomorrow night to lay out t'other crown, and since I cannot find the substance will imitate the shadow of a fine lady. Since I saw you I have met with the most terrible accident that could possibly befall me, with respect to a fruitless passion which I have some time nourished unknown both to the object, and the rest of my ac-

---

4. Lady Penelope Barry (ca 1707–86), m. Hon. James Cholmondeley (1708–75) (MANN i. 152, n. 38; Collins, *Peerage*, 1812, iv. 32–4); her husband's brother had married HW's elder sister, Mary. She eloped in 1731 and was living in Paris without her husband in 1741 (Hist. MSS Comm., *Hastings MSS*, ed. Bickley, 1928–47, iii. 7; MANN i. 139, 152). On 29 Jan. 1737 OS Lady Lucy Wentworth wrote to her father: 'Lady Pen Cholmondly is come to town but where she is I can't tell' (*Wentworth Papers*, ed. J. J. Cartwright, 1883, p. 531).

5. 'Great preparations are making at the Theatre in the Haymarket for a masquerade for next week' (*Daily Adv.* 19 Jan.). It took place on the 27th (ibid. 27 Jan.).

6. HW had been in London from late October 1736 until at least 16 Jan. 1737 OS when Gray wrote to him there from Cambridge (GRAY i. 115, 125–6). In 1736

he had been at Cambridge in early January, but had left for London before the 29th, while in 1738 and 1739 he was not at Cambridge at all (ibid. i. 8, 145–61; *Correspondence of Gray, Walpole, West and Ashton*, ed. Toynbee, Oxford, 1915, i. 62).

7. A sack, a type of woman's dress (OED *sub* 'sack' *sb* 4; *post* 1 Feb. 1737; MANN i. 170, n. 3). The Countess of Hertford wrote to the Countess of Pomfret 3 June 1741 OS, 'Few unmarried women appear abroad in robes, or sacques; and as few married ones would be thought genteel in anything else' (Frances, Countess of Hertford and Henrietta Louisa, Countess of Pomfret, *Correspondence*, 1805, iii. 203).

8. Lady Isabella Montagu (d. 1786), m. 1 (1723) William Montagu, 2d D. of Manchester; m. 2 (1743) Edward Hussey (after 1749, Hussey Montagu), cr. (1762) Bn and (1784) E. of Beaulieu.

quaintance, and almost to myself. I met my Cloe[9] t'other day at a third house, where grand and pretty free[10] and elate with mirth and gaiety she inconsiderately let drop an expression too gross for me to name, and almost for you to imagine; more nasty ideas than Swift himself could have inspired me with crowded into my mind, expelled in the twinkling of an eye all the twinklings of a two years' passion, and left there in its room a strong garrison of anti-venereal thoughts which I much question if I shall ever be able to dislodge, so that I am at present, without a compliment,

Yours, my dear Horry, much more than hers,

STREPHON II

PS. I went to Major Feaubert's manage[11] this morning after having absented myself three weeks, and unluckily found it empty, this day being the Conversion of St Paul;[12] to this I shall beg leave to sign, not improperly,

HENRY CONWAY

9. Possibly Lady Caroline Fitzroy (1722–84), m. (1746) William Stanhope, styled Vct Petersham, 2d E. of Harrington, 1756. Conway continued his friendship with her to the point of there being a kind of unspoken agreement between them, but, put off by her free and vulgar behaviour, he never reached the point of proposing. See *post* 24 March 1740 OS, 20 July 1744 OS, 5 Aug. 1744 NS.

10. The MS has been erased and written over, but this seems to be the reading.

11. I.e., riding-school (OED). This establishment, known as the Royal Academy or Royal Riding School following an annual crown grant from 1691, was founded in the 1680s by Solomon Foubert, a Huguenot refugee. After his death (1696), it was continued by his son Henry (d. 1743), naturalized in 1702 as Henry de Foubert. The Academy, which stood in what is now Regent Street at Foubert's Place, ceased to exist in 1768 or 1769 and the main building was demolished in 1813. For an account of its history and the Foubert family, see W. H. Manchée, 'The Fouberts and their Royal Academy,' *Proceedings of the Huguenot Society of London*, 1937–41, xvi. 77–97, esp. pp. 82–7. Further details and lists of its scholars in 1738 and 1739 are in the *Wentworth Papers*, pp. 536, 540–1.

12. 25 Jan. Although this is one of the more important saints' days observed by the Church of England, it is not clear why Foubert's Academy would be empty because of it.

To CONWAY, ca Thursday 27 January 1737 OS

Missing; answered *post* 1 Feb. 1737 OS. HW presumably received Conway's letter of the 25th on the 26th and Conway, this reply on either the 28th or the 30th (GRAY i. 56, headnote).

From CONWAY, Tuesday 1 February 1737 OS

Printed for the first time from the MS now WSL, formerly Rutnam. Dated by the postmark and the assumption that the masquerade described below is the one mentioned in the preceding letter.
Address: To Horatio Walpole Esquire at King's College Cambridge.
Postmark: 1 FE.

I RECEIVED my dear Horry's letter with a great deal of pleasure, and was exceedingly entertained, even at second hand, with your musical performance, though at the same time I could not help being a good deal astonished;[1] and (had not miracles long since ceased) should almost have been induced to impute the wonders therein wrought to the concurrence and prevalency of some supernatural power; for how the ears of an hundred people could be fed, or rather could not be cloyed, with the scrapings and screamings I have framed an idea of from the description you give of your concert is to me quite inconceivable, and, I think, only not a miracle. Kerwood[2] earnestly exhorts you not to frequent that devilish concert upon any consideration; he is convinced that it abounds with diabolical spells and enchantments. Some fiend, he says, lurks in each fiddle, and your harpsichord contains a legion of imps, and that you are in imminent danger of a thousand charms, which it is impossible for any human sagacity to know the force and efficacy of: for my own part (though I would not advise you to do a rash thing), yet I think if you have nothing to fear but from the charms of your concert you may safely venture there.

1. That HW was 'learning music' is suggested by West's letter to him of 18 April 1737 (GRAY i. 133), but it came to nothing. 'I know but little in music,' he wrote West (ibid. 233) and always described himself as unmusical.

2. Perhaps John Kyrwood of Letton, Herefordshire, who m. (1735) the widow of HW's uncle Galfridus (GM 1735, v. 681; Collins, *Peerage,* 1812, v. 653).

You desired an account of the masquerade: I heartily wish you had not wanted one; but am glad however that you know the means of preventing that want another time, and hope you will not fail to use them, when you find how little it is satisfied by a dull recital of facts, barely diverting to one upon the spot: masquerades like many other things lose prodigiously in carrying, and especially if they meet with a bad vehicle, are so miserably jumbled and confused by that time they arrive at the end of a fifty miles' journey, that it is morally impossible to form any idea of or receive any entertainment from 'em. This, however, will serve to inform you that it was pretty full and that not of the worst company; in short there was nothing wanting to complete the entertainment but the company of King George and Horry Walpole; to anybody else I dare not, and to you I hope I need not, tell which I most wanted there. The part I acted there (sad metamorphosis!) was that of a lady. We love to flatter our vanity, you know, not a little, so that I can't help troubling you with a few of my own adventures. In the first place I picked all my peacock's plumes out of my sister Jenny's[3] wardrobe which I ransacked without reserve; when I was sufficiently decorated, it was necessary, they said, for the sake of my reputation, to put myself under the protection of some married lady; this I willingly submitted to, and was no sooner got there than I was surprised with a thousand extravagant encomiums upon my shape and beauty, for which I was entirely obliged to a loose sack and black silk mask, which, however, soon gained me a great many admirers. The first that addressed me was a ghostly father of the Dominican order, who after much lewd conversation, many promises of spiritual absolutions and temporal rewards, finding I was not to be prevailed upon, delivered me over to the secular arm in the person of an officer upon guard. He immediately invested me, and after several vigorous attacks, finding he could not carry me by storm, made a blockade of it, and indeed he effectually cut off all verbal commerce between me and the rest of the company by hindering me, though I did not attend to him, from hearing a single word from anybody else; at last I withdrew the garrison and left him to take possession, if he pleased, of the empty citadel. I could lengthen out this detail to the consumption of all the paper in my bureau, and I'm sure of

3. Hon. Jane Conway (1714–49), Conway's half-sister (MANN i. 274, n. 32; Mis-   cellanea genealogica et heraldica, 1890, 2d ser., iii. 58).

your patience, but I shall have so much regard to both, as to add no more than that I am, dear Horry,

Yours sincerely,

H. CONWAY

Selwyn[4] desires his compliments, as also Lord Holderness[5] and Barret.[6]

To LORD CONWAY, ca Thursday 3 February 1737 OS

Missing; mentioned *post* 8 Feb. 1737 OS.

To CONWAY, ca Thursday 3 February 1737 OS

Missing; answered *post* 8 Feb. 1737 OS.

From CONWAY, Tuesday 8 February 1737 OS

Printed for the first time from the MS now WSL, formerly Rutnam. Dated by the postmark and the reference to the assault by the Duchess of Manchester's negro servant (below, n. 14).
   Address: To Horatio Walpole Esquire at King's College Cambridge.
   Postmark: 8 FE.

Dear Horry,

I HAVE sent the letters forward as you desired, the one to my brother,[1] and the other to George Montague,[2] from whom two or three posts ago I received one of the most diverting letters[3] I

4. John Selwyn (ca 1709–51), the younger; M.P. Whitchurch 1734–51; George Selwyn's brother.
   5. Robert Darcy (1718–78), 4th E. of Holdernesse.
   6. Thomas Barrett Lennard (1717–86), 17th Bn Dacre, 1755; HW's lifelong friend and occasional correspondent.

1. Francis Seymour Conway (1718–94), 2d Bn Conway; cr. (1750) E. and (1793) M. of Hertford; HW's cousin. He had left England on his grand tour 17 June 1736,

and may have been at Rheims with George Montagu at this time (GRAY i. 166, n. 34; MONTAGU i. 9). HW's letter to him is missing.
   2. George Montagu (ca 1713–80), HW's correspondent, who was at Rheims. HW's enclosed letter is missing, but another of 20 March 1737 OS (MONTAGU i. 9–11) contains HW's reflections on the 'amour' discussed below.
   3. Conway's correspondence with Montagu has not been recovered.

HON. FRANCIS SEYMOUR CONWAY,
MARQUESS OF HERTFORD, BY JOHN ASTLEY

ever saw. Among other things and to satisfy the curiosity I expressed in a former one to him, to know the particulars of his amour, he has given me a full and satisfactory account of it; but I doubt will not think me a proper person to trust a love tale with,[4] for I have really abused his confidence most horribly, and in return for ecstasies and transports have sent him two or three pages of serious remonstrances and friendly advice, which doubtless will give great umbrage to a lover basking in the full sunshine of fruition;[5] but I have endeavoured to gild the pill, which cannot but be very nauseous, by introducing my discourse with reflections upon the happiness of his present situation, and then proceeded to draw inferences, and forewarn him of the calamities it may bring upon him: how it will go down I don't know. You may see from what has been said that he is no Platonic; in short, he is over head and ears in an affair which may probably lead him into great difficulties, not to say danger. He has found a hole to creep in at, but I heartily wish he may not be in the case of the weasel in the fable;[6] such delicious viands are prodigiously fattening! He is now carrying on an intrigue with a lady, as he says, of the first rank in Rheims; and if she has any relations or friends who think her virtue and reputation worth their regarding, they will certainly think it incumbent upon them either to compel him to marry her or cut his throat. Wretched dilemma! in short, the only clue which will lead him out of this labyrinth is in my opinion a journey from Rheims.[7] But to change the subject before I tire it out, the enclosed is, as you'll see, a translation of *Intermissa Venus Diu,* by Mr Pope,[8] which, though a pretty thing upon the whole, in two or three places falls vastly short of the orig-

4. 'Cato's a proper person to entrust
   A love-tale with'
   (Addison, *Cato* II. v).
HW also echoes this passage to Mann 4 Jan. 1745 OS (MANN ii. 562).
   5. 'Fruition' has been lightly crossed out in pencil and 'success' written above in another hand.
   6. Conway is apparently thinking of Æsop's fable of the mouse and the weasel, but it is the mouse, not the weasel, who is trapped in the corn-basket by over-eating.
   7. Montagu considered doing so, for he asked HW to join him and Lord Conway on a trip to Italy (HW to Montagu 20 March 1737 OS, MONTAGU i. 9).

8. Pope's *First Ode of the Fourth Book of Horace Imitated.* The version sent to HW, which is missing, was probably a manuscript, since the earliest printed version known (apparently unauthorized) appeared in the *Whitehall Evening Post* 26 Feb. – 1 March 1737 OS, and the authorized edition was not published until 9 March 1737 (Pope, *Imitations of Horace,* ed. John Butt, 1953, p. 148). Conway's comments on the poem make it clear that the version sent to HW was closer to that in the newspaper than to the authorized edition, although not quite the same (see below, nn. 9–12).

inal, particularly 'the glorious reign of my Queen Anne'[9] has not half the spirit and energy as *'regnum bona Cynaræ';*[10] there is indeed this to be said in his defence, that he was ashamed, I suppose, to own any passion prior to that he long entertained for his Patty;[11] and therefore could not follow the author's steps so closely in that particular; in the close of the poem too, Patty's shooting along the Mall, and swiftly gliding by the canal,[12] are really very insipid in comparison of the Latin

> *Te per gramina Martii*
> *Campi, te per aquas, dure, volubiles.*[13]

Swimming and running were the usual exercises of the Roman youth which makes the images grand and lively, and the words are infinitely sweeter and more expressive. This indeed is to be said in favour of the translation that a poet must be very much at a loss to find any exercises of Mrs Blount's that could be brought in to heighten and enliven the poem as those in the original do; then the author's passion for his Patty is innocent at least if not laudable, whereas the avowing a passion for a youth (though not an uncommon thing with the Greek and Roman poets), is so notoriously impious and contrary to nature, as well as morality and religion, that it is impossible not to be offended at it. There is no news stirring but a cruel and bloody murder committed upon the body of a housemaid by a young black, formerly in the service of the

9. Line 4. This line reads 'As in the gentle reign of my Queen Anne' in the authorized edition, and 'As in the glorious reign of good Queen Anne' in the newspaper version. A third reading in a MS copy by Joseph Spence, now WSL, is the same as the one Conway gives here; but the Spence copy omits the 'Patty' passage (below, n. 11) and therefore was not the copy sent to HW. For the text of the Spence copy, see Maynard Mack, 'A Manuscript of Pope's Imitation of the First Ode of the Fourth Book of Horace,' *Modern Language Notes*, 1945, lx. 185–8.

10. Correctly 'bonæ / sub regno Cynaræ' (ll. 3–4) ('under the reign of the good Cinara').

11. Pope's Patty was Martha Blount (1690–1762); the reference to her in the poem was suppressed in the authorized

edition, but l. 37 of the newspaper version reads 'But why? ah, Patty, still too dear.' The Spence copy gives this line as 'But why, ah tell me, still too dear' and the authorized edition as 'But why? ah tell me, ah too dear.'

12. 'And swiftly shoot along the Mall
    Or softly glide by the canal
    Now shown by Cynthia's silver ray
    And now, on rolling waters
        snatched away'   (ll. 45–8)
The newspaper version is the same except for 'by' instead of 'on,' and 'washed' instead of 'snatched' in l. 48, and the Spence copy, except for 'now' instead of 'and' in l. 45.

13. Lines 39–40: 'now through the Campus Martius's fields, now through the whirling waters, O thou hard of heart.'

Duchess.[14] I should affront you and your passion if I were to name her since it is impossible but the first female grace that occurs to you must be her. But I forgot it was not a murder, for the woman is now as much, though not so well, alive as

Your humble servant,

H. C.

PS. If your reason for asking when there is a masquerade be the one I imagine, I am very sorry to tell you that I am informed there will be but one more and that not till after Lent:[15] I hope my information is not authentic. I will inquire further and also let you know when the next ridotto is, which in the opinion of some has charms even preferable to those of a masquerade.[16]

N.B. Our Duchess[17] never fails to be there. Item. The Duke[18] hates 'em.

---

14. Of Manchester. 'Yesterday [1 Feb.] a black [Jeffery Moratt], formerly a servant to . . . the Duke of Manchester, got into the house of the . . . Marquis of Lindsey . . . in Little Brook Street by Grosvenor Square, the family being out of town, and nobody but an ancient woman in it, whom he knocked down with a poker, which, with striking violently at her, he broke; after which he endeavoured to cut her throat with a knife, but missed her windpipe. He left her for dead, and then went and opened an escrutore, but the woman recovering a little, went to the window, and broke a square of the sash, whom the chairmen in the street seeing bloody, immediately went to her assistance. The black, finding he was likely to be taken, got up one of the chimneys, from whence they brought him down by burning straw. He was immediately carried before Lord Carpenter, who committed him to Newgate. The woman is much cut and bruised, but being under the care of Mr MacCullock, a surgeon, 'tis hoped she will do well' (*Daily Adv.* 2 Feb.). A similar account is in the *London Evening Post* 1–3 Feb. The woman was first reported to have died the following day, but later to be 'much better' and still later to have 'taken a fever' (*Daily Adv.* 3 Feb.; *London Evening Post* 3–5, 5–8 Feb.). Moratt was condemned to death for the robbery only on 19 Feb., but died before his execution (GM 1737, vii. 122, 186).

15. There was another 21 Feb. as Conway learned a few days later (*post* 15 Feb. 1737 OS).

16. The distinction between ridottos and masquerades seems to have been that at the ridotto a concert preceded the ball (see Charles Burney's account of the first ridotto in England in his *General History of Music*, ed. Mercer, 1935, ii. 995); masking was optional at a ridotto (Sir George Grove, *Dictionary of Music and Musicians*, 5th edn, ed. Blom, 1954–61, vii. 84), and it was generally a more select and decorous affair than a masquerade.

17. Of Manchester.

18. William Montagu (1700–39), 2d D. of Manchester.

To CONWAY, ca Saturday 12 February 1737 OS

Missing. Conway received it Monday, 14 Feb. (*post* 15 Feb. 1737 OS); it was probably written the preceding Saturday.

From CONWAY, Tuesday 15 February 1737 OS

Printed for the first time from the MS now WSL, formerly Rutnam. Dated by the postmark and the reference to the death of the Lord Chancellor.

Address: To Horatio Walpole Esquire at King's College Cambridge.

Postmark: 15 FE.

Dear Horry,

IF the tedious scrawl I sent you deserved a thousand thanks, a million, I'm sure, at least are due to you for the kind epistle yesterday's post conveyed to me, and for which I own myself doubly obliged to you; for as it is generally allowed, that a favour gratefully acknowledged is in some measure returned, so an acknowledgment, where in reality no favour is received, must consequently beget an obligation, which in the present case was so prodigiously enhanced by the many kind professions of friendship and the engaging frankness with which your last was penned that I am conscious how very unable I am to make a suitable return. Not diffidence but a real knowledge of my own weakness has demonstrated to me that I am entirely incapable of keeping up the ball with equal vigour and activity, but if anything can aid my faint efforts towards the not letting it entirely drop, 'tis the commodious footing our commerce is now established upon: I say established, for you may be sure I shall readily and joyfully close with the proposals made in your last; for to speak the dictates of a heart glad to inform you how much and how sincerely it is devoted to your service, is the greatest pleasure and satisfaction I can possibly receive from the active part of our correspondence; I mean the part I bear in the colloquy, which nevertheless is not comparable to that I enjoy in the passive, and especially in those kind assurances you give me that that tie is mutual which I find so radically established in one party. You were disappointed, you say, when you found the poem enclosed in my last[1] was not what it first appeared to be, mine; had it, it could not possibly have been what it was. I know what pleasure you must feel in the sweet vice versa of clasping a John for an empty Joseph, instead of an empty Joseph for a John,[2] so heartily congratulate you upon your agreeable disappointment; you think your having never seen any poetical production of mine is not a reason you should not; I own, I think it is one of the many; if I had broke the tie and made one circle in the water 'tis ten to one another would succeed to it; but as the case stands at present I have not turned my thoughts much to poetry, since the happy times of my being *sub regno boni Georgii* (my hinting that I am not now *sub regno boni Georgii* seems a paradox, but I believe I need not solve it to you)[3] I find I am provided of a safe vessel to embark in, and shall not in haste turn Icarus and trust to such Dedalean mechanism as the fond conceits of a very young, but more imperfect, scholar. I am almost sorry to anticipate a piece of bad news which cannot remain long unknown to you, the death of my Lord Chancellor.[4] How good and how great a man he was, and how generally lamented he dies,[5] I need not tell you, so shall only add that I am with greatest sincerity, dear Horry,

Your most affectionate coz and humble servant,

H. C.

All the pillars and posts between this and Ludgate Hill inform me there is a masquerade on Monday next:[6] so give an humble brother leave to tell it you.

1. Pope's *First Ode of the Fourth Book of Horace Imitated*.

2. The key to this puzzle seems to be 'empty Joseph,' where 'Joseph' means 'a long cloak, worn chiefly by women in the eighteenth century when riding' (OED sub 'Joseph,' 2): HW is to be congratulated on exchanging something strong and solid (Pope's verses) instead of something weak and empty (Conway's).

3. Although he now was in the King's army, the King was not in his favour—owing to his hoping for a better commission. See *post* 2 July 1737, n. 3.

4. Charles Talbot (1685 – 14 Feb. 1737), cr. (1733) Bn Talbot; lord chancellor 1733–7.

5. According to the *London Evening Post* 12–15 Feb. 'no man has died in this last century so generally lamented as his Lordship.'

6. 21 Feb. It was advertised, 'At the King's Theatre in the Hay-Market, this day, being the 21st of February, will be a ball. Being the last this season' (*Daily Adv.* 21 Feb.).

My kind compliments to Dodd,[7] and heavy complaints for his having entirely let our correspondence[8] drop, which you may tell him should not have languished through my means.

To CONWAY, ca Saturday 19 February 1737 OS

Missing; received by Conway just before he went to the masquerade on Monday, 21 Feb.; answered *post* 26 Feb. 1737 OS.

From CONWAY, Saturday 26 February 1737 OS

Printed for the first time from the MS now WSL, formerly Rutnam. Dated by the postmark and the reference to the masquerade.
Address: To Horatio Walpole Esquire at King's College Cambridge.
Postmark: 26 FE.

Dear Horry,

I FEASTED heartily upon the good supper you sent me, but (pardon me to say it) was nevertheless very far from having a belly-full, and could have digested with a great deal of ease and eat with a great deal of pleasure another sheet of paper full of such delicious viands. Well! by that time my food was digested, I put on a couple of awkward vestments, a frowzy tied wig and a swinging gold-laced hat, and thus accoutred went to the masquerade.[1] You'll be at a loss now to know what character I personated, and really from my dress one would not easily imagine; I literally did not know till I was called doctor by somebody, that I was one, and I do not yet very well know which I am obliged to for my degree—a venerable tied wig (if such it may be called, which instead of being tied hung over my shoulders in graceful ringlets) or the person who

7. John Dodd (1717–82), of Swallow-field, Berks, HW's contemporary at Eton and King's, Camb.; M.P. Reading, 1741, 1755–82 (SELWYN 26, n. 6; Namier and Brooke ii. 326). John Nichols records that Dodd 'was no scholar; but he was a favourite of many ingenious and clever men. . . . He was generous, open-hearted, and convivial,—friendly, and hospitable to a fault' (*Illustrations of the Literary History of the Eighteenth Century*, 1817–58, i. 502).
   8. None of this has been recovered.

1. Presumably that of 21 Feb. (*ante* 15 Feb. 1737 OS, n. 6).

HON. HENRY SEYMOUR CONWAY,
BY BARTHOLOMEW DANDRIDGE

christened me one, but whichever it was I took the hint, and wrought many wonderful cures, but the only perfect and effectual ones (I doubt the phrase) were of such as were troubled with a curiosity to know who their benefactor was.—But Selwyn is starving in hackney coach at the door, so I am, dear Horry,

Yours,

H. C.

To CONWAY, ca Saturday 5 March 1737 OS

Missing; answered ca 8 March 1737 OS.

From CONWAY, ca Tuesday 8 March 1737 OS

Printed for the first time from the MS now WSL, formerly Rutnam. The date, based on a fragmentary postmark, is somewhat uncertain. Although the reference to Dodd's expected visit to London would suggest a date in early April (see below, n. 2), a postmark of 8 April, a Friday, is unlikely and a letter of that date seems incompatible with Conway's letter to HW of 7 April 1737 OS.

Address: To Horatio Walpole Esquire at King's College Cambridge.

Postmark: ⟨8 MR⟩.

Dear Horry,

YOUR letter threw me into the vapours, by robbing me at once of all the pleasing hopes I had conceived of seeing you shortly in town; the damp it gave me sunk my spirits like the quick-silver in a barometer down to my very shoes; your friends in town make use of me as one of those instruments, and know punctually by looking on or talking with me what likelihood there is of your coming to this part of the world. I met Selwyn this morning, who looking pretty earnestly in my face, wished me joy of your coming to town, and indeed not quite, I hope, without reason; less penetration than he is master of would have perceived a very considerable alteration in my countenance; to be short, I had just met Captain Jones[1] who

1. Perhaps Hugh Jones, Capt. in the army, 1710, in the 32d Foot, 1726, the only Capt. Jones in the army in 1740 (Society for Army Historical Research,

told me Dodd was coming hither within these five or six days;[2] this greatly revived my sinking spirits. As I very well knew that though your heart is very obdurate and not to be moved by the potent charms of this place, that still it is but steel and as such may possibly be attracted by the great magnetic power of the body that is moving townward; to whom I beg my compliments and those also of another creditor of his; I mean my brother who writes me word he has wrote two letters to him without having received any answers.[3] The lady that fell out of the window,[4] I dare say, broke her leg, and I think it was the least her hypocrisy deserved. Your story of the Templar put me in mind (not from any similitude of the characters) of our friend Charles.[5] He has been very ill but is now recovered, and gives his service to you. Selwyn and I supped t'other night at Mr Good's;[6] our company was Mr Hardin,[7] Mr Burchett,[8] and Mr Green[9] beside ourselves. We were very merry, and drank your health; I say we, for I actually drank a glass or two of wine, which made Selwyn prophesy that I should relapse into my pristine state of jollity; but I have such perfect confidence in my own resolution, that his predictions have very little or no weight with me; for though I do take up the sword[10] I have no design of throwing away the keys, as it is reported of Pope Julius[11] (who assumed that name in memory of the great hero who formerly bore it). He was of an exceeding warlike disposition, more so a good deal than suited with his hierarchical

The Army List of 1740, Sheffield, 1931, p. 41), who was probably the Capt. Jones, 'an experienced officer, well known in the army,' who died in 1742 (*London Magazine* 1742, xi. 361).

2. Dodd does not seem to have come to London until early April, when Ashton wrote to West 5 April 1737 OS that HW had accompanied Dodd and Whaley part of the way to London, but was expected back at Cambridge that night (*Correspondence of Gray, Walpole, West and Ashton*, ed. Toynbee, Oxford, 1915, i. 131–2).

3. None of Lord Conway's correspondence with Dodd has been recovered.

4. This and the story of the Templar mentioned in the next sentence are unexplained in the absence of HW's letter.

5. Charles Lyttelton (1714–68), Dean of Exeter, 1748; Bp of Carlisle, 1762; antiquary; friend and correspondent of HW. He was at this time a student at the Middle Temple, whence he was called to

the bar in 1738 (John Hutchinson, *Catalogue of Notable Middle Templars*, 1902, p. 152).

6. Perhaps Francis Good (d. 1739), lower master at Eton 1717–34 (GM 1739, ix. 383; R. A. Austen-Leigh, *Eton College Register 1698–1752*, Eton, 1927, p. xxii). Neither he nor the other guests at this dinner are otherwise mentioned in connection with HW or Conway.

7. Not identified.

8. Possibly William Burchett (ca 1694–1750), an assistant at Eton ca 1718–28; vicar of Clewer 1729–50; perhaps canon of Windsor 1739–50 (Austen-Leigh, op. cit. 52).

9. Possibly John Greene (b. 1719), son of Maurice Greene, organist of St Paul's and professor of music at Cambridge, who was at Eton 1728–35 (ibid. 147).

10. That is, enter the army.

11. Giuliano della Rovere (1443–1513), pope, as Julius II, 1503–13.

station; it happening once that in order to engage with a French army he was obliged to cross the Tiber; as he was going over he threw St Peter's keys into the river and called for St Paul's sword: with which he made a sacrifice of his religion to his ambition, or revenge, I don't know which; perhaps both: for these Popes are shrewd fellows at killing two birds with one stone. It is no uncommon thing for 'em to destroy infidels, and fill their own insatiable coffers with the same zealous crusade, and to refine gold in the same fire that has burned heretics in the name of the Lord; many other instances there are of their pure and disinterested love for the Church and her cause. But you'll think I have but little for you if I add any more than that I am

Yours sincerely,

H. C.

I will not forget, as I own I hitherto have done, to send your silver.[12] I suppose the coach will be the best way of conveying it. Selwyn desires his compliments *cum multis aliis quos nunc perscribere longum est.*

To CONWAY, March 1737

Missing; answered *post* 22 March 1737 OS.

From CONWAY, Tuesday 22 March 1737 OS

Printed for the first time from the MS now WSL, formerly Rutnam. Dated by the postmark and the literary references.
Address: To Horatio Walpole Esquire at King's College Cambridge.
Postmark: 22 MR.

Dear Horry,

I HAVE got the leaf-silver, as you desired, and will send it with some things your mamma[1] is going to pack up for Cambridge: I don't know whether there is a sufficient quantity or not; if you

---

12. See *post* 22 March 1737 OS.   1. Catherine Shorter (ca 1682–1737), m. (1700) Sir Robert Walpole.

want more, or anything else in town, you need but let me know it, and I shall serve you with the greatest pleasure.

'Tis so long since you asked me, that I am ashamed to say I have not read *The Spleen*,[2] but by inquiring for it I have heard of some other pieces lately published, particularly, a poem by Sommerfield[3] (who wrote *The Chase*),[4] entitled, I think, *The Elbow Chair;*[5] I have not ventured into it, nor design it till I have heard more of it; if it is upon a level with the rest of our modern productions I think one is in great danger of falling asleep in it: which leads me naturally to my last night's dream. *Tibi quisque facit.*[6] Petr. The images in the following were so lively and natural, as well as a good deal more uniform and connected than the confused, irregular ideas of which our dreams are generally composed that I could not help communicating it to you, more to give myself ease, than, I doubt, it can possibly afford you pleasure; I was, methought, at the public representation of *The Orphan*[7] at the Drury Lane Theatre (I have already apprised you of its[8] being extremely natural and lively, so you must not be astonished when you find that there [was] no one incident in the whole course of my vision but what might very probably have happened to anybody but you or I; Selwyn may be

2. By Matthew Green (1696–1737), advertised as 'this day is published' in *London Evening Post* 19–22 Feb. and *Daily Adv.* 23 Feb. HW quotes several passages from it in his letter to Montagu 20 March 1737 OS (MONTAGU i. 10–11). Green was admired by Gray, who also calls him one of HW's 'favourites' (GRAY ii. 35, 39).

3. An error for William Somerville (1675–1742), poet.

4. Published in 1735.

5. No poem with this title was published by Somerville at this time. Conway may have heard of his 'The Wicker Chair,' which seems to have been circulating in manuscript. This, apparently written between 1708 and 1710, was published in a considerably revised form as *Hobbinol, or The Rural Games* in 1740; the earlier version was not printed until 1802 when F. G. Waldron published it in his *Shakespearean Miscellany*, ostensibly from Somerville's manuscript. For a discussion see R. D. Havens, 'William Somervile's Earliest Poem,' *Modern Language Notes*, 1926, xli. 80–6.

6. Petronius Arbiter, *Satyricon* CIV (or *Fragmenta* XXX, as in Bücheler's edn, Berlin, 1882):
'Somnia, quæ mentes ludunt volitantibus umbris,
Non delubra Deum, nec ab æthere numina mittunt,
Sed sibi quisque facit'
('Dreams which deceive the mind by fleeting shadows,
Neither the shrines of the gods nor the deities from the upper world send,
But each makes them for himself').
HW had three editions of Petronius (Hazen, *Cat. of HW's Lib.*, Nos 1539, 2207:30, 2253); the last two are now WSL.

7. By Thomas Otway (1652–85), revived at Drury Lane 15 March 1737 OS and performed again 20 April (John Genest, *Some Account of the English Stage*, Bath, 1832, iii. 496; *Daily Adv.* 12, 15 March; *London Stage* Pt III, ii. 648, 660).

8. Apparently the dream, not *The Orphan*.

excepted too if he pleases). Milward[9] performed his part, which was
that of Castalio, to a miracle; Mrs Cibber[10] is obliged to her visionary self for acting considerably better than her material self ever did,
but not to tire you with a circumstantial detail of incidents, I will
pass over the catastrophe of the play in order to come at that of my
dream. I went, methought, after the play with some jolly dogs to
the tavern. We were hardly seated when a certain Lord, lately come
from abroad, made his entrance; the first person he addressed himself to was a certain officer who commonly attends at great taverns,
and who followed him up, of course, to receive his commands, which
were to introduce some ladies; the fellow had not been gone three
minutes when two or three silk gowns rustled in, sounding the sig-
nal to a venereal combat. The young hero advanced with uncommon
intrepidity, and attacked 'em so vigorously that they retired with
some precipitation. I was astonished to see him use 'em so boister-
ously, but it seems he insisted upon such as he had not seen before.
After a succession of twenty or thirty several females who were all
rejected for the same reason, I hinted that perhaps it might be no
easy matter to find such as his Lordship wanted, as his acquaintance
was pretty general among the fair sex; but he wiped off all aspersions
of that kind by assuring me, with the most solemn asseverations, he
was not such a rover as I thought him and that his number of mistresses within these two months had not exceeded twenty: at last
a fresh bevy came in which were seized by several of the company
with the most fervent eagerness and after toying a little each retired
with his respective lady. I could not help reflecting how very different the scene now before me was from that I had just before been
a spectator of; in the first we see an ardent, and yet honourable lover
making the enjoyment of one adored woman the point in which all
his wishes centered, in the other people bringing themselves upon
a level with the brute creation, who without any desire for a particular object, act purely to satisfy their bestial lust, entirely ex-
cluding the more refined sensations of the mind. Whichever gate
my vision flew out at, you may be sure my principles are not shaken,
but that I still remain the same

H. C.

9. William Milward (ca 1702–42), actor
(*Daily Adv.* 8 Feb. 1742; GM 1742, xii.
107).

10. Susannah Maria Arne (1714–66), m.
(1734) Theophilus Cibber; actress. She
played Monimia in *The Orphan* (Genest,
op. cit. iii. 496).

To Conway, ca Saturday 2 April 1737 OS

Missing; answered *post* 7 April 1737 OS.

From Conway, Thursday 7 April 1737 OS

Printed for the first time from the MS now WSL, formerly Rutnam. Dated by the postmark and the reference to Glover's *Leonidas*, published 1 April (below, n. 4).

Address: To Horatio Walpole Esquire at King's College Cambridge.

Postmark: 7 AP.

Dear Horry,

THE verses you sent me[1] gave me a great deal of pleasure, and I think both copies so pretty that it would not be doing 'em the justice they deserve to affront either with a determination in favour of the other preferably to it; and I hope I shall not be thought to derogate from the lustre of the Planets, when I say that Luna[2] appears to me more eminently bright than all or any of their corps (the Sun is out of the question).

I agree with you entirely in your opinion of *King Charles;*[3] I see it in the light of a large edifice raised upon the feeble support of five or six small columns, bending under the weight of it, and the author, who is an obscure man and has nothing to depend upon but the success of this attempt, seems to be placed under this ruinous building and in dangerous likelihood of being crushed with the fall of it; this indeed and the rest of the things which have been lately published are almost bad enough to prejudice one against all modern productions, but there has lately appeared a poem[4] which in spite of that prejudice will command your attention, and they say

1. 'Planetæ sunt habitabiles' by Jacob Bryant (1717–1804) of King's College and 'Luna habitabilis' by Gray (GRAY i. 128, n. 2). HW also sent copies to West, who criticizes them in his letter of 18 April 1737 OS (ibid. i. 128–30).

2. I.e., Gray's verses.

3. *King Charles the First. An Historical Tragedy*, by William Havard (?1710–78), actor and dramatist, first performed at Lincoln's Inn Fields 1 March 1737, was published 23 March 1737 OS (John

Genest, *Some Account of the English Stage*, Bath, 1832, iii. 513; *Daily Adv.* 22, 23 March; *London Stage* Pt III, ii. 643). HW wrote on the title page of his copy (Hazen, *Cat. of HW's Lib.*, No. 1818:6:2): 'By Havard the Player.'

4. *Leonidas*, by Richard Glover (1712–85), published 1 April 1737 OS (*Daily Adv.* 1 April). HW was reading it by the 5th (*Correspondence of Gray, Walpole, West and Ashton*, ed. Toynbee, Oxford, 1915, i. 132; Hazen, op. cit., No. 1616).

extort your approbation; for my own part, I have read too little of it
to give any judgment of my own as yet, but have heard so much
said in favour of it that I believe I may venture to recommend it.
It takes its title from the name of the hero, who is Leonidas; the
action is the famous battle fought by the Grecians against Xerxes
near the Straits of Thermopylæ: the first book, which is the only one
I have read, seems to have but one fault, which is that it consists almost entirely of speeches, and as I hear, the poem continues the
same through the whole. This arises necessarily from the short time
of the action, which is less perhaps than ever was allowed to an epic
poem, and the few incidents which are not sufficient to supply matter for a long narration. *Verum ubi plura nitent in carmine non
ego paucis offendar maculis.*[5] The style is really very pretty, the
similes apt and lively, and though it has not all the energy of
Homer, Virgil, or Milton, nobody can say with justice, *nervi defi-
ciunt animique.*[6] The author is a very young man indeed (as Mr
Barret says), so we may hope this will not be his last essay; his name
is Glover, he is a merchant in the City,[7] and a friend of my Lord
Cobham[8] to whom he has inscribed his poem; this is the best account I can give you of him and his piece. I suppose you will not
long defer satisfying your curiosity further about him; but if your
Cambridge bookseller have not got it yet, let me know and I will
send it to you the first opportunity. You are always so good as to
inquire after my sister Jenny; I wish I could say I found any great
alteration in her since she has applied to Ward,[9] but really the cure
advances very slowly as yet, and I am sorry to say it, scarce sensibly. She desires you will accept of her compliments in return for
your kindness. I am, dear Horry,

Yours sincerely,

H. C.

My service to Dodd and Mr Whaley.[10]

5. Horace, *Ars poetica* ll. 351–2 ('Truly
when more things shine in a poem, I
shall not be offended by a few blemishes').

6. Ibid. ll. 26–7 ('They are deficient in
force and fire').

7. Glover had entered his father's business as a Hamburg merchant.

8. Sir Richard Temple (1675–1749), 4th
Bt, cr. (1714) Bn and (1718) Vct Cobham,
one of the principal opponents of Sir
Robert Walpole.

9. Joshua Ward (1685–1761), quack
doctor, whose 'drop and pill' was immensely popular and harmful.

10. John Whaley (1710–45), fellow of
King's 1731–45, HW's and Dodd's tutor
at King's (GRAY i. 5 and n. 20; COLE ii.
299, n. 7). Conway was apparently unaware that they were in or approaching
London (*ante* 8 March 1737, n. 2).

To CONWAY, ca Saturday 30 April 1737 OS

Missing; implied *post* 5 ?May ?1737 OS.

From CONWAY, ?Thursday 5 ?May ?1737 OS

Printed for the first time from the MS now WSL, formerly Rutnam. The date is tentative owing to the defective state of the postmark and apparent inconsistencies between this letter and that of 10 May 1737 OS. Nevertheless, this seems the most probable date for several reasons. (1) The '5' in the postmark is clear, and also part of what may be 'M' or 'A.' If 'M,' the letter would have to be May, not March, since other dateable letters make it clear that Conway was in London in late February and early March 1737, the only early March that HW seems to have been in residence at Cambridge. (2) Although from internal evidence Conway seems to be mailing the letter on a Tuesday and 5 May 1737 OS was a Thursday, Tuesday 5th April can be eliminated because Conway was in London at the end of March (*ante* 22 March 1737) and wrote HW on 7 April (*ante* 7 April 1737). (3) The absence of any definitely dateable letters between 7 April and 10 May 1737 OS makes a visit in this period likely. Gray wrote West from Cambridge 22 May 1737, 'Mr Conway has been here about a fortnight, and the little Insensible was neither struck with King's Chapel, nor moved with Trinity Quadrangle, nor touched with the Senate House, and even talked of Oxford, as he was walking on Clarehall Walks' (Leonard Whibley, 'A New Letter by Gray,' *TLS* 23 Oct. 1937, xxxvi. 776; MS now WSL). It seems that Conway arrived back in London Wednesday 27th April, visited his sister in Twickenham Thursday, wrote a 'long scrawl' on Saturday but missed the post, then wrote this letter the following Tuesday and mailed it on Thursday 5th May.

    Address: To Horatio Walpole Esquire at King's College Cambridge.
    Postmark: 5 ⟨MA⟩. PENY POST PAYD W T ⟨H⟩.

Dear Horry,

YOU have arraigned, I see, tried and condemned me as guilty of the most consummate negligence, in omitting so long the tender of my hearty thanks for the numberless favours I received from you; I wish I were able to return, as I am ready to acknowledge 'em, and I assure you I should think myself void of all civility, not to say worse of it, if I were the least backward in that duty. Yet conscious as I am of my innocence, my case is at present extremely perplexing; the uneasiness of lying under the suspicion I have incurred is intolerable, and yet I cannot without the utmost concern enter upon

my defence, since I know there can't possibly be any degrees between my being quite clear and entirely unpardonable, I mean, if
I had really been remiss in giving acknowledgments of the obligations you have laid me under, I should not have the least reason to
expect a pardon even of your good nature: but the causes of your
having not received a letter from me before were these. As you may
imagine I could not stay long in town before I went to make my
sister Jenny a visit.[1] I chose Thursday for the jaunt, without considering that it was post day; thus passed the first opportunity.[2] On
Saturday night I came up into my room and wrote you a long scrawl,
but by the mistake of an hour it was too late to send it by the post
before I had finished it: by the third post[3] since my coming to town
you have this, which I hope will be accepted with my compliments
to you and to all those who were so civil to me during my stay at
Cambridge.[4] I heartily wish it had been a little longer as you'll
guess when you hear how I travelled up. *Imprimis,* Ashton[5] can tell
you how we were packed up, six of us, and squeezed together like
Mrs Dodd's[6] prunellos;[7] for my own part I was comfortably jumbled
cheek by jowl with an immense, fat, loquacious, brandy-faced female, and she had a dear coz with her, just such an elephantess as
herself, and in every respect equal to her bating a little of the beautiful vermilion that diffused itself over her countenance. The rest
of our company were males, two striplings, a Cantab this, and that
an attorney; these with a huge humdrum left-elbow friend composed our junto. Before we had got a mile I found myself enveloped
with a wave of fat, under which the motion of the coach had

1. She was apparently at Twickenham
(*post* 10 May 1737 OS).

2. If our dating is correct, Conway had
reached London from Cambridge on
Wednesday 27 April; Tuesday the 26th
and Thursday the 28th were both post
days (see *ante* 25 Jan. 1737 OS, headnote).

3. I.e., Tuesday, 3 May; but Conway
seems to have missed it again, since the
postmark is the 5th.

4. See above, headnote.

5. Thomas Ashton (1716–75), divine;
HW's correspondent. Gray's letter to
West 22 May 1737 mentions Ashton as
being at Cambridge: 'I am qualified with
full and ample powers to treat with you
in the names of HW and A. . . . I depend upon seeing you here next month:

we have indeed nothing to show you, but
three old faces, that you have been long
used to, tho' perhaps you may find something new even in them . . . we can't
keep [our] best looks and manners long, so
make haste, I charge you' (Whibley, loc.
cit.). At the end of the letter Gray ap-
pends messages from Walpole and Ashton. On 5 April and 7 July 1737 Ashton
was at Cambridge (*Correspondence of
Gray, Walpole, West and Ashton,* ed.
Toynbee, Oxford, 1915, i. 129, 143, 146).

6. Perhaps John Dodd's mother, Margaret Glaseour, m. Randall or Randolph
Dodd (Lady Constance Russell, *Swallow-
field and Its Owners,* 1901, p. 226).

7. A variety of prunes.

nestled me, but peeping out I saw the fair nymph, who had overwhelmed me, distill from her urn, or tea-canister, as some will have
it, cherry brandy, and after every sweet mouth, and fasting, five-o'th'-
clock-in-the-morning breath had been applied to it, *itur ad me;*[8] but
I had not thoughts of imbibing anything but pure æther, and it was
not without some difficulty that I drew in a sufficient quantity of
that, for being within the atmosphere of her body, the air was so
impregnated with pinguious[9] particles, that I was hardly able to
respire; here I must beg your attention to a short episode, the subject of which is a tragic scene that passed between the two cousins,
for the sight of the brandy vessel reviving in their minds the
memory of a poor deceased dram-bottle, which being the property
of the one, was crushed I suppose by the brawny bum of the other,
a smart squabble ensued, and I don't know to ⟨what⟩ unhappy
heights their animosities might have been carried to [*sic*], had not a
fortunate jolt shook all remembrance of their grudge and the cause
of it out of their noddles. After this one of the ladies, fainting, took
out a bottle of vivifying asafœtida, the grateful effluvia of which
regaled all our nostrils most agreeably, as well as a bottle of hartshorn, which was soon after broken in the coach to the public emolument of us all. I believe one of 'em was Amalthæa[10] incog. and
what I took for a simple pocket a cornucopia, for it disembogued itself successively of twenty different stores, as raisins, almonds, ap-
ples, oranges, etc., etc. I am, dear Horry,

Yours,

H. C.

To CONWAY, ca Saturday 7 May 1737 OS

Missing; answered *post* 10 May 1737 OS.

8. Also to me.
9. Fatty, oily.
10. Zeus's nurse, owner of a she-goat whose broken horn was filled with fruit (Ovid, *Fasti* v. 115ff.).

From CONWAY, Tuesday 10 May 1737 OS

Printed for the first time from the MS now WSL, formerly Rutnam. Dated by the postmark and the mention of *Leonidas*.
Address: To Horatio Walpole Esquire at King's College Cambridge.
Postmark: 10 MA.

Dear Horry,

NOT to keep you in suspense, I will begin my letter with the fullest answers I am able to give to the questions in your last. You were so good as to make an inquiry into my sister Jenny's health the first; I cannot give you quite so satisfactory an account of it as I did in my last to you,[1] since she has had some returns of her disorder since she came to town, which I believe are in a great measure owing to her conduct. She is not, you know, the wisest manager when she is ill, nor the most cautious when she is well. At present she is much better than when she was in town before her going to Twickenham, though I doubt not quite so well as when she was there; we walked twice 'round the Park this morning and I am in hopes if she continues to use a good deal of exercise, it will facilitate, at least, if not entirely effect a cure; she has some thought of going into Warwickshire,[1a] but her great love of the town will, I am afraid, outweigh all the views of amendment in her constitution, which she may reasonably expect from the country air and exercise; I have thrown all the persuasion I am master of into the scale, and that in the most serious manner I was able, but I have not much to expect from their effect upon her; she allows 'em indeed to have a great deal of gravity but very little weight.

George Montague is not coming over; after a considerable cessation caused by my belief of his quick return, I design to write to him next post. I have not asked Sir Robert about *Leonidas* yet, but as I have not heard him mention it, I fancy he has not read it. He was talking to me today about my commission; he heard, he says, from you of my brother's kind concern for me, and desired you to tell my brother that there has not one commission in the Horse been

---

1. Perhaps in the 'long scrawl' mentioned *ante* 5 ?May ?1737 OS which Conway wrote on his return from visiting his sister at Twickenham but did not mail to HW because it was too late for the post.

1a. Presumably to Ragley, the family seat (see *post* 6 April 1746 OS, n. 2).

given away this year; there is one now vacant in the Duke of Argyle's,[2] and which Sir Robert says he'll get for me if I choose it; but there are some collateral circumstances which attend it,[3] that prevail with me rather to wait for another vacancy, than accept this, notwithstanding the advantage of an early rank; he begs you to assure my brother that he will not fail to get me in as soon as possible. I fancy you are the best judge what will be the most convenient way of conveying the monkey[4] to town. Pray tell Dodd and Mr Cole[5] I am obliged to 'em for the favour. The quantity of silver you want, which I think is two ounces, will be two or three months amassing; and I think is as dear this way as on the leaves, so if you please I will send you half a dozen books or whatever quantity you want as I sent it before. I am, dear Horry,

Yours eternally,

HEN. CONWAY

To CONWAY, mid-May 1737 OS

Missing; answered *post* ca 20–24 May 1737 OS.

From CONWAY, ca Friday 20 – Tuesday 24 May 1737 OS

Printed for the first time from the MS now WSL, formerly Rutnam. Dated by the reference to the preparation of the bill 'to restrain the licence of the stage'; leave to bring in such a bill was granted 20 May and the bill was presented and read for the first time 24 May (below, n. 5).
   Address: To Horatio Walpole Esquire at King's College Cambridge.
   Postmark: 2[?] MA.

Dear Horry,

I HAVE forwarded your letter.[1]—If I were to write a bare answer to your last, the few preceding words contain a full one; but I shall beg leave to go a little further, and be so bold as to join

2. The Royal Horse Guards (the Blues), of which John Campbell (1680–1743), 2d D. of Argyll, was Col. 1715–17, 1733–40, and 1742.
   3. Conway discusses these *post* 2 July 1737 OS when explaining why he had decided to reject this commission.
   4. Presumably the 'Pug' whose arrival in

London is discussed *post* 31 May 1737 OS.
   5. Rev. William Cole (1714–82), antiquary; HW's correspondent. He was at Eton and King's with HW.

———

   1. Perhaps to Lord Conway on the subject of Conway's commission (*ante* 10 May 1737 OS).

a little of the critic's part with that of the correspondent; upon so short a work you'll imagine my observations will not be very numerous. I have but one to make; and yet I doubt I shall not be able to contract that into so narrow a space but that, like some commentators, I shall be more voluminous than the author; and what is more odd my criticisms increase in proportion to the brevity and not length of the work that is the subject of them; this paradox would seem unsolvable, if I did not tell you that 'tis brevity alone, that I think worthy of animadversion in your letter: and this, which in some correspondents would perhaps be the most agreeable quality, is in you a fault, and the greatest you can possibly be guilty of; I freely own I cannot so entirely divest myself of all selfish views as to be contented with an 'I am well and I hope you are well, and so fare you well,' and though this gives me a great deal of satisfaction, I can't say but it receives a great addition from the sentiments with which your epistles are dictated, and the pleasing style in which they are dressed. The town has been favoured lately with the translations or rather imitations of two epistles of Horace:[2] they are pretty much liked, especially the last—*Cum tot sustineas*.[3]—They abound with a great deal of severe satire and that very personal; so much so that I think it has disgusted even those who are not at all interested; *Fuit intactis quoque cura conditione super communi*.[4]—There is a bill now preparing to be brought into the House to restrain the licence of the stage,[5] which is arrived to such an insufferable degree

---

2. Pope's *Second Epistle of the Second Book of Horace Imitated*, first advertised as 'this day is published' 28 April 1737; and his *First Epistle of the Second Book of Horace Imitated*, first advertised 19 May 1737 (*Daily Adv.* 28 April, 20 May; *London Evening Post* 17–19 May; Maynard Mack, 'Pope's Horatian Poems: Problems of Bibliography and Text,' *Modern Philology*, 1943, xli. 34, n. 12; R. H. Griffith, *Alexander Pope: A Bibliography*, Austin, Texas, 1922–7, i pt ii. 354, 361; the date of publication for the *First Epistle* given as 25 May in the last work from G. A. Aitken, 'Notes on the Bibliography of Pope,' *Transactions of the Bibliographical Society*, 1914, xii. 139, follows a later advertisement in the *Daily Gazetteer*). These Epistles are mentioned in Gray to West 22 May (Leonard Whib-

ley, 'A New Letter by Gray,' *TLS* 23 Oct. 1937, xxxvi. 776).

3. The opening words of Horace, *Epistles* II. i.

4. Horace, *Epistles* II. i. 151–2 ('Even those untouched cared about the common cause').

5. Leave to bring in this bill (the Licensing Act) was granted 20 May; it was presented and read the first time 24 May; read the second time and committed 25 May; discussed in committee on the 26th; reported, amended, and ordered engrossed on the 27th, and passed by the House of Commons on 1 June; its passage through the Lords was equally swift and it was returned to the Commons on the 8th without amendment, and received the royal assent on the 21st (*Journals of the House of Commons* xxii. 889–93, 896, 901).

of insolence, that they have not scrupled in a late play[6] to represent the King and Prince upon the stage. Such indecency certainly calls for the notice and animadversion of the legislature; and is really of the most dangerous consequence to the state; when the sovereign and the chief magistrates are publicly exposed in that light and contemptible manner, it must greatly lessen the authority of the government, and may by the increase of such a liberty tend to the subversion of it. I am, dear Horry,

Yours sincerely,

H. C.

Selwyn gives his service to you and my sister Jenny desires her compliments and a great many thanks for your kind inquiries after her: I beg mine to all friends at Cambridge; and I desire you would tell Dodd he has not made good his promise of writing to me: you gave me no answer about the silver.

From CONWAY, Tuesday 31 May 1737 OS

Printed for the first time from the MS now WSL, formerly Rutnam. Dated by the postmark and the assumption that the 'Pug' of this letter is the monkey mentioned *ante* 10 May 1737 OS.
Address: To Horatio Walpole Esquire at King's College Cambridge.
Postmark: 31 MA.

Dear Horry,

PUG is arrived very safely in town; and had she been used as tenderly and civilly here as she was upon the road might have been now in a state of perfect health; but unfortunately since her arrival she has been very roughly treated by a boisterous shaggy dog, an inseparable friend and companion of Tom Pudden;[1] I have made strict inquiry into the cause and rise of the quarrel, but as there are always parties formed on these important occasions, I have not been able to get a fair and impartial account of the transaction. Pudden

---

6. Probably *The Golden Rump*, which was never acted or printed, but was used as the occasion for the Licensing Act; see the accounts collected in Cobbett, *Parl. Hist.* x. 319–41, and D. E.

Baker, I. Reed, and S. Jones, *Biographia Dramatica*, 1812, ii. 267–8.

1. Not identified.

maintains the innocence of his dog; others on the contrary affirm, with great plausibility too, that he offered unpardonable incivilities to the lady; those who pretend to be best informed tell the affair with the following circumstances: they say that he was so uncourtly as to attempt great freedoms with her at the first interview, and that without saying the least word in order to break the matter to her, or making so much as the common compliments of congratulation upon her arrival in town; the fair on the other hand knowing that the Cambridge beauties are not usually attacked with such forward petulance, secure as she thought under the protection of her sex and virtue, punished his impertinence with a severe box on the left ear; but he, naturally choleric, and not used to meet with such rustic coyness amongst the females (having spent greatest part of his youthful days in town), could not brook the affront and instead of cringing at the feet of his cruel mistress, like some passive lovers, flew upon her with the most impetuous violence, and gave her a smart gripe on her forehead. The Fates have dealt kindly by her and mankind in preserving her life, while her beauty is so much impaired by the accident, that I may venture to say it will not be very destructive for the future.

I am, dear Horry,

Your sincere friend,

H. C.

From CONWAY, Saturday 11 June 1737 OS

Printed for the first time from the MS now WSL, formerly Rutnam. Dated by the postmark and the reference to the Hon. Catherine Conway's illness.

Address: To Horatio Walpole Esquire at King's College Cambridge.

Postmark: 11 IV.

Dear Horry,

I AM sorry to preface my letter with a piece of bad news, such at least as cannot but appear so to me; the smallpox broke out upon my sister Kitty[1] the day before yesterday. You may guess by the

1. Hon. Catherine (or Catharine or Katharine) Conway (1709 – 14 June 1737), Conway's half-sister (*Miscellanea genealo-* *gica et heraldica,* 1890, 2d ser., iii. 25, 58). 'On Tuesday morning [14 June] died after a few days illness at the Earl of Claren-

common course of the distemper that I cannot as yet give you a clear account of the sort; she has both Doctor Hollins[2] and Dr Bloxome[3] with her; they say they are not yet ⟨ab⟩le to determine whether it will be a good or bad sort, but by the symptoms and the number already come out, they imagine it will be neither the best, nor worst, but rather a mixed sort. The pains in her head and back, which were pretty violent, decrease gradually; her throat is somewhat sore; she sleeps very well; and, as far as it is possible to judge when the distemper is so little advanced, seems in a fair way to have all the success we can desire; as to life I mean; which so nearly concerns me, that it makes the other consideration of ladies[4] in this disease appear so very trifling, as not require anything upon it were I able to give any guess at the event.

You'll excuse me if I add no more than what Selwyn and Lord Holderness have insisted upon my saying—that both of them would have writ to you before had not business prevented one, and illness the other. I am, dear Horry,

Yours sincerely,

H. C.

My service to Dodd, and other friends; I received his letter.

To CONWAY, June 1737

Missing; 'letters' mentioned *post* 23 June 1737 OS.

don and Rochester's house in St James's Square, the Hon. Mrs Catherine Conway, sister to the Right Hon. the Lord Conway, now abroad on his travels' (*London Evening Post* 14–16 June; GM 1737, vii. 371).

2. John Hollings (ca 1683–1739), M.D., 1710; physician-general to the army and physician in ordinary to the King.

3. Probably Noel Broxholme (ca 1686–1748), M.D., 1723; physician to the Prince of Wales (DNB, corrected by references cited MANN iii. 250, n. 27). See HW's comments on him in a letter to Montagu 25 July 1748 (MONTAGU i. 66), where HW spells his name Bloxholme.

4. Disfigurement.

From CONWAY, Thursday 23 June 1737 OS

Printed for the first time from the MS now WSL, formerly Rutnam. Dated by the postmark and the reference to the Hon. Catherine Conway's death.

Address: To Horatio Walpole Esquire at King's College Cambridge.

Postmark: 23 IV.

Dear Horry,

NOTHING but so extraordinary an emergency as I have lately sighed under[1] should have kept me so long silent, especially when the affectionate letters I have received from you called for the earliest acknowledgments I could make of your kindness—which was so great that, had I consulted my own interest only, or could I have done it without giving you any share in it, I should have chose to communicate to you every pang I felt, every tear I shed for the loss of so deserving a woman, so kind a sister, and so agreeable a companion: I should have been happy in an opportunity of mitigating my own care could I have done it without augmenting yours, but the knowledge of your consummate good nature, as well as the repeated assurances of concern which you made me in your last, not only immediately, but mediately through me for her loss, convince me it was impracticable.—Thus denied that alleviation, I sequestered my mind from all commerce and conversation, which at another time, on a less sorrowful occasion, might have amused and diverted, if not delighted it; I shut myself up with my sister Jenny the first week; this you may imagine was giving an entire loose to my concern; but as my melancholy was not so excessive as hers, I was in hopes of bringing hers down upon a level with my own, but I found the contrary was rather the case; and in our griefs, when blended, as in liquors, the strongest prevailed; and as in them time causes the spirit to evaporate and the strength to diminish, our outward show of concern is in a great measure lessened, though we cannot but still retain a lively image of the loss we have sustained. The first squall of passion is indeed abated, but a more settled and even care still keeps our minds ruffled, and that not on the surface only.

1. His half-sister Catherine's death on 14 June.

—I cannot pretend at present to amuse you with any diverting subject: *Nostri quid agant nisi triste libelli?*[2]—So conclude

Yours ever most affectionately,

H. C.

Tell Dodd I will certainly answer his letter soon; and desire he would accept of my compliments in the meantime.

To LORD CONWAY, late June 1737

Missing; a letter of condolence on the death of the Hon. Catherine Conway, mentioned *post* 2 July 1737 OS.

To CONWAY, late June 1737

Missing; mentioned *post* 2 July 1737 OS.

From CONWAY, Saturday 2 July 1737 OS

Printed for the first time from the MS now WSL, formerly Rutnam. Dated by the postmark and the references to the death of Catherine Conway.
Address: To Horatio Walpole Esquire at King's College Cambridge.
Postmark: 2 IY.

Dear Horry,

I COULD almost wish I had it in my power to break your injunction in relation to detaining your letter to my brother, writ, as you inform me, with the charitable intent of condoling with him on the unexpected stroke of his sister's death; I mean, I wish an account of that fatal event had not been already sent by me to Mr Bowman;[1] which, if it has not yet, must certainly reach Geneva

---

2. 'What can our letters be about, unless it be the sad' (Ovid, *Tristia* 5. 1. 47).

1. Walter Bowman (d. 1782), antiquary, was Lord Conway's travelling tutor and,

long before yours can possible arrive. If that sad truth can admit of
any alleviation, if any artful softenings of diction, any happy turns
of expression can give the least mixture of sweet to that bitter
draught, I know no hand I should sooner pitch upon to mix the
cup than your own; as it is, I shall take the first opportunity of
forwarding it, which will be this night's post; I could not answer to
him deferring a moment the pleasure he will receive from it; I know
by experience with what healing skill you touch a brother's heart
bleeding with the stroke of that shaft that took a beloved sister from
him and the world forever. Whilst the common herd of correspondents (to whom I am conscious of my too near alliance), like un-
skillful chirurgeons bungling with those sad instruments, the usual
dull compliments of condolence always enlarge the wound they attempt to close.

After the great kindness I have received both from you and my
brother with respect to my going into the army as soon as possible
in order to the having it in my power to meet him in France, it will
be incumbent upon me to give my reasons for not accepting the
cornetcy that is vacant in the Duke of Argyle's regiment: and first,
instead of forwarding, it will entirely obstruct and subvert my design of going into France; for if we consider in the first place what
a strict preserver of discipline he is naturally; in the next, what an
invincible and unparalleled regard he has for Sir Robert[2] and of
course anybody that bears any relation to or has any dependence on
him; thirdly, that he has a minion[3] of his own with whom he wants
to fill up this vacancy, and that he is so much averse to my having
this commission that he has threatened to throw up his own if
it is given me; it is more than probable that he would confine me for
two years not only in England but to the most disagreeable situation in England—country quarters—where it will be in his power to
behave in a rigid disagreeable manner, and subject me perhaps to

many years later, travelling tutor to his
son Lord Beauchamp (DNB, supplemented
by *post* 24 March 1739 NS and 11 Oct.
1760).

2. Argyll had been a leader of the
opposition to Sir Robert Walpole since
1733.

3. Probably either Hugh Forbes or
George Eyres, whose commissions as cor-
nets in Argyll's regiment are dated 18

July 1737 OS, or Henry Rolt whose commission is dated 12 Aug. 1737 OS (Society
for Army Historical Research, *The Army
List of 1740*, Sheffield, 1931, p. 6). According to this army list, Conway had
been commissioned a lieutenant in Lord
Molesworth's Dragoons (16th/5th Lancers)
on 27 June 1737 OS (ibid. 65), but this
letter suggests that that commission must
have been antedated.

some of his dear countrymen[4] who have always an ungovernable itch after command, and sometimes not the most gentle method of exercising it; in short, an Englishman among a company of Scotch is like a genius surrounded with an herd of dunces; they stick together in a most profound confederacy, and when they can pick a hole in his garment, take pains to widen it; when they cannot, will either make, or suppose o⟨ne⟩[5] to accuse him of; in having such company there might be this advantage, that I should have no company at all; I should be as much alone as they would let me; but there is commonly that agreeable quality in bad company that when they see themselves avoided the ⟨mean⟩ fail to pursue. I speak this in general of that part of the Scotch that are in the army; I doubt not there are many worthy exceptions. A part of what I have said may perhaps be ill grounded, and half the difficulties I have raised only imaginary, but if your own judgment will extract what is real, probable at least, out of this rude hypothesis, I believe you will think it sufficient to make me persevere in my resolution of not accepting it. Excuse my tedious impertinence and believe me

Yours ever,

H. C.

From CONWAY, late August 1737

Missing; Conway doubtless wrote a letter of condolence to HW on his mother's death 20 August.

---

4. Conway's implication that Argyll's regiment was staffed chiefly by Scots does not seem to be borne out by the list of officers in 1740 (ibid. 6).

5. MS torn.

From CONWAY, Saturday 10 September 1737 OS

Printed for the first time from the MS now WSL, formerly Rutnam. Dated by the postmark and the reference to the duel at Florence.

Address: To Horatio Walpole Esquire at King's College Cambridge.

Postmark: 10 SE.

Dear Horry,

NOT to be worse than my word, I give you this short trouble to inform of what further account I have had of the affair at Florence,[1] and am happy that I can give you so favourable an one: Mr Wright[2] was the only man killed,[3] who by the character I hear

---

1. This affair, which seems to have been more or less suppressed in London, is fully described in a letter from Charles Fane, British Resident at Florence, to Newcastle 26 Aug. NS: 'Denis Wright, often mentioned in letters to your Grace from hence, was unfortunately killed by Mr Fotheringham a gentleman of Scotland and of a family extremely well-known by all the people of that country who are at present here. Both of these were present at a public dinner amongst the English here on the 18th instant and had drank exceedingly when Mr Fotheringham proposed playing at cards to my Lord Middlesex: Wright who had long since attached himself particularly to my Lord endeavoured to dissuade his Lordship from that proposal, and persevered to do it with so much warmth as to give offence to Mr Fotheringham, and from words they soon came to blows; they were then however parted and Wright went downstairs, but soon after unluckily returning into the room where Mr Fotheringham continued, the latter caught up an hanger and ran towards him. My Lord Middlesex stopped him, and put himself betwixt them. Mr Fotheringham finding himself stopped, threw the hanger over my Lord's shoulder and gave Wright a deep wound in the body, after which Wright with the same hanger notwithstanding the attempts of Lord Middlesex to prevent it struck Fotheringham on the head and cut through part of his skull as is related in the enclosed account given by the physician who attended them.

... Poor Wright two days after expired of his wounds, on which the government conniving at his departure, Fotheringham withdrew to Lucca where he now is, without other dangerous symptoms than the extreme melancholy into which he is fallen on account of so unfortunate an accident. I am informed that Wright after having expressed great concern for having wounded Fotheringham, signed the day before his death a paper which he sent to Fotheringham assuring the world that no rancour or enmity had ever subsisted between them before this unlucky affair, which he therefore could impute to no other cause than the transports of a sudden passion heightened by excess of drinking' (S.P. 98/40, ff. 179–80, received in London 3 Sept. OS). A slightly earlier and incomplete report had been sent by a Mr Rhodes to John Couraud, under-secretary of state, on 20 Aug. NS (S.P. 98/40, f. 175; received in London 24 Aug. OS). The fray is also mentioned in a letter from W. Bristow to the Countess of Denbigh, Venice, 4 Sept. NS (Hist. MSS Comm., *Denbigh MSS,* 1911, p. 221).

2. Denis Wright (d. 1737), described in the medical report on his death as about 50 years old (S.P. 98/40, f. 181). A description of Fotheringham's petition for a royal pardon for the murder gives the name as Dennis Wright or M'Intyre (A. J. Warden, *Angus or Forfarshire,* Dundee, 1880–5, v. 19).

3. One report, current in London at this time, stated that a Capt. Ponsonby had also been killed (*Dublin News Letter*

of him[4] will not be much missed; the man that killed him was one Fotheringay;[5] my Lord Middlesex,[6] Lord Sandwich[7] and Lord Sherrard Manners[8] bore no part in the fray though they were all present.[9] Fotheringay has made his escape[10] so that the thing will have no worse consequence than the death of Wright. I wish [I] could have the pleasure of hearing that you are arrived safely at Cambridge[11] before I go,[12] but as our departure is now fixed for Monday I cannot expect that happiness. Mrs Grosvenor[13] and Molly[14] give their duty and respects to you. If I added anything more I should be too late for the post so beg you'll excuse me and believe me with greatest sincerity, dear Horry, your most affectionate friend

H. C.

Selwyn gives his service.

13–17 Sept. OS, *sub* London 8 and 10 Sept.).

4. W. Bristow describes him as 'homme de peu de reputation, depuis longtemps en Italie et depuis un an toujours avec Lord Middlesex' (*Denbigh MSS*, loc. cit.). The frequent references to him in the dispatches from Florence alluded to by Fane (above, n. 1) have not been found in the microfilms available to the editors.

5. Correctly Fotheringham. He is perhaps Thomas Fothringham or Fotheringham (d. 1790), of Pourie or Powrie, Angus (Burke's *Landed Gentry*, ed. L. G. Pine, 1952, p. 904); the family, predominantly Jacobite at this time, had long been prominent in Angus (Warden, op. cit. iii. 404–7, v. 16–21). Warden describes his petition for a royal pardon for the 'unpremeditated murder' of Wright which apparently gives his name as Thomas, but thinks it only 'probable' that he was connected with the Powrie family (ibid. v. 19–20); no other reference to this petition has been found.

6. Charles Sackville (1711–69), styled E. of Middlesex 1720–65; 2d D. of Dorset, 1765.

7. John Montagu (1718–92), 4th E. of Sandwich.

8. Lord Sherard Manners (ca 1713–42), M.P. Tavistock 1741–2.

9. Their presence is confirmed by Rhodes's letter to Couraud 20 Aug. NS, which also mentions Lord Raymond as a witness (S.P. 98/40, f. 175).

10. He had retired to Lucca with the connivance of the Florentine government (above, n. 1).

11. HW had just returned to Cambridge 'out of a house which I could not bear' (HW to Charles Lyttelton 18 Sept. 1737 OS) because of the death of his mother 20 Aug.

12. To Ireland; 'On Monday [12 Sept.] Edward Walpole, Esq. and Mr Conway, brother to the Lord Conway, set out together for Ireland' (*Dublin Gazette* 20–4 Sept., *sub* London, 13, 15, 17 Sept.).

13. Anne Grosvenor (1679–1750), friend of Lady Walpole; under-housekeeper (1738) and housekeeper (1739) of Somerset House (GRAY i. 220, n. 17).

14. Unidentified. Possibly the Hon. Mary Townshend (*post* 31 Oct. 1741 OS, n. 23).

From Conway, ca Wednesday 28 September 1737 OS

Printed for the first time from the MS now WSL, formerly Rutnam. Dated by Conway's statement that he arrived in Dublin 'on Saturday last' (see below, n. 1); the date stamp is a London postmark, the date that the letter passed through London. News from Dublin dated 28 Sept. and 1 Oct. was printed in the *London Evening Post* 11–13 Oct.; Conway's letter probably arrived in the same post which brought these items.

Address: To Horatio Walpole Esquire at King's College Cambridge England.
Postmark: 12 OC DUBLIN.

Dublin.

Dear Horry,

I ARRIVED here on Saturday last:[1] in this time you may imagine I have not been able to inform myself of many particulars either with respect to this town or its people, especially as I had all my acquaintance to make when I came here. The town itself seems to be in no respect equal to London: not half so big, half so grand, half so clean, half so rich; there is an appearance of poverty and beggary in most parts, and I think nothing splendid or magnificent in any, at least in those that I have seen. The people are extremely civil, and hospitable; I find no fault with them but that they are too much so; wherever you go, they think there is no other way of entertaining you well but that of stuffing you up to the eyes, and in order to carry it off they never fail to drench you with a bottle of wine. As I hate drinking I made it my business to inquire if there was no set of company that was free from this excess; surely I thought I shall be sheltered from it by creeping within the shadow of a broad beaver or episcopal robe; I will not say how much I was disappointed, but really our primates and prelates are as jovial a set of men as any in the country; the broad thumb of a bishop worn flat with turning over Bibles and Fathers can upon occasion hold a glass most tenaciously; and as Venus and Bacchus enjoy a joint empire here, they don't scruple to own their subjection to the one while they are making themselves slaves to the other: a primate[2] will toast

1. Edward Walpole, with whom Conway was travelling, arrived at Dublin on Saturday, 24 Sept. (*Dublin News Letter* 24–27 Sept. OS).

2. The current primate of Ireland was Hugh Boulter (1672–1742), Bp of Bristol 1719–24, Abp of Armagh and primate of Ireland 1724–42.

his nymph with all the gaiety of one-and-twenty. With this they are most of them men of great learning and parts, good preachers and such as make a very considerable figure in their function.

I need not wish you better in point of health than when I saw you but I hope to hear that the uneasiness of your mind3 is somewhat abated: if I thought you could bear our company with tolerable patience I should wish you here; I don't know a better antidote to thought and reflection than the jollity of wine and Irish friends; how much self-interest I have in such a wish I need not tell you, as I hope you are not ignorant that nobody would be [more] happy in your company than your affectionate friend

H. C.

I beg my service to Dodd and Mr Whaley: other friends.

To CONWAY, early November 1737

Missing; answered *post* ca 20 Nov. 1737 OS.

From CONWAY, ca Sunday 20 November 1737 OS

Printed for the first time from the MS now WSL, formerly Rutnam. Dated by the reference to the reports that the Queen was 'past recovery.' The news of the crisis in the Queen's health on 12 Nov. reached Dublin on the 19th (see below, n. 2); news from Dublin as late as the 19th was printed in the *London Evening Post* 26–9 Nov. The date stamp is a London postmark.

Address: To Horatio Walpole Esquire at King's College Cambridge England. Free Edward Walpole [in Edward Walpole's hand].

Postmark: 28 NO.

Dear Horry:

I AM much obliged to you for your kind letter and especially that part of it, for which you seem quite unnecessarily to make an excuse, and call it rattling me off. I assure you it appears to me all panegyric; at least, if there is anything bitter in your poem1 it is so artfully concealed in the pleasant vehicle that conveys it, that I

---

3. Because of his mother's death.

1. Missing. HW did not transcribe a copy of it in his MS *Poems*.

am unable to distinguish where it lies. To say that I have that laudable spirit of jealousy and emulation which ought to fire the breast of a dragoon is certainly a compliment, and, to say the truth, a much greater than I deserve; I have read the histories of Cæsar and Alexander without heaving one ambitious sigh, much less have I ever conceived any jealousy of the fame acquired by my heroic countryman; nor have I been forward to form any bloody design against our neighbour France, and though I could be assured that he had the justice of Aristides, the policy of Ulysses and the magnanimity of Leonidas, I should not think it incumbent upon me, as wearing a cockade, to use my endeavours in order to the punishing him for being great and good, which doubtless are crimes of a high nature in the eyes of an officer, and the suppressing 'em a true military principle.

I should not discover this my weakness to you but that I know you will be so good as not to divulge a secret which I have imparted to you in confidence, and which if known must entirely spoil my fortune in the army and ruin me in the opinion of my brother soldiers. I cannot help, too, disowning any title to the pretty compliment you make me in the end of your poem; I might perhaps by taking great pains to be impertinent acquire the character of a scholard at quarters, or so, but despair of any esteem amongst the learned except from their good nature. I am sorry to hear that you have not yet got the better of your grief, but not without hopes that time with the assistance of your own prudence and the just reflections you are able to make upon the unprofitableness of your concern will extricate you from it. Don't think what a mother you have lost but how good a father you still have, than whom as nobody is more able, so I am sure nobody is more willing to make you happy. By our last packets we hear that the Queen is past recovery.[2] I am extremely concerned at the news, as I know how necessary she was, especially at this time.[3] Another account came, too, that tells us Sir Robert has a fit of the gout at Houghton;[4] I am sure he'll want much

---

2. Queen Caroline d. 20 Nov. 1737; her life had been despaired of on the 11th and reports to this effect had reached Dublin on the 19th (*Dublin News Letter* and *Dublin Journal* 15–19 Nov.).

3. The Queen had been one of Sir Robert's principal allies.

4. This report was untrue. An express had been sent to Sir Robert at Houghton on the 11th; he arrived in London on the 14th and visited the Queen at her bedside (John, Lord Hervey, *Memoirs*, ed. Sedgwick, 1931, iii. 883, 898).

to ⟨see⟩ the Queen before she dies, and the impossibility of their meeting, if that account be true, may perhaps be of ill consequence. I will conclude with repeating my wishes that you were with us in Dublin, as I am sure no place is more calculated for the dispelling of grief. I hardly believe that there is one set of very grave men in the whole city, nor yet does their gaiety often run to any vicious extravagance. I really question if there is a town in the world so large and populous as Dublin, guilty of so little wickedness of any kind. I am, dear Horry,

Yours sincerely,

H. C.

To CONWAY, ca Thursday 8 March 1739 OS

Missing; answered *post* 24 March 1739 NS. Since Conway, who was in France, wrote by the first post after receiving this letter, it must have been written about the 8th OS.

From CONWAY, Tuesday 24 March 1739 NS

Printed for the first time from the MS now WSL, formerly Rutnam. Dated by the reference to HW's imminent departure for Paris: he and Gray left Dover at noon 29 March NS and reached Calais by five o'clock; they proceeded to Boulogne 30 March NS (GRAY i. 162, n. 1).

Address: À Monsieur Monsieur Walpole cavalier anglais recommandé au maître du Lion d'Argent auberge à Calais pour y être conservé jusqu'à son arrivée d'Angleterre. À Calais.

Tuesday, 24.

Dear Horry,

YOUR letter arrived so late that it was impossible you should receive an answer to it at London if you set out near the time you proposed: I now write by the first post since I received yours and am in some fear that this will come too late even to meet with you at Calais; if what it contains could have been of service to you upon the road I shall be sorry; if not I should be glad it came as much too late as possible since I shall have the pleasure of seeing you so much sooner. I desired Mr Bowman to give you the directions enclosed;[1] I think there is nothing material to be added to them; you must order your chaise to be well greased every night at least, or oftener if there is necessity; take care that your servants don't put any contraband goods about the chaise. If you are two in the chaise they will oblige you to pay as much for two horses as if you put in three, so that it is better commonly to order them beforehand to put in three;[2] but if the roads are very good they'll go as well with two. As to the money I fancy you'll not find any great difficulty about that as it is much upon the same footing with ours. A louis is near of the same value as an English guinea, a six-livre piece as a crown, a three-livre piece as a half crown, a piece of 24 sols as a shilling, and one of twelve as a sixpence. A louis is worth 24 livres or four great crowns. A great crown or six-livre piece six livres. A livre is worth 20 sols. The common change that you will meet with are twelve-sous pieces, pieces of one sol and a half and liards or farthings.

Yours, dear Horry,

H. C.

I can't guess who the gentleman is that comes with you;[3] but I have some suspicion that I shall see an old acquaintance though you were not so kind as to tell me so. My brother gives his service.

[Enclosure]

Directions for Mr Walpole's Journey

If any of his servants is acquainted with the route particular directions for so short a way are of little use. At the custom house of Calais order every piece of baggage wherein there is nothing necessary on the road to be sealed with the custom house mark or lead called *plombé*. With this at Nampont and Montreuil baggage passes unopened and enters easily into Paris with a written *passavant*,

1. Printed below.
2. HW followed this advice (Thomas

Gray, *Correspondence*, ed. Toynbee and Whibley, Oxford, 1935, i. 99).
3. It was Gray.

marking the pieces so sealed. But the seat of the chaise and all other open things are still liable to be searched, and all tea, coffee, chocolate, tobacco and things new are liable to seizure, but all passes easily if either declared at Calais and in the *passavant* marked for use, or where questions are asked on the road by answering that gentlemen never are stopped and searched especially as the *passavant* shows the baggage to have been searched already and nothing left out for sale but for use on the road. The solidity of such an answer is irresistible when politely supported by a piece of money. For search being made nothing is paid, the *foulons* obey order, do their duty, that's their recompense. The same method is used at the gates of Paris. On all such occasions strangers should talk with great assurance, but with greater civility.

Grandsire at the Lyon d'Argent and the other chaise merchants seldom are well provided with chaises proper for purchase. By accident sometimes they have good ones but their best are only to be bought by the advice of a connoisseur. The hire of a double chaise to Paris is 3 louis, the hirer standing to all reparations from the receipt to the delivery, wherefore all pieces of harness, tackle and everything belonging to it ought to be in good order. A double chaise pays 4 livres 10 sols postage each post. That is for 3 horses at 30 sols each, but in good roads runs best with only two. Each saddle horse pays 20 sols, the same as horses for single chaises, which only pay 2 livres a post at the rate of two horses at 20 sols each. Wherefore 2 single chaises run as cheap as one double; and by dividing of baggage go lighter and faster. Two trunks and one portmantle is a sufficient load for a double chaise.

To run easily, overnight prepare something cold for eating all next day, for there's no stopping for hot dinners. The places for lying at are Bologne, Montreuil, Abbéville, Amiens, Breteuil, St Just, Clermont, Chantilly, Lusarche and any other place near Paris. By setting out from Calais in the morning, the route is divided so as to be at Montreuil, Amiens and Clermont. By setting out after dinner, so as to lie at Boulogne, L'Ecu de Brabant at Abbéville and at Clermont; but to reach Clermont the third day one must in a double chaise be betwixt 11 and 12 hours on the road; wherefore set out as early as possible in case of accidents. By being early one always may manage so as to walk on foot through Bologne, while the chaise makes the circuit of the upper town, and fetch a peep into the cathedral. There was a Roman pharo at the point, now demolished. The situation of Montreuil is pretty. At Abbéville to see the woollen manufacture of Van Robeis stop near the gate and take a guide while the chaise goes to the post-house. At Amiens the cathedral is a good gothic piece. By making 4 days of it the Duke of Bourbon's house and gardens at Chantilly may be seen at leisure.

This road is cheap compared to England, but dear for France. Inns are paid as in England because frequented only by English. But the paying for beds is a gross imposition. Travellers bespeak what they want and bargain beforehand when they think it worth while.

As for the posts, there are post-books to be bought at Calais. Without them no master dares impose. The regulation for the postilion is 5 sols, but they are paid 10. We give 'em 2, 3 or 4 sols more for their proper drink money as they deserve it. Where the post-house is good it is best lying there for ready service in the morning. In bad roads for a double chaise sometimes they'll put four horses; the payment of the fourth horse is but 20 sols and both this and the second postilion is arbitrary as the case requires. Send a servant before to prepare the horses, first come first served. In case of a dispute with the postmaster call for his printed orders. With a postilion money is the only reason at least till one is used to France.

At Paris drive to the Petit Hôtel d'Entragues,[4] rue de Condé, Fauxbourg St Germain, against the Hôtel de Provence. There an apartment consisting of 6 pieces is hired from the first of March. Send to my Lord or Mr Conway[5] or Mr Bowman at the Hôtel de Bretagne, rue Croix des petits Champs. The landlady has the direction. If none of them be in the way, she will order supper, etc. The same servant who was with Mr Montague[6] is ready for Mr Walpole. There are no apartments to be found near the Hôtel de Bretagne, and with equipages at Paris every place is near.

I have forgot the treasure and curiosities of St Dennis but at

4. By 21 April NS Gray and HW were lodged at the Hôtel de Luxembourg, rue des Petits Augustins, faubourg Saint-Germain (Gray to Ashton 21 April 1739 NS, in Gray, op. cit. i. 106).

5. Gray describes his and HW's arrival in Paris on Saturday 4 April in a letter to West 12 April NS: 'On Saturday evening we got to Paris, and were driving through the streets a long while before we knew where we were. The minute we came,

voilà Milors Holdernesse, Conway, and his brother; all stayed supper, and till two o'clock in the morning' (ibid. i. 102).

6. George Montagu, who was travelling with Lord Conway when they invited HW to accompany them to Italy ca Feb. 1737; see HW to Montagu 20 March 1737, MONTAGU i. 9. In Aug. 1739 Montagu and George Selwyn joined HW's party in Rheims (GRAY i. 180 and n. 18).

night they are not to be seen, and being so near town strangers see 'em in parties at more leisure. Any part of baggage that cannot be brought with the chaise may be sent with the Calais coach, and under a direction will be found here either where the coach sets up or at the custom house. But a servant must see it registered in the books of the coach at Calais after it is sealed by the custom house.

HW writes in 'Short Notes' that 'after a stay of about two months' at Paris, he and Gray 'went with my cousin Henry Conway to Rheims in Champagne, stayed there three months, and passing by Geneva, where we left Mr Conway, Mr Gray and I went by Lyons to Turin over the Alps' (GRAY i. 8–9).

At the end of April 1739 Lord Conway returned to London (ibid. i. 166, n. 34), and Gray, HW, and Conway stayed together in Paris until 1 June, when they departed for Rheims (ibid. i. 166, n. 44). On 7 Sept. the three left Rheims, travelling south toward Dijon, where they arrived 9 Sept. (see Gray, *Correspondence*, ed. Toynbee and Whibley, Oxford, 1935, i. 116–17 and nn. 2, 3). After four days they went on to Lyons (GRAY i. 180, n. 20). Their journey continued through the Dauphiné and Savoy, and on 30 Sept. HW wrote West from Aix-les-Bains (ibid. i. 181). Reaching Geneva 2 Oct. (ibid. i. 183), HW and Gray 'stayed about a week [there], in order to see Mr Conway settled' (Gray to Philip Gray 25 Oct. NS, Gray, op. cit. i. 123), and then departed for Lyons, whence they reached Turin the evening of 7 Nov. 1739 NS (GRAY i. 9, n. 49, 188, n. 1).

To CONWAY, ca Sunday 8 November 1739 NS

Missing; written from Turin, probably soon after HW's arrival there.

From Conway, Wednesday 18 November 1739 NS

Printed for the first time from the MS now WSL, formerly Rutnam. Dated by the reference to the 'rape of poor Tory.'

[Geneva], 18th.

FULL of the grief I feel for the rape of poor Tory[1] you'll excuse me, dear Horry, if I write you a very dull letter; it shan't be a letter of condolence, nor will I seal it with black wax, but like its author it shall carry its sadness not [in] its habits but in its countenance and in the very heart and bowels. But is it possible that it should be true? Poor little soul! Swallowed like Tom Thumb by a wolf of more than ordinary size? You painted it with such eloquence that it would have drawn tears from a stone. His being on the top of a vast precipice; running just before the horses' heads; its being broad sunshine; the size of the wolf etc. seem to be circumstances maliciously chosen to make me not p—ss this ten days. You don't conceive that immediately? But the same old nurse who would send things to heaven for being too good to stay on earth would tell you *the more you cry,* etc. *Défendez-vous au moins de croire que je badine;* and consider that one's never so figurative as when one's agitated by violent passions; this all our English tragedies may teach you. I had like to have forgot the fir-grove which is certainly a circumstance which fills the mind with horror, and prepares it for the great event that follows, and that little bark pierced my heart with grief! and was more moving than if he had made a dying speech of an 100 pages. I beg to know if you design him an apotheosis *à la payenne* or a canonization *à la bonne catholique?* His exit was so extraordinary that I can't be content unless you make it miraculous: which is not difficult; for instance, suppose you make Diana transgress the laws of chastity and send a wolf, which are certainly her dogs, and as much her humble servants without doubt as the eagle is Jupiter's, to invite him *à la vainqueure.* Perhaps the dear little jetty rogue enjoys the post of cup-bearer and is at this moment giving *à boire* to her Chastity. Console yourself with this idea. For me,

1. HW's black spaniel, given him by Lord Conway in Paris, had been seized by a wolf 'on the top of one of the highest Alps, by the side of a wood of firs' on 5 Nov. NS (GRAY i. 189–90; see also Gray to Mrs Gray 7 Nov. 1739 NS in Thomas Gray, *Correspondence,* ed. Toynbee and Whibley, Oxford, 1935, i. 125–6).

I am now perfectly c⟨onv⟩inced of the fact and desire you'll direct to him *chez* Diana. Tell him I was just going to write to him before his preferment but that at present I am afraid he will be too proud of his company to receive a letter from the humblest of mortals.

You ask me if I am solving a problem or getting into my chaise? I may tell you neither, in one sense, since I am much more agreeably employed in writing to my dear Horry; don't take this as a compliment for I assure you it would not be worth your taking if you knew how little inclination I have at present either for one or t'other; in another sense I can say I am doing both for I am solving problems *en attendant,* till I receive a letter which I expect to call me away, not so much on account of the war[2] for you know our laurels don't grow in winter; in the spring I'll ride post to get a sprig of the first that grows and if I don't find a mistress at whose feet to lay it you may assure yourself of it or at least promise yourself a leaf or the trimmings of the garland. For ne⟨ws⟩ I refer you to the gazettes which are the only fountains I draw from at present: as for those of my correspondents, they flowed with such violence, as I believe I told you one post, that since that they seem all dried up. I can tell you however for certain that the Duke of Manchester is dead[3] and that there was actually a fracas;[4] the circumstances are still undistinguishable, from a cloud of various reports.

As to us we live a sort of a as it were, a *vie nonchalante,* and I can retort upon you, *je m'ennuie un peu dans ce pays-ci;* we have societies which may be shaken in a bag with your conversations and for public spectacles, the English are to act a play, two plays. You'll guess I'm not of 'em; you guess right for several reasons and first because I don't expect to stay here. Alsworth[5] is here and does Phocias.[6] You know the play; *Macbeth* is the other: I find such

2. England had declared war on Spain 23 Oct. 1739 OS.

3. On 21 Oct. 1739 OS at Bath (*Daily Adv.* 23 Oct.). Mrs Delany writes Lady Throckmorton 26 Sept. 1739, 'There is not a couple in London but grow happily indifferent in six months! and if they drag the chain as many years, *what joy it is to part!* A present instance is the Duchess of Manchester; her Duke is dying, and do you think she'll spoil her eyes with crying? No, no; she has better employment for them' (Mary Granville,

Mrs Delany, *Autobiography and Correspondence,* ed. Lady Llanover, 1861–2, ii. 62).

4. Unexplained.

5. Richard Neville Aldworth (after 1762, Neville) (1717–93), HW's contemporary at Eton (MANN iv. 7, n. 2; Namier and Brooke ii. 15).

6. In *The Siege of Damascus* by John Hughes (1677–1720). An account of the plays by Aldworth himself is in [W. Coxe], *Literary Life . . . of Benjamin Stillingfleet,* 1811, i. 75–80.

pleasure in writing to you that did not my watch and my paper and my conscience admonish me I should never have done.

Yours ever.

Service to Grey.

PS. Tell me dear whether you're in earnest about tosh.[7] You fright I!

I don't hear from poor Selwyn. This really concerns me.

From Conway, ca Thursday 25 February 1740 NS

Printed for the first time from the MS now wsl, formerly Rutnam. Dated by the reference to the departure of the French cardinals for Rome (below, n. 16).

Address: À Monsieur Mons. Walpole recommandé à Mons. Monsieur Man[1] chargé des affaires de sa Majesté Britannique à Florence.

Postmark: [Illegible].

Paris.

Dear Horry,

I DON'T know what fatuity has hindered me from writing to you, for I have thought of nothing else these six weeks; which is, I think, about the time that I wrote to you last.[2] I don't know if I even told you of my journey to England;[3] you'll not be sorry to hear it; so I won't tell you my little chagrins thereupon nor my little reasons against it. I sustained a short combat, one would think only in order to yield upon better terms, for my brother writes me word there's a troop of dragoons waiting for me in England;[4] *me voilà capitaine de dragons!* I am a-going over to fight like a *tigre;* you

7. Unexplained.

1. Horace Mann (1706–86), cr. (1755) Bt; British diplomatic representative at Florence 1738–86; HW's correspondent. He was promoted to Resident 24 April 1740 OS (Mann i. p. xxxi).

2. HW says *post* 6 March 1740 NS that he received his last letter from Conway at Genoa (where he was 20–28 Nov. 1739 NS; see Gray i. 192, n. 1); this was pre-

sumably Conway's letter of 18 Nov. 1739 NS.

3. That is, his forthcoming return to England; he reached London by 6 March 1740 OS.

4. Conway had been commissioned lieutenant in Lord Molesworth's Dragoons (now the 16th/5th Lancers) 27 June 1737 OS (*ante* 2 July 1737 OS, n. 3), but nothing further has been found about his apparent promotion to captain at this time.

know I have promised you a sprig of my first laurels; but upon condition that you come and receive it from my hand. If you have a mind for a Spanish lady or two or a few *diamants* or pearls or gold or silver or any other trifles of that kind you may have 'em all at the same price.—Seriously, tell me, dear Horry, when you think of returning. I own I have malice enough to wish they'd make you captain of dragoons. I have however some hopes from the Parliament.[5] Either one or t'other Minerva must aid me in this case; and I am indifferent whether you choose to serve your country in the chamy or the togue.[6] Apropos I have seen Sir John Shadwel[7] who seems to me very odd and his wife[8] very stiff; and Mrs Molly[9] very pretty and Miss T'other[10] very ugly but very good, and all good sort of people. This puts me in mind of an accident that I had t'other day there which made us laugh extremely; you know they call Sir John sudden death; we were talking at table about illness and death and such subjects, and it came into my head (you must know it was the day after I received the news of my dragoonery) to cry up sudden death, and talked so much upon it that I made everybody die with laughing but Sir John, who grew grave in proportion as they grew merry. They talk much of you and like you of all things. Lord! Horry, how happy you'll be; the Pope[11] has done you the favour to die just as you're arriving at Rome,[12] but I doubt you'll lose more on the side of the carnival than you'll get by the Conclave; people say

5. That is, Conway hoped that HW's election to Parliament at the forthcoming general election would force him to return to England. HW, elected May 1741, did not return to England until Sept. of that year ('Short Notes,' GRAY i. 11 and nn. 69, 71).

6. Apparently 'in the army or the senate,' 'chamy' signifying the chamois doublet of the soldier and 'togue' the toga of the Roman senator (OED).

7. Sir John Shadwell (1671–1747), Kt, 1715; M.D., 1700; physician extraordinary to Queen Anne and physician in ordinary to George I and II. He had withdrawn from practice in 1735 and retired to the Continent where he remained until 1740. HW had met him and his family in Italy (MANN i. 185, n. 18).

8. Ann Binns (ca 1681–1777), m. (1725) Sir John Shadwell, Kt (ibid. viii. 283).

9. Not further identified. She is mentioned several times in letters from W. Bristow to Lady Denbigh when the Shadwells were at Naples in 1737 (Hist. MSS Comm., *Denbigh MSS*, 1911, pp. 212, 217–18). See also MANN i. 185–6 and n. 18.

10. Not identified.

11. Lorenzo Corsini (1652 – 6 Feb. 1740 NS), pope as Clement XII 1730–40. The news of his death reached Paris on the 14th and was formally announced at Versailles on the 21st (Charles-Philippe d'Albert, Duc de Luynes, *Mémoires . . . sur la cour de Louis XV*, 1860–5, iii. 141; René-Louis de Voyer, Marquis d'Argenson, *Journal et mémoires*, ed. Rathery, 1859–67, ii. 424; *Mercure historique* 1740, cviii. 340).

12. HW and Gray left Florence for Rome 21 March NS and arrived on the 26th (GRAY i. 203, n. 2, 205).

here that the Cardinal's[13] to be made Pope[14] but that he's not to go over but to depose the purple in a week; two of our old Cardinals[15] are set out. I doubt if they'll arrive at Rome for this violent fr⟨ost⟩[16] will in all probability snip those two old withered plants as the wolf did poor Tory on the top of mount what d'y call it? Poor dear Tory! I never think of you without a sigh! But I'm going to buy a little *Jack Fredrick*[17] and then I shall think of you no more. Talking of Fredrick, Charles[18] is here and Mr and Mrs Leth.[19] Tell me news of my Lord Lincoln;[20] I'll be very good and write you all the news in the world. Adieu! Lord Scarborough[21] died suddenly t'other night while his servant was gone to fetch a chair.

Compliments to Grey.

Direct to me at my brother's in Grosvenour Street and tell me all sorts of things.

---

13. André-Hercule de Fleury (1653–1743), cardinal; minister of Louis XV.

14. This report was current by 18 Feb. NS and continued to spread during the next few weeks (Argenson, op. cit. ii. 426, iii. 1–2, 7–8).

15. Armand-Gaston-Maximilien de Rohan (1674–1749), cardinal, 1712; and Henri-Oswald de la Tour d'Auvergne (1671–1747), cardinal, 1737. Cardinal Tencin was already at Rome and the other French cardinals, Fleury, Polignac, and Potier de Gesvres, did not attend the Conclave (MANN i. 21, n. 19; Luynes, loc. cit.; Argenson, op. cit. ii. 424; *Mercure historique* 1740, cviii. 340–1). D'Auvergne left for Rome 23 Feb. NS and Rohan on the 25th (Maurice Boutry, *Intrigues et missions du Cardinal de Tencin*, 1902, p. 191).

16. For details of the extreme cold of the winter of 1740 in France, see Emmanuel, Duc de Croÿ, *Journal inédit*, ed. Grouchy and Cottin, 1906–7, i. 23–4.

17. John Frederick (1708–83), 4th Bt, 1770; M.P. New Shoreham 1740–1, West Looe 1743–61; commissioner of Customs 1761–82 (Namier and Brooke ii. 473–4). He had been on his grand tour with his brother Charles in 1737–9 and had met HW and Conway in Paris in April 1739

(GRAY i. 166 and n. 39). The joke is unexplained.

18. Charles Frederick (1709–85), K.B., 1761; M.P. New Shoreham 1741–54, Queenborough 1754–84; clerk of the deliveries of the Ordnance 1746–50; surveyor-general of the Ordnance 1750–82 (Namier and Brooke ii. 472–3; *post* 6 Oct. 1748).

19. Probably Smart Lethieullier (1701–60), antiquary, F.R.S., F.S.A., who formed collections and made drawings of antiquities while travelling on the Continent; he m. (Feb. 1726) Margaret (ca 1707–53), dau. of William Sloper of Woodhay, Berks (see COLE ii. 238–9; C. H. Iyan Chown, 'The Lethieullier Family . . . ,' *Essex Review*, 1927, xxxvi. 3, 12).

20. Henry Fiennes Clinton (after 1768, Pelham Clinton) (1720–94), 9th E. of Lincoln; 2d D. of Newcastle, 1768. He was still at Turin, where he remained until 15 Sept. 1740 NS (SELWYN 1, n. 3).

21. Richard Lumley (ca 1688 – 29 Jan. 1740 OS), 2d E. of Scarbrough, had committed suicide. The Cts of Hertford to the Cts of Pomfret 4 Feb. 1740 OS gives virtually the same details (Frances, Countess of Hertford and Henrietta Louisa, Countess of Pomfret, *Correspondence*, 1805, i. 188–9).

To CONWAY,[1] Sunday 6 March 1740 NS

Printed from *Works* v. 3–4.

Florence, March 6, 1740 NS.

HARRY, my dear, one would tell you what a monster you are, if one were not sure your conscience tells you so every time you think of me. At Genoa, in the year of our Lord one thousand seven hundred and thirty-nine, I received the last letter from you;[2] by your not writing to me since, I imagine you propose to make this leap year. I should have sent many a scold after you in this long interval, had I known where to have scolded; but you told me you should leave Geneva immediately. I have dispatched sundry inquiries into England after you, all fruitless. At last drops in a chance letter to Lady Sophy Farmor[3] from a girl at Paris, that tells her for news, Mr Henry Conway is here. Is he indeed? and why was I to know it only by this scrambling way? Well, I hate you for this neglect, but I find I love you well enough to tell you so. But, dear now, don't let one fall into a train of excuses and reproaches; if the god of indolence is a mightier deity with you than the god of caring for one, tell me, and I won't dun you; but will drop your correspondence as silently as if I owed you money.

If my private consistency was of no weight with you; yet is a man nothing who is within three days journey of a Conclave? nay, for what you knew I might have been in Rome. Harry, art thou so indifferent, as to have a cousin at the election of a pope without courting him for news? I'll tell you, were I anywhere else, and even Dick Hammond[4] were at Rome, I think verily I should have wrote

1. Second son of Francis, first Lord Conway, by Charlotte Shorter his third wife. He was afterwards secretary in Ireland during the viceroyalty of William fourth Duke of Devonshire; groom of the Bedchamber to George II and to George III; secretary of state in the year 1765; lieutenant-general of the Ordnance in 1770 [1767]; commander-in-chief in 1782; and a field marshal in 1793. This correspondence commences when Mr Walpole was 23 years old, and Mr Conway two years younger. They had gone abroad together with Mr Gray in the year 1739, had spent three months together at Rheims, and afterwards separated at Geneva (HW).

2. *Ante* 18 Nov. 1739 NS.

3. Lady Sophia Fermor (1721–45), m. (1744) John Carteret, 2d Bn Carteret, 1st E. Granville, 1744. She was at Florence with her family from 20 Dec. 1739 NS until 13 March 1741 NS (GRAY i. 227, n. 18; MANN i. 4, n. 18).

4. Richard Hamond (d. 1776), HW's first cousin (MONTAGU i. 26, n. 12).

to him. Popes, cardinals, adorations, coronations, St Peters! oh, what costly sounds! and don't you write to one yet? I shall set out in about a fortnight,[5] and pray then think me of consequence.

I have crept on upon time from day to day here;[6] fond of Florence to a degree: 'tis infinitely the most agreeable of all the places I have seen since London: that you know one loves, right or wrong, as one does one's nurse. Our little Arno is not boated and swelling like the Thames, but 'tis vastly pretty, and, I don't know how, being Italian, has something visionary and poetical in its stream. Then one's unwilling to leave the Gallery,[7] and—but—in short, one's unwilling to get into a post-chaise. I am as surfeited with mountains and inns, as if I had eat them. I have many to pass before I see England again, and no Tory to entertain me on the road! Well, this thought makes me dull, and that makes me finish.

Adieu!

Yours ever,

HOR. WALPOLE

PS. Direct to me, (for to be sure you will not be so outrageous as to leave me quite off) recommandé à Monsieur Mann, ministre de sa Majesté Britannique à Florence.

From CONWAY, Thursday 6 March 1740 OS

Printed for the first time from the MS now WSL, formerly Rutnam.
Address: À Monsieur Monsieur Walpole.

London, Mar. 6, OS.

IF I have not heard from you, my dear Horry, this age,[1] I attribute it to my ill fortune which has not let me rest a moment this God knows when. You guess I am here, or rather imagine I have been here a vast while; for I have been a vast while coming here, beside

---

5. HW left Florence on the 21st (GRAY i. 203).

6. HW and Gray had been at Florence since 16 Dec. 1739 NS (ibid. i. 9, n. 52).

7. The Uffizi.

---

1. Conway had not yet received HW's letter of 6 March NS.

my natural alacrity *en fait de* journey; I have met with frosts and
God knows what to detain me. Dear Horry, I found poor Selwyn
almost dying, so ill that he saw nobody; judge of my concern when
I have not yet seen him since I came: they think him, however,
now out of danger and I hope to see him today. He has had a violent pleuritic fever. Here's no news; no news but news of balls and
operas and gaiety. Some time ago thirteen *jeunes seigneurs,* among
which was my brother, gave a magnificent ball at the Opera
House. Sir Robert was there and the Duke of Dorset[2] and, in short,
twenty or thirty people of the first quality. And on Monday next
fourteen *jeunes seigneurs* of which number I also shall have the
honour of being give just such another. The Duchess of Norforlk[3]
gave one *très magnifique* on Monday last when she entertained one
half of the town and affronted the other. In short, they have had
so many balls and things and drew poor Jack[4] into 'em that I believe that contributed to his illness. I was at the opera t'other night;
it's at the Little Haymarket House and all the world goes there;[5]
Moscovita's[6] a pretty woman and does not sing ill: Caristini[7] sings
charmingly and there's another man[8] whom I don't like; in short,
it's much better than I expected, and still more better than the
opera at Paris. You'd hardly guess where I was last night; even at

2. Lionel Cranfield Sackville (1688–1765),
7th E. of Dorset, cr. (1720) D. of Dorset.

3. Mary Blount (ca 1702–73), m. (1727)
Edward Howard, 9th D. of Norfolk.

4. John Selwyn the younger.

5. The Italian opera in England had
collapsed from lack of financial support
in 1738. Operas were revived on a modest
scale at the Little Theatre in the Haymarket 1 Dec. 1739 OS, where they continued through the winter. The opera
returned to the King's Theatre in the
autumn of 1741 under the patronage of
Lord Middlesex and others (Charles Burney, *General History of Music,* ed. Mercer, 1935, ii. 818–38; MANN i. 190–1; *post*
26, 31 Oct. 1741 OS). Conway had heard
Merode e Selinunte, a pasticcio, which
premiered 22 Jan., and was performed
most recently on 1 and 4 March (Burney,
op. cit. ii. 827; *Daily Adv.* 1, 3, 4 March;
London Stage Pt III, ii. 816, 823).

6. Usually spelled Muscovita, Lord
Middlesex's mistress. She was the prin-

cipal woman at this time (Burney, op.
cit. ii. 827; MANN i. 191 and n. 16), and
presumably the 'Signora Panichi' listed as
singing the role of Filea in the 1740
edition of *Merode* (*London Stage* Pt III,
ii. 816). HW dissents from Conway's
opinion *post* 23 April 1740 NS.

7. Apparently Giovanni Carestini (ca
1705–60), male contralto who had sung
in England 1733–5. He is generally stated
to have left England permanently in 1735,
but Burney mentions 'Carestini' as 'head
man' of the opera in 1739 and 1740 (op.
cit. ii. 782–3, 793, 826–7; Sir George
Grove, *Dictionary of Music and Musicians,* 5th edn, ed. Blom, 1954–61, ii.
60–1; *Enciclopedia dello spettacolo,* Rome,
1954–62, iii. 33–5).

8. Probably Giovanni Battista Andre-
oni (d. 1797), male soprano (MANN i.
248 and n. 17); Burney, in his description of the opera in 1740, mentions 'An-
dreoni a servant for all work' (op. cit. ii.
827).

Sir William Windam's;⁹ it was really a pretty contrast. I dined at Sir Robert's and passed the evening with my Lady Blanford.¹⁰ All the world was there, that is, all the Opposition world: the Duke of Argyle, Lord Cobham, Mr Cooke,¹¹ Mr Stanhope,¹² etc., and the Duchess of Queensborough¹³ and Lady Cobham¹⁴ and all the world. Lady Denbigh¹⁵ whom I saw at Paris made me go there. Fleethood's house¹⁶ is shut up¹⁷ and there's a new farce¹⁸ at Rich's¹⁹ where all the world goes. I have not seen it yet.

There is a parcel of trumpery news for you; nobody talks of anything else. The war and all that is never mentioned. Sir Robert is perfectly well and everybody else that you know: I have not seen your brothers²⁰ yet. Lord Annandale²¹ has been dying but is better. I long to know what you've heard and seen at the Conclave, and where you've been and how you divert yourself. Compliments to Grey. Adieu!

9. Sir William Wyndham (?1688–1740), 3d Bt, a prominent opponent of Sir Robert Walpole.

10. Maria Catherina de Jong (ca 1697–1779), m. 1 (1729) William Godolphin, styled M. of Blandford; m. 2 (1734) Sir William Wyndham, 3d Bt; later a friend of HW.

11. George Cooke (ca 1705–68), M.P. Tregony 1742–7, Middlesex 1750–68; prothonotary in the Court of Common Pleas; 'a prominent Tory lawyer' whom HW elsewhere describes as 'a pompous Jacobite' (MANN iv. 223, n. 15; J. B. Owen, Rise of the Pelhams, 1957, p. 324).

12. Probably Hon. John Stanhope (1705–48), M.P. Nottingham borough 1727–34, Derby borough 1736–48; Chesterfield's brother.

13. Lady Catherine Hyde (ca 1701–77), m. (1720) Charles Douglas, 3d D. of Queensberry.

14. Anne Halsey (d. 1760), m. Sir Richard Temple, 4th Bt, cr. (1714) Bn and (1718) Vct Cobham.

15. Isabella de Jong (1693–1769), m. (ca 1718) William Feilding, 5th E. of Denbigh; Lady Blandford's sister. She was later a friend of HW, who wrote down some 'Anecdotes told me by Lady Denbigh Nov. 3d 1768,' ed. W. S. Lewis, Farmington, 1932.

16. The Theatre Royal in Drury Lane, of which Charles Fleetwood (d. 1747) was patentee 1734–45 (GRAY i. 143, n. 18).

17. Yet performances at Drury Lane are regularly advertised in the Daily Adv. at this time. See also London Stage Pt III, ii. 823 ff.

18. Probably Rich's Orpheus and Eurydice, first performed 12 Feb. 1740 OS, described as 'a new dramatic entertainment of music and grotesque dancing'; it was a great success (see John Genest, Some Account of the English Stage, Bath, 1832, iii. 618–20; D. E. Baker, I. Reed, and S. Jones, Biographia Dramatica, 1812, iii. 107; London Stage Pt III, ii. 819–20 et seq.).

19. Covent Garden Theatre, of which John Rich (ca 1682–1761), pantomimist, was manager 1732–61.

20. Robert Walpole (1701–51), cr. (1723) Bn Walpole; 2d E. of Orford, 1745; and Edward Walpole (1706–84), K.B., 1753.

21. George Johnston (after 1744, van den Bempdé) (1720–92), 3d M. of Annandale. He became insane a few years later. His illness is mentioned in the Daily Adv. 4 March.

To Conway, ca Tuesday 15 March 1740 NS

Missing; answered *post* 24 March 1740 OS. It was probably written soon after HW received Conway's letter of ca 25 Feb. 1740 NS and would have had to have been written about 15 March NS for Conway to answer it 24 March OS, since it took about three weeks for letters to go from Florence to London. HW also mentions in his letter of 23 April NS that he had recently written two 'long' letters to Conway and so did not hasten to answer Conway's letter of 6 March OS.

From Conway, Monday 24 March 1740 OS

Printed for the first time from the MS now WSL, formerly Rutnam. Dated by Conway in the letter.

Address: À Monsieur Monsieur Walpole chez Monsieur Mann resident du roi d'Angleterre à Florence.

Postmark: WP [in circle; there is also another illegible circular postmark that appears on several subsequent letters].

C'EST avec un plaisir très sensible, mon cher ami, que je viens d'entendre la nouvelle de votre nomination à l'ordre de l'Hibou.[1] Je me fais une vraie satisfaction de vous rendre tous les compliments dont vous m'honorez au sujet de ma dragoonerie et ce n'est pas seulement par un motif de gratitude que je vous dise: que j'aimerais mieux que vous fassiez, ce que vous êtes, chevalier de cet ordre respectable, que si je l'étais moi-même; c'est aussi avec une sincerité sans égale que je souhaite, que vous soyez de tous les chevaliers de l'Hibou le premier; et le plus digne de cet honneur. Je ne doute nullement que vous n'ayez donné les preuves les plus convainçantes de votre sagesse pour mériter la protection de cet oiseau sacré, ministre, et en même temps image de la sagesse. Il y a déjà longtemps que vous êtes favori d'Appollon; je crains que vous n'alliez l'abandonner; car je ne connais pas comment vous pouvez l'être en même temps de l'un et de l'autre; d'ailleurs on vous réprochera un grand défaut de goût si vous sacrifiez ce joli garçon-là, avec sa belle chevelure d'or et toutes ses brillantes beautés, à une

1. Unexplained in the absence of HW's missing letter of ca 15 March 1740 NS, to which this letter is a reply. Our guess is that the missing letter was similar to the one HW wrote to West, 27 Feb. 1740 NS, in which he describes the 'frantic' and prolonged gaieties of the Carnival at Florence (GRAY i. 200–1).

triste vieille cassée des fatigues de la guerre et de la politique. Enfin vous n'avez qu'à choisir; chéri, à présent de tous les deux vous ne pourrez pas l'être toujours. La cour de Minerve est défendue aux partisans d'Appollon. Écrivez-moi de laquelle vous voulez être derénavant[2] afin que je vous traite en homme sage ou en bel esprit. Adieu!

Dear Horry,

I thank you ten thousand times for your charming long letter, and all your histories of cardinals, and earthquakes,[3] and carnivals and natural curiosities and unnatural ones; and Lord Granby's[4] bons mots; and Prince Beauvau[5] and Baron Stosch[6] and all the charming variety of your two sheets. You tell me so much and I have so little to tell you that I am almost ashamed to say anything: here's no politics talked of but the war, and nothing of the war but the taking Porto Bello:[7] it's reckoned a considerable thing and has been thought of consequence enough to address the King with congratulations thereupon.[8] Admiral Vernon[9] in speaking to the Governor of Panama[10] or I forget what great Spaniard, called the Queen of Spain[11] an Italian madwoman.[12] Guess what a fury she'll be in!

2. Probably coined from English 'deraign' (O.F. 'deraisne,' 'deresne') meaning 'challenge,' 'dispute.' Here it would mean 'champion' (OED).

3. There had apparently been an earthquake at Modena 'of no great consequence' sometime in February (*Pue's Occurrences* 25–29 March 1740 OS, quoting an item from the London papers of 20 March which in turn quoted letters from Italy of 24 Feb.).

4. John Manners (1721–70), styled M. of Granby; eldest son of 3d D. of Rutland; army officer; M.P. Grantham 1741–54, Cambridgeshire 1754–70. HW had met him at Genoa in Nov. 1739 (SELWYN 1).

5. Charles-Just de Beauvau (1720–93), Prince de Beauvau; son of the Princesse de Craon; HW's correspondent; Maréchal de France, 1783 (MANN i. 11, n. 43).

6. Baron Philipp von Stosch (1691–1757), collector; British secret agent at Florence (ibid. i. 9, n. 31).

7. News of the capitulation of Porto Bello on 22 Nov. 1739 reached London 13 March 1740 OS (ibid. i. 5, n. 25).

8. The joint address was voted 17 March OS and presented on the 18th

(*Journals of the House of Lords* xxv. 484, 485, 487; *Journals of the House of Commons* xxiii. 502, 503, 504; GM 1740, x. 142–3).

9. Edward Vernon (1684–1757), Vice-Adm., 1739; Adm., 1745; dismissed, 1746; M.P. Penryn 1722–34, Portsmouth 1741, Ipswich 1741–57; in command of the expedition to the West Indies.

10. Dionisio Martínez (or Martines) de la Vega (d. 1741), governor of Cuba, 1724; President of Panama, 1735 (*Enciclopedia universal ilustrada*, Barcelona, [1907–30], xxxiii. 542; J. B. Sosa and E. J. Arce, *Compendio de historia de Panamá*, [Panama City], 1911, p. 156; Edward Vernon, *Vernon Papers*, ed. Ranft, Naval Records Society, 1958, pp. 42, 43).

11. Elizabeth Farnese of Parma (1692–1766), m. (1714) Philip V of Spain.

12. Vernon had concluded a letter to the President: 'Health and prosperity to all true Spaniards that may lament sacrificing the true interest of their country to the ambition of an Italian Queen'; this in turn provoked an angry letter from the President (C. H. Hartmann, *Angry Admiral*, 1953, p. 32; Vernon, op. cit. 42–3).

The Governor of Porto Bello[13] was to march out drums beating and colours flying,[14] but instead of that his own soldiers had plundered the town and were run away. And behold my Governor who walks out with a white feather in his hat, attended by a little black boy:[15] it put me in mind of 'Enter the King and two fiddlers solus.'

This is the chit-chat: as to the more serious part of it I have heard little and thought less of it. Will you hear a little of dancing and such things? Since our ball[15a] we had a great one at the Duke of Bedford's[16] where I had like to have been in a sad scrape. All the dancers of our ball were invited; and by consequence danced with the same partners as before; but I, like a blockhead, engaged myself with Lady Car[oline] Fitzroy;[17] where as I told you I was to dance with Lady Car[oline] Lenox.[18] After being in a violent fluster for fear of affronting Lady Car[oline] and the Duchess of Rich[mond][19] and after many negotiations I got off and danced with Lady C[aroline] Len[ox]. Congratulate me thereupon! The night after the Bedford ball, we go seven or eight of us from the opera to the tavern. You'll want to know who we were: the Duke and Duchess of Bedford,[20] Lady Cardigan,[21] Lady Albemarle,[22] Lady Car[oline] Pierpoint,[23] Lord Holderness, Lord John and George Sackville,[24] Mr Deemer.[25] My brother and I supped and danced. Last night being Sunday the 23 of March, we danced an impromptu after supper

13. Who signed himself Francisco Martines de Retes (ibid. 36, 41) but the name is elsewhere given as Don Francisco Javier Martínez de la Vega y Retes and as Francisco Javier de la Vega Retez (C. F. Duro, *Armada española*, Madrid, 1895–1903, vi. 254; Sosa and Arce, op. cit. 157).

14. According to the terms of capitulation (Vernon, op. cit. 35, 36; *London Gazette* No. 7892, 11–15 March OS).

15. A somewhat similar account of this incident is in an 'extract' from a letter from Porto Bello in GM 1740, x. 146.

15a. On 10 March OS (*ante* 6 March 1740 OS).

16. John Russell (1710–71), 4th D. of Bedford.

17. See *ante* 25 Jan. 1737 OS, n. 9.

18. Lady Georgiana Caroline Lennox (1723-74), m. (1744) Henry Fox, cr. (1763) Bn Holland; cr. (1762) Bns Holland, *s.j.* Conway had not mentioned this to HW when he mentioned the ball *ante* 6 March 1740 OS.

19. Lady Sarah Cadogan (1706–51), m. (1719) Charles Lennox, 2d D. of Richmond; Lady Caroline's mother.

20. Hon. Gertrude Leveson Gower (1715–94), m. (1737) John Russell, 4th D. of Bedford.

21. Lady Mary Montagu (ca 1711–75), m. (1730) George Brudenell, 4th E. of Cardigan, cr. (1766) D. of Montagu.

22. Lady Anne Lennox (1703–89), m. (1723) William Anne van Keppel, 2d E. of Albemarle.

23. Lady Caroline Pierrepont (d. 1753), m. (1749) Thomas Brand, of The Hoo, Herts, HW's friend and correspondent (MONTAGU i. 150).

24. Lord John Philip Sackville (1713–65), M.P. Tamworth 1734–47; and Lord George Sackville (after 1770, Germain) (1716–85), cr. (1782) Vct Sackville; army officer and politician.

25. Joseph Damer (1718–98), cr. (1753) Bn Milton and (1792) E. of Dorchester.

HON. FRANCIS SEYMOUR CONWAY,
MARQUESS OF HERTFORD, BY BARTHOLOMEW DANDRIDGE

till 3 o'clock at the Duchess of Norfolk's, and tonight we have a *grandissimo* ball at Sir Thomas Robinson's.[26] I told you that last night being Sunday the 23 of March we danced at the Duchess of Norfolk's and that tonight, which is Monday, the 31st of March, we dance at Sir Thomas Rob[inson]'s. Now lest the critics of future ages should go to war about this point of chronology, I must inform you that on Monday the 24 of March I began this letter; that I had not time to finish it then; that on Thursday I let the post slip by, a neglect unknown to me before, and that I now give you the continuation and conclusion of it on this present Monday the 31st of March. I'll tell you more of this ball soon, at present I can only say that he has invited near 200 persons; whereof his house will not hold the moiety. I say he has asked 200 souls but he certainly designed they should leave their bodies at home. He asks three or four and twenty couple of dancers, whereas his room, according to his own account, will hold twelve (provided the women dance without hoops and the men in their waistcoats); and by consequence, says he, there will be room to spare. What I say about waistcoats and hoops I take to be literally true, for the ball room is so narrow that it cannot admit anything that has the name of pannier though it were but a work basket. I went yesterday to Hampton Court, where I lamed myself. I am still lame and God knows how I shall dance!

I find an inclination to say a great deal more to you, but I find also, unluckily for me, and fortunately for you that I have already said too much and that I have entered into a ridiculous detail of an uninteresting story about a dance, with the circumstances that an old woman would relate a ball that was given in the time of good King Charles; how she was the finest dancer of ⟨her⟩ time; how she was taken out to dance a saraband by such a Duke and how she made a slip at the beginning of the dance and let a fart in trying to recover herself; and how she danced out of time; and all in confusion; and ended abruptly and forgot to make her curtsy. You'll laugh to see how much I resemble this old woman, *mutate nomine de te, fabula narratur,*[27] resolved to hobble through my two sheets of paper, out of a sort of gratitude as people think to be polite by

---

26. 'Long' Sir Thomas Robinson (?1702–77), cr. (1731) Bt; M.P. Morpeth 1727–34; commissioner of Excise 1735–42; governor of Barbados 1742–7.

27. Horace, *Satires* I. i. 69–70 ('Change the name, the tale is told of you').

the length of their compliments. I should be inconsistent if I did not finish as abruptly.

I told you, I believe,[28] that Selwyn was quite recovered.

To CONWAY, Saturday 23 April 1740 NS

Printed from *Works* v. 5–6.

Rome, April 23, 1740 NS.

AS I have wrote you two such long letters[1] lately, my dear Hal, I did not hurry myself to answer your last;[2] but chose to write to poor Selwyn[3] upon his illness. I pity you excessively upon finding him in such a situation: what a shock it must have been to you! He deserves so much love from all that know him, and you owe him so much friendship, that I can scarce conceive a greater shock. I am very glad you did not write to me till he was out of danger; for this great distance would have added to my pain, as I must have waited so long for another letter. I charge you, don't let him relapse into balls; he does not love them, and, if you please, your example may keep him out of them. You are extremely pretty people to be dancing and trading with French poulterers and pastry-cooks, when a hard frost[4] is starving half the nation, and the Spanish war ought to be employing the other half. We are much more public-spirited here; we live upon the public news, and triumph abundantly upon the taking Porto Bello.[5] If you are not entirely debauched with your balls, you must be pleased with an answer of Lord Hartington's[6] to the Governor of Rome.[7] He asked him what they had determined

28. Not in any letter that has survived. Conway had told HW *ante* 6 March 1740 OS that John Selwyn was believed out of danger but that he had not yet seen him.

---

1. *Ante* 6 March 1740 NS and the missing letter of ca 15 March 1740 NS.

2. *Ante* 6 March 1740 OS; HW would not yet have received Conway's letter of 24–31 March 1740 OS.

3. John Selwyn, elder brother of George Augustus Selwyn. He died about 1750 (HW). HW's letter is missing.

4. For some details of the 'Great Frost' of 1740, see GM 1740, X. 35.

5. HW had apparently learned of the capture of Porto Bello in a letter from Mann received about 16 April NS (MANN i. 5, n. 25).

6. William Cavendish (1720–64), styled M. of Hartington 1729–55; 4th D. of Devonshire, 1755.

7. Monsignore Filippo Manente Buondelmonte (1691–1741), governor of Rome 1739–41 (ibid. i. 8, n. 19). HW tells this same anecdote to Mann 23 April 1740 NS (ibid. i. 7–8).

about the vessel[8] that the Spaniards took under the cannon of Civita Vecchia, whether they had restored it to the English? The Governor said, they had done justice. My Lord replied, 'If you had not, we should have done it ourselves.' Pray reverence our spirit, Lieutenant Hal.

Sir, Moscovita is not a pretty woman, and she does sing ill; that's all.

My dear Harry, I must now tell you a little about myself, and answer your questions. How I like the inanimate part of Rome you will soon perceive at my arrival in England; I am far gone in medals, lamps, idols, prints, etc. and all the small commodities to the purchase of which I can attain; I would buy the Coliseum if I could: judge. My mornings are spent in the most agreeable manner; my evenings ill enough. Roman conversations are dreadful things! such untoward mawkins as the princesses! and the princes are worse. Then the whole city is littered with French and German abbés, who make up a dismal contrast with the inhabitants. The Conclave is far from enlivening us; its secrets don't transpire. I could give you names of this cardinal and that, that are talked of, but each is contradicted the next hour. I was there t'other day to visit one of them, and one of the most agreeable, Alexander Albani.[9] I had the opportunity of two cardinals[10] making their entry: upon that occasion the gate is unlocked, and their eminencies come to talk to their acquaintance over the threshold. I have received great civilities from him I named to you, and I wish he were out, that I might receive greater: a friend of his[11] does the honours of Rome for him; but you know that it is unpleasant to visit by proxy. Cardinal Delci,[12]

8. The *Sea Horse* from Falmouth; see ibid. i. 8, n. 20.

9. Alessandro Albani (1692–1779), cardinal, 1721; librarian of the Vatican 1761–79; collector. HW had visited him 20 April NS (ibid. i. 9).

10. Philipp Ludwig (1699–1747), Graf von Sinzendorff, cardinal, 1727, Bp of Breslau, 1732, and Silvio Valenti (1690–1756), cardinal, 1738, papal secretary of state 1740–56, made their entries into the Conclave 19 April (ibid. i. 11, n. 46, ii. 55, n. 5; Maurice Boutry, 'Le Cardinal de Tencin au Conclave de Benoît XIV,' *Revue d'histoire diplomatique*, 1897, xi. 390).

11. Conte Alessandro Petroni (ca 1704–

71), chamberlain and Master of the Horse to Clement XIV (MANN i. 9 and n. 26).

12. Ranieri Pannocchieschi d'Elci (1670–1761), cardinal, 1737, was one of the three principal candidates of the Corsini faction in April and was proposed again in July (*Enciclopedia italiana*, Rome, 1929–39, xxvi. 202; *Genealog. hist. Nachrichten*, 1740–1, 1st ser. ii. 238–9, 730; ibid., 1762–3, 3d ser. i. 332–8; Michael Ranft, *Merkwürdige Lebensgeschichte aller Cardinäle*, Regensburg, 1768–81, iii. 344–8; Boutry, op. cit. xi. 399). HW may, however, have him confused with Cardinal Cenci, whom he describes *post* 5 July 1740 NS as 'the only

the object of the Corsini faction,[13] is dying; the hot weather will probably dispatch half a dozen more. Not that it is hot yet; I am now writing to you by my fireside.

Harry, you saw Lord Deskfoord[14] at Geneva; don't you like him? He is a mighty sensible man. There are few young people have so good understandings. He is mighty grave, and so are you; but you can both be pleasant when you have a mind. Indeed one can make you pleasant, but his solemn *Scotchery* is a little formidable: before you I can play the fool from morning to night, courageously. Good night. I have other letters to write,[15] and must finish this.

Yours ever,

HOR. WALPOLE

To CONWAY, ca Sunday 15 – Friday 20 May 1740 NS

Missing; written from Rome and answered by Conway *post* 9 June 1740 OS. Letters from Rome to London seem to have taken about a month (e.g., Conway replied to HW's letter of 23 April NS on 14 May OS).

one he [Corsini] could have ventured to make Pope,' and who was in poor health, which does not seem to have been true of d'Elci.

13. The faction of cardinals created by Clement XII, headed by his nephew Neri Maria, Marchese Corsini (1685–1770), cardinal, 1730 (GRAY i. 208, n. 9), which opposed the 'vecchi' faction of cardinals of earlier creation, headed by Annibale Albani (1682–1751), cardinal, 1711; chamberlain, 1719 (MANN i. 16–17 and nn. 10, 12).

14. James Ogilvy (ca 1714–70), styled Lord Deskford 1730–64; 6th E. of Findlater, 1764. HW elsewhere describes him as a 'sensible Scotchman with much knowledge, though 'twas difficult to say whether he sought more to acquire it or to show it. He seldom laughed, but when he related his own sayings, but that often' (HW's *MS Commonplace Book of Verses*, p. 29). HW had met him for the first time in Rome (DALRYMPLE 151).

15. The only other letter of this date which has been recovered is to Mann (MANN i. 6–12).

From CONWAY, Wednesday 14 May 1740 OS

Printed for the first time from the MS now WSL, formerly Rutnam. Dated by the reference to the King's departure for Gravesend 'yesterday morning' (below, n. 5).

Dear Knight,

YOUR reproach[1] about French poulterers and pastry-cooks is groundless and unjust *quo ad me* for I was not in England while the frost lasted; I don't answer for what I should have done if I had, but I was not, and so! You say you're mad after antiquities and that the inanimate part of Rome pleases you as much as the living does little; I rejoice to hear it because I think from what I have heard of Rome, it is in that way only to be made agreeable; I could wish myself with you perhaps as much as you wish yourself here, and am troubled when I think that our occupations have not been less distant from one another of late than our persons, or rather my occupation has been doing nothing and I begin now to be as heartily tired of it as ever I was with doing anything, which is saying a great deal. You can't imagine how that exhortation of Pliny's to his friend which I dropt upon lately struck me and how much I wish to obey it: *Proinde tu quoque strepitum istum inanemque discursum et multum ineptos labores, ut primum fuerit occasio relinque teque studiis vel otio trade, satius est enim, ut Attilius noster dixit; otiosum esse quam nihil agere.*[2] 'Tis prodigious the nothings I have done; the dances I have danced, the games I have played, the visits I have made and the follies I have committed. I don't believe I have read five hours in ten weeks that I have been over; you can't think with what pleasure I should bury myself with you in antique dirt; I'd even serve the apprenticeship of medals[3] under you. Do you know that I should tread upon those sacred hills that you inhabit with awe and could club a tear with you over Virgil's or Tully's tomb? for though unlearned I am an amateur of everything in the shape of science,

1. In his letter *ante* 23 April 1740 NS.
2. Pliny, *Letters* I. ix, with a slight omission: 'Relinquish then also at the first opportunity such noise and commotion, such empty pursuits and very absurd exertions, and devote yourself to study, or even idleness; as our Attilius said, "Truly it is better to be at leisure than to be active and accomplish nothing." '
3. When Conway visited Florence in 1751, he took a 'course of medals' in the Uffizi Gallery (MANN iv. 297 and n. 5).

and have a particular veneration for antiquity though I know it only *par reputation*. . . .[4]

Well! our good King, God bless him, grows madder every day than another. You will hardly believe me when I tell you he is gone to Hanover.[5] The Walmouden[6] and he have packed up their alls and sat out yesterday morning for Gravesend. She's in a vast fuss about it and cries for fear they should think she was occasion of it. We begin to be treasonable already[7] and I wish we don't become ten times more so; the wit blossoms already on the occasion; *voici* the first epigram that is come out this spring. It's a short dialogue between a patriot and a courtier.

> Cour. speaks: I'll tell you news will make you curse:
> The King does cross the main.
> Pat.: I'll tell you something ten times worse!
> The King comes back again.

Now for a piece of City wit: *qui vaut bien le vôtre*. They say they knew the King was so bold that if there was a war he'd certainly go abroad and *expose* himself.[8] The regency is left as usual in the hands of thirteen of the wisest heads in the Council.[9] Princess Mary's[10] wedding was celebrated on Thursday, and everybody very fine. Felton Hervey[11] takes it into his head to be in love with her and cries from morning to night about her going, which is pleasant

4. About two-thirds of a line is crossed out and cannot be deciphered.

5. George II's decision to visit Hanover was first known about 1 May; he formally declared his intention in Council on the 12th and set out for Gravesend on the 13th (Hist. MSS Comm., *Egmont Diary*, 1920–3, iii. 131, 140; *Daily Adv.* 2, 14 May; GM 1740, x. 260).

6. Amalie-Sophie-Marianne von Wendt (1704–65), m. (1727) Oberhauptmann Gottlieb Adam von Wallmoden; cr. (1740) Cts of Yarmouth; George II's mistress. She had set out for Gravesend with her suite on the 12th May (*Daily Adv.* 13 May).

7. For the reaction to the King's journey see *Egmont Diary*, iii. 133, 140–2.

8. 'Lord Chesterfield said, upon the King's going abroad this year . . . that his Majesty kept his word, for he had often said, *if there should be a war, he would go and expose himself*' (ibid. iii. 141–2).

9. The final list of the Regency in GM 1740, x. 260 and in the newspapers gives sixteen names, but the *Daily Adv.* had reported on the 13th that 'we hear they [the Regents] are thirteen in number, consisting of all the great officers of the Kingdom.' As Conway says, the usual arrangement on the King's absence was to appoint the principal members of the Cabinet Council as lords justices.

10. Mary (1723–72), of England, m. (1740) Friedrich II, Landgrave of Hesse-Cassel. The ceremony, performed 8 May OS in the Chapel Royal at St James's Palace, is described in the *Daily Adv.* 10 May and the *Egmont Diary*, iii. 137–8.

11. Hon. Felton Hervey (1712–73), 10th son of 1st E. of Bristol; M.P. Bury St Edmunds 1747–61; equerry to Queen Caroline 1736–7; groom of the Bedchamber to the Duke of Cumberland 1737–56.

sure. Monsieur Donep[12] who is come to fetch her is called the Man here. I mention this only to introduce a stroke of Lady Townshend's.[13] She asked a gentleman if that was the man that was to put it into the Princess;—she meant his leg.[13a] But by the by nobody did for she was married only by contract[14] and the Duke[15] was proxy; all the lords and counsellors signed it; you understand me, I mean Privy ones.[15a] You must have heard before this time that the Duke of Argyle is turned out;[16] and a furious fury he's in as you may imagine: he came to Court and had audiences of the King and all sorts of things, but upon his refusing the command the King offered him which was that of one camp and insisting upon a general command he was turned out. This happening just at this juncture gives occasion to a ridiculous story. They say the King came to Sir Rob[ert] and said, 'Let me go to Hanover'; and he said no, he could not, and the King said 'Pray do,' and he said no; in short, after entreating a great while in vain, the King said, 'I'll turn out the Duke of Argyle if you'll let me go,' so he said, 'Well, then you may, but don't stay long.' All this passing in the style of a boy's asking to go to mictum is mighty foolish. The Duchess of Argyle[17]

12. August Moritz von Donop (ca 1694–1762), Hessian army officer and diplomatist (*Genealog. hist. Nachrichten*, 1763–4, 3d ser. ii. 509–10; *Repertorium der diplomatischen Vertreter aller Länder*, Vol. II, ed. Friedrich Hausmann, Zurich, 1950, pp. 181, 185, 187, 374). He had been expected in London since mid-March, but did not arrive until 2 May (*Common Sense*, 15 March 1740 OS, which spells his name 'Donness'; *Daily Adv.* 5 May).

13. Etheldreda (*or* Audrey) Harrison (ca 1708–88), m. (1723) Charles Townshend, 3d Vct Townshend; HW's friend and occasional correspondent.

13a. An allusion to an apocryphal account of the marriage of Henry VIII and Anne of Cleves, according to which the King's proxy symbolically consummated the match by putting his leg into bed with Anne. See *post* 20 Aug. 1775, n. 15.

14. 'His Grace the Duke of Newcastle, one of his Majesty's principal secretaries of state, read the marriage contract between her Royal Highness the Princess Mary, and his Serene Highness the Prince of Hesse, which was in writing; his Royal Highness the Duke of Cumberland being

procurator for his Serene Highness, the Princess Mary and the Duke of Cumberland both signed the contract in the Chapel Royal. After which his Grace the Archbishop of Canterbury read his Majesty's assent to the aforesaid contract, which was in Latin' (*Daily Adv.* 10 May).

15. William Augustus (1721–65), cr. (1726) D. of Cumberland.

15a. That is, all who had been sworn of the Privy Council.

16. Argyll's increasing opposition had culminated in a violent attack on the ministry during the debate on the state of the nation 15 April 1740 OS; his speech was printed soon afterwards in *The Conduct of . . . the D–ke of Ar–le for the Four Last Years Reviewed*, 1740, pp. 33–57, and reprinted in Robert Campbell, *Life of . . . John, Duke of Argyle*, 1745, pp. 325–38. On the 25th he demanded a general command but instead was dismissed from all his posts on or about 30 April OS (BM Add. MSS 32693, ff. 232, 249).

17. Jane Warburton (ca 1683–1767), m. (1717) John Campbell, 2d D. of Argyll.

distressed me terribly t'other night at Lady Townshend's: upon Miss Walpole's[18] coming into the room, she asked me who that was. I told her Miss Walpole; she asked 'What Miss Walpole?' Somebody said, 'Sir Robert's daughter,' and she said, 'I did not know he had even a daughter so old.' Here her inquiries ceased to my surprise and great satisfaction for I thought she would know all about her.[18a] You know these things confuse me, *pour peu qu'on y prenne d'intérêt.*

I saw Spangle[19] at Court, and have seen Mrs Grosvenor several times. She hears from you often,[20] and is happier about it than one can conceive. You are very good to her and she deserves it: I saw Hester Thrower[21] there and she talked to me of Mrs Whaley[22] whom I know a little and twenty other people that I never heard of. Well, Horry, I seem to have told you a vast many comical things. I look upon my letter [as] a sort of journal which contains a great many excellent facts thrown together without style or order. If you have any friend more out of the way of news than yourself, I fancy you may make a very clever letter with these materials: Lord Granby, for instance, who, I hear, is gone to Constantinople.[23] But to conclude after all these pleasant stories I am going to tell you so melancholy a one about myself that your heart will ache for me. Nothing less than going to Ireland, to my regiment,[24] to reviews, to nonsense and to drinking and eating and poverty and misery and beggary. Pity me, dear Horry, I have such a prospect of hurry and journey and restlessness before me as cracks my brain. I go into Ireland, that you conceive; and then come back, I believe, to stand for some place or other,[25] I don't know what, and then rioting all the winter. In short, I can't bear it and I hate myself and everybody else; everybody but you, my dear Horry. No, I'll hate you, too, for being so easy (I don't say merry) while I am so sad. Adieu.

Ta to Grey.

18. Lady Maria (Mary) Walpole (ca 1725–1801), m. (1746) Col. Charles Churchill; HW's half-sister.

18a. I.e., that she was illegitimate.

19. Not identified; possibly a nickname.

20. None of HW's letters to Mrs Grosvenor have been recovered.

21. Not identified; possibly a nickname, although the name exists in Suffolk.

22. Not identified; perhaps John Whaley's mother.

23. A few details of Granby's eastern travels are given in W. E. Manners, *Some Account of the . . . Marquis of Granby,* 1899, pp. 9–10.

24. See *ante* ca 25 Feb. 1740 NS, n. 4.

25. Conway was elected for Higham Ferrers at the general election of 1741.

From CONWAY, Monday 9 June 1740 OS

Printed in full for the first time from the MS now WSL, formerly Rutnam. Printed in part, *Rockingham Memoirs* i. 371–2; reprinted, *Colburn's United Service Magazine*, 1880, lii pt i. 167–8. Dated by the reference to the going into mourning 'yesterday' for the King of Prussia (below, n. 7).

YOU can't imagine, my dear Horry, how glad I am to hear you live so comfortably and divert yourself so well. Your ball,[1] I've a notion, was mighty fine, and I fancy your *disgrazio* of the English did not affect you extremely. But you have the most Jacobitical penetration into the pedigree of the Stuarts. What don't we all know (I'm sure we are told so), that the nurse clapped in her own great robust infant in the place of a little sickly Majesty who died? Fye! Horry, come away from that generation of Jacobites, fly by night! *return, ungrateful Englishman, back to your native climes again.*[2] By the by, I beg to know seriously when you design we should see you; we long for't more than I am able to tell you, and for my part I feel that I shall grow grave and importunate about it if you don't give me some hopes in your next. I told you[3] that my evil destiny had condemned me to pass this summer in Ireland. We actually set out, my brother and I, either on Friday next, or this day sennight. We stay two or three days at the Duke of Bedford's[4] and then my sister[5] and Mr Bowman take us up to continue our journey.[6] We went yesterday into mourning for his late Majesty of Prussia;[7] the present King[8] has writ a letter with his own [hand] to

1. As described in HW's missing letter of ca 15–20 May 1740 NS. It was probably the ball at the Villa Patrizi in honour of the Prince and Princesse de Craon and the Venetian ambassador Foscarini on 14 May NS. The Pretender, his sons, and the diplomatic corps were also at it (MANN i. 25 and nn. 10, 11).

2. Not found; possibly penned by Richard West in a missing letter to HW and Gray; see *post* ca 23 Aug. 1740.

3. *Ante* 14 May 1740 OS.

4. Woburn Abbey, Beds.

5. Hon. Anne Seymour Conway (d. 1774), m. (1755) John Harris. HW's

letter *post* 5 July 1740 NS makes it clear that it was she and not Conway's half-sister Jane who was making the trip to Ireland.

6. The Dublin papers mention Lord Conway's arrival there on 27 June OS (*Dublin Gazette, Pue's Occurrences, Dublin Newsletter,* 24–28 June 1740 OS).

7. Frederick William I (1688 – 31 May 1740 NS), K. of Prussia 1713–40. News of his death reached England 30 May OS; the Court went into mourning 8 June (*Daily Adv.* 31 May, 3, 9 June).

8. Frederick II (1712–86), the Great, K. of Prussia 1740–86.

Monsieur Algarotti[9] to this effect: 'Venez mon cher Algarotti; mon sort est changé. Je puis à présent jouir de mes amis—ne me faites pas longtemps perdre ce plaisir. J'ai de l'impatience à vous revoir. Frederick Roi.'[10] All this is mighty pretty and romantic and one would [think] they had been friends from the cradle, for kings don't condescend to these familiarities with subjects but upon extraordinary occasions; but behold all this friendship is the growth of one week or fortnight that Algarotti stayed with him on his road to Petersburgh with Lord Baltimore.[11] I must send you *Admiral Hosier's Ghost*[12] though it should stand you in half a crown, because all the world is crying out about it in some way or other. The Patriots cry it up and the Courtiers cry it down and the hawkers cry it up and down 'till they make one deaf; for my part I had rather hear your opinion about it than tell my own; but I have not the patience to wait for and so must tell you that I like it extremely and think it mighty solemn and mighty poetical; several men of sense that I have seen are of the same opinion; judges, and not party mad. Now as I take you for a very indifferent politician (you understand me, I mean a man of indifference in party matters), and think you far from an indifferent judge I hope you'll join with us. You

9. Francesco Algarotti (1712–64), cr. (1740) Count by Frederick the Great; man of letters (GRAY ii. 165, n. 29). He was living in London at this time, intimately connected with Lord Hervey, and made no secret of his summons from the new King, which he obeyed 6 June OS (Robert Halsband, *Life of Lady Mary Wortley Montagu*, Oxford, 1956, pp. 187, 196–7). Halsband's chapters X–XII and XV contain a thorough account of the complicated and curious relations between Algarotti and Hervey, Lady Mary Wortley Montagu and Frederick the Great.

10. The text of this letter, 3 June 1740 NS, as given in Frederick's *Œuvres*, ed. Preuss, Berlin, 1846–57, xviii. 15, is merely 'Mon cher Algarotti, mon sort a changé. Je vous attends avec impatience; ne me faites point languir. Federic.' HW gives another version, quite close to Conway's in this letter, in his *MS Commonplace Book of Verses*, p. 41.

11. Charles Calvert (1699–1751), 5th Bn

Baltimore. Algarotti had accompanied him on his mission to Russia in May 1739. On their return they had visited Frederick at Rheinsburg 20–25 Sept. 1739 NS (Frederick, however, calls it an eight-day visit), and both of them made a considerable impression upon him. Frederick immediately began a passionate correspondence with Algarotti, whom he dubbed 'cygne de Padoue,' and wrote an 'Épitre à milord Baltimore, sur la liberté' which he sent to Voltaire (Frederick II, op. cit. xiv. pp. xiv, 71–6; xvi. 378; xvii. 33; xviii. pp. ix, 3ff; xxvii pt iii. 120; Voltaire, *Correspondence*, ed. Besterman, Geneva, 1953–65, ix. 251; Halsband, op. cit. 177, 183–4).

12. By Richard Glover, first advertised as 'this day is published' in the *Daily Adv.* 21 May. Hannah More describes an evening party in 1785 at which Glover sang the ballad while HW listened with 'much complacency' (MORE 229). The SH records do not show that HW owned a copy.

know the history of his lying a vast while before Porto Bello[13] and losing almost all his crew. Adieu dear Horry.

Yours ever,

H. CONWAY

PS. This is the last verse which I could not send you in print because I must have sent you a sheet of paper more,[14] but can assure you it's genuine and really a part of the enclosed.

> All your country's foes subduing,
> When your patriot friends you see,
> Think on vengeance for my ruin,
> And for England sham'd in me.

It's Glover's.

Adieu once more! Service to Grey.

Monday, June 9th.

I forgot in my paragraph of Prussia news to tell you that the poor young monarch is gone author-mad and has sent for Voltaire[15] and God knows who.[16] N.B. He writes princely Prussian sonnets himself.

I shall always write to you *chez Monsieur Mann* if you don't send me some other direction.

13. In 1726–7, during which most of Hosier's crew died of a fever (DNB *sub* 'Hosier').

14. The four lines that follow appear on p. 7 of the 1st edn; by detaching them and the title page, Conway had to send only two leaves (pp. 3–6).

15. Frederick's letter to Voltaire, 6 June 1740 NS (Voltaire, op. cit. x. 144–5), although very friendly, was not precisely a summons. Voltaire paid a brief visit to Berlin in November 1740 (ibid. x. 328–30; T. Besterman, *Voltaire*, 1969, pp. 256–7).

16. Frederick had already sent for his former tutor Duhan, the philosopher Wolff, and Maupertuis (ibid. x. 145n).

To Conway, Tuesday 5 July 1740 NS

Printed from *Works* v. 8–12. From Conway's reply below (*post* before 23 Aug. 1740 OS), it would appear that the text was 'edited' by the removal of phrases and sentences before it was printed in *Works*.

Re di Cofano, vulg. Radicofani,[1] July 5, 1740 NS.

YOU will wonder, my dear Hal, to find me on the road from Rome: why, intend I did to stay for a new popedom, but the old eminences are cross and obstinate, and will not choose one,[2] the Holy Ghost does not know when. There is a horrid thing called the *mal'aria*,[3] that comes to Rome every summer and kills one, and I did not care for being killed so far from Christian burial. We have been jolted to death; my servants let us come without springs to the chaise, and we are wore threadbare: to add to our disasters, I have sprained my ankle, and have brought it along, laid upon a little box of baubles that I have bought for presents in England. Perhaps I may pick you out some little trifle there, but don't depend upon it; you are a disagreeable creature, and may be I shall not care for you. Though I am so tired in this devil of a place, yet I have taken it into my head, that it is like Hamilton's Bawn,[4] and I must write to you. 'Tis the top of a black barren mountain, a vile little town at the foot of an old citadel:[5] yet this, know you, was the residence of

1. A frontier town of Tuscany, 36 miles SE of Siena, on the principal road from Rome to Florence. HW and Gray had spent the night of 23 March NS there on their way to Rome (MANN i, endpaper; GRAY i. 205).

2. Benedict XIV was not elected until 17 Aug. 1740 NS.

3. 'At Rome there is what they call the Mala Aria (and what we should call a bad air) at a particular part of the summer. They have great superstition about it; and are so exact, as to name the very day it comes in. The country about Rome is almost a desert, scarce half the ground is ever cultivated, and there is sometimes not a house to be seen for 5 or 6 miles together. This is one great occasion of the Mala Aria, which lies over Rome in July and August, and in some part for 40 miles around it'

(Joseph Spence to Mrs Spence, 23 Aug. [1732], BM Egerton MSS 2234, f. 62). The true cause of malaria was not discovered until the late 19th century.

4. A large estate in co. Armagh, about 25 miles from the Conway estates around Lisburn and the subject of Swift's 'The Grand Question Debated. Whether Hamilton's Bawn should be turned into a Barrack or a Malt-House,' written in 1729 and published in 1732 (Swift's *Poems*, ed. H. Williams, 2d edn, Oxford, 1958, iii. 863–73).

5. Originally a monastery, but fortified in the 12th century and virtually destroyed by an explosion in 1735 (GRAY i. 205, n. 11). See also Thomas Gray, *Correspondence*, ed. Toynbee and Whibley, Oxford, 1935, i. 145, for a further description of the barrenness and desolation of the place.

one of the three kings that went to Christ's birthday; his name was
Alabaster,[6] Abarasser, or some such thing; the other two were kings,
one of the East, the other of Cologn. 'Tis this of Cofano, who was
represented in an ancient painting, found in the Palatine Mount,
now in the possession of Dr Mead;[7] he was crowned by Augustus.
Well, but about writing—what do you think I write with? Nay, with
a pen; there was never a one to be found in the whole circumference
but one, and that was in the possession of the governor, and had
been used time out of mind to write the parole with: I was forced
to send to borrow it. It was sent me under the conduct of a serjeant
and two Swiss, with desire to return it when I should have done with
it. 'Tis a curiosity, and worthy to be laid up with the relics which
we have just been seeing in a small hovel of Capucins on the side of
the hill, and which were all brought by his Majesty from Jerusalem.
Among other things of great sanctity there is a set of gnashing of
teeth, the grinders very entire; a bit of the worm that never dies, preserved in spirits; a crow of St Peter's cock, very useful against Easter;
the crisping and curling, frizzling and frowncing[8] of Mary Magdalen,
which she cut off on growing devout.[9] The good man that showed us
all these commodities was got into such a train of calling them the
blessed this, and the blessed that, that at last he showed us a bit of
the blessed fig tree that Christ cursed.

---

6. Balthazar. This legend, to which HW
also alludes in his letter to West 22
March 1740 NS (GRAY i. 205), is apparently either his own invention or of
purely local origin; it is particularly
curious since Balthazar is almost always
represented as a negro.

7. Dr Richard Mead (1673–1754), physician and collector. HW is alluding to a
fragmentary Roman painting, found on
the Palatine, which Mead had acquired
before 1740; it was believed at this time
to represent Augustus, M. Agrippa, Maece-
nas and Horace, but the figure to whom
the crown was being given was missing;
for contemporary descriptions and engrav-

ings, see George Turnbull, *Treatise on
Ancient Painting,* 1740, pp. 172–3 and
plate 3; idem [compiler], *Three Disser-
tations, One on the Characters of Augustus, Horace, and Agrippa . . . by the
Abbé Vertot,* 1740, p. xiv and plate facing
p. 1; and idem, *A Curious Collection of
Ancient Paintings,* 1744, p. 11 and plate 3.

8. HW to Bentley 28 Aug. 1755 (CHUTE
248–9) attributes this phrase to the Puri-
tan pamphleteer William Prynne, but it
has not been found in his works.

9. Conway's reply indicates that HW
had also mentioned being shown the Virgin's maidenhead, damaged, and the King
of Cofano's breeches pocket.

Florence, July 9.

My dear Harry,

We are come hither, and I have received another letter from you
with *Hosier's Ghost*.[10] Your last[11] put me in pain for you, when you
talked of going to Ireland; but now I find your brother and sister go
with you, I am not much concerned. Should I be? You have but to
say, for my feelings are extremely at your service to dispose as you
please. Let us see: you are to come back to stand for some place; that
will be about April. 'Tis a sort of thing I should do too; and then we
should see one another, and that would be charming: but it is a
sort of thing I have no mind to do; and then we shall not see one
another, unless you would come hither—but that you cannot do:
nay, I would not have you, for then I shall be gone.—So! there are
many *ifs* that just signify nothing at all. Return I must sooner than
I shall like. I am happy here to a degree. I'll tell you my situation.
I am lodged with Mr Mann,[12] the best of creatures. I have a terreno
all to myself, with an open gallery on the Arno, where I am now
writing to you. Over against me is the famous Gallery;[13] and, on
either hand, two fair bridges.[14] Is not this charming and cool? The
air is so serene, and so secure, that one sleeps with all the windows
and doors thrown open to the river, and only covered with a
slight gauze to keep away the gnats. Lady Pomfret[15] has a charming
conversation once a week.[16] She has taken a vast palace[17] and a vast
garden, which is vastly commode, especially to the cicisbeo-part of
mankind, who have free indulgence to wander in pairs about the

10. *Ante* 9 June 1740 OS.

11. *Ante* 14 May 1740 OS.

12. Afterwards Sir Horace Mann. He
was at this time Resident at Florence
from George II (HW). HW was staying
at this time at the Casa Ambrogi, Via de'
Bardi; Mann did not lease his later residence, the Casa Manetti, Via San Spirito,
until 1 Aug. 1740 NS (Gray i. 237, n. 4).

13. The Uffizi.

14. The Ponte Vecchio and the Ponte
alle Grazie.

15. Henrietta Louisa, wife of Thomas
Earl of Pomfret (HW). Hon. Henrietta
Louisa Jeffreys (ca 1700–61), m. (1720)
Thomas Fermor, 2d Bn Leominster, cr.
(1721) E. of Pomfret. She, her husband,

and her two eldest daughters lived at
Florence from 20 Dec. 1739 NS to 13
March 1741 NS (ibid. i. 227, n. 18; Mann
i. 4, n. 18). For HW's character of her,
see Gray ii. 247–8.

16. Usually on Fridays (Robert Halsband, *Life of Lady Mary Wortley Montagu*, Oxford, 1956, p. 202).

17. The Palazzo Ridolfi, which Lady
Pomfret had leased in May. She describes
it and the gardens, which contained
about eight acres, in a letter to Lady
Hertford 29 May 1740 NS (Frances, Countess of Hertford and Henrietta Louisa,
Countess of Pomfret, *Correspondence*,
1805, i. 227–31; Mann i. 59, n. 7).

arbours. You know her daughters: Lady Sophia[18] is still, nay she must be, the beauty she was: Lady Charlotte[19] is much improved, and is the cleverest girl in the world; speaks the purest Tuscan like any Florentine. The Princess Craon[20] has a constant pharaoh and supper every night, where one is quite at one's ease. I am going into the country with her and the Prince[21] for a little while,[22] to a villa of the Great Duke's.[23] The people are good-humoured here and easy; and what makes me pleased with them, they are pleased with me. One loves to find people care for one, when they can have no view in it.

You see how glad I am to have reasons for not returning; I wish I had no better.

As to *Hosier's Ghost,* I think it very easy, and consequently pretty; but, from the ease, should never have guessed it Glover's. I delight in your, 'the Patriots cry it up, and the Courtiers cry it down, and the hawkers cry it up and down,'[24] and your laconic history of the King and Sir R[obert] on going to Hanover, and turning out the Duke of A[rgyll].[25] The epigram[26] too you sent me on the same occasion is charming.

Unless I sent you back news that you and others send me, I can send you none. I have left the Conclave, which is the only stirring thing in this part of the world, except the child that the Queen of

18. Afterwards married to John Lord Carteret, who became Earl of Granville on the death of his mother in the year 1744 (HW).

19. Afterwards married to William Finch, brother to [Daniel Finch, 7th] Earl of Winchelsea (HW). Lady Charlotte Fermor (1725–1813), m. (1746) Hon. William Finch (MANN i. 4, n. 23). 'Lady Charlotte was agreeable enough in her person, and extremely so in her manner; never spoke improperly; never despised company of her own age or under it, though always capable of entertaining those above it. Her sincerity and justness of expression were only inferior to the modesty of her delivery' (HW's MS *Commonplace Book of Verses,* p. 29).

20. The Princess Craon was the favourite mistress of Leopold the last Duke of Lorrain, who married her to Monsieur de Beauvau, and prevailed on the Emperor to make him a prince of the

Empire. They at this time resided at Florence, where Prince Craon was at the head of the Council of Regency (HW). Anne-Marguerite de Ligniville (1686–1772), m. (1704) Marc-Antoine de Beauvau, Prince de Craon (MANN i. 3, n. 8).

21. Marc de Beauvau (1679–1754), Prince de Craon; President of the Council of Regency to the Grand Duke of Tuscany 1737–49 (ibid. i. 9, n. 27).

22. This excursion apparently did not take place, since HW told West 2 Oct. 1740 NS that he had not yet visited any of the Grand Duke's villas (GRAY i. 230).

23. The Craons usually spent the summer at the Petraia (MANN i. 390, n. 2); there were seven other villas of the Grand Duke in the immediate vicinity of Florence (GRAY i. 230, n. 3).

24. *Ante* 9 June 1740 OS.

25. *Ante* 14 May 1740 OS.

26. Ibid.

Naples[27] is to be delivered of in August. There is no likelihood the Conclave will end, unless the messages take effect which 'tis said the Imperial and French ministers have sent to their respective Courts for leave to quit the Corsini for the Albani faction;[28] otherwise there will never be a pope. Corsini has lost the only one he could have ventured to make pope, and him he designed; 'twas Cenci,[29] a relation of the Corsini's mistress. The last morning Corsini made him rise, stuffed a dish of chocolate[30] down his throat, and would carry him to the scrutiny. The poor old creature went, came back, and died. I am sorry to have lost the sight of the pope's coronation, but I might have stayed for seeing it till I had been old enough to be pope myself.

Harry, what luck the Chancellor[31] has! first, indeed, to be in himself so great a man;[32] but then in accidents: he is made chief justice and peer,[33] when Talbot is made chancellor and peer: Talbot dies in a twelvemonth,[34] and leaves him the Seals at an age when others are scarce made solicitors:[35]—then marries his son[36] into one of the first families of Britain, obtains a patent for a marquisate and eight thousand pounds a year after the Duke of Kent's[37] death: the Duke

27. Maria Amalia (1724–60) of Saxony, m. (1738) Charles VII, K. of Naples, K. of Spain as Charles III, 1759. Her first child Maria Elisabeth was born 6 Sept. 1740 NS, and died two years later (Isenburg, *Stammtafeln* ii. taf. 50).

28. John Walton's (i.e., Baron Stosch's) dispatches from Florence 9 and 16 July 1740 NS (S.P. 98/43, ff. 58, 61) mention that the French and Imperial ministers had sent to their respective courts for further instructions. The Imperial ambassador extraordinary to the Conclave was Scipio Publicola (d. 1747), Principe di Santa Croce; and the French, Paul-Hippolyte de Beauvilliers (1684–1776), Duc de Saint-Aignan (MANN i. 3, n. 10, 12, n. 52; SELWYN 59, n. 7).

29. Seraphino Cenci (1676 – 24 June 1740 NS), Abp of Benevento, 1733, cardinal, 1734, had been proposed to the Conclave by Corsini in March and remained a strong candidate of that faction throughout April (*Genealog. hist. Nachrichten*, 1740–1, 1st ser. ii. 99–102, 239; Michael Ranft, *Merkwürdige Lebensgeschichte aller Cardinäle*, Regensburg, 1768–81, ii. 289–91; Maurice Boutry, 'Le

Cardinal de Tencin au conclave de Benoît XIV,' *Revue d'histoire diplomatique*, 1897, xi. 392).

30. This detail is confirmed by *Genealog. hist. Nachrichten*, 1st ser. ii. 102.

31. Philip Yorke (1690–1764), cr. (1733) Bn and (1754) E. of Hardwicke; lord chancellor 1737–56.

32. HW soon changed this opinion when he became convinced that Hardwicke had been in league with Newcastle to 'betray' Sir Robert Walpole (*Mem. Geo. II* i. 158–61).

33. In Nov. 1733.

34. Not until Feb. 1737 (*ante* 15 Feb. 1737 OS and nn. 4, 5).

35. Hardwicke was 46 when he became lord chancellor.

36. Philip Yorke (1720–90), styled Vct Royston 1754–64; 2d E. of Hardwicke, 1764; m. (22 May 1740 OS) Lady Jemima Campbell (1722–97), Marchioness Grey, *s.j.*, 1740.

37. Henry Grey (1671 – 5 June 1740 OS), 12th E. of Kent, cr. (1706) M. and (1710) D. of Kent, had received a patent as Marquess Grey 19 May 1740 OS, with a special remainder to his granddaughter

dies in a fortnight, and leaves them all! People talk of fortune's wheel that is always rolling: troth, my Lord Hardwicke has overtaken her wheel, and rolled along with it.

I perceive Miss Jenny[38] would not venture to Ireland, nor stray so far from London; I am glad I shall always know where to find her within three-score miles. I must say a word to my Lord,[39] which, Harry, be sure you don't read. 'My dear Lord, I don't love troubling you with letters, because I know you don't love the trouble of answering them; not that I should insist on that ceremony, but I hate to burthen anyone's conscience. Your brother tells me he is to stand member of Parliament: without telling me so, I am sure he owes it to you. I am sure you will not repent setting him up; nor will he be ungrateful to a brother who deserves so much, and whose least merit is not the knowing how to employ so great a fortune.'

There, Harry, I have done. Don't suspect me: I have said no ill of you behind your back. Make my best compliments to Miss Conway.[40]

I thought I had done, and lo, I had forgot to tell you, that who d'ye think is here?—Even Mr More![41] our Rheims Mr More! the fortification, hornwork, ravelin, bastion[42] Mr More! *which is very pleasant sure.* At the end of the eighth side, I think I need make no excuse for leaving off; but I am going to write to Selwyn, and to the lady of the mountain;[43] from whom I have had a very kind letter. She has at last received the Chantilly brass. Good night: write to me from one end of the world to t'other.

Yours ever,

Hor. Walpole

and heiress, Lady **Jemima Campbell** and the heirs male of her body (GEC).

38. Miss Jane Conway, half-sister to Henry Seymour Conway. She died unmarried in 1749 (HW).

39. Francis Lord Conway, afterwards Earl and Marquis of Hertford, elder brother to H. Seymour Conway (HW).

40. Afterwards married to John Harris, Esq., of Hayne in Devonshire (HW).

41. See a letter to Mr West, dated Rheims, 20th July, 1739 (HW). This letter (GRAY i. 177–80) contains an account of a

visit by this gentleman, who is not otherwise identified, to HW, Gray, and Conway. See also MANN i. 123, n. 42.

42. HW quotes More as saying that 'our ships are our bastions, and our ravelins, and our hornworks' (GRAY i. 180).

43. Possibly Selwyn's mother, Mary Farrington (ca 1690–1777), m. (ca 1708–9) Col. John Selwyn; she lived at Matson, on Robins Wood Hill, which is described in HW to Bentley Sept. 1753 as 'lofty enough for an Alp' (CHUTE 152). Both of HW's letters are missing.

From CONWAY, before Saturday 23 August 1740 OS

Printed for the first time from the MS now WSL, formerly Rutnam. Dated approximately by Conway's comment that he is to go to the assizes at Carrick-
fergus on 'Saturday next' (below, n. 7).

Address: À Monsieur Monsieur Walpole recommandé à Monsieur Mann resident du roi d'Angleterre à Florence.

Postmark: [Illegible].

[?Lisburn].

THANK you, my dear Horry, ten thousand times for your charming, long, magnificent letter, no part of which (delightful as it
all was) gave me so sensible a pleasure as your telling me you were
on your return from Rome, which I hope I may understand of your
coming home, without straining the teat to flatter the great interest
I have in it: but then you add some time after that you are sure
you must come home sooner [than] you desire; though this seemed a
sort of comment upon t'other, yet I balanced some time whether I
was to be pleased with it or not; you'll forgive me if I found any
inclination to triumph in a thing that you look upon as a misfortune; but in return I may venture to assure you that this is the only
misfortune could happen to you without giving your friends in
England at least as much concern as I doubt your present one will
give them pleasure, however they may dally with you or flatter you
with feigned condolences. 'Tis thus we are made! my dear Horry,
and though having lain myself so lately under the same compulsion,
I could not help having a little feeling for you, yet I soon found
means to give it a turn in my own imagination that authorized me
to indulge the great propensity I had to be pleased; I easily supposed
that all the dismal apprehensions that you have formed in prejudice
to poor England would be agreeably disappointed; and that a
thousand pleasures would rise up which you have scarce suffered
yourself to form an idea of. If he finds, says I, no open galleries on
the Arno, yet a thousand open hearts will stand ready to receive him
and he'll forget the Arno *on the pleasanter banks of the Thames.*[1]
I thought a great deal more in the same style, and if I had had the
least grain of poetical genius I would have put 'em into a poem
with a thousand conceits about the *mal'arias,* thunders, lightnings,

1. Apparently a line from a song.

earthquakes, hurricanes, gnats, bugs, scorpions, *Hornwork Mores²*
etc. concluding with so inviting a description of England that you
should have ordered your chaise before you got to the end of it.
At present, after lamenting much *la petitesse de mon génie,* I have
nothing to say, but to exhort you in the words of your more poetical
friend:³

> Return, ungrateful Englishmen
> Back to your native climes again.

After all I wish you don't find out that this [is] but a bad copy of
my countenance, except that part of it which relates to the pleasure
I promise myself in seeing you than which nothing is more sincere;
but if my encomiums upon England don't seem forced at least
I am sure at present I should gladly make the exchange for Italy
without bating an ace of the *mal'arias,* thunders, scorpions or what
you will. Your naïve description of your Gallery had more effect
upon me, I doubt, than all I could have said of England would
have had upon you; and not only that but everything in Italy; for
entre nous I am a little Italy mad;⁴ but I am ashamed to own it because I know so little either of its antiquities, language, paintings,
sculptures, history or anything else belonging to it that I am afraid
my desire of seeing it would be looked upon as a childish curiosity,
which perhaps may have some part in it; though I languish to know
Italian and to read the Ariosto and the Tasso and such dear people, whom I have now only read or heard of. Then for medals,
paintings, history I have a furious desire to know something about
them; and then I want to travel and do a thousand things which I
almost despair of which is terrible. Don't I put you in mind of little
George,⁵ your nephew, with all his wants of ten thousand men and a
hundred thousand lions with a proportionable quantity of swords
and pistols and hangers? I should delight in being with you even in
your King *Alablaser's* vile citadel: and as for your governor and
his pen if you and some more friends were with me I should not
trouble him much. Your relics delight me above all things, but when
you talked of the Virgin's maidenhead being damaged I began to be

2. See *ante* 5 July 1740 NS and n. 41.

3. Possibly West; see *ante* 9 June 1740 OS, n. 2.

4. Conway did not visit Italy until the late autumn of 1751.

5. George Walpole (1730–91), styled Vct Walpole 1745–51, 3d E. of Orford, 1751.

in great pain where it would end and was much relieved by his Majesty's breeches pocket. You are so kind as to say you have some little feelings at my service;[6] I can never call for 'em at a more proper season than the present and I am sure they never can be disposed of in a more charitable manner than for the relief of a poor friend, who beside other innumerable sufferings, is on Saturday next (if he lives so long) condemned to go to the assizes at Carickfergus[7] in the County of Antrim and then and there to be barbarously and inhumanely set up as candidate for the ensuing election of a member to represent the said county.[8] Mem. he has with great difficulty obtained hopes of his being excused from acting as foreman of the Grand Jury, and then we go to England[9] and soon after comes on another more terrible setting up.[10] I don't yet perfectly know upon what footing. If I guess right this may in some measure affect your Worship. *Proximus ardet Ucalegon,*[11] and I don't know but what our situations resemble one another in more points than one. I am going [to] be *loaded* with honours that I am so far from coveting at present that I am afraid I shall hardly be able to obey Horace's injunction to his friend: *æquam memento rebus in arduis, servare mentem.*[12] 'Tis thus, my dear Horry, that we are hurried down the stream of life, always looking one way and rowing another.[13] Here am I obliged to give a forced preference to a situation that the world thinks more honourable, when I should think myself

6. 'My feelings are extremely at your service to dispose as you please' (*ante* 5 July 1740 NS).

7. These were scheduled to begin on Friday, 22 Aug. OS (*Pue's Occurrences* 28 June – 1 July 1740 OS).

8. Conway's unanimous election as M.P. for Co. Antrim (where his brother owned large estates) did not take place until 19 Oct. 1741 OS, and he does not seem to have taken his seat in the Irish House of Commons until 7 Oct. 1755. Since he was standing for the vacancy created by the death of John Upton after the prorogation of the last session of the Irish Parliament, it was necessary to wait for the opening of the next biennial session in Oct. 1741 for the formality of issuing the writ for the new election (*Journals of the House of Commons . . . Ireland,* Dublin, 1753–71, vii. 203, 213, 219; ix. 239; *Pue's Occurrences* 3–6 May 1740 OS;

Dublin Newsletter 13–17, 24–27 Oct. 1741 OS; Rowley Lascelles, *Liber munerum publicorum Hiberniæ,* [1852], i pt i, 'Parliamentary Register of the Commons,' p. 1). At this period, general elections in Ireland took place only at the death of the sovereign.

9. The departure of Lord Conway and his sister for England on 29 Oct. 1740 OS is mentioned in the *Dublin Newsletter* 28 Oct. – 1 Nov., but Conway is not included in the list of passengers.

10. I.e., for the English House of Commons. Conway was returned on the Wentworth interest for Higham Ferrers in Dec. 1741.

11. Virgil, *Æneid* ii. 311–12 ('Ucalegon burns next door').

12. Horace, *Odes* II. iii. 1–2 ('Remember in arduous circumstances to keep an even mind').

13. This is a figure used by Plutarch.

more happy in following inclinations that would lead me a more private but a pleasanter way, and I believe make me a better and, if anything would, an abler man: I don't pretend to be so philosophical as to divest myself of all ambition but I can't help thinking that deserving honours without being in possession of them is more honourable and of course satisfies a right ambition more than being loaded like a herald with badges that belong to other people. But I find I grow dry and grave to a degree as well as selfish for I have talked of nothing where dear I has not been concerned for though I have mentioned you, dear I is never more concerned than in what regards dear you. Now I have been racking my brain to find out some news, or to think of some subject or other worth entertaining you with; but in vain, for news I have none and as for a description of the place and people where I am, which is the natural topic of travellers, I have not the impudence to send an account of Ireland into Italy; if I catch you in Lapland or Tartary you shall have a fair description of it, but one must be an Irishman to send it anywhere else. My brother thanks you for your little epistle,[14] and bids me assure you that though his idleness prevents him from being your constant correspondent, nobody is more sincerely your constant friend and servant; he bid me say modest things for him in regard to his letters and that it was a proof of the friendship he professed to you to save you the trouble of so many trifles and impertinences: but if I should enlarge any more upon it I should do his compliments wrong and besides it's a ridiculous thing for me who can hardly and very awkwardly *me tirer d'affaire* of my own correspondences to pretend to carry 'em on for anybody else, so that I don't care to go farther for my best friends than a postscript, love, service or the like. Now you begin to be mightily tired of me, I've a notion; and so I'll relieve you with an imitation of Horace which has been much liked and then conclude if I can. The subject is Gen. Churchill's[15] having the Duck Island given him[16] as you'll

14. The paragraph included *ante* 5 July 1740 NS.

15. Charles Churchill (ca 1679–1745), Lt–Gen., 1739; M.P. Weymouth and Melcombe Regis 1701–10, Castle Rising 1715–45; an intimate friend of Sir Robert Walpole (Selwyn 20, n. 8).

16. Churchill had become deputy ranger of Hyde and St James's Parks in

Dec. 1739 (GM 1739, ix. 661). Duck Island is situated in the latter; previous 'governors' had been St-Évremond in the reign of Charles II and Stephen Duck, who had been appointed by Queen Caroline (H. B. Wheatley and Peter Cunningham, *London Past and Present*, 1891, ii. 294).

see; the author unknown.[17] Now as you mayn't have the ode in your memory and as I have and as it is very short, I'll set it down to save you the trouble of turning over a Horace.

> O Venus, regina Cnidi Paphique,
> Sperne dilectum Cypren, et vocantis
> Thure te multo Glyceræ decoram
>   Transfer in ædem.
> Fervidus tecum puer, et solutis
> Gratiæ sonis properentque nymphæ
> Et parum comis sine te Iuventus
>   Mercuriusque.

> O Venus, joy of men and gods,
> Forsake for once thy blest abodes,
>   And deign to visit my land!
> On thy fond vot'ry kindly smile,
> Quit Paphos and the Cyprian Isle
>   To reign o'er my Duck Island.

> Thee, Goddess, thee my pray'rs invoke,
> For thee alone my altars smoke;
>   Oh! treat me not with rigour!
> Thy wanton son bring with thee too,
> My dying embers he'll renew,
>   And gird my back with vigour.
> Bring too the Graces to my arms,
> Girls that are prodigal of charms,
>   Of ev'ry favour lavish;
> Melting and yielding let them be,
> Consider I am sixty-three,
>   And that's no age to ravish!

> Let florid youth attend thy train,
> Much wanted by thy crazy swain;
>   And gentle Venus, prithee,

17. The poem, an imitation of Horace, *Odes* I. xxx, was written in Dec. 1739 by Charles Hanbury Williams (1708–59), K.B., 1744; poet, wit, and diplomatist; later HW's correspondent. According to HW this poem was 'the first thing that made him [Williams] known as a poet of great genius and wit' (SELWYN 313). There is a copy in Williams's MSS, now WSL, lxix. f. 8, and a transcript is in HW's *MS Poems*, p. 39. It was printed GM 1741, xi. 48 and in Williams's *Works*, ed. Jeffery, 1822, i. 234–6. There are slight verbal differences between all these versions.

To crown thy gifts and ease my pain,
Since Ward[18] has labour'd long in vain,
Let Mercury come with thee.

Tell me if you are critic grave enough to be angry with the pun at the end of it or if you like it or how? Write to me *d'abord* and tell me good news about your coming; I'd rather hear that than the Conclave for I don't *care a fig* what old woman ties St Peter's keys to her apron string. I am, dear Horry, yours as much as ever, more if possible. Adieu! Poor Selwyn's ill! but I don't know any particulars; I have writ very pressingly and hope to have a good account of him, for he's too good to suffer.

To CONWAY, Sunday 25 September 1740 NS

Printed from *Works* v. 12–14.

Florence, September 25, 1740 NS.

My dear Hal,

I BEGIN to answer your letter the moment I have read it, because you bid me; but I grow so unfit for a correspondence with anybody in England, that I have almost left it off. 'Tis so long since I was there, and I am so utterly a stranger to everything that passes there, that I must talk vastly in the dark to those I write; and having in a manner settled myself here, where there can be no news, I am void of all matter for filling up a letter. As, by the absence of the Great Duke,[1] Florence is become in a manner a country town, you may imagine that we are not without *démêlés;* but for a country town I believe there never were a set of people so peaceable, and such strangers to scandal. 'Tis the family of love, where everybody is paired, and go as constantly together as parakeets. Here nobody

18. Joshua Ward, the quack doctor (*ante* 7 April 1737 OS, n. 9). In a note to his transcript of these verses, HW comments: 'General Churchill was the great patron of Ward's Drop, in opposition to the physicians. Governor Hart's son having taken it and caught cold, it flew into his head and distracted him. The Queen hearing of this, said to Mr Chur-chill one day in the Drawing-Room, "Oh! Mr Churchill, I hear the Drop has made a man mad."—"Yes, Madam." "Yes! why, is it true?" "Yes, Madam." "Why, who is it?"—'Dr Meade, Madam" ' (HW's *MS Poems*, p. 39).

1. Francis I (1708–65), Emperor 1745–65; Grand Duke of Tuscany 1737–65.

hangs or drowns themselves; they are not ready to cut one another's throats about elections or parties; don't think that wit consists in saying bold truths, or humour in getting drunk. But I shall give you no more of their characters, because I am so unfortunate as to think that their encomium consists in being the reverse of the English, who in general are either mad, or enough to make other people so. After telling you so fairly my sentiments, you may believe, my dear Harry, that I had much rather see you here than in England. 'Tis an evil wish for you, who should not be lost in so obscure a place as this. I will not make you compliments, or else here is a charming opportunity for saying what I think of you. As I am convinced you love me, and as I am conscious you have one strong reason for it, I will own to you, that for my own peace you should wish me to remain here. I am so well within and without, that you would scarce know me: I am younger than ever, think of nothing but diverting myself, and live in a round of pleasures. We have operas, concerts, and balls, mornings and evenings. I dare not tell you all one's idlenesses; you would look so grave and senatorial, at hearing that one rises at eleven in the morning, goes to the opera at nine at night, to supper at one, and to bed at three! But literally here the evenings and nights are so charming and so warm, one can't avoid 'em.

Did I tell you Lady Mary Wortley[2] is here? She laughs at my Lady Walpole,[3] scolds my Lady Pomfret, and is laughed at by the whole town. Her dress, her avarice, and her impudence must amaze anyone that never heard her name. She wears a foul mob, that does not cover her greasy black locks, that hang loose, never combed or curled; an old mazarine blue wrapper, that gapes open and discovers a canvas petticoat. Her face swelled violently on one side with the remains of a pox,[4] partly covered with a plaister, and partly with white paint, which for cheapness she has bought so coarse, that you

2. Lady Mary Pierrepont (1689–1762), m. (1712) Edward Wortley Montagu; letter-writer. She had been staying with Lady Pomfret at Florence since 22 Aug. NS and remained until 16 Oct. (Robert Halsband, *Life of Lady Mary Wortley Montagu*, Oxford, 1956, pp. 201, 205).

3. Margaret Rolle (1709–81), m. 1 (1724) Robert Walpole, cr. (1723) Bn Walpole,

2d E. of Orford, 1745; m. 2 (1751) Hon. Sewallis Shirley; HW's sister-in-law. She was living at Florence with Samuel Sturgis, with whom she had eloped in 1734.

4. That this is the word omitted from *Works* and later printings is clear from Conway's reply *post* ca 30 Nov. 1740 OS. Halsband, op. cit. 204, questions the accuracy of this description of Lady Mary.

would not use it to wash a chimney.—In three words I will give you her picture as we drew it in the *Sortes Virgilianæ*—⁵

Insanam vatem aspicies.⁶

I give you my honour, we did not choose it; but Gray, Mr Cooke,⁷ Sir Fr[ancis] Dashwood⁸ and I, and several others, drew it fairly amongst a thousand for different people, most of which did not hit as you may imagine: those that did I will tell you.

For our most religious and gracious King:⁹

Di, talem terris avertite pestem.¹⁰

For one that would be our most religious and gracious King:¹¹

Purpureus veluti cum flos succisus aratro
Languescit moriens, lassove papavera collo
Demisere caput, pluvia cum forte gravantur.¹²

For his son:¹³

Regis Romani; primus qui legibus urbem
Fundabit, Curibus parvis et paupere terra
Missus in imperium magnum.¹⁴

For Sir Robert:

Res dura et regni novitas me talia cogunt
Moliri, et late fines custode tueri.¹⁵

I will show you the rest when I see you.

Hor. Walpole

5. The passages that follow and seventeen others are given, with notes, in HW's MS *Commonplace Book of Verses*, pp. 1–2, where he dates them Aug. 1740.

6. *Æneid* iii. 443 ('You shall look upon an inspired prophetess').

7. Edward Coke (1719–53), styled Vct Coke 1744–53; M.P. Norfolk 1741–7, Harwich 1747–53. He had been at Florence from late June to 6 Aug. 1740 NS (Frances, Countess of Hertford, and Henrietta Louisa, Countess of Pomfret, *Correspondence*, 1805, ii. 6, 41).

8. (1708–81), 2d Bt; 4th Bn Le Despenser, 1763. He was at Florence until the beginning of October 1740 (ibid. ii. 116; Lady Pomfret's journal, Finch MSS D411, *sub* 6 Sept. and 1 Oct. 1740 NS, reference kindly supplied by Professor Robert Halsband).

9. George II.

10. *Æneid* iii. 620 ('Ye gods, avert such a pest from the earth').

11. I.e., the Old Pretender.

12. Ibid. ix. 435–7 ('As when a purple flower, cut by the plow, languishes dying; or as poppies, with weary neck, bow the head, when weighted by chance with rain').

13. The Young Pretender.

14. Ibid. vi. 810–12 ('The Roman king, who, sent to great authority from little Cures and a poor land, shall first found the city by laws').

15. Ibid. i. 563–4 ('Hard circumstances and the newness of my kingdom force me to do such things and protect my frontiers far and wide with guards').

To Conway, October 1740

Missing; answered ca 30 Nov. 1740 OS together with HW's letter of 25 Sept. NS.

From Conway, ca Sunday 30 November 1740 OS

Printed for the first time from the MS now WSL, formerly Rutnam. The postscript, which is written in the upper right corner of the first page of the MS, is dated 30 Nov.; several passages in this letter are clearly a reply to HW's of 25 Sept. 1740 NS, while others answer a missing letter received later.

Dear Horry,

I WAS in the country when your letter came, but the moment I came to town I set an honest gentleman with a wooden leg to work about your country dances,[1] which are at last finished and I hope will please you, or rather, please the ladies you design to oblige with 'em, for I imagine you don't interest yourself much about 'em; if you are still at Florence, as I don't doubt but you are, make my excuses to the ladies for the delay they have suffered and lay all the fault upon the fiddler. You may tell 'em for their farther satisfaction that some of these dances were new last winter and that the rest, beside those you named, are chosen by one of the best dancers and the best fiddler in town. By the best dancer you are not to imagine I mean myself, no, I did not think it became me, who am one of the worst in the world at these things, to depend upon my own judgment in a point of such importance. You mentioned some concern about Selwyn in your last;[2] I am happy to have the pleasure of telling you that nobody at present has less title to your concern; he has been at Tunbridge this summer and God knows what they have done to him there, but he has actually suffered a perfect metamorphose; he is returned sleek and well-looking, full of spirits and jolly and his complexion so clear and rubicund that one would not know him. You would think he had changed his skin, and has so

---

1. Requested in HW's missing letter of Oct. 1740.

2. HW's concern was doubtless occasioned by Conway's mentioning *ante* before 23 Aug. 1740 OS that 'poor Selwyn's ill! but I don't know any particulars.'

like Virgil's *simile* snake *mala gramina pastus*³—vid. H. Legge⁴—
that one would not know one from t'other; and as you say of yourself he is so changed within and without that you would scarce
know him. So that you, too, will not know one another when you
meet and have all your acquaintance to form over again. That's a
false thought and a foolish one, by the by, but it's all one; the folly
of it will make you laugh; and one had better laugh at a foolish
thing than be grave at a wise one: I have a notion Lady Mary⁵ diverts you a good deal in that way; she makes you laugh at her follies
and I fancy her wisdom will never make either herself or anybody
else grave. But then she's so clever with her follies that I don't doubt
but she adds to your amusements and pleasure, lively as they are; I
want to know if she's paired yet; I have a notion she's one of your
barren birds that choose to live single because they cannot get a
mate; for her greasy locks and her canvas petticoats, and her whitewash and her stinks and her poxes will have more power to repel
her lovers than her wit will have to attract 'em, and so she'll always
be acting the part of an electrical body gaining hearts at a distance
and drawing 'em towards her only to send 'em away faster than they
came. Pray make my compliments to Lord and Lady Pomphret; and
to the young ladies; is Lady Sophy as pretty and as agreeable as ever?
or do you think her as much so as I did when I had the pleasure of
seeing her at Paris?⁶ I like the verses you sent me⁷ so well that I
own I can't help having my doubts about their being quite extempore; tell me who's they are; whether they're yours or Grey's or
whose? I don't doubt but the young lady I last mentioned may be as
likely as any of the Nine to have inspired those thoughts; as to
Zelinda's being in England,⁸ that's nothing, for poets transport both
themselves and everybody else just where they will *modo [me]
Thebis, modo ponit Athenis*.⁹

3. *Æneid* ii. 471 ('fed on poisonous
herbs').

4. Hon. Henry Legge (after 1754 Bilson
Legge) (1708–1764), chancellor of the Exchequer 1754–5, 1756–61; from ca 1735 to
1739 he had been Sir Robert Walpole's
private secretary (Namier and Brooke iii.
30). The phrase 'vid. H. Legge' is written
below the word 'simile.'

5. Lady Mary Wortley Montagu.

6. The Pomfrets had visited Paris in
late Jan. and early Feb. 1739 (Frances,

Countess of Hertford, and Henrietta
Louisa, Countess of Pomfret, *Correspondence*, 1805, i. 54); Conway was there
with his brother at that time.

7. HW's 'To Zelinda, from Florence';
there is a copy in HW's *MS Poems*, pp.
30–2, printed below, Appendix 2.

8. The hero of HW's verses had been
wandering about Europe in a vain attempt to forget Zelinda at home.

9. Horace, *Epistles* II. i. 213 ('Sets me
down now at Thebes, now at Athens').

And now I'm upon the topic of verses I'll tell you that that ode[10] has never been given to Legge, nor have I ever seen anything of his[11] at all equal to it. Broxolm[12] and Pultney[13] are named and Lord Chesterfield,[14] of course. I own from what I have seen of their several productions I should think it Pultney's. He has writ an ode lately in Lord Lovel's[15] name to Lord Chesterfield[16] which has some strange inadvertencies in it such as *lyric lyre* and *verdure ever green*[17] but it's pretty enough in the main: I got a sight of it but it's very hard even to have that, and copies, impossible; I believe on account chiefly of an expression relating to the Royals, where he says let's keep 'em since we have them.[18] The only good things I have seen or heard of lately are both bawdy: one a description of Merryland[19] and the other a song on Admiral Vernon[20] full of *double entendres* and good in the way. I have good mind to write it down. *La voici!*

> Two gossips were merrily met
> One morning at nine before noon,
> And they were resolv'd on a whet
> To put their sweet voices in tune;
> Away to the tavern they went
> Joan fill up her glass and began;
> Poor girl, if thou'rt merrily bent
> Ne'er sham it but give me thy man.

10. The verses by Charles Hanbury Williams enclosed in Conway's letter *ante* before 23 Aug. 1740 OS.

11. Nothing further is known of Legge's verses.

12. Dr Broxholme (*ante* 11 June 1737 OS, n. 3), who was noted as a wit as well as a physician. HW elsewhere mentions 'a pretty correspondence of Latin odes that passed between him and Hedges' (MONTAGU i. 66).

13. William Pulteney (1684–1764), cr. (1742) E. of Bath; M.P. Hedon 1705–34, Middlesex 1734–42; leader of the opposition to Sir Robert Walpole.

14. Philip Dormer Stanhope (1694–1773), 4th E. of Chesterfield.

15. Thomas Coke (1697–1759), cr. (1728) Bn Lovel and (1744) E. of Leicester; friend and neighbour of Sir Robert Walpole.

16. *An Epistle from Lord L[ove]l to Lord C[hesterfiel]d, by Mr P[ulteney]*, 1740.

17. 'Beneath the spreading oak we'll sit / And thumb the lyric lyre' (p. 1); 'How beauteous is this rival scene! / With constant verdure ever green' (p. 2).

18. 'Let honest men together join, / And since we have it, keep that line, / Fixt by the Revolution' (p. 6).

19. *A New Description of Merryland*, printed at Bath with a preface dated 20 Oct. 1740, and advertised as 'this day is published' in the *Daily Adv.* 6 Nov. By the end of the month it had gone through four editions and a piracy (ibid. 10, 17, 27, 28 Nov.). A modern limited edition was published in New York in 1932. The copies in the Yale University Library are attributed to Thomas Stretzer.

20. This is printed as 'The Gossips-Toast,' with some verbal differences and one additional stanza in *Vernon's Glory. Containing Fifteen New Songs, Occasioned by the Taking of Porto-Bello and Fort Chargre*, 1740, pp. 19–22.

2.

I'll give, Joan, a man o' my word
    A man who was ne'er known to flinch
As brave and as keen as his sword,
    I warrant a man ev'ry inch.
Oh! he is the prettiest fellow,
    You'll know him without any name.
'Twas he who so storm'd Port Bello;
    For he's a true cock of the game.

3.

Soon he made such a hole in her walls
    That nothing before him cou'd stand,
He plied her with such cannon balls,
    And mounted the breach sword in hand;
Resistless he enter'd the fort
    And saw her submit to his pleasure.
He only desir'd the sport
    And car'd not a fig for the treasure.

4.

To the ladies who fell in his hands
    He show'd himself courteous and civil
Still ready and at their commands
    Though freckled and tann'd like the Devil.
Then Port Bello he leaves to find out
    The joys which new conquests afford
But e'er he cou'd take t'other bout
    His mast was brought low by the board,

A common mischance, Joan, you know;
    But he was so active and clever
It was up in an instant, I trow
    As stout and as well fixt as ever;
So to vex their Italian damn'd Queen
    (For he hates an Italian like Hell)
He goes and bum-bards Carthagene,
    Then puts into his Porto Bell.

5.

Thou hast toasted a jewel, quoth Joan,
    I love him thou know'st as my eyes;
His courage through all the world's known;
    Him how the Czarina would prize!

Cou'd she once his abilities prove,
　　I'll warrant she'd keep him employ'd,
From her soul such a servant she'd love
　　Nor e'er with his service be cloy'd.

6.

But the knight does not love him I doubt
　　Because he can do more than he,
What a pity such e'er shou'd be out,
　　He serves when he's in with such glee!
Then a f＿t for the insolent Don
　　An English wife loves to be free.
I'll do as I like with my own,
　　No Spaniard shall ever search me.

7.

Let his Worship for our borough stand
　　Not a sixpenny piece shall he give;
Cou'd I choose of all men in the land,
　　He my member shou'd be while I live:
I speak it, dear girl, from my heart,
　　Wou'd England with more did abound
Like him who can play a man's part,
　　All patriots both upright and sound!

8.

Him in triumph again may I see!
　　In glory each day may he rise!
Oh! Long, very long may he be,
　　The dearest delight of my eyes!
The Admiral Heaven defend,
　　For though wicked courtiers may scoff,
Poor England must be at an end
　　Shou'd he for our sins be cut off.

You see it's a dialogue between two gossips and if you have a mind
to sing it, it goes to the same tune with an old song that begins
like it.[21] I have not marked any of the equivokes because if they have
any fault they are rather too plain. I have read your verses since and
I recall all I said about Lady Sophy's inspiring 'em: whoever Zelinda

21. According to ibid. 19, it was sung to the tune of 'An Old Woman Cloathed in Grey.' This tune and a discussion of various versions, none of which seems to correspond very closely to this ballad, are in William Chappell, *Old English Popular Music*, ed. Wooldridge, 1893, ii. 120–1.

is I dare say there is no similitude in their characters. I had forgot inconstant and promiscuous love[22] and twenty things; upon reading 'em again, too, I find 'em more incorrect than I thought they were, but I still think 'em pretty and extraordinary for extempore. Adieu. You'll have an hundred bundles but I'll try to enclose your dances as well as I can. Service to Grey. When shall one see you?

The country dances are directed to Mr Mann for fear you should be gone. Nov. 30.

To Conway, early January 1741 NS

Missing; answered *post* 19 Jan. 1741 OS.

From Conway, Monday 19 January 1741 OS

Printed in full for the first time from the MS now wsl, formerly Rutnam. First printed in part, *Rockingham Memoirs* i. 377–8; reprinted, *Colburn's United Service Magazine,* 1880, lii pt i. 177–8.

Address: À Monsieur Monsieur Walpole recommandé à Monsieur Mann resident du roi d'Engleterre à Florence.

Postmark: [Three illegible marks].

Mon[day], Jan. 19, OS.

Dear Horry,

I DID indeed perceive and with great regret that you had left me off, but I did [not] know till t'other day that you complained of me to Selwyn, I think it was, that you were seriously angry with me for not writing, which indeed I did not at all suspect because the last I wrote to you, was an age ago,[1] as you may find by the date

---

22. Each gay alcove, voluptuous recess
  Where glowing dames their gaudy knights caress,
  Now these, now new ones to my sick'ning eye
  Presented scenes of foul inconstancy;
  Such as—Oh Heav'n! that that pure breast should prove
  The wanton harbour of promiscuous love.

1. *Ante* ca 30 Nov. 1740 OS. HW could not have received this letter before early January 1741 NS, and apparently replied to it immediately in the missing letter acknowledged below. The last letter he had received from Conway before that was apparently that of *ante* before 23 Aug. 1740 OS to which he had replied 25 Sept. NS. Sometime in the late autumn, therefore, he had apparently written to John Selwyn (in a missing letter) com-

if there is evr'a one, for my letters are not always dated. However that be I will fairly own that I am in the wrong, not for writing too late then but for not writing since, but I insist upon it that you confess in your turn that you might have writ, though it had been but to scold me, before you received my letter, and you may know that I was preparing to be angry at you when I received yours, so I hope we shall sheath our animosities on each side and conclude like Peacham and Lockit: 'Brother, brother we are both in the wrong,'[2] for I would not upon any account have our letters upon the ceremonious footing of visiting turn about like ladies of quality, nor our correspondence proceed, as I think you once observed to me, move for move, like a game at chess. Let it rather be a game at comet, where we are to play four or five cards together if it be necessary. I own I never play a card without hopes of making you play another but I shall never insist upon your playing card for card when you find it inconvenient, any more than I do upon your following suit, for though you have played sense to nonsense from the beginning of our correspondence and seemed as it were to trump all my cards, you never heard me complain of it, did you? For I seem to be playing at the noble amusement of my Lady's hole, where I have always the good luck to get a king for an ace.

But shall one never see you, dear Horry? Sure Florence must have some strange enchanting power, perhaps some hidden charms that we are not acquainted with. Are you in love there or what is it? If I don't hear you are removed before this gets to you I shall despair of seeing you. If our spring can't invite you here nor your flaming summers drive you from Italy I shall give you over. But now is the time that young Englishmen come like herrings in shoals from all parts of the world; a new scene is opening[3] where everybody will crowd either as actor or spectator. What swarms to see the new play! or rather the old farce acted by a new set of players. Whichever I am it would not be worth my while to come five mile for it, I shall be so indifferent a spectator, and if you will, so indifferent an actor, or rather no actor at all. I shall in all probability play no other part than that of a mute, and only help to crowd the stage and keep those

plaining of Conway's silence. Conway, on his side, had received no letter from HW between the missing one of October 1740, to which he replied ca 30 Nov. OS and the one he acknowledges here,

2. *The Beggar's Opera* II. x.
3. I.e., a general election, and with it a new Parliament,

warm that are to play greater roles. I want much to know what you think of all this and if you feel a feel or how? I own I feel as if I had rather be out of the scrape and yet it is my own fault if I am in it. But I am like those people who run into a quarrel out of curiosity and often get a black eye or a broken pate for their pains. Poor Sir Robert is to lose his head immediately, as they say, about which he seems to trouble his head very little. But I must tell you a good thing of Lady Thanet's[4] before I go any farther; Lord Bat—st[5] told her at the Bath that he had Sir Robert's head in his pocket. 'Are you sure of it?' says she. 'Oh yes,' says he, 'Nothing surer.' 'Why, then,' says she, 'you can't possibly do so well as to put it upon your shoulders.' On Wednesday, I think, they bring in a motion for an address to remove him, into the House of Lords:[6] then there comes the Place Bill;[7] and God knows what besides that will quite ruin him. This is the whole extent of my politics: I have no more time or else I'd talk to you a little more. Service to Grey: and best compliments to Signor Potaphæ.[8] I am ashamed I have not answered his letter. Adieu! The Conwayhood salutes you.

4. Lady Mary Saville (1700–51), m. (1722) Sackville Tufton, 7th E. of Thanet.

5. So in the MS; Conway alludes to the anecdote *post* 16 Feb. 1741 OS as involving Lord Bathurst: Allen Bathurst (1684–1775), cr. (1712) Bn and (1772) E. Bathurst, an active opponent of Sir Robert Walpole. The anecdote also appears in a MS book of anecdotes collected by the 2d Vct Palmerston early in his career and possibly learned from his grandfather, a contemporary of these events (Brian Connell, *Portrait of a Whig Peer*, 1957, p. 33); the gentleman is given there, too, as Lord Bathurst.

6. The motion to remove Sir Robert Walpole was not brought in until 13 Feb. 1741 OS, when it was debated in both Houses. Conway gives an account *post* 16 Feb. 1741 OS.

7. Leave to bring in a bill 'for the better securing the freedom of Parliaments, by limiting the number of officers in the House of Commons' was granted 22 Jan. OS; it was read for the first time on the 27th, for the second time and committed on the 29th, debated in committee on 5 Feb., reported and engrossed on the 10th, passed on the 12th, and thrown out by the House of Lords on their second reading 26 Feb. (*Journals of the House of Commons* xxiii. 610, 618, 624, 634, 643, 648; *Journals of the House of Lords* xxv. 611–12). There seem to have been no significant debates at any point.

8. Presumably Conway's misreading of Patapan, HW's dog given him by Madame Grifoni; see also *post* ca 21 Feb. 1741 OS.

From CONWAY, Thursday 12 February 1741 OS

Printed for the first time from the MS now WSL, formerly Rutnam. Dated by the following letter, which it obviously precedes.

Address: À Monsieur Monsieur Walpole recommandé à Monsieur Mann resident du roi d'Engleterre à Florence.

Postmarks: [Two illegible marks].

Thursday, Feb. 12, OS.

Dear Horry,

AT this moment I can scarcely take up the pen I am under such affliction for poor Selwyn's illness, and I don't know how I can excuse myself to you for taking such pains to give you concern and to be the messenger of bad news, but you are so good that I know you will indulge me in endeavouring to alleviate my sorrow by sharing it with you, who I know are formed to feel for others and who I flatter myself take some little part in everything that regards me. Besides as you love him yourself, you might think it unkind in me not to apprise you of it for fear you should be shocked with the sudden news of his death which I have too much reason to apprehend will happen ere you receive this; his disorder has advanced with such rapidity that it must now be near a crisis and the doctors think his symptoms very bad. On Wednesday last I saw him at Lady Hervey's,[1] and yesterday (but a week afterwards) I saw him in such a condition as I cannot bear to think on. He has his senses but by intervals, talks a great deal incoherently. He calls often for his friends, and has asked very often for me! Dear Horry, you pity me, I'm sure, when you think how good a friend I shall lose: I saw him yesterday; he expressed great joy at seeing me and talked pretty sensibly but at intervals was very incoherent. They don't care anybody should go to him so I am not sure that I shall see him again. Adieu! dear Horry; I hardly know [what] I have said, my concern has interrupted me so. If he is better I will not fail to let you know next post.

---

1. Mary Lepell (1700–68), m. (1720) John Hervey, summoned to Parliament (1733) as Lord Hervey of Ickworth.

From CONWAY, Monday 16 February 1741 OS

Printed from the MS now WSL, formerly Rutnam. First printed, *Rockingham Memoirs* i. 378–82; reprinted, *Colburn's United Service Magazine*, 1880, lii pt i. 178–80.

Address: À Monsieur Monsieur Walpole recommandé à Monsieur Mann resident du roi d'Engleterre à Florence.

Postmark: [Illegible].

London, Feb. 16, 1741.

Dear Horry,

'TIS with great pleasure, you'll believe, that I fulfill my promise of letting you know if there was the least sign of amendment in poor Selwyn, whom I gave you so melancholy an account of last post; I wish I could make this more satisfactory to you and myself by telling you he was quite out of danger, but as his distemper seemed to be at such a crisis that I believe nobody thought he would live four-and-twenty hours, the least change for the better gives us room to hope: he has had some rest, they have given him the bark, and yesterday they tell me, he was pretty free from his delirium. These are good signs, but yet I am not so sanguine as to flatter myself that he is by any means free from danger.

You are so much his friend and so much mine that I am sure you will be glad of this account, and will add some to the numberless wishes that are sent up every day for his recovery, and which nobody can fail to form that knows him or knows his merit.

I designed to have contented myself with giving you this account but when I am conversing with you I am tempted *nescio qua dulcedine*[1] always to exceed the bounds which for your sake I prescribe myself at setting out. But I should really be to blame if I did not give you some account of your father's victory on Friday[2] in both Houses, that seemed to resemble Cimon's triumphs *over land and wave.*[3] They made a motion to address his Majesty desiring that he would be graciously pleased to remove the Right Honourable Sir Robert Walpole from his council. But after scheming the whole winter, holding council upon council and junto upon

1. Virgil, *Georgics* iv. 55 ('I know not by what delight').

2. 13 Feb. 1741 OS.

3. 'Like Cimon, triumph'd both on land and wave' (Pope, *Dunciad* i. 86), in allusion to the victories of Cimon (d. 449 B.C.), Greek general.

junto, rallying the debris of last winter's secession,[4] and raking together the whole hotch-potch, that mingled mass of Jacobites, Tories, Whigs, Republicans etc. men of all principles and of no principles, in order to give a total overthrow before next winter, calling out of their graves a dozen or two of *veteres, vieti, veternosi senes*,[5] who have been buried for ages in the country, drowned all party feuds in October[6] and tobacco, and even forgot there was such a thing as politics; after all this you may well imagine they were wiser than ever and nothing less than Sir Robert's head (which you know Lord Bathurst has kept in his pocket some time)[7] was to pay for it. Nay they had calculated to a man by how many votes he was to lose it.[8] What would you think was Sir Robert's majority after this? 290 to 106 in the House of Commons and I think 90 odd to 40 odd amongst the Peers.[9] The first who opposed the motion in the House of Commons was Lord Cornbury;[10] then Mr Southwell[11] and Mr. Herley.[12] Above 70 of their sure men left the House before the

---

4. Many of the Opposition members had seceded from the House of Commons 9 March 1739 OS after failing to carry an address against the Convention of the Pardo. The manœuvre failed, and they returned at the beginning of the next session in Nov. 1739 (W. Coxe, *Memoirs of Sir Robert Walpole*, 1800, pp. 85–8, 125).

5. An adaptation of Terence, *Eunuchus* l. 688: 'Hic est vietus vetus veternosus senex' ('this is a withered, ancient, lethargic old man').

6. October ale.

7. Conway had related this anecdote to HW *ante* 19 Jan. 1741 OS.

8. The Opposition was said to have expected 219 votes (*Hardwicke Corr.* i. 253).

9. The vote in the House of Lords was 89-47 or, including proxies, 108-59 (Cobbett, *Parl. Hist.* xi. 1062, 1215; Coxe, op. cit. iii. 564).

10. Henry Hyde (1710–53), styled Vct Cornbury 1723–51; summoned to the House of Lords as Bn Hyde of Hindon, 1751; M.P. Oxford University 1732–51. At this time he usually voted with the Opposition. His speech is not given in the report of the debates in the *London Mag-*

azine, March–April 1742, xi. 105–21, 157–83 (reprinted, Cobbett, op. cit. xi. 1224–1303), on which the eighteenth-century collections of debates were based, but it does appear in Dr Johnson's version of the debate in GM, April 1743, xiii. 173–5 (reprinted Cobbett, op. cit. xi. 1372–4), where he does not appear as the first opponent of the motion; it is also mentioned in Sir Dudley Ryder's report of the debates printed Sedgwick i. 91–5. He objected to the irregular nature of the Opposition attack.

11. Edward Southwell (1705–55), secretary of the Council in Ireland 1730–55; M.P. Bristol 1739–54; a country Whig who usually voted with the Opposition (G. F. Russell Barker and A. H. Stenning, *Record of Old Westminsters*, 1928, ii. 870; J. B. Owen, *Rise of the Pelhams*, 1957, p. 67, n. 6). His speech is not given in the accounts of the debate, but he is mentioned as opposing the motion in Coxe, op. cit. iii. 564, Cobbett, op. cit. xi. 1388, and Sedgwick i. 94.

12. Edward Harley (?1699–1755), 3d E. of Oxford, 1741; M.P. Herefordshire 1727–41; brother of Lord Treasurer Harley whose impeachment had been directed by Sir Robert Walpole. Identical versions

question;[13] in short you never saw people so totally discomfited. But observe the conduct of their leader;[14] he sits still waiting till Sir Robert should make his speech and withdraw,[15] that he might attack him when he was gone with a new charge, but the whole House called upon him by name and made him get up; which he did at last in a furious passion and spoke very ill, they say:[16] for Mr Pulteney, he attacked him almost entirely upon a thing which unluckily was transacted during the seven[17] years that Sir Robert was out of all employment, relating to the army debentures. But Sir Robert declared to me the day after that his speech[18] which was of an hour and a half was entirely made in answer to what Pulteney said; and that he did not make the least use of any notes which he had taken, or of the plan he had laid down before. I did not hear the debate, but am told they never were driven to such shifts. Some

of his speech appeared in the *London Magazine* 1742, xi. 167–8 (reprinted Cobbett, op. cit. xi. 1268–9) and GM 1743, xiii. 173 (not reprinted), where it precedes Cornbury's. His grounds were the same as the latter's. The generosity of his opposition to the motion is praised in *Hardwicke Corr.* i. 252.

13. This is an exaggeration. A list of those who withdrew, printed in Coxe, op. cit. iii. 563, contains 44 names; a letter from John Orlebar to Rev. Henry Etough 14 Feb. 1741 OS also states ' 'tis supposed that thirty or forty of the Tories did not vote at all. . . . 'Tis computed that there were once near 450 members in the House; but upon the division there were only 106 for the Address, and 290 against it; which, with the tellers and Speaker, make but 401' (ibid. iii. 564). See also Cobbett, op. cit. xi. 1388 and Hist. MSS Comm., *Egmont Diary*, 1920–3, iii. 192.

14. Pulteney.

15. After the motion had been made and seconded there was a long debate as to whether Sir Robert Walpole should withdraw, but the motion to that effect was dropped without a division. This part of the debate does not appear in the accounts based on the *London Magazine*, but many of the 'speeches' delivered are in Dr Johnson's account GM 1743, xiii. 74–[8], 115 (reprinted Cobbett, op. cit. xi. 1328–35). See also Sir Robert Walpole's

own account of the debate in Coxe, op. cit. iii. 562.

16. The two versions of Pulteney's speech (Cobbett, op. cit. xi. 1269–84, from *London Magazine*; and ibid. xi. 1379–84, from GM) are radically different: the former is a long and reasoned criticism of the whole course of Walpole's policy in which the affair of the army debentures, mentioned below, takes only a minor place (xi. 1281–2); the latter is much briefer and more violent, omits all the detail on foreign policy, and is specific only on the affairs of the army debentures.

17. Sir Robert Walpole was out of office for only three years, from April 1717 until June 1720. Many of the army debentures were issued during this period but they were redeemed in 1727, when he was again at the Treasury, to the great profit of those who speculated in them.

18. There are three versions of this, one printed in Coxe, op. cit. iii. 564, 'taken from Parliamentary minutes in the handwriting of Sir Robert Walpole, etc.', reprinted Cobbett, op. cit. xi. 1284n–96n, and the versions from the *London Magazine* and GM (ibid. xi. 1284–1303, 1384–7). The former of these is closer to that given by Coxe than the latter, which in turn answers the GM's version of Pulteney's speech more closely.

said it was sufficient reason that he had been minister almost twenty years.

> Quem tamen inveniet tam longa potentia finem?[19]

This was their chief complaint; and indeed they are to be pitied not because he has been in power so long, but because they have been out. Poor Lord Carteret[20] was dragged into it head and shoulders, he has been distracted between shame on one side and fear on the other this great while; his enmity to the Duke of Argyle[21] drives him one way and his hatred of Sir Robert another; two minutes after he had made the motion he rubbed his periwig off and has not ceased biting his nails and scratching his head ever since. If you want to know their situation at present read Milton's description[22] of Satan and his crew of fallen angels; some are threatening; some silent and gloomy; some reasoning apart; but all overwhelmed with flames, and disappointment, and all in the dark as to everything but their own unhappiness.

So much for politics. If I go on any farther you'll think I have caught the contagion and am grown as politically mad as any of my countrymen, but you must know for all this that nobody is so indifferent in party matters. I seldom think about 'em, and when I do I sometimes think one in the wrong and sometimes t'other, but commonly both; when I am angry at either side I rail and for that moment am Courtier or Patriot just as it happens; but in the generality of my conversation I am a perfect Atticus.[23] I converse with people on both sides, and as I don't love to trouble my head about affairs that I have nothing to do in, politics are the last subject I choose to talk of.

19. 'What end will such long power find nevertheless?' The source of this quotation has not been found.

20. John Carteret (1690–1763), 2d Bn Carteret; 1st E. Granville, 1744; a leading opponent of Sir Robert Walpole since 1730. He moved the address for Walpole's removal in the House of Lords. Three versions of his speech, considered the best he ever made, are in Cobbett, op. cit. xi. 1047–85, 1047n–51n, 1153–70.

21. The antagonism between Argyll and Carteret over the Porteous Riots in Edinburgh in 1736 appears in Lord Hervey's *Memoirs of the Reign of George II*, ed.

Croker, 1884, iii. 39–40, 99–106. Argyll's open disaffection with the Opposition party after Sir Robert Walpole's fall is discussed by Richard Glover in *Memoirs of a Celebrated Literary and Political Character* (1814, pp. 13–14): 'the Duke treated [Carteret] with many terms of abhorrence, styling him his enemy . . . walked up and down exclaiming against Carteret.'

22. *Paradise Lost*, Book I.

23. T. Pomponius Atticus (109–32 B.C.) managed to keep on good terms with the leaders of all parties during the Roman civil wars.

I hear we are to see you soon,[24] so I have heard this great while and yet one does not see you; but you have sent away your clothes and so can't stay; *probatum est*: besides here will be a seat in Parliament[25] warmed by some fat Court backside, that will grow cold before you come. Be sure, don't play the Lot, nor the Orpheus, nor the fool so much as to cast a look back on Florence when you are set out; nor once think of your Gallery or the Arno or your beauties *de ce pays-là* nor any such thing, for if you do you're gone, you relapse infallibly for two or three years at least. Shut your eyes all the way through Germany[26] and proceed straight hither without turning either to the right or to the left. You can't imagine how I long to give a dish of tea in my snug lodgings and to talk to you of a thousand things. Adieu!

Since I began this I hear that the doctors think Selwyn much better, and that there are great hopes of him. How often do I mutter, 'When shall we three meet again?' Pray come soon that I may enjoy that wish, and then depart in peace upon my third pilgrimage to that unholy land, that land of bulls.[27] Besides I may be drowned, you know, in going and then there is such fighting and such warring over the face of the earth that one cannot call one's life one's own. What a madman peaceable people would think one for bartering such an inestimable property for the value of £200 per annum[28] and the ridiculous title of Captain of Dragoons. Goodbye! captain or no captain, alive or dead, I shall always be sincerely yours. Service to Grey: and to my Persian friend and likeness.[29] The family make their compliments.

---

24. HW had received instructions from his father shortly before 21 Feb. 1741 NS (and which had therefore been sent well before this letter was written) to 'leave Italy as soon as possible' to avoid being trapped by Spanish troops (HW to Spence 21 Feb. 1741 NS).

25. HW was returned for Callington 14 May 1741 OS ('Short Notes,' GRAY i. 11, n. 71).

26. There is no other evidence that HW considered returning through Germany; his father had given him permission to spend some time in France on his way home (HW to Spence 21 Feb. 1741 NS).

27. Ireland. This expedition did not take place, probably because of Conway's promotion to the Guards (*post* ca 25 July 1741 OS, n. 14).

28. The pay of a captain of dragoons in 1748 was 15s. 6d. per day, which is closer to £300 than £200 per annum ('An Abstract of the Daily Pay of His Majesty's Land Forces and Marines' in *Court and City Register*, 1748, facing p. 153).

29. This is perhaps another reference to Patapan.

From CONWAY, ca Saturday 21 February 1741 OS

Printed for the first time from the MS now WSL, formerly Rutnam. Dated approximately by Conway's reference to criticisms begun 'two days' after the publication of Middleton's *History of the Life of . . . Cicero* on 19 Feb. 1741 OS (below, n. 3). Since HW replies to this letter 25 March NS, it could not have been written much later than 21 Feb. OS.

Address: À Monsieur Monsieur Walpole recommandé à Monsieur Mann resident du roi d'Engleterre à Florence. Pd 1s. 3d.

Postmark: [Two illegible].

Dear Horry,

I SHALL ruin you in letters, but I know you interest yourself so much about poor Selwyn that I can't let you hear about him too often, and I am sure you will not think this dear, whatever it costs you, since it brings you the good news of his recovery, which, as you may know from the letters I wrote to you before, is one of the most extraordinary that ever was known; he lay under a continued high fever for, I think, twelve days together, and was light-headed great part of the time; this, with eight blisters that they put on him, and some of which run still, you may imagine has reduced him very low, but he is otherwise quite well. He gets up every day, but is forced to lie upon a couch all the time; yesterday he tried to sit in a chair but was forced to have recourse to his couch after sitting there about an hour; he eats chicken and pudding etc. and gathers strength slowly but just perceivably every day.

He desired me yesterday to give his service to you and to tell you that he has received your letter[1] and will answer as soon as ever he is able. You can't imagine how happy Mr and Mrs Selwyn[2] are about his recovery and in short how happy everybody is that knows him. I saw nobody that did not seem anxious about him and which is extraordinary, in this particular case I believe the whole town and even the Court itself were sincere.

At last Middleton's book[3] is come out and the whole town is at

1. Missing.

2. Col. John Selwyn (1688–1751), M.P. Truro 1715–21, Whitchurch 1727–34, Gloucester city 1734–51; m. (ca 1708–9) Mary Farrington (ca 1690–1777), Bedchamber woman to Queen Caroline (MANN i. 329, n. 9, 339, n. 33).

3. *The History of the Life of Marcus Tullius Cicero,* by Conyers Middleton (1683–1750), D.D., author and controversialist; HW's correspondent and the chief influence in his life at Cambridge. The book was published by subscription 19 Feb. 1741 OS (DALRYMPLE 6, n. 3). For

this moment a-reading it; for my part it's so long[4] and I'm so idle that I believe I shall keep it for the country, or perhaps take it with me to Ireland and make poor Tully suffer a worse banishment from my friendship than he did before from the utmost rage of his enemies. But what will delight you above all things is that they began a critic upon it before they had had time to read it, actually in two days;[5] and I wish it mayn't cost me two months; but those people are voracious! and make no more of a pair of large quarto volumes! This fellow puts me in mind of the country man that was for banishing Aristides because he was tired of hearing him called the Just;[6] for to be sure nothing could provoke him to such an extravagance but the character with which this book came out; but indeed to be good or to be liked is the greatest fault a book can have with these gentlemen.

Adieu!

Family compliments!

Grey and Potaphur

To CONWAY, Saturday 25 March 1741 NS

Printed from *Works* v. 6–8.

Florence, March 25, 1741 NS.

Dear Hal,

YOU must judge by what you feel yourself of what I feel for Selwyn's recovery, with the addition of what I have suffered from post to post. But as I find the whole town have had the same sentiments about him (though I am sure few so strong as myself) I will not repeat what you have heard so much. I shall write to him tonight,[1] though he knows without my telling him how very much I love him. To you, my dear Harry, I am infinitely obliged for the

HW's connection with it, see *post* 25 March 1741 NS and nn. 23, 28, and the references in DALRYMPLE.

4. Two volumes quarto.

5. The earliest printed notice of the book yet found is the favourable review beginning in *The Publick Register: or,*

the *Weekly Magazine*, 28 Feb. 1741 OS. Conway may be referring to verbal criticisms.

6. Plutarch, *Aristides* vii. 6.

1. HW's letter is missing.

three successive letters[2] you wrote me about him, which gave me double pleasure, as they showed your attention for me at a time that you knew I must be so unhappy; and your friendship for him.

Your account of Sir Robert's victory[3] was so extremely well told, that I made Gray translate it into French,[4] and have showed it to all that could taste it, or were inquisitive on the occasion. I have received a print by this post that diverts me extremely; *The Motion*.[5] Tell me, dear now, who made the design, and who took the likenesses;[6] they are admirable: the lines[7] are as good as one sees on such occasions. I wrote last post to Sir Robert, to wish him joy; I hope he received my letter.[8]

I was to have set out last Tuesday, but on Sunday came the news of the Queen of Hungary[9] being brought to bed of a son;[10] on which occasion here will be great triumphs, operas and masquerades,[11] which detain me for a short time.

I won't make you any excuse for sending you the following lines;[12] you have prejudice enough for me to read with patience any of my idlenesses.

Inscription
For the Neglected Column
In the Place of St Mark at Florence

Escap'd a race,[13] whose vanity ne'er rais'd
A monument, but when themselves it prais'd;

2. *Ante* 12, 16 and ca 21 Feb. 1741 OS.

3. On the event of Mr Sandys's motion in the House of Commons to remove Sir Robert Walpole from the King's presence and councils forever (HW). Conway's account is *ante* 16 Feb. 1741 OS.

4. This translation has apparently not survived.

5. This famous satiric print, published 21 Feb. OS, is fully described in British Museum, *Catalogue of Prints . . . Political and Personal Satires*, 1870–1954, iii pt i. 369–72 (No. 2479); and M. D. George, *English Political Caricature*, Oxford, 1959, i. 89–90 (reproduction, Plate 26).

6. Mrs George, op. cit. i. 90, n. 1, 115, n. 1, suggests that George Townshend, later famous for his caricatures, may have been responsible although he was only 18 at the time.

7. These are printed in full in British Museum, op. cit. iii pt i. 369–70.

8. Missing.

9. Maria Theresa (1717–80), m. (1736) Francis of Lorraine, Grand Duke of Tuscany 1737–65, Emperor 1745–65; Queen of Hungary 1740–80.

10. Joseph (13 March 1741 NS – 1790), Emperor (as Joseph II) 1765–90.

11. The Florentine celebrations for Joseph's birth are mentioned briefly in Giuseppe Conti, *Firenze dopo i Medici*, Florence, 1921, p. 218.

12. The verses that follow were omitted from *Works* and subsequent reprintings and a note substituted explaining that they had been printed in HW's *Fugitive Pieces* (*Works* i. 17–18). They are printed here from HW's copy in his *MS Poems*, pp. 27–8, with his notes as they appear there; these differ slightly from those in the printed versions.

13. The family of Medici (HW).

Sacred to truth oh! let this column rise,
Pure from false trophies and inscriptive lies!
  Let no enslavers of their country here
In impudent relievo dare appear:
No pontiff by a ruin'd nation's good
Lusting to aggrandize his bastard-brood:
Be here no Clement,[14] Alexander[15] seen;
No pois'ning Cardinal,[16] or pois'ning Queen:[17]
No Cosmo, or the Bigot-Duke,[18] or He[19]
Great from the wounds of dying liberty.
No Lorrainer[20]—one lying arch[21] suffice
To tell his virtues and his victories:
Beneath his influence how commerce[22] thriv'd,
And at his smile how dying arts reviv'd:
Let it relate, e'er since his rule begun,
Not what he has, but what he should have done.
  Level with Freedom, let this pillar mourn,
Nor rise till the bright blessing shall return;
Then tow'ring boldly to the skies proclaim
Whate'er shall be the happy hero's name,
Who, a new Brutus, shall his country free,
And like a God, shall say, let there be Liberty!

My dear Harry, you enrage me with talking of another journey to Ireland; it will shock me if I don't find you at my return: pray take care and be in England.

14. Cardinal Julio de' Medici [1478–1534], afterwards [1523] Pope Clement VII (HW).

15. Alexander de' Medici [1511–37], the first Duke of Florence, killed by Lorenzino de' Medici [Lorenzo di Pier Francesco de' Medici, 1514–48] (HW).

16. Ferdinand the Great [1549–1609], was first Cardinal and then [1587] became Great Duke, by poisoning his elder brother, Francis I [1541–87] (HW). HW's note in *Fugitive Pieces* adds 'and his wife Bianca Capello [1548–87].' The poisoning reports are doubtful.

17. Catherine de' Medici [1519–89], wife [1533] of Henry II King of France (HW). While she approved certain political assassinations, there is no evidence that she practised poisoning.

18. Cosmo III [1642–1723] (HW).

19. Cosmo [1519–74] the Great enslaved the republics of Florence and Siena (HW).

20. Francis 2d Duke of Lorrain, which he gave up to France against the command of his mother, though a princess of France [Élisabeth-Charlotte de Bourbon d'Orléans (1676–1744)], and against the prayers of all his subjects, and had Tuscany in exchange (HW).

21. The triumphal arch erected to him [1739] without the Porta San Gallo at Florence (HW).

22. Two inscriptions over the lesser arches call him Restitutor Commercii et Propagator Bonarum Artium, as his equestrian statue on horseback trampling on Turks, on the top, represent[s] the victories that he was designed to have gained over that people, when he received the command of his father-in-law the Em-

I wait with some patience to see Dr Middleton's Tully, as I read the greatest part of it in manuscript;[23] though indeed that is rather a reason for my being impatient to read the rest. If Tully can receive any additional honour, Dr Middleton is most capable of conferring it.

I receive with great pleasure any remembrances of my Lord and your sisters; I long to see all of you. Patapan[24] is so handsome that he has been named the silver fleece; and there is a new order of knighthood to be erected to his honour, in opposition to the golden. Precedents are searching, and plans drawing up for that purpose. I hear that the natives pretend to be companions, upon the authority of their dog-skin waistcoats; but a council that has been held on purpose has declared their pretensions impertinent. Patapan has lately taken wife unto him,[25] as ugly as he is genteel, but of a very great family, being the direct heiress of Canis Scaliger, Lord of Verona: which principality we design to seize *à la prussienne;*[26] that is, as soon as ever we shall have persuaded the republic of Venice,[27] that we are the best friends they have in the world. Adieu, dear child!

Yours ever,

HOR. WALPOLE

PS. I left my subscriptions for Middleton's Tully with Mr Selwyn;[28] I won't trouble him, but I wish you would take care and get the books, if Mr S. has kept the list.

---

peror's, armies—but he was prevented by some fevers. He has since been chosen emperor, in 1745 (HW).

23. HW mentions 'the specimen which you were so good as to show me at Cambridge' in his letter to Middleton ca 1 Sept. 1739 NS (DALRYMPLE 7).

24. A dog of Mr Walpole's (HW).

25. A puppy by this mating, which HW gave to Mann, is mentioned in Mann to HW 21 Aug. 1741 NS (MANN i. 112) and Chute to HW 22 Aug. 1741 NS (CHUTE 4), with much joking about his 'titles' and 'all the regards that are due to the honourable house of which he is the estimable first fruits, though a little irregularly produced.'

26. As Frederick the Great had seized Silesia in Dec. 1740.

27. Which had controlled Verona since 1405.

28. George Augustus Selwyn (1719–91), wit and politician; HW's correspondent; John Selwyn's brother. HW had sent a list of subscriptions to Middleton's book to England by him in Sept. 1739, containing orders for copies for Lords Holdernesse and Conway, H. S. Conway, Thomas Brand, and three copies for himself (HW to Middleton ca 1 Sept. 1739 NS, DALRYMPLE 7, 8). One of HW's copies is Hazen, *Cat. of HW's Lib.*, No. 315; he probably gave the other two away.

To Conway, ca Wednesday 19 – Friday 28 July 1741 NS

Missing; answered *post* 6 Aug. 1741 OS. It was probably written from Genoa where HW was ca 19–28 July NS.

From Conway, ca Thursday 23 July 1741 OS

Printed for the first time from the MS now wsl, formerly Rutnam.
Address: À Monsieur Monsieur Walpole recommandé à Monsieur Charles Selwyn[1] Rue Ste-Appoline à Paris. Franc à Paris.
Postmark: 23 IY.
Memoranda (by HW):

navis hispanæ magister dedacorum pretiosus emptor[2]

the rill that in sweet murmurs trembles down the hill[3]

who stupid stare on the rich chariot's charms
the garter'd shield and blazonry of arms.
stupet in titulis et imaginibus[4]

Inscript[ion] for Runny Mead[5]

To the souls of those heroes

p. 4. One would think Milton had lived all his life in Hell.[6]

a woman to be married going to take a great affair in hand[7]

find—some quiet bank that wants the wandering wind
vagis caretque ventis[8]

1. Charles Selwin (ca 1716–94), banker in Paris, who had been a member of the Alexandre Alexander banking firm but had gone into business under his own name sometime in 1741 (GRAY i. 239, n. 12).

2. Horace, *Odes* III. vi. 31–2 ('the master of some Spanish ship, lavish purchaser of shame').

3. Any use that HW may have made of this line and of the others here has not been discovered.

4. Horace, *Satires* I. vi. 17 ('stupefied by titles of honour and emblems of rank'). The English couplet above is obviously an imitation of this line.

5. Nothing further is known of this; presumably it was a satiric inscription for Runnymede, the scene of Magna Carta.

6. An allusion to p. 4 of the MS of *ante* 16 Feb. 1741 OS.

7. HW repeats this to Mann and Lincoln on 13 Sept. 1741 OS (MANN i. 142; SELWYN 21).

8. Apparently an adaptation of Horace, *Odes* III. xxix. 23–4: 'caretque ripa vagis taciturna ventis' ('and the quiet bank wants the wandering wind'). The preceding line is obviously an imitation. The rest of the memoranda have not been identified.

Tu seras bien attrapé, mon Ami,
Tu seras bien_____

as common as the tale that once has rung
On G_____9 sieve-like ears or leaky tongue

Austere flaps his leaden wing.

Dear Horry,

AFTER the alarm you gave us by the first news of your illness,[10] and the anxiety we have remained under ever since by your continued silence, you can't imagine with what satisfaction I saw an account of your entire recovery in a letter to Mrs Grosvenour.[11] I read in her countenance a great deal of good news from you before she had spoke a word, and thought myself very fortunate in happening to call upon her the very morning after she had received your letter, which saved me perhaps some days inquietude about you: we were very apprehensive about [you] and I own I think had great reason for our fears; I thought on the consequences of a violent disorder, though in appearance past, with the addition of a hot climate and the usual tenderness of your constitution as dangers not at all to be slighted; I was ingenious too in tormenting myself and drew even from your silence to me a new cause of anxiety. I am sorry you had so just an excuse for it and can assure you however a line or two when you have leisure to think of so idle a correspondent would confirm my happiness and be a piece of charity very well bestowed. I am uncertain whether this will find you or no; Mrs Grosvenor does not seem to have any great dependence upon it; however, I send it as a venture which if it succeeds may make me rich in obtaining an answer from you and I shall be otherwise easy enough about the fate of it, since I hope you don't want this to convince you of my happiness upon this occasion. I assure you nothing should have prevented my writing before but an utter ignorance where or how to direct to you.

Great revolutions have happened of late both public and pri-

9. HW has written in letters above the dash that might be 'ag.'

10. HW had fallen ill of 'a kind of quinsy' at Reggio about 20 May NS and was 'given over for fifteen hours' ('Short Notes,' GRAY i. 10). See also Spence's account of HW's illness ibid. i. 10, n. 62; and MANN i. 51. HW had begun to improve by the 25th and was out of danger by the 27th (ibid.). The letters in which HW told of his initial recovery are all missing, but they apparently reached England about 6 June OS (GRAY i. 243, 246).

11. Missing.

vate. We have rejoiced for the taking of Carthagena and mourned for the loss of it;[12] many are turned out and many advanced, some deaths and some weddings, my brother married[13] and I a colonel in the Guards![14] I have not time to be more particular at present; I am in London, your family in the country.[15] I have the whole town to myself, see nobody, know nobody, and do nothing but learn mathematics and fortifications. Judge how melancholy! Adieu. Service to Grey.[16]

H. C.

From CONWAY, Thursday 6 August 1741 OS

Printed from the MS now wsl, formerly Rutnam. First printed (misdated 1740), *Rockingham Memoirs* i. 372–5; reprinted (similarly misdated) *Colburn's United Service Magazine*, 1880, lii pt i. 171–3. The references to the death of Lord Augustus Fitzroy, to HW's being in France, and to the miscellaneous news items mentioned by Conway all indicate that the letter belongs in 1741, not 1740; also, 6 Aug. 1740 OS fell on a Wednesday, not a Thursday.

Th[ursday], Aug. 6.

Dear Horry,

YOU cannot imagine how happy you make me with that charming old stock of friendship that you say you have kept in lavender for me; it's a treasure that I value more than I can express, and

12. Reports that Vernon had taken Cartagena on 1 April OS reached London on 17 May OS, and information that the English had retired after heavy losses arrived 18 June OS (*Daily Adv.* 18 May, 20, 22 June; see also *Vernon Papers,* ed. Ranft, Naval Records Society, 1958, pp. 204–34).

13. To Lady Isabella Fitzroy (1726–82) on 29 May. The Countess of Hertford wrote the Countess of Pomfret 3 June 1741 OS, 'My Lord Conway and my Lady Bell Fitzroy were married last week' (Frances, Countess of Hertford and Henrietta Louisa, Countess of Pomfret, *Correspondence,* 1805, iii. 295).

14. The *Daily Adv.* 15 May describes Conway as 'appointed captain-lieutenant of the first regiment of Foot-Guards [later the Grenadier Guards], in the room

of Captain-Lieutenant Hemmington [Hemington].' Conway's appointment as captain-lieutenant is dated 14 Feb. 1741 OS in the regimental records; he was also appointed lieutenant-colonel in the army at the same time (Sir F. W. Hamilton, *Origin and History of the First or Grenadier Guards,* 1874, iii. 447–8; Namier and Brooke ii. 244).

15. The newspapers in mid-June had reported that Sir Robert Walpole intended to go to Houghton for a month at the beginning of July (*Daily Adv.* 15 June).

16. HW's quarrel with Gray at Reggio ca 14 May NS was not generally known to his friends in England, although HW seems to have written to Ashton about it (GRAY i. 247).

without any unreasonable doubts of your gratitude or constancy I would have given the world to have insured it when we parted; but affection would be no longer affection if it was not attended with some anxiety, if it ceased to be that *res solliciti plena timoris:*[1] how did I know but that in these cursed piratical times I might have been robbed of it? and what redress could I have had? To think of making new ones instead of it would be like that old Roman loggerhead[2] that Velleius[3] makes honourable mention of, who threatened the people if they lost the old Corinthian statues that they should find[4] new one[s] in their stead; indeed I must have recourse to better times than these if I would find another friendship worthy to succeed it. I won't make you any compliments; it's none, God knows, to tell you that I love you if possible more than ever, and can forgive you anything but doubting of it. So you see, my dear Horry, I am ready for your coming; you shall find your old apartment in my heart in the best order in the world to receive you; it has no need of dusting or brushing up I assure you; I hope you meant no such thing by saying you writ your last only to announce yourself! But you require a history of the present times of me; indeed you apply to the very worst person in the world; I know nothing of politics, *imprimis,* which is a great article in modern history; as to scandal and common news to be sure I hear it as others do now and then but then I am *plenus rimarum;*[5] it comes in at one ear literally and out at t'other. I have no sort of retention, and but very moderate intelligence of late, for I see nobody. Would you believe it? Horry, I have been hitherto in this dreary city all this live-long summer, but I can't bear summer people, and so I live a good deal alone; I now and then go to Chelsea[6] as you may suppose, once a week or so; then I have a metamorphosed *quondam* country sister[7] whom you have heard of; this with two or three dropping-in acquaintance makes my world, so if you have a mind to hear the history of that I can give it you, but for the great one I know nothing of it. As to myself I have a thousand idle hours, which with

1. Ovid, *Heroides* i. 12 ('thing filled with anxious fear').

2. Lucius Mummius (fl. 154–42 B.C.), surnamed Achaicus, the conqueror of Corinth. The anecdote is in Velleius's *Historiæ Romanæ* i. 13.

3. Gaius Velleius Paterculus (ca 19 B.C.–*post* 30 A.D.), Roman historian.

4. I.e., provide.

5. Terence, *Eunuchus* 1. 105 ('full of cracks').

6. Presumably to see Sir Robert Walpole at Orford House.

7. Probably his half-sister Henrietta (see *post* 29 Aug. 1746 OS).

Strephon's Complaint.

to the tune of N'est dans le Voisinage.

There lives not far on yonder Plain
  The Brightest of the Female Train;
Ye shepherds of your hearts beware
  For oh! she's false as she is Fair!
A thousand times I've heard her own
  Her heart was mine & mine alone,
She'll swear the very same to you;
  Fool that I was to think her True!

2.

Last night beneath yon Beaches shade
You, Venus, heard the vows she made,
That light & day should sooner part
  Than strephon from his Cloe's heart;
And yet this very morn was seen
  When Damon came upon the Green
Which way her am'rous Glances Flew
  Fool that I was to think her True!

3.

E'en Celadon that Piping swain
  The Dullest Lout upon the Plain,
She heard, & with his Sing-song art
  He dearly bought her Fickle Heart.

'STREPHON'S COMPLAINT' BY HORACE WALPOLE

some small study and a thousand idle amusements pass as fast at least as I wish 'em to do; Lord, Horry, I have at last begun to draw; you'll not be sorry to hear that; I shall confine myself chiefly or rather entirely to perspective, views of buildings, landscapes etc. I feel as if I should take to it mightily and only regret having begun so late. I have a notion Lens[8] is dead, so I have taken a good old German,[9] who was recommended to me by my master of mathematics (for you must know I am in the midst of that and fortifications). He seems to be good at that kind of drawing and has done some views of parts of London which I really think pretty. It must be owned he smells a good deal of tobacco, but time will get the better of that, I hope. He diverts me with talking like my Lord Grantham,[10] and is as solemn as he can be for his life. I almost wish I had stayed for your advice, but now the affair is done I hope for your approbation; as to my performances, which are as yet only two small landscapes, if you'll take my opinion, they are moderate for the first, neither very bad nor good, but nothing tending towards a genius. So I must depend upon time and my old German's instructions and yours when you come over: which I beg you'll do incessantly. What should you do there? You hate France, and England loves you. As for your loving it I want to know how that stands, but I am sure it will divert you when you come; it's a pleasant animal; one may laugh at it as much as one will, but if one grows grave there's no living here. Your ballad[11] is extremely pretty and I think you have done it great injury to put it up in that halfpenny form, with such a title and a frontispiece that I could have done myself.— But it's hard to plague you with so tedious a letter and not relieve you with one paragraph of news; here's a paper just come in;[12] I'll read it and if I can find anything for you, you shall have it:—nothing but foreign news; letters from The Hague and Paris *à la main's* but they say that you French are going to declare war against us immediately, and are marching your troops towards our Electoral Dominions;[13] it does not signify; I am sure the war must be general.

8. Bernard Lens (1682–1740), miniature-painter and water-colourist; HW's drawing-master ('Short Notes,' GRAY i. 7 and n. 28; COLE ii. 222–3 and nn. 6–7.

9. Unidentified, as is Conway's master of mathematics.

10. Henry d'Auverquerque (ca 1672–1754), cr. (1698) E. of Grantham, a cousin

(by illegitimate descent) and a favourite of William III.

11. Apparently, from what Conway says about the 'frontispiece,' HW's 'Strephon's Complaint,' the MS of which is now WSL. It is printed below, Appendix 3.

12. Not identified.

13. Hanover. All the papers at this

The body politic of Europe is in strange disorder and a great deal of bad blood must be let out before it can possibly come to itself again, so the sooner the better. There has been an earthquake at Naples[14] and a storm of hail at Geneva,[15] according to custom; and the Turkish ambassador[16] at Petersburg made a good figure a-horseback though he is but a short, slender man about sixty years of age; this, with the marriage of a great silk dyer to Miss——,[17] a young lady of great beauty, merit, and fortune, and the death of an eminent distiller in Cornhill is all that I find worth your notice. Upon Lord Augustus's[18] death there has been a sort of negotiation about my coming in for Thetford but I don't know what will come on it.[19] I am very easy about the event of it, thanks to Jupiter, and can leave it to him without the least pain. Adieu, dear Horry. Service to Grey.

To CONWAY, September 1741

Missing; written from Paris where HW had arrived ca 30 Aug. 1741 NS.

time were full of reports about the movements of French troops towards and into Germany.

14. No reference to this has been found.

15. 'They write from Geneva, that on the 5th instant [5 July NS], they had so dreadful a storm of hail, that they do not think they can possible [sic] recover the damage done to the vines these three years to come, nor the chestnut trees in nine years; and that the hail stones lay two foot deep on the ground' (*London and Country Journal* 6 Aug. 1741 OS; see also *Daily Adv.* 29 July 1741 OS).

16. Hāǧǧī Mehmed Paša (*Repertorium der diplomatischen Vertreter aller Länder*, Vol. II, ed. Friedrich Hausmann, Zurich, 1950, p. 409). Conway is referring to some description of his state entry into St Petersburg on 29 June OS (10 July NS). The fact of the entry is mentioned in the *Daily Adv.* 25 July, but no details are given. The very sentence that Conway is paraphrasing occurs, however, in the account in the *Mercure historique* for Aug. 1741, cxi. 196–7: 'Cet ambassadeur,

quoique de petite taille et maigre, avait fort bonne mine à cheval: il est agé d'environ 60 ans.' The *Mercure* transliterates his name as 'Eminy Mehemet Bacha.'

17. Neither this nor the following item has been found. The *London Evening Post* 4–6 Aug. reported, 'On Monday last was married . . . Mr John Horncastle, a wholesale linen-draper . . . to Miss Warren . . . an agreeable young lady, with £3000 fortune.'

18. Lord Augustus Fitzroy (1716–28 May 1741), naval officer; M.P. Thetford 1739–41. News of his death, which occurred at Jamaica, reached London 23 July 1741 OS (Collins, *Peerage*, 1812, i. 218; *Daily Adv.* 27 July).

19. The negotiations fell through; Lord Henry Beauclerk was returned for Thetford 29 Dec. 1741 OS in the place of Lord Augustus Fitzroy, while Conway was returned for Higham Ferrers 28 Dec. 1741 OS in the place of Henry Finch who had elected to sit for Malton.

From CONWAY, ca Wednesday 9 September 1741 OS

Printed for the first time from the MS now WSL, formerly Rutnam. Dated approximately by the London postmark; since Conway was in Gloucestershire, the letter must have been written at least a day or two earlier.

Address: À Monsieur Monsieur Walpole recommandé a Monsieur Charles Selwyn banquier dans la rue Ste-Appoline à Paris.

Postmark: 10 SE.

Dear Horry,

AS to commissions I have none to trouble you with only to beg you will bring yourself over with what expedition you may[1] and to take particular care you don't suffer in the voyage. I would not have some of my polite friends know that I have so little to say to Paris; I don't know whether I should be received in some houses if I was known to suffer a friend of mine to come from Paris without so much as a Birthday suit[2] or a pair of ruffles, but so it is; and I am proud to own it to you. I care not a fig for anything in Paris but yourself and comp[any]. Yes; I have some remains of a passion for poor Knight,[3] who was very civil to me, and I beg you'll give my compliments to him. I was in hopes I should have been in town at your arrival and should have gone a little *au devant* a day or so if you would have let me; but you know what a family creature I am: and in short I have put off my journey hither from week to week and day to day so long that I was at last forced to yield to their frequent invitations, which indeed were come to the degree of insistings. So here I am, that is, at Sandywell,[4] and here we live the prettiest country life in the world—walk, ride, shoot, play at comet[5] and do twenty pretty things—all amongst ourselves; for we have as little

1. HW was already at Calais, waiting for fair weather to take him to England (MANN i. 140).

2. For the King's Birthday. HW had had one made in Paris (see *post* 31 Oct. 1741).

3. Probably Robert Knight (d. 1744), cashier of the South Sea Company, who had fled to the Continent in 1721 after the Bubble burst, and who eventually became a banker in Paris (MANN i. 126, n. 24, 459, n. 19).

4. Sandywell or Sandiwell Park, Glos, a few miles southeast of Cheltenham. The property had been purchased by Lord Conway's father but was later sold by Lord Conway himself (Ralph Bigland, *Historical . . . Collections Relative to the County of Gloucester*, 1790–92, i. 484–5).

5. The French game of *comète*, first popularized by Louis XV about 1730. It was played with cards which were distinguished by various numbers of stars. From HW to Mann 22 Oct. 1741 OS it would appear that it had only recently become popular in England (MANN i. 173 and n. 12).

communication with the creatures about us as possible. But I hope
to see you soon for all that, and will though I elope and fly by
night, for I long to see you. I told you we don't live much with our
neighbours and of course we are not like to be very popular. At my
brother's first coming down they thought they should have been
devoured by monsters that left their caves every day to stare at
Lady Conway who was forced to do the honours and sat like Daniel
in the lion's den, expecting they'd eat her up every moment. I am
in some doubt whether this will find you at Paris, so for that reason
and because I have no earthly thing to tell you, I shall conclude. All
the little knowledge I have of people and things shall be entirely at
your service when I see you. It will do perhaps well enough by
way of question and answer but I really have nothing of importance
enough to make a figure in the shape of narration. So adieu! My
brother desires his love to you and my sisters theirs as far as may be
decent.

My brother says he shall be infinitely obliged if you'll bring him
over fourteen pair of *manchettes brodées* and as much of *galon de
mousquetaire* as will lace him a coat and waistcoat: one lace only
round the coat and two on the sleeve. A broad lace.

To Lord Conway, ca Tuesday 15 September 1741 OS

Missing; mentioned in Conway to HW ?19 Sept. 1741 OS. It presumably
announced HW's arrival in England; he reached London 14 Sept.

From CONWAY, Saturday ?19 September 1741 OS

Printed for the first time from the MS now WSL, formerly Rutnam. The date is somewhat uncertain, although it was clearly written very soon after HW's arrival in London. The following Saturday is most likely.

Address: ⟨To H⟩oratio Walpole Esquire ⟨at the⟩ Right Honourable Sir Robert Walpole's ⟨in⟩ Downing Street London.

Postmark: [illegible] SE. FAIRFORD.

Saturday.

Dear Horry,

I CAN'T tell you how happy I am that you are returned or how miserable I am that I could not be in town to meet you; for I long to see you and to know both the present state and ancient history of you, your health, your spirits, how are they? what feels do you feel upon standing on English ground? These are questions that I may ask now but must resolve myself when I see you—I must study you to find out how you like us. Then such cartloads of virtu! medals and pictures; a buckle of one hero and a button of another, things that I am miserably ignorant of, God knows; but I'll hear the history of it all with great attention, like country people that see the Tombs at Westminster Abbey and admire the profound knowledge of the sexton, and like 'em all as much as you please since I shall comprehend 'em as little. My brother was vastly obliged to you for your letter and so elevated upon the receipt of it that he immediately formed the most extravagant hopes from your goodness, even of seeing you at Sandywell. I know you'd think me both mad and a fool if I pretended to indulge myself in any such flattering prospect. I know that the country can have no charms for you; I won't tell you what air, what walks, what prospects, or what diversions we have, nor inform you how many coveys of partridges or bevys of quails lie in the neighbourhood; but this I must say in our favour: you'll pass a few days in great tranquillity and rest yourself to a miracle after your journey; you'll neither be molested with smoking country gentlemen nor chattering country ladies; you'll be in a family that loves you and will do everything they can to make themselves supportable to you for three or four days or so; for longer we cannot think of. Nay, for my part I don't think of that; I durst not hope it because I know I shall be disappointed. Then you'll see a new place; I am violently tempted to tell you it is one of the finest in Europe and I don't know whether I should resist my inclination to leasing¹ in this occasion, if I had not a stronger inducement in reserve. You'll see Lady Conway and I assure you she is worth coming farther to see. I am sure you'll both admire and love her when you know her; and be surprised to see in one of fifteen all the sense and prudence of the ripest age joined to the simplicity of her own. I'll say no more but, dear Horry, make us happy if you can. I know one may as well move mountains as bring you into the country; but if faith (which I own is very little able to do it in the present case) will move mountains why should not charity? Your own charity, I know nobody has so much, and you really can't find more worthy objects (in one sense, I mean) to exercise it upon; however you are disposed I am resolved to see you soon and will certainly make but a short stay here if you give me no hopes in your next. Adieu! I wrote a letter to you lately to Paris,² I am afraid too lately to find you there. I am only afraid because there were some trifling commissions for you from my brother. Tell me where you are and where you are to be!

All our loves and services!

---

1. Lying; now an obsolete word; the last example given in OED from common usage is 1731.

2. *Ante* ca 9 Sept. 1741 OS.

To Conway, ca Monday 21 September 1741 OS

Printed from *Works* v. 14–15. The date is uncertain. Mrs Toynbee argued for placing it in November on the assumption that Conway's letter to Gray must have been written on the death of Gray's father 6 Nov. 1741 OS (*Notes and Queries*, 1897, 8th ser., xii. 493; Toynbee i. 132, notes), but Conway's letter could have been merely welcoming Gray home. It is also probable that HW had written Conway of his quarrel with Gray and that Conway wished to show Gray that it would not affect their friendship. It seems clear from Conway's letters (which were unknown to Mrs Toynbee) that this letter is in answer to Conway's of ca 9 Sept. and apparently to that of ?19 Sept. (below, nn. 2, 3, 7). It is also clear from the general contents of the present letter that it was written shortly after HW reached London on 14 Sept., not after an interval of nearly two months; nor is it conceivable that he would have waited so long to write Conway. Since this letter answers Conway's letters of ca 9 and ?19 Sept., it cannot be earlier than 20 Sept.

London, 1741.

My dearest Harry,

BEFORE I thank you for myself, I must thank you for that excessive good nature you showed in writing to poor Gray.[1] I am less impatient to see you, as I find you are not the least altered, but have the same tender friendly temper you always had. I wanted much to see if you were still the same—but you are.

Don't think of coming before your brother; he is too good to be left for any one living: besides, if it is possible, I will see you in the country. Don't reproach me, and think nothing could draw me into the country:[2] impatience to see a few friends has drawn me out of Italy; and Italy, Harry, is pleasanter than London. As I do not love living *en famille* so much as you (but then indeed my family is not like yours), I am hurried about getting myself a house;[3] for I have

1. Conway's letter to Gray is missing and is not mentioned in either of his preceding letters to HW, but HW may have learned of it from common friends in London. Gray had reached London at the very beginning of September, about two weeks before HW arrived (Thomas Gray, *Correspondence*, ed. Toynbee and Whibley, Oxford, 1935, i. 187).

2. This seems to be a reply to Conway's remarks *ante* ?19 Sept. 1741 OS

that he knew 'the country can have no charms for you,' and 'I know one may as well move mountains as bring you into the country.'

3. This scheme did not materialize; on 19 Oct. OS HW wrote to Mann that he was fitting up an apartment in Downing Street (MANN i. 171), and apparently wrote in similar terms to Conway about the same time; see Conway's reply to a missing letter, *post* 26 Oct. 1741 OS.

so long lived single, that I do not much take to being confined with . . .⁴

You won't find me much altered, I believe; at least, outwardly. I am not grown a bit shorter, or a bit fatter, but am just the same long lean creature as usual. Then I talk no French, but to my footman; nor Italian, but to myself. What inward alterations may have happened to me, you will discover best; for you know 'tis said, one never knows that one's self. I will answer, that that part of it that belongs to you, has not suffered the least change—I took care of that.

For virtu, I have a little to entertain you: it is my sole pleasure.— I am neither young enough nor old enough to be in love.

My dear Harry, will you take care and make my compliments to that charming Lady Conway,⁵ who I hear is so charming, and to Miss Jenny, who I know is so? As for Miss Anne,⁶ and her love *as far as it is decent;*⁷ tell her, decency is out of the question between us, that I love her without any restriction. I settled it yesterday with Miss Conway,⁸ that you three are brothers and sister to me, and that if you had been so, I could not love you better. I have so many cousins, and uncles and aunts, and bloods that grow in Norfolk, that if I had portioned out my affections to them, as they say I should, what a modicum would have fallen to each!—So, to avoid fractions, I love my family in you three, their representatives.

Adieu, my dear Harry! Direct to me at Downing Street. Goodbye!

Yours ever,

Hor. Walpole

---

4. A name or passage has been omitted in *Works,* indicated by asterisks.

5. Isabella Fitzroy, daughter of Charles Duke of Grafton (HW).

6. Miss Anne Conway, youngest sister of Henry Seymour Conway (HW).

7. HW is echoing a phrase from *ante* ca 9 Sept. 1741 OS.

8. Since it appears from the preceding sentences that Conway's sister Anne and his half-sister Jane were with the family at Sandywell, this must be his only other unmarried half-sister, the Hon. Henrietta (or Harriet) Seymour Conway (d. 1771), later HW's occasional correspondent (Collins, *Peerage,* 1812, ii. 561; *Miscellanea genealogica et heraldica,* 1890, 2d ser., iii. 57).

To Conway, ca Friday 23 October 1741 OS

Missing; Conway's reply, *post* 26 Oct. 1741 OS, seems to have been written almost immediately upon receiving the letter.

From Conway, Monday 26 October 1741 OS

Printed from the MS now WSL, formerly Rutnam. First printed (misdated 1740) *Rockingham Memoirs* i. 375–7; reprinted (similarly misdated) *Colburn's United Service Magazine*, 1880, lii pt i. 175–7. The year is clearly 1741 from the contents. This letter measures 4⅛ by 6½ inches when folded.

Monday, Oct. 26.

LOOK here, Horry, here's just such a bit of paper as you writ to me upon and if I can help it I won't write a word more upon it. I have just writ to Selwyn[1] and told him that I had received your note and would answer it soon, but it's now come into my head to do it this minute, that I may scold you for the shortness of your last; before my resentment is cooled, for you know I am soon appeased; indeed, Horry, if one did not love you better than anybody, and you did not write better than other people one could never forgive you. But I had forgot; those are the very reasons why I should be the most angry with you. So know that nothing but a vehement long letter can ever make it up betwixt us. I must tell you too that you must write it soon for we have fixed our journey for this day fortnight. And I feel as if I should like to meet upon the best terms imaginable with you. For to say the truth (don't tell Horry Walpole of it) I long [to] see you. Indeed I heartily wish I had been at the unpacking of your virtu,[2] for I love to see pretty things though I don't understand 'em. And for your Tiberius,[3] Vespasian[4] and Octavia[5] I honour them; and most obsequiously kiss

1. This letter is missing.
2. HW wrote to Mann 19 Oct. 1741 OS that he had been 'opening all my cases from the custom house the whole morning' (MANN i. 170).
3. Nothing of Tiberius is mentioned in the list of antiquities that HW sent to Middleton 9 April 1743 OS (DALRYMPLE 12–14).

4. A bust of Vespasian in basalt, which HW had purchased at Cardinal Ottoboni's sale at Rome in May 1740. It eventually stood at the right of the fireplace in the Gallery at SH (GRAY i. 214, 232, n. 15; DALRYMPLE 12, nn. 4–5).
5. Perhaps the gold medal of Antony 'with the head of Octavia the reverse,' which HW discusses in his letter to Mid-

their hands, if they have any. What closet have you fitted up? Are you in your old apartment or is it t'other charming green closet?

Pray tell Mrs Leneve[6] I like her *bouts rimés* much and should be glad to hear from her the true history of *Quoties, Domine?* Have you heard anything of the duel between Winnington[7] and Augustus Townshend?[8] It's charming! But don't say anything of it from me if you have not because Selwyn told me of it and bid me not let it go out of the family,[9] of which family I reckon you are. I hear his M. is come over[10] full of his H. treaty[11] and that he expects great applause for it from the Parliament. It's whispered too that he is like to be disappointed. Have you seen Lord Bolingbrook's pamphlet?[12] What do you think of it? You are, or are to be a politician, but for me I trouble myself with no such thing. Have you seen or heard anything about the opera? I believe it's too late for you to subscribe now, but I hope you intend to go there very often. You must know I am a director,[13] a director! well I give you leave to make what reflections you please upon me, but don't say a word for I am now trying to get my name out. Was there ever such an oaf in the world! Do scold me I beseech you, Horry, for that will really be some punishment to me. I may be ruined too, for what I know; and

---

dleton 9 April 1743 (DALRYMPLE 14 and nn. 26–28).

6. Mrs Isabella Leneve [ca 1686–1759], a gentlewoman of a very ancient family in Norfolk, who had been brought up by Lady Anne Walpole, aunt of Sir Robert Walpole, with his sister Lady Townshend, and afterwards had the care of Sir Robert's daughter Lady Maria, after whose marriage with Mr Churchill, she lived with Mr Walpole to her death. She had an excellent understanding and a great deal of wit (HW's note to his letter to Mann 13 Dec. 1759). See also MONTAGU i. 62, n. 27 and MANN ii. 36, n. 37.

7. Thomas Winnington (1696–1746), politician and wit; M.P. Droitwich 1726–41, Worcester 1741–6.

8. Hon. Augustus Townshend (1716–46), HW's cousin (DNB *sub* Charles Townshend, 2d Vct Townshend). HW gives an account of the duel in his letter to Mann 22 Oct. 1741 OS (MANN i. 172–3).

9. Selwyn's sister Albinia (d. 1739) had

married (1730) the Hon. Thomas Townshend (1701–80), Augustus's half-brother.

10. The King had reached England from Hanover on 19 Oct. OS (*Daily Adv.* 20, 21 Oct.).

11. George II, as Elector of Hanover, had concluded a convention of neutrality with France 27 Sept. NS, promising to withhold troops from joining the Austrians and to vote for the Bavarian Elector as Emperor. This contradicted England's alliance with Maria Theresa (MANN i. 133, n. 10). For the immediate reaction to it, see ibid. i. 187.

12. No pamphlet attributed to Bolingbroke was published at this time and it is not clear to what Conway is referring unless it is to *The Groans of Germany*, advertised as published 'this day' in the *Daily Adv.* 21 Oct., and sometimes ascribed, but probably erroneously, to James Ralph (MANN i. 187, n. 34).

13. See *post* 31 Oct. 1741 OS, n. 51.

forced to elope some fair evening; you'd hear nothing of me till you see my name in the paper for a bankrupt and a description of my person. What d'ye think we do with ourselves here? We breakfast together, then part commonly and remain in our respective apartments, till dinner: unless the day serves for walking, but of those we have very few. And those few we make fewer by our little inclination to walk, the country is so dirty and so dismal. At four we dine, and after dinner read some stupid ⟨book⟩ till supper, for we have a tolerable learned library here, but the worst for a lady's entertainment that ever was: all this is melancholy enough, but one shall see you in a fortnight, my dear Horry, and that makes everything supportable. Adieu! my compliments to all your house. So you can't bear Mrs Woffington.[14] Yet all the town's in love with [her]. To say the truth I am glad to find somebody to keep me in countenance for I think she is an impudent Irish-faced girl.

To CONWAY, Saturday 31 October 1741 OS

Printed from a photostat of the MS in the Pierpont Morgan Library. First printed Toynbee i. 114–18. Miss Berry bequeathed it to Sir Frankland Lewis, on whose death it passed to his widow, Lady Theresa Lewis. She left it to a son of her first marriage, Sir Thomas Villiers Lister. Mr Morgan acquired it, along with HW's letters to the Berrys and other Walpoliana, from his widow.

London, Oct. 31, 1741.

My Dearest Harry,

YOU have made me infinitely happy but infinitely impatient for Monday sennight. I have wished for you more particularly this week, and wanted you all at Sir Thomas Robinson's[1] and the Birthday.[2] You have already had accounts I suppose of the former from

---

14. Margaret ('Peg') Woffington (ca 1714–60), actress, first appeared in London in Nov. 1740 and performed at Drury Lane for the season of 1741–2. HW calls her 'a bad actress' in his letter to Mann 22 Oct. 1741 OS (MANN i. 176).

1. His ball, described below and in HW to Mann 2 Nov. 1741 OS (MANN i. 183–5), took place 23 Oct. (ibid. i. 174). Conway describes an earlier one *ante* 24 March 1740 OS.

2. The King's Birthday, 30 Oct. OS.

Lady Caroline[3] and Mr Selwyn but I will say my bit about it too; I told Lady Caroline I would; besides I made a list of most of the people, and will tell you some of the company which was all extremely good; there were none but people of the first fashion, except Mr Kent,[4] Mr Cibber,[5] Mr Swiny,[6] and the Parsons family[7] and you know all these have an alloy. Kent came as governess to Lady Charlotte Boyle,[8] Cibber and Swiny have long had their freedom given them of this end of the town, and the Parsons's took out theirs at Paris. There were an hundred and ninety-seven people, yet no confusion; he had taken off all the doors of his house, and in short distributed everybody quite to their well-being. The dancers were the two Lady Lenox's[9] (Lady Emily Queen of the Ball, and appeared in great majesty from behind a vast bouquet), Lady Lucy Manners,[10] Lady Ankram,[11] Lady Lucy Clinton,[12] Ladies Harriot[13] and Anne Wentworth,[14] Sophia and Charlotte Farmor, and Camilla Bennet;[15] Miss Pelham,[16] Lord! how ugly she is! Misses Walpole,[17]

3. Lady Caroline Fitzroy, Lady Conway's sister; HW says below that she did not dance.

4. William Kent (?1686–1748), painter, sculptor, architect, and landscape-gardener (Margaret Jourdain, *The Work of William Kent*, 1948, addendum).

5. Colley Cibber (1671–1757), actor and dramatist; poet laureate since 1730.

6. Owen Mac Swinny (d. 1754), dramatist.

7. Sarah Parsons, m. James Dunn, called Comte Jacques O'Dunne; Anne Parsons (d. 1769), m. (1754) Sir John Hinde Cotton, 4th Bt; and John Parsons. They were the son and daughters of Humphrey Parsons (ca 1676–1741), lord mayor of London, 1730, 1740, 'a Jacobite brewer, who lived much in France and had somehow or other been taken notice of by the King' (HW's note to his letter to Mann 2 Nov. 1741 OS, MANN i. 185, n. 14, which see for the above identification).

8. Lady Charlotte Elizabeth Boyle (1731–54), m. (1748) William Cavendish, styled M. of Hartington, 4th D. of Devonshire, 1755. Kent was a close friend and associate of her father, the Earl of Burlington.

9. Lady Emilia Mary Lennox (1731–1814), m. 1 (1747) James Fitzgerald, 20th E. of Kildare, cr. (1761) M. of Kildare

and (1766) D. of Leinster; m. 2 (1774) William Ogilvie; and her sister Lady Caroline Lennox (*ante* 24 March 1740 OS, n. 18). The ball was given in Lady Emily's honour (MANN i. 174).

10. (ca 1717–88), m. (1742) William Graham, 2d D. of Montrose, 1742.

11. Lady Caroline Darcy (d. 1778), m. (1735) William Henry Ker, styled E. of Ancram 1722–67, 4th M. of Lothian, 1767. HW told Mann that she was the only married woman who danced (ibid. i. 184).

12. (1721–63) (Collins, *Peerage*, 1812, ii. 213).

13. Lady Henrietta (Harriet) Wentworth (d. 1786), sister of the 2d E. of Strafford, m. (1743) Henry Vernon (DU DEFFAND iv. 364, n. 11).

14. Lady Anne Watson Wentworth (d. 1769), dau. of the E. of Malton, m. (1744) William Fitzwilliam, 3d E. Fitzwilliam.

15. (d. 1785), m. 1 (1754) Gilbert Fane Fleming; m. 2 (1779)—Wake, apothecary of Bath (MANN i. 184, n. 9, and *London Chronicle* 9–12 Oct. 1779, xlvi. 345).

16. Catherine Pelham (1727–60), eldest surviving dau. of Henry Pelham, m. (1744) Henry Fiennes Clinton, 9th E. of Lincoln, 2d D. of Newcastle-under-Lyne, 1768.

17. HW's half-sister, later Lady Mary Churchill.

Leneve,[18] Churchill,[19] Parsons,[20] Maccartny,[21] Pultney,[22] Mary Town-shend,[23] Newton[24] and Brown.[25] The men Lord John Sackville, Lord Ankram,[26] Holderness, Ashburnham,[27] Howard,[28] Hartington, and Castlehaven,[29] Mr Colebrook,[30] Poulett,[31] Churchill,[32] two Town-shends,[33] Parsons,[34] Vernon,[35] Carteret,[36] Col. Mcguire,[37] and a Sir Will[iam] Boothby.[38] For the rest of the company you shall see the list when you come to town. Lord and Lady Euston[39] and Lady Caroline did not dance. A supper for the lady dancers was served at twelve, their partners and waiting tables with other supper stood behind. Oh I danced country dances, I had forgot myself. The ball ended at four.

18. Elizabeth Le Neve (1720–?54), m. (between 1743 and 1748) Hugh Pigot, later Adm.; niece of 'Mrs' Isabella Le Neve (MANN ii. 36, n. 35; *post* 30 July 1754).

19. Harriet Churchill (1726–77), natural dau. of Gen. Charles Churchill, m. 1 (1747) Sir Everard Fawkener; m. 2 (1765) Hon. Thomas Pownall (MANN i. 184, n. 13).

20. Presumably the elder of the Parsons sisters (above, n. 7).

21. Probably Frances Macartney (d. 1789), m. (1748) Fulke Greville; poetess; the 'Fanny' of HW's 'The Beauties' (BERRY i. 47, n. 41; GM 1789, lix pt ii. 763), although it is uncertain which of the four Macartney sisters was the eldest.

22. Anna Maria Pulteney (1727–42) (SELWYN 89, n. 25).

23. Hon. Mary Townshend (ca 1720–76), m. (1753) Lt-Gen. Hon. Edward Cornwallis; HW's cousin and occasional correspondent (*East Anglian* 1903–4, n.s. x. 348; Collins, *Peerage*, 1812, ii. 554).

24. Not identified; HW may have mistaken the name since there seems to be no "Miss Newton' who could be described as of 'the first fashion' at this time.

25. Probably one of the two daughters of Sir Robert Browne, Bt; the younger died unmarried in 1755 (MONTAGU i. 170 and n. 12; HW to Bentley 17 July 1755, CHUTE 236).

26. William Henry Ker (ca 1710–75), styled E. of Ancram 1722–67, 4th M. of Lothian, 1767.

27. John Ashburnham (1724–1812), 2d E. of Ashburnham.

28. Thomas Howard (ca 1714–63), styled Lord Howard 1731–43, 2d E. of Effingham, 1743.

29. James Tuchet (1723–69), 7th E. of Castlehaven.

30. Robert Colebrooke (1718–84), M.P. Maldon 1741–61; minister to the Swiss Cantons 1762–4 (MANN i. 185, n. 15).

31. Presumably one of the three younger sons of the 1st E. Poulett: Peregrine (1708–52); Vere (1710–88), 3d E. Poulett, 1764; or Anne (1711–85) (Collins, *Peerage*, 1812, iv. 13–14).

32. Charles Churchill (?1720–1812), natural son of Gen. Charles Churchill; later HW's brother-in-law.

33. These were most probably two of HW's Townshend cousins, sons of the 2d Vct, and not the two elder sons of the 3d Vct, who were rather young for this affair.

34. John Parsons (above, n. 7).

35. Not identified; there were several Vernons of about the right age and social position.

36. Hon. Robert Carteret (1721–76), styled Bn Carteret 1744–63, 2d E. Granville, 1763.

37. Probably Hugh Maguire (d. 1766), an Irish Catholic officer in the Austrian service who abjured his religion and became a Lt-Col. in the British army in 1742 (SELWYN 84, n. 13). See also *post* 24 Oct. 1742 NS.

38. (1721–87), 4th Bt.

39. George Fitzroy (1715–47), styled E. of Euston, m. (10 Oct. 1741 OS) Lady Dorothy Boyle (1724–42). The marriage was already in chaos; see MANN i. 174–5.

Now for the Birthday; there were loads of men, not many ladies, nor much finery. Lord Fitzwilliams[40] and myself were the only two very fine.[41] I was in a great taking about my clothes; they came from Paris and did not arrive till nine o'clock of the Birthday morning.[42] I was obliged to send one of the King's Messengers for them and Lord Holderness's suit to Dover. There were nineteen suits came with them; do you know I was in such a fright lest they should get into the news, and took up the *Craftsman*[43] with fear and trembling. There was the greatest crowd at the ball I ever saw. Lady Euston danced country dances with the Duke.[44] My Aunt Horace[45] had adapted her gown to her complexion, and chose a silk all broke out in pink blotches. By the way was ever anything so terrible as Lord Holderness's face? Poor Lady Ankram's will be as bad in a twelve-month. She, the Duke of Kingston,[46] Lord Middlesex, and Lady Albermarle[47] are dreadfully altered. You can't think what an altera-tion towards old I find among my acquaintance.

Harry, you must come and be in love with Lady Sophia Farmor; all the world is or should be. But I had cried her up so much be-fore she appeared[48] that she does not answer everybody's expecta-tion. No more will the opera[49] tonight, for Amorevoli[50] is ill and does not sing; his part is to be read. They had certainly much better have stayed till Tuesday, but for fear of disappointing people, I fear they will disappoint them. I am not to be there, for Dodd has got a fever with the heat of the ball last night, so I shall not leave him. Indeed, my dear Harry, I will not scold you about the opera, but I should have been glad, I own, that you were not in the direc-tion.[51] I doubt much of the success; and even should it succeed,

40. William Fitzwilliam (1720–56), 3d E. Fitzwilliam.

41. HW told Mann 2 Nov. 1741 OS that he and Fitzwilliam 'were far the most superb' (ibid. i. 185).

42. HW also mentions this to Mann, ibid.

43. The principal Opposition journal. It appeared on Saturdays.

44. Of Cumberland.

45. Mary Magdelaine Lombard (ca 1695–1783), m. (1720) Horatio Walpole, cr. (1756) Bn Walpole of Wolterton (MANN ii. 47, n. 2). HW's references to her are usually unflattering.

46. Evelyn Pierrepont (1711–73), 2d D. of Kingston.

47. Lady Anne Lennox (1703–89), m.

(1723) William Anne van Keppel, 2d E. of Albemarle.

48. Lady Sophia and her family had returned to London from the Continent in early October (MANN i. 165, 169–70; SELWYN 28).

49. Which was opening for the season with *Alexander in Persia* (MANN i. 183, n. 3; *London Stage* Pt III, ii. 939).

50. Angelo Amorevoli (1716–98), tenor (MANN i. 80, n. 16; SELWYN 5; *Enciclo-pedia dello spettacelo*, Rome, 1954–62, i. 500–1). He had a fever (MANN i. 185, 190).

51. HW expresses a similar concern for Conway in his letter to Mann 5 Nov. 1741 OS and gives a list of the other directors (ibid. i. 190–1).

gentlemen, and they very young gentlemen, are mighty apt not to understand economy and management. Do, get out of it, if possible.

Good night, I have nothing more to tell you now, but I shall have a quantity to say to you. My loves to all your family.

Yours ever,

H. W.

From CONWAY, Tuesday 31 July 1742 NS

Printed in full for the first time from the MS now WSL, formerly Rutnam. First printed in part *Rockingham Memoirs* i. 382–3; reprinted in part *Colburn's United Service Magazine*, 1880, lii pt i. 320–1. The year is clearly 1742 when Conway was stationed at Ghent; in subsequent years he left for the Continent much earlier and was not at Ghent in July.

July 31.

Dear Horry,

IDLE as I am and idle as you know me I don't doubt but you expect by this time a long letter brim-full of a thousand pretty stories, relations of my travels, descriptions of places, people etc., for which reason to prevent your farther disappointment, I must begin by advertising you that neither from what I have seen or done you are to expect the least entertainment; if I was publishing an account of my voyage and had only the world to deceive you should hear of trees bearing fishes, of miraculous gudgeons, flying serpents and even Flying Dutchmen; but as I think it inconsistent with the friendship that subsists between us and with the standing order of correspondence to depart from the letter, you must take it just as I found it; and have this at least to comfort you, that a barrenness of incidents and want of variety in both things and places will reduce it to a very small compass. First we crept over the sea in four tedious days,[1] and from thence stepped immediately into a bi-

1. The date of Conway's departure from England is uncertain. He says *post* 29 Aug. 1742 NS that he wrote the present letter when he had 'scarce arrived' at Ghent; he seems to have been at least a week en route. He was joining his company in the brigade of Guards which had left England 26 May 1742 OS as part of the 'Pragmatic Army' being assembled in Flanders (Sir F. W. Hamilton, *Origin and History of the First or Grenadier Guards*, 1874, ii. 105).

lander,[2] which bilander is a certain vast fresh-water machine, answering the idea that I have of the Ark, and filled with just such a motley complement: Dutch, English, German, Flemish, civil, military, male, female, dogs, cats etc., but all in appearance of the unclean kind. In this agreeable conveyance we were dragged by two lean Flanders mares, up a narrow canal and through a melancholy, flat, undiversified country[3] to Bruges, a clean, old-fashioned town that has nothing to be said either for or against it but the neatness of the streets; and puts me in mind of [a] cleanly old woman: smug and insipid. I'm afraid you'll not be struck with this idea! Here we saw nothing, or at least nothing that I can or care to remember but Sir Harry Englefield's[4] sister[5] in a convent of English nuns; she is vastly handsome and we were all that day violently in love with her. The next we changed our amphibious vehicle for its counterpart upon wheels, very improperly called a diligence, which brought us five or six leagues in twice as many hours to Ghent where we arrived as you may imagine *plus ennuyés que fatigués,* and tired of nothing so much as the great tranquillity and ease of our journey. Now, dear Horry, I know you interest yourself enough about me to have some curiosity about a place I am to pass the next century in; for so appears to me the vast period of time that lies betwixt me and England; I was going to say betwixt you and me but I am resolved not to think that the case as long as ever I can help it: and yet I don't know with what face I can invite you to such a miserable place; for miserable indeed it is by all I have heard or seen of it beyond anything you can imagine. *Imprimis* we have no sort of society or commerce whatsoever with the people; and to console us, if that be really a loss, no earthly thing that pretends to the name of diversion or amusement: both without and within the walls, a perfect desert; not a place to ride or walk in. I have lived hitherto with

2. Lt-Col. Charles Russell, who made a similar trip from Ostend to Bruges a few weeks earlier, describes a bilander as 'very like one of our west country barges' (Hist. MSS Comm., *Frankland-Russell-Astley MSS,* 1900, p. 214).

3. Lt-Col. Russell describes the trip between Ostend and Bruges as 'twelve miles through a very flat country, not a house worth £50 and scarce a tree (except a willow) or a hedge all the way' (ibid.).

4. Sir Henry Englefield (d. 1780), 6th Bt.

5. Probably either the Rev. Mother Martha Englefield (ca 1711–93), professed as a nun ca 1728, who died at the Prinzenhof, Bruges; or Mary Winefred Englefield (ca 1717–77), professed ca 1735, and later abbess of the English Benedictines at Dunkirk (*Publications of the Catholic Record Society,* 1913, xii. 23, 40).

Lord and Lady Ancram,[6] which has made it tolerable, but how my time will pass when I shall be reduced to do as they do here, which is in the most literal sense doing nothing, is a thing I have no imagination of. You won't believe me when I tell you that they saunter about the streets and *lounge* at a coffee house or tavern door all day long; I have already wished a thousand times I had been taken by the privateers, and carried to St Sebastian's.[7] I should at least have had retirement there, been at liberty to think and perhaps been allowed the use of books, pen, ink and paper: every article of which I'm afraid will hardly be permitted me here. Well! I set out tomorrow for Bruxelles and Antwerp with Lord and Lady Ancram who are going into Holland. I shall see new things and new places and am resolved not to think of Gant till I see it again; which that some happy accident may avert is my serious prayer. In the meantime you see how honestly I deal with you; yet not so very disinterestedly perhaps neither for when I tell you of the miseries of Ghent, I lay open my own to you and bold as my expectations of relief from you may be, I think nothing too much to hope from your charity and good nature. They talk now of our encamping, God knows with what grounds; whatever happens, however my stars dispose of me, I shall wish at least to see you and if that can't be, draw some consolation in my state of separation from the hope that I am not quite forgot by my friends, by such I mean as I desire should remember me and such as I cannot forget. Adieu! I need not tell you how forward you stand in that rank nor how much I am my dear Horry's

Sincere friend and servant,

H. C.

Direct à Monsieur, Monsieur Conway, Lieutenant Colonel dans les troupes de sa Majesté Britannique à Ghent.

6. Lord Ancram, like Conway, was a Capt. and Lt-Col. in the 1st Regiment of Guards (Hamilton, op. cit. iii. 448).

7. The many English prizes being taken there are mentioned in the *Daily Adv.* 8 July 1742 OS.

To CONWAY, ca Sunday 1 August 1742 OS

Missing; Conway calls it a 'note' in his reply 29 Aug. 1742 NS. From the last paragraph in Conway's reply, it seems likely that this was written before HW left for Houghton with his father 5 Aug. OS (MANN ii. 8): otherwise Conway would have known that HW was there.

From CONWAY, Wednesday 29 August 1742 NS

Printed for the first time from the MS now WSL, formerly Rutnam. The year is clearly 1742, when Conway was stationed at Ghent.

Aug. 29 NS.

Dear Horry,

IF I was not sure that you have justice and gratitude enough to make it unnecessary, I should begin this by telling you that I am without vanity the best creature in the world. I was scarce arrived here when without regard to that family rubric which you mentioned and in manifest violation of the laws of brotherhood I wrote you a long letter over the heads of several that were above you in the list of relation: and though I have received nothing from you but a note which you are indeed modest enough not to call a letter, I am now set down to write to you in the best humour in the world with you and not knowing when or where this letter may end: I own your excuse of packing hurry[1] would have been well enough imagined if yours had not been accompanied with one to Lord Bury[2] which to my mortification looked fuller and blacker than mine.

1. HW and his family were packing for removal from Downing Street by mid-July and were staying at Chelsea before the end of the month (MANN i. 494–5, ii. 7).

2. George Keppel (1724–72), styled Vct Bury 1724–54, 3d E. of Albemarle, 1754. He began his military career as an ensign in the Coldstream Guards 1 Feb. 1738 OS, but moved to the Royal (1st) Dragoons as a Capt.-Lt 25 April 1741 OS, where he became 'Capt. of a troop' in Nov. 1741; on either 14 April or 14 July 1743 OS he returned to the Coldstream Guards as a Capt.-Lt (C. T. Atkinson, *History of the Royal Dragoons*, Glasgow, [1934], pp. 153, 480; Daniel MacKinnon, *Origin and Services of the Coldstream Guards*, 1833, ii. 480; *London Magazine*, 1741, x. 570). He had probably recently arrived at Ghent, since the Royals did not go overseas until Aug. 1742 (Atkinson, op. cit. 153). HW's correspondence with him has not been recovered. At the time of his succession to the title HW described him as 'a great friend of mine' (MANN iv. 460).

At pater ut gnati sic nos debemus amici
Si quid sit vitium non fastidire.[3]

I feel myself, in short, vastly averse to falling out with you and besides have been so often guilty myself on the same head that between one and t'other I should scold very awkwardly. But don't
think I shall always be so tame. I know the value of your letters, nay
of every line that comes from you, too well, not to be seriously hurt
when I am not paid to the last syllable; nay, I expect much more
from you than you can possibly think of from me, in proportion to
the inequality of our circumstances; and besides change is not at all
at par between England and Flanders: our coin is really not current amongst you civilized people. To hear what tents and mar-
quees, what pickets and mangers, what coffers[4] and canteens[5] we are
preparing for our camp would certainly be very amusing news to
you! And *à propos* to all that, you can't think, my dear Horry, with
what infinite regret I see my hopes of meeting you here diminish
daily by the approach of a campaign.[6] To invite you to Gant is almost more than is consistent with the affection I have for you; and
I am far from forming so wild and so unfriendly a wish as that of
seeing you in a winter's camp which to a man in red is certainly no
disagreeable thing but to one in brown would be the devil. This
to one read in causes and effects would seem a strange paradox;
but is to be resolved by this short question: *ambitione tremes?*[7]—To
a man swelling with ambition linen houses[8] and hard fare even in
the wettest country in the world and in the wettest season are things
more desirable than the luxury of palaces, *et venere et canis et*
pluma sardanapali.[9] Then to be lord in one's own little dwelling!
and sovereign of a territory about 100 yards square with the government of 70 or 80 subjects! These are sweets that even Houghton
Hall could not afford me. You see, I'm grown military *à brûler;* I

---

3. Horace, *Satires* I. iii. 43–4 ('At any
rate, we should deal with a friend as a
father with his child, and not be fastidious
about some blemish').

4. A type of fortification; see OED *sub*
'coffer, 6.'

5. The earliest use of this word in this
sense of military provision shop given
in OED is from 1744.

6. No campaign took place in 1742,
although it was generally believed until

late in the autumn that the army assembled at Ghent would invade French
Flanders or at least besiege Dunkirk.

7. Properly *tremis:* 'Do you tremble with
ambition?'

8. I.e., tents.

9. Juvenal, *Satires* x. 362 ('and the
loves and the feasts and the down cush-
ions of Sardanapalus'). Conway has clearly
written 'canis,' not 'cenis,' but it must be
a slip.

have already dreamt a thousand golden dreams of honour and achievements and God knows what! and built castles in the air innumerable, new Lisles[10] and Dunkerques which I take and raze in the twinkling of an eye; this with some more substantial edifices that I build upon paper, makes almost my whole occupation. In the meantime, my dear Horry (honour apart), I languish to see you and the rest of my friends in England, I won't own with what impatience and with what weakness.

> *Cum repeto tempus quo tot mihi cara reliqui*
> *Labitur ex oculis nunc quoque gutta meis!*[11]

even as much as any man can have who is not in love; for of that you have acquitted me long ago. And now I talk of love; how go on the *amourettes* twelve miles from London?[12] I don't know whether you have broke your heart yet in the pursuit of her, but I'm sure I've almost cracked my brain to find her out: and *au bout du conte* if your endeavours have not been more successful than mine I am afraid it can't hold out much longer in the ruinous state I left it. Tell me news of it, [I] beseech you, for I'm really in pain for you: you could hardly bear an absence of 12 miles and how you'll support one of 80 I am not able to conceive. Of this you said not a word in your last, nor of twenty things equally important for me to know, and yet had the assurance to tell me you knew nothing.—Of revolutions in Christendom or of those at St James's, of strange events, of robberies, of marriages, of deaths and burials, you might indeed know nothing. But how and what you do and see and hear? These are the points where my curiosity is levelled, and the smallest passages or most frivolous circumstances of your life will be worth reams of gazette. For the rest, they are fine monsters, as Mr Dorrington[13] says, very pretty monsters; but, generally speaking, either interest or amuse me in a very small degree.

I beg my duty and respects to Lord Orford and compliments to Lady Mary and Mrs Laneve, making no doubt but you are with 'em

10. I.e., Lille.

11. Ovid, *Tristia* I. iii. 3–4, with 'tempus' substituted for 'noctem' ('When I recall the time I relinquished so many things dear to me, even now from my eyes the teardrops fall').

12. Neither this passage nor the further discussion of the subject *post* 26 Sept.

1742 NS reveals the object of HW's admiration.

13. Perhaps either Theophilus Dorrington (d. 1715), controversialist and voluminous author; or his son Theophilus (d. 1768), treasurer of the East India Company.

at Houghton: in my present situation I durst not say I wish myself
with you, nor you with me, but indeed, dear Horry, I feel myself, if
possible, more than ever your affectionate

Friend and servant,

H. C.

Remember that I am going into camp, where our correspondence
will be more slow and more difficult than at present. *Ainsi, plus de
poulets, s'il vous plaît.*

To CONWAY, ca Monday 23 August 1742 OS

Missing. From what can be deduced of its contents from Conway's reply
post 15 Sept. 1742 NS, it seems to have contained much of the same material
as HW to Lincoln 23 Aug. 1742 OS (SELWYN 32–3).

From CONWAY, Saturday 15 September 1742 NS

Printed from the MS now WSL, formerly Rutnam. First printed *Fraser's
Magazine*, 1850, xli. 632. The year is clearly 1742, when Conway was stationed at
Ghent.

Address: To the Honourable Horatio Walpole junior Esquire at the Earl of
Orford's at Houghton in Norfolk. Pour l'Engleterre.

Postmark: SE [illegible].

Sept. 15, NS.

Dear Horry,

I HAVE just read your letter over and over and forward and backward in order to conjure up some human spirits, for really without some extraordinary aid I have not the power to produce a word
in any shape whatever, unless it be in very peevishness of heart and
in order to swear and grumble at everything that I hear and see and
do and everybody. This place dear Horry, grows worse and worse,
by continuing always the same; *cela s'entend* I mean becomes more
unsupportable; one really does not live here, one's dying a slow
death: I fancy myself in the Inquisition roasting the soles of my feet

or having a drop of water dribble upon my forehead. They live, my
dear Horry, as I told you before in coffee-houses and at shop doors
and in streets and in stables from morning till night. Now as nobody is more fond of idleness than myself, or loves loitering less,
this drives me home, where I lead my days in a chintz nightgown
reading both morning and evening and becoming the most regular,
painstaking correspondent in spite of my teeth. You bid me write to
you sometimes! I should always do it with real pleasure but at
present I neither can nor dare do otherwise, for if a post fails to
bring me letters from England I don't recover it in a month. In the
meantime I wither and mould like an old store-pippin for want of
air, exercise, and amusement. I am convinced you won't know me
when I come back; I feel myself under the circumstances of decay at
this moment, it is not that I study hard God knows! yet I read two
or three hours every morning and evening; but I am peevish and
ill-natured and fret and fume and with this do no earthly thing. I
neither walk, nor ride, nor eat nor drink, nor sleep nor talk which
however are such ingredients as one can't well spare out of the
'cup of life,' as Prior[1] calls it. And apropos to writing if you have any
Christian charity left for your cousin you'll write to me often, for
I really live not by bread (as I have told you) but by every word
that comes from my friends in England. Yet at last our comedy is
arrived,[2] and this is to become, *dit-on,* the gayest town in the world.
Of this I see no appearance. As for the comedy it's a good troop
enough and I design to frequent 'em. *Cela dissipe!* You are the best
creature in the world, dear Horry, to talk of coming here and for
the encampment, if there was nothing between us but that, I believe I should be happier than I'm like to be for some months: yet

1. Matthew Prior in 'Henry and Emma,
A Poem, Upon the Model of The Nut-
brown Maid':
'O impotent estate of human life!
Where hope and fear maintain eternal
    strife:
Where fleeting joy does lasting doubt
    inspire;
And most we question, what we most
    desire.
Amongst thy various gifts, great heav'n,
    bestow
Our cup of love unmix'd; forbear to
    throw
Bitter ingredients in . . .' (ll. 167–73).

2. No English company of players in
Flanders has been identified. Lt-Col.
Charles Russell wrote from Ghent 24 Nov.
1742 NS, 'This place is extremely dull, no
public place of any sort but the playhouse,
and that of no use except as a coffee-house,
for if one understood the language never
so well, not one word could one hear distinctly enough to be able to understand
what was said. The coffee-houses are so
bad that I never go to one' (Hist. MSS
Comm., *Frankland-Russell-Astley MSS,*
1900, p. 221).

they talk of encampment as much as ever and our generals look as black and as big as if there was really something to be done. In the meantime I am ruined with buying old lumbering cart-horses and such a pack of camp trumpery as would amaze you, and if all this comes to nothing, as I suspect shrewdly it won't, as far as one decently may I shall wish our old generals hanged for ruining me in such a simple way.

I wish the Mayor's feast[3] may make you as happy as any venison-eating alderman in the Corporation; and that your times may mend! Pray wish for me a little; I would have you do more; but it's too unreasonable to torment you any longer on that head and then such obstacles! Selwyn's listing himself diverts me. Pray tell Mrs Selwyn that a water-drinker is in no danger, for nobody lists without being made drunk first.

I have seen your chapter of preferments,[4] printed here and the additional one: which is not bad neither, a pompous edition and a new title, *The Vision.*—Pray read Cibber's letter to Pope.[5] There's some scurrility in't; not quite undeserved, some truth, some humour, some folly. Poor Colley! he'll certainly suffer for it.[6]

Adieu! dear Horry, all sorts of compliments.

Believe me truly yours,

H. C.

To CONWAY, ca Sunday 5 September 1742 OS

Missing; answered *post* 26 Sept. 1742 NS. This is a reply to *ante* 29 Aug. 1742 NS.

3. 'If I am very good, and learn my *patois* well, I am promised that I shall go to the Mayor's feast at Lynn—there's joy!' (HW to Lincoln 23 Aug. 1742 OS, SELWYN 33).
4. HW's *The Lessons for the Day. Being the First and Second Chapters of the Book of Preferment*, 1742, was published in London 5 Aug. OS. Only the 'Second Chapter' was by HW; see MANN i. 491–3 and notes, and Hazen, *Bibl. of*

HW 18–22. Nothing further is known of this Flemish edition.
5. *A Letter from Mr Cibber to Mr Pope, Inquiring into the Motives that might induce him in his Satirical Works to be so frequently fond of Mr Cibber's Name*, advertised as 'this day is published' in *Daily Adv.* 23 July 1742 OS. HW had already read it by 29 July (MANN ii. 8).
6. Pope substituted Cibber for Theobald as the hero of the *Dunciad*.

From CONWAY, Wednesday 26 September 1742 NS

Printed from the MS now WSL, formerly Rutnam. First printed, *Fraser's Magazine*, 1850, xli. 633; also printed from the MS, *Rockingham Memoirs* i. 384–6; reprinted *Colburn's United Service Magazine*, 1880, lii pt i. 321–2. The postmark is the date of the arrival of the letter in London; the year is clearly 1742, when Conway was stationed at Ghent.

Address: To the Honourable Horatio Walpole Esquire at Houghton in Norfolk. Pour l'Engleterre.

Postmark: SE 18.

Ghent, Sept. 26.

Dear Horry,

I DELIGHT in your disowning your *amourette* twelve miles out of London! Do you forget all that passed in Chelsea summer-house[1] on that head and in Chelsea parlour too? But if you do, I am sure Mrs Leneve does not nor Lady Mary neither, who were both as tired with the subject as you were delighted with it. Yes twelve miles out of London, Horry, and yet you are in the right to commend London too. I know your beauty was a little out of its sphere at that time, gone to shine and do mischief in some country village; but its satellites accompanied it too, for I remember you made frequent excursions about that time, in spite of all the dust and heat in the world. I'm not so simple, my dear Horry. I know that people *like* London as Doctor Bentley[2] said of Applepy[2a] but nobody *loves* London for London's sake, but green girls and quadrille matrons. So don't think to get off by a vile quibble about residency and inhabitance like a vile election witness; you had in short an *amourette* in the forms, and a sighing and a walking in the park and a galloping about in chaises. All this I'm sure of, and you have a great deal of confidence to deny it. Then as to acquitting you of feels, I never was farther from it; have not you made songs and read romances?[3] Can you deny this too? However to show my generosity, I'll tell you how far I'll go: of constancy I will acquit you and that's the last

1. This octagonal structure, built by Sir Robert Walpole at one end of the terrace on the Thames at Orford House, Chelsea, is illustrated in Hugh Phillips, *The Thames about 1750*, 1951, pp. 164–5; see also J. H. Plumb, *Sir Robert Walpole: The Making of a Statesman*, Boston, 1956, p. 206 and Plate 5.

2. Richard Bentley (1662–1742), scholar and critic. The occasion of the remark has not been found.

2a. I.e., Appleby.

3. Conway also alludes to HW's former fondness for romances *post* 25 Oct. 1743 NS, 18 April 1745 NS, and 10 Aug. 1745 NS.

word with you. I like your *gross* refusal of Dick Hammon's party (as you call it). Had he really the face to ask you to go a-shooting with him? I believe you'd hardly go a-shooting with our twelve-mile friend! 'Tis as if Sir Thomas Robinson had asked one to go to Barbadoes[4] with him! You surprise me with what you say about winter; I have certainly made some strange blunder in my letter,[5] for I never dreamt of wintering here. I should have hanged myself if I had long ago. I suppose I call this winter because of the badness of the weather; or if I reckoned by the length of time I have passed here, Christmas would have been come long ago.

Majesty swears he will come over and make us encamp and use us to fatigue:[6] then Prague is not taken and they say it grows more and more uncertain whether it will or not;[7] the French say it will not and thereupon little Bossu[8] grows as pert as a pear-monger and pretends to demand categorical answers to his foolish questions. The Hagers are asleep still, though Lord Stair[9] is come over to jog 'em again. Yet they dream something of campaigns and preparations and stretch a little as if they might wake some time or other.[10] There's the conversation of this place and the wisdom of it and the everything of it for one really has no other ideas here.

I like your idea of St Austin and his paradise,[11] and I have a notion Ghent would make a very good paradise; for if four gates and four rivers make a place delightful *à plus forte raison* four-and-twenty gates and four-and-twenty rivers which this place has at least.

I am just where I was when I writ to you last, same life, same ennui; I have formed no sort of alliance or connection: I don't

4. Robinson had been appointed governor of Barbados 22 Jan. 1742 OS (MANN i. 301, n. 46); he reached the island 8 Aug. 1742 OS (DNB).

5. HW had apparently misinterpreted Conway's comment *ante* 29 Aug. 1742 NS that he would not form 'so wild and so unfriendly a wish as that of seeing you in a winter's camp.'

6. For the reports about the proposed royal expedition to Flanders current at this time see MANN ii. 48, n. 10, 61 and n. 5.

7. Reports that the Austrians had converted the siege of Prague into a mere blockade reached London the same day as Conway's letter (see MANN ii. 47–8, n. 6a, 61, n. 9b; *Daily Adv.* 20 Sept. OS), and

so were probably already current at Ghent.

8. Probably François de Bussy (1699–1780), French minister to England since 1740 (MANN ii. 131, n. 21). Conway is reporting the rumours circulating at Ghent.

9. John Dalrymple (1673–1747), 2d E. of Stair, at this time ambassador to Holland and commander-in-chief of the Allied forces in Flanders. He had been in London for consultation at the end of August but set out for Holland 2 Sept. OS (ibid. ii. 48, n. 7).

10. A hope which proved unfounded at this time.

11. Unexplained in the absence of HW's letter.

know how it is some people are made so that they form friendships in a moment and stick like burrs to the first person they meet, and I believe they are the happiest for they never feel anything for the loss or absence of friends. Theirs grow like the Hydra's heads; they have a continual supply; John or Thomas is the same thing to them; and Nature has excused 'em from the painful constant *desiderium* of absent friends or the worse sufferings from lost ones. Adieu! Dear Horry. *Je m'en tiens à mes anciens;* and never was more sincerely or with greater

Affection yours.

Compliments.

To CONWAY, ca Monday 20 September 1742 OS

Missing; answered *post* 29 Sept. 1742 OS.

From CONWAY, Wednesday 29 September 1742 OS

Printed from the MS now WSL, formerly Rutnam. First printed, *Fraser's Magazine,* 1850, xli. 634–5. Although Conway is usually consistent in using New Style dating on the Continent, the 'OS' in the date-line of the present letter is clear and is confirmed by the reference to Carteret's visit to The Hague, where he did not arrive until 5 Oct. NS.

Sept. 29, OS.

Dear Horry,

THOUGH I can't brag much of my good humour I really laughed at several things in your letter as you recommend to me, and laughed *tout de bon* as much as one decently can by one's self. But there's a certain laugh that accompanies ill humour as well as good, and I think one never finds one's self so much disposed to laugh at the follies of mankind as when one is out of humour; at least they never appear so ridiculous; for as to being angry with their follies without they hurt one I think one must be rather ill-natured than ill-humoured: and yet I own I have been inclined to be peevish with some follies of late; things at least that I suspect shrewdly will turn out follies at last, but then they did hurt me and, what's worse, do hurt me and, I am afraid, will hurt me some time longer. Indeed, Horry, I am ashamed to own with how little temper I bear an exile which I both sought and wished for myself; a misfortune which I suffer in common with thousands, and which I once thought and indeed under certain circumstances may still prove an advantage. But that *may* has so little of probability in it, according to my poor opinion at present, that I really think it hardly worth having; and so much for that.—So it is, my dear Horry, with many thousand things in life, which appear charming in prospect, but change their nature when carried into execution: nothing so delightful and so jolly as Flanders and a campaign! And what does all this jollity sink into? Into Ghent; into quarters in the most detestable town in the world; into the loss of one's friends and of all one loved and liked in England, with no shadow of an advantage, hitherto at least, to balance it. You say you pity me, and I assure you, as unacceptable a thing as pity generally is, I heartily thank you for it; I'm not a bit above it. However, your pity really extends a little too far; pity me at Ghent as much as you please, but as to the rest, though I own your prophecy is true *à la lettre,* and that I actually have passed and do pass many a tedious hour, I really would not, be it habit, be it vanity, be it prejudice, I would not change my profession for any other I know; and yet at the same time I had rather be a scrivener, an exciseman, what you will, than a mere soldier and command armies; for your mere soldier I take to be as far removed from humanity as any wild beast in Libya, unknowing, unpolished, unsociable, with savage manners, narrow principles, and a weak head to govern a strong heart. He thinks all life confined to the army, and hardly knows that there exist human creatures wearing brown coats or black gowns; and even within the verge of his own profession his pride and ambition make him hate all above him and despise all below him. He loves you furiously, but would cut your throat at any time to give half-a-dozen fools like himself an opinion of his courage. He loves his country too in general, vehemently, but hates every individual in it; and is through conscience and duty professed enemy to all mankind besides.

You know that Lord Carteret is gone to The Hague[1] and that

---

[1]. Carteret left London 19 Sept. OS, arrived at The Hague 5 Oct. NS, and reached England on his return 6 Oct. OS (MANN ii. 61, n. 9, 70, n. 12).

the King's voyage is put off till his return,[2] from whence I suspect we shall neither see his Majesty nor the French this year. I know this is the last infidelity, I know I am even heretical *à brûler* on this point, but so it is; there appears to me so little reason in any scheme I have heard of, that I believe in none. But then the secret is kept inviolably, and we are to find ourselves upon the point of doing some great action before we know where we are; we are not to be encamped now, but cantooned; which cantooning, if you should chance not to be acquainted with it, is being quartered up and down in villages near one another so as to be assembled in a moment; and these villages are actually named at present: for example the right wing, say they, is to lie at Dixmude and thereabouts; the left at Courtrai; and the *corps de bataille* at a place called Rousselaer;[3] all these between us and Dunkirk.

You endeavour to comfort me by saying you are as dull at Houghton as I can be at Ghent, and I'm vastly obliged to you for good intention, but it is not possible that Houghton should be half so bad. Houghton's the country and a little solitary and all that, but Ghent's another kind of dulness. Ghent's pert as well as dull; Ghent's a garrison, my dear Horry, and I really believe the worst garrison in the world; Ghent's populous and yet unsociable; peopled like the deserts of Arabia with tigers, bears, and wolves. Give me some comfort and tell me when the Parliament meets;[4] all my hopes depend upon that. I languish for it to a shameful degree. Give all proper compliments, and believe me,

Yours sincerely.

2. Newcastle had told Lord Bath 18 Sept. OS that the King's trip 'may *possibly* depend . . . upon the accounts Lord Carteret shall bring, and the representations he shall make' (ibid. ii. 61, n. 5). This proved true, and the trip was abandoned on Carteret's return, although HW had already heard that it was given up before Carteret reached London (ibid. ii. 69–70; J. B. Owen, *Rise of the Pelhams*, 1957, pp. 138–9).

3. Rousselaere or Roulers, 13 miles NW of Courtrai.

4. Parliament met 16 Nov. OS; Conway, as an M.P., would be given leave to return to England while it was sitting.

From CONWAY, Wednesday 24 October 1742 NS

Printed for the first time from the MS now WSL, formerly Rutnam.

À Calais ce 24 d'octobre.

Mon cher Horry,

JE crains fort vous devenir à la fin ennuyeux à force d'être ponctuel; cela ne m'aurait pourtant pas empêché de vous écrire par la dernière poste (tant j'ai envie de vous tourmenter) si ce n'était pour l'embarras qui attend la veille d'un voyage; jeudi je partis de Gand pour accompagner Milady Ancram; qui s'est embarquée ce matin pour Douvre. Voilà donc des excuses du côté et de l'autre. Si vous êtes d'humeur à me trouver impertinent, je vous prie de vouloir bien accepter la première, et de trouver la dernière aussi méchante qu'il vous plaira si par hazard mes lettres ont le bonheur de ne vous pas êtres ennuyeuses. Je pourrais aussi vous assurer par parenthèse: qu'il ne m'est guère arrivé de faire des excuses pour être trop ponctuel, et qu'il y a fort peu de gens au monde qui pourraient me mettre dans le cas d'en demander, si vous voulez savoir d'où m'est venue la fantaisie de vous écrire en mauvais français plutôt qu'en anglais passable; je vous dirai premièrement que je suis en France, puis que depuis quelques jours m'étant accoutumé à jaser français avec des hôtesses et filles de cabaret, ce français tel qu'il est me vient assez naturellement: d'ailleurs craignant fort comme je viens de dire de vous ennuyer; j'ai voulu cacher les défauts d'un style qui doit vous être devenu trop familier en l'habillant de nouveau, avec le temps comme je me sens chaque jour plus d'inclination à vous parler; si je me trouve assez fortifié des sages instructions de Mr Angelo Cori[1] je tâcherai de vous sauver un peu d'ennui en vous écrivant un italien qu'assurément vous n'entendrez pas tout Florentin que vous êtes.

Me voici donc à sept lieues de Douvre! que ne sentais-je pas, mon cher petit cousin, en regardant ces charmants Rochers Blancs, quelle extase à voir ces côtes qui ne sont qu'à vingt lieues de Londres? et de quel regret ne me trouvais-je accablé de me les voir défendues en-

1. Angelo Maria Cori, prompter to the opera, who also taught Italian, and from whom Conway (and perhaps HW) had taken lessons (MANN i. 170 and n. 7, 254, n. 32).

core cinq ou six semaines, qui sont à moi commes ces semaines mysterieuses de l'écriture sainte, qui valent des centaines d'années.

Vous voilà toujours à Houghton,[2] n'est-ce pas? Je ne demande pas de quelle façon vous vous y amusez de peur que vous ne me disiez qu'il vous est arrivé quelque surcroît d'ennui. On me dit pourtant que Milady B.[3] n'ayant plus si bonne opinion du pouvoir de certaines gens; travaille à présent par d'autres voies à rétablir le Chevalier[4] dans son poste ou à faire donner un regiment au Col. M-g-re,[5] qui étant plus jeune colonel que moi a eu la rare modestie de faire présenter deux placets à S. M. pour demander un regiment. Ce soin dit-on l'empêchera de sortir de Londres. Et à propos de ces certaines gens dont je parlais; ne dit-on pas que le Pr.[6] va les persécuter dans la séance prochaine avec plus de chaleur que jamais? Cela passe le raillerie; aussi cela me fâche-t-il extrêmement, je vous assure; je vous prie d'en être très faché aussi. Mais serieusement, n'étant plus M. vous le verrez devenir plus aimable de jour en jour. Priez le . . .[7] d'accepter mes devoirs; ne manquez pas non plus de faire mes baisemains à votre sœur, à la poule d'Inde[8] et à toute la boutique si vous voulez. Je ne mets pas cela ensemble au moins! car pour Lady M[ary] c'est assurément la plus aimable fille du monde. Vous savez déjà que nous ne faisons plus la guerre cet hiver-ci; le R[oi] est enragé dit-on de ce qu'on ne veut pas lui laisser faire la plus grande sottise du monde, aussi n'aura-t-il rien à quoi donner de ses coups de pieds royals qu'à son malheureux chapeau ou tout au plus à ses ministres qui peut-être ne le valent pas.

Savez-vous par hazard où est à présent le petit Legge, j'avais promis de lui écrire: ce que je n'ai pas fait autant par paresse que pour

2. HW left Houghton for London 25 Oct. OS (ibid. ii. 88).

3. From what follows, apparently Margaret Cecil (ca 1696–1782), m. Sir Robert Brown, cr. (1732) Bt.

4. Sir Robert Brown (d. 1760), cr. (1732) Bt; M.P. Ilchester 1734–47, had been dismissed as paymaster of the Works in favour of Sir Charles Gilmour 14 July 1742 OS (ibid. i. 493 and nn. 15, 16).

5. Probably Col. Maguire (ante 31 Oct. 1741 OS, n. 37), whom HW later mentions as having been much admired by Lady Brown, and who had obtained a lieutenant-colonelcy 15 Feb. 1742 after abjuring his religion (SELWYN 84; W. J.

Hardy, 'Lady Cathcart and her Husbands,' *St Albans and Hertfordshire Architectural and Archæological Society Transactions*, 1897–8, n.s. i pt ii. 121).

6. Possibly the Prince of Wales. The allusion seems to be to some rumour that he was going to oppose the new ministry as he had Sir Robert Walpole's; this, however, did not prove true (J. B. Owen, *Rise of the Pelhams*, 1957, p. 149).

7. A word, probably some term for Lord Orford, has been crossed out.

8. Perhaps a nickname for Mrs Leneve, who is usually included in Conway's compliments.

n'avoir pas su son addresse. Je l'aime pourtant fort c'est pourquoi je serais charmé que je puisse faire la paix avec lui avant que j'écrirai. Adieu! mon très cher Horace, après tant d'excuses et de précautions, je sens bien que je dois vous avoir fort ennuyé. Pardonnez-moi je vous prie, et surtout ne manquez pas de prendre votre revanche. Je l'attendrai avec toute l'impatience possible.

From CONWAY, Tuesday 21 May 1743 NS

Printed from the MS now WSL, formerly Rutnam. First printed (misdated 1742) *Fraser's Magazine*, 1850, xli. 631. That the correct year is 1743, when Conway was with the army in Germany, is clear from the contents and the following letter.

Address: To the Honourable Horatio Walpole Jun. in Arlington Street London. Pour l'Angleterre. Par la Hollande.

Postal marking: From Cleve. [Illegible] 16.

Memoranda (by HW, in pencil, doubtless for a missing letter; all the headings are crossed out, which is proof that HW used them):

Wootton[1]   Lord Conway
Zink[2]   Lord Hartington
Hazard[3]   Mrs Grosvenor
Chenevix[4]

Nuis,[5] May 21.

Dear Horry,

I'M afraid I promised to write to you as soon as I landed,[6] but I assure you though I had the best intentions in the world to execute my promise I literally had not a single moment more than

1. John Wootton (ca 1682–1764), animal and landscape painter. He had recently painted Patapan (G. E. Kendall, 'Notes on . . . John Wootton,' *Walpole Society*, 1932-3, xxi. 24–5, which supplements and corrects MANN ii. 220 and n. 25).

2. Christian Friedrich Zincke (1685–1767), enamel-painter, who did a series of members of the Walpole family for Sir Robert Walpole (OSSORY ii. 110, n. 19).

3. Perhaps Peter Hazard or Hasert, cabinet-maker in Great Queen Street, St Giles-in-the-Fields, between 1724 and 1744 (Sir Ambrose Heal, *London Furniture Makers*, 1953, p. 78).

4. Paul Daniel Chenevix, proprietor of a 'great toyshop' in the Haymarket, and husband of the Mrs Chenevix who occupied SH before HW took it. He apparently died in Feb. 1743 (MANN ii. 366, n. 12).

5. Apparently Neuss, in Rhenish Prussia, 80 miles from Utrecht on the direct route to Cologne. To reach it from Utrecht they must have had to travel day and night.

6. Conway may have been with the group of officers who left London with the Hon. George Boscawen, also an officer in the 1st Regiment of Guards, 3 May OS (*Daily Adv.* 4 May OS; Sedgwick i. 475).

served me for the shortest of notes[7] to my brother just to say that I was on this side the water. Since that we have been travelling like couriers without a moment's respite; we went the first night to Rotterdam, the next to Utrecht, travelled all last night, and are now obliged to lie here for want of horses. All our apprehensions of *parties bleus*[8] are vanished and we are now pursuing our journey like true knights errant without a thought of the difficulties we are to encounter. In the first place we are now in the heart of a barbarous country without a word of the language either ourselves or servants, with that utterly ignorant of the road and under no small distress as you may imagine about money, eating, drinking, etc. I have hitherto seen nothing that is worth mentioning: Rotterdam indeed is a pretty town but without variety; for when one has seen one street with its canal, its shipping, its quays, and rows of trees, one has seen it all. The same I believe may be said of the whole country: there's the most tiresome sameness in everything—in the towns, prospects, and people. I will say nothing of the *agréments* that I meet with to cover this multitude of *ennuis,* because I know you won't believe me if I do; and if I tell you I have none you'll tell me as you have done already that it's my own fault, and won't even have the charity to pity me. But I desire you will; for indeed I never wanted it more. I have not yet mustered up my campaign spirits, nor half forgot the friends I left behind me. The metamorphose from civil to military is hardly begun yet, and I am now in that sort of purgatory between one life and t'other that makes it the duty of my friends to pray night and day for my deliverance.

They say here that the Dutch have certainly voted 20 thousand men,[9] which it is thought will bring things to a quick determination for if the French are inclined to attack us, they will do it before the Dutch can join us[10] and for our attacking 'em they will have so fortified their camp at Hailbron[11] before they can have joined us that

7. Missing.

8. There was apparently some danger of their being intercepted by raiding parties of French hussars in the course of their journey.

9. 'Hague, May 17 [NS]. The grand affair of the march of the 20,000 men for succouring the Queen of Hungary passed this day in the assembly of the States General, to the great joy of all well-wishers of the common cause, and to-

morrow it is to pass the resumption there' (*Daily Adv.* 11 May OS). Further details of the vote of the troops are given in letters from The Hague published in the *Daily Adv.* during the following week.

10. The first of the Dutch troops did not join the Allied army until 10 Sept. NS (*post* 11 Sept. 1743 NS, n. 4).

11. Heilbronn, where some French troops had reportedly encamped around 6 May NS (*Daily Adv.* 2, 7 May OS), al-

it will be imprudent either to attack 'em or to leave 'em behind us. Pray let me hear from you. I shall be at Frankfort[12] in three or four days so I'd have you direct to me there immediately. The safest way is to get your letter sent from the Secretary's office by Lord Stair's packet: inquire about that. Adieu!

Compliments to all your family.

To CONWAY, ca Friday 20 May 1743 OS

Missing; answered *post* 9 June 1743 NS, where it appears from the next to last paragraph to have been written before HW left London for Houghton.

From CONWAY, Sunday 9 June 1743 NS

Printed from the MS now WSL, formerly Rutnam. First printed, *Rockingham Memoirs* i. 387–90; reprinted *Colburn's United Service Magazine,* 1880, lii pt i. 324–5.

Camp I don't know where
not far from where we were before[1]
June 9, NS.

Dear Horry,

I AM glad to get a moment to write to you, for we are now upon that violent military footing and so much in earnest that they never let one rest. The night before last between ten and eleven o'clock we received orders to strike our tents at midnight and march at break of day: which accordingly we did[2] and after

though they do not in fact appear to have done so; see the detailed account of the movements and cantonments of the detachment of French troops in the vicinity of Heidelberg at this time in *Oesterr. Erbfolge-kreig* v. 285–9.

12. Conway's regiment was encamped near Höchst, 6 miles west of Frankfurt (Hist. MSS Comm., *Frankland-Russell-Astley MSS,* 1900, p. 236).

1. The Guards and most of the other English troops had crossed to the south bank of the Main 3–5 June NS and encamped near Kelsterbach; the redeployment described below took them about three miles further southwest along the south bank (*Oesterr. Erbfolge-krieg* v. 292; Hist. MSS Comm., *Frankland-Russell-Astley MSS,* 1900, pp. 239, 241; *Daily Adv.* 11 June OS).

2. 'Yesterday morning six British regi-

marching backward and forward all day came to take possession of the ground where we now are with the three battalions of Guards and two regiments of Foot. It's an advantageous post situated upon an hill and surrounded by woods. The French had their head-quarters at D'Armstad last night[3] which is about three leagues[4] from us. Twenty battalions which had repassed the Rhine are now come over again[5] and are marching towards us. Our generals imag-ine they will attack us immediately, and are in a great fluster. The troops are moving up here both English and Hanoverian—some are already encamped.[6] We have abundance of parties posted in the woods and about, our picket guard lies out upon the ground and in short we are as much upon the *qui vive* as can be. I know you don't know what a picket guard is: so I'll tell you because in these war-like days it's necessary to know a little of terms in order to read gazettes and correspond with one's friends. The picket guard is a certain number of men in every regiment who lie all night under arms, in short always ready in case of a sudden alarm, but com-monly in their tents. The spirits of our men is surprising: they de-sire nothing so much as to fight and never appear so elated as when they think they are going to it. Yesterday morning as we were drawn up to march, I saw a man of my company who has been ill a great while looking like all the ghosts and skeletons you can imagine; he said he was ill the day before but that the news of this march had cured him and given him new spirits. You must know the suddenness of this march and the circumstances of break of day and no drums beating made all us young soldiers fancy we were to fight immediately. By this time I imagine I have heartily surfeited you with military nonsense. I must add however that the Prince of

ments marched at daybreak without sounding drum or trumpet, and were followed by six pieces of cannon' (ibid. 8 June OS, *sub* Frankfurt 9 June NS). Detailed descriptions of the troop move-ments and battle alarm discussed here are in a letter from Lt-Col. Russell to his wife, 2 June OS, *Frankland MSS*, pp. 242–3; and *Oesterr. Erbfolge-krieg* v. 293–5.

3. A slight exaggeration; on the 8th the main body was still at Lorsch, Noailles slightly north at Zwingenberg, and only an advance guard at Eberstadt, slightly south of Darmstadt (ibid. v. 293).

4. About ten miles.

5. Conway seems to be mistaken about the movements of the French troops. The main body under Noailles crossed the Rhine at Worms 4–6 June; on 5 June NS the detachments stationed near Heidelberg started north (after crossing the Neckar, not the Rhine); the two forces united at Lorsch on the 7th and marched north towards the Pragmatic Army on the 9th (ibid. v. 289, 293).

6. The army remained in order-of-battle from 8 to 10 June NS, but the French came no closer than six miles. During the night of the 10th, the Allies recrossed the Main and the French with-drew (ibid. v. 293–5; MANN ii. 248, n. 2).

Conti[7] has certainly been beat in Bavaria[8] with a loss of about two thousand men;[9] the progress of Prince Charles[10] in that country is prodigious.[11] He was polite enough to send the Prince of Conti his own baggage[12] which had been taken. They[13] look upon their affairs as very desperate and that is what drives 'em to the thoughts of attacking us. We have been told that they have positive orders for it and that the whole army has taken the sacrament thereupon. This is the creed at present amongst our great people, but for myself I am still infidel enough to think they are in no such hurry and that our armies may meet and look at one another without offence.

You can't think how sorry I am for poor Moustache[14] and for Dolly and Neddy Townshend.[15] The first not on my own account but on yours and poor Pat's,[16] and the others for their own. I agree with you entirely in everything about Lord Cornbury, in everything but the similitude that your partiality for me has traced between our characters.[17] Indeed, Horry, I am as sensible of the amiableness of his as I am ashamed of the nothingness of my own. However, dear Horry, I am not less happy in your partiality than I should be vain of your judgment in my favour if I thought it unbiased. You bid me in your last think of the comfort of knowing there are those who will hear my complaints and pity 'em. To think that I am remembered by my friends with some sympathy for all my ennuis and my cares and perhaps with some little regret for my absence is indeed the only thing that can make it supportable and by much the greatest happiness I am capable of in my present situation. Adieu, dear Horry, you can't think how sensible I am of all your kindness and what comfort I shall always have in hearing from you. I won't

7. Louis-François de Bourbon (1717–76), Prince de Conti.

8. At Deggendorf 27 May NS (MANN ii. 249, n. 16).

9. According to the official French casualty lists the killed and wounded numbered only 32 officers and 448 men and the prisoners of all ranks 115 (ibid. ii. 249, n. 17).

10. Charles-Alexandre (1712–80) of Lorraine; governor-general of the Austrian Netherlands.

11. He had won an important victory at Simbach near Braunau 9 May NS and had taken some fortified places since (ibid. ii. 230 and nn. 1–2, 234 and nn. 5–7, 12–14, 249).

12. For further details of this incident, see ibid. ii. 249, n. 18.

13. The French.

14. Apparently one of HW's dogs.

15. HW's cousins: Hon. Dorothy Townshend (ca 1714–76), m. (19 May 1743) Rev. Hon. Spencer Cowper; and Hon. Edward Townshend (ca 1719–65) (DNB sub Charles Townshend; East Anglian, 1903–4, n.s., pp. 348–9; GM 1779, xlix. 271; Daily Adv. 21 May OS). The nature of their misfortune has not been found.

16. Patapan.

17. HW had apparently compared Conway favourably with Cornbury in his missing letter.

begin to pity you till I know you are at Houghton[18] and then only because I know you expect it. However I think myself obliged in gratitude to answer any sum of compassion you shall draw for my demands are so large upon you.—Compliments to Lord Orford and Lady Mary. Oh! and Mrs Leneve, etc.

I believe I told you to direct to me *au Quartier Général de l'armée de sa majesté Britannique près de Frankfort en Almagne.* You should say too *dans le premier bataillon des Gardes Anglaises.*

To CONWAY, ca Friday 10 June 1743 OS

Missing; answered *post* 8 July 1743 NS. It was probably written immediately after receiving Conway's letter of 9 June NS; see HW to Mann 10 June OS (MANN ii. 247–9) for his concern created by Conway's reports of the probability of an immediate battle.

From CONWAY, ca Sunday 30 June 1743 NS

Missing; mentioned *post* 8 July 1743 NS; presumably written soon after the battle of Dettingen and from what Conway says of it probably similar to his letter to his brother of 30 June NS: 'On Thursday last the 26 [27 June] we marched at daybreak from our camp at Aschaffenberg, the Guards making the rear guard of the army, which in a retreat is look[ed] upon as the post of honour but proved quite the contrary on this occasion by throwing us entirely out of the action. . . . Our brigade which I told you made the rear guard with another of Hanoverians and a few horse marched off to the right to avoid being flanked by the French cannon and were posted upon a hill with a large wood between us and the rest of the army. This wood covered the right flank of our army and the river was on the left. . . . As soon as the attack began the Guards were missed and sent for in great haste but being ill conducted by our guide the enemy were retired before we came upon the plain, where we had the honour of sharing the victory by passing one of the wettest and coldest nights I ever felt upon the ground amongst the slain and wounded of both sides. . . . You can't imagine how terrible it was not to be engaged; and yet to have had hitherto more fatigue than the rest and been put always upon what is called the post of honour' (MS now WSL; printed *Colburn's United Service Magazine,* 1880, lii pt i. 460–2). Similar accounts of the inactivity of the Guards are in the letters of Conway's fellow Guards' officer, Lt-Col. Russell, to his wife, 18 and 19 June OS, Hist. MSS Comm., *Frankland-Russell-Astley MSS,* 1900, pp. 251–4.

18. HW left London for Houghton with his family 23 May OS (MANN ii. 232, n. 19).

To Conway, Saturday 25 June 1743 OS

Missing; answered *post* 27 July 1743 NS; Conway did not receive it until about 24 July NS. It congratulated him on his escape at Dettingen.

From Conway, Monday 8 July 1743 NS

Printed for the first time from the MS now wsl, formerly Rutnam. The postmark is the date of arrival in London.

Address: To the Honourable Horatio Walpole Jun. at the Right Honourable Lord Orford's at Houghton in Norfolk, Angleterre.

Postmark: IY 6. AB.

Camp at Hanau,[1] July 8 NS 1743.

Dear Horry,

I CAN never thank you enough for the goodness of your last, nor ever deserve half so much by anything but the sincere return I make to all the kindness and affection you express. Of that merit I am indeed a little vain and if you knew to what degree I possess it perhaps you might not think yours quite thrown away. I told you in my last how little you would have had to fear for your friends in the Guards if you had known our situation t'other day. I told you, too, what I fancy you will not agree with me in and may perhaps not easily believe, that we thought ourselves heinously ill-treated by the great care that was taken of our persons. I am almost ashamed to own to you that I had the smallest spark of such a resentment about me; it sounds so like pretending to heroism and love of danger, but I hope, dear Horry, you will do me the justice to acquit me of all that fantastical merit and attribute it all to as human a feeling as even fear itself, to the vanity of having my share in the good things that were done and the glory that was gained. Perhaps you may despise this too, but one does not live in camps without catching the contagion of 'em; this makes one consider how little true merit there is in the world, this very little vanity, mean as it appears abstractedly considered, had I don't doubt the greatest share in the suc-

1. To which the Allied army had retired immediately after the battle of Dettingen.

cess of the day. Yet 'tis surely something to behave well in the hour of danger, 'tis[2] something to be considered, I don't say by the world, but by one's friends; don't you feel that a little? and won't you let me wish a little for such a satisfaction? Indeed, Horry, I am as easy about advancement and even gain as most people. Colonel or lieutenant colonel, with five hundred or a thousand per annum, is pretty indifferent to me. I am vain enough to think I can despise all the trappings and *colifichets* that are the usual marks of honour, but then I am fond of my own weaknesses and even proud of 'em to a degree. I have those whom I esteem and of course those whom I would fain be esteemed by. If this ambition be a fault 'tis at least I hope a pardonable one; and an error I am so in love with that I shall not easily believe one can wish too much or bid too high to satisfy it. Adieu, dear Horry. Broglio[3] is arrived at the Necker[4] within four or five days march of Noailles's[5] army. As to the rest, things remain *in statu quo;* Prince Charles follows Broglio, I believe at about two days march distance.[6] His hussards are up with him, about four thousand of 'em, who harass his army extremely.[7]

Yours sincerely.

Compliments to your family.

To CONWAY, July 1743

Missing; answered *post* 27 July 1743 NS.

2. 'And' before and 'surely' after ' 'tis' crossed out here in the MS.

3. Victor-François (1718–1804), Duc de Broglie; Maréchal de France, 1759; commander of the French army in Bavaria.

4. Broglie's army reached the Neckar at Wimpfen 5–8 July NS (*Oesterr. Erbfolge-krieg* v. 320), although a Paris *à-la-main* of 10 July NS reported that detachments of his troops had begun to reach Heidelberg, somewhat farther on, on the 4th (*Daily Adv.* 5 July OS).

5. Adrien-Maurice (1678–1766), Duc de Noailles; Maréchal de France. His army was encamped in the vicinity of Offenbach near Frankfurt (ibid. *sub* Frankfurt 7 July NS).

6. Rather more than that; most of his army was still south of the Danube, which it did not cross until the 9th-10th; it reached the Neckar 17 July NS (*Oesterr. Erbfolge-krieg* v. 328).

7. Details of this are ibid. v. 320–1.

From CONWAY, Saturday 27 July 1743 NS

Printed from the MS now WSL, formerly Rutnam. First printed, *Rockingham Memoirs* i. 391–2; reprinted *Colburn's United Service Magazine,* 1880, lii pt i. 463–4. The postmark is the date of arrival in London.
Address: To the Honourable Horatio Walpole Jun. in Arlington Street London. Angleterre.
Postmark: IY 27. AB.

Camp at Hanau, July 27, NS.

Dear Horry,

I AM ashamed to say I am now to thank you for two letters, yet the first of the 25th of June I did not receive till about three days ago. It was vastly kind and deserves a thousand thanks, but if you would not be angry I would tell you 'twas horrid to be so congratulated for one's escape from dangers one had not been in. I see by your last you won't let one feel anything of the kind, so I shall say no more upon that subject and even repent of what I said in my last; you'll think me such a fool! But, dear Horry, by the by how can you try to spoil one so? I am vastly inclined to think well of myself already, but that I meet with so many rubs every day, so many mementos of my own *pauvreté,* and if you don't abate a little of your goodness for me you'll really make me as vain as I am foolish. To say I am too good for a soldier!—I remember a man, Horry, who was born a footman, and to whom nature had given extraordinary talents for that station: he might even have made a tolerable *valet-de-chambre,* but that his friends persuaded him he had parts suited to the stage. He applied to Mr Rich,[1] obtained a diadem for his first appearance; had the misfortune not to please, fell down all the ranks of the theatre from a king to a snuff-candle and starved.

I should never have done if I told you all the sights I have seen today:[2] Prince Charles, Kevenhuller,[3] a Croat, a pandour[4] etc. The

---

1. John Rich, manager of Covent Garden.

2. At a review of the army, held in honour of the visitors (Hist. MSS Comm., *Frankland-Russell-Astley MSS,* 1900, p. 268).

3. Ludwig Andreas (1683–1744), Graf Khevenhüller; field marshal, 1737 (MANN i. 80, n. 25).

4. 'The name borne by a local force organized in 1741 by Baron Trenck on his own estates in Croatia to clear the country near the Turkish frontier of bands of robbers; subsequently enrolled as a regiment in the Austrian army, where, under Trenck, their rapacity and brutality caused them to be dreaded over Germany, and made *Pandour* synonymous in West-

first is about thirty year old, a good soldier-like appearance, and in the countenance not unlike Lord James Cavendish,[5] neither short nor tall and fattish. Kevenhuller is a little ordinary-looking man, with a sharp face,[6] and something of Justice Deveil[7] upon the whole. A pandour is something like a hussard, but a Croat the likeness of no earthly creature; savage beyond all description, and then a perfect magazine of all sorts of implements military and civil; so they are both. Guns and swords and daggers and pistols and arrows and knives and forks and spoons, and belts and pouches and cartridges to the end of the chapter. They came the day before yesterday and go away tomorrow; what they have concerted or whether anything I know not.[8]—I begin to grow impatient to know whether we shall have anything more to do or not. Tell me what you think in England. I am for forcing the French to excellent terms; but then, dear Horry, how I long to be with you, and how I despair of it for ages! I would even now with this prospect of peace compound for three months. I can't bear to think of it! Make my compliments to all your family; I would write to assure Lord Orford of my duty, but that I could not hope to give him any amusement and am afraid of being troublesome. Adieu.

To CONWAY, July–August 1743

Missing; answered *post* 21 Aug. 1743 OS; written from London where HW was from shortly before 19 July OS until shortly after 14 Aug. OS (MANN ii. 275, 291).

ern Europe with "brutal Croatian soldier" ' (OED; MANN i. 144, n. 4).

5. (d. 1741), army officer; M.P. Malton, 1741 (ibid. i. 197, n. 5). Lt-Col. Russell makes the same comparison, but also notes resemblances to Lady Harriet Campbell and the late Duke of Hamilton (*Frankland MSS*, p. 269).

6. 'His stature is rather low, but a good look and a fine piercing eye, very much denoting the able man he has since proved himself to be' (ibid.).

7. Thomas De Veil *or* Deveil (ca 1684–1746), Kt, 1744; J.P. for Middlesex, Essex, Surrey, Hertfordshire, Westminster, and the Tower of London and its liberties; one of the most active London magistrates (*Memoirs of the Life and Times of Sir Thomas Deveil, Knight*, 1748; *London Magazine*, 1746, xv. 534; *Daily Adv.* 8 Oct. 1746 OS; W. A. Shaw, *Knights of England*, 1906, ii. 287).

8. There is an account of their discussions in *Oesterr. Erbfolge-krieg* v. 330.

From CONWAY, Wednesday 21 August 1743 NS

Printed for the first time from the MS now WSL, formerly Rutnam. The post-mark is the date of arrival in London.

Address: To the Honourable Horatio Walpole, Jun., in Arlington Street, London, Angleterre.

Postmark: AV 20. AB.

Camp at Bibreck,[1] Aug. 21, 1743.

Dear Horry,

IT'S true I write from the army, and an army upon the banks of the Rhine, but seriously if it was not for the name of it I should be just as diverting a correspondent upon the banks of the Severn or Humber; for sure of all dull places an inactive camp is the dullest, and I am so afraid you should expect something from me! You can't imagine how I hate you for putting yourself upon a foot of having nothing to say from London—it can't be—even in the ruins of all society there one finds something worth talking of, something or other that has some connection with what used to interest one; but here 'tis quite otherwise. We deal only in the grand and if that fails we have no earthly resource, no sort of fund for tittle-tattle but to tell you of his Majesty's looks,[2] what hero died by his royal frown or revived by his smiles, or whose hand my Lord Carteret squeezed hard-est, what general wore the blackest wig or the wisest face, or whose queue, or whose roll of grievances was longest, are such circum-stances as I can't help thinking would be even tiresome! and yet what better can one expect from a land flowing with jack-boots and campaign periwigs? But to tell you something at least that may look like news, tomorrow we pass the Rhine, with what design or whether with any God knows! Some deserters from the French hussars who came in yesterday said the French army was marching towards us;[3] but to this we don't seem to give great credit. In the

1. Biebrich, on the Rhine 3½ miles south of Wiesbaden, where the British troops had encamped 15 Aug. NS after leaving the camp at Hanau on the 10th; they were there until 21 Aug. NS (*Oesterr. Erbfolge-krieg* v. 336–7; Hist. MSS Comm., *Frankland-Russell-Astley MSS,* 1900, pp. 276–7).

2. George II and Carteret had been

with the army since 19 June NS (MANN ii. 247, n. 26).

3. This was not true; during the pre-vious week the French army had retired from the vicinity of Speyer to the areas between Landau and Weissenburg on the Alsatian border (*Oesterr. Erbfolge-krieg* v. 337–8).

meantime about ten thousand of their army watch Prince Charles to prevent his passing[4] and will do it I fancy unless he takes the trouble of marching down to our bridges which perhaps you mayn't know are just below Mayence.[5] Our first day's march is little more than crossing: his Majesty is to be lodged in a convent of Carthusians[6] where we, his guards, shall attend him. You have heard of our new knights: Honeywood,[7] Campbel,[8] Cope[9] and Ligonier.[10] I have nothing new to tell you of 'em. I did not even see 'em dubbed.—You do me justice indeed, dear Horry, when you imagine I think of you when I wish to return, I cannot tell you how much, nor how much I am dear Horry's

H. C.

Compliments dans les formes.

4. Prince Charles and his army had been in the vicinity of Breisach on the Rhine near Freiburg since 14 Aug. NS (ibid. v. 335, 342–3).

5. Mainz; that is, the bridges at Biebrich, where the Pragmatic Army was now crossing.

6. 'The King is to have his quarters in the Carthusian convent, about half a mile from Mayence, in a fine high situation, so we shall have dry ground for our brigade to encamp on' (*Frankland MSS,* p. 279).

7. Sir Philip Honywood (d. 1752), K.B., 1743; Gen. of Horse, 1743; Col. of the King's Regiment of Horse Dragoons, 1732; of the King's Regiment of Horse (First Dragoon Guards), 1743 (MANN ii. 260, n.

22). He and the others mentioned were nominated K.B. 12 July 1743 OS (W. A. Shaw, *Knights of England,* 1906, i. 169). There was talk of making them and others knights-banneret, reviving that extinct order, but the idea was dropped (MANN ii. 268 and n. 12).

8. Hon. Sir James Campbell (ca 1667–1745), K.B., 1743; Lt-Gen., 1742; Col. of 2d Dragoons.

9. Sir John Cope (d. 1760), K.B., 1743; Lt-Gen., 1743; Col. of the 7th Dragoons; later commander-in-chief in Scotland during the '45.

10. Sir John Louis Ligonier (1680–1770), K.B., 1743; cr. (1757) Vct and (1766) E. Ligonier.

From CONWAY, Wednesday 11 September 1743 NS

Printed for the first time from the MS now WSL, formerly Rutnam. The year is clearly 1743 from the contents; the postmark is the date of arrival in London, OS.

Address: To the Honourable Horatio Walpole, Jun., in Arlington Street, London, Angleterre.

Postmark: SE 12. AB.

Camp at Worms,[1] Sept. 11, NS.

Dear Horry,

THOUGH it is an age since I have heard from you, and though you ought by this time to have received two letters[2] from me, I would not have you think I write on purpose to scold; I own I am not without inclination to do it if I would indulge myself, but you have been so very good to me before that I don't think myself quite *en droit* to quarrel with you. Besides I know the difference that ought to be made between a correspondent in town and one at Houghton, and now I hear you are returned there, I write to tell you that I shall be vastly disappointed if you are not as good as ever. In the meantime I don't know whether I should wish you to have diverted yourself too much, you'll have so much to regret. But how was it? Were things right and the people there that should be? —For me I am tired of telling you of the uncertainties we are in: one day marching to attack the French lines,[3] the next going into Lorraine, and the next back to Flanders, in short, more wavering and more in the dark than ever.—The Dutch are at last arrived, that is, the first division,[4] and they told us at first would all be here this

1. Where the Pragmatic Army had been encamped since 30 Aug. NS (*Oesterr. Erbfolge-krieg* v. 340).

2. *Ante* 27 July and 21 Aug. 1743 NS. The last letter Conway had received from HW was the missing one of the end of July or beginning of August OS that he acknowledges *ante* 21 Aug. NS.

3. The first French line at this time was between Landau and Germersheim, south of Speyer, and the second along the river Lauter, the northern boundary of Alsace (ibid. v. 337–8). Repeated reports from the Pragmatic Army at this time, printed in the London papers, told

of its impending or actual advance towards these lines (*Daily Adv.* 12 Sept. OS *sub* Worms 11 Sept. NS, 13 Sept. OS *sub* Düsseldorf 17 Sept. NS, 17 Sept. OS *sub* Frankfurt 19 Sept. NS, 21 Sept. OS *sub* Worms 20 Sept. NS), but it did not begin to move south until 25 Sept. NS (*post* 25 Sept. 1743 NS).

4. 'We have a new bridge laid across the Rhine for the Dutch, one column of whom arrived yesterday and are encamped over against us, the rest being expected on Friday or Saturday. Some say they will return without crossing the river at all, it being thought there will

week; at present they say not till the latter end of the month. They remain on t'other side of the water till they are all come up and even then some people doubt of their passing.—You will have heard by this time of Prince Charles's attempt to pass:[5] he was possessed of an island,[6] and had encamped a good many of his troops there, but most of 'em have been since obliged by the enemy's cannon to retire and the few that remain lie constantly *ventre à terre,* so I imagine cannot hold it long.[7]—Prince Waldeck,[8] who commanded another attack,[9] made at the same time, had actually passed, but not being supported was obliged to retire over his bridge,[10] leaving five companies of grenadiers in some little forts which they had taken, and which they defended very bravely till they were retaken by the French after three repulses, who attacked 'em the fourth time sword in hand, and killed 'em all to a man[11]—and this was the most considerable part of his loss. I can't help thinking his passage now more doubtful than ever.—You can't imagine, dear Horry, how sorry I am to hear Lord Orford has been out of order[12] and how much I long to hear from you that he is better.—You may expect to hear a great deal of so extraordinary an event as Lord Stair's resignation;[13] but I really am so little acquainted with the circumstances that you

be nothing for us to do, either here or elsewhere' (Lt-Col. Russell to Mrs Russell, Worms, 31 Aug. OS, Hist. MSS Comm., *Frankland-Russell-Astley MSS,* 1900, p. 286).

5. The Rhine at Breisach 3–4 Sept. NS. There is a detailed account of these unsuccessful attempts in *Oesterr. Erbfolgekrieg* v. 342–51. The reports reaching the Pragmatic Army, some of which Conway summarizes here (see also *Frankland MSS,* pp. 286–7), as well as those printed in the English newspapers (*Daily Adv.* 5 Sept. OS *sub* Paris 9 Sept. NS [the first report to reach England], 8 Sept. OS *sub* Freiburg 5 Sept. NS, 12 Sept. OS *sub* Hague 13 and 15 Sept. NS), confuse and telescope two separate attempts to cross at different places and occasionally add still further erroneous details from various feints made at other points at the same time.

6. Rheinach (*Oesterr. Erbfolge-krieg* v. 347).

7. Reports reached Worms on the 13th NS that Prince Charles had withdrawn

from the island, but in fact he held it until mid-October when he retired to winter quarters (ibid. v. 368; *Daily Adv.* 14 Sept. OS *sub* Worms [1]3 Sept. NS).

8. Karl August Friedrich (1704–63), Fürst von Waldeck; field marshal, 1746 (MANN iii. 240, n. 11).

9. At Rheinweiler, some 23 miles south of Breisach, 3 Sept. NS (*Oesterr. Erbfolge-krieg* v. 348–9).

10. Waldeck's troops had crossed by boats, not a bridge (ibid.); the bridge was involved in Prince Charles's attempt at Breisach.

11. This is something of an exaggeration; Waldeck lost about 400 men, killed, wounded, or captured (ibid.).

12. He had had a bad fall in July (MANN ii. 277), but seems to have recovered by this time.

13. Stair had resigned his command 4 or 5 Sept. NS (*Oesterr. Erbfolge-krieg* v. 354; GEC). Reports to this effect were current in London by the 6th OS (*Daily Adv.* 6 Sept. OS).

would have but little satisfaction in my account. He has presented a memorial[14] to the King which one does not see here yet, but which a little time will make public both here and in England. However one does not talk politics by the post; make all sorts of compliments for me and believe me sincerely

Yours,

H. C.

To CONWAY, September 1743

Missing; answered *post* 25 Sept. 1743 NS.

From CONWAY, Wednesday 25 September 1743 NS

Printed for the first time from the MS now WSL, formerly Rutnam. That the letter was written on the 25th is clear from the details of the advance of the army. The postmark is the date of the letter's arrival in London.

Address: To the Honourable Horatio Walpole in Downing Street,[1] London, Angleterre.

Postmark: SE 27. AB.

Camp at Frankendal,[2] Sept. 25, NS, 1743.

NO, dear Horry, I am far from being angry with you and farther yet from suspecting you of neglecting me. I know you are too good, yet I own I began to think it an age since I had heard from you and of course had wished a long time to have a letter. 'Tis not that I would have friends correspond with all the exactness of merchants and think it necessary to give one another immediate advice, when their last of such a date came to hand. I don't expect you should always send an answer the post after you receive one's letter; a post or two is nothing, and if you should be irregular enough to

14. *The Memorial of the E— of S—, Presented When His Resignation Was Accepted* (MANN ii. 130, n. 3). A 7-page folio edn, 1744, now WSL, has the MS endorsement: 'Tom's Coffee House, Nov. 9, 1743.'

1. Conway made a similar slip on a letter to Sir Robert Walpole in 1744; see *post* 6 Oct. 1744 OS and 28 Oct. 1744 NS.

2. Frankenthal, where the Pragmatic Army marched from Worms 25 Sept. NS (*Oesterr. Erbfolge-krieg* v. 363).

write the post before it would be still better; in short, I like to hear often from you, I can never think often enough, so, as often as you can write without giving yourself trouble, I shall be vastly glad to receive a line, a word, anything just to let one know you are well. Your longest letters are the most agreeable; your shortest are infinitely so, and when you have what you call nothing to say, that nothing gives me more pleasure than the somethings of fifty other people. So, in spite of all excuses, I shall expect a little sacrifice of your indolence now and then. You know my situation; you tell me I have need of all my patience. It has indeed held out to a miracle; yet I own I find it pretty much *délabrée* at present and was it not for the constant repairs made by letters from England, would have been worn out long ago. Well, Horry, contrary to expectation we are now afoot again. Yesterday came out a sudden order for our march, we knew not where; today we are come to a town called Frankendal, which is about two leagues' march and so far on our road towards Spires,³ whither to go farther we don't know but, somewhere, march again tomorrow. Dear Horry, we are going farther from England! We may beat the French, perhaps, but that thought I own would even damp the joy of a victory with me. If we should be once seriously engaged, God knows when one may see you. Pity me, pray, and if I should be doomed to a longer banishment wish me to think if possible less on England; wish me a new stock of patience and at least all the poor reparation that laurels can make for the loss of one's friends!—I hope Lord Orford is quite recovered. Give my duty to him and best compliments to Lady Mary and Mrs Leneve and believe [me] dear Horry's most sincerely

H. C.

3. Speyer, where the army arrived 27 Sept. NS (ibid. v. 364; *Daily Adv.* 28 Sept. OS *sub* 29 Sept. NS). Noailles had withdrawn his first line from the vicinity of Landau to behind the Lauter 20–22 Sept. NS; when the news reached the Pragmatic Army at Worms, it was decided to advance (*Oesterr. Erbfolge-krieg* v. 360, 363).

From CONWAY, Friday 25 October 1743 NS

Printed from the MS now WSL, formerly Rutnam. First printed, *Rockingham Memoirs* i. 392–4; reprinted *Colburn's United Service Magazine*, 1880, lii pt i. 464–5. The postmark is the date of the letter's arrival in London.

Address: To the Honourable Horatio Walpole, Jun., in Arlington Street, London, Angleterre.

Postmark: OC 17.

Oct. 25, 1743 NS.

Dear Horry,

YOU'll wonder how I can be arrived at The Hague without having let you hear a word of my journey[1] and communicating to you the vast joy I feel upon my escape, and the great part you bear in it. But the hurry of my journey, together with the hurry of my spirits was so prodigious that I have either forgot or neglected half of the things necessary to be done upon the occasion. I am now at The Hague as I told you; where I am under promise to stay some days with Lord Holdernesse,[2] by whose means I obtained my *congé*. Lord Holdernesse they say is going to be married here;[3] for me, remember I say nothing of it: the lady's name is Doublet.[4] I saw her all day yesterday, dinner at Mr Trevor's,[5] and cards and supper at Lord Stair's,[6] and I assure [you I] think her both pretty and agreeable to a degree. Lord Stair has not yet taken his leave here, but does not interfere with any sort of business or politics whatever: he talks of going the beginning of next week.[7] In the meantime whist *lui tient lieu de tout*. He en-

1. The Pragmatic Army had begun to retire towards winter quarters 10–11 Oct. NS; Conway left the army on or shortly before 17th Oct., perhaps on the 16th, when the King left the army at Mainz, since Conway says below that he started his trip from Mainz (*Oesterr. Erbfolgekrieg* v. 367; Hist. MSS Comm., *Frankland-Russell-Astley MSS*, 1900, p. 296; *Daily Adv.* 15 Oct. OS *sub* Mainz 17 Oct. NS).

2. Who had been with the army since 23 June NS in attendance on the King as one of his lords of the Bedchamber (*Frankland MSS*, p. 248).

3. He was, 29 Oct. NS.

4. Mary Doublet (ca 1721–1801); she had a fortune of £50,000 (*Genealog. hist.*

Nachrichten, 1743–4, 1st ser. v. 847–8; *Daily Adv.* 1 Nov. OS).

5. Robert Trevor (after 1754, Hampden) (1706–83), 4th Bn Trevor, 1764; cr. (1776) Vct Hampden; envoy to Holland 1739–46.

6. 'The Earl of Stair had on the 24th several foreign ministers, and other persons of distinction, to supper with him, amongst whom were the Marquis de St Gilles and his Lady' (*Daily Adv.* 24 Oct. OS *sub* Hague 27 Oct. NS).

7. Stair had been at The Hague since 25 Sept. NS; he took his formal leave 31 Oct. NS and reached London 27 Oct. OS (MANN ii. 324, n. 14; *Daily Adv.* 25 Oct. OS *sub* Hague 31 Oct. NS; 28 Oct. OS).

tertains too with his usual magnificence, and in short may very probably be prevailed upon by his amusements and his indolence to stay something longer than he intends. I mention this because if he holds his resolution I think it just possible I may come over with him.—I hear he stays in London this winter, but on peril of his regiment and government[8] is not to make any stir in the political world, but play at whist *tout de bon* all winter long.—I hear the Duke of Argyle[9] is succeeded in his honours and estate by his worthy brother,[10] from whom they fall to Jack Campbel[11] when he shall have puddled[12] away his days amongst toads, spiders, and projectors.[13]

The Hague looks like a capital and is very pretty; but the society savours more of a large country town, consisting of one general circle where all know one another, from whence the communication of news is so regular that you have not made water five minutes before the whole town is acquainted with it, with this, incessant eating, drinking and cards, and a French comedy, *Voilà la Haye!* You'll say I form my opinion very soon, and so I do but in short this is my opinion, and whether it's right or wrong signifies not three halfpence either to you or me.

We fell down the Rhine from Mentz to Cologne which took up almost three days, during which time we were amused with many of the finest prospects but particularly the most rude and romantic, the most Salvator Rosa[14] that ever you saw, even passing the Grande Chartreuse by Chamberri,[15] and the Savoy Mountains; such noble horrors of rocks and woods and ancient castles perching upon the summits of pointed rocks! with all the fury of the Rhine finding its

8. Stair was Col. of the 6th Dragoons and governor of Minorca.

9. Who had died 4 Oct. 1743 OS.

10. Lord Archibald Campbell (1682–1761), cr. (1706) E. of Ilay; 3d D. of Argyll, 1743. He had been one of Sir Robert Walpole's strongest supporters, but was now suspected of 'treachery' in his fall (SELWYN 287, n. 5).

11. John Campbell (ca 1693–1770), 4th D. of Argyll, 1761; subsequently Conway's father-in-law.

12. 'To busy oneself in an untidy or disorderly way; to "muddle" or "mess" about' (OED).

13. HW elsewhere relates that the 3d D. of Argyll 'had a great thirst for books; a head admirably turned to mechanics;

was a patron of ingenious men, a promoter of discoveries, and one of the first great encouragers of planting in England; most of the curious exotics which have been familiarized to this climate being introduced by him' (*Mem. Geo. II* i. 277–8). Lady Louisa Stuart, in her 'Memoir' of John, Duke of Argyll also mentions the 3d Duke's interest in 'philosophical experiments, mechanics, natural history' (Coke, *Journals*, i. p. xxiv).

14. (1615–73), painter.

15. Which Conway had visited with HW and Gray 29 Sept. 1739 NS. HW had then compared the scenery in the mountains of Savoy with the paintings of Salvator Rosa which he greatly admired (GRAY i. 181 and n. 2).

way or rather forcing a passage through a ridge of mountains. I longed to loll over an Ariosto,[16] or be buried in some endless rom⟨anc⟩e of your acquaintance,[17] *Clelia*[18] or *Cleopatra*[19] or *Amadius of Gaul.*[20]

Adieu, dear Horry, I hope I shall find you in town;[21] I hope so for your sake and my own, and it's really an indecent time to be starving on those bleak plains! I am very sorry to hear Lord Orford has had a fall,[22] but hope it has had no consequence; pray give my duty to him and my best compliments to Lady Mary, Mrs Leneve, and all friends.

Adieu.

H. C.

Conway and other military members of Parliament spent the winter in England, returning to Flanders on transports carrying English troops, which left about 15 May 1744 OS and reached Ostend about 17 May OS (28 May NS) (see *post* 3 June 1744, n. 4). Lt-Col. Charles Russell wrote from headquarters at Beerlegem, 23 May 1744 OS, 'All who came by the last transport are at Bruges, including seven general officers, Boscawen and all the members of Parliament . . .' (Hist. MSS Comm., *Frankland-Russell-Astley MSS,* 1900, p. 314). And on 30 May 1744 OS he wrote, 'Our people are now all come, and we are very strong in officers . . .' (ibid. 317).

---

16. Ludovico Ariosto (1474–1533), author of *Orlando Furioso.*

17. Conway alludes to HW's reading of romances *ante* 26 Sept. 1742 NS, *post* 18 April 1745 NS, and 10 Aug. 1745 NS.

18. *Clélie,* by Madeleine de Scudéry (1607–1701), translated into English 1655–8. HW mentions reading it in a letter to Montagu 6 May 1736, but there is no other record of his copy (MONTAGU i. 3 and n. 3).

19. *Cléopâtre,* by Gautier de Costes [or Coste] de la Calprenède (1614–63). HW's

copy of the last two (of twelve) parts, Leyden, 1658, is Hazen, *Cat. of HW's Lib.,* No. 1224. HW speaks of it with contempt in his strictures on La Calprenède's *Cassandre* in a letter to Mme du Deffand ca 21 Dec. 1773 (DU DEFFAND iii. 436–7), but see *post* 18 April 1745 OS and 24 Oct. 1746 OS.

20. *Amadis de Gaule,* a 15th-century prose romance.

21. HW had returned to London shortly after 3 Oct. OS (MANN ii. 315).

22. In July (*ante* 11 Sept. 1743 NS, n. 12).

From CONWAY, Wednesday, 3 June 1744 NS

Printed for the first time from the MS now WSL, formerly Rutnam. HW received this letter 29 May OS (MANN ii. 448, where it is confused with the letter of 26 May 1745 NS, which is misdated 21 May 1744 NS; that letter was misdated thus when printed in *Rockingham Memoirs* i. 395–6, and also redated incorrectly 21 May 1745 NS when reprinted in *Colburn's United Service Magazine*, 1880, lii pt ii. 212–13. When we edited HW to Mann 29 May 1744 OS, the present letter had not been recovered).

Ghent, June 3d NS, 1744.

Dear Horry,

I OUGHT to make excuses for not writing before, but you know the confusion and hurry of such a journey,[1] and I assure you ours has been greater than ordinary. We have been hurried, alarmed, put to flight,[2] our baggage given for lost, ourselves not far from it; yet after all safely arrived I may almost say at the army, since I believe there remains not the least difficulty in our way thither; it is about 3 leagues from hence and between us and Oudenard.[3] I would fain tell you everything that I know about us and our situation, but I have heard so much and yet so little, that I can properly say I know, that my account, especially in the hurry I write, will be as confused as one could wish.—First, as to ourselves we had a good voyage,[4] etc., some alarms at Ostend,[5] but yet no obstruction till we got to Bruges; there we heard of our old friend the Count de Saxe[6] sent with a

1. From Dover to Ostend to Bruges and then to Ghent; see below, n. 4.
2. See below and n. 7.
3. The Allied army had advanced early in the week from its camp at Assche, slightly to the west of Brussels, to the vicinity of Beerlegem 'within two leagues of Oudenarde and three of Ghent' (Hist. MSS Comm., *Frankland-Russell-Astley MSS*, 1900, p. 314; *Daily Adv.* 29 May OS).
4. Conway, together with the other officers who were members of Parliament, had gone to Flanders on the transports with recruits and drafts from the English regiments which left about 15 May OS. The English newspapers reported that the transports reached Ostend on the 18th or 19th OS (29th or 30th NS), but a French intelligence report that they arrived on the 28th NS seems more probable in view

of the subsequent events between their arrival and this letter (J.-L.-A. Colin, 'Les Campagnes du Maréchal de Saxe,' *Revue d'histoire rédigée à l'État-Major de l'armée (section historique)*, May 1903, x. 985, n. 3; *Daily Adv.* 11, 15, 24, 28, 31 May OS).
5. They probably heard reports similar to those printed in the *Daily Adv.* 28 May OS *sub* Ostend 27 May NS: 'Parties of the enemy from time to time appear in this neighbourhood, even at our gates, but without committing any outrages. . . . The French have taken possession of some posts upon the canal between Bruges and Ghent, whereby the navigation between these two cities is almost wholly interrupted.'
6. Hermann-Maurice (1696–1750), Comte de Saxe; Maréchal de France, 1744; 'our

strong party to intercept us, but with such uncertain intelligence, that we thought it more becoming to look upon it as an idle story with which of all places in the world camps are most infested; so the morning after we arrived we set out from Bruges, with our recruits and draughts to the number of about 400, and had marched almost 4 leagues, which is near half way hither, in great security and on the French side of the canal, when somebody that was a little advanced before our party came back, as I don't know 'em, I may say in a great fright, and told us the French were marching in a strong body and just going to attack us, and soon after we learnt from some of our own hussars that there was actually a detachment of 4,000 lying to intercept us, upon which it was immediately resolved to retire, and by good luck we made our retreat in excellent order and without the least molestation.[7] This made us draw in our horns a little so we contented ourselves with staying all the next day at Bruges in order to know something more of the strength etc. of the enemy. When I say *we* lay still I mean our party, for Churchill[8] and I amused ourselves by going out with a party of hussars and dragoons to reconnoitre: however, we saw none of the French but 3 straggling hussars whom, after a little course in company with some of our own, we took without difficulty or resistance on their part. We went a little too late for 'em. They had been that morning in all about 4,000, as we were informed by the prisoners, within a league and half of the town and were then retired; from which time we have heard or seen no more of 'em. All our party is now arrived here in safety and they are gone back I suppose to their army, part of which is now actually employed in the siege of Menin,[9] which must be taken if not very soon relieved as the garrison is only of 1100 men.[10] Our army approaches by degrees and if we receive our reinforcements[11] it's

friend' because he had been in command of the abortive French invasion of England the past winter.

7. This incident occurred 1 June NS; detailed contemporary accounts from the French side in Colin, op. cit. x. 986–8, give the French force as about 3,800 infantry and 1200 horse. Further details are in the *Daily Adv.* 30 May OS *sub* Ghent 4 June NS, where the chronology is somewhat inaccurate. The affair is also mentioned *Frankland MSS*, pp. 314, 316, 318.

8. Presumably Charles Churchill Jr, later HW's brother-in-law, at this time a Capt. in his father's (the 10th) Regiment of Dragoons (SELWYN 85, n. 20).

9. The French, with some 30,000 men, had invested Menin 17–18 May NS; the siege began on the night of the 28th and the place surrendered 4 June NS (MANN ii. 448, n. 3).

10. Other estimates of the garrison vary between 1200 and 1500 (*Oesterr. Erbfolgekrieg* vi. 353; *Frankland MSS*, p. 315).

11. At this time the Allied army num-

thought we may be able to raise the siege. I cannot exactly tell the distance of Menin from hence, but they say you may hear the cannon from our ramparts that look that way and from the camp very distinctly.[12] We heard yesterday from a Dutch courier that the twenty thousand Dutch were already advanced, I think, as far as Antwerp[13] and that they would be joined immediately by a body of 15,000 Prussians;[14] this is so very good and I doubt so very unlikely that I cannot credit it. They say the French have declared war in form against the Dutch,[15] as they did it before in effect by attacking Menin.[16] This is, I would fain say in few words if I could bring you to think so, an account of our present situation; our Maréchal[17] has sent his plate, they say, to Antwerp and is tucked up for the greatest undertakings. Tomor[row] if possible I shall be with him and from thence I intend to tell you more things.—Adieu, dear Horry, think of me I beseech you and don't fancy it's clever to say you have no news, etc. I insist upon hearing from you and often; say anything, I don't care what.— And believe me, ever yours most affectionately

H. C.

I need not tell you to make my compliments to Lord Orford, Lady Mary, Mrs Leneve. Adieu!

bered about 55,000, the French about 87,000 (MANN ii. 448, n. 5; *Daily Adv.* 28 May OS *sub* Brussels 1 June NS).

12. Lt-Col. Russell wrote to his wife the same day from the camp at Beerlegem that Menin being 'but six leagues from us, and the wind setting fair made us yesterday hear a cannonading all day long' (*Frankland MSS*, loc. cit.).

13. This was not true; the States General were still debating about sending them in late May, although a French agent reported from Ghent 5 June NS that the Allies were expecting 10,000 Dutch troops from the camp at Breda (MANN ii. 449, n. 6; *Daily Adv.* 26 May OS, *sub* Hague 27 May NS).

14. This was not true; Frederick had earlier refused to provide 10,000 troops at George II's demand on the grounds

that it was far from clear that the French were the aggressors in the war. The diplomatic correspondence relating to this event was currently being released at The Hague and some misunderstanding of it may have given rise to this rumour (*Daily Adv.* 22 May OS, *sub* Hague 22 May NS, 1 June OS, *sub* Hague 29 May NS, 4 June OS, *sub* Hague 2 June NS).

15. This was not true: France never did formally declare war on the Dutch.

16. Which the Dutch garrisoned under the Barrier Treaty of 1715 (R. Geike and I. A. Montgomery, *The Dutch Barrier*, Cambridge, 1930, p. 290).

17. George Wade (1673–1748), field marshal, 1743; commander-in-chief of the British forces in Flanders. Conway was one of his aides-de-camp.

To Conway, ca Friday 1 June 1744 OS

Missing; answered *post* 1 July 1744 NS. Since Conway there complains that the letter was written 'an age' ago and was an 'immense' time on the road, it seems probable that HW had answered Conway's previous letter promptly; this surmise is strengthened by what can be deduced of the contents of HW's letter.

From Conway, Wednesday 1 July 1744 NS

Printed for the first time from the MS now WSL, formerly Rutnam. The postmark is the date of the letter's arrival in London.

Address: To the Honourable Horatio Walpole, Jun., in Arlington Street, London. Pour l'Angleterre.

Postmark: IV 25 AB.

Beirleghem,[1] July 1st 1744.

My dear Horry,

I AM ashamed to find what an age it is since you wrote your last. However, I have some excuse from the immense time it was on the road and for the remainder I would have as little as possible charged to negligence and nothing to neglect, of which it is really no compliment to say I am incapable towards you.—I am vastly obliged to you for the fears you are so kind to say you had about my getting safe to the army and would fain think myself so for my share of those you express about the event of this battle which you foretell[2] and which, by the way, for a man who knows nothing is really an extraordinary piece of knowledge, for on this side the water I do assure you we think of nothing less: Ypres[3] has followed the example of Menin, made much the same defence and surrendered upon the same conditions;[4] when I say the same defence I mean as to the time for they really showed more spirit and sold it somewhat dearer to the

1. The modern spelling is Beerlegem.
2. HW's expectations of a battle were probably based on a false report from the newspapers which he relayed to Mann 29 May OS to the effect that the Allied army had crossed the Scheldt and intended to force the French to a battle (Mann ii. 448 and n. 4).

3. Which Saxe had invested 6 June NS, immediately after the surrender of Menin; it capitulated 25 June NS (Mann ii. 456, n. 6; *Oesterr. Erbfolge-krieg* vi. 374).
4. The two capitulations, which resemble each other but are not identical, are printed *Mercure historique* 1744, cxvi. 689–93; cxvii. 105–9.

French. The Prince of Hesse-Philipstall,[5] who commanded there, is a man of great bravery and, I believe, could not bring himself to act quite so tamely as their High Mightinesses would have had him.[6] He made one or two sallies in which the French lost a good many men as is reported[7] though of that we know nothing with certainty. The French are now besieging Fort Knocke[8] which is about 2 leagues from Ypres, and they say have sent two more detachments to invest Farnes and Nieuport[9] but this is mere report, and as likely at least to be false as true. Our embarkation[10] arrived the day before yesterday at Ostend and we expect will be at Ghent tomorrow. This is all the news I shall tell you at present because it's rather more than I know, and though after making you know so much in spite of your teeth, it's coming off but shabbily especially from this fountain of news, yet I really have no more and I know the dignity of a letter from the army too well to stuff it with fables; how do I know but, if you had not gone to Lady Caroline Fox's,[11] my news might reach the

5. Wilhelm (1692–1761), Prinz von Hesse-Philippsthal, who spent his life in the Dutch service; governor of Ypres 1732–44 (Genealog. hist. Nachrichten 1762–3, 2d ser. xiii. 464–6). According to Isenburg, Stammtafeln i. taf. 103, he became Landgraf of Hesse-Philippsthal-Barchfeld in 1722, but the full obituary cited above does not mention this accession to sovereign power.

6. The French account of the siege of Ypres in the Mercure historique 1744, cxvii. 105 says 'le Roi n'aurait pas pris cette ville si facilement sans une espèce de révolte des habitants, qui ont forcé le commandant à capituler, après s'être défendu en lion.'

7. Details of the siege of Ypres are in Oesterr. Erbfolge-krieg vi. 367–74; sallies by the defenders are mentioned ibid. vi. 371–2 and 372–3. See also the accounts of the defence in the Daily Adv. 18 June OS, sub Hague 23 June NS, 23 June OS, sub Hague 23 June NS, 25 June OS, sub Brussels 25 June NS, and 28 June OS, sub Brussels 29 June NS.

8. Or Knoque, which had been invested 27 June and surrendered 29 June NS after a sixteen-hour siege (J.-L.-A. Colin, 'Les Campagnes du Maréchal de Saxe,' Revue d'histoire rédigée à l'État-Major de

l'armée (section historique), July 1903, xi. 1; Oesterr. Erbfolge-krieg vi. 376; Mercure historique 1744, cxvi. 693, 707; Daily Adv. 27 June OS, sub Ostend 30 June NS).

9. The French did not invest Nieuport, but besieged Furnes which surrendered 10 July NS (Colin, op. cit. xi. 2–3, 32; Mercure historique 1744, cxvii. 109).

10. According to HW, six English regiments and 6000 Dutch were expected to leave England 12 June OS; some of these, including the Dutch, were delayed, and the four regiments that reached Ostend 29 June NS were detained there in expectation of a French siege and did not join the rest of the army until the middle of the month (MANN ii. 449, nn. 6, 7, 457; Hist. MSS Comm., Frankland-Russell-Astley MSS, 1900, pp. 324, 327).

11. Lady Caroline Lennox (see ante 24 March 1740 OS, n. 18) had secretly married Henry Fox 3 May 1744 OS and run off with him on the 8th, an event that enraged her parents and caused a great furor in London society; see HW to Mann 29 May 1744 OS, MANN ii. 450–1; Earl of Ilchester, Henry Fox, 1920, i. 104–10; Earl of Ilchester and Mrs Langford-Brooke, Life of Sir Charles Hanbury-Williams, 1929, pp. 80–2. Williams wrote to Fox that on the night of Lady Caroline's flight, 'Hor-

ears of the Chancellor of the Exchequer[12] from thence diffuse itself through the whole mass of ministry and produce some measure of government, which God forbid I should ever have upon my conscience.—So I find you amuse yourself exceedingly with Vauxhall and your pretty parties upon the water;[13] I'm glad your taste is so much improved; how you used to despise those junketing bouts! By the way, I hear you have sold yourself body and soul to the new Knight[14] and to the Bunbury-Bums;[15] your old friends complain they never see you. I told Cornwallis[16] your message and he said he'd write. Lord Bury[17] I have hardly seen but he's very well. After telling you an age ago I had nothing to say I think I may conclude without farther apology. I am glad to hear Lord Offord is quite recovered.[18]

ace Walpole came up into the box where I was at the Opera, and told me he had heard the news, and that he understood 'twas made a point of by the Duke and Duchess [of Richmond] for their friends not to visit you: and that therefore he desired to know the first moment he might pay his compliments to Lady Caroline and yourself, and that he would do it' (ibid. 81).

12. Henry Pelham, who with his brother, the Duke of Newcastle, had treated the marriage as a state crisis. See the references cited in the preceding note and the letters quoted in Princess Marie Liechtenstein, *Holland House*, 1874, i. 57–66.

13. These are not mentioned in any letter that has been recovered.

14. Sir Charles Hanbury Williams, who had been invested K.B. 28 May 1744 OS (W. A. Shaw, *Knights of England*, 1906, i. 169). HW's first known letter to him is a missing one of 16 June 1744 OS (Selwyn 47), written shortly after Williams had left London for the summer.

15. Apparently the circle around Susannah Bunbury (1700–64), m. William Handasyd; later (ca 1756–64) housekeeper at Windsor. Richard Rigby told Williams 21 June OS that he and HW often spent their evenings with Mrs Handasyd and her daughter, and HW mentions dining with her in a letter to Williams 7 July OS (ibid. 57 and n. 43; see also Montagu i. 111 for HW's affection for

her). HW, however, complained to Williams 26 June 1744 OS that he was bored with all his new acquaintance except Rigby (Selwyn 51).

16. Hon. Edward Cornwallis (1713–76), army officer; M.P. Eye 1743–9, Westminster 1753–62; lt-governor of Nova Scotia 1749–52, governor of Gibraltar, 1762–76; groom of the Bedchamber, 1747–63; at this time a major in the 20th Foot. Sometime in 1744 HW composed a mock petition for him to the King, joking about his inability to pronounce the letter *r* (HW's *MS Commonplace Book of Verses*, pp. 39–40, where HW has also recorded a few biographical data and anecdotes about him). HW speaks of him as a close friend in a letter to Mann 29 Nov. 1745 OS (Mann iii. 175), but told Montagu 14 Dec. 1752 that Cornwallis was then 'too busy in the Bedchamber to remember me!' (Montagu i. 145). One letter from Cornwallis to HW, 18 Dec. 1745 OS, has been recovered.

17. Who was now a Capt.-Lt in the 2d (Coldstream) Regiment of Guards, where he had moved from the 1st (Royal) Dragoons in 1743 (C. T. Atkinson, *History of the Royal Dragoons*, Glasgow, [1934], pp. 153, 480; Daniel MacKinnon, *Origin and Services of the Coldstream Guards*, 1833, ii. 480–1).

18. Lord Orford had been 'extremely ill from a cold' caught while fishing with Princess Amelia about the middle of May, but HW reported 29 May OS that he was again 'quite well' (Mann ii. 449).

I beg you'll give my duty to him and compliments to Lady Mary. Tell her I'm sorry to hear operas are over forever,[19] and beg to know what is to be the fashionable diversion next winter.—By this time I suppose you are drawing towards Houghton,[20] where I wish you much amusement. Adieu.

Queen Brunette salutes King Pat.

From CONWAY, Monday 6 July 1744 NS

Printed for the first time from the MS now WSL, formerly Rutnam.
Address: To the Honourable Horatio Walpole, Jun., in Arlington Street, London. Pour l'Angleterre.

Beirleghem, Monday, July 6, 1744.

Dear Horry,

I BELIEVE I ought to make you some excuse for troubling you again so soon after my last, but a messenger going out today I could [not] resist the temptation of being one of the first to tell you that yesterday an account came that Prince Charles has actually passed the Rhine;[1] it's true this does not come regularly from him, but is so authentic that Duke d'Aremberg[2] sent an aide-de-camp to the Marshal[3] with it the moment he had received it. It comes from the postmaster-general at Mentz to him at Brussels.[4]—It's dated 2d of this month N.S. and is in substance as follows.—Monsieur: J'ai

19. No operas were performed at the King's Theatre, Haymarket, from 16 June 1744 OS to 7 Jan. 1746 OS (*London Stage* Pt III, ii. 1208–9; Charles Burney, *General History of Music*, ed. Mercer, 1935, ii. 843). The opera had been in serious financial difficulties since the 1743 season (MANN ii. 293–4 and n. 22).

20. HW did not go to Houghton until mid-August, although his father went 24 June OS (SELWYN 49, 72; MANN ii. 498). Before Conway left London HW had already decided to remain in London until August (ibid. ii. 442).

1. Prince Charles, with the principal

body of the Austrian army crossed the Rhine near Philippsburg, south of Speyer, 30 June–3 July NS (*Genealog. hist. Nachrichten* 1744–5, 1st ser. vi. 593–7; *Oesterr. Erbfolge-krieg* v. 437–43), but this news had not yet reached the Allied army. The crossing described below, quite accurately, is that of a smaller detachment in the vicinity of Mainz (ibid. v. 444–5). See also *Mercure historique* 1744, cxvii. 72–6.

2. Léopold-Philippe-Charles-Joseph de Ligne (1690–1754), Duc d'Arenberg, commander-in-chief of the Austrian forces in Flanders (MANN ii. 79, n. 3).

3. Wade.

4. Not identified.

l'honneur de vous marquer que le Prince Charles a passé le Rhin
cette nuit à une lieue d'ici, à Weissenau, et 4,000 pandours et hussards à Walff5 à 2 lieues d'ici. Il y a plusieurs français tués et l'on dit
qu'ils ont pris douze pièces de canon dans l'isle appartenant à mon
frère.—Personne ne sort de la ville et pourtant l'on voit jeter
les ponts du côté de la Ste Croix, et toute la campagne est pleine
de troupes.—Monsieur de Bernclau6 qui a commandé l'armée du
Prince Charles, est arrivé cette nuit à Trebur avec le gros de l'armée
et passera encore aujourd'hui.—A very odd sort of letter as you perceive but one passes over the style in consideration of such news. It
was writ early in the morning of the 2d and of course he passed the
night from the first to the 2d.—These places are one, 2 leagues below
and t'other, one above Mentz as I apprehend, on the Rhine. This
puts us in the greatest spirits imaginable. It quite changes the face of
affairs and we now hope to finish the campaign as gloriously as it was
unhappily begun. Besides this Mr Trevor writes us word that the
States have actually ordered 11 battalions and 22 squadrons to join
us immediately,7 some of which we expect here in a very few days.
I'm sorry to add to this that Count Nassau,8 nor Gen. Cronstom9
have yet had any advice of this that we know; but he writes so positively that I think it's hardly possible to doubt of it.—Our news from
Italy, too, is very great. The Spaniards in retiring precipitately from
Oniglia have had 12 battalions of foot, one of miquilets10 and a
regiment of dragoons entirely cut to pieces by the militia of Pié-
mont.11 This secures that country, I believe, in a great measure and

5. Walluf.
6. Johann Leopold Pernklö (1700–46),
Freiherr von Schönreuth, called Bernklau
or Bärnklau; Austrian general (ibid. iii. 41,
n. 9; Constant Wurzbach, *Biographisches
Lexikon des Kaiserthums Oesterreich*, Vienna, 1856–91, i. 117–18).
7. Lt-Col. Russell mentions two days
earlier that 'we hear that our Marshal
has just had a letter saying that the
Dutch are sending six thousand foot and
four thousand horse immediately to join
us' (Hist. MSS Comm., *Frankland-Russell-
Astley MSS*, 1900, p. 324).
8. Willem Maurits (1679–1753), Graaf
van Nassau, Heer van Ouwerkerk, commander-in-chief of the Dutch troops with

the Allied army (*Genealog. hist. Nachrichten* 1753–4, 2d ser. iv. 637–41; *Nieuw Ne-
derlandsch Biografisch Woordenboek*, Leyden, 1911–37, i. 1369–70).
9. Isaac Kock (1661–1751), Baron Cron-
ström, second in command of the Dutch
troops with the Allied army (ibid. i. 654–
6; *Genealog. hist. Nachrichten* 1751–2, 2d
ser. ii. 709, 909–29).
10. Miquelets, Spanish mountaineers. According to OED the word was not used for
guerrilla troops until the Peninsular war.
11. This false report, with some variations of detail, is also given in *Frankland
MSS*, p. 325; *Daily Adv.* 30 June OS; and
HW to Mann 29 June OS, MANN ii. 466.
The Spanish troops, which had advanced

binds the King of S[ardinia].[12] We hear too from Veletri that the Spaniards and Neapolitans have been repulsed by Lobkowitz[13] in attempting to force their passage.[14]—We expect a courier from Prince Charles every hour; in the meantime we know no particulars of what passed farther than what I have told you. We know no more which way he will move—whether towards Alsace or Lorrain.[15] Whichever way he moves the French will be obliged to send him[16] reinforcements from hence[17] as Coigni's[18] army is certainly too weak to stand before him unless it be behind the lines that guard the passage into Alsace. Our troops from England[19] were at Bruges on Friday from whence they were to march yesterday morning and we expect every minute to hear they are arrived at Ghent:—here ends my news and with it my letter for we're such thorough soldiers, we breath nothing but war, talk of nothing else, I don't say think of nothing else, for notwithstanding I feel as much as anybody can do from these great events, I don't find myself so absorbed by 'em as to be a bit less sensible to the interesting trifles of my own little system of friends and connections on your side the water. For this reason I beg to explain what I find you chose to misunderstand in a former letter of mine[20] where you make me insist upon your writing news; no: I told you your not having news to tell should be no excuse for not writing. I told you you could never want news to send me, when the

to Oneglia 6 June NS, had retired abruptly on the 17th because of a change in strategy, and were safely back in Provence, despite some harassment by the Piedmont militia, by the 19th (Spenser Wilkinson, *Defence of Piedmont 1742–1748*, Oxford, 1927, pp. 130, 132; *Oesterr. Erbfolge-krieg* viii. 447–8).

12. Charles Emmanuel III (1701–73), D. of Savoy and K. of Sardinia, 1730. He was allied with Austria and England by the Treaty of Worms, 1743, but had continued to threaten to accept Franco-Spanish offers.

13. Johann Georg Christian (1686–1753), Fürst von Lobkowitz; field marshal (MANN i. 205, n. 29).

14. Another false report, probably based on a garbled report of the successful Spanish attack on 'Notre Dame des Anges near Velletri' 17 June NS (ibid. ii. 459–60 and n. 2; *Oesterr. Erbfolge-krieg* viii. 247–61).

15. Prince Charles attacked the French lines along the Lauter that guarded the passage into Alsace.

16. I.e., send against him; Conway's sentence structure is sometimes faulty.

17. The French, who learned of the passage on the 6th, dispatched reinforcements under the Duc d'Harcourt on the 10th and a further large detachment under the King himself and Noailles on the 16th (J.-L.-A. Colin, 'Les Campagnes du Maréchal de Saxe,' *Revue d'histoire redigée à l'État-Major de l'armée (section historique)*, July 1903, xi. 16–17, 19, 30).

18. François de Franquetot (1670–1759), Comte (Duc, 1747) de Coigny; Maréchal de France, 1734; commander of the French army on the Rhine (La Chenaye-Desbois viii. 608–9; NBG).

19. For these see *ante* 1 July 1744 NS, n. 10.

20. *Ante* 3 June 1744 NS.

smallest trifles relating to yourself or my friends would be news as acceptable and as interesting for me as battles, victories and alliances. Adieu. Remember this and let me hear from you when you have leisure.

H. C.

All sorts of compliments!

To CONWAY, Friday 29 June 1744 OS

Printed from the MS now WSL; first printed Wright i. 351–3. The MS passed into the possession of the Waldegraves; it was acquired from the present Earl in 1948 by WSL.

Arlington Street, June 29, 1744.

My dearest Harry,

I DON'T know what made my last letter so long on the road: yours[1] got hither as soon as it could. I don't attribute it to any examination at the Post Office: God forbid I should suspect any branch of the present administration of attempting to know any one kind of thing! I remember when I was at Eton, and Mr Bland[2] had set me any extraordinary task, I used sometimes to pique myself upon not getting it, because it was not immediately my school business: what, learn more than I am absolutely forced to learn! I felt the weight of learning that, for I was a blockhead, and pushed up above my parts.

Lest you maliciously think I mean any application of this last sentence anywhere in the world, I shall go and transcribe some lines out of a new poem,[3] that pretends to great impartiality, but is evi-

1. *Ante* 1 July 1744 NS, postmarked in London 25 June OS. Although HW heard of Prince Charles's crossing of the Rhine 'from the Secretary's office' on the day that he wrote this letter (MANN ii. 466), the tone of the third paragraph shows that it was written before that news arrived.

2. Henry Bland (ca 1703–68), D.D., 1747; prebendary of Durham, 1737; HW's

tutor at Eton ('Short Notes,' GRAY i. 4–5 and n. 12).

3. *Discord: or, One Thousand Seven Hundred and Forty-Four. By a Great Poet Lately Deceased*, advertised as 'this day is published' 23 June OS. The author is unknown, but Henry Fox thought it might be by Whitehead (SELWYN 49, n. 16). HW's copy is Hazen, *Cat. of HW's Lib.*, No. 280).

dently wrote by some secret friend of the ministry. It is called Pope's —but has no good lines but the following. The plan supposes him complaining of being put to death by the blundering discord of his two physicians Burton[4] and Thompson:[5] and from thence makes a transition to show that all the present misfortunes of the world flow from a parallel disagreement: for instance in politics:

> Ask you what cause this conduct can create?
> The doctors differ that direct the state.
> CRATERUS[6] wild as THOMPSON rules and raves:
> A slave himself, yet proud of making slaves:
> Fondly believing that his mighty parts
> Can guide all councils, and command all hearts;
> Give shape and colour to discordant things,
> Hide fraud in ministers and fear in kings.
> Presuming on his power, such schemes he draws
> For *bribing iron,*[7] and giving Europe laws
> That camps and fleets and treaties fill the news,
> And succours unobtain'd, and unaccomplish'd views.
>
> Like solemn BURTON, grave PLUMBOSUS[8] acts;
> He thinks in method, argues all from facts;
> Warm in his temper, yet affecting ice,
> Protests his candour, e'er he gives advice.
> Hints, he dislikes the schemes he recommends;
> And courts his foes—and hardly courts his friends.
> Is fond of power and yet concern'd for fame;
> From different parties would dependants claim;
> Declares for war, but in an awkward way;
> Loves peace at heart, which he's afraid to say:
> His head perplex'd, although his hands are pure;
> An honest man—but not a hero sure!

I beg you will never tell me any news, till it has passed every impression of the Dutch Gazette; for one is apt to mention what is wrote to one; that gets about, comes at last to the ears of the ministry, puts them in a fright; and perhaps they send to beg to see your letter:

4. Simon Burton (ca 1690 – 11 June 1744), M.D., 1720.

5. Thomas Thompson (d. 1763), a well-known quack (MONTAGU i. 66, n. 27; MANN iii. 249–50 and n. 24).

6. Carteret, from *cratera,* a vessel for mixing wine and water.

7. This is nonsense (HW).

8. Henry Pelham, or leaden. HW thought this character of him 'especially' admirable (SELWYN 49).

how you know one should hate to have one's private correspondence made grounds for a measure—especially for an absurd one, which is just possible.

If I was writing to anybody but you who know me so well, I should be afraid this would be taken for pique and pride—and be construed into my thinking all ministers inferior to my father: but my dear Harry, you know it was never my foible to think over-abundantly well of him—why I think as I do of the present great geniuses—answer for me, Admiral Matthews,[9] great British Neptune, bouncing in the Mediterranean, while the Brest Squadron is riding in the English Channel,[10] and an invasion from Dunkirk every moment threatening your coasts, against which you send for six thousand Dutch troops,[11] while you have twenty thousand of your own in Flanders,[12] which not being of any use, you send these very six thousand Dutch to them, with above half of the few of your own remaining in England; a third part of which half of which few you countermand, because you are again alarmed with the invasion, and yet let the six Dutch go, who came for no other end but to protect you.[13] And that our naval discretion may go hand in hand with our military: we find we have no force at home; we send for fifteen ships from the Mediterranean[14] to guard our coasts, and demand twenty from the Dutch. The first fifteen will be here perhaps in three months: of the twenty Dutch, they excuse all but six, of which six they send all but four;[15] and of your own small domestic fleet, five

9. Thomas Mathews (1676–1751), Vice-Adm. of the Red and commander-in-chief of the Mediterranean fleet since March 1742 (MANN i. 405, n. 11). The first part of this sentence alludes to events in Feb.–March 1744, the last part to the current situation.

10. In Feb. 1744; for its movements until it was dispersed by the great storm of 25–6 Feb. OS, see ibid. ii. 398 and n. 1, 402 and n. 8, 407 and n. 6, 423 and nn. 4–5. HW also wrote to Mann 18 June 1744 OS that 'the Brest squadron is making just as great a figure in our channel, as Matthews does before Toulon and Marseilles' (ibid. ii. 463).

11. These were sent for in Feb. 1744 and arrived in mid-March OS (ibid. ii. 400, nn. 13–14).

12. In winter quarters. Troops were sent for from Flanders during the invasion

crisis but were unable to embark before the storm ended the invasion threat (ibid. ii. 394 and n. 14, 408, 416, 423).

13. Six British regiments and the 6000 Dutch had been supposed to leave for Flanders 12 June OS, but in the face of reports of another French invasion attempt from Dunkirk only four regiments sailed immediately, reaching Ostend 18 June OS (ante 1 July 1744 NS, n. 10). The Dutch, however, followed them on the 24th OS (MANN ii. 449, n. 6).

14. The ships had been ordered home 24–5 May OS; they arrived in mid-September (ibid. ii. 458 and n. 14a, 477 and n. 7).

15. The British had requested 20 ships of the Dutch 14 April OS; the Dutch had replied by 11 June OS that they could supply only six, but these reached Spithead 12 July OS (ibid. ii. 458 and nn.

are going to the West Indies,[16] and twenty a-hunting for some Spanish ships,[17] that are coming from the Indies. Don't it put you in mind
of a trick, that is done by calculation? Think of a number; halve it:
double it: add ten: subtract twenty: add half the first number: take
away all you added: now what remains!

That you may not think I employ my time as idly as the great men
I have been talking of,[18] you must be informed that every night constantly I go to Ranelagh, which has totally beat Vauxhall. Nobody
goes anywhere else; everybody goes there. My Lord Chesterfield is
so fond of it, that he says he has ordered all his letters to be directed
thither.[19] If you had never seen it, I would make you a most pompous description of it, and tell you how the floor is all of beaten
princes; that you can't set your foot without treading on a Prince
of Wales or Duke of Cumberland.[20] The company is universal:
there is from his Grace of Grafton[21] down to children out of the
Foundling Hospital; from my Lady Townshend to the Kitten;[22] from
my Lord Sandys[23] to

Your humble cousin and sincere friend,

HOR. WALPOLE

15–16). HW's statement that they were, in
fact, sending only two is probably based
on some current rumour.

16. This was reported in the *Daily
Adv.* 31 May OS, but seems to be without
foundation.

17. This seems to be another unfounded
rumour. The *Daily Adv.* 27 June OS had
carried a report that 'a fleet of twenty
men of war are now ready to sail from
Spithead on a secret expedition' as well
as news that some Spanish warships
loaded with treasure were en route from
Cuba, but no attempt to intercept them
was made or apparently even contem-
plated.

18. The MS reads 'off.'

19. Lady Townshend wrote a week
earlier: 'Lord Chesterfield is grown so
excessively fond of Ranelagh that he goes

there every night and declares that he
designs to live there soon altogether' (to
Lady Denbigh 22 June OS, Hist. MSS
Comm., *Denbigh MSS*, 1911, p. 250).

20. Their most recent visits had been
23 and 27 June (*Daily Adv.* 25, 28 June
OS).

21. Charles Fitzroy (1683–1757), 2d D. of
Grafton.

22. (d. 1745), a prostitute, who was
about to become Dick Edgcumbe's mistress (SELWYN 56, n. 33, 66 and n. 3, 90).

23. Samuel Sandys (1695–1770), cr.
(1743) Bn Sandys; chancellor of the Exchequer, 1742–3. HW held him in particular contempt; see especially his 'Verses
Addressed to the House of Lords, On Its
Receiving a New Peer,' which he wrote at
the time of Sandys's peerage (MANN ii.
357–8).

From CONWAY, Saturday 18 July 1744 NS

Printed for the first time from the MS now WSL, formerly Rutnam. Dated by its position as a reply to HW's letter *ante* 29 June 1744 OS, by HW's reply to it *post* 20 July 1744 OS, and by the reference to the 'grand council of war' in progress, which took place 18 July NS (below, n. 3). The postmark is the date of the letter's arrival in London.

Address: To the Honourable Horatio Walpole in Arlington Street, London.
Postmark: IY 1 <?7>. AB.

Dear Horry,

IT'S pleasant to be forbid telling news when one has none to tell because one has the merit of obedience without the pain [of] keeping a secret. But by your care lest my letters should become a measure of government one would imagine you had received my last, for it's hardly possible to conceive that anybody should have so strange an imagination but myself. However, as I find you have a mind to be thought a good friend of the ministry, I shall now alter my tone and tell you that I have a better opinion of their parts and intelligence than to think they will give any attention to my nonsense if it should fall into their hands, which Heaven forbid! The verses you sent are so good and at the same time such arrant flattery to the ministers that, not to rob Mr Pope, I should really guess they were your own. The characters are very just and the similitude with those of the two doctors happy enough. I owned if you had not cautioned me against it I should have suspected you of malice a little in calling yourself a blockhead as I could not possibly understand it *à la lettre*.

I am sorry to find we agree so little in our politics, especially about the troops that you seem to envy us so much, for I own myself so selfish as to have lost all apprehensions of an invasion from the moment I left England and have contracted such an avidity for reinforcements that I could almost drain you to the last man; we really want 'em prodigiously and the great revolution that is begun in the affairs of Europe[1] will be but half effected at best, perhaps quite lost, unless we are able to do something, or to maintain ourselves at least

1. By Prince Charles's passage of the Rhine, which had caused the French to lessen their pressure on Flanders by sending reinforcements to their eastern frontiers.

here. The Dutch seem to be a little awake at present[2] and if we were just to take that opportunity to fall asleep, perhaps we mayn't soon find 'em so well disposed again. I should really fancy you had learnt your politics from some of the ladies at Ranalagh Gardens you are so vastly cautious; you would give up the Mediterranean, give up Flanders and not even suffer us to take a Caracca ship, and all for fear of an invasion which I believe the French think much less of than you.

We are now holding a grand council of war;[3] I don't know about what; if I hear anything of their deliberation that is worth your knowing I assure you you shall hear it in spite of your teeth. And do you know, by the by, that it's quite shocking to a man in Flanders to forbid him telling you news; it's all our dependence and the only chance we have of amusing you; swearing and talking bawdy, in which our humour chiefly consists, will not bear writing so well. You know we are no adepts at essays and for the history of our private life God knows it won't bear description. But, dear Horry, not by way of amusing you I must tell you a melancholy story of myself, which is nothing less than that I am absolutely ruined. My fortune of very small that it was is sunk to nothing at all at present,[4] and not the least prospect I doubt of seeing it mend. But *patienza!* I know a man may bustle through the world without it and as to the mere matter either of pride or conscience I really believe few people bear such a stroke with less concern than myself; with regard to one particular thing[5] which you'll guess without my naming I now begin to think

2. For the Dutch reinforcements supplied at this time, see *Oesterr. Erbfolge-krieg* vi. 400–1. Lt-Col. Russell wrote from Beerlegem 18 July NS, 'that the Dutch from England will be in Ghent tomorrow, and that some battalions from Holland are within five leagues of us, all which will sometime or other make up twenty thousand . . . they say they will assist us only in case we are attacked, but if we should act offensively, then they will not join us' (Hist. MSS Comm., *Frankland-Russell-Astley MSS*, 1900, p. 327).

3. There is an account of this council, which took place 18 July NS, in *Oesterr. Erbfolge-krieg* vi. 406–8. It was rather inconclusive.

4. When Conway was considering the purchase of a regiment the next year, he mentions his fortune as consisting of a 'little South Sea stock' worth about £1500 and producing some £60 a year (Conway to Lord Conway, 4, 11 Aug. 1745 NS, MSS now WSL, printed *Colburn's United Service Magazine*, 1880, lii pt ii. 320–24). Conway may have had a financial loss as a director of the opera; see *ante* 26, 31 Oct. 1741 OS, 1 July 1744 NS, n. 19, and MANN i. 190–1, ii. 226, 293–4.

5. Marriage to Lady Caroline Fitzroy. Conway had been in love with her since 1741 (MANN i. 221); the Countess of Hertford wrote the Countess of Pomfret 9 April 1741 OS, 'My Lord Conway is very soon to be married to Lady Bell Fitzroy; and the town says that Lady Caroline is resolved to make a double alliance, by

so seriously of it that I am upon the point of taking the most disagreeable resolutions for my own sake partly, but most for that of another person to whom without such a prospect as God knows I am from having at present in any degree I may perhaps be doing a daily injury; I know I ought to do this whatever it costs me. I feel, too, how hard it is to do it and in that dilemma know not how to resolve anything: perhaps, too, that which is designed most for her advantage might have a contrary appearance and that is the thing in the world I certainly would most cautiously avoid. Pray don't mention to anybody what I say upon this head; I could not help saying it to my dear Horry from whose friendship and good sense I expect both advice and consolation.

I hear from other people that your family is gone to Houghton[6] to which you leave me quite in the dark by not mentioning 'em at all.—I saw <a> letter t'other day from your father to the Marshal[7] and I own I was a li<ttle mo>rtified to find there was not the least mention made of me in it, it is n<ot> material to be sure and perhaps what I [ought] not to expect, but if he had but asked if he was content with me or hoped that I behaved well in his family, the least word of that kind would have showed some kindness. I beg you won't say anything of this remark of mine, because however the thing may be in itself my animadversion may be improper, as nothing is so ridiculous as to claim an attention that one is not entitled to.—

There is one thing I should be glad to know; I sometimes imagine he may think it an omission that I never write to him, which I should certainly if I dreamed of his looking upon it in that light or did not rather imagine he might think it forward or troublesome. Adieu.

H. C.

Oh. Here's Stanley[8] here. He's really a good-humoured creature. He asks after you and said he'd write you a postscript in my letter but he has forgot it so it's no matter.

marrying his younger brother' (Frances, Countess of Hertford and Henrietta Louisa, Countess of Pomfret, *Correspondence,* 1805, iii. 51–2).

6. Lord Orford had gone to Houghton 24 June OS (SELWYN 49).

7. Missing.

8. Hans Stanley (1721–80), diplomatist and politician; M.P. St Albans 1743–7, Southampton 1754–80. HW wrote to Sir Charles Hanbury Williams 14 Aug. 1744 OS: 'Mr Stanley came from the army last Wednesday' (ibid. 71).

To Conway, Friday 20 July 1744 OS

Printed from *Works* v. 15–18.

Arlington Street, July 20, 1744.

My dearest Harry,

I FEEL that I have so much to say to you, that I foresee there will be but little method in my letter; but if upon the whole you see my meaning, and the depth of my friendship for you, I am content.

It was most agreeable to me to receive a letter of confidence from you, at the time I expected a very different one from you; though, by the date of your last, I perceive you had not then received some letters, which though I did not see I must call simple, as they could only tend to make you uneasy for some months. I should not have thought of communicating a quarrel[1] to you at this distance; and I don't conceive the sort of friendship of those that thought it necessary. When I heard it had been wrote to you, I thought it right to myself to give you my account of it—but, by your brother's desire, suppressed my letter, and left it to be explained by him, who wrote to you so sensibly on it,[2] that I shall say no more; but that I think myself so ill used, that it will prevent my giving you thoroughly the advice you ask of me; for how can I be sure that my resentment might not make me see in a stronger light the reasons for your breaking off an affair, which you know before I never approved?

You know my temper is so open to anybody I love, that I must be happy at seeing you lay aside a reserve with me, which is the only point that ever made me dissatisfied with you. That silence of yours has, perhaps, been one of the chief reasons that has always prevented my saying much to you on a topic which I saw was so near your heart. Indeed, its being so near was another reason; for how could I expect you would take my advice, even if you bore it? But, my dearest Harry, how can I advise you now? Is it not gone too far for me to expect you should keep any resolution about it; especially in absence, which must be destroyed the moment you meet again? And if you ever should marry and be happy, won't you reproach me with

1. Apparently someone had written to Conway about HW's quarrel with Lady Caroline Fitzroy; HW alludes to it in a letter to Sir Charles Hanbury Williams

19 Sept. 1744 OS (SELWYN 82, 83). See also Conway's brief reference to it near the end of his reply *post* 5 Aug. 1744 NS.

2. Lord Conway's letter is missing.

having tried to hinder it?—I think you as just, and honest, as I think any man living. But any man living in that circumstance would think I had been prompted by private reasons. I see as strongly as you can, all the arguments for your breaking off; but indeed the alteration of your fortune adds very little strength to what they had before. You never had fortune enough to make such a step at all prudent: she loved you enough to be content with that; I can't believe this change will alter her sentiments, for I must do her the justice to say, that 'tis plain she preferred you with nothing to all the world. I could talk on upon this head; but I will only leave you to consider, without advising you on either side, these two things: whether you think it honester to break off with her after such engagements as yours (how strong I don't know), after her refusing very good matches[3] for you, and show her that she must think of making her fortune; or whether you will wait with her till some amendment in your fortune can put it in your power to marry her.

My dearest Harry, you must see why I don't care to say more on this head. My wishing it could be right for you to break off with her (for, without it is right, I would not have you on any account take such a step) makes it impossible for me to advise it; and therefore I am sure you will forgive my declining an act of friendship, which your having put in my power gives me the greatest satisfaction. But it does put something else in my power, which I am sure nothing can make me decline, and for which I have long wanted an opportunity. Nothing could prevent my being unhappy at the smallness of your fortune, but its throwing it into my way to offer you to share mine. As mine is so precarious, by depending on so bad a constitution, I can only offer you the immediate use of it. I do that most sincerely. My places still (though my Lord W. has cut off three hundred pounds a year[4] to save himself the trouble of signing his name ten times for

3. Possibly this refers to a missing letter from Conway; see also *post* 5 Aug. 1744 NS.

4. In his 'Account of my Conduct Relative to the Places I Hold under Government' HW writes, 'Before my father's quitting his post, he, at the instance of my eldest brother, Lord Walpole, had altered the delivery of exchequer bills from ten pounds to an hundred pounds. My deputy, after that alteration made, observed, that, as usher of the Exchequer, who furnishes the materials of Exchequer bills, on which, by the table of rates in the Exchequer, I had a stated profit, I should lose ten per cent which he represented to my father; who, having altered them to oblige my brother, would not undo what he had done; but to repair the prejudice I had suffered, Sir Robert, with his wonted equity and tenderness, determined to give me £2000 in lieu of what I lost, and would have added that legacy in a codicil to his will:—but

once) bring me in near two thousand pounds a year.[5] I have no debts, no connections; indeed no way to dispose of it particularly. By living with my father, I have little real use for a quarter of it. I have always flung it away all in the most idle manner. But, my dear Harry, idle as I am, and thoughtless, I have sense enough to have real pleasure in denying myself baubles, and in saving a very good income to make a man happy for whom I have a just esteem and most sincere friendship. I know the difficulties any gentleman and man of spirit must struggle with, even in having such an offer made him, much more in accepting it. I hope you will allow there are some in making it. But hear me: if there is any such thing as friendship in the world, these are the opportunities of exerting it, and it can't be exerted without 'tis accepted. I must talk of myself to prove to you that it will be right for you to accept it. I am sensible of having more follies and weaknesses and fewer real good qualities than most men. I sometimes reflect on this, though I own too seldom. I always want to begin acting like a man and a sensible one, which I think I might be if I would. Can I begin better, than by taking care of my fortune for one I love? You have seen (I have seen you have) that I am fickle, and foolishly fond of twenty new people: but I don't really love them: I have always loved you constantly: I am willing to convince you and the world, what I have always told you, that I loved you better than anybody. If I ever felt much for anything, which I know may be questioned, it was certainly for my mother. I look on you as my nearest relation by her, and think I can never do enough to show my gratitude and affection to her. For these reasons, don't deny me what I have set my heart on—the making your fortune easy to you.[6]

this happening only two days before his death, when he was little capable of making that codicil, my brother Lord Walpole engaged, at my father's desire, to pay me £400 a year; which not long after my brother redeemed for the intended £2000' (*Works* ii. 364).

5. In March 1745, when his father died, HW says that he received an additional £1300 per year in income, and that his total income was 'about £3300 a year clear' ('Short Notes,' GRAY i. 15). These figures would agree with his estimate of £2000 here. HW held the offices of usher of the Exchequer, worth between £900 and £1800 a year, and comptroller of the Pipe and clerk of the Estreats, worth about £300 together (ibid. i. 7–8 and nn. 36, 39).

6. According to *Works* 'the rest of this letter is wanting.'

From CONWAY, Wednesday 5 August 1744 NS

Printed from the MS now WSL, formerly Rutnam. First printed, *Rockingham Memoirs* i. 399–403.

Elsighem, Aug. 5, 1744.

My dear Horry,

I AM quite at a loss where to begin or how to thank you for all the vast goodness and friendship of your last; I know it is out of my power to do even that as I ought. Judge then how unhappy I must be in seeing it so impossible for me to do anything that can deserve the name of the smallest return for such an abundance of kindness! I know the little value set upon words on such occasions and therefore shall endeavour to trouble you with as few as possible. I know they are common to art and honesty, yet I flatter myself there is a simplicity in the genuine overflowings of a heart full of real gratitude that is not to be counterfeited: if there is, that I'm sure will speak for me on this occasion; besides I know amongst all your goodness for me you have had some opinion of my sincerity and if you have the least of the goodness of my heart you cannot doubt of my feeling everything that gratitude and friendship can make one feel for a real obligation. Nor is my joy inferior to either; a joy, my dear Horry, not arising from any thought of advantage that I intend to draw from it, but from the knowledge of having such a friend and seeing a proof of such goodness as I thought had no longer existence but in romances, a mere creature of the brain and that had long been banished from the hearts of men.

I have no alloy to my satisfaction on this occasion but the difficulty I have in refusing an offer pressed in so kind a manner and from one whom I know not only sincere in his intentions, but, from an excess of goodness, even desirous of putting himself to inconvenience on my account. But, dear Horry, how very unworthy should I think myself of that goodness if I were capable of accepting it? I see the art you use to lessen the value of the obligation by saying you have no use for it, and setting in a ridiculous light the manner in which you dispose of it. But as to the first, I know your income is by no means such an one as can bear an encumbrance of that kind; it's true, it's vastly more than is necessary for your sustenance; so is mine, and so is Tom Barny's,[1] but the inconvenience is retrenching; leaving the routine in which one set out, or living below one's rank and the expenses of the company one lives with: if you or I had been born a ditcher, we should have thought it no sort of hardship to live upon bread and cheese and bacon, and a plum pudding once a week, but as it is, our ideas, our appetites and our train of life is otherwise formed, and what would be luxury in one station is penance in another. But as to the other article, my dear Horry, look round the world, see of what kind the expenses of others are and then see if yours deserve the name you give 'em. Half the money in England is sacrificed to the vices of the first owners and the encouragement of it in others, to French vintners, French cooks and French whores, without enumerating all the train of follies that almost absorbs the other; while yours is disposed in a manner equally useful to society and honourable to yourself by encouraging in your sphere those arts that humanize mankind, or by supporting those with your charity who are real objects of compassion. I am too sensible of my own incapacity to make half so good an use of it and I should both rob them of the effects of your generosity and you of the pleasure of exercising it. I could use many other arguments; may not you think one time or other of changing your situation, may not you have a family to provide for? As to my own part, the thought of dependence is, I assure [you], by much the lightest argument with me against it, because I know you well enough to know you'd take care I should forget it; besides my mind begins to be formed a little to dependence. I find it is my lot and I must endeavour to bear it with as little reluctance as possible, and as this would be only a change of dependence, I could certainly place it nowhere so well as upon one whom I even feel a pleasure in being obliged to, as I would be bound to him by all possible ties. I hope then, my dear Horry, you will forgive my refusing you now perhaps the only request I shall refuse you in my life; and as I know the steadiness of your desire to serve me, I cannot help making it mine to you that you will not think of pressing me any more upon this head, as my resolution is absolutely fixed and as that is the only sort of acknowledgment I cannot make on this occasion.

1. HW's servant, who had accompanied him to Italy, and was now at Bath 'patching together some very bad remains of a worn-out constitution.' He had died or retired by 1753 (MANN i. 101 and n. 20, ii. 498, iv. 396).

As to the other affair[2] about which I wrote to you, I thank you a thousand times for the interest you take in it; but am sorry to find any consideration should make you think it necessary to use the least reserve on that subject which, as my situation at present is not such as makes it necessary, I beg you will avoid for the future. As to engagements, I really have none with her but such as may be construed to arise from the circumstances you mention, and as her honour is by no means hurt by our intercourse, I don't look upon mine as absolutely bound, especially considering the light in which we stand at present, the difficulties that oppose themselves to our marriage and the inconvenience arising to her from it at best; and as to the matches refused, it must be owned that they were such as indeed were advantageous in regard to fortune, but such as in every other light she ought in prudence to refuse. Thus much on this side the question; on the other an acquaintance carried on like ours, with a knowledge of each other['s] inclinations, may strictly be looked upon as a sort of engagement. I find you have no great opinion of my resolution, and indeed my behaviour on some occasions relating to this affair, which I fancy you may have known something of, has not been such as could give you a very great one. But at present with regard to that I really think, at least at present, that I am capable of keeping one, if I thought it absolutely necessary; and as to bearing what may be said, I do assure you, my dear Horry, it is impossible for you to say anything upon it that I should either imagine proceeded from any motive but that of serving me (I have too good proof of your love!) or remember afterwards to the prejudice of our friendship in any degree. What you mention, our happiness afterwards, is certainly the grand point; and as it is one of such infinite consequence, I expect from your friendship that you will say everything to me that you think or know that may relate to it without concealing the least tittle that you think it better for me to hear. You know, I believe, the doubts I have formerly had on that head, and though I cannot accuse her of anything lately that could revive 'em, you know 'tis easier to revive 'em, than to form such; and 'tis impossible to promise oneself that they would not grow again and even more strongly in another situation. I shall say no more: you see I speak very freely to you, and beg above all things you will use no

2. With Lady Caroline Fitzroy.

sort of reserve to me. By what you said I should imagine she was concerned in the affair that passed lately between you and Shane[3] which I assure you is the first I have heard of it, if it was so.

We have at length passed the Scheld,[4] which is looked upon as our Rubicon, and are now advanced within about three leagues of the enemy's camp.[5] Tomorrow's march will bring us pretty near 'em[6] but with the Lys between us, so that I fancy no consequence will immediately follow from it. Adieu. Another time I'll write to you more fully of these things.

H. C.

To CONWAY, ca Monday 6 August 1744 OS

Missing; answered *post* 2 Sept. 1744 NS. From Conway's reply it would seem that this was probably written before HW had learned of Frederick II's invasion of Bohemia.

3. Apparently a nickname for Conway's half-sister, the Hon. Jane Conway. Conway uses the same name in writing to his brother 4 Aug. 1745 NS: 'Adieu, my dear brother, tell Shane I have received hers' (MS now WSL). HW mentions his quarrel with her to Sir C. H. Williams 19 Sept. 1744 OS: 'I was only sorry Miss E. was innocently drawn into it by those two fools Lady Caroline Fitzroy and Jenny Conway' (SELWYN 82).

4. 31 July NS (*Oesterr. Erbfolge-krieg* vi. 422).

5. At Courtrai, about 8 miles from the English troops at this moment (ibid. vi. 425).

6. Contrary to expectation, the Allied army did not advance towards Courtrai but turned south on the 6th and encamped near Estaimbourg about 6 miles north of Tournai (ibid. vi. 429).

From CONWAY, Wednesday 2 September 1744 NS

Printed from the MS now WSL, formerly Rutnam. First printed, *Rockingham Memoirs* i. 403–5.

Address: To the Honourable Horatio Walpole, Jun., in Arlington Street, London.

Memoranda (by HW):[1] Miss T[ownshend]
                    Mr Chute
                    Mr Ashton
                    Sir Ch. Williams
                    Mr Edgcumbe
                    Mr Conway
Another list of five items has been heavily deleted and is illegible.

Chateau d'Anstain,[2] Sept. 2d 1744.

Dear Horry,

NOTHING is so true as what you prophesy about us;[3] I did not quite think so when I received yours, but I assure [you] I am now almost convinced that we neither shall nor can do anything. Thanks to the King of Prussia, Prince Charles has repassed the Rhine,[4] the French are coming back again, and we shall shortly be just where we were some months ago. I am in such a rage at that anointed highwayman, that filthy King of Prussia, that I could tear him to pieces. I want to have him poisoned, massacred, racked; noth-

1. This is apparently a list of letters received or written. 'Miss T.,' 'Mr Ashton,' and 'Mr Conway' have been crossed out. Of the persons mentioned we know that HW had received Chute's letter of 15 Aug. 1744 NS by 1 Sept. OS (MANN ii. 506), but his answer has not been found (CHUTE 51–3); he had received two letters from Sir Charles Hanbury Williams, both missing, to which he replied 19 Sept. OS; he received letters from Richard Edgcumbe of 10 Aug. and 10 Sept. OS, but his replies have not been recovered (SELWYN 65–7, 78–83); and he would have received the present letter from Conway about 30 Aug. OS. We have no record of correspondence with Ashton or Miss Mary Townshend in 1744: but HW apparently wrote about Mary Townshend in his letter of ca 13 Sept. to Conway; see Conway's answer *post* 7 Oct. and n. 13. This letter to Conway parallels HW's letter of 19 Sept. OS to

Sir C. H. Williams, in which he tells of visiting the Townshends's seat in Norfolk, Raynham Hall.

2. Anstaing, southeast of Lille, headquarters of the British forces since 10 Aug. NS; they remained there until 29 Sept. NS (Hist. MSS Comm., *Frankland-Russell-Astley MSS*, 1900, pp. 331, 341).

3. Presumably that there would be no battle with the French; HW wrote to Mann 6 Aug. 1744 OS that he was 'convinced' there would be none (MANN ii. 496).

4. 23 Aug. NS at Beinheim; the French army learned of it the 28th (ibid. ii. 505, n. 2a; J.-L.-A. Colin, 'Les Campagnes du Maréchal de Saxe,' *Revue d'histoire rédigée à l'État-Major de l'armée (section historique)*, Aug. 1903, xi. 291). Frederick II had re-entered the war by invading Bohemia, and Prince Charles had been recalled to help defend that front.

ing could satisfy me about him—don't you feel just the same? Is there any bearing it? I hate politics of all things—they are now upon that abominable footing—to see all the affairs of Europe take a new face just as the phlegm or gall of one foolish fellow is uppermost! It sets the world in so ridiculous a light, and so depreciates the dignity of human nature, that there is no seeing it with patience. And yet I think it ought to give one patience too, for it teaches one that there is nothing in this great world that deserves a moment's care or a moment's dependence: kings, empires, states, ministries, and armies, all appear to me now in the light of fine raree-shows, that one may divert oneself a little with, provided one has no interest in 'em; but from the moment you have that, the scene changes and they become a group of tyrants, fools, pickpockets, and butchers. Yet through this crowd of villainy one must be content to bustle, and the best way to get through it is to think of it as little as possible. One should take the world as one does a dose of physic, hold one's nose and not taste it a bit if possible.5 I speak now of the great world, I mean the public, for my ideas of private life are very different. I think it's impossible to make the first a foundation for one solid satisfaction, and I think the other, well managed, affords a thousand.—And apropos to that, I thank you a thousand times for all your goodness in your last, but you shock me when you talk of determining to live so as to have it in your power to do things for me which your goodness inclines you to do, but which I have already told you I could never think of accepting. No, my dear Horry, don't think of it, I beseech you, and as the benefit is intended for me, oblige me more by resolving to live in all respects in the way that is most agreeable to yourself, for I do assure you I never should be easy a moment if I thought you changed the least tittle in your way or your schemes of life on my account.—My

5. Conway gave vent to similar reflections in a letter to his brother 22 Aug. 1744 NS: 'You see how this great world is the sport of chance and how the powers of Europe seem to be playing a game at whist for empire. Sometimes one side has a good hand and the game is their own . . . next minute it's just the contrary . . . then they cut in and cut out and change partners. *Dieu sait comment!* It's really a miserable affair; and to one who reflects seriously upon it the most mortifying proof of human little-ness: today we are drunk with joy, we fire our guns, P. Charles has passed the Rhine, and we think ourselves at the gates of Paris! Tomorrow what? All this fair fabric is destroyed: no miracle, no missionary from heaven to stop our career but the fumes of champagne or of his own gall have turned the head of as mere a mortal as you or me and he says it shall be otherwise! My comfort is he must come to be hanged and so much for him' (MS now WSL).

fortune is certainly small; it's nothing at all; so is that of a thousand people that I see every day of equal rank with myself; and I shall make it my business to adapt my views and my desires to it. As to one certain point,[6] you know that was not the only difficulty I had upon it and in the end who knows but I may be as happy as I am, as if things had taken quite another turn. You know I was always a sort of philosopher, for which you laugh at me, but it really has its use, and I really hope to be one time or other the better for it.—By this time you are at Houghton;[7] I want to know how you amuse yourself there; do you think it possible one should wish to be with you there? I assure [you] I do extremely. I wish it for itself very much and for your company; and I wish it too by way of not being here; this is really dreadful! For diversion, would you think it? we do no earthly thing[8] but play at whisk with the Marshal quite *en famille* every evening.[9] He is vastly good, but you feel what that is. Adieu! dear Horry; we can do nothing I doubt and heaven knows how I long to have this farce over.

My compliments to Lord Orford and Lady Mary, to Mrs Leneve, etc.

To CONWAY, ca Thursday 13 September 1744 OS

Missing; answered *post* 7 Oct. 1744 NS. Conway mentions that HW complained of his 'campaign of three weeks' at Houghton, which indicates that the letter was written about three weeks after HW arrived at Houghton ca 22 Aug. OS. The content of this letter apparently parallels HW's letter of 19 Sept. OS to Sir Charles Hanbury Williams (SELWYN 80–3).

6. Marriage.
7. HW left London for Houghton 20 Aug. OS and arrived ca the 22d (DAL-RYMPLE 23; SELWYN 72).
8. The MS reads 'think.'
9. Lt-Col. Russell wrote to his wife two days later that Wade's table 'at best is a bad one, and scarce any of the general officers dine there unless they can't avoid it. Yesterday, I was obliged to go by invitation of the aides-de-camp, but it was doing penance' (*Frankland MSS*, pp. 337–8).

From CONWAY, Wednesday 7 October 1744 NS

Printed for the first time from the MS now WSL, formerly Rutnam. The post-mark is the date of the letter's arrival in London.

Address: To the Honourable Horatio Walpole, Jun., in Arlington Street, London. Pour l'Angleterre.

Postmark: OC 1. AB.

Huysse,[1] Oct. 7, NS.

Dear Horry,

I PERCEIVE your campaign of three weeks is almost as tiresome to you as ours of God knows how many months, I hate to count 'em. I have told you already how differently I should have thought of it, but about ours at least I believe there could not possibly be two opinions; but that you should grow tired of the country just when you have found out that you love it, that's new and diverts me vastly, as well as your solitary coursing![2] You'll certainly become a prodigious sportsman. I assure you I think this quite serious and am under some apprehensions of seeing you buried in the country, quite swallowed up like poor Tory[3] by those human bears called country gentlemen. It's true you pretend you can't bear the company[4] but when one has a thorough taste for anything one easily grows to like those who follow it, and that this is your case, that you are quite gone in it is plain. Most people carry on the farce of hunting as we do that of fighting—for mere glory and in order that the world should see what fools they are—but when a man is capable of enjoying it by himself I look upon his case to be quite desperate; however, I have some hopes from your going to town so soon;[5] the winter may civilize you a little.—I thought our blossom of war had fallen some time, I mean in Flanders, but of late it has taken all of a sudden to blow again with this *Été de St Martin,* and flourishes to a degree; you

1. 11 miles SW of Ghent.
2. 'I have found riding so necessary for my health, which was very poor when I came out of town, that I go a-coursing constantly every morning and by letting nobody go with me but my own footman who knows no more of it than I do, I have imprinted a mysterious awe upon it, and pass for a whimsical gentleman that loves nothing but solitary country

diversions' (HW to Sir C. H. Williams 19 Sept. 1744 OS, SELWYN 80–1).
3. For this incident see *ante* 18 Nov. 1739 NS and n. 2.
4. For HW on the subject of country gentlemen, see his letter to Chute 20 Aug. 1743 OS (CHUTE 42–4).
5. HW returned to London the second week of October (*post* 6 Oct. 1744 OS; MANN ii. 518).

know what a bloody resolution we marched with t'other day to Pont d'Espierre,[6] and now we are following 'em God knows whither; we are advanced within a league of Deynse upon the Lys, which post they have abandoned,[7] and now have collected their whole force at Courtrai. Tomorrow, I believe, we shall pass the Lys and I suppose march towards Courtrai at least,[8] where it seems to be uncertain whether they will stay or not.[9]—They give us great hopes of the Czarina[10] but I believe nothing can be expected from her this campaign.[11] And so ends my chapter of politics.

Poor Lady Thingum![12] was ever such a foolish girl! and how all the old virgins who have choked bastards by the dozen will crow and peck at her? *Cela fait pitié!* And I'll warrant her good mother tells her she'll be damned a thousand times for so enormous a crime, and her sensible father-in-law forgot it the next day!

I agree with you entirely about Molly Townshend.[13] I think noth-

---

6. This battle alarm occurred 1 Oct. NS, but the Allied army found the enemy gone (*Oesterr. Erbfolge-krieg* vi. 470; Hist. MSS Comm., *Frankland-Russell-Astley MSS*, 1900, p. 342).

7. On 4 Oct. NS, after advancing to a point slightly north the previous day; the Allied army had advanced towards Deynse on the 6th (*Oesterr. Erbfolge-krieg* vi. 471, 476).

8. The army did not move again until 15 Oct. NS, when it began retiring towards winter quarters (ibid. vi. 477).

9. The French abandoned Courtrai 9 Oct. NS for lack of forage (ibid. vi. 476).

10. Elizabeth (1709–61 OS), Empress of Russia 1741–61, had moved towards a rapprochement with England and the Allies after the disgrace of La Chétardie, the French ambassador, in June (for which see MANN ii. 494–5 and nn. 3–6). In late Sept. NS it was known in Holland that she had promised to supply 12,000 troops, and rumours of their 'speedy' marching were current; at the beginning of October the Russian minister to the States General confirmed his mistress's intention of honouring her commitment and the British minister at Brussels 'declared in public that the Court of Russia has not only granted to his Britannic Majesty the succour of 12,000 men stipulated by treaty [that of 1742], but that it

will also furnish the Queen of Hungary with a like number of troops' (ibid. ii. 499, n. 10; *Daily Adv.* 22 Sept. OS *sub* Hague 27 Sept. NS, 29 Sept. OS *sub* Petersburg 15 Sept. [?OS], 1 Oct. OS *sub* Hague 6 Oct. NS, 4 Oct. OS *sub* Brussels 5 Oct. NS).

11. Conway is correct; Russia pleaded the lateness of the season as an excuse for delaying the troops and contented herself with exorting the Elector of Saxony to assist Maria Theresa (MANN ii. 512, n. 8a; GM 1744, xiv. 566). No Russian troops were actually sent until 1748, too late to be of use (*post* 29 April 1748 NS, n. 13).

12. The *dramatis personæ* of this scandal have not been identified. A paragraph in the *Daily Adv.* 1 Oct. OS may relate to it: 'The waiting-woman of a lady of quality near Blyth in Yorkshire is committed to Nottingham Gaol, with another woman, an accomplice, for the murder of a bastard child, which they put into a bandbox and threw into a fish pond, where it was lately found.'

13. Hon. Mary Townshend (*ante* 31 Oct. 1741 OS, n. 23). HW writes 19 Sept. OS to Sir C. H. Williams about a visit to the Townshends's seat in Norfolk, Raynham Hall (SELWYN 81–3), and possibly wrote a similar account to Conway in his letter of ca 13 Sept. OS.

ing is so clever and so good-natured. I agree with you a good deal about t'other[14] too; he's very good-natured!

I writ to your father last post;[15] I thought it was better to do it, at least that there could be no harm in it.

At present I am full of curiosity to know how all this will end, and particularly to be at some certainty about our coming over: I believe our affairs will not be of very long duration and, as the Parliament meets soon,[16] flatter myself it will not be very long before I see you, which I assure you, my dear Horry, I long to do more than ever, to thank you for all your goodness and to give you all possible proofs how sincerely I am obliged to you. I assure you I dread Marshal Onslow[17] as much as you can possibly do, but even that I can forget when I think of returning to my friends. Adieu!

Yours affectionately,

H. C.

To CONWAY, Saturday 6 October 1744 OS

Printed from *Works* v. 18–19.

Houghton, Oct. 6, 1744.

My dearest Harry,

MY Lord[1] bids me tell you how much he is obliged to you for your letter, and hopes you will accept my answer for his. I'll tell you what, we shall both be obliged to you if you will enclose a magnifying glass in your next letters; for your two last[2] were in so

14. Perhaps one of the Townshends.
15. The letter, which Conway inadvertently addressed to Downing Street, is missing; see *post* 6 Oct. 1744 OS and 28 Oct. 1744 NS.
16. Parliament had been further prorogued 20 Sept. OS until 27 Nov. OS (GM 1744, xiv. 505), but the news of this delay had perhaps not yet reached Flanders.
17. Arthur Onslow (1691–1768), M.P. Guildford 1720–7, Surrey 1727–61; Speaker of the House of Commons 1728–61. HW, who frequently ridiculed Onslow at this

time, had written to Sir Charles Hanbury Williams 19 Sept. OS that he hoped the exercise he was following at Houghton would make him 'strong enough to go through a winter of Waller, Admiral Vernon and the Speaker' (SELWYN 81).

1. Sir Robert Walpole, first Earl of Orford (HW).
2. *Ante* 2 Sept. and 7 Oct. NS. Conway's handwriting is especially small in these letters; see *post* 28 Oct. NS.

diminutive a character, that we were forced to employ all Mrs Leneve's spectacles, besides an ancient family reading-glass with which
my grandfather[3] used to begin the psalm, to discover what you said
to us. Besides this, I have a piece of news for you: Sir Robert Walpole, when he was made Earl of Orford, left the ministry, and with it
the palace in Downing Street;[4] as numbers of people found out three
years ago, who not having your integrity were quick in perceiving the
change of his situation. Your letter was full as honest as you; for,
though directed to Downing Street, it would not, as other letters
would have done, address itself to the present possessor. Do but
think if it had! The smallness of the hand would have immediately
struck my Lord Sandys[5] with the idea of a plot; for what he could
not read at first sight, he would certainly have concluded must be
cipher.

I march next week towards London, and have already begun to
send my heavy artillery before me, consisting of half a dozen books
and part of my linen; my light horse commanded by Patapan follows
this day sennight. A detachment of hussars surprised an old bitch
fox yesterday morning, who had lost a leg in a former engagement;
and then having received advice of another litter being advanced as
far as Dasingham,[6] Lord Walpole commanded Captain Riley's[7] horse
with a strong party of fox-hounds to overtake them: but on the approach of our troops the enemy stole off, and are now encamped at
Sechford common, whither we every hour expect orders to pursue
them.

My dear Harry, this is all I have to tell you, and to my great joy,
which you must forgive me, is full as memorable as any part of the
Flanders campaign.[8] I do not desire to have you engaged in the least
more glory than you have been. I should not love the remainder of
you the least better for your having lost an arm or a leg; and have
as full persuasion of your courage as if you had contributed to the
slicing off twenty pair from French officers. Thank God, you have
sense enough to content yourself without being a hero; though I

3. Col. Robert Walpole (ca 1650–1700).
4. Conway had made a similar slip in
his letter to HW *ante* 25 Sept. 1743 NS.
5. Samuel Sandys, made chancellor of
the Exchequer on the resignation of Sir
Robert Walpole in February 1741 [*sic*],
and afterwards created Lord Sandys (HW).

He was now of course living in Downing
Street.
6. Dersingham, Norfolk.
7. Not identified.
8. Mr Conway was now with the Allied
army in Flanders (HW).

don't quite forget your expedition a-hussar-hunting the beginning of this campaign.⁹—Pray, no more of those jaunts! I don't know anybody you would oblige with a present of such game: for my part, a fragment of the oldest hussar on earth should never have a place in my museum; they are not antique enough: and for a live one, I must tell you I like my raccoon infinitely better.

Adieu, my dear Harry! I long to see you.—You will easily believe, the thought I have of being particularly well with you is a vast addition to my impatience; though you know it is nothing new to me to be overjoyed at your return.

Yours ever,

HOR. WALPOLE

From CONWAY, Monday 19 October 1744 NS

Printed for the first time from the MS now WSL, formerly Rutnam.
Address: To the Honourable Horatio Walpole, Jun., in Arlington Street, London, Angleterre.
Postmark: OC 22.

Dronghen,¹ Oct. 19, 1744.

Dear Horry,

I HAVE no right to trouble you again but that it seems a long time to me since I have writ or heard from you,² nor nothing to tell you but what I suppose you know already, that at last our tedious, loitering campaign is over; most of our troops are already gone into garrison³ and tomorrow we shall bring up the rear and march into Ghent where the Marshal intends staying about a fortnight and where I doubt I must stay that fortnight with him.⁴ Afterwards I fancy he will go to The Hague and as I believe he will not want us there, I hope about that time to be preparing for my journey homewards; and shall expect to find you by that time at least in town, if

9. Conway describes this expedition *ante* 3 June 1744 NS.

1. Dronghem, where the English troops had moved 15 Oct. NS (*Oesterr. Erbfolgekrieg* vi. 477).

2. Conway would not yet have received HW's letter of 6 Oct. 1744 OS.

3. The English troops began the march to winter quarters at Brussels, Ghent, and Bruges on 17 Oct. NS (ibid. vi. 478).

4. Wade released Conway 30 Oct. NS (*post* 31 Oct. 1744 NS).

you are not there already. But I suppose you will be one of the first housed. I was extremely sorry to hear by one Mr Gardiner[5] who is of a Norfolk family that your father has been out of order[6] but I hope it is not of consequence; he says that he talks of staying at Houghton all the year but as I hear nothing of it from you I am in hopes that is not true.

Amidst all my desire to return I think with more dread of Marshal Onslow every day than another; here's such work for our polemic geniuses in Parliament that I'm sure they'll wear us out before the winter is half over; besides, I suppose we shall be pulled to pieces for not fighting by the mob great and small. I hear even the ministry are Arembergians[7] and if so we shall have a blessed time of it! Mr Trevor says we had better have sacrificed five or six thousand men though no good consequence had been expected from it than not, and if the same Christian spirit reigns throughout, it's easy to guess what turn things will take, if the Duke d'Aremberg can persuade the ministry that he was always for action and the Mars[hal] against it, and they are so fighting mad as to wish for it upon such terms. I own I am far from believing the first and can less agree with the reasonableness of murthering five thousand Englishmen to secure the power or even the necks of any one or any five or six in the world; I look upon soldiers as men and not as beasts of burthen, and I could wish that those who think so lightly of their merit or their service were to make a trial of what they undergo—but I beg pardon for tormenting you with any of this stuff before your time: God knows you are doomed to hear enough of it.

---

5. Possibly a relative of the Rev. John Gardiner who was chaplain to Lord Walpole at Crostwight, east Norfolk, and rector of Great Massingham (R. W. Ketton-Cremer, *Norfolk Portraits*, 1944, p. 110; R. A. Austen-Leigh, *Eton College Register 1698–1752*, Eton, 1927, p. 136).

6. HW told Mann 26 Nov. OS that Lord Orford had 'this whole summer been troubled with bloody water upon the least motion' (MANN ii. 538 and n. 20).

7. The joint command of the troops in Flanders had been split by dissensions during the entire campaign, each group—English, Austrian, and Dutch—blaming the others for the failure to achieve success. The summary of the campaign in *Oesterr. Erbfolge-krieg* vi. 479–81 distributes the blame about equally among all parties, but the English writers blame Arenberg rather than Wade for the repeated delays. See, for example, C. T. Atkinson, *History of the Royal Dragoons*, Glasgow, [1934], p. 162; J. W. Fortescue, *History of the British Army*, 1910–30, ii. 106–7; Evan Charteris, *William Augustus, Duke of Cumberland*, 1913, pp. 158–9. Conway's fears of Parliamentary attacks, however, proved groundless, since the dismissal of Granville in November and the subsequent reorganization of the ministry removed the chief grievances of the Opposition.

You have heard me talk some time of coming somewhere a little nearer the Parliament House and I am in a manner resolved to execute it this winter. As you were to be the first of my friends in town I had thoughts of troubling you to find me out a convenient lodging or rather a little snug and very cheap house if one could find such a thing about Pall Mall on towards you in St James's Street: but my old lodgings are taken till Christmas, I think, so it will be time enough when I come to town, I suppose, to go about it. I shall have some regret in leaving Mr Smith[8] but it's such a journey from the House that it's terrible. Adieu, dear Horry, I long vastly to see you and shall count the moments with impatience till my return; so believe me in the meantime

Sincerely and affectionately yours,

H. C.

From CONWAY, Wednesday 28 October 1744 NS

Printed for the first time from the MS now WSL, formerly Rutnam. The postmark is the date of the letter's arrival in London.

Address: To the Honourable Horatio Walpole, Jun., in Arlington Street, London, Angleterre.

Postmark: OC 22.   GAND.

Oct. 28, 1744.

My dear Horry,

YOU tell me the strangest things in the world; sure you joke; it's impossible I should have directed my letter to Downing Street! However, what you say upon that is literally true; I love and respect Lord Orford exactly as I did Sir Robert Walpole and exactly the same in Downing Street as in Arlington Street or in any other part of the world and I hope it does not sound like bragging of any extraordinary honesty when I say that my regard for him or for any of my friends does not depend upon change of place, in any sense, or upon loss of it. What Lord Sandys would have taken my letter for, provided it was not a compliment to him, I am very indifferent, but I hope Lord Orford took it for what it was meant: a sincere profession

8. Conway's landlord. The change of lodging apparently did not take place, since Conway mentions leaving books with Mr Smith *post* 18 April 1745 OS.

of my regard for him and if that was intelligible in it I am quite easy about the rest; for the story that I told was really not worth deciphering. But the reason of my writing so small a hand was that I had used myself to take down the orders of the day in a small book and in a very great hurry, which had made me take up that hand for convenience. I don't know whether I am much more intelligible at present but at least I think my hand is, without vanity, something larger.[1]

As to the affair of Dasingham which you write me word of, I don't know which to applaud more, the conduct of the leader or the ability of the historian. But I assure you I am a little in pain about the event; you speak as if you were to be yourself upon the expedition[2] and after the idea you have already given me of your sportly genius I think it would not be quite impossible to persuade one you have been a-fox-hunting; but God forbid! Dear Horry, content yourself with coursing, or, if you will, let even that alone. I do not desire to have you engaged in the least more glory than you have been; I should not love the rest of you the least better for having lost an arm or a leg, or have as full a persuasion of your courage as if you had been at the death of fifty brace of foxes or broke your neck in the cause!

By this time, I suppose, you are come or coming to town; I am glad to think I shall find you there, though as yet I don't know when I shall come. I cannot decently think of leaving the Marshal before he goes, which I doubt will not be sooner than a fortnight. I wish you could see a letter that I send to Lady Mary by this post; if you should be at Houghton I desire you will not hint that you know anything of it but it's really curious; it's writ by one Mrs Mary Doyne, an officer's servant here, who is such a mistress of the epistolary style that several gentlemen have employed her to write. It is a sort of journal or rather history of the campaign, and I assure you quite a masterpiece.

Adieu, dear Horry. I long for nothing more than to see you and to assure you how sincerely I am

Yours ever,

H. C.

1. It is at least twice as large.
2. HW writes to Sir C. H. Williams 19 Sept. 1744 OS, 'How I shall do tomorrow, when I begin hunting, I can't tell' (SELWYN 81).

From CONWAY, Saturday 31 October 1744 NS

Printed for the first time from the MS now WSL, formerly Rutnam. The post-mark is the date of the letter's arrival in London.

Address: To the Honourable Horatio Walpole, Jun., in Arlington Street, London, Angleterre.

Postmark: OC 27.

Memoranda (by HW, probably notes for an otherwise missing letter):

Lord Granville	D. of Newcastle[2]	Lord Litchfield[3]	Capt. Thomas[5]
D. of Richmond[1]	Som[erset] House	Mr Tilson[4]	Mr Chomley[6]

Ghent, Oct. 31, 1744.

Dear Horry,

YOU'LL be surprised to hear from me again so soon but some little alteration having happened in my schemes since I wrote last I could not help letting you know it; I told you, I believe, in my last that I had not thought it decent, having no particular business to plead, to ask the Marshal to let me go, but yesterday he told me of himself he wondered I had not thought of going yet and upon my answering that I had not thought proper to ask while I thought he had any commands for me here, he replied very good-naturedly that he desired my modesty might not hinder me from doing as I liked, upon which I immediately resolved to set out if I could conveniently in a few days; he has writ for his yacht some time so that if he should happen to go himself within a week I should still wait for him, but I fancy it will be longer before he goes,[7] especially as he has not been out of his room almost since his arrival here and though he is

---

1. Charles Lennox (1701–50), 2d D. of Richmond.

2. Thomas Pelham Holles (1693–1768), 2d Bn Pelham, cr. (1715) D. of Newcastle.

3. George Henry Lee (1718–72), 3d E. of Lichfield, 1743. He was the centre of some conversation at this time for his approaching marriage (16 Jan. 1745 OS) in the face of his mother's opposition to Dinah Frankland, since he was fourth in descent from Charles I while Miss Frankland was fourth in descent from Cromwell (GEC vii. 646, n. *e* and references there cited).

4. Possibly the Rev. George Tilson (ca 1715–78), a contemporary of HW's at Eton and Cambridge, chaplain at Hampton

Court, chaplain of the Royal Dragoons 1748–60 (Venn, *Alumni Cantab.*; C. T. Atkinson, *History of the Royal Dragoons,* Glasgow, [1934], p. 506).

5. Possibly John Thomas who from Capt. in the 10th regiment of Foot became Lt in the Coldstream Guards 12 July 1739 OS, Capt.-Lt 17 Feb. 1748 OS, Capt. 28 Nov. 1749 OS, Maj. 1762, Lt-Col. 1763, Lt-Gov. of Fort St Philip, Minorca, 1777 (Daniel MacKinnon, *Origin and Services of the Coldstream Guards,* 1833, ii. 480–1; Hist. MSS Comm., *Frankland-Russell-Astley MSS,* 1900, p. 366).

6. Perhaps the Hon. Robert Cholmondeley (see *post* 14 Aug. 1747 NS, n. 5).

7. Wade did not return to London until 25 Nov. OS (*Daily Adv.* 27 Nov. OS).

not at present very ill, it must take some time before he can think of undertaking his journey. I need not repeat how real a pleasure I shall have in finding myself among my friends nor how particular an one in seeing my dear Horry and thanking him a thousand times for all his goodness and friendship, which I wish I could pay in any other coin than that of the most sincere acknowledgments and gratitude. I long to talk to you of a thousand things, too, as my situation at present is really a little bizarre though I assure you all considered, I have not many uneasy moments about it. I have, thank God, a little natural stock of philosophy that I hope will always put it out of the power of fortune, I mean as far as regards fortune only, to make me unhappy. And for the rest, time perhaps may make everything easy in some shape or other.

Adieu, dear Horry. Having troubled you so very lately I fancy you'll not be sorry that I am obliged to finish. I have no doubt about finding you in London. So, dear Horry,

Jusqu'à revoir,

Yours sincerely,

H. C.

From CONWAY, Thursday 18 April 1745 OS

Printed from the MS now WSL, formerly Rutnam. First printed, *Rockingham Memoirs* i. 406–8; reprinted *Colburn's United Service Magazine*, 1880, lii pt i. 473–4. The year is supplied by the letter *post* 14 May NS, which this one obviously precedes.

Memoranda:
35	– 10	– 6
80	– 1	– 6
115	– 12	– 0

The signature 'R. Walpole' is also written a number of times on the blank sheet, as though someone were trying to copy a frank or signature.

Dover, April 18.

Dear Horry,

I DON'T know whether you'll thank me for writing from this cursed place, where I find no earthly thing to tell you and can write nothing but complaints, but if I have nothing to say on one hand I have so little to do on t'other, that I don't know how I could answer passing so many idle hours without letting my friends hear something of me and if I have no hopes of amusing you, I know you will excuse my trying to amuse myself by writing to you, though it be a little at your expense. I was so fortunate as to arrive here the very day that the wind changed to the east,[1] after continuing in the west for two months successively, and have the comfort of hearing from most of the sailors here, that it is likely to continue in this quarter a fortnight or three weeks. To add to the agreeableness of this situation, the army is now actually in the field,[2] and in all probability marched to the relief of Mons, which they say has been some time invested by the French,[3] and consequently it is not very unlikely that there may be some action[4] before we get up to it. I am not fonder of broken bones than my neighbours but yet really am very uneasy in this situation, and wish a thousand times I had never heard of Mr Pelham, the Parliament, and the no-business that kept me so long in London,[5] though I must have the gratitude to own I was as much obliged to 'em then as I am angry at 'em now and at myself for being so. Don't you pity me excessively with all my distresses and *ennuis* about me, and no sort of amusement or occupa-

1. Which it did on 12 or 13 April; from the 13th until the 27th it blew generally from the northeast, when it again changed to westerly for a few days (*Daily Adv.* April *passim*). Conway seems to have managed to sail on the 20th, however (Richard Lyttelton to Sir Thomas Lyttelton 23 April OS, quoted in Maud Wyndham, *Chronicles of the Eighteenth Century*, 1924, i. 132–3).

2. This does not seem to be true; at a council of war 29 April NS (the day of this letter) it was decided to march towards Tournai, and the army began to move on the 30th NS (F. H. Skrine, *Fontenoy*, 1906, p. 142; GM 1745, xv. 223, 246).

3. Conway seems to have been misled by reports from the army similar to that sent to England by the D. of Cumberland 23 April NS: 'By all the intelligence I have from different parts, the real design of the enemy is to besiege Mons' (quoted Skrine, op. cit. 141). In reality the Duke had been deceived by a French feint towards Mons covering their real advance towards Tournai (ibid. 138, 141).

4. Conway reached the army in time to take part in the battle of Fontenoy, 11 May NS. He had recently been made an aide-de-camp to the D. of Cumberland by HW's influence: 'When Lord Orford was on his death bed, I prevailed on him to send for Mr Poyntz and make it his last request to the Duke [of Cumberland] to make him [Conway] his aide-de-camp, which the Duke on his [Conway's] former votes [against the army] had great aversion to do' (HW's *MS Political Papers*, f. 64). For further details of Conway's adverse votes, see *post* 6 March 1746 OS and n. 5.

5. Conway had probably been detained by the Parliamentary inquiry into the conduct of Mathews, Lestock, and others at the Battle of Toulon, which was finally decided 11 April OS by voting an address to the King recommending courts martial for the two admirals, six captains, and several other officers (MANN iii. 25–6 and notes; 32–4 and notes).

tion to divert me from 'em? I have been vastly obliged to your Abelard,[6] and with that melancholy companion have visited all the cliffs upon the coast, till I was ready to take a lover's leap from some of 'em in arrant despair. But they are rather too high, and without one could be taken up by some kind shepherdess at bottom and recovered, there would be no joke in it. Besides, it would be shameful just at the opening of a campaign to have so very little patience as not to live at least till one crossed the water, that it might be said one *died abroad*. That sounds tolerably even in these unheroic days, but I don't think we have any taste for the romantic, and I fancy I should make just the same figure in a newspaper as some poor love-sick housemaid that drowns herself in Rosamond's Pond.[7] And you, Lord, how you'd despise one; I really believe instead of lamenting your cousin you'd laugh at me for being such a fool, for it's a long time since you were romantic. I remember you buried in romances[8] and novels; I really believe you could have said all the *Grand Cyrus's*,[9] the *Cleopatra's*,[10] and *Amadis's* in the world by heart, nay, you carried your taste for it so far that not a fairy tale escaped you. *Quantum mutatus!*[11] But one thing I comfort myself with, you have laid up a vast stock of romance, and one day or other, when you fall in love, it will all break out; and then Lord have mercy upon you! I would not have you come within ten miles of Dover.

I desire you'll write to me and tell me all the news you know, that I may have something to say to you if I am destined to stay here. We hear of great news from Bavaria,[12] but only by the papers, so that's not to be depended upon. Tell Lady Mary I hope she has received the books for our library; I left 'em with Mr Smith,[13] and a book of plays that I borrowed of you.

6. HW had probably given Conway a copy of John Hughes's *Letters of Abelard and Heloise*, which had reached a seventh edition by 1743 (DNB *sub* 'John Hughes').

7. In St James's Park, filled up in 1770 (H. B. Wheatley and Peter Cunningham, *London Past and Present*, 1891, iii. 168–9).

8. Conway alludes to HW's fondness for romances *ante* 26 Sept. 1742 NS, 25 Oct. 1743 NS, and *post* 10 Aug. 1745 NS.

9. *Artamène, ou le Grand Cyrus*, 10 vols, 1649–53, a romance by Mlle de Scudéry. HW mentions it somewhat contemptu-

ously to Montagu 22 March 1762 (MONTAGU ii. 22).

10. For this romance, see *ante* 25 Oct. 1743 NS, n. 19.

11. Virgil, *Æneid* ii. 274 ('what a change').

12. Reports, still unconfirmed but true, that the Elector of Bavaria had been forced into a neutrality with Austria were published in the *Daily Adv.* 15 April OS. See also MANN iii. 34 and n. 14, 37–8 and nn. 10–12.

13. Conway's landlord (*ante* 19 Oct. 1744 NS).

Do you know Mr Hardenberg?[14] I live with him and Lord Charles Hay;[15] they are very civil and good-natured, and if we don't amuse one another much, I attribute it quite to the dullness of the place and the uneasiness of our situation. Adieu!

Yours ever,

H. C.

To CONWAY, ca Monday 22 April 1745 OS

Missing; implied by Conway's mention of 'all the dignity of distress that you talk of,' *post* 14 May 1745 NS and by his reference to Patapan's death, which occurred ca 19 April OS.

From CONWAY, Friday 14 May 1745 NS

Printed from the MS now WSL, formerly Rutnam. First printed, *Rockingham Memoirs* i. 408–9; reprinted *Colburn's United Service Magazine*, 1880, lii pt ii. 210–11. The postmark is the date of the letter's arrival in London.

Address: To the Honourable Horatio Walpole in Arlington Street, London, Angleterre.

Postmark: MA 11. AB.

Ath, May 14 NS, 1745.

Dear Horry,

AFTER all my delays and distresses at Dover, I was certainly in the greatest luck imaginable to come up time enough for the battle.[1] I don't doubt, too, but you'll think that of escaping from it,

14. Presumably one of the five surviving sons of Christian Ludwig von Hardenberg (1663–1736), all of whom were Hanoverian courtiers, officials, or army officers (*Genealogisches Staatshandbuch,* Frankfurt-am-Main, 1835, lxvi. 471–6); it is not clear, however, which of these was in England at this time. For the family, see also Chesterfield's *Letters,* ed. Dobrée, 1932, iii. 617; *Gothaisches Genealogisches Taschenbuch der Gräflichen Häuser,* Gotha, 1876, xlix. 345–6; Wilhelm Rothert, *Hannover unter dem Kurhut 1646–1815,* Hanover, 1916, pp. 405–30, 495–6;

and frequent references throughout *Genealog. hist. Nachrichten.*

15. (ca 1700–60), 3d son of 3d M. of Tweeddale; Maj.-Gen., 1757; M.P. Haddingtonshire 1741–7 (MANN i. 356, n. 25), since 7 April 1743 OS a Capt. and Lt-Col. in the 1st Foot Guards (Sir F. W. Hamilton, *Origin and History of the First or Grenadier Guards,* 1874, iii. 448). He was wounded at Fontenoy; see *post* 14 May 1745 NS.

————

1. Of Fontenoy, 11 May NS.

and escaping without the least accident, was at least equal to it; and to say the truth, notwithstanding all the dignity of distress that you talk of and the ambition of making a romantic corpse, it is a piece of fortune I am far from despising; to another now I should strike up immediately, and relate in a high, historic style, all the exploits of the day, but as I know you as unheroical as you own yourself unsentimental, I shall content myself with very few words on that head. We marched out of our camp at daybreak and began to form on the plain, which was the field of battle, before five o'clock, from which time their cannon began playing upon us and did not cease till half an hour after one, though we were engaged several hours with small arms; this plain rose gradually towards a fortified village[2] of the enemy, in the centre of it, and had a wood[3] on the right, from both which their chief batteries played. Some of our battalions advanced beyond the village and over the top of the rising,[4] but were so miserably galled by the cannon, at the same time that they were engaged with their line, that our troops, after rallying several times, were forced to retire, but they not caring to pursue us, we lost not a single man in our retreat, and that night brought off all our baggage. As to the behaviour of the Duke,[4a] of which I was witness the whole time, I can say I never saw more coolness nor greater intrepidity than he showed throughout the whole, exposing himself wherever the fire was hottest, and flying wherever he saw our troops fail, to lead 'em himself and encourage 'em by his example.[5] His horse received three wounds, and he one spent ball on his arm which only made a slight bruise but did him no hurt. Of us poor Ancram[6] and Lord Cathcart[7] are both wounded but in a very good way; for myself the balls had the same complaisance for me as for the Duke; one only hit my leg after all its force was gone,[8] and my horse which I rid all day received

---

2. Fontenoy.

3. The Forest of Barry.

4. The famous encounter between the English and French Guards (F. H. Skrine, *Fontenoy*, 1906, pp. 169–73 and sources there cited).

4a. Of Cumberland.

5. This description of the Duke's conduct is borne out by all contemporary reports.

6. Who, like Conway, was a Capt. and Lt-Col. in the 1st Guards and one of the Duke of Cumberland's aides-de-camp;

he was 'severely wounded by a musket ball' (ibid. 129, n. 9).

7. Charles Schaw Cathcart (1721–76), 9th Bn Cathcart. He was a Capt. in the 20th Foot, a lord of the Bedchamber and aide-de-camp to the Duke of Cumberland; he was shot in the face (ibid. 130, n. 12; GEC).

8. Conway had particularly distinguished himself in the battle. HW told Mann that he and Lord Petersham were the 'most commended'; his company was almost totally destroyed (only twenty-four

only a slight wound in the leg. Lt-Gen. Campbell[9] and Gen. Ponson-bey[10] are killed, and in general we have lost a vast number [of] of-ficers. Of the company that came over with me, two, Col. Douglass[11] and young Ross[12] were killed, Lord G. Sackville[13] and Lord Ch. Hay[14] wounded, but both I hope in a good way. There—I did not think I should have said so much, and I am sure you're vastly tired of it: our loss in the right wing amounts, I think, to 5822 killed and wounded, and in the left, who I doubt did not do quite so well,[15] between 1500 and 2000.[16] Poor Berkeley[17] is killed, whom I lament excessively. Col. Montagu[18] too is killed, and was very lucky in it, for his thigh was first broke, and the moment they took him up to carry him off, a cannon ball took off his head; the Major[19] too is wounded. The Duke has just sent for me, so I must conclude.

Yours, dear Horry, most sincerely.

What are all deaths to poor Patapan![20]

men survived) and he himself was for some time engaged single-handedly with two French grenadiers (MANN iii. 43 and n. 13; Sir F. W. Hamilton, *Origin and History of the First or Grenadier Guards*, 1874, ii. 122; P. Yorke to Horatio Walpole, Sr, 4 May OS, printed in Lord Stanhope, *History of England*, 1839-44, iii. Appendix, p. lxi; *post* 1 July 1745 OS, n. 24).

9. Hon. Sir James Campbell (*ante* 21 Aug. 1743 NS, n. 8).

10. Hon. Henry Ponsonby (d. 1745), Maj.-Gen., 1743; Col., 1735, of the 37th Foot (MANN iii. 43, n. 4).

11. Hon. Robert Douglas (ca 1703-45), Col. in the 3d Regiment of Foot Guards; M.P. Orkney and Shetland 1730-45.

12. Hon. Charles Ross (1721-45), Capt. in the 3d Regiment of Foot Guards; M.P. Ross-shire 1741-5.

13. At this time Lt-Col. in the 28th Foot; he was shot in the breast.

14. He had been severely wounded in the arm (and at first reported killed) at the encounter with the French Guards on the crest of the hill above Fontenoy (above, n. 4; Hamilton, op. cit. ii. 120-1, 125).

15. The left wing included the Dutch, who had retreated early in the battle.

16. Reports of the Allied casualties at the battle vary between 7300 and 7500 (MANN iii. 44 and notes).

17. Henry Berkeley (d. 1745), ensign, 1741, and Lt and Capt. 1744, in the 1st Regiment of Foot Guards (ibid. i. 459, n. 18; Hamilton, op. cit. ii. 125, iii. 449).

18. Edward Montagu (d. 1745), Lt-Col. of the 31st Foot; George Montagu's brother (MANN iii. 43, n. 8). See also HW's letter to Montagu ca 11 May 1745 OS, MON-TAGU i. 11-12.

19. Charles Montagu (d. 1777), K.B., 1771; another brother of George Mon-tagu, at this time a major in the 11th (Sowle's) Regiment (ibid. i. 31, n. 14; Skrine, op. cit. 368). A third brother, Christopher, an army chaplain, also died about this time, although it is not clear that he was killed in the battle (MANN iii. 43, n. 8).

20. Who had died ca 19 April OS (ibid iii. 39).

To CONWAY, ca Saturday 4 May 1745 OS

Missing; a 'kind little letter' answered *post* 26 May 1745 NS. It was probably written shortly after the first reports of the battle of Fontenoy reached England 4 May OS.

From CONWAY, Wednesday 26 May 1745 NS

Printed from the MS now WSL, formerly Rutnam. First printed (misdated 1744), *Rockingham Memoirs* i. 395–6; reprinted (misdated 21 May), *Colburn's United Service Magazine*, 1880, lii pt ii. 212–13. The date is determined by the reference to the capitulation of Tournai.

Address: To the Honourable Horatio Walpole in Arlington Street, London, Angleterre.

Lessines, May 26, NS.

Dear Horry,

I THANK you for your kind little letter, which indeed had so much goodness in it that it easily covered all the fault of its extreme conciseness, the only fault that yours can ever have with me. As to your joy upon the occasion[1] I should be ungrateful to find fault with that after you have told me I had some share in it; and I assure you, you do me too much honour to think me so stiff a patriot as not to be sensible to such feels. I felt 'em here in the safety of some that are with us and I own I find myself capable of carrying 'em so far, that I am afraid I could see the balance of Europe shake with tolerable philosophy if the quiet possession of my friends and attachments were secured to me. I wish all the world happy with all my heart but they will give me leave to wish myself so too, I would even sacrifice a great deal to make 'em really so but not to nourish the pride of any system or any faction great or little in the universe. I am not even ashamed to say to a friend (in the midst of a camp) that I look upon peace as the *summum bonum*. I only wish 'em all of one mind in politics and religion and I believe the world would be much happier and much better if they were all good Mussulmen or good Frenchmen than in this jarring chaos of systems and

1. Fontenoy.

religions, kingdoms, republics, states, provinces, parties, sects, and factions.

I hear your prediction about our friend[2] and, as you call her, my disciple, is accomplished, and that things are almost settled to her present satisfaction, only he is to undergo the ordeal trial of one campaign before he can approve himself worthy, but this I dare say is of his own seeking and I'll do her the justice to think she'd take him as he is without any such chimerical probation. As to the Earl, I fancy he'll wear his willow with a Christian resignation, for he seems to have been growing cool for some time as fast as t'other grew hot; however it be I really wish her very happy and should be glad to hear ⟨he⟩ was like to make her so; I don't know him at all.

As to our military affairs I shall not trouble you much with them. By all accounts the actual loss of the enemy in the late engagement was greater than ours,[3] and for farther consolation we hear the French and even their King himself extol the English bravery to the skies. We are promised recruits immediately[4] and are by no means dispirited by our disappointment. Tournai has capitulated[5] and eight days are given to the Governor[6] to consider whether he will give up the citadel.[7] I hear you have been at Houghton;[8] what could tempt you to such an extravagance? Give my compliments to all friends,

2. The following letter makes it clear that this alludes to Lady Caroline Fitzroy and George Townshend; the 'Earl,' an unsuccessful suitor, has not been identified. HW writes about this romance to Sir C. H. Williams 30 May 1745 OS: 'When he [Frederick Campbell] is to fetch Mr Townshend's picture, she [Lady Townshend] looks at Lady Caroline. Poor Lady Caroline! She is forced now to romp with Spitzer, the hussar-dog' (SELWYN 84). An obscure paragraph in Conway's letter to his brother 30 May 1745 NS may refer to the same affair: 'I hear of strange revolutions in the family. God knows where it will all end! I sincerely wish it may be well, and fancy the mystery will not be long in clearing up. I hear a certain gentleman, who has long had on one boot, does not seem inclined to pull on t'other; from whence I have strong suspicions matters will not remain long in suspense' (*Colburn's United Service Magazine*, 1880, lii pt ii. 215; MS now WSL).

3. French casualties seem to have been over 7,000 but somewhat less than the Allies' (MANN iii. 44, nn. 15, 16).

4. Two English regiments, drafts from the battalions of Guards, and other recruits sailed from Gravesend on the day of this letter and others were expected to go in a few days (ibid. iii. 52, n. 3).

5. 23 May NS, after involved negotiations with the French (documents quoted in F. H. Skrine, *Fontenoy*, 1906, pp. 219-21).

6. Johan Adolf (d. 1747), Baron van Dorth; Gen., 1743 (MANN iii. 52, n. 1).

7. He was ordered to defend it; the siege was resumed 1 June NS and it held out until 20 June NS (ibid. iii. 52, n. 2, 61, n. 5; *post* 21 June 1745 NS).

8. HW also mentions this 'expedition' *post* 1 July 1745 OS, but there are no other references to it. It may have been in connection with his negotiations to have Rigby made M.P. for Castle Rising by his brother Robert, which led in turn to HW's quarrel with his brother Edward (FAMILY 14-21).

particularly Miss Townshend⁹ if you see her. Does she talk of retiring? Adieu!

Yours dear Horry sincerely,

H. C.

To CONWAY, Monday 27 May 1745 OS

Printed from *Works* v. 19–21.

Arlington Street, May 27, 1745.

My dear Harry,

AS gloriously as you have set out, yet I despair of seeing you a perfect hero! You have none of the charming violences that are so essential to that character. You write as coolly after behaving well in a battle, as you fought in it. Can your friends flatter themselves with seeing you one day or other be the death of thousands, when you wish for peace¹ in three weeks after your first engagement,² and laugh at the ambition of those men who have given you this opportunity of distinguishing yourself? With the person of an Orondates,³ and the courage, you have all the compassion, the reason, and the reflection, of one that never read a romance. Can one ever hope you will make a figure, when you only fight because it was right you should, and not because you hated the French, or loved destroying mankind? This is so un-English, or so unheroic, that I despair of you!

Thank Heaven, you have one spice of madness! Your admiration

9. Presumably Hon. Mary Townshend; see *post* 27 May 1745 OS, nn. 15, 17, 1 July 1745 OS, 30 Aug. 1745 NS.

---

1. See *ante* 26 May 1745 NS.
2. The battle of Fontenoy, where Mr Conway greatly distinguished himself (HW).
3. The hero of La Calprenède's *Cassandre*: 'The gods had endowed him with all the most excellent parts, that can render a person accomplished; his face was marvelously handsome, and through a beauty which had nothing of effeminate, one might observe something so martial, so sparkling, and so majestic, as might in all hearts make an impression of love, fear,

and respect at once; his stature exceeded that of the tallest men, but the proportion of it was wonderfully exact, and all the motions of his body had a grace, and liberty that was nothing common; his age seemed to be then about six or seven and twenty' (English trans., 1652, pt i. 3). HW told Mme du Deffand ca 21 Dec. 1773 that he had been unable to finish *Cassandre* (DU DEFFAND iii. 436–7). The only edition of *Cassandre* recorded in HW's library is Vols 3, 4, and 5 of Sir Charles Cotterell's translation, 1725, which HW apparently purchased after 1766 (ibid. iii. 437, n. 3; Hazen, *Cat. of HW's Lib.*, No. 367).

of your master[4] leaves me a glimmering of hope that you will not be always so unreasonably reasonable. Do you remember the humorous lieutenant, in one of Beaumont and Fletcher's plays,[5] that is in love with the King? Indeed your master is not behind hand with you;[6] you seem to have agreed to puff one another.

If you are all acting up to the strictest rules of war and chivalry in Flanders, we are not less scrupulous on this side the water in fulfilling all the duties of the same order. The day the young volunteer[7] departed for the army (unluckily indeed it was after the battle),[8] his tender mother Sisygambis,[9] and the beautiful Statira,[10] a lady formerly known in your history by the name of Artemisia,[11] from her cutting off her hair on your absence,[12] were so afflicted

4. William, Duke of Cumberland, to whom Mr Conway was aide-de-camp (HW). Conway's admiration appears *ante* 14 May 1745 NS and was doubtless expressed in his other letters to England.

5. *The Humorous Lieutenant*.

6. The Duke of Cumberland's praise of Conway at this time has not been found, but he was pressing for a regiment for Conway in July (*post* 25 Oct. 1745 NS, n. 4).

7. Identified by Wright as 'George, afterwards Marquis Townshend'; see *ante* 26 May 1745 NS, n. 2. The Hon. George Townshend (1724–1807), 4th Vct Townshend, 1764; cr. (1787) M. Townshend.

8. George Townshend's appointment as 'captain of a troop of horse in General Cope's regiment [7th Dragoon Guards] in Flanders' was announced in the *Daily Adv.* 19 April 1745 OS. On 8 May OS he was appointed aide-de-camp to Lt-Gen. Lord Dunmore, and on 29 May OS he was made a captain in Bligh's (20th) regiment of Foot (C. V. F. Townshend, *The Military Life of Field Marshal George, First Marquess Townshend*, 1901, pp. 73, 78–9). Townshend accompanied Lord John Murray whose departure for Flanders is reported in the *Daily Adv.* as Wednesday 15 May OS (*Daily Adv.* 16 May; C. V. F. Townshend, op. cit. 52). In a letter of 4 May OS Philip Yorke writes Horatio Walpole, Sr, 'Lord Dunmore and the officers who went with him had not joined the army' before the battle of Fontenoy (Lord Stanhope, *History of England*, 1839–44, iii. Appendix, p. lxi); and the D. of Cumberland's 'Orders' apparently do not mention Lord Dunmore before 19 May

NS (A. N. Campbell-Maclachlan, *William Augustus, Duke of Cumberland*, 1876, pp. 133–4; see also FAMILY 12).

9. Lady Townshend. Historically, Sisygambis was the mother of Darius III; she was captured but well treated by Alexander the Great. She also plays a prominent part in *Cassandre* and in Lee's *Rival Queens* which is based upon it.

10. Lady Caroline Fitzroy. Historically both the wife of Darius, a legendary beauty, and their daughter, whom Alexander married, were named Statira. Although both women appear in *Cassandre*, only the daughter, who is the principal heroine of the play and the object of Oröondates' exploits, is named there, and the mother's beauty is attributed to her; the mother remains essentially a background figure. Statira also appears in Lee's *Rival Queens*.

11. A queen of Caria, remarkable for her beauty and her excessive grief for her dead husband; see Valerius Maximus iv. 6.

12. No other reference to this affecting scene has been found, except in Conway's answer, *post* 21 June 1745 NS. HW to Montagu 13 July 1745 OS gives another example of the former violence of Lady Caroline's fondness for Conway, quoting a Mrs Comyns as saying that 'Lady Caroline Fitzroy . . . gave the mob ten guineas to demolish my house, because her Ladyship fancied I got women for Colonel Conway.' HW commented that he intended 'to have infinite fun with his [Conway's] prudery about this anecdote, which is full as good as if it was true' (MONTAGU i. 19).

and so inseparable, that they made a party together to Mr *Graham's*[13] (you may read *Iapis*[14] if you please) to be blooded. It was settled that this was a more precious way of expressing concern than shaving the head, which has been known to be attended with false locks the next day.

For the other princess[15] you wot of, who is not entirely so tall as the former, nor so evidently descended from a line of monarchs[16]— I don't hear her talk of retiring. At present she is employed in buying up all the nosegays in Covent Garden, and laurel leaves at the pastry-cooks', to weave chaplets for the return of her hero.[17] Who that is, I don't pretend to know or guess. All I know is, that in this age retirement is not one of the fashionable expressions of passion.

HOR. WALPOLE

From CONWAY, Monday 21 June 1745 NS

Printed from the MS now WSL, formerly Rutnam. First printed (misdated 1744) *Rockingham Memoirs* i. 397–9; reprinted (correctly dated) *Colburn's United Service Magazine*, 1880, lii pt ii. 215–17. Conway misdated the letter 1744; it is a reply to HW's *ante* 27 May 1745 OS and also mentions the capitulation of the citadel of Tournai, which occurred 20 June 1745 NS.

Address: To the Honourable Horatio Walpole, Jun., in Arlington Street, London, Angleterre.

Postmark: IV 19. AB.

Lessines, June 21, NS, 1744 [1745].

Dear Horry,

I WOULD fain fancy I deserve all the compliments you make me but notwithstanding my opinion of your excellent judgment and great love of truth, I can't find in myself all those good qualities

13. A celebrated apothecary in Pall Mall (HW). Daniel Graham (d. 1778), apothecary to the King from before 1723 until ca 1762 (MORE 28, n. 6).

14. Son of Iasus, loved by Apollo, who taught him the arts of healing and prophecy; he cured Æneas of a wound (Virgil, *Æneid* xii. 391–421).

15. The Hon. Mary Townshend; a reply to Conway's question *ante* 26 May NS as to whether she talked of retiring. Conway in his reply *post* 21 June NS does not seem

to be sure of whom HW is speaking; but see also *post* 1 July OS and 30 Aug. NS.

16. Lady Caroline was a great-granddaughter of Charles II.

17. Probably the Hon. Edward Cornwallis (*ante* 1 July 1744 NS, n. 16), whom she married in 1753; he was promoted in 1745 to Lt-Col. in Col. Thomas Bligh's (20th) regiment of foot, which was in Flanders (MANN iii. 177 and n. 37; Namier and Brooke ii. 256; *post* 30 Aug. 1745 NS).

that you attribute to me, especially that unreasonable reasonableness that you are so good as to give me. I own I feel myself so divested
of it that I have no idea what I can have done or said to impose upon
you so grossly; if you knew all the ridiculous weaknesses I feel, even
you would allow me to be unreasonable enough o' conscience; nay
I dare not confess 'em all to you for fear you should think me too
much so. I know you are no great friend to reason so am the less
vain of your compliment; yet in return for it am willing to give
up my reason to merit your good opinion, and fairly disclaim all
title to it; only just keep so much of it as is sufficient to show me the
insignificancy of it and to make me wish for less, unless it be the
reason of the Stoics that teaches us to be indifferent to everything.
This world is not made for reason, and a man who follows it strictly
is sure to be disappointed, whereas he that forsakes it has perhaps
not above ten or twenty to one against him; for me I am very unreasonable I own and very whimsical in my desires and therefore I
think it is barely possible I may be happy one time or other, but if I
am not to be so in the way I desire I assure you neither honour, nor
interest, nor regiments, nor generalships, nor kingdoms can give it
me. You told me before I was unreasonably reasonable, now tell me
if I don't appear reasonably unreasonable? In the first place I heartily
wish the campaign over and yet when it is, may possibly be as far
from my happiness as I am at present; if so, why then I shall wish it
begun again. Such uncertain creatures are we; almost every season
and every circumstance of our life makes a new man of us; so I fancy
others are because so I feel myself, happy today because I flatter myself with some prospect of success, as unhappy tomorrow because some
trivial accident has damped those hopes, and both perhaps with
equal or with the least reason imaginable. All mankind, without they
are very reasonable or very stoical indeed, have some point in view,
some wish to the accomplishment of which all their views and all
their endeavours tend. Whatever you offer 'em that is foreign to that
may perhaps console 'em a little but cannot satisfy 'em:

> That cruel something unpossest
> Corrodes and leavens all the rest.[1]

I won't enter too far into this discussion, but from this I fancy many
men draw a great deal of merit they have little or no real title to;

1. Matthew Prior, 'The Ladle,' ll. 165–6.

'tis with our passions as with our sight, fix it firmly upon one object and you'll find you hardly perceive any other. It is not that one wants sensibility but one wants attention to 'em; thus much for myself. I don't insist upon your understanding nor believing me, if you have not a mind; it will serve as matter of speculation at least, and so serves very well for the purpose of correspondence; however I am glad to hear our friend Artemisia[2] wants neither sensibility nor attention: of the first I should never suspect her, and for the other, provided she chooses her time well, 'tis no great matter, you'll say. Attentions to the absent are like those to the dead, mere pageant and ceremony and more becoming a Mogul lady than an European princess. I was very vain of the cutting of the hair but that bleeding party I own is very grand and quite puts my vanity out of countenance, notwithstanding which I assure you my rival[3] and I are very well together. I hear he knows all about me, and in return I assure you, whatever I hear about him will not now give me a moment's uneasiness. I sincerely wish her well and happy and only hope we may now be more so separately than we could have been together. As for the other person you mention,[4] if I know who it is, I am not ashamed to say I love her very sincerely but in such a way as to wish her very happy while I am in Flanders, I assure you; so pray make ⟨her⟩ my compliments; if you see her tell her I am vastly obliged to her for thinking of me sometimes, that it cannot be oftener than I think of her, and th⟨at⟩ I hope by this time all schemes of retirement are quite laid aside.

I am afraid the citadel of Tournai is taken or upon the point of being so.[5] What change this will cause with us I don't yet know. Adieu! dear Horry, yours affectionately,

H. C.

Compliments to Lady Mary and Mrs Leneve.

PS. Since I wrote this I hear the citadel of Tournai is given up, on condition that the garrison shall not serve anywhere till the 1st of January, 1747.[6]

2. See *ante* 27 May 1745 OS.
3. George Townshend.
4. The Hon. Mary Townshend, *ante* 27 May 1745 OS.
5. It had surrendered the preceding day; see postscript.

6. For an account of the capitulation on 20 June NS by the acting governor of Tournai, see F. H. Skrine, *Fontenoy*, 1906, pp. 222–3. See also the account of the surrender in *Mercure historique* 1745, cxix. 115–17.

To CONWAY, Monday 1 July 1745 OS

Printed from *Works* v. 21–3.

Arlington Street, July 1, 1745.

My dear Harry,

IF it were not for that one slight inconvenience, that I should probably be dead now, I should have liked much better to have lived in the last war[1] than in this; I mean as to the pleasantness of writing letters. Two or three battles won, two or three towns taken, in a summer, were pretty objects to keep up the liveliness of a correspondence. But now it hurts one's dignity to be talking of English and French armies, at the first period of our history in which the tables are turned. After having learnt to spell out of the reigns of Edward the Third and Harry the Fifth, and begun lisping with Agincourt and Cressy, one uses one's self but awkwardly to the sounds of Tournay and Fontenoy. I don't like foreseeing the time so near, when all the young orators in Parliament will be haranguing out of Demosthenes upon the imminent danger we are in from the overgrown power of King Philip. As becoming as all that public spirit will be, which to be sure will now come forth, I can't but think we were at least as happy and as great when all the young Pitts[2] and Lytteltons[3] were pelting oratory at my father for rolling out a twenty years peace, and not envying the trophies which he passed by every day in Westminster Hall. But one must not repine; rather reflect on the glories which they have drove the nation headlong into. One must think all our distresses and dangers well laid out, when they have purchased us Glover's[4] oration for the merchants,[5] the Admiralty for the Duke of Bedford,[6] and the reversion of secretary at war for Pitt, which he will certainly have,[7] unless the French king should happen

1. The War of the Spanish Succession.
2. William Pitt (1708–78), cr. (1766) E. of Chatham.
3. George Lyttelton (1709–73), 5th Bt, 1751; cr. (1756) Bn Lyttelton.
4. The author of *Leonidas* (HW).
5. Glover drafted the petition of the merchants of London presented 20 Jan. 1742 OS and afterwards (2 March) summarized the evidence for the petitioners in a two hour speech before the House of Commons (MANN i. 295 and nn. 7–9, 353–4; Hist. MSS Comm., *Egmont Diary*, 1920–3, iii. 258).
6. John Russell (1710–71), 4th D. of Bedford, had become first lord of the Admiralty 25 Dec. 1744 OS in the 'Broad-Bottom' ministry following Granville's dismissal.
7. Pitt had asked for the secretaryship of war in Dec. 1744, but had been refused; the King continued to resist his

to have the nomination; and then I fear, as much obliged as that Court is to my Lord Cobham and his nephews,[8] they would be so partial as to prefer some illiterate nephew of Cardinal Tencin's,[9] who never heard of Leonidas or the Hanover troops.[10]

With all these reflections, as I love to make myself easy, especially politically, I comfort myself with what St-Évremond[11] (a favourite philosopher of mine, for he thought what he liked, not liked what he thought) said in defence of Cardinal Mazarin, when he was reproached with neglecting the good of the kingdom that he might engross the riches of it: 'Well, let him get all the riches, and then he will think of the good of the kingdom, for it will all be his own.'[12] Let the French but have England, and they won't want to conquer it. We may possibly contract the French spirit of being supremely content with the glory of our monarch, and then—why then it will be the first time we ever were contented yet.

We hear of nothing but your retiring,[13] and of Dutch treachery:[14] in short, 'tis an ugly scene!

I know of no home news but the commencement of the Gaming Act,[15] for which they are to put up a scutcheon at White's for the

appointment to this office, but he became a joint vice-treasurer of Ireland 22 Feb. 1746 OS and paymaster of the forces 6 May 1746 OS (MANN ii. 551-2 and n. 21; J. B. Owen, *Rise of the Pelhams*, 1957, pp. 248-9, 285-6, 289-90, 292-3, 301).

8. Pitt, Lyttelton, and the Grenville brothers.

9. Pierre Guérin de Tencin (1679-1758), cardinal, 1739; French chargé d'affaires at Rome 1721-4, 1739-41; minister of state, 1742; the chief promoter of the current Jacobite plots.

10. Pitt had been particularly violent in his opposition to retaining Hanoverian troops in the winter of 1743-4 (MANN ii. 383 and n. 13; Owen, op. cit. 201, 212).

11. Charles de Marguetel de Saint-Denis de Saint-Évremond (1613-1703).

12. This quotation has not been found in Saint-Évremond, but it is close in spirit to his ironical defence of Mazarin in his letter on the Treaty of the Pyrenees (Saint-Évremond, *Œuvres mêlées*, ed. Giraud, 1865-6, ii. 21-38). HW owned the 5th edn of Saint-Évremond's *Works*, Amsterdam, 1739 (Hazen, *Cat. of HW's Lib.*, No. 948).

13. Mr Conway was still with the army in Flanders (HW). The Duke of Cumberland had unwillingly retreated from Lessines to Gramont 30 June NS after the Dutch had insisted on strengthening various garrisons and thereby had reduced his field army (F. H. Skrine, *Fontenoy*, 1906, pp. 224-6; *Oesterr. Erbfolge-krieg* ix. 146).

14. The defection of the principal Dutch engineer at Tournai, Hertsell, at the beginning of the siege is described in a letter from the Hon. Philip Yorke to 'Old' Horace Walpole 27 May 1745 OS in Lord Stanhope's *History of England*, 1839-44, iii. Appendix, pp. lxv-lxvi. The Duke of Cumberland wrote Harrington 25 June NS, 'A very small sense of honour would have put such a garrison out of the reach of so mortifying a capitulation. What the articles of it call the "honours of war" must, after such a defence, be looked upon as an insult, and be called . . . the mean hire of treachery and cowardice' (Skrine, op. cit. 223).

15. 18 Geo. II, c. 34: 'An act to explain, amend, and make more effectual the laws in being, to prevent excessive

death of play; and the death of Winnington's wife,[16] which may be an
unlucky event for my Lady Townshend.[17] As he has no children, he
will certainly marry again; and who will give him their daughter,
unless he breaks off that affair, which I believe he will now very
willingly make a marriage article? We want him to take Lady Charlotte Fermor.[18] She was always his beauty, and has so many charming
qualities, that she would make anybody happy. He will make a good
husband; for he is excessively good-natured, and was much better to
that strange wife than he cared to own.

You wondered at my journey to Houghton; now wonder more, for
I am going to Mount Edgecumbe.[19] Now my summers are in my own
hands,[20] and I am not obliged to pass great part of them in Norfolk, I
find it is not so very terrible to dispose of them up and down.[21] In
about three weeks I shall set out,[22] and see Wilton and Doddington's[23]
in my way. Dear Harry, do but get a victory, and I will let off every
cannon at Plymouth; reserving two, till I hear particularly that you
have killed two more Frenchmen with your own hand.[24] Lady Mary[25]
sends you her compliments; she is going to pass a week with Miss
Townshend[26] at Muffits;[27] I don't think you will be forgot. Your

and deceitful gaming; and to restrain and
prevent the excessive increase of horse-
races.' It went into effect 24 June 1745 OS
and, among other provisions, forbade rou-
lette.

16. Love Reade (d. 25 June 1745 OS),
m. (1719) Thomas Winnington (DNB *sub*
'Winnington').

17. Who was Winnington's mistress
(MANN i. 173 and n. 6a; SELWYN 45–6).

18. This did not take place; Lady
Charlotte married the Hon. William
Finch 9 Aug. 1746 OS, about four months
after Winnington's death.

19. Near Plymouth, to visit his friend
Dick Edgcumbe.

20. Because of his father's death, 18
March 1745. HW wrote Mann 29 April
1745 OS, 'I shall only make short excursions in visits; you know I am not fond
of the country, and have no call into it
now! My brother will not be at Houghton
this year; he shuts it up, to enter on
new, and there very unknown, economy:
he has much occasion for it!' (MANN iii.
39–40).

21. HW had recently returned from a
visit of 'near three weeks' with Rigby at

Mistley, Essex (MONTAGU i. 14; MANN iii.
60; SELWYN 86).

22. HW left London 8 Aug. and returned 5 Sept. OS (MANN iii. 92, 101;
SELWYN 94).

23. Eastbury, near Blandford, Dorset,
seat of George Bubb Dodington (1691–
1762), cr. (1761) Bn Melcombe. For the
house, see ibid. 71, n. 26.

24. Alluding to Mr Conway's having
been engaged with two French grenadiers
at once in the battle of Fontenoy (HW).

25. Lady Mary Walpole, youngest
daughter of Sir R. Walpole, afterwards
married to Charles Churchill, Esq. (HW).

26. Daughter of Charles Viscount
Townshend, afterwards married to Edward Cornwallis brother to Earl Cornwallis and groom of the Bedchamber to
the King (HW).

27. Muffetts, near Hatfield, Herts, a
seat of Rev. Hon. Spencer Cowper, who
had married Miss Townshend's sister
Dorothy; the Cowpers had been there
since Jan. 1745 (Spencer Cowper, *Letters*,
ed. Hughes, 1956, pp. 39–48, Surtees Society, Vol. CLXV).

sister Anne has got a new distemper, which she says feels like something *jumping* in her. You know my style on such an occasion, and may be sure I have not spared this distemper. Adieu!

Yours ever,

HOR. WALPOLE

From CONWAY, Tuesday 10 August 1745 NS

Printed for the first time from the MS now WSL, formerly Rutnam. The postmark is the date of the letter's arrival in London.

Address: To the Honourable Horatio Walpole, Jun. in Arlington Street, London, Angleterre.

Postmark: AV 5. AB.

Vilvorde, Tuesday, August 10 NS, 1745.

Dear Horry,

THOUGH I think you told me in your last that you were tired of our correspondence, the reason you gave for it was so very extraordinary that I am resolved not to believe it; if you had told me I was dull as a post and that there was no sort of amusement in my letters I should have no difficulty in the world in believing you, but that you should pretend to complain because we don't beat the French and that nothing but news of victories will go down with you, there's no bearing it. You might for aught I know have some pleasure in the stories of Agincourt and Cressi in your infancy as you say; if ever you were heroically inclined it was in those very early days, but you soon fell from your taste for those substantial honours to the imaginary glories of *Amadis* and *Cassandra*, from whence it dwindled gradually into *Zaide*[1] and the *Princess of Cleves*[2] and lost itself entirely in the *Égaremens*[3] and *History of Marianne;*[4] so own, dear Horry, that provided you and your friends are safe and at their

1. *Zayde, histoire espagnole,* 1670–1, chiefly by Mme de la Fayette; HW's copy is Hazen, *Cat. of HW's Lib.,* No. 1005.

2. *La Princesse de Clèves,* 1678, also by Mme de la Fayette.

3. Probably *Les Égarements du cœur et de l'esprit,* by Claude-Prosper Jolyot de

Crébillon (1707–77). HW's copy of The Hague, 1736, edn is Hazen, op. cit. No. 1026.

4. *La Vie de Marianne,* 1731–41, by Pierre Carlet de Chamblain de Marivaux (1688–1763). HW's copy of the 1742 edn is Hazen, op. cit. No. 997.

ease, can eat, drink, sleep and laugh as usual, that you don't care
sixpence who beats or is beaten, wins or loses, what revolutions happen or what monarch governs us from almighty Jove to the Log of
Wood,[5] and I'll agree if you please that my letters are the stupidest in
the world; nay, I'll own it without for I am dull myself to the last
degree in every sense of the word, inveterately so, and past all hopes
of cure till I can think of coming to England for my recovery; I have
the *mal du pays* to such a degree there's no bearing it absolutely. My
only comfort is that the time must come; I actually perceive it advance a little. There are as many minutes in the hour and hours in
the day as there are when one is happier, which makes me sure that
in two months it will be the 10th of October about which time I
hope we shall think a little of winter quarters. This is not a country
for a winter campaign, thank God; and there are certain things here
called equinoctial rains which make the country impracticable and
send the poor soldiers in flocks to the hospital. I shall be very sorry
for 'em and hope they'll all recover, but I must own shall not pray
heartily for fair weather. They say the King of France is going to
Paris;[6] the siege of Ostend is now, I believe, begun;[7] our troops and
stores are arrived there[8] and as I have great confidence in the defence
Monsieur de Chanclos[9] will make, I think this may possibly be the
last operation of the campaign. The French parties advance of late
very near us;[10] we have had several little skirmishes but I believe they
think of nothing less than attacking us. Our four battalions of Austrians are come in[11] and we have now fortified the canal[12] so as to

5. 'King Log: the log which Jupiter in
the fable made king over the frogs' (OED
sub 'log').

6. He was still with the army in
Flanders at the end of the month (*post*
30 Aug. 1745 NS).

7. Ostend was virtually invested by 7
Aug. NS, but the siege did not begin in
earnest until 18 Aug. because of delays
in the arrival of the French artillery;
Ostend capitulated 23 Aug. (H. Pichat,
*La Campagne du Maréchal de Saxe dans
les Flandres*, 1909, pp. 141, 145–7;
Oesterr. Erbfolge-krieg ix. 168–72).

8. From England by ship between 7
and 9 Aug. NS (ibid. ix. 169, n. 4;
MANN iii. 78, n. 4).

9. Charles-Urbain (1686–1761), Comte
de Chanclos de Rets Brisuila, seigneur de

Leves; general in the Austrian service;
governor of Ostend, 1738; field marshal,
1754 (*Biographie nationale. . . . de Bel-
gique*, Brussels, 1866–1944, iii. 424–7; *Genealog. hist. Nachrichten* 1762–3, 2d ser.,
xiii. 169–72).

10. 'The French parties come quite into
our suburbs, and yesterday they took two
coaches with the persons in them, but a detachment of hussars were set after them
and brought them back' (*Daily Adv.* 3
Aug. OS, *sub* Brussels 7 Aug. NS).

11. Their arrival on 8 Aug. NS is mentioned ibid. 6 Aug. OS *sub* 'Camp of the
Allies in Brabant' 8 Aug. NS; Pichat, op.
cit. 157; and *Oesterr. Erbfolge-krieg* ix.
175.

12. The Vilvorde or Willebroek canal
between Brussels and the Schelde.

fear nothing there[13] and of course secured the country on that side as far as Antwerp. We have lost two bilanders full of Dutchmen in one of our skirmishes[14] amounting to about 140 men, but that's no great loss; the Major[15] who commanded 'em was killed and four men; the rest of the party and 300 English, in all about 600 men designed as a reinforcement for Dendermonde,[16] were forced back to Antwerp from whence they were going up the Scheld. Lord Bury was out yesterday with a reconnoitring party of 500 horse.[17] They were fired at by some infantry in a village where they passed and lost two men and two horses and two or three more wounded but the Colonel who commanded, not thinking it advisable to attack 'em, the affair ended so. Adieu, dear Horry, Ned[18] and all our friends are well. A good journey to Mount Edgecumb, what a rage! Compliments to Lady Mary and Miss Townshend if you see her. I should be glad to know the state of her resolutions about the winter, whether one is to see her, or that she goes to her abominable hermitage. *J'espère qu'il n'en est plus question.*

Adieu! Yours, dear Horry, affectionately,

H. C.

To CONWAY, Wednesday 7 August 1745 OS

Missing; Conway in his reply *post* 30 Aug. 1745 NS mentions it as having been written the night before HW left for Mount Edgcumbe.

13. 'Our works along the canal are quite finished, and our front is covered by good entrenchments' (*Daily Adv.* loc. cit.).

14. At Saint-Amants (or St-Amand) on the night of 4–5 Aug. NS; details, from the account of the skirmish sent to the States General by Prince Waldeck, are in Pichat, op. cit. 133–5. According to this, three bilanders were lost, 180 Dutch were made prisoners and eleven were killed; Conway's other details are accurate.

15. Major Harel (ibid.).

16. Which the French had invested 3 Aug. NS; the siege began on the 8th and it surrendered on the 13th (ibid. 132, 137–9; *Oesterr. Erbfolge-krieg* ix. 164–8).

17. No further details of this skirmish have been found.

18. Cornwallis.

From CONWAY, Monday 30 August 1745 NS

Printed for the first time from the MS now wsL, formerly Rutnam. The postmark is the date of the letter's arrival in London.
Address: To the Honourable Horatio Walpole, Jun., in Arlington Street, London, Angleterre.
Postmark: AV 27. AB.

Vilvorde, August 30, 1745.

Dear Horry,

I OWN I did not think you had the courage to undertake such a voyage. I know how you talk of such things for ages without even a design of putting 'em in execution, but for the present I own my incredulity has hardly the least ground left to work upon. That packing up and setting out tomorrow,[1] as you say, are such proofs as it would be great impertinence for me to contest, but I really believe you don't know where you are going. It's to the very end of the world and I don't fancy you can possibly be back till towards the end of next winter. I wish the world mayn't put a bad construction upon it and say you are running away from the invasion, as my Lady Erby,[2] I think it was, intended to do by going to China; or rather, I suspect you of being in the plot with Miss Townshend and intending to leave this wicked world and giving yourself up to a religious life. Your fits of devotion are not very frequent but extremely violent when they come;[3] however, if you do not intend to deceive us I am very glad to hear you have sent to exhort her against the wicked resolution she seemed to have almost half taken of staying in the country; I am afraid in using my name you did not choose the best argument in the world but I assure [you] you could say nothing too strong for me upon the subject, without supposing that you have your family rage of imagining I am [in] love with her; and to prove the contrary to you I do assure you I love her excessively and there

1. HW left London for Mount Edg-cumbe 8 Aug. OS (*ante* 1 July 1745 OS, n. 22).

2. Probably Dorothy Paget (d. 1734), m. (by 1706) Edward Irby, cr. (1704) Bt. HW, however, says the remark was the 'late Duchess of Bolton's [Henrietta Crofts (d. 1730), m. (1697) Charles Powlett, 2d D. of Bolton],' made 'when Whiston told her the world would be burnt in three years' (to Montagu 1 Aug. 1745 OS, MONTAGU i.

22; repeated in *Walpoliana*, ed. John Pinkerton, [1799], i. 15–16).

3. Cole mentions that when HW first came to Cambridge he was 'of a religious enthusiastic turn of mind . . . even so much as to go with Ashton, his then great friend, to pray with the prisoners in the Castle' (John Nichols, *Literary Anecdotes of the Eighteenth Century*, 1812–15, v. 569).

are very few of my friends I shall see again with such pleasure, and of the few elect I really do not feel as if I could by any means spare any.—Count Wallis[4] and I think of you both very often; and since your new expedition and her danger of falling into a cloister, with as many doubts and fears as you can possibly think of your friends militant on this side the water. We have two or three comfortable deserters here of late that have told us the King of France was going home immediately[5] and that towards the middle of next month their troops would begin to go into cantonment which is the step immediately preceding winter quarters;[6] the first from all accounts is true and for the other, though I have no hopes in the world of it, I could have kissed 'em for telling news that sounded so agreeable; I am not sure I should not grow tired of a successful campaign but an unlucky one is sure of all things the most abominable. By the by, why Count Wallis, pray?[7] You can't imagine how you puzzled us with the title and with your discussion upon it in his letter.[8]

As to invasions or other news I can tell you none. The French by this time, I believe, having taken Nieuport[9] are moving this way, I mean the detachment that has been that way to join the army here, after which we shall soon know what their intentions are, as the season is now too far advanced for delays if they intend doing anything of consequence.[10] Sir John Ligonier sets out today to meet the King at Helvoetsluys.[11] Yesterday a French party who conducted some prisoners of ours hither was suffered by an Austrian captain to pass through one of [the] posts on the canal and so through our camp to Mackling;[11a] the officer was put in arrest; but he excuses himself by saying a general of ours was by and by not objecting he thought he

---

4. A nickname given by HW to Ned Cornwallis who later married Mary Townshend; see below, n. 7.

5. Louis XV left the army 1 Sept. NS (H. Pichat, *La Campagne du Maréchal de Saxe dans les Flandres*, 1909, p. 173, n. 1).

6. This was Saxe's intention at this time, but at the insistence of the King and ministry, the campaign was prolonged until mid-October (ibid. chap. iv).

7. HW was probably punning on the Grafen von Wallis, a distinguished Austrian military family (Constant von Wurzbach, *Biographisches Lexikon des Kaiserthums Oesterreich*, Vienna, 1856–91, lii. 255–71).

8. HW's letter to Cornwallis is missing.

9. Nieuport, besieged since 28 Aug. NS, surrendered 5 Sept. (Pichat, op. cit. 152–5; *Oesterr. Erbfolge-krieg* ix. 172–4).

10. The last action of the campaign was the siege of Ath (28 Sept.–7 Oct. NS).

11. The D. of Cumberland wrote to Newcastle 27 Aug. NS that he had sent Ligonier to meet the King at Utrecht, and a letter from Harrington to Cumberland from Helvoetsluys 28 Aug. NS makes it clear that Ligonier had already seen the King (F. H. Skrine, *Fontenoy*, 1906, pp. 258–9). George II was returning from Hanover to England because of the Jacobite rising in Scotland.

11a. Probably Mechlin.

consented to it which is true enough.¹² Adieu, dear Horry; I hope you divert yourself excessively at Mount Edgecumb. In the meantime, I long every hour more to see you where you'll do it more.

Yours ever affectionately,

H. C.

Lord Bury's and Ned's compliments.

From CONWAY, Monday 25 October 1745 NS

Printed for the first time from the MS now WSL, formerly Rutnam. The postmark is the date of the letter's arrival in London.

Address: To the Honourable Horatio Walpole, Jun., in Arlington Street, London, Angleterre.

Postmark: OC 25.

Williamstadt, Oct. 25th NS.

Dear Horry,

I WRITE to let you know that I am coming over to you, but God knows when; I am got as far as this upon my way, but move so slowly and so irregularly that I can hardly fancy myself nearer my journey's end; by being made master of others I am no longer so of myself; in short, [I] have the misfortune to be tied to the most disagreeable command in the world; I have been for this week past travelling by land and water with such a pack of ragamuffins as you have no conception of, a general gaol delivery of all the prisoners of seventeen or eighteen regiments.¹ If I had not had the prayers of all good Christians in my favour there would have been no outliving it. Three days was I shut up with 'em in a bilander, of which my share was one fourth of a cabin four foot square divided between myself and Gennet² and two Dutch skippers. The first night our two friends were invited out to supper in a neighbouring boat and I was in hopes they intended to make that their rendezvous but next morning was agreeably surprised before I was up to wake and find 'em and several

12. No other details of this incident have been found.

———

1. The English prisoners of war, who had been released by the French in mid-

September; for some details of their previous history, see F. H. Skrine, *Fontenoy*, 1906, pp. 256–7, 263–4, 281–2.

2. Possibly the servant mentioned *post* 28 Jan. 1759 and n. 3.

of their friends drinking tea and geneva and smoking in my little bedchamber; at last this charming scene ended and I arrived two days ago at this place which is a little Dutch, Dutchissime town; the most abominable place I ever knew, where I die of ennui and impatience that increases every day and with it a prospect, I doubt, of staying here a week longer; which I own I am not in spirits enough even on my approach to England to bear with much moderation; things are in so disagreeable a situation there[3] that I can't promise myself the peaceable enjoyment of my friends during the few short months we are allowed to stay there, and I look upon myself rather as coming over to make a winter campaign with you. This I must own I shall feel very sensibly if it be my fate, nor can any honours or advantages though they should rain upon me make it up to me. These weaknesses to you, dear Horry, who have your share in causing 'em I am not ashamed to own. From the world and from the military world in particular I would fain conceal 'em; but one can't think nor wish as one would and, notwithstanding all the art with which the world abounds, nature has just power enough left to make men unhappy. I'll tell you what my case is at present. The Duke (whose goodness to me I can never be grateful enough for) is now pushing for a regiment for me;[4] you know how great a thing that is; and yet I own I dread to hear I have obtained it because it's gone to Scotland[5] where I must expect to follow it immediately and pass the winter; or if this should not be, he[6] has ordered us all to bring horses over and intends, I believe, taking the field;[7] all this makes me melancholy; but the thoughts of seeing you and some of my friends soon, though but for a moment, gives me some cheerful intervals at least; I would fain dwell upon such thoughts only but you know how impossible that is. Adieu! Believe me, dear Horry,

Yours with great truth, and affection—

3. As a result of the Jacobite capture of Edinburgh and the defeat of the British troops at Prestonpans 21 Sept. OS.

4. In July the D. of Cumberland had recommended that Conway succeed Francis Ligonier as Col. of the 48th Foot. This did not take place, but Conway obtained the 48th Foot in April 1746, following Ligonier's death after the battle of Falkirk (Skrine, op. cit. 235–6; Conway to Lord Conway 4 Aug., 11 Aug., 13 Sept.

NS in *Colburn's United Service Magazine*, 1880, lii pt ii. 320–6, MSS now WSL; Robert Beatson, *Political Index*, 3d edn, 1806, ii. 240; *post* 6 March 1746 OS).

5. The 48th Foot had left Flanders directly for Newcastle about 27 Sept. NS (C. T. Atkinson, 'Jenkins' Ear, the Austrian Succession War and the 'Forty-Five,' *Journal of the Society for Army Historical Research*, 1943–4, xxii. 292).

6. That is, the Duke of Cumberland.

7. He did so.

Because of fears for the safety of England, ten battalions embarked from Flanders 20 Sept. 1745 NS, and other regiments followed at intervals. The embarkation of infantry was to be completed by 22 Oct. NS, and of cavalry and train by 29 Oct. NS. On 1 Nov. NS a fleet of transports and ordnance ships was ready to sail from Hellevoetsluis. Apparently Conway left Vilvorde about 18 Oct. NS; the Duke of Cumberland issued his final orders from his headquarters at Vilvorde 21 Oct. NS, arriving in London 29 Oct. NS (18 Oct. OS), where he stayed until ca 25 Nov. OS (C. T. Atkinson, 'Jenkins' Ear, the Austrian Succession War and the 'Forty-Five,' *Journal of the Society for Army Historical Research*, 1943–4, xxii. 291–3; A. N. Campbell-Maclachlan, *William Augustus, Duke of Cumberland*, 1876, pp. 240–2, 244; MANN iii. 166–7; *Daily Adv.* 19 Oct., 25 Nov. OS).

Prince Charles had captured the town and castle of Carlisle 15 Nov. OS, and had marched to Preston by 27 Nov. OS (MANN, loc. cit.; W. B. Blaikie, *Itinerary of Prince Charles Edward Stuart*, Edinburgh, 1897, p. 28). On that day the Duke of Cumberland with his staff (including Conway) arrived at Lichfield to take over the command of the army under Sir John Ligonier (*post* 30 Nov. 1745 OS, n. 1).

From CONWAY, Saturday 30 November 1745 OS

Printed from the MS now WSL, formerly Rutnam. First printed, *Rockingham Memoirs* i. 410–11; reprinted *Colburn's United Service Magazine*, 1880, lii pt ii. 471–2. The postmark is the date of the letter's arrival in London.

Address: To the Honourable Horatio Walpole, Jun., in Arlington Street, London.

Postmark: LITCHFIELD. 2 DE.

Litchfield, Nov. 30th 1745.

Dear Horry,

I HAVE hardly had a moment to write yet, and only pretend now to tell you in three words that we are hitherto safe and sound;[1] our troops are almost all come up; one battalion of Guards came in here this morning, another is expected today, and the last tomor-

---

1. The D. of Cumberland and his staff, including Conway, arrived at Lichfield 27 Nov. OS (Evan Charteris, *William Augustus Duke of Cumberland*, 1913, pp. 224–5; *Daily Adv.* 2 Dec. OS).

row;[2] the rebels are come to Warrington,[3] which is about forty-four or five miles, I think, from this place; yet I hardly think they'll venture an engagement, because they seem to have lost time and been irresolute in their motions. As soon as we are assembled, I fancy tomorrow or next day, we shall advance.[4] If they should do the same, the affair will be soon decided betwixt us, and I hope entirely determined; if not, we are in some hopes Marshal Wade may be able to oppose their retreat;[5] which they seem to think of if the accounts are true that we have heard of their having left one hundred men in the Castle of Carlisle,[6] and since sent twenty wagons of cheese and biscuit thither under a guard. We had some idea they might think of trying to slip us and march towards London, through Derbyshire,[7] but they are now quite out of that road. They can't think of Chester while we are so near and I can't think 'em mad enough to go into Wales, where both the armies must block 'em up, and therefore they must, in my opinion, either engage us or retire immediately; all this makes me happy in a prospect of seeing the affair soon ended, which of all things I most wish, having very little apprehension of their success.

2. Two Guards battalions had been ordered to leave London 23 Nov. OS and march to Lichfield, arriving 3 Dec.; and a third battalion (from the 2d Regiment of Guards) was ordered to leave on the 25th and reach Lichfield 4 Dec. However, expresses from Lancashire and Lichfield dated 30 Nov. and 2 Dec. indicate that at least one regiment had arrived by the 30th, and all three by 1 Dec. (Daniel MacKinnon, *Origin and Services of the Coldstream Guards*, 1833, i. 377–8, ii. 341–3; *Daily Adv.* 2 Dec. OS; MANN iii. 167, n. 17).

3. The Jacobite army reached Wigan 28 Nov. OS, but instead of continuing directly south to Warrington, turned east to Manchester, where it arrived on the 29th and remained on the 30th (W. B. Blaikie, *Itinerary of Prince Charles Edward Stuart*, Edinburgh, 1897, pp. 28–9, Scottish History Society XXIII). For current reports that the rebels were at Warrington, however, see a letter from Col. Joseph Yorke (another of the D. of Cumberland's aides-de-camp) to his father from Lichfield, 30 Nov. 1745 OS, in

George Harris, *Life of Lord Chancellor Hardwicke*, 1847, ii. 197, and letters from Warrington, 28 Nov. OS and Stafford, 30 Nov. OS in the *Daily Adv.* 2, 4 Dec. OS.

4. The D. of Cumberland, misled by a Jacobite feint towards Wales, advanced to Stafford 2 Dec. OS, but when he learned that the main army had gone to Derby, retreated south until he was at Meriden Common near Coventry on the 6th, and between the Jacobites and London (Blaikie, op. cit. 30, 31; Charteris, op. cit. 228–31).

5. Wade was in command of the army on the east coast, based on Newcastle-upon-Tyne, from which he had advanced to Persbridge by the 28th (Blaikie, op. cit. 28).

6. The Young Pretender did leave a garrison of unstated size at Carlisle (John Murray of Broughton, *Memorials*, ed. Bell, Edinburgh, 1898, p. 248n, Scottish History Society XXVII).

7. This was their intention, but the D. of Cumberland was misled by the feint towards Wales (above, n. 4).

We lay a night at Lord Strafford's[8] on the road, and passed almost a whole day there. They were vastly polite, and would have us come though we had sent an excuse at night, because it was so late. In answer to it he sent us his coach and said he should stay supper, so there was no refusing, though it was twelve o'clock before we got there. There was Lady Lucy,[9] a Miss Cockburn,[10] and Mr Vernon,[11] who set out early the next morning for town. It's a bad house, and I think a disagreeable place. Make my compliments to Lady Mary and Mrs Leneve. Let me hear from you, and believe me,

Ever yours,

H. C.

Direct to me at the Duke's quarters at Litchfield or elsewhere.

To CONWAY, ca Friday 6 – Monday 9 December 1745 OS

Missing; answered *post* 13 Dec. 1745 OS. The date is uncertain, but from the reference to HW's 'anxiety,' it would seem likely to have been written between the arrival of the news in London (6 Dec. OS) that the Young Pretender was at Derby and the news of the rebels' retreat, which HW knew by 9 Dec. OS (MANN iii. 178–9). It would have taken HW's letter several days to reach Conway on his march north.

8. Boughton Park, near Northampton, one of the seats of William Wentworth (1722–91), 2d E. of Strafford; HW's friend and correspondent. Strafford's father had purchased the house from Lord Ashburnham in 1717; in 1889 it was the property of Mr Howard Vyse, who inherited it through Lady Lucy Howard, Strafford's sister (Coke, *Journals,* i. 1, n. 2).

9. Lady Lucy Wentworth (d. 1771), m. (1747 *or* 48) Sir George Howard, K.B.; Lord Strafford's sister (Collins, *Peerage,* 1812, iv. 279–80; Joseph Foster, *Pedigrees of the County Families of Yorkshire,* 1874, ii. *sub* Wentworth; *Whitehall Evening Post* 13–16 Feb. 1748 OS.

10. Jane Cockburn, dau. of a protégé of the 2d D. of Argyll, who had been brought up with his family. On her father's death, she became companion to the Ds of Argyll and later was maintained by the Duke's daughters. For an account of her by Lady Louisa Stuart, see Coke, op. cit. iv. 455–6. She presumably was at Boughton with Lady Strafford, who was a dau. of the D. of Argyll.

11. Henry Vernon (1718–65), of Hilton Place, Staffs; M.P. Lichfield 1754–61, Newcastle-under-Lyme 1761–2 (GRAY i. 166, n. 43). He had married Lord Strafford's sister, Lady Henrietta Wentworth, in 1743.

From CONWAY, Friday 13 December 1745 OS

Printed from the MS now WSL, formerly Rutnam. First printed, *Rockingham Memoirs* i. 411–13; reprinted *Colburn's United Service Magazine*, 1880, lii pt ii. 472–4.
Address: To the Honourable Horatio Walpole in Arlington Street, London.

Wiggan, Dec. 13.

Dear Horry,

I AM extremely obliged to you for the anxiety you express in your last on our account, and think I cannot at present make a better return to it than by taking the first opportunity to let you know that your friends are all well, and for some time at least I think out of the way of danger; it's true we are at present in pursuit of the rebels, with a strong body of cavalry of both armies, and some infantry;[1] but they are got so much ahead of us,[2] that it is very doubtful whether we shall be able to overtake 'em.[3] However, I think the step we have taken is very right,[4] and though we should not be able to attack 'em, it seems incumbent upon us to wait on 'em out of the kingdom, and at least make their retreat as little commodious to 'em as possible. They marched from Preston this morning, and are at Lancaster to-night. This place is about ten miles from the former, and our advanced parties, I fancy, will be tonight beyond Preston. I have a strong idea that as soon as we appear, it will put 'em in a good deal of consternation, and perhaps occasion a desertion amongst 'em; for they are in great apprehensions of our cavalry, and are besides low in spirits, and much harassed. They talk of halting at Carlisle to receive their reinforcements from the north; but I believe our march

1. The D. of Cumberland with all his cavalry and 1000 foot, including mounted infantry, left Meriden in pursuit of the Jacobite army on 8 Dec. OS and marched steadily north (W. B. Blaikie, *Itinerary of Prince Charles Edward Stuart*, Edinburgh, 1897, p. 31, Scottish History Society XXIII).

2. As Conway says below, the Jacobites marched from Preston to Lancaster 13 Dec. OS (ibid.).

3. The Duke's advance guard did overtake the Prince's rear guard at Clifton 18 Dec. OS, but in an indecisive skirmish the Jacobites beat off the loyal troops and continued their retreat (ibid. 31–2).

4. Conway is probably referring to the pressure from London for a halt to the pursuit. On 10 Dec. OS the D. of Cumberland at Macclesfield received orders from the Cabinet of 8 Dec. to remain at Coventry; these were followed by orders of the 12th to return with the army to London, but these were in turn followed by orders of the 14th (received on the 16th) to continue the pursuit if he thought fit (Evan Charteris, *William Augustus Duke of Cumberland*, 1913, p. 236).

will puzzle 'em excessively, and very likely make 'em stagger in that resolution; as it will be impossible, I should imagine, for those reinforcements to join 'em before we reach Carlisle, and, of course, have it in our power to intercept 'em. Marshal Wade is marched back[5] with the main body of his army; and if they[6] stay at Carlisle will join us there. Our men are in very good health and spirits, and horses in excellent order, so that if they should stand before us, I should have no doubt of success, as they cannot defend themselves against the force of our cavalry.

I thank you for your reproof about my reflection on the slowness of the Marshal's proceeding;[7] and though I don't remember what, or to whom it was, I must own it could not be right, as the fact on which it was grounded was not true—at least in the light I put it, which, however, was as we had been informed, and so far, I think, my reflection was excusable; the horse who had been advanced did halt at or near Richmond about the time I mentioned,[8] while the foot were continuing their route, I must still say very deliberately, towards Ferrybridge, where they halted three entire days.[9] I must own I think there is a great fault in their proceedings, and I am the readier to say it, because I know that the fault is far from being all or even the chief part of it in the Marshal. I know that he is obstructed and hampered in every step he takes by a dead weight of Dutch troops[10]

5. Wade had advanced as far as Wakefield 10 Dec. OS intending to intercept the Young Pretender, but finding that the Jacobite army was several days' march ahead, returned to Newcastle with his foot, although he sent his cavalry on, which joined the Duke's at Preston 13 Dec. (Blaikie, op. cit. 31).

6. The Jacobites.

7. According to HW, Conway had been sent by the Duke of Cumberland to Wade 'to hasten his march upon the back' of the rebels (to Mann 9 Dec. OS, MANN iii. 179). Since Conway says he does not remember to whom he made the reflection, it was presumably not made in a missing letter to HW and does not appear *ante* 30 Nov. 1745 OS. Col. Joseph Yorke expresses the same opinion in writing to Hardwicke 4 Dec. OS: 'I am sorry Marshal Wade has been so dilatory in his march westward; for had he not made four days' halt at Richmond, he

would have prevented all this by coming behind 'em some time ago; and tho' he could not perhaps have reached 'em with his foot, yet his cavalry might have perpetually harassed and have forc'd 'em into our jaws' (*Hardwicke Corr.* i. 474–5).

8. Wade's cavalry was at Darlington and Richmond by 25 Nov. OS (James Ray, *Compleat History of the Rebellion*, Bristol, 1750, pp. 145–6).

9. Wade's infantry reached Ferrybridge, Yorks, 8 Dec. OS, but were at Wakefield by the 10th (Blaikie, op. cit. 30, 31).

10. The 6000 Dutch troops which had arrived in England in mid-September (MANN iii. 109 and n. 13; SELWYN 97 and nn. 16, 17). For similar comments on them by Gen. Oglethorpe, see a letter from the Abp of York to Lord Hardwicke, 4 Dec. 1745 OS, George Harris, *Life of Lord Chancellor Hardwicke*, 1847, ii. 199.

and their generals,[11] whom he must drag after him, and therefore he cannot act with that expedition and spirit that he ought, and that the times and our present circumstances require.

As to what regards the reflection coming from me, I have really a great esteem for the Marshal, and am far from forgetting that he behaved with great civility to me while I was under him;[12] but yet I can't think those obligations of a nature to prevent my giving my opinion to my friends upon his conduct in an affair so interesting as that of his present command; and I assure you, I should do the same of any person in the world in that situation; I mean with that decency that is due from one of my rank to his; and in confidence to my friends only, where one accustoms one's self to speak with free-dom one's sentiments upon most things without imagining they are ever to be called in question; and as for opening of letters, I don't suspect that in the number that pass through the offices mine are like to make any impression, or even to incite a curiosity of knowing to whom they belong. However, dear Horry, I take your reproof as I am sure it was meant: it's a liberty I love my friends should use with me. I think it's a proof of friendship, and therefore could not dislike it from any, but least of all from one of whose goodness I have had so many marks.

We march again tomorrow morning, and I fancy shall hardly make a halt till we come up with them, or see 'em at least to our *ne plus ultra*.[13] Adieu; give my best compliments to Lady Mary, Mrs Leneve, and all friends. Ned Cornwallis has just joined us with his regiment and is of our expedition.[14]

Yours sincerely,

H. C.

11. They were under the command of Count Nassau (*ante* 6 July 1744 NS, n. 8).

12. Conway had been one of Wade's aides-de-camp in 1744 (*ante* 3 June 1744 NS and n. 17).

13. The Scottish border.

14. Cornwallis was Lt-Col. of Bligh's (the 20th) Foot (MANN iii. 177, n. 37). His letter to HW from Preston 18 Dec. mentions 'this is the sixth day's march without a halt with a thousand volunteers from the army and Bligh's regiment.'

From CONWAY, Friday 7 February 1746 OS

Printed for the first time from the MS now WSL, formerly Rutnam.

Perth,[1] February 7.

Dear Horry,

BY this time you have long since heard of all our cheap conquests and bloodless victories.[2] I have little new to tell you but that we have continued our pursuit to this place with all sorts of success but that of overtaking our enemy who flies too fast to give us any hopes of doing that with any effect; from this place they divided into three bodies or rather two principal ones,[3] the Highlanders for the most part taking the King's Road[4] to the mountains and Lord John Drummond's[5] that of the eastern coast towards Montrose etc. They give out that they are to join again about Inverness,[6] attack Lord Loudon[7] there and after taking that and recruiting their army to return southwards; but these things are in general looked upon as mere brags for besides that their spirits are *aux abois* and that their men are enough inclined to run home with the plunder they have got it's almost or rather, I believe, quite impossible they should subsist to-

1. Where the D. of Cumberland and his staff arrived 6 Feb. OS (W. B. Blaikie, *Itinerary of Prince Charles Edward Stuart*, Edinburgh, 1897, p. 39, Scottish History Society XXIII). Conway had remained with the Duke in the northwest of England until the fall of Carlisle and had returned with him to London in early January. On receipt of the news of the battle of Falkirk the Duke had been appointed to command in Scotland 25 Jan. OS and, accompanied by Conway, had left immediately for Edinburgh, where they arrived 30 Jan. 'The ministry would have kept back Mr Conway, as being in Parliament; which when the Duke told him he burst into tears, and protested that nothing should hinder his going—and he is gone' (HW to Mann 28 Jan. 1746 OS, MANN iii. 204 and n. 12; *History and Antiquities of Carlisle*, Carlisle, 1838, pp. 77–8).

2. When the Jacobites learned of the D. of Cumberland's approach, they abandoned the siege of Stirling Castle 29 Jan.

OS and retired northward so that the Duke, instead of having a battle, made a virtually unimpeded progress through Stirling to Perth. The news of the retreat was known in London 5 Feb. (Blaikie, op. cit. 37–9; MANN iii. 208 and notes).

3. This decision was made at a council of war 2 Feb. OS. The third (and smallest) group was Lord Ogilvie's regiment and the Farquharsons, who, being near their own country, took a middle route to visit their homes (Blaikie, op. cit. 38).

4. One of the roads built by Wade after 1726 when he was commander-in-chief in Scotland.

5. Lord John Drummond (1714–47), titular 4th D. of Perth, 1746. He and Lord George Murray took the Lowland regiments and the horse along the coast road (ibid.).

6. This was their intention (ibid.).

7. John Campbell (1705–82), 4th E. of Loudoun, who had raised some 2000 loyal troops in the vicinity of Inverness.

gether in the mountains and indeed if you saw 'em you'd easily believe it. I wonder you don't come for after your jaunt to Cornwal it is but a step farther to visit the Highlands; only think what joy in the months of January and February to pass over the poetical banks of the Tweed and Tay or trace the revolutions in Scotland from the glorious field of Prestonpans[8] through the yet disputed ground of Falkirk[9] and Sherifmuir,[10] up to their source at Dunsinane and Scone, that awful seat of regality which lies but a mile from hence and which I have some thoughts of seeing today. Does not this excite your curiosity? and is't possible that indolence should have such an ascendant over you that you should prefer the lazy satisfaction of living with your friends in ease and luxury, to check noble enjoyments, which are seasoned to us by constant fatigue and by all imaginable inclemencies of climate and season, not to mention dirt, inconvenience of lodging, want of provision[11] and a thousand little accidents that do not leave but to make our life still more desirable. Indeed, I beg all your pardons but in this situation my friends must excuse me if I do all in my power to forget 'em, if possible totally and in time, if I am but so happy as to stay here, I don't at all despair of it, for I'm sure I see nothing here that ought to put me a bit in mind of the things and places I have left.

You know that we have taken the famous Jenny Cameron,[12] who is something of a beauty only a little antiquated; if she had been a day under forty we should all [have] been in love with her. I wish you could see Lady Kilmarnock's[13] letters to her husband which we

8. Where the Jacobites had defeated the English under Cope 21 Sept. 1745 OS.

9. Where the Jacobites had again defeated the English under Hawley 17 Jan. 1746 OS.

10. Sheriffmuir, where an indecisive battle took place between the Jacobites and the loyal troops 13 Nov. 1745.

11. The D. of Cumberland and the army were detained at Perth for two weeks by want of supplies (Evan Charteris, *William Augustus Duke of Cumberland*, 1913, p. 253).

12. Jean or Jeanie Cameron (ca 1699–1772), of Glendessary, m. —O'Neal, from whom she was divorced. She was taken at Stirling and imprisoned at Edinburgh Castle until released on bail in Nov. 1746.

Her alleged career as a camp-follower of the Young Pretender is mostly a fabrication (Compton Mackenzie, *Prince Charlie and His Ladies*, New York, 1935, pp. 49–50; Robert Chambers, *History of the Rebellion*, 1869, pp. 251–2 n.; Robert Forbes, *The Lyon in Mourning*, ed. Paton, Edinburgh, 1895–6, i. 292–3, Scottish History Society XX–XXII; *The Prisoners of the '45*, ed. Seton and Arnot, Edinburgh, 1928–9, i. 69, 213; ii. 82–3, Scottish History Society, 3d ser., XIII–XV; MANN vi. 453).

13. Lady Anne Livingston (1709–47), m. (1724) William Boyd (1705–46), 4th E. of Kilmarnock. Her letters had presumably been seized at Callendar House, near Falkirk, her ancestral seat, since the D. of Cumberland wrote to the Lord Justice Clerk, Falkirk, 1 Feb. 1746 OS: 'One cir-

have taken by the bushel. She's a very ugly fat woman about fifty[14] or upwards, devoured with the scurvy and other disorders, and so fond as nothing ever was but your agreeable aunt,[15] I am sure. She writes just such fond fiddle-faddle letters, half of which are composed of soft endearing expressions such as life, honey, jewel, only joy and love, etc., with every now and then a rapture wishing him folded in those scurvy arms or clasped to that fat breast, with earnest prayers for health, preservation and a quick return; the other half filled with little domestic concerns and housewifely wants such as a pair of shoes or new clogs, a little brandy and lemons, a night cap or a pair of garters, all which are intermixed with her endearments, paragraph after paragraph, without the least connection. In one I remember after telling him she had a fistula *in ano* and been exposed to a man to have it cut, with many other griefs and disorders both of mind and body, particularly the disobedience of a son[16] and long absence of her beloved Lord under which she is going to sink, she begs in a postscript that he will send her a few *rubans!* Is not she charming? and does not this give one a blessed idea of matrimony? Yet to this perhaps may we all be reserved and God knows if some of us don't wish it in our hearts. However, it's pretty in its beginnings at least and I long to see how it sits upon Lady Mary;[17] but when? Nay, God knows, but see it I certainly shall. The lawyers cannot detain them[18] nor these pitiless mountains us forever; to be fair I have great hopes our pilgrimage is almost accomplished. While I am writing, I hear that our best intelligences talk of nothing but the dispersion of these wretches and that his Highness is going towards the coast where the French are preparing to embark,[19] from all which it's plain we have nothing more to do here and from which I am

cumstance is particular, that Lady Kilmarnoch, who till last night had always stayed at Callenden [sic] House, went off with them [the rebels]' (*London Gazette Extraordinary* 5 Feb. 1746 OS). HW mentions the letters to Montagu 5 Aug. 1746 OS (MONTAGU i. 41–2), but no other reference to them has been found.

14. Actually, in her late thirties.

15. The wife of 'Old' Horace Walpole (*ante* 31 Oct. 1741 OS, n. 45).

16. James Boyd (after 1758, Hay) (1726–78), Kilmarnock's 2d but only surviving son, styled Lord Boyd ca 1728–46; 15th E. of Erroll, 1758. Since he remained loyal to

the Hanoverians and fought in the 21st Foot against the Jacobites, he was allowed to succeed to the family estates, although not to the forfeited titles.

17. Lady Mary Walpole; she and Charles Churchill were married 22 Feb. OS (*Daily Adv.* 26 Feb. OS).

18. For the legal difficulties about the fortunes of Lady Mary and Churchill, see MANN iii. 104, n. 18.

19. Reports similar to these appeared in the *London Gazette Extraordinary* 10, 13 Feb. 1746 OS, *sub* Edinburgh and Perth 5 Feb.

willing to conclude we shall not stay long. Adieu! Make London as merry as ever you can for our reception. I shan't expect to stay long amongst you[20] (that's a melancholy thought, by the by!) but I would fain pass the little time that's given me as well as possible that I may have some happiness to live upon when I am banished again.

I hear of little news from amongst you but Mr Pit's being secretary at war[21] and Sir William Young's[22] being advanced into a sort of lucrative annihilation; God knows how the public will come off in these scrambles but for them I fancy neither will have much reason to complain.

Compliments to Lady Mary etc. Lord Bury is yours. Ned[23] is stopped at Edinburgh. Adieu!

H. C.

To CONWAY, February 1746 OS

Missing; implied *post* 19 Feb. 1746 OS, where Conway discusses a request from HW to recommend Edward Cornwallis to the D. of Cumberland.

20. Because he would be sent back with the army to Flanders once the rebellion was over.

21. The Cobhamite faction, with the support of the Pelhams, had been insisting on Pitt's appointment, but on 6 Feb. the King refused to accept him (MANN iii. 209 and n. 18; J. B. Owen, *Rise of the Pelhams*, 1957, pp. 292–4).

22. Sir William Yonge (ca 1693–1755), 4th Bt; M.P. Honiton 1715–54, Tiverton 1754–5. He was secretary at war, but his removal to the vice-treasurership of Ire-

land to make room for Pitt had been expected since November (MANN iii. 155 and n. 14). His transfer finally took place, under somewhat different circumstances, in May (ibid. iii. 256 and n. 15a).

23. Cornwallis. Bligh's regiment (the 20th Foot) of which he was still, apparently, commanding Lt-Col., had been expected at Edinburgh 1 Feb. OS, where it was assigned to garrison duty at the Castle (*London Gazette* No. 8507, 1–4 Feb. OS, *sub* Edinburgh 30 Jan.; *Daily Adv.* 18 Feb. OS *sub* Edinburgh 10 Feb.).

From CONWAY, Wednesday 19 February 1746 OS

Printed for the first time from the MS now WSL, formerly Rutnam. The post-mark is the date of the letter's arrival in London.

Address: To the Honourable Horatio Walpole, Jun., in Arlington Street, London.

Postmark: 26 FE.

Perth, Wednesday, F[ebruary] 19.

Dear Horry,

I BEGIN by that which I fancy will give you most pleasure which is that Lord Bury has already spoke to the Duke about Ned's affair[1] and that he has promised in the most obliging manner to mention it to the King. You know I believe that I interest myself sincerely for him and therefore though I should have been happy myself in any opportunity of showing my esteem for him as well as a particular one in obliging you, I was very glad Lord B. undertook the affair as I know nobody has more interest with the Duke and could by no means flatter myself that my application would have been of equal weight; and I am farther happy in thinking that with his merit in the situation he's in[2] and with such recommendation he'll stand a very fair chance. I have hardly seen him since I left you, only one night at Berwick,[3] his regiment lying at Edinburgh, where I fancy it may possibly remain some time.

I am a little angry with you all in town for not giving me some account of the strange revolutions that have happened amongst you, for I have yet only had the disagreeable news of the first change[4] in

1. Presumably a regiment. It may already have been known that Brig.-Gen. Bligh, Col. of the 20th Foot, was going to succeed to the colonelcy of the 12th Dragoons (as he did in April) and Cornwallis may have been pressing to succeed him. If so, the suit was unsuccessful, for Lord George Sackville became Col. of the 20th Foot 9 April 1746 OS and Cornwallis seems to have remained Lt-Col. until 1749, when he was given command of the troops going to Nova Scotia and made a colonel. He finally received a regiment (the 40th Foot) in 1750 (DNB sub 'Bligh'; Robert Beatson, *Political Index*, 1806, ii. 194, 218, 235; GM 1749, xix.

189; *Court and City Register*, 1748, p. 143).

2. Lt-Col. commanding the regiment.

3. Presumably 27 Jan. OS, when the D. of Cumberland was on his way to Edinburgh (*Daily Adv.* 31 Jan. OS).

4. The resignation of the entire Pelham ministry 10–11 Feb. 1746 OS and the succession of Granville and Bath. For this crisis, see J. B. Owen, *Rise of the Pelhams*, 1957, pp. 295–7 and HW to Mann 14 Feb. 1746 OS, MANN iii. 210–13 and notes. The news reached the D. of Cumberland and his staff at Edinburgh 15 Feb., where they were staying briefly for a conference (D. of Cumberland to

a very short letter from my brother. 'Tis the most insolent trick of fortune that I believe she ever ventured to play, amongst us at least, and not at all inferior to her pranks amongst the Turks and Asiatics; for me *je n'y comprends goutte,* and should have been much obliged to anybody that would have given me some sort of light into transactions so sudden and so mysterious; I conceive the general cause but how it could proceed so silently to such a crisis and unite so many discordant interests and parties, I have no notion—much less how the second turn[5] was brought about with a velocity that looks like magic. I would have given something to see that week's levees, with all the variety of hopes, fears, triumphs and dejections that composed 'em and above all to have met our two ministers[6] of Brentford[7] coming down the back stairs.

I was surprised at a friend of mine[8] a good deal: that's enough to say, but not at all so at a relation of ours[9] who, I hear, has come post from the west just in time to hear he had nothing better to do than return. You love to laugh and make one laugh; pray let me hear a little of these affairs.

Our army is now in motion[10] and the last of us will leave this

Newcastle 16 Feb. 1746 OS, BM Add. MSS 32706, f. 157; George Harris, *Life of Lord Chancellor Hardwicke,* 1847, ii. 219–20).

5. The abandonment of the attempt by the new ministers to form an administration 12 Feb. and the formal restitution of the old ministers on the 14th. The news that the *status quo* had been restored was announced by the D. of Cumberland to his aides-de-camp at breakfast 17 Feb. OS (ibid. ii. 220–1).

6. Lord Bath and Lord Granville (HW).

7. In Buckingham's *Rehearsal* II. iv, the physician and the gentleman usher usurp the throne simply by announcing that they have done so.

8. Duke of Grafton (HW). This may be an allusion to some sort of inaccurate account of Grafton's conduct during the ministerial crisis. He did not resign as lord chamberlain with the Pelhams, although he intended to do so the day the new ministry collapsed. Knowledge of his intention, however, had come as a surprise to Granville, probably because Grafton was a personal friend of the King's and so would reasonably be expected to remain in office under the circumstances (*Private Correspondence of Chesterfield and Newcastle 1744–46,* ed. Sir Richard Lodge, 1930, p. 117; MANN iii. 211).

9. Lord Cholmondeley (HW). George Cholmondeley (1703–70), 3d E. of Cholmondeley; HW's brother-in-law. He was another personal friend of the King's; the King had resented Cholmondeley's removal from lord privy seal to vice-treasurer of Ireland in 1744 and had proposed him as secretary of state in an abortive attempt to overthrow the Pelhams in Sept. 1745 (Owen, op. cit. 244, 281–2; MANN ii. 551). Under these circumstances, Cholmondeley may very well have expected a major office in the new administration. He does not, however, appear to have come to London during the crisis, but to have remained at Chester with the troops (Stair to Newcastle 24 Feb. 1746 OS, BM Add. MSS 32706, f. 207).

10. The van of the army had advanced to Dundee 14 Feb.; other units followed during the week, and the Duke himself left Perth 21 Feb. OS (*Daily Adv.* 25, 27 Feb., 4 March OS).

place the day after tomorrow; I have been dismally disappointed about returning and find it grew more distant every day just when I thought we were upon the point of setting out; with this we lead the most tiresome life imaginable. Judge of the state of my spirits! Adieu! Let me hear from you and believe me most

Sincerely dear Horry yours

H. C.

Compliments to Lady Mary and Mrs Leneve.

To CONWAY, ca Thursday 27 February 1746 OS

Missing; probably written in reply to *ante* 19 Feb. OS, which arrived in London 26 Feb.; answered *post* 3 March OS.

From CONWAY, ca Thursday 27 February 1746 OS

Missing; HW says *post* 6 March 1746 OS that he received a letter from Conway 'last night' from Aberdeen; the D. of Cumberland reached Aberdeen 27 Feb. OS (W. B. Blaikie, *Itinerary of Prince Charles Edward Stuart*, Edinburgh, 1897, p. 40), and Conway would have had to have written promptly for the letter to reach London by 5 March.

From CONWAY, Monday 3 March 1746 OS

Printed for the first time from the MS now WSL, formerly Rutnam. From internal evidence, March 1746 has to be the correct month; Conway apparently misdated the letter '4' March, since the first Monday of March 1746 OS fell on the 3d.

Address: To the Honourable Horatio Walpole in Arlington Street, London.
Memoranda (by HW): Mr P.¹

Moneyed interest hid its head—storm that hung over the capital—Religion and the Funds. A maxim uncontroverted the less you trust to fortune the better. A scandalous rebellion and Popish Pretender. Caprice in public credit. Avarice, combinat. and cabal——disappointed avarice. Disappointed ambition that melancholy tomorrow.

[There is also a long list of illegible names in pencil on the cover.]

Aberdeen, Monday, M[arch] 4 [3].

IT is indeed, I doubt, pretty much as you say and after thinking myself upon the point of returning from the moment almost that I left you, I am now come to have hardly the least glimmering hope left of seeing you for ages. The Duke himself is likely to stay a great while but I for my sins, I doubt, condemned to stay a great while longer. I mean if that should succeed for me on which you have congratulated me by anticipation² and which is certainly not done yet or at least was not then, yet by what I hear it is in a very fair way, though not without some small difficulties; if they should happen to be too strong you know I shall not want consolations, amongst which the thought of seeing my friends sooner is such an one that I hardly dare own how great it is or how near it would come to an equivalent: these are weaknesses which we warriors ought to be ashamed of and which of all people in the world are the most

1. These may be notes of a speech by either Pelham or Pitt in the otherwise unrecorded debates in the House of Commons 10 and 11 March 1746 OS on the methods of raising supplies for the year, in which the government supporters defeated Sir John Barnard and the Opposition by a majority of 99 (*Private Correspondence of Chesterfield and Newcastle 1744–46,* ed. Sir Richard Lodge, 1930, pp. 128, 129; *Journals of the House of Commons* xxv. 89–90). One account of the debate in the committee on the 10th mentions that 'Mr Pitt made a florid oration

in favour of the Court, which has made him the ridicule of everyone, and was very severely handled by Sir John for personal reflections against him' (Hist. MSS Comm., *Hastings MSS,* 1928–47, iii. 55). The illegible list of names on the cover may also be connected with these debates. HW would probably have received this letter about the 10th or 11th if it came by the post from Aberdeen.

2. That is, on his obtaining a regiment, presumably the succession to the colonelcy of the 48th Foot. See also *post* 6 March 1746 OS.

improper for us: we ought to be no other than a mere military engine with heads and hearts like bullets and battering rams, all solid and impenetrable, and of all misfortunes in the world it's the greatest for us to think of anything out of the verge of our own profession, to be connected with anything, or to feel for anything.—The rebels at present are using all sorts of means to increase their army and have succeeded so far as to raise some new men and bring back some of those that had left 'em but they are so scattered at present in different bodies that it's impossible to talk with any certainty of their numbers, and still less so of their designs. Sometimes they are going to attack Fort Augustus and Fort William, sometimes marching after Lord Loudon and sometimes entrenching themselves to defend the Spay; nay, they'd make one believe they are doing all at once. As soon as we can march this mystery will begin to clear up, and I am apt to believe their projects will all vanish with it. Their affairs seem to me pretty desperate; disappointed of the reinforcements from France,[3] their communication with it at present almost cut off if not entirely,[4] and the chief part of their men raised by compulsion, if they should ever bring 'em to face us I think there is no great doubt of the event.

Pray tell Lady Mary that without saying any pretty things upon her marriage I wish her joy very seriously and very sincerely and I think she'll be happy for what in this world seems a very odd reason, because she deserves to be so, but with her temper and some other qualities that I could name without flattery I believe she can hardly fail.

Poor Uncle John![5] I am not very sorry he's dead as you may imagine, so shall say no melancholy things about it. I delight in your interview with Er[asmus][6] vastly and what a number of doleful dirges you are to expect from Arthur![7] Adieu, dear Horry. I don't know whether you are going to be married or not but I wish as you say

3. Possibly an allusion to the capture, 21 Feb. OS, of two French ships with part of Fitzjames's regiment (MANN iii. 222, n. 9).

4. Twenty-two ships under Adm. Byng were patrolling the coast of Scotland (H. W. Richmond, Navy in the War of 1739–48, Cambridge, 1920, ii. 189); nevertheless two French ships with troops had reached Aberdeen 21 and 22 Feb. OS, a few days before the loyal troops reached that

place (London Gazette No. 8515, 1–4 March OS).

5. John Shorter, the eldest brother of HW's and Conway's mothers. This letter establishes the date of his death, which was previously unknown.

6. Erasmus Shorter (d. 1753) (MONTAGU i. 156).

7. Arthur Shorter (d. post 1746); for him and Erasmus see also post 29 Aug. and 24 Sept. 1746 OS.

I was,—to anything but Scotland, of which I can hardly bear the honeymoon, and have not found it in any respect like Lord Dumfreis's[8] lodgings. Pray pity me vastly, I am dismally dispirited.

Yours, etc.,

H. C.

PS. We are to have a ball[9] here tonight; only think of it!

To CONWAY, Tuesday 4 March 1746 OS

Missing; mentioned by HW *post* 6 March 1746 OS as a 'long letter' written on Tuesday; probably the letter answered by Conway *post* 19 March 1746 OS.

To CONWAY, Thursday 6 March 1746 OS

Printed for the first time from photostats of two MS copies in different hands kindly supplied by the late Sir John Murray.

London, March the 6th 1746.

My dear Harry,

AS I wrote you a long letter on Tuesday I have little else to say than to contradict the account I gave you of its being resolved to send ten thousand of our national troops abroad; Damer[1] was my author for it, and told it me in a manner that made me easily believe it: and indeed from whence so great a mistake could arise I am yet at a loss to conceive as Mr Ellison[2] was his author for it: he mentioned particularly the two regiments of dragoons; and the num-

---

8. William Dalrymple Crichton (1699–1768), 5th E. of Dumfries; 4th E. of Stair, 1760.

9. There is an account of this ball in Evan Charteris, *William Augustus Duke of Cumberland*, 1913, p. 260, based on the description in *The Life of John Metcalf, commonly called Blind Jack of Knaresborough*, who was fiddler for the occasion.

1. Probably Joseph Damer (1718–98), cr. (1753) Bn Milton and (1792) E. of Dorchester; M.P. Weymouth and Melcombe Regis 1741–7, Bramber 1747–54, Dorchester, 1754–62. His son John eventually married Conway's daughter.

2. Probably Cuthbert Ellison (1698–1785), Gen., 1772; M.P. Shaftesbury 1747–54 (SELWYN 156, n. 11).

ber of Foot, but said the particular corps amongst them was not yet absolutely determined. As it was likely to come from Lord Stair's[3] I gave entire credit to it, but upon asking Mr Pelham I find it not so: when it was resolved to keep the Hessians longer in Scotland,[4] the King himself mentioned it; but nothing is determined or done in it.

I received yours last night from Aberdeen, and am sorry to see your stay in Scotland is likely to be much longer than I expected; I do not believe the rebels intend to fight you, nor do I believe they intend immediately to disperse; France is too evidently concerned in the continuance of it, not to dispose of men or money enough to keep up their spirits a little longer; any time gained is of infinite consequence to her views and progress in the Netherlands; I doubt let our ships do what they will they cannot entirely prevent the French succours, and as long as they are paid, there will be Highlanders in rebellion.

With respect to the regiment I will tell you all that has passed about it; at least that I am acquainted with, and that I believe I may safely say is the whole; when the King mentioned it to Mr Pelham I was in the country; upon coming to town I found I had been desired to call at Mr Pelham's, as soon as I returned or it was convenient: which I did the evening I came: Mr Pelham told me the King had mentioned the Duke's particular recommendation of you for one of the vacant regiments to him; had been pleased himself to say you was a brave young fellow, and a good officer, and felt himself disposed to do it: but said fairly at the same time he must own he had one difficulty that remained with him; which was a fondness that you had shown by a vote or two you had given for popular bills and which he was apprehensive might extend to your whole way of thinking upon matters of that kind: I told Mr Pelham that I believed your way of thinking in matters of government was as just as any man's, and could consequently not think nay was convinced, you

---

3. Ellison had been a Lt-Col. on the staff of the army under Stair formed to resist the expected French invasion in 1744 (GM 1744, xiv. 169); he may have been one of Stair's aides-de-camp.

4. About 6000 Hessian troops arrived at Leith 8 Feb. OS to replace the Dutch auxiliaries (W. B. Blaikie, *Itinerary of Prince Charles Edward Stuart*, Edin-

burgh, 1897, p. 88, Scottish History Society XXIII). They were ordered back to Flanders about 20 Feb. OS in the belief that the rebellion was over, but the order was countermanded almost immediately when it became apparent this was not the case (MANN iii. 222 and nn. 11–17).

could not at present look upon the prerogative as an object to be so much apprehended, as to wish its weight lessened by a heap of popular bills and which were really never proposed but as an engine of party: that as to the vote you had given for a place bill,[5] it was given by a young man when he first came into the world, but I was convinced not as a pledge of any such extravagant ideas: he told me he had wrote to the Duke and mentioned the King's difficulty about it, and asked me if I thought it best to write to you upon it; I told him if he had already done it to the Duke I thought it was unnecessary: that I knew your way of thinking was such that his Majesty would if he was acquainted with it have no objections to it; and that I was absolutely certain you intended as much to support him and his government as any honest man, and would I was sure be ready to tell the Duke so when he mentioned it to you.

From CONWAY, Wednesday 19 March 1746 OS

Printed from the MS now WSL, formerly Rutnam. First printed, *Rockingham Memoirs* i. 413–15; reprinted *Colburn's United Service Magazine,* 1880, lii pt ii. 475–6. This may have been received 24 March OS, when an express from the D. of Cumberland, Aberdeen, 19 March, arrived in London (*London Gazette* No. 8521, 22–5 March OS).

Address: To the Honourable Horatio Walpole, Jun., in Arlington Street, London.

Aberdeen, Wednesday, March 19.

Dear Horry,

I HAVE been writing to you every day for some time past and have been constantly hindered by some foolish thing or other; the three last days I have been out upon an expedition against the rebels[1] as foolish as anything because it ended in nothing. I am much obliged to you for your history of the late administration[2] which pleases me

5. Probably in March 1742, during Conway's first session of Parliament. No division lists for these debates have been found. HW comments elsewhere that Conway had 'set out upon a plan of [un]fashionable virtue, had provoked the King and Duke by voting against the army at the beginning of the war' (*Mem. Geo. II* i. 41). See also *ante* 18 April 1745 OS, n. 4, for Conway's votes against the army.

1. To Strath Bogie; Conway describes it in more detail further on in the present letter.

2. Probably in HW's missing letter of 4 March OS.

much better than one that I have seen since in the shape of I don't know what;3 something of Tom Thumb, which is mighty stupid, in spite of all the advantages of the subject. Pray who's my slow friend— the Duke of Gr[afton]?4 I imagine so by our cordiality. And by the by I hear my quick friend his daughter5 has had a violent squabble with Lord R[obert] Bertie;6 as you have a good hand at such stories I beg you'll let me hear the particulars, which I fancy must be curious.—I have seen a scurrilous print7 in which she is introduced which is mighty low and stupid; one of the persons I don't know.

I hear of nothing but gaieties and gallantries amongst you which is shocking considering that I have now for some [time] given up all hopes of seeing you for ages; indeed I doubt not till next winter, for if I get the re[giment] I know it will be here and consequently I am fixed here till that time at least and perhaps longer, at least so my fears tell me; and I am so imprudent as to have been uttering these fears in all my letters till my brother has actually chid me and I must own he's in the right for it may have a bad construction put upon it as if I was indifferent to the service and not sufficiently sensible of the obligation I have to the Duke on that account; but perhaps the thing may not be so near as we thought; I imagined it was actually done and that blowing over perhaps it may now be some time before it is determined; so I shall in the meantime suspend both my joys and my fears on that head. But exclusive of that I doubt our stay is likely to be long here, considering the obstinacy of the rebels and the resolutions of the Duke to see the rebellion entirely finished, which with all the *désagréments* that attend it I can't help entirely applauding, and I am in hopes that the motions we shall soon make will con-

3. Probably 'The Surprising History of a Late Long Administration: Showing the Wonderful Transactions, the Wise Negotiations, the Prudent Measures, and the Great Events of that Most Astonishing Period,' by Titus Livius junior, advertised as 'this day is published, in folio' in the *Daily Adv.* 10 March OS. No copy has been seen by the editors, but it seems to have been the only pamphlet on the abortive ministry.

4. For other references to Grafton's torpidity, see MANN ii. 82; *Mem. Geo. II* i. 181; and (probably) SELWYN 27.

5. Lady Caroline Fitzroy.

6. (1721–82), Gen. 1777; lord of the

Bedchamber; M.P. Whitchurch 1751–4, Boston 1754–82 (MONTAGU i. 85, n. 43). Nothing is known of his relations with Lady Caroline.

7. Probably 'Taste A-La-Mode, 1745,' published 12 Sept. 1745 (British Museum, *Catalogue of Prints . . . Political and Personal Satires*, 1870–1954, iii pt i. 588–9 [No. 2774]). See the reproduction in G. Paston [Emily Morse Symonds], *Social Caricature in the Eighteenth Century*, 1905, Plate VI, opp. p. 10; Lady Caroline is presumably the young woman on the left lifting her skirts in a provocative manner and being ogled by a young man.

tribute greatly towards it; our vanguard is now advanced within 12 miles of the Spay[8] where they are, and as soon as the wind which is more obstinate than the rebels will let our supplies come up we shall all move on there. The party that I told you I had been upon was to take a post called Strathbogie,[9] where there had lain for some days past a body of the rebels that called themselves 1500 or 2000 but were I believe about 800.[10] Gen. Bland[11] who commands the vanguard consisting at present of four battalions of Foot,[12] two of cavalry[13] and the Campbells[14] marched on Monday morning early thither in hopes to have surprised that post and had like to have succeeded for the rebels did not know of our approach nor begin to move out of the town till our advanced party was within sight. They had been out in the morning attempting to surprise a post of ours[15] and were

8. That is, the vanguard of the loyal troops were in Strath Bogie while the Jacobites under Lord John Drummond were concentrated along the Spey, 12 miles away.

9. Strath Bogie is a valley rather than a post.

10. 'His Royal Highness having received intelligence on Sunday the 16th instant, that Roy Stewart was at Strathbogie, with about one thousand foot and three score hussars, sent Colonel Conway with orders to Major-General Bland to attempt to surprise them, and if he should not succeed in that, to attack them' (London Gazette No. 8521, 22–5 March OS, which contains the official report of the action sub Aberdeen 19 March OS). Both figures for the Jacobite force are probably exaggerated; an account by one of the Jacobites involved, written two years later, relates that 'upon the 17th there had come about 3000 of Cumberland's men, commanded by General [Bland], to Strathbogie, 12 miles from Spey or Fochabers, and dispossessed Roy Stewart and Abachie Gordon's battalions, a part of Lord Elcho's troop of guards and a few of the hussars, amounting in whole to about 500 men, who formed the Prince's advance guard, and made a safe retreat without the loss of one man after they were within musket shot of the 3000 men . . . and when they joined Lord John Drummond at Spey, the whole of them would not have been above 900 or 1000

men at that time' (Robert Forbes, The Lyon in Mourning, ed. Paton, Edinburgh, 1895–6, ii. 213–14, Scottish History Society XX–XXII). Further details of the whole incident are in the anonymous 'Memoirs of the Rebellion in 1745 and 1746, so far as it Concerned the Counties of Aberdeen and Banff,' Origins of the 'Forty-Five, ed. Blaikie, Edinburgh, 1916, pp. 154–5, Scottish History Society, 2d ser. II).

11. Humphrey Bland (ca 1686–1763), Major-Gen., 1745; Lt-Gen., 1747; later (1753) commander-in-chief in Scotland (GM 1747, xvii. 497).

12. The Royals (1st), Barrell's (4th), Price's (14th), and Cholmondeley's (34th) (London Gazette No. 8520, 18–22 March OS, sub Aberdeen 14 March OS).

13. Cobham's Dragoons (10th Hussars) and Kingston's Light Horse, one of the volunteer regiments raised in the summer and fall of 1745, and disbanded in Sept. 1746 (ibid.; C. T. Atkinson, 'Jenkins' Ear, the Austrian Succession War and the 'Forty-Five,' Journal of the Society for Army Historical Research, 1943–4, xxii. 293, 296).

14. The Argyllshire militia, commanded by Lt-Col. Campbell, which had joined the government troops 16 Jan. 1746 OS and disbanded 17 Aug. OS (W. B. Blaikie, Itinerary of Prince Charles Edward Stuart, Edinburgh, 1897, pp. 36, 64, Scottish History Society XXIII).

15. At Clate, which had been occupied the night before by the loyal Grants,

returned about an hour, when they saw us advancing and then marched off with great precipitation, so we got the post very cheap at least which is an important one, though we acquired no great honour; we pursued them about 2 miles beyond the town with some of Kingston's Light Horse, a few dragoons and some of the Campbells but Gen. Bland, fearing we should engage too far in a country we did not ⟨know⟩, especially as night was coming on and our troops were fatigued with a long mar⟨ch⟩ ordered us to return.[16] One of Kingston's thought he wounded Roy Stewart[17] by a shot in ⟨the⟩ arm and a fellow who came to Strathbogie since says he is dead of the wound, which at least seems to confirm a little the belief of his being wounded. He stayed in the rear I believe chiefly to reconnoitre our party. This is all the mischief we pretend to have done. However the men found a good hot dinner in most of the quarters which the rebels were just sitting down to and perhaps were very well contented to get without fighting for it. Adieu, dear Horry, I have no more news to tell you.

Yours affectionately,

H. C.

although they had moved on for greater safety to Castle Forbes, which the Jacobites did not dare attack that morning ('Memoirs of the Rebellion in . . . Aberdeen and Banff,' op. cit. 153–4).

16. 'On Monday the 17th, Major-General Bland marched towards Strathbogie and was almost within sight of the place, when the rebels had the first notice of his approach: upon which they abandoned the town, and fled with the utmost precipitation towards Keith. Our vanguard pushed the rear of the rebels a good way beyond the river Deveson; but as the night was coming on, and the evening was wet and hazy, Major-General Bland ordered the troops to quit the pursuit, notwithstanding which the volunteers, viz. the Marquis of Granby, Colonel Conway, Captain Halden, and several others, continued to pursue the rebels at least two miles; whose panic was so great, that it was concluded they would not halt long in a place, till they had passed the Spey' (*London Gazette* No. 8521, 22–5 March OS, *sub* Aberdeen 19 March OS).

17. John (called John Roy) Stewart (1700–52); had joined the Young Pretender at the beginning of the rebellion and served as colonel of the 'Edinburgh regiment.' 'It is reported from among the rebels that Roy Stewart was killed by a shot he received from one of the Duke of Kingston's men' (ibid.). The rumours were untrue; what actually happened is described by the author of the 'Memoirs of the Rebellion in . . . Aberdeen and Banff,' op. cit. 155: 'Among these last [the Jacobite rear-guard], was Hunter of Burnside, who for a good way kept within speech of the party under Major Crawford and the volunteers that pursued them but managed his horse with so much dexterity, turning so oft and so nimbly, that they could not aim at him rightly; at length one of the Campbells shot so near him as made him start aside and gallop off, and as the forces took him for Roy Stewart, this gave occasion to the story of that gentleman being either killed or wounded.'

Is Mrs Leneve with you? My service to her.

I had forgot Mr Mann.[18] Nothing but the Duke's desiring it shall make me employ any other, but as I think he employs him himself there's no likelihood of that.

To CONWAY, ca Thursday 20 March 1746 OS

Missing; answered *post* 30 March 1746 OS; it probably replied to Conway's *ante* 3 March 1746 OS.

To CONWAY, ca Friday 28 March 1746 OS

Missing; answered *post* 6 April 1746 OS; it seems to be an answer to Conway's of 19 March OS.

From CONWAY, Sunday 30 March 1746 OS

Printed from the MS now WSL, formerly Rutnam. First printed (misdated 20 March), *Rockingham Memoirs* i. 415–17; reprinted (correctly dated), *Colburn's United Service Magazine*, 1880, lii pt ii. 476–7.

Address: To the Honourable Horatio Walpole, Jun., in Arlington Street, London.

Aberdeen, Sunday, March 30.

Dear Horry,

YOU are very good to pity us, and as far as pity can go in cases so desperate as ours, I can give your good nature the satisfaction of knowing it does console us, but as you say, to combat so many demons under all the various forms of High and Low landers, friends and enemies, to combat at the same time with all that climate, country, and air can afford of disagreeable, and with it the worst of all devils, a thorough ennui and inquietude, in twenty different shapes

---

18. Galfridus Mann (1706–56), army clothier; Sir Horace Mann's brother. HW had obviously reminded Conway to employ him as clothier for his regiment when he obtained it.

of regrets, mortification, and desire, is more than I believe any patience is well able to sustain. However, one must make the best of it,
and having little or no matter for it, [we] here draw all our consolation from the charity and good nature of our friends, who, I hope,
too can afford us a thought now and then without interrupting too
much the scene of gaiety that I hear flourishes so in London, and
which I assure you I am far from envying you, though I can't help
regretting it. I assure you I hear even with pleasure how your diversions go on, and that you have sent all your discontents and fears to
Scotland, the proper seat of 'em. This I would have, and provided
you think of us sometimes, 'tis all we expect. Poor Lady Chapman.[1]
I am sorry to hear her gaiety has had so unfortunate a catastrophe;
and poor Sir John! I pity him more, for I hear he is like to have his
impotence as public as his wife's lewdness has long been. How could
he be such a fool as to meddle with her?—I hear Miss Vane[2] has run
away with Mr Hope.[3] Queer. Is it possible? But indeed I am convinced there is nothing a girl won't run away with: it's the greatest
joy they have. I hear there have been fifty quarrels between Lady
Townshend and Lady Car[oline]:[4] between the latter and his Grace
a dismal one, and an irreparable breach between Lady T[ownshend]
and Mr W[innington]. These things are all diverting, and I am vastly
glad to hear the town has so much spirit. Plays, operas, and masquerades, and balls are vulgar diversions; but quarrels, scandal, and
gallantries, charming—don't you think so? As for us, we grow duller
and duller. The rebels have crossed the Firth of Cromarty in boats,[5]
favoured by a fog, in consequence of which Lord Loudon's fine army

1. Rachel Edmondson (d. ?1764), m. (1736) Sir John Chapman (ca 1710–81), 2d Bt; M.P. Taunton 1741–7. No other de-tails of the scandal have been found.

2. Lady Anne Vane (d. 1776), m. 1 (20 March 1746 OS) Hon. Charles Hope Weir (divorced, 1757); m. (2) Hon. George Monson (*Scots Peerage* iv. 494; Collins, *Peerage*, 1812, iv. 526; *Annual Register* 1776, p. 227).

3. Hon. Charles Hope Weir (1710–91), M.P. Linlithgowshire 1743–68. Miss Vane was his second wife; he had assumed the name of Weir after his first marriage, but seems to have used it irregularly (*Scots Peerage* loc. cit.). 'Last week Charles Hope Weir, Esq., brother to the Earl of Hop-ton, was married to Miss Vane, eldest

daughter of the Hon. Henry Vane, Esq.' (*Daily Adv.* 25 March OS).

4. Fitzroy. No details of these quarrels have been found.

5. The Jacobites under Perth crossed the Firth of Dornoch (not Cromarty) by boat 20 March OS, captured some of Loudoun's troops and dispersed the others (W. B. Blaikie, *Itinerary of Prince Charles Edward Stuart*, Edinburgh, 1897, p. 42, Scottish History Society XXIII; *London Gazette* No. 8523, 29 March – 1 April OS, *sub* Aberdeen 26 March OS; *Daily Adv.* 8 April OS *sub* Edinburgh 31 March). Several other contemporary ac-counts are in *More Culloden Papers*, ed. Duncan Warrand, Inverness, 1923–30, v. 39–47.

is, I doubt, entirely dispersed. The last accounts from Fort William look as if they were giving over their design upon that place,[6] and everything looks as if they were going north towards Sutherland, etc., where it will be happy if we can pen 'em up.

Adieu, dear Horry. You see how stupid I am and how little I have to tell you.

Yours ever,

H. C.

You don't say a word of Lady Mary. Pray give my compliments; and to Churchill. I intended to have writ and wished him joy, but I think it's too late now.

From CONWAY, Sunday 6 April 1746 OS

Printed from the MS now WSL, formerly Rutnam. First printed, *Rockingham Memoirs* i. 417–20; reprinted, *Colburn's United Service Magazine*, 1880, lii pt iii. 66–9. This letter may have been sent with the express from the D. of Cumberland, Aberdeen, 6 and 7 April OS, which reached London 15 April OS (*London Gazette* No. 8527, 12–15 April OS).

Address: To the Honourable Horatio Walpole, Jun., in Arlington Street, London.

Aberdeen, Sunday, Ap[ril] 6th.

Dear Horry,

I DON'T know what you mean by glory and triumph. I am conscious of no title to anything of the kind, not even as they are often bestowed, without being acquired and I assure you I have less taste for them since I have been sent here to hunt after 'em, where we have little chance to find 'em, and where, I must own between friends, I doubt the fairest sprig of laurel would hardly have tempted me to come, upon condition of remaining in this exile so long as I

---

6. 'There are no certain accounts relating to Fort William' (*London Gazette* No. 8524, 1–5 April OS, *sub* Aberdeen 31 March OS). The Jacobites had blockaded Fort William 24 Feb. OS and besieged it 20 March, but raised the siege and retired 3 April (MANN iii. 228, n. 3).

There is an account of events there from 14 March in the *London Gazette* No. 8526, 8–12 April; and, in greater detail, in C. L. Kingsford, 'The Highland Forts in the "Forty-Five,"' *English Historical Review* 1922, xxxvii. 371–9.

have done, and much less so long as I am afraid I am condemned to
stay.

I hear now of another regiment vacant, yet my fate with regard to
that still remains in suspense.[1] I don't know whether my friends, and
even I myself (for which I had some reason too) have not been too
sanguine in our expectations. You know I have a sort of jumble of
hopes and fears on that head, which are all in their full height at
present, and so will continue till the affair is decided; and, I must
own, neither my love of money nor desire of being recorded by the
parson of Ragley,[2] nor hardly by yourself, have weight enough to
overbalance my desire of seeing and living a little with my friends.

Pray, since when have you set yourself the task of becoming our
hist[or]iographer? I am mighty glad to hear it, because in less able
or less partial hands I could not hope to make any figure at all.—As
to my picture at Eckardt's[3] (and which I suppose is now to be copied
en taille douce for my frontispiece), I can say now what I never could
before, that I wish ten times more than you can to sit again and have
it finished. However, for the print it may do very well as it is, the
armour being much more to the purpose than the face of the hero,
and it being a pretty indifferent thing to posterity whether my eye-
brow is more or less arched or the hollow over my eye more or less
conspicuous: and apropos to posterity etc. to talk in the style of my
own country, if I find that I am to live here long, I assure you I shall
die very soon; so you may be preparing your history for the press.
Besides, I should be curious to see it before I die, and should be glad
to know what shape it is to appear in, whether memoirs, containing
the adventures of my private life, or a grand history of my public one
only; or whether military or civil or both, because on all these heads

1. Conway was gazetted colonel of the
48th Foot 15 April 1746 OS (*London
Gazette* No. 8527, 12–15 April OS), although according to the regimental list
in Robert Beatson, *Political Index*, 1806,
ii. 240, his commission is dated 6 April,
the very day of this letter. Two other
regiments with a vacancy were the 20th
Foot to which Lord George Sackville was
appointed colonel 9 April, and the 37th
Foot to which Lewis Dejean was appointed colonel 3 April (ibid. ii. 218, 233;
Richard Cannon, *Historical Record of the
Twentieth or the East Devonshire Regiment of Foot*, 1848, pp. 13–14, 65).

2. Warwickshire, chief seat of the Conways. Although they rarely resided there
at this time since the house was unfinished, most of them, including Conway
himself, were baptized and buried there in
Arrow parish church (*Miscellanea genealogica et heraldica*, 1890, 2d ser. iii. 1–4,
23–6, 40–1, 56–8, esp. pp. 2, 58).

3. John Giles Eccardt (d. 1779),
painter, who did portraits of many of
HW's friends. His portrait of Conway
(see illustration) later hung in the Library
at SH ('Des. of SH,' *Works* ii. 444); it was
bought SH xx. 18 by Lord Waldegrave.

Eckardt.

W. Greatbatch, sculp.

THE HON^{BLE} HENRY SEYMOUR CONWAY.

GENERAL CONWAY.

Walpole's Cousin & Correspondent.

FROM THE ORIGINAL FORMERLY IN THE COLLECTION AT STRAWBERRY HILL.

London, Published by Richard Bentley, 1857.

I could give you many useful hints, being acquainted with sundry curious particulars of my own story, that nobody in the world knows but myself, nor ever would but for the fair opportunity you promise me of seeing 'em make a figure in the world. And indeed, I believe the principal part of my achievements are of this kind, so that it is absolutely necessary I should be consulted, especially as the *Gazettes* will furnish you but very sparingly; so great is the negligence and inattention of those people.

As to a certain lady[4] (whose connection with my history I don't insist upon your inserting, unless you have a mind to do it for the instruction of your children by an episode like the Island of Calypso, for instance, or rather I should say the story of Antiope[5]) as to her, I don't know how it will sound if you mention it in my history, but nothing was ever greater than my tranquillity on hearing what you tell me confirmed;[6] and as I really wish her well, I should be glad she's married, but I think I have seen better prospects of harmony and happiness.[7]

Adieu, dear Horry! We march tomorrow,[8] that's something; but as it's yet a vast way to John of Groat's House, I don't know when we shall turn our faces to London; so continue to pity us as much as you please, and I know of course you'll try to comfort one.—Yours. Ned[9] is here.

Pray tell Miss Townshend[10] I am vastly glad to hear of her recovery, and advise her against that quantity of screaming relations, for fear of a relapse.

PS. Since I wrote, the *Sheerness* is come in with the *Hazard* sloop, formerly in our service, and now a privateer in the French.[11] He

4. Lady Caroline Fitzroy.

5. Either Antiope, beloved of Zeus, mentioned in Homer and later legend, or Antiope, an Amazon married to Theseus (Plutarch, *Theseus* 26–7); either character would be applicable to Lady Caroline.

6. Presumably her approaching engagement to Vct Petersham, although HW does not mention it as 'settled to the consent of all parties' until June 1746 (MONTAGU i. 30).

7. Petersham was as gallant as Lady Caroline.

8. The departure of the army from Aberdeen was delayed until the 8th

(postscript; *London Gazette* No. 8527, 12–15 April OS, *sub* Aberdeen 7 April).

9. Cornwallis. Bligh's regiment, which he was commanding, reached Aberdeen 25 March OS (ibid. No. 8523, 29 March – 1 April OS).

10. The Hon. Mary Townshend.

11. The *Hazard* had been captured by the Jacobites at Montrose 24 Nov. 1745 OS, and renamed the *Prince Charles* snow (W. B. Blaikie, *Itinerary of Prince Charles Edward Stuart*, Edinburgh, 1897, p. 28, Scottish History Society XXIII; Robert Forbes, *The Lyon in Mourning*, ed. Paton, Edinburgh, 1895–6, iii. 18–21,

chased her a vast while, and at last drove her on the northern shore,[12] after a sort of running fight of three or four hours. The crew and troops aboard all landed, in all near 200, with four or five-and-twenty officers, French and Spanish; but meeting with about 70[13] of Lord Loudon's regiment under the Captains Sir Harry Monro[14] and Maccoy[15] with 20 militia, they were attacked by them, and after losing six[16] I think killed, the rest were taken,[17] and are now brought here by the *Sheerness*. They had at least £8000 in specie[18] with 'em, which they had landed, and was taken by Lord Loudon's men, who were so vastly rich by it they did not know what to do with it; but they made a division, and sent 500 as a present to the captain[19] of the *Sheerness*, and gave some more to some volunteers that were with 'em; but on arriving here they offered to lend it to the Duke for the use of the army, who has accepted of it.—It was by the oddest accidents in the world that all this happened, for this party were some of Major Maccinzie's,[20] who surrendered himself at Dornoch,[21] on the

Scottish History Society XX–XXII). It had been recaptured 25 March 1746 OS and arrived at Aberdeen with the *Sheerness* on the evening of 6 April. Details of the capture are in the *London Gazette* No. 8527, 12–15 April OS, *sub* Aberdeen 6 April and Edinburgh 9 April; Conway's account differs slightly from these as indicated in subsequent notes.

12. At Tongue on the northern shore of Sutherland.

13. 80, according to the *Gazette* accounts.

14. Sir Harry Munro (ca 1720–81), 7th Bt; M.P. Ross-shire, 1746–7, Tain burghs 1747–61.

15. Hon. George Mackay (ca 1715–82), of Skibo, M.P. Sutherland 1747–61, Capt. in one of Loudoun's independent companies.

16. One account in the *Gazette* says 'three or four' were killed and 'eight' dangerously wounded; the other that five were killed.

17. 156 officers, soldiers, and sailors were taken prisoner; a list of most of the officers is in the *London Gazette* No. 8527, 12–15 April OS.

18. One of the accounts in the *London Gazette* gives the sum as '£12,000 and upwards,' the other, 'said to be 12,500 guineas'; one Jacobite account says 'most

people say 10,000 pounds' (Forbes, op. cit. ii. 271). Further details of the distribution of the money are in the *Daily Adv.* 15 April OS.

19. Lucius O'Brien (d. 1771), Capt., 1745; Rear-Adm., 1770 (John Charnock, *Biographia Navalis*, 1794–8, v. 405–11; John Hardy, *Chronological List of the Captains*, 1779, p. 40; GM 1771, xli. 571).

20. 'Capt. William M'Kenzie, who has long served in Russia' was appointed 'major of the new Highland Reg. to be commanded by the E. of Loudon' in July 1745 (GM 1745, xv. 389). He was apparently William Mackenzie (d. 1770), grandson of the 4th E. of Seaforth and father of the 1st Bn Seaforth (cr. 1797), although the genealogical sources conflict (GEC xi. 587; *Scots Peerage* vii. 510; Collins, *Peerage*, 1812, viii. 599; *More Culloden Papers*, ed. Duncan Warrand, Inverness, 1923–30, v. 30). There are other references to him in the accounts of the surrender at Dornock (*ante* 30 March 1746 OS, n. 5); in *Culloden Papers*, ed. H. R. Duff, 1815, pp. 412–13; and in the 'Narrative by John Lord Macleod,' in William Fraser, *The Earls of Cromartie*, Edinburgh, 1876, ii. 397.

21. 20 March OS (*ante* 30 March 1746 OS, n. 5).

rebels passing the Firth,—but having then made their escape, they tried to join Lord Loudon, who was marched for the Isle of Skie,[22] but found themselves intercepted and were saving themselves by marching northward when they met with these people; so that by the same accident they got so much money and honour and secured themselves by going aboard the man-of-war.

Besides this, the *Sheerness* took another small armed vessel with military stores at the Orkneys in her way round.[23] This capture will distress the rebels greatly, as they are in prodigious want of money. —We have at last accounts that they have raised the siege of Blair[24] upon the approach of the Hessians, and that many of the Athol men have left them thereupon.[25] I hear of no damage done of either side at this siege, but one man I think killed; for the rebels kept at due distance, only firing their cannon against the walls, which are immensely thick. I write this on Monday, our march being deferred today, but tomorrow I fancy we shall move.

To CONWAY, ca Thursday 10 April 1746 OS

Missing; answered *post* 18 April 1746 OS.

22. Loudoun and the other refugees from Dornoch reached Skye 26 March OS (*More Culloden Papers,* v. 51).

23. 'The captain of the *Sheerness* also picked up, in the Orkneys, a ship of Boston in New England, commanded by one Sinclair, who had some arms and ammunition on board, and had put himself into the power and service of the Pretender. His mate and men had before quitted him; and upon the *Sheerness's* coming into the harbour of Stromness, he, and the Highlanders who were with him, got off in a boat, but Capt. O'Brien has brought off the ship, with what arms and ammunition were on board' (*London Gazette* No. 8527, 12–15 April OS, *sub*

Aberdeen 6 April). Further details of the defection of the ship are in the *Daily Adv.* 8 April OS, *sub* Edinburgh 1 April.

24. 'We hear from Dunkeld, that the rebels . . . raised the siege of Blair, and retired with the greatest precipitation upon the approach of the troops sent to relieve that place' (*London Gazette* No. 8527, 12–15 April OS, *sub* Aberdeen 7 April). Blair had been besieged since 17 March OS, but the siege was raised 2 April; for an account of the siege, see *Scots Magazine* 1808, lxx. 330–3, 410–13.

25. If this means that the Atholl men had deserted the Jacobites, it does not appear to be true.

From CONWAY, Friday 18 April 1746 OS

Printed from the MS now WSL, formerly Rutnam. First printed, *Rockingham Memoirs* i. 420–22; reprinted *Colburn's United Service Magazine*, 1880, lii pt iii. 73–5. This may have been sent with the detailed account of the battle by the D. of Cumberland, Inverness, 18 April, which reached London 26 April (*London Gazette Extraordinary* 26 April OS).

Address: To the Honourable Horatio Walpole, Junior in Arlington Street, London.

Inverness, Apr[il] 18.

Dear Horry,

YOU accuse me of not telling you news: I am going to make up for my omissions by such news as I hope will content you. We have beat the rebels,[1] beat 'em in a set battle, and I assure you *de la bonne manière,* losing very few of our own and destroying a good number of those vermin. You have heard how they ran away from us at the Spey;[2] they did the same at Nairn[3] (the place we encamped at before our last march): we were almost out of breath with running after 'em, and had lost all hopes of meeting with 'em. The truth was their people were not come in;[4] the Young Pretender still lay at this place waiting for the junction of the clans who were dispersed

1. At Culloden 16 April OS. Conway's account of the battle is very close to that in the D. of Cumberland's letter, Inverness, 18 April OS, mentioned in the headnote. Another account from the government side is in a letter from Col. Yorke to his father, Inverness, 18 April OS, in George Harris, *Life of the Lord Chancellor Hardwicke,* 1847, ii. 222–8.

2. On 12 April OS; an account of the events at the crossing of the river is in the *London Gazette* No. 8528, 15–19 April OS, *sub* Speymouth 13 April: 'Major-General Huske was detached in the morning with the 15 companies of Grenadiers, the Highlanders and all the cavalry, and two pieces of cannon, and his Royal Highness went with them himself. On our first appearance the rebels retired from the side of the Spey towards Elgin; whereupon the Duke of Kingston's Horse immediately forded over, sustained by the Grenadiers and Highlanders, but the rebels were already got out of their reach before they could pass. The Foot waded over as fast as they arrived; and though

the water came up to their middles, they went on with great cheerfulness.'

3. Which the army reached 14 April OS. Lord Albemarle wrote to the D. of Richmond from there on the 15th: 'At this town (whether insolence in them or whether they did not expect us so soon I can't tell) we heard they proposed waiting for us; the Duke immediately sent the cavalry forwards, who not only drove them out of it but four miles beyond, where having taken a few prisoners they were forced to stop for want of the Foot coming up to sustain them' (E. of March, *A Duke and His Friends,* 1911, ii. 498). For an account of these events from the Jacobite side, see Robert Forbes, *The Lyon in Mourning,* ed. Paton, Edinburgh, 1895–6, ii. 273–4, Scottish History Society XX–XXII.

4. Lord George Murray, in describing the projected night attack on the Duke of Cumberland (below, n. 6), mentions that 'the objection to it was that a great many of the army had not as yet joined, particularly Keppoch, the Master of

all over the country. At Nairn we halted one day[5] to refresh our troops as well as to inform ourselves of the posture and countenance of those gentlemen, and heard that they were assembled, had marched out of this place, and drawn themselves up in order of battle on a moor on this side of Inverness, expecting we should march that day; from all which it was pretty clear they intended to give us battle. The night before we marched they sent a strong detachment to surprise our camp, who marched back without attempting anything.[6] On the 16 we marched and found, by deserters and other intelligence on the march, that they were posted on a great moor near Lord President's[7] house, called Cullodden House, and on our left as we march to Inverness. This moor lies in a high mountainous country, and we imagined their design was to come down and attack our flank on the march, whereupon we bore up upon the hills to the left, and our advanced guard soon discovering them drawn up in order of battle, our march was ordered so as to come just upon their front, which was so well executed that we came up exactly over against 'em and in the best order imaginable. They began the cannonading but were so well answered by our artillery, which was divided between the intervals of the front line, that in about ten minutes we saw that their centre began to be in some confusion. At the same time we perceived that the Highlanders, who were drawn up very deep on each flank, began to move forward in columns to attack us, and on our left they actually made some impression on Barrel's regiment,[8] attacking 'em sword in hand and mixing with 'em. But that regiment, as well as Monro's,[9] plying 'em well with their bayonets, and the second line keeping its order and advancing to sustain them, they were soon repulsed with great loss. At the same

Lovat, Cluny, Glengyle, the Mackenzies, and many of the recruits of Glengary and other regiments, which were all expected in two or three days, and some of them sooner' (Forbes, op. cit. i. 255). See also James Dennistoun, *Memoirs of Sir Robert Strange*, 1855, i. 55–6.

5. 15 April.

6. For this projected night attack, see Forbes, op. cit. i. 255–60 and Dennistoun, op. cit. i. 55–9.

7. Duncan Forbes (1685–1747), lord president of the court of session, 1737; M.P. Ayr burghs 1721–2, Inverness burghs 1722–37.

8. The 4th Foot, commanded by Wil-

liam Barrell (d. 1749), Lt-Gen., 1739 (MANN iii. 248, n. 10). It was on the left of the English line. Seventeen men of the regiment were killed and 108 wounded (*London Gazette Extraordinary* 26 April OS).

9. The 37th Foot, formerly commanded by Sir Robert Munro (ca 1684–17 Jan. 1746), 6th Bt. The colonelcy had just been given to Lewis Dejean (*ante* 6 April 1746 OS, n. 1; *London Gazette* No. 8527, 12–15 April OS). Fourteen men of the regiment were killed and 68 wounded (*London Gazette Extraordinary* 26 April OS).

time a party of the Campbels with our cavalry on the left coming up almost unperceived upon their flank, put their right in entire confusion and made vast slaughter. On our right, perceiving that the clans were coming down in columns, the Duke ordered Pulteney's[10] regiment and Kingston's Horse up from the reserve to strengthen that flank,[11] whereupon seeing that we rather out-flanked 'em and that our men kept up their fire, they never ventured to come amongst us but sheered off and soon joined in the *déroute* that was begun on the left and in the centre and which now became quite general. From this time it was nothing but pursuit. They left all their cannon,[12] and our cavalry did their duty very well in the pursuit, sparing very few that came in their reach. I believe they have lost between two and three thousand men,[13] of which the major part are left on the field. All the French pickets surrendered prisoners,[14] and some of the Horse are come in since.[15] Lord Kilmarnock[16] and Lord Lewis Drummond[17] with some more of their chiefs are taken,[18] and I believe a good many killed.[19] Brigadier Stapleton[20] is wounded and taken. On

10. The 13th Foot, commanded by Lt-Gen. Henry Pulteney (1686–1767), brother of the E. of Bath (MANN vi. 560, n. 6).

11. 'When we were advanced within 500 yards of the rebels, we found the morass upon our right was ended, which left our right flank quite uncovered to them; his Royal Highness thereupon immediately ordered Kingston's horse from the reserve, and a little squadron of about sixty of Cobham's [10th Dragoons] which had been patrolling, to cover our flank; and Pulteney's regiment was ordered from the reserve to the right of the Royals [1st Foot]' (*London Gazette Extraordinary* 26 April OS).

12. A list is in ibid.

13. 'By the best calculation that can be made, 'tis thought the rebels lost 2000 men upon the field of battle, and in the pursuit' (ibid.).

14. A list of the French officers who surrendered is in the *Gazette Extraordinary*, which also gives the total number of French prisoners as 222.

15. 'On the 17th, as his Royal Highness was at dinner, three officers, and about sixteen of Fitz James's regiment, who were mounted, came and surrendered themselves prisoners' (ibid.).

16. 'Lord Kilmarnock, on foot by himself, fell on his face and begged him with quarter, which was granted him with difficulty' (Col. Yorke to Lord Hardwicke, 18 April OS, Harris, op. cit. ii. 227).

17. Louis Jean Edward Drummond, called Lord Lewis Drummond (1709–92), 2d son of the 2d D. of Melfort in the Jacobite peerage; acting commander of the French 'Royal Scots' (or Lord John Drummond's regiment) (*Scots Peerage* vi. 70, ix. 135). He lost his leg at Culloden; he was sent to London in June, but treated as a French prisoner of war (*Prisoners of the '45*, ed. Seton and Arnot, Edinburgh, 1928–9, i. 328–9, ii. 164–5, Scottish History Society, 3d ser., XIII–XV).

18. A list of the rebel officers taken prisoner is in the *London Gazette Extraordinary* 26 April OS.

19. Some of these are mentioned in the dispatch in the *Gazette Extraordinary* and others 'who (the rebels themselves say) were killed in the battle' are listed at the end.

20. Walter Valentine Stapleton (d. 1746), Irish officer in the French service, who commanded the Irish brigade in the '45. He died of his wounds at Culloden (*Prisoners of the '45*, i. 236, 327, 330–1, iii. 330–3; Richard Hayes, *Bio-*

our side the loss is very inconsiderable, not amounting to above 200 killed and wounded,[21] amongst whom are very few officers and nobody of distinction but Lord Robert Kerr[22] killed and Col. Rich[23] wounded. Bury[24] will be with you perhaps before this reaches you, and tell you all these things much better than I can. Adieu! dear Horry, in vast haste,

Yours ever,

H. C.

Ned and all friends are well.

To CONWAY, ca Friday 25 April 1746 OS

Missing; implied in the postscript to *post* 7 May 1746 OS, but apparently written before HW had received Conway's letter of 18 April.

graphical Dictionary of Irishmen in France, Dublin, 1949, p. 291).

21. The official casualty list gives 50 killed, 259 wounded, and one missing, 'rank and file . . . officers included' (*London Gazette Extraordinary* 26 April OS, where there is also a list of the officers killed and wounded).

22. Lord Robert Ker (d. 16 April 1746), Capt. of grenadiers in Barrell's regiment (MANN iii. 248, n. 11).

23. Sir Robert Rich (1717–85), 5th Bt,

1768; Maj.-Gen., 1758; Lt-Gen., 1760; at this time Lt-Col. in Barrell's regiment (ibid. i. 486, n. 15; iii. 248, n. 20). He lost a hand at Culloden.

24. Who had been sent post with the news immediately after the battle; he was delayed by weather and did not reach London until the morning of 24 April OS, but the news had already arrived from Edinburgh at noon on the 23d (ibid. iii. 247 and nn. 3–5).

From CONWAY, Wednesday 7 May 1746 OS

Printed from the MS now WSL, formerly Rutnam. First printed, *Fraser's Magazine*, 1850, xli. 635–6; also printed from the MS in *Rockingham Memoirs* i. 422–5, where the last paragraph from *ante* 19 March 1746 OS is mistakenly appended; reprinted (with the same error), *Colburn's United Service Magazine*, 1880, lii pt iii. 205–8.

Address: To the Honourable Horatio Walpole, Junior, in Arlington Street, London.

Postmark: 16 MA. [There also appears to be a very faint MY 10.]
Memoranda (by HW):[1]

At Duke of St Albans's[2]	In the Castle
Picture of Duchess of Mazarine[3]	Anne Duchess of York[7]
Earl of St Albans[4]	The Beauties[8]
G.V.D. of Buckingham[5]	
Last Earl of Oxford[6]	
à toute la belle compagnie	Altar-ation
célestine.	All-tar[10]
Vow of Chast. of Countess of	
Warw. in Ed. 3[9]	

1. These memoranda are written in scattered groups on the cover.

2. Burford House, Windsor, built for Nell Gwyn by Charles II and occupied at this time by her grandson Charles Beauclerk (1696–1751), 2d D. of St Albans. It was purchased by George III in the 1770s and still exists as the Gray Block in the Royal Mews (T. E. Harwood, *Windsor Old and New*, 1929, pp. 122–7). HW had visited George Montagu at Windsor between 16 and 22 May OS (MANN iii. 254; MONTAGU i. 25 and n. 1). The present location of the following portraits is unknown to the editors.

3. Hortense Mancini (1646–99), m. (1661) Armand-Charles de la Porte, Duc de Mazarin. The portrait was by Carlo Maratti; HW eventually owned a copy of it, which he hung in the Great North Bedchamber at SH (ibid. ii. 54 and n. 20; 'Des. of SH,' *Works* ii. 496).

4. Henry Jermyn (ca 1604–84), cr. (1643) Bn Jermyn and (1660) E. of St Albans.

5. George Villiers (1628–87), 2d D. of Buckingham.

6. Aubrey de Vere (1627–1703), 20th E.

of Oxford, father-in-law of the 1st D. of St Albans.

7. Anne Hyde (1638–71), m. (1660) James, D. of York, later James II.

8. By Sir Peter Lely (1618–80), now at Hampton Court. About a month later HW asked Montagu to try to find someone to copy the pictures (MONTAGU i. 34–5). See also HW to Dalrymple 23 Feb. 1764 (DALRYMPLE 96–7) on his unsuccessful attempts to have them copied as part of his projected edition of Gramont's *Mémoires* (MONTAGU i. 118).

9. Philippe de Ferrers (d. 1384), m. (before 1353) Guy de Beauchamp, eldest son of Thomas de Beauchamp, 11th E. of Warwick, who died before his father. On her husband's death she took a vow of chastity that included 'tout le belle [c]ompaigne celestine.' The vow is given in William Dugdale, *Baronage*, 1675–6, i. 235. Since her husband died before his father she was never Countess of Warwick. HW's copy of Dugdale's *Baronage*, 1675–6, is Hazen, *Cat. of HW's Lib.*, No. 590.

10. This appears to be a charade.

Mulier Formosa super-knee

No. 20 30£   Alum Stalum non est Malum
    to Edward Ironsides   Beerum clerum est Sincerum
  295   Vinum Finum est Divinum[12]
    40. Minors & Boldero
  210
     James Colebroke[11]
  100£

Inverness, Wednesday, May 7th.

Dear Horry,

I WISH I was at London, and you at Inverness, that I might find something to say to you, but in such places and such a life as ours what can one have to talk of but swords and firelocks, marches and dispositions, and is not it better to say nothing? When we have a battle or the smallest skirmish to treat you with, you're sure to have it; but I know you too well and have too much consideration for you to torment you with all the fiddle-faddle stuff that makes the body of our news and conversation. In short, it's unreasonable of you, most unreasonable indeed, to complain of a soldier in the heart of a dismal northern campaign for not writing news or being entertaining. It's a mercy we can write at all, and if we don't tell you bad news, I thi⟨nk you⟩ ought to be mighty well contented—however, to stop your mouth for some little time at least, I wrote you ⟨immediately⟩[13] not only an account of our victory, but I assure you a much longer account than I wrote anybody and if I continue in the same style, I have a notion [I] should soon tire you out of your complaints, and make you own that it is in writing as in other things, *Il vaut mieux rien écrire qu'écrire des riens,*[14] unless one had Madame Sévigné's,[15] your favourite, or your own turn, to say 'em agreeably; besides, they must be an agreeable kind of nothings that are capable

---

11. These are all London bankers: Edward Ironside (d. 1753), F.S.A., lord mayor, 1753, a partner in the banking-house of Ironside and Belchier, Lombard Street, which existed 1729–56; Minors and Boldero, another firm in Lombard Street 1742–60, and later under other names; and James Colebrooke (1680–1752), 'a great money scrivener in Threadneedle Street' (F. G. Hilton Price, *Handbook of London Bankers*, 1890–1, pp. 17, 41–2, 92,

117; DNB *sub* Edward Ironside [ca 1736–1803]; SELWYN 114, n. 7). The numbers and prices suggest an auction.

12. This appears to be a 'counting-out rhyme.'

13. Piece torn out of MS.

14. Conway is adapting a passage from Pliny's *Letters* I. ix which he quoted to HW *ante* 14 May 1740 OS.

15. Marie de Rabutin-Chantal (1626–96), m. (1644) Henri, Marquis de Sévigné.

of such a turn. But to think of the dry transactions of our camp turned by such a clumsy hand as mine! 'Twould really make you sick, and I say again I have too much consideration for you.

Yet the history of our female captives I know would have flourished in your hands, and made a very good romance, serious or comic, as you happened to be disposed. Lady Macintosh,[16] as they call her, because she is wife to the laird of that name, is very young, and they say very handsome—I have not seen her yet. She left her husband, who is in Lord Loudon's regiment, and led out her men, or rather his, and I believe she was in the battle. Since her being taken, she has suffered no farther confinement than that of being obliged to live with her laird, which I believe with the addition of two lovers that visit her constantly, the poor woman finds grievous enough. These are the old President whom you remember at your father's,[17] and is now as old again, and Colonel Cockayne,[18] whom perhaps you have seen, both seriously enamoured. She was said to be the first in the good graces of the Young Gentleman,[19] but I believe had only the name of it, for he is generally reckoned quite indifferent to women, and I believe a true Italian in all respects.[20] Her favoured lover seems to have been one Macgillivra,[21] whom she laments much

16. Anne Farquharson (1723–84 *or* 87), known as 'Colonel Anne,' m. Angus *or* Æneus Mackintosh (ca 1702–70) of Mackintosh, 3d Lord Mackintosh in the Jacobite peerage. He raised a company for the government in the Black Watch; his wife raised his clan and others for the Young Pretender, whom she also saved from capture at Moy House in Feb. 1746. She was arrested there a day or two after the battle, but released a few weeks later by her husband's influence. The fullest account of her is in Compton Mackenzie, *Prince Charlie and His Ladies*, New York, 1935, pp. 49–70. See also, for additional factual data, *Prisoners of the '45*, ed. Seton and Arnot, Edinburgh, 1928–9, i. 310, 317–18, iii. 100–4, Scottish History Society 3d ser. XIII–XV; Burke, *Landed Gentry*, 1937, pp. 751, 1484; *Scots Magazine* 1770, xxxii. 398; 1784, xlvi. 167; GM 1770, xl. 345; *Origins of the '45*, ed. Blaikie, Edinburgh, 1916, p. 101, n. 2, Scottish History Society 2d ser. II.

17. Forbes as lord advocate for Scotland had been in effect secretary of state for Scotland from 1725 to 1737. He had

returned to Inverness from Skye 25 April OS (*London Gazette* No. 8533, 3–6 May OS).

18. Thomas Cockayne (d. 1749), at this time Lt-Col. in Pulteney's [13th] Foot; Ensign, 1716; Capt., 1735; Maj. before 1743, when he was secretary to Gen. Honywood; adjutant-general to Wade, 1744; aide-de-camp to Albemarle in 1747 (Society for Army Historical Research, *Army List of 1740*, Sheffield, 1931, p. 26; GM 1744, xiv. 339, 1749, xix. 476; Hist. MSS Comm., *Frankland-Russell-Astley MSS*, 1900, pp. 297, 408). The regimental lists in the *Court and City Register* give his Christian name as John, but the other sources all give Thomas. He had commanded the detachment that took Lady Mackintosh prisoner (Mackenzie, op. cit. 65–6; Robert Forbes, *The Lyon in Mourning*, ed. Paton, Edinburgh, 1895–6, ii. 189, Scottish History Society XX–XXII).

19. The Young Pretender.

20. There seems to have been little gossip about him on this score.

21. Alexander Macgillivray (d. 16 April 1746), of Dunmaglas, chief of his clan and

(he was killed at the battle), and asks if he did not make a fine corpse? Lady Ogilvie[22] I believe I told you of;[23] she's very young too, and rather handsome, but so foolish and so insensible of her condition that my pity for her was soon worn out. Yet she really is much of a heroine, and might make a very fine figure in romance amidst all her misfortunes, and such as one would think should affect a woman most as the loss of a young husband, not dead but in great danger at least,[24] and the fear of imprisonment or death. She seems to feel only for the loss of the battle and the ruin of their cause, though she has told me in confidence that she was yet sure the Prince would come to the throne. In short, she has been so very indiscreet, and talked treason to everybody so outrageously, that the Duke now lets her see nobody, which she ⟨takes so much⟩ to heart that yesterday I was told she was fallen very ill. Lady Kinloch[25] and Lady Gordon[26] are ⟨set at⟩ liberty; and in their room we hear that Sir James,[27] husband to the first, is taken, as is Lord Tullibardin;[28] I think he surrendered himself. The Young Pretender is gone towards the west coast,[29] where he landed, and yesterday we had an account of two

Lt-Col. of Lady Mackintosh's regiment, led the Mackintoshes at Culloden (*A List of Persons Concerned in the Rebellion*, Edinburgh, 1890, p. 376, Scottish History Society VIII; *Origins of the '45*, p. 101 and n. 1).

22. Margaret Johnstone (1724–57), m. David Ogilvie (1725–1803), styled Lord Ogilvie, titular E. of Airlie, 1761. She was captured at Kilihuntley after Culloden and later imprisoned in Edinburgh Castle, from whence she escaped 21 Nov. 1746 and joined her husband in France (*Prisoners of the '45*, iii. 238–41).

23. Not in any letter that has been found. Conway may have written HW another letter immediately after that of 18 April OS, since HW told Mann 25 April OS that 'Mr Conway says, he hears' that the Young Pretender was wounded at Culloden (MANN iii. 248). No such statement appears in Conway's letter of 18 April OS.

24. Ogilvie escaped to France via Norway; he was eventually pardoned in 1778 and returned to England.

25. Janet Duff (1710–51), sister of the 1st Lord Braco (later 1st E. Fife), m. (1730) Sir James Kinloch, 3d Bt (Alistair and Henrietta Tayler, *Book of the Duffs*,

Edinburgh, 1914, i. 87, 98–101; *Prisoners of the '45*, ii. 324–5).

26. Hon. Janet Duff (1727–58), dau. of 1st Lord Braco (later 1st E. Fife), m. 1 (1745) Sir William Gordon, 3d Bt, m. 2 (1753) George Hay of Mountblairy (Tayler, op. cit. i. 130–7; *Prisoners of the '45*, ii. 232–3).

27. Sir James Kinloch (d. 1776), 3d Bt, was captured 29 April 1746 OS, sent to London and on 15 Nov. 1746 OS attainted and condemned to death; he was reprieved by the influence of his brother-in-law Lord Braco, but remained in custody until 1748 when he was released on condition he remain in England (ibid. ii. 324–5; *London Gazette* No. 8535, 10–13 May 1746 OS, *sub* Inverness 5 May).

28. William Murray (1689–9 July 1746), styled M. of Tullibardine, attainted in 1716, cr. (1717) D. of Rannoch in the Jacobite peerage. He surrendered near Dumbarton 27 April 1746 OS (ibid. No. 8533, 3–6 May OS, *sub* Edinburgh 30 April; *Prisoners of the '45*, iii. 378–81).

29. On the day of this letter the Young Pretender was hiding on the island of Euirn (Iubhard) in Loch Shell off the Isle of Lewis in the Outer Hebrides; he had left the mainland 26 April OS (W. B.

French men-of-war going into Loch Moidart[30]—we suppose in order to take him off. A twenty-gun ship[31] and I think a small sloop or two[32] followed 'em in and engaged 'em some time, but, finding 'em too strong for 'em, were obliged to stand out again.[33] Orders are sent to larger ships[34] to sail immediately and endeavour to intercept 'em: one, they say, is a good deal disabled, and even our small ones intend to lie by and wait for their coming out. We have another piece of ship-news, which, if it proves true, is very great, and the authority is very good too, for the ship that brings the account from the West Indies to the Duke of Newcastle spoke to one of ours off the Orkneys, who sent the report to the commodore here.[35] It is that a twenty-gun ship of ours in company with a privateer has taken the fourth galleon,[36] the richest of 'em all, and worth a million in bullion.—

Blaikie, *Itinerary of Prince Charles Edward Stuart*, Edinburgh, 1897, pp. 47, 49, Scottish History Society XXIII).

30. What follows is a slightly confused account of events off Borradale in Loch Nanuagh 29 April – 3 May 1746 OS (ibid. 47–8). Details from the government side are in the *London Gazette* No. 8536, 13–17 May OS, and No. 8538, 20–24 May OS, and from the Jacobite, in David, Lord Elcho, *A Short Account of the Affairs of Scotland*, ed. Charteris, Edinburgh, 1907, pp. 439–43. See also MANN iii. 270. The Young Pretender had, of course, missed the ships, although the report was circulated that he had escaped on them on the 4th (*London Gazette* loc. cit.).

31. The *Greyhound* (ibid. No. 8536, 13–17 May OS).

32. The *Baltimore* and the *Terror* (ibid.).

33. On 3 May. 'I crossed pretty close to the commodore, gave him a broadside, and then stood to the other. The sloops followed my example, and we were engaged till nine o'clock when our masts and rigging were so much shattered, that the sloops were not capable of keeping under sail, which was the only means we could propose to annoy them by, as we were inferior to them in strength. One of the French ships [*Bellona*] carried 34 guns, 24 of which were 9 pounders. The other [*Mars*] carried 32, 22 of which were 9 pounders. Wherefore, after lying at anchor some time and having repaired

our damages as well as we could, we made sail and . . . are now refitting' (account of Capt. Noel of the *Greyhound*, ibid.). The account in Elcho, loc. cit., is essentially the same.

34. The *Raven* and *Furnace* sloops and the *Serpent*, of which only the *Raven* had joined by the 6th, by which time the French ships had left (*London Gazette* No. 8538, 20–24 May OS).

35. Thomas Smith (d. 1762), Capt., 1730; Commodore, 1744; commander-in-chief at Leith and on the coast of Scotland, 1746; Rear-Adm., 1747; Vice-Adm., 1748; Adm., 1757.

36. 'Commodore Smith received yesterday advice from Capt. Jefferys, of the *Scarborough*, dated Deer Sound, in the Orkneys, the 27th past, that a ship from New England was put in there, sent express from the governor to his Grace the Duke of Newcastle, with an account, that one of his Majesty's twenty-gun ships, with a privateer, had taken a galleon, which was by far the richest prize that had been made since the war began, she having on board a million sterling in bullion' (*London Gazette* No. 8535, 10–13 May OS, *sub* Inverness 5 May; Robert Beatson, *Naval and Military Memoirs of Great Britain*, 1804, i. 324–5). Sandwich wrote Bedford 12 May 1746 OS, 'she is a Spanish register ship, and has above a million sterling registered on board; the lucky ship is not named, nor do I understand the express is come to town; but if

We hear of no rebels together anywhere, so that I fancy our remaining work will be pretty easy. The day before yesterday 100 Mcphersons (I've a notion they were) surrendered themselves with their arms,[37] and were brought in here by the Grants. We are preparing for our march, which I fancy will be in a few days,[38] a shocking journey into the heart of the Highlands, but it's all one. I mind much more the time than the conditions of my pilgrimage, and nothing shocks me now but that I am not to see you till November: that's the term I set myself, and it's a dreadful one. Adieu! Compliments to Lady Mary and Churchill, Mrs Leneve, etc.

Yours ever,

H. C.

PS. I am glad the Duchess of Q[ueensberry's][39] windows were broken with all my heart, and think she deserved more for her foolish obstinacy. I am only sorry a certain house in L[eicester] Fields[40] did not suffer as I hear it deserved.

To Conway, ca Friday 9 May 1746 OS

Missing; answered *post* 21 May 1746 OS.

the account is true, I suppose it must be one on the Carolina station' (*Bedford Corr.* i. 101).

37. They were not Macphersons but tenants of a branch of the Grants who had joined the rebellion; the incident is described in letters from Sir Archibald Grant to Sir James Grant, Inverness, 8 May 1746 and from Ludovick Grant to Newcastle (William Fraser, *The Chiefs of Grant*, Edinburgh, 1883, ii. 262, 266–7).

38. The main body of the army left for Fort Augustus 23 May (*London Gazette* No. 8540, 27–31 May OS).

39. Lady Catherine Hyde (ca 1701–77), m. (1720) Charles Douglas, 3d D. of Queensberry. She had apparently refused to illuminate her house for the victory at

Culloden. 'The mob were so enraged at those that did not light up candles on Thursday night [24 April], that they broke all the windows of empty houses, and of those who were in the country, all over the City and Liberty of Westminster' (*Daily Adv.* 26 April OS).

40. Leicester House, residence of the P. of Wales, who was in opposition. One report mentions that 'the King as soon as he had heard Lord Bury's account [of the victory at Culloden] ordered him to the P[rince], who sent him word that he was engaged in a party a-hunting and desired him to be with him by . . .' (Hist. MSS Comm., *Hastings MSS*, 1928–47, iii. 56, where the MS breaks off as indicated).

From CONWAY, Wednesday 21 May 1746 OS

Printed for the first time from the MS now WSL, formerly Rutnam.
Address: To the Honourable Horatio Walpole, Junior, in Arlington Street, London.

Inverness, Wednesday, May 21.

Dear Horry,

WHILE you make excuses for not writing I think I ought to make you twice as many for writing; you hate old news; I have no new, nothing in the shape of it to tell you nor no scandal nor no secrets and am besides as dull, as melancholy and as unamusing as one can well be even at Inverness, even as unamusing as every thing and person here appears to me. I have but one secret in the world,[1] which I should be very glad to tell you but that I have sworn to conceal it some time longer and I am not quite sure it would entertain you if I told it you; it is a very profound one which you'll think very strange when I tell you it's in the possession of 14 people,[2] nay of fifteen already, and the greater burthen to me because it has cost me a great [deal] of time, trouble and inquiry to come at so that you see I pay you no very great compliment in being impatient to tell it you but being sworn most solemnly to the contrary and it being of a nature that I can't trust my best friend with, so [we] must both bear it as we can for some time longer. Perhaps at last you'll hear it from other hands before I have an opportunity of telling it you. However, if it will be any satisfaction to you to be let a little farther into the nature of it I think I may go so far as to tell you that it is the sentence of a general court martial of which I was a member (for my mortification) it having amused us any morning this week past from 8 to one.—It is upon the governors of this place[3] and two

1. The decision of the court martial on Major Grant, described below.
2. The order setting up the court martial on 7 May OS lists fourteen members (printed in A. N. Campbell-Maclachlan, *William Augustus, Duke of Cumberland,* 1876, p. 306). The fifteenth was presumably the Duke himself.
3. The principal trial was that of Major George Grant (d. 1755), of Culbin, governor of Fort George at Inverness (William Fraser, *Chiefs of Grant,* Edinburgh,

1883, i. 329, where no mention is made of the inglorious conclusion of his career). 'Major Grant, deputy governor of Fort George, has been tried by a general court martial for abandoning the same to the rebels [on 20 Feb. OS], and has been adjudged to be dismissed from his Majesty's service, and rendered incapable of ever holding any military office or employment under his Majesty' (*London Gazette* No. 8540, 27–31 May 1746 OS, *sub* Inverness, 19 and 22 May). The sen-

other officers here whose trials have come in by way of episode; and one of whom, Capt. Minchin[4] is broke for being drunk during the siege; that I may tell you for it is published and as well known at present as the generality of my news, being in public orders.—As to the rest I know nothing in the world, none of the Pretender's secrets nor of any of his friends, not even where they are, or what they propose to do with themselves. Of ourselves I know no more, not even the interesting secret so well expressed in *The Rehearsal*,[5] 'How long we here shall stay; how soon shall go.' Two brigades are already gone, one to Perth and the other to Fort Augustus.[6]

I am glad to hear Bathiani[7] is not yet beat; it seems to me a miraculous escape; but Antwerp is gone[8] and I suppose the Dutch will sign a neutrality and not let any troops land upon the Continent. If so we may amuse ourselves with our wooden walls and sea expeditions and I don't doubt but the Duke of B[edford] and Admiral Vernon[9] will soon take all the Indies, in which case I would e'en give up the Old World at once and go bag and baggage and settle ourselves in the new one. I think this a very good scheme, I assure you and if my friend the Duke of B[edford] has not yet proposed it in Council I would have your friend Mr P[elham] make himself popular by being beforehand with him.

I am at present very busy about my regiment where I have cut out amusement for myself for four or five months to come and don't intend seeing any of you till the winter, yet I own I don't give you up

tence was published in formal orders 7 June (Campbell-Maclachlan, loc. cit., where some of the other sentences of the court martial are also printed). For Grant's conduct of the siege, based on the records of the court martial in State Papers, Scotland, see C. L. Kingsford, 'The Highland Forts in the "Forty-Five",' *English Historical Review* 1922, xxxvii. 369–70.

4. Lt (not Capt.) Minchin of Guise's Regiment (6th Foot); for his part in the siege, see ibid.

5. By George Villiers, 2d D. of Buckingham:

'Sir, if you please, we should be glad to know,

How long you here will stay, how soon you'll go?' (IV. i)

6. 'Brigadier Mordaunt is already at Perth, with the Royal's, Pulteney's, and Sempil's regiments. . . . Major-General Bland is sent forward with three battalions to Fort Augustus, for which place his Royal Highness proposes to begin his march tomorrow' (*London Gazette* loc. cit.).

7. Karl Joseph (1697–1772), Fürst von Batthyáni, joint commander of the Allied army in Flanders (MANN iii. 23, n. 7, 240).

8. The Allies withdrew from Antwerp 16 May NS (5 May OS), the town surrendered 19 May NS, and the citadel 31 May NS (ibid. iii. 255, nn. 9–10).

9. Both of whom were advocates of global rather than European warfare. Conway seems to have been unaware that Vernon had been removed from his command in Dec. 1745 and dismissed the service 11 April OS (ibid. iii. 188, 244, n. 33).

without infinite regret, but what signifies regret? In short, I look
upon it as my fate and the fine I pay for my advancement. So as I
said before with infinite regret till September at least, adieu. Pity me
sometimes and believe me most sincerely and affectionately

Yours,

H. C.

Let me know what becomes of you.

From CONWAY, Tuesday 12 August 1746 OS

Printed for the first time from the MS now WSL, formerly Rutnam.
Address: To the Honourable Horatio Walpole, Jun., in Arlington Street,
London.
Postmark: AU 16. 22 AV.

Fort Augustus, Tuesday, Aug. 12.

Dear Horry,

IT seems an age to me since I have heard from you yet you have
generally been so good to me in writing that I don't venture to
complain, and especially at present with so many people in town,[1]
so much diversion and so many things to see, to hear and to talk of,
I can easily make an excuse for you, besides which the post is not
quite to be depended upon and may have done either me or you injustice. However, as I am far from waiting regularly for your letters
before I write I should have done it long ago if I had not been upon
a tedious expedition[2] since I wrote to you and since that at Fort
William, all which will very little bear description and could not
give you the least amusement, as I missed of my errand, met with
no adventures, and for the country through which I passed I can
only say that it was one continued scene of rocks, bogs and mountains for a fortnight's marching successively with little more variety
than one would see in the Western Ocean. Yet after travelling so far

1. Because of the trial of the rebel
lords.
2. Conway had been in command of a
party searching for the Young Pretender
in Morar and Knoydart 13–25 July OS
(*The Albemarle Papers,* ed. C. S. Terry,
Aberdeen, 1902, i. 10–12).

after the Young P[retender] I can at present give no farther intelligence of him than that he's thought to be still in the country.[3]—I saw lately the examination of one Oneil[4] who wandered with him a great while, which contains his history almost entirely and circumstantially enough from the day of the battle to the time of his landing in the Isle of Skie, during which period he met with some adventures curious enough, running many risks of being taken and suffering great hardships; he was three times[5] in sight of some of our men-of-war in an open boat, and forced to skulk behind rocks till they were past; once Capt. Scot[6] landed within two miles of him with a party and at another time he was so hard run and had so little hopes of escaping that he was just going to send this Oneil to Gen. Campbell[7] to surrender himself. At first Sullivan[8] and one McDon-

---

3. On the day of this letter the Young Pretender was at Glenmoriston, about five miles from Fort Augustus (W. B. Blaikie, *Itinerary of Prince Charles Edward Stuart*, Edinburgh, 1897, p. 64, Scottish History Society XXIII).

4. Felix O'Neil *or* O'Neille, Capt. in Lally's French-Irish regiment, 1744. He had been sent to Scotland with dispatches in March 1746; he joined the Young Pretender shortly after Culloden and remained with him until 28 June OS; he was captured soon after and confined at Edinburgh until Feb. 1747 when he was released on parole and eventually exchanged. Biographical details are in *Origins of the 'Forty-Five*, ed. W. B. Blaikie, Edinburgh, 1916, p. 230, n. 1, Scottish History Society 2d ser. II; idem, *Itinerary*, p. 53. His 'declaration,' Fort Augustus, 7 Aug. 1746 OS, which Conway follows below, is printed in *The Albemarle Papers*, i. 71–6; two variant copies of a narrative by him, written a year or so later and not always in harmony with his 'declaration,' are in Robert Forbes, *The Lyon in Mourning*, ed. Paton, Edinburgh, 1895–6, i. 102–8, 365–75, Scottish History Society XX–XXII.

5. 6 May, 10 May, and 15 June (Blaikie, *Itinerary*, pp. 49–51). 'In their passage [6 May] they met two English men-of-war, which obliged them to put into an uninhabited island . . . they went from thence [10 May] still southwards, and were chased by a sloop of war in amongst the rocks off the Harries, where they remained three hours till she was gone. . . . in their passage thither [to Loch Boisdale, 15 June] they met two English men-of-war, whom they avoided by getting behind a rock, where they remained near two hours' (O'Neil's 'declaration,' *Albemarle Papers*, i. 73–5).

6. Caroline Frederick Scott (d. 1755), Capt. (after Nov. 1746, Major) in Guise's Regiment [6th Foot], Lt-Col. 29th Foot, 1749; engineer-general of the East India Company's forts in India and commander of the troops there, 1752. He had conducted the defence of Fort William in March 1746 and was now active in the searching parties for the Young Pretender. See C. L. Kingsford, 'The Highland Forts in the "Forty-Five",' *English Historical Review*, 1922, xxxvii. 371–81, *Albemarle Papers* i. 270, and *London Evening Post* 26–8 June 1755.

7. Later 4th D. of Argyll. This happened 24 or 25 June: 'They stayed at the place fixed upon all the next day without hearing from her [Flora Macdonald], which made them think she had deceived them; having no hopes of escaping, he was just going to send Capt. O'Neille to General Campbell to surrender himself, when the guide returned with a message from Miss Flora' (O'Neil's 'declaration,' *Albemarle Papers*, i. 75; Blaikie, *Itinerary*, pp. 52–3). O'Neil does not mention this in his later narratives.

8. John William O'Sullivan (b. ca 1700),

ald,[9] a priest, brother, I think, to Lochiel,[10] were with him; afterwards he and Oneil remained a great while alone.[11] They lived a month or five weeks upon a mountain called Carisdale;[12] I think it is in the island of Uist; and in a small cottage. Another time they passed four days in an uninhabited island,[13] living only upon dried fish, and in this manner has that wretch crept about from rock to rock and hole to hole in continual apprehension. When he parted with Oneil he put on woman's clothes and put himself under the care of a Miss Flora McDonald,[14] a young girl who is since taken.[15] She would not let Oneil go with 'em, so they went alone into the Isle of Skie, where he changed his clothes again and went alone to one McDonald,[16] a factor of Sir Alexander's,[17] told him that he trusted his life with him and hoped he would not discover him; but that he was so unhappy he did not much care whether he lived or died, with all which the man was so touched that he received him kindly, though as Sir Alexander pretends (who told me this himself),[18] he was a good friend to

one of the 'seven men of Moidart' who accompanied the Young Pretender to Scotland at the beginning of the rebellion; he remained with him until 20 June. His narrative of the 'Forty-Five' is printed in Alistair and Henrietta Tayler, *1745 and After*, 1938, pp. 45–216, as is all the known biographical data on him.

9. Allan Macdonald, chaplain of Clanranald's regiment and the Young Pretender's confessor, remained with him until the beginning of May; biographical details are collected in *Origins of the 'Forty-Five*, p. 228, n. 2; see also Blaikie, *Itinerary*, p. 49.

10. Allan Macdonald is described as a clansman of Ranald Macdonald of Clanranald, but no other details of his genealogy appear to be known (ibid.). Lochiel was not a Macdonald but a Cameron.

11. Conway has misunderstood the declaration, which is rather vaguely phrased; O'Neil was rarely alone with the Prince.

12. Coradale in South Uist, where the Young Pretender remained 15 May – 5 June (Blaikie, *Itinerary*, pp. 50–1). 'They went to Corridale, a mountain in South Uist, where they remained near a month in a shieling of one McGachans, and were subsisted by him and some of the people of the country' (O'Neil's 'declaration,' *Albemarle Papers*, i. 74).

13. Euirn (Iubhard), 6–10 May (Blaikie, *Itinerary*, p. 49). 'In their passage they met two English men-of-war, which obliged them to put into an uninhabited island, where they remained four days, having no provisions but some dried fish which they found on the rocks' (O'Neil's 'declaration,' *Albemarle Papers*, i. 73–4).

14. Flora Macdonald (1722–90), m. (1750) Allan Macdonald of Kingsburgh.

15. Shortly after she left the Young Pretender 1 July (Blaikie, *Itinerary*, p. 54).

16. Alexander Macdonald (ca 1688–1772), of Kingsburgh (Alexander Mackenzie, *History of the Macdonalds*, Inverness, 1881, pp. 267–71). Conway's version of events on Skye, which he learned from Sir Alexander Macdonald, is understandably inaccurate. Lady Margaret Macdonald, Sir Alexander's wife, sent Kingsburgh to assist the Young Pretender, who 'changed his female clothes in a wood for a Highland dress' after he left Kingsburgh's house 30 June (Blaikie, *Itinerary*, p. 54).

17. Sir Alexander Macdonald (1711–23 Nov. 1746), of Sleat, 7th Bt. He had remained loyal to the government.

18. Sir Alexander, who was at Fort Augustus, had apparently told Conway a version of the incident similar to the one he sent to Duncan Forbes 29 July: 'He (the Pretender) accosted him [Kings-

the government. This man is also since taken; from Skie the P[retender] came into Morar[19] and there joined the Laird of Morar, another McDonald[20] who gave him into other hands and from that time I can give no farther account of him.[21]

Tomorrow we march towards our winter quarters, winter being, I assure you, already begun in this agreeable climate; mine are to be at Stirling where I shall be in eight days and in about two or three months more would fain flatter myself I shall have the pleasure of seeing you. If you remember, I told you when I was coming away I looked upon ⟨it as⟩ an affair of about three weeks. You see how long they have been and may guess ⟨how⟩ they have appeared to me. However, having borne it so long I must e'en try to eke out my ⟨pati⟩ence a little longer and content myself with the hopes of passing the winter amongst you, which I would fain think nothing but another rebellion can disappoint me of.

We have no earthly news here but a duel that has been fought between a Capt. Hamilton[22] and a Capt. Fitzgerald,[23] who quarrelled six years ago in the West Indies and the former being just arrived in England set out immediately for this place to fight Fitzgerald and has had the satisfaction of running him twice through the body, one of which wounds is through his lungs, yet the surgeon says he may recover. Adieu! Compliments to Lady Mary and Ch[urchill], Mrs Leneve, etc.

---

burgh] with telling him that his life was now in his hands, which he might dispose of; that he was in the utmost distress, having had no meat or sleep for two days and two nights, sitting on a rock beat upon by the rains; and when they ceased, ate up by flies; conjured him to show compassion but for one night' (quoted in A. M. W. Stirling, *Macdonald of the Isles*, 1913, pp. 85–6). The whole incident, in a slightly garbled version, was known to the government in London by 22 July (SELWYN 103).

19. The Young Pretender had reached the mainland from Skye 5 July and arrived at Morar on the 8th (Blaikie, *Itinerary*, pp. 55–6).

20. Allan Macdonald (d. 1756); for him see *Origins of the 'Forty-Five*, p. 81, n. 2; *Prisoners of the '45*, ed. Seton and Arnot, Edinburgh, 1928–9, iii. 44–5, Scottish History Society 3d ser. XIII–XV.

21. From Morar, the Young Pretender went to Angus Macdonald of Borradale. The last intelligence the army had apparently obtained of his movements had been from the capture of his guides, the Mackinnons, almost immediately after they left him at Borradale 10 July (Blaikie, *Itinerary*, p. 56). It was this intelligence which had led to the organization of Conway's searching party to Morar and Knoydart (above, n. 2).

22. Not identified. No other reference to this duel has been found.

23. Perhaps the Capt. Fitzgerald of Dejean's Regiment (37th Foot) 'left sick at Fort Augustus' according to a return of absent officers 6 Sept. OS (*Albemarle Papers*, i. 206).

To Conway, August 1746 OS

Missing; a 'shadow of a letter' mentioned *post* 29 Aug. 1746 OS.

To Conway, Saturday 23 August 1746 OS

Missing; mentioned *post* 29 Aug. 1746 OS.

From Conway, Friday 29 August 1746 OS

Printed for the first time from the MS now WSL, formerly Rutnam.

Stirling, Aug. 29.

Dear Horry,

AS to the clothing, I don't immediately recollect that I know such a person in the world as Mr Wilson,[1] much less that I have promised to him or to anybody but Mr Mann to have that of my regiment, so that you may depend upon it, I shall not break that I gave him and you. In a little time I shall write to my agent[2] to settle matters with him, the time of making the contracts now almost coming on.

I have besides that shadow of a letter about that affair received yours of the 23d. I have also received another ghost of a letter from you, which disappointed me much; in short, a letter from my good dowager sister[3] directed in your handwriting, a phenomenon which I am at a great loss to account for as I told you in a former letter if you received it.[4] She lives in the country; I don't believe you see her often; she can write and knows, I suppose, how to direct to me; after

1. William Wilson, an army clothier, who gave evidence to the Committee on the State of His Majesty's Land Forces and Marines in the spring of 1746 (*Reports from Committees of the House of Commons*, 1803–6, ii. 87).

2. Henry Taylor (d. 1758) of Charles Street, Westminster, was Conway's regimental agent in 1748 and presumably at this time (*Court and City Register*, 1748, pp. 145, 146; GM 1758, xxviii. 197).

3. Probably his elder half-sister the Hon. Henrietta Seymour Conway (ca 1711–71), HW's correspondent (Collins, *Peerage*, 1812, ii. 561; GM 1771, xli. 239). She was in the habit of asking HW to frank her letters for her; see *post* 11 April 1760 and 27 April 1764.

4. This is not mentioned in any surviving letter.

all which how you come to direct her letters passes my comprehension —but of that somewhat too much.

I pity you sincerely for the negotiation you have undertaken but console myself with thinking you'll be paid for your trouble by the honour of accommodating the most difficult of all disputes and of bringing peace into a most divided brotherhood.[5] But you can't imagine how you surprise me by telling me Arthur is in town. I had no notion that anything but the Pretender's being crowned there could bring him so far and then that he would only be dragged up to expire in peace after seeing that glorious day. Poor man, what can you do with him with all his miseries and all his complaints? But you are retiring to Windsor![6] You know this is not the first I have heard of your taking a house in the country and used to think you whimsical, but this sudden fit of old age and poverty are such arguments as won't bear an answer. I actually pity you but hope, however, that your infirmities won't prevent your passing the winter in town. In summer, you may be as old and as asthmatical as you please. You guess rightly enough about me. I have never had a fit of sickness since I was ten years old nor one fit of old age in my life; if anything I think I rather grow foolisher than wiser; so, in short, whether the Highland air has sharpened my appetite for it I don't know but certain it is that I never longed more childishly for London in my life. I hope to see you well settled there before two months are passed, and am, dear Horry, most sincerely and affectionately

Yours,

H. C.

To Conway, ca Monday 15 September 1746 OS

Missing; written from Windsor; answered *post* 24 Sept. 1746 OS.

5. HW was attempting to reconcile his and Conway's uncles, Arthur and Erasmus Shorter. See also *post* 24 Sept. OS.
6. HW took a house within the precincts of the Castle. His house-hunting at Windsor is outlined in MONTAGU i.

39, 40, 44 and n. 2. See also Thomas Gray, *Correspondence*, ed. Toynbee and Whibley, Oxford, 1935, i. 236; 'Short Notes,' GRAY i. 16. HW moved there 19 Aug. (MONTAGU i. 45; MANN iii. 298).

From CONWAY, Wednesday 24 September 1746 OS

Printed for the first time from the MS now WSL, formerly Rutnam.

Sterling, Sept. 24.

Dear Horry,

I HAVE received not without some surprise yours dated from Windsor, for though your talking of taking of a house in the country and even your taking it did not astonish me very much, I must own I never thought you'd go so far as to live in it; however, my comfort is that it being now but the month of September, before November you'll be tired of it and we shall see you in the winter quite recovered of this fit of poverty, old age and love of retirement and relapsed on the other hand into your old bigotry for town. But if you are really in earnest about being old and poor you must come here, this especially if you have any disposition to be dull. This place is calculated for the old, the poor and the dull; for the rich could not spend their money here, and here's no society for the gay nor entertainment for the young, so that one might indeed grow rich if one stayed here long but *en revanche* should infallibly become both old and dull.

I have a notion you have undertaken an Herculean labour in endeavouring to reconcile the differences of our two good uncles[1] and for every one that you are so lucky as to finish I dare say twenty grow in the place. However, it's a Christian design and I heartily wish you may perfect it that they mayn't be left to drive you out of town whenever my good stars shall think it time to bring me into it. But of all strange things, what you tell me of Arthur's being without miseries is the most strange; when I saw him he was made up of stone, gravel, gout, rheumatism, ruptures etc., with more whinings and pinings and greater disorders of mind than body. Pray give my duty to him as a part of what in his state of whining used to be near and dear. I want to know how it fares with his Jacobitism and how he bears the misfortunes of his friends?

Your Corona Carduana[2] is something like a crown of thorns and

---

1. Erasmus and Arthur Shorter, whose differences may have been related to settling the estate of their older brother John; see *ante* 3 March, 29 Aug. 1746 OS.

2. Crown of thistles.

such I assure it has been in the obtaining and will be in the wearing to those that are to wear it in this country. For my part I'd give up any crown in the world rather than wear it here. I know this shocks your taste for royalty but to show you we can moralize at Stirling[3] as well as Windsor, I think all crowns crowns of thistles and would not give up the free social pleasures incompatible with majesty for all the pomp and power that attend it: but perhaps I do you wrong and though you take your pictures and bronzes out of the world with you, you may have left your taste for those other toys behind you.—Are you really philosophical? I want much to know, 'tis such a change in you since I last heard the history of your sentiments that I scarce know how to believe it; and yet your sentiments and mine, dear Horry, have undergone some strange revolutions since the youthful days we passed together[4] at the foot of that hill you mention, the very remembrance of which makes me as old and as philosophical as you can be and with all my laughing it would be the greatest satisfaction imaginable to me to be able now to spend some weeks with you in the contemplation and enjoyment of that scene, which indeed, as you say, has something of melancholy in it but a melancholy that I envy compared to the disagreeable melancholy I am, I doubt, for some time condemned to here.

I wish I could hear news of the Parliament's meeting;[5] that would give me some hopes of a release. Perhaps you don't wish the same; however, let one know when you hear anything of it for there's no describing the dreadful ennui of this place.

Adieu, yours affectionately,

H. C.

Are you quite alone?

---

3. Stirling had been one of the favourite residences of the Scottish monarchs.
4. At Eton.
5. At this time Parliament was pro- rogued to 30 Sept. OS; on that day it was further prorogued to 18 Nov. OS, when it met (*Journals of the House of Commons* xxv. 188).

To Conway, Friday 3 October 1746 OS

Printed from *Works* v. 23–4.

Windsor still,[1] Oct. 3, 1746.

My dear **Harry,**

YOU ask me if I am really grown a philosopher. Really I believe not; for I shall refer you to my practice rather than to my doctrine, and have really acquired what they only pretended to seek, content. So far indeed I was a philosopher even when I lived in town, for then I was content too; and all the difference I can conceive between those two opposite doctors was, that Aristippus loved London, and Diogenes Windsor: and if your master the Duke, whom I sincerely prefer to Alexander, and who certainly can intercept more sunshine, would but stand out of my way, which he is extremely in, while he lives in the Park here,[2] I should love my little tub of forty pounds a year, more than my palace *dans la rue des ministres,*[3] with all my pictures and bronzes, which you ridiculously imagine I have encumbered myself with in my solitude. Solitude it is, as to the tub itself, for no soul lives in it with me; though I could easily give you room at the butt end of it, and with vast pleasure; but George Montagu, who perhaps is a philosopher too, though I am sure not of Pythagoras's silent sect,[4] lives but two barrels off; and Ashton,[5] a Christian philosopher of our acquaintance, lives at the foot of that hill which you mention with a melancholy satisfaction that always attends the reflection. Apropos, here is an ode[6] on the very subject, which I desire you will please to like excessively: . . . .

1. In the summer of the year 1746 Mr Walpole had hired a small house at Windsor (HW).

2. 'The Duke is here at his Lodge with three whores and three aide-de-camps; and the country swarms with people. He goes to races, and they make a ring about him, as at a bear-baiting' (Gray to Wharton, 11 Sept. 1746 OS, Gray, *Correspondence,* ed. Toynbee and Whibley, Oxford, 1935, i. 239–40). The Duke had been made Ranger and Keeper of Windsor Forest and Great Park 12 July 1746, and had taken up residence in the Lodge (later Cumberland Lodge) in Windsor Great Park.

3. Arlington Street. HW wrote to Montagu 1 Dec. 1768: 'From my earliest memory Arlington Street has been the ministerial street' (MONTAGU ii. 271).

4. Candidates for admission to Pythagoras's cult were especially tested for their ability to maintain silence.

5. Ashton had become a fellow of Eton 20 Dec. 1745 OS (R. A. Austen-Leigh, *Eton College Register 1698–1752,* Eton, 1927, p. 9).

6. Gray's *Ode on a Distant Prospect of Eton College:* the text that HW sent to Conway is omitted in *Works.*

You will immediately conclude, out of good breeding, that it is mine, and that it is charming. I shall be much obliged to you for the first thought, but desire you will retain only the second, for it is Mr Gray's, and not

Your humble servant's,

HOR. WALPOLE

From CONWAY, Saturday 18 October 1746 OS

Printed for the first time from the MS now WSL, formerly Rutnam.

Sterling, Oct. 18.

Dear Horry,

YOU tell me that you are not really become a philosopher, but if you are as content as you say I think you are really a philosopher and much more really so than all the boasted professors of philosophy from Pythagoras down to the mere modern hermits, for I doubt if any of 'em were content. For me, I assure you I am far from being a philosopher, that is, I am far from being content, but if living a dismal, solitary, uncomfortable life and disliking cordially the little glimpse of the world that I see here is being a philosopher, then am I an excellent one. In short, like you I am a mixture of Aristippus and Diogenes, for to the doctrines and inclinations of Aristippus I join the practice of Diogenes; what sort of a philosopher that makes I leave you to determine. However, I fancy I could make a much better at that butt end of a tub which you are so kind as to offer me and though the vicinity and example of the Duke might go near to discompose one's philosophy a little as to the decorum, I fancy it would not at all disqualify one for a member of your sect. By the by, apropos to your complaint, I hear my master does indeed take up more of your sunshine every day than another for they write me word he grows fat *à vue d'oeil*. I am really sorry for it for besides the encumbrance to one destined to an active life it brings a thousand distempers and dangers with it.

The Ode that you sent in obedience to your injunction I do indeed like excessively and in return having little to amuse you with send you a poem,[1] which I think has some nature and passion in it, but which you are at full liberty to like or dislike as you please for I picked it up in the Highlands last winter and look upon it as a sort of curiosity being, as I was told, the growth of that frozen climate. Pray are you and Grey well together again?[2] I thought that breach was quite irreconcilable. Adieu. Make my compliments to both your neighbour philosophers and believe me, dear Horry,

Most sincerely yours,

H. C.

To CONWAY, Friday 24 October 1746 OS

Printed from *Works* v. 24–5.

Windsor, October 24, 1746.

WELL, Harry, Scotland is the last place on earth I should have thought of for turning anybody poet: but I begin to forgive it half its treasons in favour of your verses,[1] for I suppose you don't think I am the dupe of the Highland story that you tell me: the only use I shall make of it is to commend the lines to you, as if they really were a Scotsman's. There is a melancholy harmony in them that is charming, and a delicacy in the thoughts that no Scotchman is capable of, though a *Scotchwoman*[1a] might inspire it. I beg both for Cyn-

1. Missing. HW assumes in his reply that it was written by Conway, but Conway denies it *post* 9 Nov. 1746 OS.

2. HW and Gray had been reconciled in early Nov. 1745 (GRAY ii. 1); Gray wrote Wharton 10 Aug. 1746, 'Mr W. I have seen a good deal . . . all is mighty free, and even friendly, more than one could expect' (Gray, *Correspondence*, ed. Toynbee and Whibley, Oxford, 1935, i. 236–7).

1. Enclosed in Conway's last letter.

1a. Caroline Campbell (1721–1803), m. 1 (as his third wife) (1739) Charles Bruce (1682 – 10 Feb. 1747 OS), 3d E. of Ailesbury; m. 2 (19 Dec. 1747) Hon. Henry Seymour Conway. At the time of her marriage to Ailesbury Mrs Delany's sister wrote:

'Her father can give her no fortune; she is very pretty, modest, well-behaved, and just eighteen, has two thousand a year jointure, and four hundred pin money: *they say* he is cross, covetous and three-score years old, and this unsuitable match is the *admiration of the old* and the *envy of the young!*' (Mary Granville, Mrs Delany, *Autobiography and Correspondence*, ed. Lady Llanover, 1861–2, ii. 54–5). HW's allusion to her in the present letter is the earliest mention yet found of Conway's attachment to her, which had obviously begun well before her husband's death; about 17 Feb. 1747 OS, seven days after Lord Ailesbury's death, Lord Pulteney wrote to Charles Hotham: 'Colonel Conway is to be married to Lady Alis-

thia's sake and my own that you would continue your *de tristibus*, till I have an opportunity of seeing your muse, and she of rewarding her: *Reprends ta musette, berger amoureux!* If Cynthia has ever travelled ten miles in fairy land, she must be wondrous content with the person and qualifications of her knight, who in future story will be read of thus: Elmedorus was tall and perfectly well made, his face oval, and features regularly handsome, but not effeminate; his complexion sentimentally brown, with not much colour; his teeth fine, and forehead agreeably low, round which his black hair curled naturally and beautifully. His eyes were black too, but had nothing of fierce or insolent; on the contrary, a certain melancholy swimmingness that described hopeless love, rather than a natural amorous languish. His exploits in war, where he always fought by the side of the renowned Paladin William of England, have endeared his memory to all admirers of true chivalry, as the mournful elegies which he poured out among the desert rocks of Caledonia[2] in honour of the peerless lady and his heart's idol, the incomparable Cynthia, will forever preserve his name in the flowery annals of poesy.

What a pity it is I was not born in the golden age of Louis XIV, when it was not only the fashion to write folios, but to read them too! Or rather, it is a pity the same fashion don't subsist now, when one need not be at the trouble of invention, nor of turning the whole Roman history into romance, for want of proper heroes. Your campaign in Scotland rolled out and well be-epitheted would make a pompous work, and make one's fortune; at sixpence a number, one should have all the damsels within the Liberties[3] for subscribers: whereas now, if one has a mind to be read, one must write metaphysical poems in blank verse, which though I own to be still easier have not half the imagination of romances, and are dull without any agreeable absurdity. Only think of the gravity of this wise age, that have exploded *Cleopatra*[4] and *Pharamond*,[5] and approve

bury [*sic*] immediately, notwithstanding my Lord is not yet buried; the only reason I can give for her violent hurry is that Mr Conway is to go [to] Flanders in a little while, and she has a mind to make sure of him whilst she can' (A. M. W. Stirling, *The Hothams*, 1918, ii. 30, letter dated by internal evidence).

2. Mr Conway was now in Scotland with the Duke of Cumberland, to whom he had been appointed aide-de-camp in

the year 1743 [1745] (HW). He had ceased to be an aide-de-camp on obtaining his regiment in April.

3. I.e., the 'Liberties of London and Westminster.'

4. *Cléopâtre*, by Gautier de Costes [*or* Coste] de la Calprenède; see *ante* 25 Oct. 1743 NS, n. 19, and 18 April 1745 OS.

5. *Faramond, ou l'histoire de France*, 1661, also by La Calprenède, left incomplete on his death.

The Pleasures of the Imagination,[6] *The Art of Preserving Health,*[7] and *Leonidas!*[8]—I beg the age's pardon: it has done approving these poems, and has forgot them.

Adieu, dear Harry! Thank you seriously for the poem. I am going to town for the Birthday,[9] and shall return hither till the Parliament meets; I suppose there is no doubt of our meeting then.

Yours ever,

Hor. Walpole

PS. Now you are at Stirling, if you should meet with Drummond's *History of the Five King Jameses,*[10] pray look it over. I have lately read it, and like it much. It is wrote in imitation of Livy, the style masculine, and the whole very sensible—only he ascribes the misfortunes of one reign to the then king's loving architecture,[11] and

In trim gardens taking pleasure.[12]

6. By Mark Akenside (1721–70), M.D., published in January 1744.

7. By John Armstrong (1709–79), M.D., published in 1744.

8. By Richard Glover; see *ante* 7 April 1737 OS.

9. The King's Birthday, usually celebrated 30 Oct., but on the 28th it was postponed to 13 Nov. (GM 1746, xvi. 557, 610). HW was going to London principally for the production of his *Epilogue to Tamerlane,* 'spoken by Mrs Pritchard, in the character of the Comic Muse, November 4, 1746' at Covent Garden (Montagu i. 48 and nn. 1, 2; 'Short Notes,' Gray i. 16 and nn. 105, 106).

10. *The History of Scotland, from the Year 1423 until the Year 1542. Containing the Lives and Reigns of James the I., the II., the III., the IV., the V.,* 1655, by William Drummond (1585–1649) of Hawthornden. HW's copy of Drummond's *Works,* Edinburgh, 1711, in which the work is reprinted as *The History of the Lives and Reigns of the Five James's, Kings of Scotland,* is now WSL (Hazen, *Cat. of HW's Lib.,* No. 1111). In 1782 HW told Lord Buchan that 'Drummond of Hawthornden is a favourite author with me' (Dalrymple 166).

11. Drummond writes that near the end of the life of James III: 'He was much given to buildings and trimming up of chapels, halls and gardens, as usually are the lovers of idleness; . . . an humour, which though it be allowable in men which have not much to do, yet it is harmful in princes; as to be taken with admiration of watches, clocks, dials, automates, pictures and statues' (*Works,* Edinburgh, 1711, p. 61).

12. 'That in trim gardens takes his pleasure' (Milton, *Il Penseroso,* l. 50).

From CONWAY, Wednesday 5 November 1746 OS

Printed for the first time from the MS now WSL, formerly Rutnam.

Sterling, Nov. 5.

Dear Horry,

I HOPE to follow my letter very soon—so soon that if I had not more mind to write than to be idle I have a very fair excuse, but besides that you are one of the few I have a pleasure in writing to, I can't in gratitude defer for a moment thanking you for all the variety of undeserved applauses that you bestow upon me in your last, nor in conscience think of robbing the true author of the verses I sent you of his share of them, though by the obscurity of the place where I picked them up I fancy I might play the plagiary pretty safely; in short, you may have what fancies you please and not only know the author but the subject, yet I can assure you the story I told you is all true and can only flatter your penetration in having guessed right that it was a Scotch woman who inspired them, which though I cannot say of my own knowledge seems at least highly probable. However, I am very glad of the mistake which has produced so pretty a piece of imagination as your romantic paragraph; which pleases me so much that I seriously long to see a whole novel, nay, if you will, a romance by the same hand and though as you say the Augustan age of Lewis XIV is no more, I dare say it would steal admirers enough from *The Art of Preserving Health* and *The Pleasures of the Imagination;* and I fancy too you are, or were at least, romantic enough not to think it a very disagreeable task and if you are as much be-Cynthia'd as you seem to think me it would be quite charming to make your mistress fall in love with the effect of your own romances.

Drummond's history I have read and think of it pretty much as you do. I wish he had continued it a little lower down, and should have been curious to see his account of poor Queen Mary in whose reign he would have found matter for better morals than the injurious reflection upon architecture that you seem so much offended with; indeed, he had enough in those he has writ for they are full of as many reverses as any I think I ever met with. It seems to have been sufficient to have the name of Stewart from the first down to the last to make them weak and unfortunate. Adieu. I hope to find you in town and settled.

Yours affectionately.

Conway was in London for the meetings of Parliament, which convened 18 Nov. OS. The Duke of Cumberland left for The Hague in Feb. 1747 (*Daily Adv.* 2, 6 Feb.; GM 1747, xvii. 99); Conway apparently followed with his regiment late in March OS, for the various corps of the Allied army 'were drawing together with all diligence' in early April (see following letter, n. 2). On 20 April NS Conway's regiment is listed in the Duke of Cumberland's 'General Orders' for the line of battle (A. N. Campbell-Maclachlan, *William Augustus, Duke of Cumberland*, 1876, p. 348).

From CONWAY, Saturday 15 April 1747 NS

Printed for the first time from the MS now WSL, formerly Rutnam. The year is supplied by the contents, which describe the military situation just before the opening of the campaign of 1747.

Haren,[1] Apr. 15, NS.

Dear Horry,

I AM ashamed I have not writ to you sooner but I have really been in such a continual hurry from the moment of my landing as has left me very little time to myself and God knows when it will cease. We are now in the full flow of it, preparing everything for taking the field immediately,[2] in short, a multiplicity of business that keeps me in a perpetual agitation of body and mind. Our troops are all in motion, assembling from all quarters. We promise ourselves a

1. Haaren or Haren, a village about 6 miles northeast of the D. of Cumberland's headquarters at Tilburg.

2. 'We are assured by a private letter from Tilbourg dated April 14 NS that Marshal Bathiani and Prince Waldeck had received their final orders from the Duke and were set out for their respective corps, which were drawing together with all diligence; and 'twas the general opinion, that the army would be formed by the 25th, and that it would soon move towards the enemy, the junction of the three bodies being to be made in their march' (*Daily Adv.* 8 April OS). The English troops apparently began to advance 21 April NS (A. N. Campbell-Maclachlan, *William Augustus, Duke of Cumberland*, 1876, p. 351; *Oesterr. Erbfolge-krieg* ix. 493).

very fine army and talk of doing great things, but what they are I cannot pretend to tell you, the plan of our operations being hitherto kept very secret.[3] In the meantime the French, I hear, talk at least as big as we do and threaten to have a vast army in the field very soon; however, the wise amongst us seem to think they gasconade a little and are full of our superiority.[4] I'll tell you more of these matters soon but at present, besides the difficulty of knowing the true state of these matters, I am so taken up in the little sphere of my own corps that I really hardly once peep out to see what's passing abroad. M. Bathiani, I hear, says the Queen's troops will be 60 thousand effective and from another hand I am told there are actually 46 of them now upon the territories of the States.[5] Lord Sandwich[6] was with the Duke t'other day but is now gone back to The Hague so that the great work of peace is for some time suspended, the reception of the ambassadors not being yet settled.[7] And so with this, my dear Horry, I conclude, being as I've told you in an equal fullness of business

3. The object at this time was the siege of Antwerp, but bad weather and French counter-movements prevented it (Evan Charteris, *William Augustus, Duke of Cumberland*, 1913, pp. 301–2).

4. Lord Sandwich wrote to Newcastle, Breda, 11 April NS, scoffing at the well-founded English fears of French superiority: 'The French certainly give out that their numbers are superior to ours but your Grace will observe that to give that idea any degree of plausibility they always count by battalions and not by effective men, and I believe in point of completeness the French battalions may in general at least be put upon the same footing as those of their enemies, which it [*sic*] allowed, cannot in my opinion give them any superiority considering the number of places they have to guard whose garrisons are included in the number of battalions that are said to be intended to serve in the Low Countries' (BM Add. MSS 32807, f. 265). Sandwich then estimates the Allied army at 116,000 effectives; and by the time it marched it was estimated at 127,000 (ibid. f. 266; *Daily Adv.* 17 April OS *sub* Tilbourg 19 April NS). In fact the Duke of Cumberland's forces barely reached 100,000 at the beginning of the campaign, only 80,000 of which were ready, while the French apparently had about 110,000 ef-

fectives (see MANN iii. 389, n. 22, 395, n. 7 and the sources there cited).

5. 'I have the best authority can be had, both that of his Royal Highness and Marshal Bathiani that there are 48,000 Austrians cantoned ever since the fifth of this month upon the territories of the Republic. . . . The Austrians when they tell us of 48,000 men that they have now in the field, at the same time declare they are to have 12,000 more to complete their contingent of 60,000 men, and I don't find that there is any doubt but that they will in a good degree be able to make good their promise' (Sandwich to Newcastle, Breda, 11 April NS, BM Add. MSS 32807, ff. 265–6).

6. At this time minister plenipotentiary to the abortive Conference of Breda. He had apparently visited the Duke 10 or 11 April NS, since he had apparently seen him when he wrote to Newcastle from Breda on the 11th (see previous note), and was back at The Hague by the 13th (*Daily Adv.* 8 April OS).

7. It never was; the Conference of Breda had been postponed for the fifth time on 16 March NS because of procedural difficulties and never reconvened, although it remained in nominal existence for two more months (Sir Richard Lodge, *Studies in Eighteenth-Century Diplomacy 1740–1748*, 1930, p. 235).

and dearth of news. I have heard very little hitherto from my friends in England which is generally one's fate before one's settled; I had a kind little letter from G. Montague[8] for which I desire you'll return him my best compliments; tell him I really am obliged to him and would write to thank him for it if I did not think he would take this way of doing it as equally well meant and less troublesome. Make my compliments to Lady Mary Churchill and Mrs Leneve, and believe me, dear Horry,

Affectionately yours,

H. C.

To CONWAY, Thursday 16 April 1747 OS

Printed from *Works* v. 26–7.

Arlington Street, April 16, 1747.

Dear Harry,

WE are all skyrockets and bonfires tonight for your last year's victory;[1] but if you have a mind to perpetuate yourselves in the calendar, you must take care to refresh your conquests. I was yesterday out of town, and the very signs as I passed through the villages made me make very quaint reflections on the mortality of fame and popularity. I observed how the Duke's head had succeeded almost universally to Admiral Vernon's,[2] as his had left but few traces of the Duke of Ormond's.[3] I pondered these things in my heart, and said unto myself, 'Surely all glory is but as a sign!'[4]

8. Missing.

1. The battle of Culloden (HW). 'Thursday 16. Being the anniversary of the victory at Culloden, was a numerous and splendid appearance of nobility, foreign ministers, gentry, etc. to pay their compliments to his Majesty on the occasion, and the evening concluded with illuminations, bonfires, etc.' (GM 1747, xvii. 198).

2. An essay on this subject from the *Mirror* 19 Feb. 1780 is quoted at some length in Jacob Larwood and J. C. Hotten, *The History of Signboards*, 1866, pp. 54–5; it states that the Duke held his po-

sition until replaced by the King of Prussia, Prince Ferdinand, and the M. of Granby during the Seven Years' War. For Vernon's head on signs see also SELWYN 29.

3. James Butler (1665–1745), 2d D. of Ormonde, who had been a popular hero during the wars of William III and the War of the Spanish Succession. One innsign in his honour survived at Gloucester until the mid-19th century (Larwood and Hotten, op. cit. 59).

4. Soon after Mr Walpole published a paper in *The World* upon this subject (HW).

You have heard that old Lovat's[5] tragedy is over: it has been succeeded by a little farce, containing the humours of the Duke of Newcastle and his man Stone.[6] The first event was a squabble between his Grace and the sheriff[7] about holding up the head on the scaffold—a custom that has been disused, and which the sheriff would not comply with, as he received no order in writing.[8] Since that the Duke has burst ten yards of breeches-strings[9] about the body, which was to be sent into Scotland; but it seems it is customary for vast numbers to rise to attend the most trivial burial.[10] The Duke, who is always at least as much frightened at doing right as at doing wrong, was three days before he got courage enough to order the burying in the Tower.[11] I must tell you an excessive good story of George Selwyn:[12] some women were scolding him for going to see the execution, and asked him, how he could be such a barbarian to see the head cut off? 'Nay,' says he, 'if that was such a crime, I am

5. Simon Frazer [Fraser (ca 1667–1747), 11th] Lord Lovat, beheaded on Tower Hill the 9th of April 1747 (HW). For his trial and execution, see MANN iii. 379–82, 386–7.

6. Andrew Stone (1703–73), Newcastle's secretary and under-secretary of state; M.P. Hastings 1741–61.

7. The sheriffs of London for 1746–7 were Thomas Winterbottom (d. 1752), lord mayor 1751–2; and Robert Alsop (d. 1785), who completed Winterbottom's term as lord mayor in 1752 (GM 1752, xxii. 289; 1785, lv pt i. 406).

8. 'Thursday 2 [April]. The sheriffs of London received a warrant, in a letter from the D. of Newcastle, for the execution of Lord Lovat on the 9th, intimating that it was expected they would expose the head at the four corners of the scaffold, as usual. The sheriffs immediately returned an answer to his Grace, that, as it had not been practised lately, they desired it might be inserted in the body of the warrant' (ibid., 1747, xvii. 197). The incident is also mentioned, in a different context, in A Candid and Impartial Account of the Behaviour of Simon Lord Lovat, 1747, p. 24.

9. Alluding to a trick of the Duke of Newcastle's (HW).

10. 'On the execution of Lord Lovat, he desired to have his body sent to his seat in Scotland, it was thought with some hope of his clan's rising at his burial where it is their custom to meet in great numbers. The Duke of Newcastle gave leave, but afterwards was persuaded to stop the body, which was buried in the Tower' (HW's MS Political Papers, f. 9). 'There is a report, that some hundreds of the Clan of Fraser intended to meet the aforesaid corpse at some distance from the burial-place of the family in Scotland, in order to attend the funeral of their chief' (Daily Adv. 17 April OS). Lord Hardwicke wrote in similar terms to Newcastle 12 April OS (BM Add. MSS 32710, f. 427).

11. 'We are informed that Mr Stephenson, the undertaker, received an order last night from the secretary of state, not to remove the corpse of the late Lord Lovat till he has further directions. Mr Stephenson was to have set out this morning with the corpse from his house in the Strand for Scotland' (Daily Adv. 14 April OS). Lovat's body was buried in the Tower 17 April OS and the bones removed to the crypt of St Peter's Chapel in 1877 (MANN iii. 386, n. 6).

12. George Augustus Selwyn (1719–91), wit; M.P. Ludgershall 1747–54, 1780–91, Gloucester City 1754–80; HW's correspondent.

sure I have made amends, for I went to see it sewed on again.'[13] When he was at the undertaker's,[14] as soon as they had stitched him together, and were going to put the body into the coffin, George, in my Lord Chancellor's[15] voice, said, 'My Lord Lovat, your Lordship may rise.' My Lady Townshend has picked up a little stable boy in the Tower, which the warders have put upon her for a natural son of Lord Kilmarnock's,[16] and taken him into her own house. You need not tell Mr T.[17] this from me.

We have had a great and fine day[18] in the House on the second reading the bill for taking away the heritable jurisdictions in Scotland. Lyttelton[19] made the finest oration imaginable; the Solicitor-General,[20] the new Advocate,[21] and Hume Campbell,[22] particularly the last, spoke excessively well for it, and Oswald[23] against it. The majority was 233 against 102. Pitt[24] was not there; the Duchess of Queensberry had ordered him to have the gout.[25]

13. After the execution Stephenson wrote Selwyn: 'I'm this moment come back from the Tower, have had some trouble in bringing him off, so that have been forced to put the hearse in an inn yard —till it is dark about 8 o'clock when if nothing extra prevents you may depend on my sending to you and favouring you with what you so much desire' (MS now WSL).

14. William Stephenson of the Strand (above, nn. 11, 13).

15. Lord Hardwicke, who presided at the trial as Lord High Steward.

16. For Lady Townshend's 'passion' for Lord Kilmarnock, see HW to Montagu 16 Aug. 1746 OS (MONTAGU i. 47) and J. H. Jesse, George Selwyn and His Contemporaries, 1882, i. 106–7.

17. Hon. George Townshend, Lady Townshend's son, now an aide-de-camp to the D. of Cumberland (A. N. Campbell-Maclachlan, William Augustus, Duke of Cumberland, 1876, p. 351).

18. 14 April OS (Journals of the House of Commons xxv. 359). The debates are imperfectly reported in Cobbett, Parl. Hist. xiv. 27–51; that on the first reading, 7 April, is given in the form of two speeches summarizing the arguments on both sides; that on the second reading is not reported; and that on the third, 14 May, consists of one speech by Lyttelton

'from his own copy' which is more probably his speech on the second reading mentioned here.

19. Sir George, afterwards created Lord Lyttelton (HW). For the enthusiastic reception of his speech, see the letters quoted in Maud Wyndham, Chronicles of the Eighteenth Century, 1924, i. 210–11.

20. William Murray [1705–93], afterwards [1756, Bn and 1776] Earl of Mansfield (HW). He was solicitor-general 1742–54, and lord chief justice of the King's Bench 1756–88.

21. William Grant [1701–64], lord advocate of Scotland [1746–54] (HW); M.P. Elgin burghs 1747–54; lord of session as Lord Prestongrange, 1754.

22. Only brother to the Earl of Marchmont (HW). Alexander Hume Campbell (1708–60), M.P. Berwickshire 1734–41, 1742–60.

23. James Oswald [1715–69], afterwards [1751–9] a lord of Trade and [1763–7] vice-treasurer of Ireland (HW); M.P. Dysart burghs 1741–7, 1754–68, Fifeshire 1747–54.

24. William Pitt, afterwards Earl of Chatham (HW).

25. In Jan. 1746 HW described Pitt as 'governed by her mad Grace of Queensberry' (MANN iii. 195). She had been in violent opposition since having been forbid the Court in 1729, but returned to

I will give you a commission once more to tell Lord Bury[26] that he has quite dropped me: if I thought he would take me up again, I would write to him; a message would encourage me. Adieu!

Yours ever,

Hor. Walpole

To Conway, Monday 8 June 1747 OS

Printed from *Works* v. 27–9.

Twickenham, June 8, 1747.

YOU perceive by my date that I am got into a new camp, and have left my tub at Windsor. It is a little play-thing-house[1] that I got out of Mrs Chenevix's shop,[2] and is the prettiest bauble you ever saw. It is set in enamelled meadows, with filigree hedges:

A small Euphrates through the piece is roll'd,
And little finches wave their wings in gold.[3]

Two delightful roads, that you would call dusty, supply me continually with coaches and chaises: barges as solemn as barons of the Exchequer move under my window; Richmond Hill and Ham Walks bound my prospect; but, thank God! the Thames is between me and the Duchess of Queensberry.[4] Dowagers as plenty as flounders

Court in June 1747, 'a point she has been intriguing these two years' (ibid. iii. 420).

26. George Keppel, eldest son of William Earl of Albemarle, whom he succeeded in the title in 1755. He was now, together with Mr Conway, aide-de-camp to the Duke of Cumberland (HW). Neither of them was any longer aide-de-camp to the Duke; Conway had surrendered the post on obtaining his regiment; Bury had become aide-de-camp to the King in May 1746 (MANN iii. 247, n. 6a) and apparently a lord of the Bedchamber to the Duke about the same time. No letters of HW's correspondence with Lord Bury have been recovered.

1. Strawberry Hill, to which HW had just moved from London (MANN iii. 414).

For its appearance at this time, see HW's drawing, reproduced ibid.

2. A famous toy shop (HW). Elizabeth Deard, m. Paul Daniel Chenevix; in 1739 the shop was on the 'Corner of Warwick Street near Pall Mall' (MANN ii. 366, n. 12). HW's agreement with Mrs Chenevix, dated 27 June 1747 OS, providing for a year's lease from 20 May 1747, is printed GRAY i. 17, n. 112.

3. 'A small Euphrates through the piece is roll'd,
   And little eagles wave their wings in gold'
(Pope, *Moral Essays*, Epistle V, ll. 29–30).

4. Who had a house at Petersham; for one of her visits to SH, see HW to Montagu 14 July 1748 OS, MONTAGU i. 61.

inhabit all around, and Pope's ghost is just now skimming under my window by a most poetical moonlight.[5] I have about land enough[6] to keep such a farm as Noah's, when he set up in the ark with a pair of each kind; but my cottage is rather cleaner than I believe his was after they had been cooped up together forty days. The Chenevixes had tricked it out for themselves: up two pair of stairs is what they call Mr Chenevix's[7] library, furnished with three maps, one shelf, a bust of Sir Isaac Newton, and a lame telescope without any glasses. Lord John Sackville *predecessed* me here, and instituted certain games called *cricketalia,*[8] which have been celebrated this very evening in honour of him in a neighbouring meadow.

You will think I have removed my philosophy from Windsor with my tea-things hither; for I am writing to you in all this tranquillity while a Parliament is bursting about my ears. You know it is going to be dissolved:[9] I am told, you are taken care of, though I don't know where,[10] nor whether anybody that chooses you will quarrel with me because he does choose you, as that little bug—[11] did; one of the calamities of my life which I have bore as abominably well as I do most about which I don't care. They say the Prince has taken up two hundred thousand pounds, to carry elections which he won't carry:[12]—he had much better have saved it to buy the Parliament after it is chosen. A new set of peers are in embryo,[13] to add more dignity to the silence of the House of Lords.

I make no remarks on your campaign,[14] because, as you say, you do nothing at all; which, though very proper nutriment for a thinking head, does not do quite so well to write upon. If any one of you can

5. Pope's villa is only a few hundred yards north of SH.

6. 'When Mr Walpole bought Strawberry Hill [1748], there were but five acres belonging to the house' ('Des. of SH,' *Works* ii. 400).

7. Paul Daniel Chenevix (d. ?1743), goldsmith, brother of Richard Chenevix, Bp of Waterford (GRAY i. 103, n. 11; MANN ii. 366, n. 12). HW identifies the room on his drawing (above, n. 1).

8. For Lord John's interest in cricket, see C. J. Phillips, *History of the Sackville Family*, [1930], ii. 79, 193, and H. S. Altham, *History of Cricket*, 1926, p. 37.

9. 18 June OS. The decision had been unexpected; see MANN iii. 412 and nn. 1, 1a.

10. Conway was returned for Penryn, a borough jointly controlled by Lord Falmouth and Lord Edgcumbe, at the general election (Sedgwick i. 217).

11. Presumably Thomas Watson Wentworth (1693–1750) cr. (1728) Bn and (1734) E. of Malton and (1746) M. of Rockingham; he controlled the borough of Higham Ferrers, from which Conway was returned in 1741. Nothing is known of his quarrel with HW.

12. For the Prince's failure in the elections, see J. B. Owen, *Rise of the Pelhams*, 1957, pp. 312–17.

13. For a list of them, with HW's comments, see MANN iii. 419 and n. 11.

14. Mr Conway was in Flanders with William Duke of Cumberland (HW).

but contrive to be shot upon your post, it is all we desire, shall look upon it as a great curiosity, and will take care to set up a monument to the person so slain, as we are doing by vote to Captain Cornewall,[15] who was killed at the beginning of the action in the Mediterranean four years ago. In the present dearth of glory, he is canonized, though, poor man! he had been tried twice the year before for cowardice.[16]

I could tell you much election news, none else; though not being thoroughly attentive to so important a subject, as to be sure one ought to be, I might now and then mistake, and give you a candidate for Durham in place of one for Southampton, or name the returning officer instead of the candidate. In general, I believe, it is much as usual—those sold in detail that afterwards will be sold in the representation—the ministers bribing Jacobites to choose friends of their own—the name of well-wishers to the present establishment, and patriots, outbidding ministers that they may make the better market of their own patriotism:—in short, all England, under some name or other, is just now to be bought and sold; though, whenever we become posterity and forefathers, we shall be in high repute for wisdom and virtue. My great-great-grandchildren will figure me with a white beard down to my girdle; and Mr Pitt's will believe him unspotted enough to have walked over nine hundred hot ploughshares, without hurting the sole of his foot. How merry my ghost will be, and shake its ears to hear itself quoted as a person of consummate prudence!—Adieu, dear Harry!

Yours ever,

HOR. WALPOLE

---

15. James Cornewall (1698–1744), Capt. R.N. 1724; M.P. Weobley 1732-4, 1737-41; killed in the Battle of Toulon 11 Feb. 1744 OS. The House of Commons had voted a monument to him at public expense (the first for a naval hero) in Westminster Abbey 28 May 1747 OS; the monument, 36 feet high, designed and executed by Sir Robert Taylor, was completed in 1755 (*Journals of the House of Commons* xxv. 397; Earl of Liverpool and C. Reade, *House of Cornewall*, Here-

ford, 1908, pp. 111–17, which corrects his birthdate in DNB and contains a full description and a reproduction of the monument).

16. Cornewall had been court-martialed and convicted of an error of judgment for his conduct in avoiding the Spanish fleet in the autumn of 1741 (H. W. Richmond, *The Navy in the War of 1739-48*, Cambridge, 1920, i. 167-8); the other instance has not been found.

From CONWAY, Monday 12 June 1747 NS

Printed for the first time from the MS now WSL, formerly Rutnam.

Camp at Bauwell,[1] June 12, 1747.

Dear Horry,

I AM quite sorry to find an appearance of all correspondence being stopped betwixt us, but God forbid it should remain so! If the post has done either me or you wrong, I hope I shall have the good luck by this to repair it, and I assure you I am as far from suspecting you, my dear Horry, of neglecting me as I am from being guilty of any real neglect to you, though I must confess I have many idlenesses upon my conscience in regard to correspondence and now might have writ oftener than I have though I have had but one letter from you since I left England. I think it is but about two months by days and hours but to my ideas a vast while more, and I think too with all our fair hopes and mighty boastings we have all the prospect in the world of passing a most tedious, idle campaign for it has turned out for us much as usual; the French as much stronger as we are weaker than our calculations made us, which reduces us very near to the mortifying necessity of acting upon the defensive, in which situation it depends entirely upon the will and pleasure of Messieurs Les Français whether anything shall be done or not; they have talked very big in the gazettes at least and were to do the greatest things when the King came to the army; he has now been there some time[2] and yet the same face of tranquillity seems to reign in their army as in ours. There is, however, a notion of their going to besiege Maestricht,[3] which if they should attempt it would probably cost us a battle to attempt the relief of it. Sometimes there have been reports of their intending to attack us here but as our situation is pretty strong I believe they'll hardly attempt it.

You told me, I remember, in your last amidst your moral reflections upon sign-posts that the Duke had supplanted many Admiral Vernons in the roads you have frequented; I doubt from many cir-

1. Or Bouwel, a few miles east of Antwerp, headquarters of the D. of Cumberland 26 May – 17 June NS (*Oesterr. Erbfolge-krieg* ix. 522, 536).

2. Louis XV had arrived at Brussels 31 May NS (ibid. ix. 525).

3. This was the French intention and led to the battle of Laffeldt 2 July NS (*post* 9 July 1747 NS).

cumstances that if we don't do something soon to refresh as you say that the Ansons[4] will soon beat the Cumberlands by as much at least as a water-hero in the eyes of true Britons is superior to a land one. This victory[5] is to make him a peer,[6] I understand, another would entitle him to a dukedom and a third very complete, I fancy, might make him King of England, to show you that glory has in it something more valuable if not more substantial than a sign-post.— You may see from what I have told you that you have no news to expect from me, but don't let that discourage you from writing even though you should have none to tell me. I want to hear of yourself, whether you are retired to your lonely tub in Windsor or still enjoying the more agreeable solitude of Arlington Street. Adieu, my dear Horry; let me hear from you soon and believe me most sincerely and affectionately

Yours,

H. C.

I give compliments to nobody for I don't know who you're with.

From CONWAY, Sunday 9 July 1747 NS

Printed for the first time from the MS now WSL, formerly Rutnam.

Maestricht, July 9, 1747.

Dear Horry,

IT was matter of real concern to me that I could not write to you immediately after the engagement[1] but the accident that befell me at the same time that it gave me greater impatience to do it and

---

4. George Anson (1697–1762), cr. (1747) Bn Anson; Admiral, 1748.

5. Of 3 May OS, off Cape Finisterre; see MANN iii. 402–3 and notes.

6. He was created a baron 13 June OS.

---

1. The Battle of Laffeldt or Laeffeld 2 July NS. Conway had been captured by the French: 'By a gentleman who came last Friday [7 July NS] from the army we have an account that Lord Robert

Sutton and Col. Conway, who were taken prisoners at the late action, were returned to the Duke's quarters on their parole. . . . Col. Conway had like to have been killed by the treachery of a French officer, who he had taken prisoner, and ordered to go by his horse's side to save his life; but the Frenchman seeing a strong party coming to attack us, he pulled the Colonel by his hair backward from off his horse, and who [Conway] had been killed by a

made it more necessary will, I hope, clear me from any suspicion of neglect which on such an occasion would, I own, be unpardonable. It's now three days since my return[2] and this is the first opportunity I have had of writing; my confinement for the three days that I was with the French was made very light to me by their civility, so that all things considered I think I have no great reason to complain of my fate. You must have heard twenty accounts of the affair so I shall say little of it; the whole consisted in the attack of the village of Lovald[3] and that of our cavalry on the left, and among all the affairs I have seen or heard of I never knew so little diversity of opinion or accounts even between the enemy and us. They own that no less than forty battalions had been repulsed with considerable loss before they took it, and that they have lost 8,000 men and 1,000 officers killed and wounded,[4] which is near double our loss,[5] and that they have lost ten pair of colours and six standards[6] they can't deny because we have got them, whereas we lost on our side only one of the former and four of the latter.[7] My regiment was a good deal engaged in the village and had the good luck to take three pair of colours for which the Duke called us good boys; that's enough for us. All your friends are well so I shall not trouble you with a

private man with his own bayonet, had not one of our sergeants killed him [the private] with his halbert, for which he [the sergeant] was presently cut to pieces' (*Whitehall Evening Post* 30 June – 2 July 1747 OS). HW gives an even more graphic account of the incident in a letter to Montagu 2 July 1747 OS (MONTAGU i. 50).

2. HW had been informed of Conway's return to Maestricht 6 July NS in a letter from Stephen Poyntz 1 July OS. The Duke of Cumberland wrote to Chesterfield 10 July NS, 'I have sent back all the French prisoners taken upon their parole, as Marshal Saxe has done by such of ours as are able to travel, and two days after the rest Sir John Ligonier returned, upon his parole likewise, with leave to stay four days, and then to go to Liège. He has had very extraordinary honours done him, and been received as well by the French King as the Marshal de Saxe, with a very surprising familiarity' (S.P. 87, Military Expeditions 23).

3. I.e., Laffeldt; in the *London Gazette Extraordinary* 2 July OS on the battle, it is called merely Val. Conway's regiment was stationed in the village.

4. 'Col. Conway brings an account that the French own the loss of 1,000 officers and 9,000 private men, but we compute it at upwards of 12,000' (Poyntz to HW 1 July OS). For several conflicting accounts of the French casualties, see *Oesterr. Erbfolge-krieg* ix. 628–9 and notes.

5. The total British, Hanoverian, and Hessian casualties, according to the *London Gazette* No. 8654, 30 June – 4 July OS, were 4,930; more complete figures in *Oesterr. Erbfolge-krieg* ix. 940–1, make the total 5,824.

6. According to the *London Gazette Extraordinary* 2 July OS, the Allies took 5 standards and 7 colours; another list in the *London Gazette* No. 8656, 7–11 July OS, of the trophies actually brought to England includes 6 standards, 7 colours, and mentions another of each not yet brought in. Still further conflicting figures of standards and colours taken at the battle are collected in *Oesterr. Erbfolge-krieg* ix. 629 and n. 5.

7. These figures are confirmed in the *London Gazette Extraordinary* 2 July OS.

black list of killed and wounded that you know nothing of and may read in the *Gazette*. Poor Harry Campbell[8] I am sure you'll be sorry for from his character if you did not know him; we have had no account of his being killed but knowing his excessive forwardness in exposing himself and having not been able to hear a word of him since the action I am afraid we have too little room to doubt of it.

Adieu, my dear Horry, I am in the hurry of a thousand letters and other things.

Most affectionately yours,

H. C.

To CONWAY, ca Thursday 2 July 1747 OS

Missing; Conway's letter *post* 14 Aug. 1747 NS seems to be a reply to a letter from HW, although Conway says *post* 5 Oct. NS that he has had no letter since that of 8 June OS. It seems unlikely that HW failed to write to him after the battle of Laffeldt.

From CONWAY, Monday 14 August 1747 NS

Printed for the first time from the MS now WSL, formerly Rutnam.

Mastricht, Aug. 14, 1747.

My dear Horry,

YOU conclude by telling me if I have not more to do than you that I am the idlest of mortals and I begin by telling you that I not only have nothing to do but do nothing and that if you have no better occupation than I have you are not only the idlest but the most *ennuyé* of all people. I have been for some time at Aix[1] and when I was quite tired of sauntering there I returned here; I am now

---

8. Capt. Henry Campbell (d. 2 July 1747 NS), of the Coldstream Guards; aide-de-camp to Gen. Ligonier and brother of Lady Ailesbury (MONTAGU i. 50 and n. 7). See also Rex Whitworth, *Field Marshal Lord Ligonier*, Oxford, 1958, p. 160 and Hist. MSS Comm., *Frankland-Russell-Astley MSS*, 1900, pp. 371, 373.

1. 'By letters from the army, we are informed that Sir John Ligonier, though sent back to us, is not yet at liberty to serve, nor yet Colonel Conway; . . . the latter is at Aix-la-Chapelle' (Col. Russell to Mrs Russell, Flushing, 25 July 1747 OS, Hist. MSS Comm., *Frankland-Russell-Astley MSS*, 1900, p. 379).

ten times more tired of this and would give anything to go and saunter anywhere else in the world. My history is that I am still a prisoner,[2] and consequently might as well be anywhere as here but they keep me with hopes of being exchanged day after day and as I squint towards England my impatience to hear some decisive answer upon the subject keeps me here. What contributes to finish my ennui is that of late there is but one single thing talked of so that one would think it was treason to open one's lips to talk of anything else: that is the siege of Bergen op Zoom[3] about which I must own, however, I have some curiosity and could hear something of it every day with pleasure at least while they continue to defend it as well as by all accounts they have done hitherto, for by our last accounts the French who have opened the trenches there now near a month have not yet been able to carry any part of the covered way, are masters of no outwork nor have been able to hurt the defences of the place. I suppose you understand these terms but if you don't you may tell 'em to anybody *hardiment* and if they don't understand 'em neither it will please them just as well. They tell me such wonders there that I can scarce believe that the Dutch are both generous and brave, that they give wine and brandy-wine and even money to the soldiers who to show as great a miracle actually behave well, *tantum mortalia pectora,*[4] etc. I beg your pardon for talking to you so long upon this subject but in short as I told you one must talk of no other. The Duke had a ball last night but I won't break the law to give you this history of that, nor indeed have I anything that tempts me much to the infringement of it unless it be a crime to tell you that I am ever, dear Horry,

Sincerely and affectionately yours.

2. The cartel concerning the exchange of prisoners was signed at Liège 31 Aug. (see *post* 5 Oct. NS, n. 9); and the Duke of Cumberland wrote Chesterfield from Richelle 31 Aug. NS, 'The affair relating to the exchange of prisoners, I may say is in a manner finished, as the Paper, a copy of which I enclose, will be signed this night at Leige, the consequence of which is, that General Ligonier and all the other officers here or elsewhere upon their parole, will be declared free, and all our troops prisoners are upon their march hither, those of Graham's Regiment will I hope by this time be arrived in England' (D. of Cumberland to Chesterfield 31 Aug. 1747 NS, S.P. 87, Military Expeditions 23).

3. Which had been invested 12 July NS and held out until 16 Sept. NS (MANN iii. 434, n. 2). Full details of the siege are in *Oesterr. Erbfolge-krieg* ix. 635–703.

4. 'Quid non mortalia pectora cogis, / Auri sacra fames' (Virgil, *Æneid* iii. 56–7) ('To what dost thou not drive mortal hearts, O accursed greed for gold').

I was very sorry indeed for poor Bob:[5] though I have had no connection with him lately I don't know [how] to excuse nor indeed to account for his strange behaviour. I hope it is not true what I have heard that he makes it worse by abusing the Guards and telling a story of his leaving them because they behaved so ill! However, I assure [you], I feel for him if he feels for himself but I feel more for his friends.

From CONWAY, Thursday 5 October 1747 NS

Printed for the first time from the MS now WSL, formerly Rutnam. HW mentions this letter to Montagu 1 Oct. 1747 OS (MONTAGU i. 52), which helps establish the date.

Camp at Richelt,[1] Oct. 5.

Dear Horry,

IT'S such an age since I heard from you that it looks actually as if our correspondence was at an end. I looked at the date of your last, from your new tub, and find it as old as the eighth of June;[2] I have writ to you since, I assure you; perhaps you have not received my letter or letters, for I know you have a great deal of goodness for me and are not so idle a correspondent as myself; your solitude,

---

5. Hon. Robert Cholmondeley (1727–1804), HW's nephew, an officer in the 3d Regiment of Guards, had been broken for cowardice at Laffeldt and sent from the army (*Frankland MSS*, p. 372). He was back in London by 23 July OS (*Whitehall Evening Post* 21–23 July OS) and later entered the church. The incident was quite successfully suppressed at the time, although a paragraph in the *General Evening Post* 23–25 July OS, apparently alludes to it: 'A certain officer who was discharged for ill behaviour at the late battle, had like, in his return home, to meet accidentally with that fate, which he had not courage enough to face honourably in the field; the chaise in which he was posting away from danger having overturned and broke his arm.' Rumour elaborated what had happened and transferred the scene of misconduct to Fontenoy and Dettingen; Boswell mentions it in his *London Journal*, ed. F. A. Pottle, 1950, p. 92, and Joseph Jekyll gives a graphic account in a letter of 18 Jan. 1831 (*Correspondence of Mr Joseph Jekyll with his Sister-in-law, Lady Gertrude Sloane Stanley, 1818–1838*, ed. Bourke, 1894, pp. 265–6).

1. Richelle, on the Maas between Maestricht and Liège, the Duke of Cumberland's headquarters from about 21 Aug. NS to sometime between 25 and 28 Sept. NS when it was shifted to Argenteau (*Daily Adv.* 22 Aug. OS *sub* Maestricht 21 Aug. NS; *London Gazette* No. 8677, 19–22 Sept. OS, No. 8678, 22–6 Sept. OS).

2. Conway had probably received at least one letter from HW since then; see *ante* ca 2 July 1747 OS.

too, has prevented my hearing of you, as that you may by this time be got to Japan for aught I know to the contrary or be partaking the diversions of Agra with the Great Mogul; wherever you are I should have some satisfaction in knowing positively you are alive and well and beg if this finds you, you'll take the first opportunity of making me easy on that head; if after all this should only end, as I hope, in your attention to your new habitation, or that you are grown more idle or more studious than ordinary I shall think myself very well off; for as to mending the affair of our correspondence I am in hopes it's now too late, and shall flatter myself instead of it with a prospect of treating of that and many other important affairs with you face to face when I shall desire to have our treaty of correspondence settled upon a new foot against our next parting.

Our affairs politically speaking are grown much worse since the times of our correspondence, particularly by the villainous desertion of Bergen op Zoom[3] but with regard to ourselves much otherwise; the King of France is gone[4] and his army, too, from our neighbourhood,[5] and even that in the Low Countries[6] is doing nothing, so that we look daily for winter quarters, and regard the whole business of the campaign as absolutely finished; grim-visag'd war for the present at least smoothes its rugged front,[7] the fires lose their lustre and even the black periwigs of our generals their horror and everything looks as peaceable and as Londonish as possible. The Duke himself gives up his hopes of any more fighting and asked me t'other day if I did not long for the meeting of the Parliament; he jokes with me sometimes about a certain affair;[8] perhaps you'll do so too, for many of my friends do, but if I had a mind I could stop your mouth by telling you I grow very serious about it, and it's worth my while I

3. Which had been taken by storm 16 Sept. NS; it was generally assumed (apparently without foundation) that treachery had had a hand in its fall.

4. Louis XV left the army 23 Sept. NS and reached Paris on the 26th (*London Gazette* No. 8677, 19–22 Sept. OS *sub* Richel, 25 Sept. NS; *Mercure historique,* 1747, cxxiii. 453).

5. The French army on the Maas had begun to retire behind the Dyle 3 Oct. NS (*Oesterr. Erbfolge-krieg* ix. 711). Details of the withdrawal as they appeared to the Allied army are in the *London Gazette* No. 8678, 22–6 Sept. OS, *sub*

Liège 25, 28 Sept. NS and Argenteau 28 Sept. NS; No. 8679, 26–9 Sept. OS, *sub* Liège 2, 5 Oct. NS and Argenteau 2 Oct. NS.

6. The army under Lowendal that had taken Bergen-op-Zoom; it was now attacking Lillo, which surrendered 12 Oct. NS (*Daily Adv.* 13 Oct. OS *sub* Antwerp 16 Oct. NS).

7. 'Grim-visag'd war hath smooth'd his wrinkled front' (Shakespeare, *Richard III*, I. i. 9).

8. His marriage to Lady Ailesbury, which took place 19 Dec. 1747 OS.

am sure, for you're a formidable enemy on those occasions; indeed, Horry, I do, I grow wondrous serious; perhaps you'll be surprised, for you think me without resolution, but if another person can be as serious as myself we shall actually commit the most serious folly in the world. I could say a vast deal in my justification but what I say goes for nothing, so should be glad to hear what you think if you'll tell one so far gone your opinion impartially; for as I value your friendship I shall always be glad of your approbation in anything of consequence: about the great or little trifles of the world I'll differ and squabble with you as much as you please. Since I began this I have heard a very disagreeable piece of news relating to myself; but which I am in hopes will somehow or other be avoided; it is that the term for which we were set at liberty by the agreement[9] being expired on the 9th I think it is, or 11th of this month,[10] and the French prisoners in England not being sent back according to promise, they demand us again. Yesterday Sir J. Ligonier received a letter[11] to tell him that M. Saxe hoped he did not forget that on

9. The 'Échange Préliminaire des officiers, soldats . . . et autres troupes légères, faites prisonniers de guerre . . .' signed at Liège 31 Aug. 1747 NS required that Frenchmen who were prisoners of war, including those captured in the Mediterranean area, 'seront rendus et renvoyés en France dans l'espace de six semaines, à compter du jour de la signature du présent, sinon et à faute d'exécution de la part de sa Majesté Britannique dans l'expiration du dit délai. Nous Commissaires de sa Majesté Très Chrétienne, protestons sous les authorisations ci-dessous, que les officiers, de quelques grades qu'ils soient, des troupes de sa Majesté Britannique et à sa solde, remis en activité en vertu du présent, seront sommés de revenir en France . . . l'activité [du dit présent acte] ne devant avoir force et vertu qu'au moyen de l'exécution de la dite clause de six semaines de délai fixé, qui ne pourra . . . être réputée comminatoire' (copy enclosed in D. of Cumberland to Chesterfield 31 Aug. 1747 NS, S.P. 87, Military Expeditions 23). Chesterfield wrote the Duke of Cumberland 4 Sept. 1747 OS (ibid.), 'Captain de Cosne has the King's orders to proceed to France with all the rest of the French prisoners here, as soon as they can

be collected from the several places, where they now are, to that of their embarkation.'

10. The Duke of Cumberland wrote Marshal Saxe 3 Oct. 1747 NS: 'Sur ce que je me suis informé au Lieutenant Colonel Cokayne touchant la date du terme fixé, il m'a dit qu'au lieu du 9e ce n'était que le 11e d'Octobre que le temps expirait. J'avoue que cette extrême précision me parait pousser l'exactitude au delà de ce à quoi je me serais attendu. Car, je sais que les ordres ont été donnés, et que les vaisseaux sont rassemblés dans les divers ports d'Angleterre aussi bien que de l'Italie, pour le transport des prisonniers de guerre. . . . D'ailleurs le Commissaire Seigneur a lui-même assuré le Lieutenant Colonel Cokayne, que si un retardement de quelques jours survenait, occasioné par les vents ou par quelque autre cause de cette nature, on n'y ferait pas attention' (copy enclosed in D. of Cumberland to Chesterfield 5 Oct. 1747 NS, ibid.). Saxe answered 4 Oct. NS that he did not blame the Duke of Cumberland for the delay in returning the prisoners but that he had hoped 'que l'on apporterait plus de diligence à leur retour' (ibid.).

11. From the Marquis du Mesnil, Liège, 2 Oct. 1747: 'Monseigneur le Comte de

such a day the term expired, and we became prisoners again; in consequence of which he offers him very politely his house at Paris. I am still in hopes that they will let us go upon our parole as they did before; if not and the affair should not be settled you may judge how unhappy I shall be. The Duke is angry at the French for being so strict, but I think he has much more reason to be so with our people[12] for neglecting or wilfully breaking their promise,[13] which has brought us into this scrape. Adieu, dear Horry; let me hear from you and believe me

Affectionately yours,

H. C.

Col. Russell wrote 14 Oct. 1747 OS from Bois-le-duc, 'Barrington and I rode over to the headquarters at Ousterwick yesterday, and there met General Ligoniere, Conway and such a vast number of my acquaintances that I had no time to go to the Guards . . . (Hist. MSS Comm., *Frankland-Russell-Astley MSS*, 1900, p. 394). On 29 Oct. 1747 OS he wrote from Breda, 'The Duke came this morning to his quarters, about four miles away, and all the regiments will be in winter quarters tomorrow

Saxe m'avait chargé de vous faire mille compliments, et en même temps de vous faire souvenir que le terme de six semaines convenu dans l'Échange pour la Remise de nos Prisonniers faits en Écosse ou ailleurs, expire le 9ᵉ de ce mois, et que cependant l'on n'a eu encore aucun avis de leur départ d'Angleterre. Comme il est aussi spécifié, Monsieur, dans le dit traité, qu'en cas d'inexécution, votre échange cesse d'être en activité, et que vous vous constituerez prisonnier où il vous sera indiqué, Monseigneur le Comte de Saxe vous offre sa maison à Paris, où il tâchera de vous dédommager en tout ce qui dépendra de lui, de la privation de votre liberté' (copy enclosed in D. of Cumberland to Chesterfield 5 Oct. 1747 NS, ibid.).

12. HW wrote Montagu 1 Oct. 1747 OS, 'our great secretary has let the time slip for executing the cartel, and the French have reclaimed their prisoners' (MONTAGU i. 52).

13. The Duke of Cumberland on 5 Oct. NS thanked Chesterfield for 'your dis-

patch of the 18th past OS in which you acquaint me, there shall be no further delay in sending back the prisoners, especially as Marshal Saxe has begun, in a manner, already to summon Sir John Ligonier to return a prisoner the day the six weeks shall be out, if our prisoners do not arrive at Callais' (D. of Cumberland to Chesterfield 5 Oct. 1747 NS, loc. cit.). Chesterfield answered 2 Oct. OS that 'there has been no neglect at all in this business here, but that whatever delay has been, has been purely occasioned by the dilatoriness of the French Court in not sending hither in time the necessary remittances of money for their officers demanded long ago' (Chesterfield to D. of Cumberland 2 Oct. 1747 OS, in ibid.). On 16 Oct. NS the Duke of Cumberland wrote Newcastle, 'Nothing new has happened with relation to the prisoners . . . and I hope if Captain de Cosne is arrived at Calais that we shall hear no more of this disagreeable affair' (D. of Cumberland to Newcastle 16 Oct. 1747 NS, in ibid.).

except the Guards, who will wait until his Royal Highness removes from headquarters' (ibid. 397; see also Cumberland to Newcastle 8 Nov. OS, BM Add. MSS 32713, f. 337). Conway presumably returned to England in mid-November when the Duke of Cumberland, General Ligonier, and other officers arrived in London (*Daily Adv.* 14 Nov. 1747 OS; GM 1747, xvii. 541). Conway was married to Lady Ailesbury 19 Dec. 1747 OS (*ante* 24 Oct. 1746 OS, n. 1). They left London with other officers about 20 March OS, and went to Rotterdam where Conway had to leave Lady Ailesbury and Lady Ancram in order to join his regiment at Breda 7 April NS (see following letter and nn. 2–4).

From CONWAY, Monday 29 April 1748 NS

Printed for the first time from the MS now WSL, formerly Rutnam. Dated by the siege of Maestricht and the christening of the young Stadtholder.

Camp at Hellenraet,[1] Ap. 29.

Dear Horry,

I AM ashamed to think how long it is since I left England,[2] when I consider how little my friends there have heard of me from that time; however, I am not without excuse, and indeed have been from the time of my landing in more hurry than I can well express. I was but just arrived at Rotterdam where I was in hopes of being able to stay a little just to see Lady Ailesbury settled in some place better than an inn, when I was called away by a sudden alarm of the Duke's being actually in the town and in his way to Breda[3] (my garrison), where it was almost necessary I should be before him; accordingly, away I posted with the reluctance that you may imagine, leaving the two ladies[4] who were now under my convoy only (Ancram being gone to the Duke) at a villainous inn. I thought myself

1. Near Roermond, the D. of Cumberland's headquarters since about 11 April NS (*Daily Adv.* 11 April OS *sub* Hellenraet 11 April NS).

2. Conway and Lady Ailesbury left London with a large party of officers about 20 March OS (*Whitehall Evening Post* 15–17, 17–19 March OS; *Daily Adv.* 18, 22 March OS).

3. These events took place 7 April NS; the D. of Cumberland left The Hague on the morning of the 7th and arrived at Breda on the morning of the 8th (ibid. 2 April OS *sub* Hague 7 April NS, 4 April OS *sub* Breda 8 April NS).

4. Lady Ailesbury and Lady Ancram; for the latter see *ante* 31 Oct. 1741 OS, n. 11.

lucky, however, in succeeding in my journey to Breda where I was ready for the reception of the Duke, who I had reason to think would not have been so well-pleased if he had not found me there. He left us the next morning and in two days more my regiment had orders to march out of garrison and accordingly began its progress with 12 more battalions under Lord Albemarle[5] for this country,[6] where in about ten days[7] we joined the Duke and his army and on our arrival found the siege of Mastricht[8] begun which indeed we had very little hopes of preventing; by the reports they have here it makes rather a better defence than was expected, but yet can't be expected to hold much longer. By our last accounts yesterday[9] the French were not yet masters of the covered way but not far from it, so that I fancy either yesterday or today in all probability it was attacked.[10] When this affair is over the French have two principal views;[11] one is marching towards Holland, for Breda, Bois-le-duc etc. and the other the siege of Luxemburgh; which is what many, I find, look upon as the most probable, as it has been always a favourite point with 'em and as they can meet with no interruption in it and how far this may weigh with Marshal Saxe's prudence I can't tell but am apt myself to think they will choose the former, as their army is now vastly superior, I doubt indeed not less than double to ours, and ours being now divided,[12] if they can find means to keep them so, and cut off any part from the rest or find an opportunity of attack-

5. William Anne van Keppel (1702–54), 2d E. of Albemarle.

6. 'It is expected that Lord Albemarle will arrive on the 18th with nine British and four Imperial battalions which marched out of Breda yesterday' (*Daily Adv.* 11 April OS *sub* Hellenraet 11 April NS).

7. That is, about 20 April NS.

8. Which had been fully invested about 12 April NS; the trenches were opened 19 April NS. For details of the siege, see *Oesterr. Erbfolge-krieg* ix. 808–21.

9. 'Ruremonde, April 28 [NS]. . . . The advices we have received here concerning the siege of Mastricht are that the French had not yet attacked the covert way; that they continued to suffer much by the bad weather; that the attack upon Wyk had been suspended by reason of the rise of the waters, which had drowned a great part of the trenches; but that they

continued that on the left of the Maese with great vigour, notwithstanding the great fire which was made from the Fort of St Pierre' (*Daily Adv.* 26 April OS).

10. It was, on the night of the 28th, but retaken by the defenders (ibid. 27 April OS *sub* Liège 30 April and Hellenraet 2 May NS). The siege came to an end 4 May NS with a temporary cease-fire, and Maestricht surrendered 7 May NS with full honours as part of the general armistice accompanying the signing of the preliminaries of the Peace of Aix-la-Chapelle 30 April NS (MANN iii. 480–1 and nn. 11 and 12).

11. All the speculations that follow came to nought because of the armistice signed the following day.

12. A secondary army of 40,000 men under the Stadtholder had been assembled at Breda (*Daily Adv.* 27 April OS *sub* Hague 3 May NS).

ing the whole or any part they may disable us utterly from showing our faces in the field the rest of the campaign, even when our succours[13] are arrived. Besides that, by acting on that side the world though nothing of this kind should be in their power, they will strike a greater terror; and I should fancy do their business better, by making the fears of some parts of our Alliance operate against the obstinacy of others. We shall grow wise at last, but God knows how dear our experience may cost us! I am afraid this year with all its frail[14] promises and its real expenses will be the most deceitful of any we have begun, with our usual pomp of hopes in the spring and I wish may not end with our usual autumnal despair, the anniversary distemper of true Englishmen. I wish I may guess wrong, for if they go to Luxemburgh 'tis the *ne plus ultra* of the campaign, as they'll leave us time to muster all our force quietly and in all probability make up such an army as may stop their farther progress, so late in the year as they must return if Luxemburgh makes any sort of defence proportionable to its strength. In short, heaven preserve us, I think we are in a woeful scrape and shall be much obliged to those, be they militant or civil, [who][15] get us out of it. This is dull stuff, my dear Horry, but you must take us as we are; we are very poor at invention, *nous autres militaires,* and the camp is the worst soil in the world either for that or the produce of anything amusing. Our lives are as uniform as our clothes and of the dullest sort of uniformity; all this you know and it's so hard for me to tell you anything you don't! Lady Ailesbury stays at Rotterdam, I mean hitherto; but Lady Ancram is gayer and has been pretty much at The Hague where all the world has been to christen the young Stadtholder.[16] The Marshal Bathiani has got the gout and the Duke is really by no means well.[17] Adieu, dear Horry, do return good for evil. I know you

13. Conway is probably referring to the 30,000 Russian troops engaged by England and Holland at the end of January 1748; they had begun to march west immediately and were at this time somewhere in western Poland or Upper Silesia; their advance was finally stopped in the Upper Palatinate in July (MANN. iii. 466, n. 1; GM 1748, xviii. 94, 141, 189, 286, 334).

14. 'Frail' written over 'mighty,' which has been crossed out.

15. MS reads 'or.'

16. Willem (8 March 1748–1806), Stadt-holder as Willem V, 1751, was christened 11 April NS (*Daily Adv.* 6 April OS).

17. For his health earlier in the month see MANN iii. 483 and n. 28. Col. Joseph Yorke wrote Hardwicke 11 April NS, 'H.R.H. is greatly to be pitied, who has the misfortune to head so unconnected an alliance. . . . Great is the load he has to bear, and stout as he is, it has greatly depressed him; for I attribute that terrible illness, which had like to have deprived us of his inestimable life, in a

are always disposed to it, and tell me a little of the agreeable things that your world affords. I am ever

With great sincerity, affectionately yours,

H. C.

My compliments to Mrs Leneve.

To CONWAY, May 1748

Missing; answered *post* 24 June 1748 NS.

From CONWAY, Monday 24 June 1748 NS

Printed for the first time from the MS now WSL, formerly Rutnam.

Camp at Nestleroi,[1] June 24.

Dear Horry,

I FIND in your last you prophesied we were coming home, yet I doubt I am farther from it now than you thought me then, and I am ashamed to think how long that is ago. If people are as impatient for the peace as you say they are and as I really believe them, too, they may yet think it long before it's concluded, for though all parties languish for it they come into it with as much seeming reluctance and as many ceremonies and delays as any modest woman consents to her own pleasure, and more too perhaps you'll think; the poor Genoese indeed, I believe, are fairly ravished and therefore the work's over the sooner with 'em,[1a] but what d'ye think of the Spaniards who are the greatest losers by the war while it lasts, the only gainers

great degree to the ruinous situation that he found affairs in, without any human probability of their being likely to mend. Thank God, he is much better, and notwithstanding the fatigue he has undergone before he was perfectly recovered, I think he gets strength daily' (*Hardwicke Corr.* i. 654).

———

1. Nistelrode, 12 miles east of Bois-le-Duc.

1a. However, by Article 6 of the pre-

by the peace and the last to come into it.[2] The Queen of Hungary like most of her sex was more proud than virtuous and thought it for her dignity to make difficulties that [s]he intended to give up knowing the dire necessity that compelled her to it,[3] and well considering what it was to continue the war without English subsidies. Sardinia[4] I don't mention as not looking upon him as a principal; the conduct of France seems to most people surprising because it appears moderate. I don't think them likely to make a foolish bargain and therefore fancy they have good reasons, indeed for them and us I think much [could] be said on both sides and have a notion we have made a pretty fair agreement; but all considered, I must believe favourable to us when we think of the immediate danger of Holland; not from the operations of the French arms only but [from] their own internal weakness, dissensions and instability.[5] I don't know indeed whether the people will be content long. As you say, I do believe they will not, because they can't be long content with anything; yet I do think for the present at least they might be satisfied. We have had a very bad war by land, I can't think made up for by our successes at sea, and therefore I should think it senseless to expect what is abstractedly called a good peace, and mad to venture at engaging farther for it when every day might make our terms worse.

I don't know what has made me so vastly political; I really believe it is because I have nothing else to say. We do nothing now but handle our firelocks, which does not make a figure in relation; the day before yesterday (the Accession) we had a general review which they say was very fine;[6] for me I saw nothing but my own regiment, which

liminary treaty of Aix-la-Chapelle, Genoa had restored to her all the territories she possessed before the war (MANN iii. 481, n. 15).

2. Spain, which gained the Duchies of Parma and Placentia for Don Philip, did not sign the preliminaries until 28 June NS (ibid. iii. 479, nn. 4–5, 485, n. 7).

3. For the Imperial protestations against the preliminaries see ibid. iii. 480, n. 6. Kaunitz, however, signed them late in May (Sir Richard Lodge, *Studies in Eighteenth-Century Diplomacy 1740–1748*, 1930, pp. 357–8).

4. Which signed 30 May NS (ibid. 359).

5. Holland had recently been swept by riots; see below, n. 9.

6. 'St Oldenroy, June 23 [NS]. Yesterday being the anniversary of his Britannic Majesty's accession to the Throne, his Royal Highness the Duke of Cumberland caused all the army to be arranged in order of battle, in two lines, near Nestelroy. After dinner the Duke, accompanied by M. de Haaren, Deputy of the States General, went to review the army, and passed before the front of each line from one end to the other; after which his Royal Highness being posted on an eminence between the two lines, the artillery fired fifty cannon; the last of which was followed by a running fire from the army, which began at the right wing of the first line, and after having run entirely through it, was continued by the second line, returning from the left to right. The same

as you may imagine I thought charming, but the Duke was in rap-
tures. I have just been in Holland for a fortnight with Lady Ailesbury, where I saw some fine Dutch paintings, a great deal of fine
china and the Stadt House[7] at Amsterdam which besides the queer-
ness of the country and the absurdity of the people is, I think, all
there is worthy of remark. I have a little sort of a bit of news which
I kept for last which is that our army is going to separate immediately
and lie in cantonments,[8] I fancy, quietly till the time is ripe for our
leaving this filthy land of frogs. I forgot to tell you that in our
journey we had like to have seen a Dutch insurrection at Harlem,[9]
where they were very busy a-pulling down excisemen's houses and
throwing their money into the canals (for it's the etiquette of a
Dutch mob never to steal anything) but they were so rude as to
have shut up their gates that they might be private and would not
let us in. Monsieur Grovestein[10] went in from the Prince of Orange[11]
to pacify 'em; they received his ambassador very civilly but said they
must do the business they were about and not have any more im-
posts; I think they only murdered three or four people and threw
a few more into the canals. I won't say a word of all this in a political light having been so tiresome at first; this mobbishness has been
epidemical and run like the disease amongst horned cattle[12] almost
all round the country; the Prince of Orange has been very ill[13]

was repeated three times, and afterwards
was followed by three loud huzzas from all
the army, exactly in the same order. Everyone who saw the army owned, that nothing was ever more perfect, as well in respect to men and horses, as to clothing,
arms, and discipline' (*Daily Adv.* 20 June
OS).

7. Now the Royal Palace.

8. 'Headquarters at Nistleroy, July 9
[NS]. We have begun this week to enter
into cantonment and, it is said, that by
the middle of the next all his Majesty's
British and Electoral troops will be under
cover' (ibid. 4 July OS).

9. Accounts of this affair, which began
about 12 June NS, and which confirm
most of Conway's details, are in *Daily
Adv.* 16 June OS *sub* Amsterdam 15 June
NS, 18 June OS *sub* Amsterdam 18 June
NS, and 24 June OS *sub* Rotterdam 28
June NS; some of these are reprinted GM
1748, xviii. 272. A more complete account

is in *Nederlandsche Jaerboeken*, 1748, ii
pt i. 433–47. The popular revolts against
the tax farmers had begun in Groningen
and Friesland in May; Haarlem had been
the first city in Holland to rise, but was
rapidly followed by most of the others.

10. Anton Sirtema, Baron van Grov-
estins, grand écuyer to the Stadtholder.

11. Willem IV (1711–51) was installed as
Stadtholder of all the provinces of Holland
11 May 1747 NS (MANN iii. 394 and n. 1).

12. Which had ravaged England from
1745, having come there from Holland
(ibid. iii. 174 and nn. 16–18).

13. 'His Highness has been of late a
good deal out of order with a violent fit
of the colic, attended with a fever for
which he has been blooded and blistered,
and is still confined to his apartment'
(*Daily Adv.* 8 June OS, *sub* Hague 14
June NS). Further details of his illness
are ibid. 22 June OS *sub* Hague 21 June
NS. He was virtually recovered by the

but is better again. I must tell you how they lie and then I'll have
done actually.—The Prince and Princess[14] in a great bed of state,
the room well lighted up, curtains all open, and nothing but a single
sheet of fine Holland over their persons, and with this all the nurses
and children,[15] four or five of them at least, in the room. This is
really propagating in state and I suppose the Stadtholder's children
must be got as well [as] born in public. Adieu, dear Horry, I've quite
wearied you.

Yours most sincerely,

H. C.

To Conway, Monday 27 June 1748 OS

Printed from the MS now WSL; first printed Wright ii. 223–5. For the history
of the MS see *ante* 29 June 1744 OS; it was marked by HW for inclusion in
Works, but was not included.

Strawberry Hill,[1] June 27, 1748.

Dear Harry,

I HAVE full as little matter for writing as you can find in a camp.
I don't call myself farmer or country gentleman, for though I
have all the ingredients to compose those characters, yet like the ten
pieces of card in the trick you found out, I don't know how to put
them together. But in short, planting and fowls and cows and sheep[2]
are my whole business, and as little amusing to relate to anybody
else as the events of a still-born campaign. If I write to anybody, I am
forced to live upon what news I hoarded before I came out of town,
and the first article of that, as I believe it is in everybody's gazette,

25th (ibid. 20 June OS *sub* Hague 25
June NS).

14. Anne (1709–59), of England, m.
(1734) Willem IV of Orange.

15. Besides the new-born son (*ante* 29
April 1748 NS, n. 16), they had one surviving daughter, Karoline (1743–87), m.
(1760) Karl, Fürst von Nassau-Weilburg.

1. This and a letter to Sir Charles Hanbury Williams written the same day (Selwyn 113) are the earliest we have to be
dated from 'Strawberry Hill,' although

HW had referred to the place by that
name in letters to Montagu 18 May 1748
(Montagu i. 56) and to Mann 7 June
(Mann iii. 486), and Gray had called it
by that name in a letter to HW written
in Aug. 1747 (Gray ii. 30). See also 'Short
Notes,' ibid. i. 17 and n. 115.

2. HW's sheep were Turkish with four
horns (Selwyn 116). For his fowls, see
Montagu i. 51. The various references to
his planting are collected in *Strawberry
Hill Accounts,* ed. Toynbee, Oxford, 1927,
pp. 36–9; see also *post* 29 Aug. 1748 OS.

must be about my Lord Coke.[3] They say, that since he has been at
Sunning Hill with Lady Mary, she has made him a declaration in
form that she hates him, that she always did and that she always
will.[4] This seems to have been a very unnecessary notification; however as you know his part is to be extremely in love, he is very
miserable upon it, and relating his woes at White's, probably at
seven in the morning, he was advised to put an end to all this history
and shoot himself—an advice they would not have given him, if he
were not insolvent: he has promised to consider of it.

The night before I left London,[5] I called at the Duchess of Richmond's who has stayed at home with the apprehension of a miscarriage:[6] the porter told me there was no Drawing Room till Thursday
—in short, he did tell me what amounted to as much, that her Grace
did not see company till Thursday, and then she should see everybody: no excuse, that she was gone out or not well. I did not stay
till Thursday to kiss hands, but went away to Vauxhall; as I was coming out, I was overtaken by a great light and retired under the trees
of Marble Hall[7] to see what it should be. There came a long procession of Prince Lobkowitz's[8] footmen in very rich new liveries, the
two last bearing torches, and after them the Prince himself in a new

3. Edward Coke, styled Vct Coke (*ante*
25 Sept. 1740 NS, n. 7), had m. (1747) Lady
Mary Campbell (1727–1811), later HW's
friend and correspondent. Lady Louisa
Stuart's narrative of this marriage is in
Coke, *Journals*, i. pp. lix–lxxii, and additional letters about it, pp. cxxiii–cxxviii.

4. Lady Mary's version of what took
place at Sunning Hill, where they had
gone 30 May 1748 OS, is in a declaration
by her and a letter of her sister's, ibid.
i. pp. cxxv–cxxviii. It does not mention
Lady Mary's position as given here, but
stresses Lord Coke's assertion 'that he
would make me as unhappy as it was
in his power.' The immediate result of
these quarrels was a duel between Coke
and the Hon. Henry Bellenden on 28 June
OS, described by HW, at this time a supporter of Coke, in a letter to Montagu 14
July OS (MONTAGU i. 59–61 and notes).

5. On or about Tuesday 7 June OS;
HW had told Montagu 26 May OS that
he was going to SH 'to settle' the following day, but he either postponed the trip

or returned to London for a few days,
since he was at Arlington Street on 7
June OS (MANN iii. 484; MONTAGU i. 57).

6. Her fears were apparently justified,
since no child of hers is recorded by
Collins at this time; HW mentions this
as her 'twenty-fifth pregnancy' (MONTAGU
i. 57), which he apparently means literally, since in discussing her last pregnancy in 1750 he says she has 'been with
child seven and twenty times' (MANN iv.
125).

7. It is shown in John Roque, *Plan of
the Cities of London and Westminster
and Borough of Southwark*, 1745, 3 C 4,
on the riverside of Vauxhall.

8. Presumably Joseph Maria Karl (1725–
1802), Fürst von Lobkowitz, field marshal,
1785, who had apparently been in England
since Jan. 1745 (MANN ii. 487, n. 6, iii. 13).
For some details of his relations with the
Venetian ambassadress and Lady Emily
Lennox in Oct. 1745, see a letter from the
latter in Brian Fitzgerald, *Emily, Duchess
of Leinster*, 1949, pp. 14–15.

sky blue watered tabbycoat with gold buttonholes, and a magnificent gold waistcoat fringed, leading Madame l'Ambassadrice de Venise[9] in a green sack with a straw hat, attended by my Lady Tyrawley,[10] Wall,[11] the private Spanish agent, the two Miss Molyneux's[12] and some other men. They went into one of the Prince of Wales's barges, had another barge filled with violins and hautboys, and an open boat with drums and trumpets. This was one of the *fêtes des adieux:* the nymph weeps all the morning and says she is sure she shall be poisoned by her husband's relations when she returns, for her behaviour with this Prince.

I know no other news, but that Mr Fitzpatrick[13] has married his Sukey Young,[14] and is very impatient to have the Duchess of Bedford come to town to visit her new relation.[15]

Is not my Lady Ailesbury weary of her travels? Pray make her my compliments, unless she has made you any such declaration as Lady Mary Coke's. I am delighted with your description of the Bedchamber of the House of Orange, as I did not see it, but the sight itself must have been very odious, as the hero and heroine are so extremely ugly. I shall give it my Lady Townshend as a new topic of matrimonial satire.

Mr Churchill and Lady Mary have been with me two or three days, and are now gone to Sunning. I only tell you this, to hint that my house will hold a married pair: indeed it is not quite large enough for people who lie like the Patriarchs with their whole genealogy,

9. Eleonora (fl. 1742–58), Contessa di Colalto, m. (1742) Cavaliere Pietro Andrea Capello (ca 1702–63), Venetian ambassador to England 1744–8 (MANN ii. 431, n. 9, v. 219). HW told Mann two years later 'I never liked anything of her, but her prettiness, for she is an idiot' (ibid. iv. 169). For her behaviour in Florence, see also ibid. iv. 174–5, and at Rome, *post* 23 Jan. 1752 NS.

10. Hon. Mary Stewart (d. 1769), m. (1724) James O'Hara, 2d Bn Tyrawley.

11. Richard Wall (1694–1778), Maj.-Gen., Spanish minister plenipotentiary to England 1747–51; ambassador 1751–4; Spanish secretary of state 1754–64 (MANN iii. 504, n. 10). Since England and Spain were still at war, he was not yet formally accredited.

12. Not identified.

13. Hon. Richard Fitzpatrick (b. ca 1719–27, d. 1796), 2d son of the 1st Bn Gowran (BERRY ii. 57, n. 26; OSSORY i. 51).

14. This lady, who died in 1759, is variously described in the peerages as 'Anne, daughter of Mr Young' (*Debrett's Peerage*, 1803, ii. 496, and 1806, ii. 680), and as 'Anne, daughter of Mr Usher of London' (John Lodge and Mervyn Archdall, *Peerage of Ireland*, 1789, ii. 347; Collins, *Peerage*, 1812, viii. 308; Kearsley's *Peerage*, 1802, ii. 398); she is called 'Susanna' in Daniel Lysons, *Environs of London*, 1792–6, iii. 252.

15. Fitzpatrick's older brother John, 1st E. of Upper Ossory, had married the Ds of Bedford's sister.

and menservants and maidservants and oxes and asses in the same chamber with them.

Adieu! do let this be the last letter and come home.

Yours ever,

H. W.

From CONWAY, Sunday 1 September 1748 NS

Printed for the first time from the MS now WSL, formerly Rutnam.

Eersel,[1] Sept. 1.

Dear Horry,

YOURS from Strawberry Hill I received; if it were not for your request in the end of it I should be ashamed to say how long ago; however, I have given you fair time, you see, and if the negotiators at Aix[2] had not been asleep it might well have been the last that passed betwixt us; besides though you seem inclined to write no more, you have not prohibited my part of the commerce, and as long as you allow the importation of my letters you must expect to be troubled with them; though God knows they're a most vile commodity, and I dare say not worth the duty you pay for them. To get out of this fine allegory, I find myself as ignorant of anything worth sending you as possible, and there is a sameness and a dullness in the sphere of our little correspondence here that passes all comprehension; and a darkness over our future prospect that is the most tiresome thing in the world; I have no comfort but in thinking the season is so far advanced that some change must soon be made and from our situation it really can't be for the worse. You'll wonder perhaps a little to hear me talk in this style and imagine having Lady Ailesbury with me I might be better content; and so I really should if I could think of keeping her here, or be perfectly easy with her situation; but in the condition she's in,[3] you may guess what that is, and at this distance from home, I really can't be a moment satisfied; especially

1. About 9 miles southwest of Eindhoven.

2. The reasons for the delay in converting the preliminaries of Aix-la-Chapelle into a definitive treaty are discussed in Sir Richard Lodge, *Studies in the History of Eighteenth-Century Diplomacy 1740–1748*, 1930, pp. 362–3. The treaty was finally concluded 18 Oct. NS.

3. Conway and Lady Ailesbury's only

as there is and has been lately a good deal of sickness in the army. I
have asked the Duke's leave for us both to go through Flanders, so
that I think to see her safe landed at Dover and then return;[4] she does
not care to go till the last moment that is proper; but for me I own
I long to have her gone and shall endeavour to hasten our passports
and move as soon as possible, though she has not yet made me Lady
Mary's agreeable declaration. I wish I could make the whole journey
with her, and should be particularly happy in the thoughts of making Strawberry Hill a visit, whatever disadvantage it or its master
might appear to after leaving this amiable country, which how I
shall bear when she's gone I have no conception, and yet feel destined
to pass a dreary month or two here. I find out that I have writ away
a long letter about myself, a tiresome subject and yet I don't know
where to find a better, being at a loss for any that can give you the
least entertainment; the generals wear their black wigs just as usual.
I vow I could not swear to you that a hair in any of them is dis-
placed. People come about in gloves and boots and gape and bow at
the Duke's levee exactly as I have known them these six years, and in
these dead times no one man distinguishes himself from another, to
give one an opportunity of saying anything of him; it's really vexa-
tious to live with such people that seem to do neither harm nor
good in their generation. It's terrible for me that am a quiet, dull
animal and regular; it would be death to you that are a lover of ex-
tremes: and I am afraid even the relation may be too much for you.
You talk of having nothing to say! Had I your Prince Lobkowitzes,
your Duchess of Richmonds, your Lord and Lady Cooks and your
Fitzpatricks to talk of I should have writ you another sort of letter.
Adieu, dear Horry, do write to me again in pity for I shall be miserably dull soon, and but a line will be a charity to me though you only
tell me the intrigues of your poultry, or describe the warfare of your
dunghill cocks. I am with the truest regard, dear Horry,

Most sincerely yours,

H. C.

Lady A. desires her compliments.

child was Anne Seymour Conway (8 Nov.
1748–1828), born at Combe Bank, Sundridge, Kent, m. (1767) Hon. John Damer

(*Scots Peerage* i. 386; Percy Noble, *Anne
Seymour Damer*, 1908, p. 1).

4. This plan was carried out; see *post*
9 Oct. 1748 NS.

To Conway, Monday 29 August 1748 OS

Printed from *Works* v. 29–31.

Strawberry Hill, August 29, 1748.

Dear Harry,

WHATEVER you may think, a campaign at Twickenham furnishes as little matter for a letter as an abortive one in Flanders. I can't say indeed that my generals wear black wigs, but they have long full-bottomed hoods which cover as little entertainment to the full.

There's General my Lady Castlecomer,[1] and General my Lady Dowager Ferrers![2] Why do you think I can extract more out of them than you can out of Hawley[3] or Honeywood?[4] Your old women dress, go to the Duke's levee, see that the soldiers cock their hats right, sleep after dinner, and soak with their led-captains till bedtime, and tell a thousand lies of what they never did in their youth. Change hats for head-clothes, the rounds for visits, and led-captains for toad-eaters, and the life is the very same. In short, these are the people I live in the midst of, though not with; and it is for want of more important histories that I have wrote to you so seldom; not, I give you my word, from the least negligence. My present and sole occupation is planting, in which I have made great progress, and talk very learnedly with the nurserymen, except that now and then a lettuce run to seed overturns all my botany, as I have more than once taken it for a curious West Indian flowering shrub. Then the deliberation with which trees grow, is extremely inconvenient to my natural impatience. I lament living in so barbarous an age, when we are come to so little perfection in gardening. I am persuaded that a hundred and fifty years hence it will be as common to remove oaks a hundred and fifty years old, as it is now to transplant tulip roots. I have even begun a treatise or panegyric on the great discoveries made by pos-

1. Hon. Frances Pelham (d. 1756), sister of the D. of Newcastle, m. (1715 *or* 1717) Christopher Wandesford, 2d Vct Castlecomer; she coined one of HW's favourite 'Strawberry proverbs' (see BERRY i. 55–6, MONTAGU ii. 311, and *post* 27 Nov. 1774). After her death HW bought some of her furniture for SH (*Strawberry Hill Accounts*, ed. Toynbee, Oxford, 1927, pp. 7, 89–90).

2. Selina Finch (1681–1762), m. (1699) Robert Shirley, cr. (1711) E. Ferrers.

3. Henry Hawley (?1679–1759), Lt-Gen., 1744.

4. Gen. Sir Philip Honywood (*ante* 21 Aug. 1743 NS, n. 7).

terity in all arts and sciences; wherein I shall particularly descant on the great and cheap convenience of making trout rivers—one of the improvements which Mrs Kerwood[5] wondered Mr Hedges[6] would not make at his country house, but which was not then quite so common as it will be. I shall talk of a secret for roasting a wild boar and a whole pack of hounds alive, without hurting them, so that the whole chase may be brought up to table; and for this secret, the Duke of Newcastle's grandson, if he can ever get a son, is to give a hundred thousand pounds. Then the delightfulness of having whole groves of hummingbirds, tame tigers taught to fetch and carry, pocket spying-glasses to see all that is doing in China, with a thousand other toys, which we now look upon as impracticable, and which pert posterity would laugh in one's face for staring at, while they are offering rewards for perfecting discoveries, of the principles of which we have not the least conception! If ever this book should come forth, I must expect to have all the learned in arms against me, who measure all knowledge backward: some of them have discovered symptoms of all arts in Homer; and Pineda[7] had so much faith in the accomplishments of his ancestors, that he believed Adam understood all sciences but politics. But as these great champions for our forefathers are dead, and Boileau[8] not alive to hitch me into a verse with Perrault,[9] I am determined to admire the learning of posterity, especially being convinced that half our present knowledge sprung from discovering the errors of what had formerly been called so. I don't think I shall

5. Cornelia Hayes, m. (1) Galfridus Walpole, HW's uncle; m. 2 (1735) John Kyrwood, of Letton, Herefordshire (*ante* 1 Feb. 1737 OS, n. 2; MONTAGU i. 15, n. 6). She seems to have been given to absurd remarks (ibid. i. 15, 74; *post* 7 Jan. 1772).

6. Perhaps John Hedges (ca 1689–1737), for whom see MONTAGU i. 66, n. 28.

7. Pineda was a Spanish Jesuit, and a professor of theology. He died 1637, after writing voluminous commentaries upon several books of the Holy Scriptures, besides an universal history of the church (HW). HW confuses two contemporaries of the same name: Juan de Pineda (1557 or 1558–1637), S.J., who wrote biblical commentaries, and Juan de Pineda (d. ca 1593), of Medina del Campo, a monk, who wrote *La Monarquía eclesiástica, ó Historia universal del mundo*, Salamanca, 1588 (*Enciclopedia universal ilustrada*,

Barcelona, [?1907–30], xliv. 1006–8; NBG). HW is quoting Pierre Bayle, *A General Dictionary Historical and Critical*, tr. J. P. Bernard, Thomas Birch, et al., 1734–41, i. 223n; he later copied the passage into his commonplace book (now WSL) of extracts from Bayle, dated 1750, f. 3. For further evidence that HW was reading Bayle at this time, see MONTAGU i. 77–9.

8. Nicolas Boileau Despréaux (1636–1711), poet and champion of the ancients in the 17th century 'quarrel of the ancients and moderns.'

9. Charles Perrault (1628–1703), writer and principal advocate for the moderns in the 'quarrel of the ancients and moderns,' during which he exchanged polemics with Boileau. For a typical epigram against Perrault see Boileau's *Odes*, ed. Boudhors, 1941, p. 48.

ever make any great discoveries myself, and therefore shall be content to propose them to my descendants, like my Lord Bacon, who, as Doctor Shaw[10] says very prettily in his preface to Boyle, *had the art of inventing arts:*[11] or rather like a Marquis of Worcester,[12] of whom I have seen a little book which he calls *A Century of Inventions,*[13] where he has set down a hundred machines to do impossibilities with, and not a single direction how to make the machines themselves.

If I happen to be less punctual in my correspondence than I intend to be, you must conclude I am writing my book,[14] which being designed for a panegyric will cost me a great deal of trouble. The dedication, with your leave, shall be addressed to your son that is coming, or, with my Lady A.'s leave, to your ninth son, who will be unborn nearer to the time I am writing of; always provided that she does not bring three at once, like my Lady Berkeley.[15]

Well! I have here set you the example of writing nonsense when one has nothing to say, and shall take it ill if you don't keep up the correspondence on the same foot. Adieu!

Yours ever,

HOR. WALPOLE

10. Peter Shaw (1694–1763), M.D.; editor of Bacon and Boyle.

11. This passage occurs in Shaw's 'General Preface' to his edition of *The Philosophical Works of Francis Bacon,* 1733, i. p. ix, not in the 'General Preface' to his edition of *The Philosophical Works of the Honourable Robert Boyle,* 1725. HW's copy of the 1738 edition of the latter is Hazen, *Cat. of HW's Lib.,* No. 1311; he does not seem to have owned a copy of the former, which was dedicated to his uncle Horace.

12. Edward Somerset (ca 1603–67), 2d M. of Worcester.

13. *A Century of the Names and Scantlings of such Inventions as at Present I can call to Mind to have Tried and Perfected,* first printed, 1663; reprinted 1746, 1748, and frequently thereafter. HW describes this 'amazing piece of folly' in *Royal and Noble Authors, Works* i. 375. His copy of the 1746 edition, with marginal markings and two notes, which he used in *Royal and Noble Authors,* is now WSL (Hazen, op. cit. No. 1608:4:3).

14. That is, his treatise 'on the great discoveries made by posterity.'

15. Elizabeth Drax (ca 1720–92), m. 1 (1744) Augustus Berkeley, 4th E. of Berkeley; m. 2 (1757) Robert Nugent, cr. (1767) Vct Clare and (1776) E. Nugent. She had given birth to triplet daughters, who did not live, 22 July OS (GM 1748, xviii. 332; *Daily Adv.* 28 July 1748 OS; the date in Collins, *Peerage,* 1812, iii. 625 is wrong).

From CONWAY, Wednesday 9 October 1748 NS

Printed for the first time from the MS now WSL, formerly Rutnam.

Eersel, October 9, 1748.

Dear Horry,

MY journey to Calais from which I am just returned has prevented my writing to you sooner in answer to your last, which I received the day, I think, before I set out. I can't see why I should call it a journey to Calais; I really went to Dover as I believe I told you I intended, though it was not actually mentioned in my furlough so that I exceeded a little as you see but it was really necessary on her account she having no creature with her [but] an awkward soldier's wife so that I have not much upon my conscience for that transgression. I am sorry our journey furnished me with nothing worth observation and that might help the terrible dullness of this place and my own a little, but it really was too good a journey to write about, being quite quiet and uniform and attended with no one accident to give life to a description. I find the French are in as great a hurry to leave Flanders as we are to get there, I mean the particulars;[1] for their Court seems to be slow enough about it so that we live still in the same doubt when any evacuations will take place. I found the Duke here upon my return which I own I neither desired nor expected,[2] with all my regard for his Royal Highness, being in great hopes things were too far settled to make his presence necessary. There is a sort of report that things are regulated for our taking possession of Antwerp and some more of the Flemish garrisons about the 15th or 20 of this month[3] and from England I am told that the peace is in all probability signed by this time;[4] but whether in one or t'other there is any truth or not we are such mysterious politicians here that I can hardly guess. The Austrian army marched away

1. Accounts of the preparations of various French generals and individuals to leave Flanders are in the *Daily Adv.* 28 Sept. OS *sub* Brussels 29 Sept. NS.

2. The D. of Cumberland had returned to London 29 Aug. OS, but left it again 10 Sept. OS for his headquarters at Eindhoven where he arrived on the 24th NS (ibid. 30 Aug., 12, 19 Sept. OS).

3. There does not seem to have been any such agreement; the French did not begin to evacuate Antwerp until 11 Dec. NS (*Oesterr. Erbfolge-krieg* ix. 838).

4. It was not signed until 18 Oct. NS (*ante* 1 Sept. NS, n. 2), although a report that it was already signed had appeared in the *Daily Adv.* 22 Sept. OS.

t'other day[5] so suddenly and so slyly that nobody knew how to account for it, the Duke nor nobody in our army having the least idea of it but the day before, and they are actually upon the march for the other end of the world—Hungary, Transylvania and God knows where. The Dutch as I understand have played as pretty near the same trick and are marched off for their respective garrisons[6] without so much as acquainting the Duke who properly commands 'em with their intentions. I neither know nor care twopence what all these things mean provided the farce would but end and one might go home in peace having made our harvest-home of laurels to plant cabbages or what else we please, for I assure you you'll see me a planter soon as well as yourself; we are all upon a country house, somewhat of which you may perhaps have heard from Churchill but if it is not that it will be another.[7] Pray, my dear Horry, tell me when the Parliament is like to meet[8] for I long to hear of it having but little dependence upon anything else for my return and I doubt it will be an age. My service to your dowagers.

Yours ever and most affectionately,

H. C.

To CONWAY, Thursday 6 October 1748 OS

Printed from *Works* v. 31–3.

Strawberry Hill, Oct. 6, 1748.

Dear Harry,

I AM sorry our wishes clash so much. Besides that I have no natural inclination for the Parliament, it will particularly disturb me now in the middle of all my planting; for which reason I have never inquired when it will meet, and cannot help you to guess—but I should think not hastily—for I believe the peace, at least the evacua-

5. The Austrian army began to retire 26 Sept. NS (*Oesterr. Erbfolge-krieg* ix. 835).

6. This does not appear to be true, although the Dutch had drastically reduced their forces on 9 Sept. NS (ibid. ix. 834).

7. Conway leased Latimers, near Ches-

ham, Bucks, in the summer of 1749 (*post* 14 Sept. 1749 OS, n. 7).

8. Parliament was at this time prorogued to 13 Oct. OS, but on that day was further prorogued to 29 Nov. OS, when it finally met (*Journals of the House of Commons* xxv. 662).

tions are not in so prosperous a way as to be ready to make any figure in the King's speech. But I speak from a distance; it may all be very toward: our ministers enjoy the consciousness of their wisdom, as the good do of their virtue, and take no pains to make it shine before men. In the meantime we have several collateral emoluments from the pacification: all our milliners, tailors, tavernkeepers, and young gentlemen are tiding to France for our improvement and luxury; and as I foresee we shall be told on their return that we have lived in a total state of blindness for these six years, and gone absolutely retrograde to all true taste in every particular, I have already begun to practise walking on my head, and doing everything the wrong way. Then Charles Frederick[1] has turned all his virtu into fireworks, and, by his influence at the Ordnance, has prepared such a spectacle for the proclamation of the peace[2] as is to surpass all its predecessors of bouncing memory. It is to open with a concert of fifteen hundred hands, and conclude with so many hundred thousand crackers all set to music, that all the men killed in the war are to be wakened with the crash, as if it was the day of judgment, and fall a-dancing, like the troops in the *Rehearsal*.[3] I wish you could see him making squibs of his papillotes,[4] and bronzed over with a patina of gunpowder, and talking himself still hoarser on the superiority that his firework will have over the Roman naumachia.

I am going to dinner with Lady Sophia Thomas[5] at Hampton Court, where I was to meet the Cardigans; but I this minute receive a message that the Duchess of Montagu[6] is extremely ill, which I am much concerned for on Lady Cardigan's[7] account, whom I grow

1. (*Ante* 25 Feb. 1740 NS, n. 19), who was clerk of the deliveries in the Ordnance 1746–50, staged the display of fireworks 27 April 1749 OS on the proclamation of the Peace (MANN iv. 47–8) and those of the D. of Richmond for the D. of Modena 15 May 1749 OS (MONTAGU i. 80–1 and n. 2). It is not clear here whether HW is referring to the former or to Frederick's preparation for a personal display.

2. Which did not take place until 25 April 1749 OS (MANN iv. 46).

3. Buckingham's *The Rehearsal* II. v.

4. Curl papers; this is the earliest use of the word given in OED.

5. Lady Sophia Keppel (1711–73), m. Gen. John Thomas (Collins, *Peerage*, 1812, iii. 733).

6. She was mother to Lady Cardigan, and daughter to the great Duke of Marlborough (HW). Lady Mary Churchill (1689–1751), m. (1705) John Montagu, 2d D. of Montagu.

7. Lady Mary Montagu [ca 1711–75], third [2d] daughter of John Duke of Montagu and wife [1730] of George Brudenell [1712–90, 4th] Earl of Cardigan, afterwards created [1766] Duke of Montagu (HW).

every day more in love with;[8] you may imagine, not her person, which is far from improved lately: but since I have been here, I have lived much with them;[9] and, as George Montagu[10] says, *in all my practice* I never met a better understanding, nor more really estimable qualities; such a dignity in her way of thinking, so little idea of anything mean or ridiculous, and such proper contempt for both!

Adieu! I must go dress for dinner, and you perceive that I wish I had, but have nothing to tell you.

Yours ever,

Hor. Walpole

From Conway, Thursday 14 September 1749 OS

Printed for the first time from the MS now WSL, formerly Rutnam. '1749' is added in another hand. That this is the correct date is shown by HW to Montagu 28 Sept, 1749 OS, where HW describes his first visit to Latimers (Montagu i. 102); from the present letter it is clear he has not yet been there.

Memoranda (by HW): 2 first Bedfords[1] buried at Cheynies,
                                    near Latimer's.
                            Sir Edw. Sandys[2]
                            K. of Denm. Orcades and Schetland[3]

8. HW later modified his estimate of Lady Cardigan after she had taken offence at passages about her grandfather, the first Duke of Marlborough, in *Royal and Noble Authors* (Montagu ii. 89, n. 14; Berry i. 105 and nn. 22–24).

9. Lady Cardigan owned a villa at the foot of Richmond Hill (More 2, n. 5).

10. Nephew to the Earl of Halifax, and elder brother of Colonel, afterwards Sir Charles Montagu, K.B. (HW).

1. John Russell (ca 1485–1555) cr. (1539) Bn Russell and (1550) E. of Bedford; and his son Francis Russell (1527–85), 2d E. of Bedford. HW discusses the Bedford tombs at Chenies, Bucks, which he visited a few days after receiving this letter, in a letter to Montagu 28 Sept. 1749 OS (ibid. i. 102 and n. 3).

2. Apparently Sir Edwin Sandys (d. 1607 or 1608), Kt 1599, who succeeded his father as lord of the manor of Latimers in

1601 (*Vict. Co. Hist. Bucks* iii. 209; GEC xi. 447). Some early Buckinghamshire antiquarians seem to confuse him with Sir Edwin Sandys (1561–1629), the well-known early Stuart statesman; see George Lipscomb, *History . . . of Buckingham*, 1847, iii. 268–9, who gives a garbled account of the Sandys tenure of the manor on the authority of Browne Willis (1682–1760); and Bryant Burgess, 'Latimers or Latimer,' *Records of Buckinghamshire* [1887], vi. 31, who partially corrects Lipscombe.

3. The Orkneys and Shetlands, ancient possessions of the kingdom of Norway, became Danish upon the union of the Scandinavian crowns in 1397; in 1468–9 they were pledged by Christian I of Denmark for the payment of the dowry of his daughter Margaret, betrothed to James III of Scotland, and since the money was never paid, they passed permanently to the Scottish crown. Denmark formally renounced its claim to the islands in 1590

Mallet-Mallock.4 Lord Ankram
Dryden's Virg. Ogilby's5
100. 500.
Board of Trade. Col. Bladen.6

Latimers,7 Sept. 14.

Dear Horry,

I WAS in hopes I should have heard from you before this time as I
think I had a sort of promise before we left town of a visit at
Latimers which I have expected with great pleasure ever since.8 I am
just now returned after a good deal of wandering and, I hope, to
settle here for some time, which makes me think it a proper one to
put you in mind of us. I know such a farmer and such a country
gentleman as you, I mean so busy a one, such a builder9 and such a
gardener must be greatly taken up and that your hours are very
sacred; however, when your affairs permit and a few days may be
stolen from your occupations, know that there is to be entered upon
immediately, if you please, a great, old house lying and being in the
County of Bucks and Parish of Chesham, about 12 miles from Ux-
bridge, which will give you a very great welcome, is in a healthful

(*Salmonsens konversations Leksikon*, 2d
edn, ed. Christian Blangstrup, Copen-
hagen, 1915–30, xviii. 615).

4. David Mallet (ca 1705–65), poet and
miscellaneous writer, had changed his
name from Malloch to Mallet in 1724. He
was much in the public eye during 1749
for his publication of Bolingbroke's *Patriot King* 3 May 1749 OS with a preface
attacking Pope; see MANN iv. 59–62.

5. Two words at the end of this line
are illegible. The note probably relates to
John Ogilby (1600–76), miscellaneous
writer, who published a translation of
Virgil in 1649; this was reissued in 1654 in
royal folio with plates by Hollar that
were borrowed by Dryden for his translation.

6. Probably Col. Martin Bladen (?1680–
1746), M.P. Stockbridge 1715–34, Maldon
1734–41, Portsmouth 1741–6; commissioner of trade and plantations 1717–46; a
staunch supporter of Sir Robert Walpole.

7. Near Chesham, Bucks, recently leased
by Conway. The house and manor, which
had been in the Cavendish family since
1615, was at this time the property of
Lord James Cavendish, on whose death in
1751 it passed to his daughter Elizabeth

(*Vict. Co. Hist. Bucks* iii. 209). The early
16th-century house was much altered by
Mrs Cavendish during her occupancy and
almost entirely rebuilt in the Elizabethan
style in the 19th century (ibid. iii. 204;
HW to Bentley 5 July 1755, CHUTE 233).
A sketch of it ca 1786 is in Burgess, op.
cit. 27; and illustrations of the 19th-cen-
tury reconstruction are ibid. 37 and Lipscomb, op. cit. iii. 268.

8. HW made this visit within two
weeks. He did not like the house, which
he described as 'large and bad, old but of
a bad age; finely situated on a hill in a
beech wood, with a river at the bottom,
and a range of hills and woods on the
opposite side belonging to the Bedfords.
They are fond of it; the view is melancholy' (HW to Montagu 28 Sept. 1749 OS,
MONTAGU i. 102).

9. HW had made alterations to the in-
terior of SH in 1748 (*Strawberry Hill Accounts*, ed. Toynbee, Oxford, 1927, pp. 1,
34). The earliest extant reference to re-
modelling SH in the Gothic manner is in
HW to Montagu 28 Sept. 1749 (loc. cit.),
but there may have been one in the missing letter to which Conway is replying.

airy situation and shall be insured to stand during your term though cotemporary with Queen Elizabeth's grandfather, is neither haunted with ghosts, rats, nor country neighbours, and if it's cold will have good fires before Michaelmas Day. I have now tried all my rhetoric and if these things don't prevail must despair of seeing you; I should have thought it madness to dream of drawing you into the country formerly at this season but should think it an affront to you now if I suspected you of leaving it for some few months. Adieu, dear Horry, let me know what hopes we have of seeing you and when for fear any accident should happen to disappoint us of your company. Lady Ailesbury desires her compliments. I should send mine to Mrs Leneve but hear she's a false nymph and has abandoned you.

Believe me most sincerely yours,

H. CONWAY

From CONWAY, Thursday 28 June 1750 OS

Printed from the MS now WSL, formerly Rutnam. First printed, *Fraser's Magazine*, 1850, xli. 638. '1750' has been added in another hand, possibly HW's; it is confirmed by the tone of the references to Latimers, where Conway and Lady Ailesbury seem well established although looking for a new house. It could not have been written in 1751 because Conway was abroad after the beginning of July, while in 1749 they do not seem to have been at Latimers as early as June.

Latimers, June 28.

Dear Horry,

I THINK I had a sort of promise from you that we should either see you soon at Latimers,[1] or at least hear from you. Being in great uncertainty what was to come of you then, and in no less impatience since to know whether your scheme for France[2] still lives, or is gathered to its worthy forerunners of our acquaintance, long since departed, all I have to say, with great deference to it, is that if it should not survive the receipt of this, Latimers is now in its bloom of beauty, but blooming, like the rose in the desert, with no soul to see and to commend it. As to us, we are alone and consequently have but little entertainment to offer you; but then you are sure to be free

1. HW finally made this visit in late July (MANN iv. 163; *post* 17 July 1750 OS).
2. HW does not mention this plan of visiting France at this time in any of his surviving letters.

from any troublesome ceremony. I am not unreasonable enough to think of tearing you from Lady Strafford,[3] Lady Montroth,[4] and all your dowagers, but just for such a reasonable time as you can steal from quadrille, and will give you fresh pleasure in returning to it. You see I don't touch upon your planting—that's sacred;[5] and besides, I really envy it you so much that I can't talk of it without pain; for all our fine schemes, Watlington[6] and Moor Park,[7] with twenty others you don't know by name, are gone, where I hope they'll meet yours for Paris: all vanished, and we condemned to this inn of an hired house, which, pretty as it is, I can't bear while it has the hateful quality of belonging to another. And really after all 'tis a shocking grievance that those who have pretty places, and won't or can't enjoy 'em, will so act the dog-in-the-manger as to keep others out of 'em. I desire you'll be watchful for our interest, and if you hear of anything that's to be sold let us know, for we are under the circumstances of the most vehement impatience, and I doubt shall be drove to some horrid violence. You know I have already tampered with you about a neighbour of yours,[8] who certainly deserves the worst, and I think can't escape unless we are satisfied soon.

I hear your brother has made great discoveries, and is likely to get well out of his most troublesome affair.[9]

Adieu, dear Horry. Let one hear of you, and believe me most sincerely yours,

H. C.

Lady Ailesbury desires her compliments.

3. Probably Anne Johnson (ca 1684–1754), m. (1711) Thomas Wentworth (d. 1739), 1st E. of Strafford; not HW's friend Lady Anne Campbell (ca 1715–85), m. (1741) William Wentworth, 2d E. of Strafford. The Straffords owned a house at Twickenham.

4. Lady Diana Newport (d. 1766), m. (1721) Algernon Coote, 6th E. of Mountrath; she lived at Twickenham Park. For HW's accounts of her drunkenness and supposed affair with Lord Hardwicke, see MONTAGU i. 135 and n. 20.

5. See *ante* 6 Oct. 1748 OS and MONTAGU i. 79.

6. Probably Watlington Park, Oxon, near Wallingford, at this time a possession of the Stonor family, 'a respectable brick edifice, on a lofty site' (J. N. Brewer,

Beauties of England and Wales, 1801–16, xii pt ii. 321).

7. Near Rickmansworth, Herts, rebuilt for Benjamin Styles between 1720 and his death in 1739. The house was finally sold by the Court of Chancery to Lord Anson in 1754. HW visited it in 1744 and again in 1760 (SELWYN 62 and references cited there in n. 29).

8. Not identified.

9. Presumably Orford's difficulties with his wife. No details of their relations at this time are known, but HW mentions shortly after his brother's death in 1751 that he had found in his papers 'her intercepted billets-doux' to Sewallis Shirley, with whom she had been living since 1746 (MANN iii. 309, iv. 247–8).

To CONWAY, July 1750

Missing; answered *post* 17 July 1750 OS.

From CONWAY, Tuesday 17 July 1750 OS

Printed from the MS now WSL, formerly Rutnam. First printed, *Fraser's Magazine*, 1850, xli. 638–9. '1750' has been added in another hand, possibly HW's; the present letter is clearly a sequel to *ante* 28 June 1750 OS.

Latimers, July 17.

Dear Horry,

THOUGH really I am a little afraid of being so familiar; you begin with such a *Sir,* and end with such an *obedient, humble servant,* that I am in doubt whether it is not fit for me to change my style too, though I am so hampered in an usage almost immemorial that I should certainly find it very difficult; for I really can scarce keep up a decent degree of ceremonial phrase with my new acquaintance; and to be formal with my old ones seems as unnatural a thing to me as to be familiar with Lord Northampton[1] or the Duchess of Dorset.[2]

I should have writ to you before to tell you what our motions were to be, but that your journey first,[3] and one of mine since, from which I am but just returned, prevented me; we look upon ourselves as fixed here till the 10th or 11th of next month, and expect nobody in the meantime that I believe you will have any objection to if you should happen to meet 'em, our only promises being from Sir John Ligonier and General Campbell,[4] and that for a few days only, except it be Mrs Weston,[5] who has not yet been here, and whom you

1. James Compton (1687–1754), 5th E. of Northampton.
2. Elizabeth Colyear (d. 1768), m. (1709) Lionel Cranfield Sackville, 7th E. of Dorset, cr. (1720) D. of Dorset. HW mentions 'the excessive reserve and silence' of both the Duke and Duchess to Mann 1 Sept. 1750 OS (MANN iv. 179).
3. HW had apparently been visiting Rigby at Mistley, Essex, since early July

and did not return to London until 24 July (ibid. iv. 163).
4. Lady Ailesbury's father, later 4th D. of Argyll (*ante* 25 Oct. 1743 NS, n. 11).
5. Perhaps the wife of Edward Weston (1703–70), HW's tutor before he went to Eton ('Short Notes,' GRAY i. 3–4 and nn. 7–9), who was married twice, first (1730) to Penelope Patrick and secondly, to Anne Fountayne (DNB).

may still meet if you please, as you were so good to say you wished. So that as to convenience it will be convenient at any time, and I can most sincerely assure you from us both, always very agreeable to see you when you can think it so.

I am much obliged to you for the care you promise to take for us about an house, which we both long for most impatiently, and really I think not quite with an unreasonable impatience neither, as the sooner we get it the longer we shall enjoy it: more time to plant and improve, and age steals on with a silent foot, you know, and upon none so fast as your planters, who, as their trees grow upwards, never think how they are hastening downwards themselves, of which tendency in myself my grey hairs admonish me daily. But for your instruction upon this subject, since you are so good as to undertake it for us, you must know that our views have been growing more ambitious daily since our scheme was first formed and whether our appetite is increased from so long a fast, or how I don't know, but from a box with a few acres, we are come to talk of elbow-room, a manor, a command, etc; in short, our eye is upon a farm of two, three, or four hundred per annum, with wood, water and prospect; these are the requisites. I should add a pleasant country, and if possible a good house, though with all this our list of articles is so long, 'tis no easy matter, I am afraid, to find them assembled. However, the house we are least solicitous about, as that may soon be mended if it's bad but the other articles, being either incorr[ig]ible in their nature, or no otherwise than in a long course of time, I own I have not spirits or patience to sit down in a miserable place and spend my money in doing what Nature has done in so many, especially as she is generally sure to please one, and one does not grow tired of her works as we do of our own.

Adieu. Believe me

Most sincerely yours,

H. C.

Lady Ailesbury desires her compliments.

To CONWAY, October 1750

Two letters missing; answered *post* 29 Oct. 1750 OS.

From CONWAY, Monday 29 October 1750 OS

Printed from the MS now WSL, formerly Rutnam. First printed, *Fraser's Magazine,* 1850, xli. 636–8. Placed in 1750 because of the references to Conway's search for a house.

Latimers, Oct. 29.

Dear Horry,

I AM sitting down to thank you for your second letter before I have had not opportunity of doing it for your former, which I really should be much ashamed of if it had been the effect of my own idleness; but first I was interrupted by company that came to us, and did not leave us till we set out on an expedition into Surrey and Hampshire, from which we returned last night. Part of our business was to see a house there,[1] which indeed is our chief business at present so that we are very unlucky in not having received your intelligence about Eversly[2] before, that we might have seen it. As it is, after thanking you and your laudable zeal for the good cause very sincerely, I am afraid I must put it to a farther trial (though, after all the trouble you have given yourself about us, I am ashamed) by begging you to ask Mr Comyns,[3] if you see him, some few particulars farther about the place, I mean that in Hampshire, for the other,[4] though it has many agreeable things about [it] and particularly being in the neighbourhood of Strawberry Hill (we are such true devotees) is by both of us reckoned much too near London. I should

---

1. Holt Forest, as appears below.
2. Eversley, in northeast Hampshire on the Berkshire border, apparently owned by Valens Comyn (see next note). The house now known as Eversley Manor, built after 1736 by Wadham Wyndam for his own residence, was known as Fir Grove until the present century (*Country Life* 1943, xciii. 528–31, 572–5).
3. Valens Comyn (d. 1751), M.P. Hin-

don 1747–51, who apparently lived at Twickenham since he is buried there (R. S. Cobbett, *Memorials of Twickenham,* 1872, p. 68). He is described in the Parliamentary lists in the *Court and City Register* as of Eversley, Hants, but the family is not mentioned in the account of the parish in *Vict. Co. Hist. Hants* nor elsewhere in connection with Hampshire.
4. Not identified.

indeed upon the strength of what you say, as you seem to imagine it[5] would do for us, have concluded you had heard some particulars of the beauties of the place, as wood, water, hill and vale, the concave and convex of Mr Kent[6] etc., and something of this kind I should be obliged to you if you'd ask him[7] for us, if you see him and have not; and what sort of country, whether wet or dry, this being the sort of examination we make of every place that comes before us; for as our intention is to buy, which is wedding a place for life, you'll own too much caution can't be used; and as to the reports of people, some of them are so very unaccountable, so misjudged, and so distant from the truth, that without it be upon the knowledge of some friend whose taste I can depend upon, after some places I have seen and heard commended, I never intend to visit any more but upon some good intelligence which makes me the more anxious about this, because if the description has pleased you, I dare say we should like it, I mean provided 'twas just; and as the price sounds pretty moderate, I should have great hopes of it's doing for us.

Lady Ailesbury writes to Miss Townshend[8] today, who lives in that country,[9] and will desire her to see it if she can, or at least inquire about it. The place which we have seen near Mr Hunter's[10] is Holt Forest,[11] which has many things agreeable in it and some otherwise, so that though we are pretty much inclined to it in general, we have made no determination.

I have not yet thanked you for the pedigree[12] and all the trouble

5. Eversley.

6. William Kent, the landscape gardener and architect.

7. Mr Comyn.

8. The Hon. Mary Townshend.

9. Miss Townshend was living at Ewhurst, near Basingstoke, Hants, by 1747; see Spencer Cowper, *Letters*, ed. Hughes, 1956, p. 79, Surtees Society CLXV.

10. Apparently Thomas Orby Hunter (ca 1716–69), of Crowland, Lincs; M.P. Winchelsea 1741–59, 1760–9; lord of the Admiralty 1756–63; lord of the Treasury 1763–5. He had purchased the site of Waverley Abbey in Farnham hundred, Surrey, near the Hampshire border in 1747 and built a house there (Owen Manning and William Bray, *History . . . of Surrey*, 1804–14, iii. 152).

11. This house cannot be identified, but it was obviously in or near Alice Holt Forest on the Surrey-Hampshire border between Farnham, Surrey, and Binsted, Hants.

12. Missing. In the absence of HW's letters, this paragraph remains obscure, but it apparently concerns genealogical researches by HW into the former lords of the manor of Latimers. The references to 'a Lord Latimer's arms' and 'that staring monument' suggest that these studies were provoked by armorial bearings on a chimney-piece or similar object. The references to Queen Elizabeth and her favourites further suggests that HW had perhaps shown the arms to be those of the Greville family who were unquestioned lords of the manor 1548–67 and who had earlier claims to it through their marriages with heiresses of the Nevills, Lords Latimer, the earlier holders of the manor. Genealogical details and details of

I doubt it has given you, for which I am afraid it will be paying you but poorly to say it gave us equal pleasure in satisfying a curiosity of a long standing, and which that staring monument did not let us forget a moment; and as people who are in the grossest ignorance of things form systems as well as those that know the most, I have asserted with a sort of confidence for some time past that they were a Lord Latimer's arms, misled by the name, the common report, and finding something of Lord Latimers in Cambden's *Life of Queen Elizabeth*,[13] though nothing about him at all to the purpose. So I am obliged to you particularly for drawing me out of my error, and not letting me expose myself or deceive my friends any longer with this fable. Soon after I received these lights from you, we had a visit from Lord and Lady Cobham,[14] to whom I had a fine opportunity of displaying my new-acquired knowledge, and letting him into this history of his nominal ancestry,[15] but could not be so unjust as to conceal the source from whence I drew my instruction. Queen Elizabeth is really more obliged to you than she could express if she were alive; but you'd complete the obligation by making out her consanguinity with the Lord Chancellor,[16] Lord Leicester,[17] and many more upon whom she cast a very favourable eye, as well as for destroying her cousinship with poor Essex,[18] when it could not save his head or that of her cousin and sister-queen,[19] where her consanguinity did not

---

the conflicting claims to the manor are in *Vict. Co. Hist. Bucks* iii. 208–9; GEC *sub* Latimer and *sub* Willoughby de Broke; Bryant Burgess, 'Latimers or Latimer,' *Records of Buckinghamshire* [1887], vi. 29–31; W. L. Rutton, 'Notes in Reference to . . . the Manor of Iselhampstead-Latimer,' ibid. vi. 55–71. The manor was, in fact, never held by Queen Elizabeth's favourite Fulke Greville (1554–1628), cr. (1621) Bn Brooke, having been sold by his father Sir Fulke Greville (d. 1606), to Miles Sandys in 1567; the Grevilles, however, were distantly related to Elizabeth through their Nevill descents.

13. The death of John Nevill (ca 1520–77), 4th Bn Latimer, n.c., is mentioned in William Camden's *Annals, or The Historie of the Most Renowned . . . Elizabeth*, 1635, p. 197. Latimers had been owned by his ancestors, but since it had passed to heiresses of the senior line in the

later 15th century (*Vict. Co. Hist. Bucks* iii. 208), he had never been connected with the manor.

14. Richard Grenville (after 1752 Grenville Temple) (1711–79), styled Vct Cobham 1749–52, 1st E. Temple, 1752; m. (1737) Anne Chambers (ca 1709–77).

15. Lord Cobham was a great-great-grandson of Miles Sandys, lord of the manor of Latimers from 1567 until his death in 1601, but neither the Sandyses nor the Temples seem to have been related to the earlier lords.

16. Sir Christopher Hatton (1540–91), K.G. 1588, lord chancellor 1587–91.

17. Robert Dudley (1532 *or* 1533–88), K.G. 1559, cr. (1564) E. of Leicester.

18. Robert Devereux (1566–1601), 2d E. of Essex; he was Elizabeth's first cousin twice removed, being a great-grandson of Anne Boleyn's sister Mary.

19. Mary, Queen of Scots.

move her so strongly. Adieu! Lady Ailesbury joins with me in many thanks and compliments.

Yours most sincerely,

H. C.

From Conway, Wednesday 14 July 1751 NS

Printed in full for the first time from the MS now wsl, formerly Rutnam. First printed (with omissions) *Fraser's Magazine*, 1850, xli. 639–40.
Memoranda (by HW): D. of Somers. and Butler.[1]

Paris,[2] July 14 NS, 1751.

Dear Horry,

I THINK I promised to write to you at my coming away, but, however that is, I feel too much inclination to it not to indulge it without I was sure it would be disagreeable to you. Journeys to Paris of late years, without they have some extraordinary events to support 'em, have not the gift of affording much entertainment, and mine was so very good and prosperous, and so barren of events, that I could scarce give you a better detail of it than you'd find in the *livre des postes*. Here are a good many English here, but hardly any of your acquaintance, I believe, besides Lord Hyde[3] and Stanley.[4] The first has taken an house, I think for nine years.[5] He has inquired after you, and I suppose would have sent compliments if I had told him I was to write to you. His house is pretty; he has laid out a good deal of money upon it, lives a good deal among the

1. Perhaps a note for some anecdote concerning Charles Seymour (1662–1748), 6th D. of Somerset; 'the proud Duke.' Several anecdotes of his pride and arrogance, some of them concerning his servants, are collected in J. H. Jesse, *Memoirs of the Court of England from . . . 1688 to the Death of George the Second*, 1843, iii. 252–5.

2. Conway was en route to Minorca to join his regiment, the 34th Foot, to the colonelcy of which he had been transferred from the 48th Foot 24 July 1749 OS.

3. Lord Cornbury (*ante* 16 Feb. 1741 OS, n. 10) had been summoned to the House of Lords in his father's barony of Hyde of Hindon 22 or 23 Jan. 1751 OS.

4. Hans Stanley (*ante* 18 July 1744 NS, n. 8). For his assiduous cultivation of HW (who never particularly cared for him), see Selwyn 71. He remained at Paris for two years (Namier and Brooke iii. 468).

5. Here a line of writing has been heavily crossed out: 'and intends I believe . . . it his chief residence.'

French, by whom he's very well received, and enters into all the gaiety of a Paris life, all which looks a design of making this his chief residence.

Stanley, I believe, is pretty much in the same resolution, but does not own (to me at least) that he is settled here for many months. Yesterday morning he came to me with a common English fiddler's hat like yours, an English frock, worsted stockings, and a long stick, walking all through the town, for he lives on the ramparts. How the French will receive a man with such a barbarous taste in dress I don't know, but I don't think him likely to conform, and if they don't take him in his own way, I have a notion he'll call 'em a parcel of puppies and leave them.

I have seen Lady Hervey[6] only once. She has been very ill and is not yet so recovered as to go into company; I fancy her turn is that of the *bel esprit* and literature. You know she has changed her principles in politics,[7] and her religious ones I have heard were in danger, but don't pretend to say it. I was invited to meet her tomorrow at Lord Hyde's at dinner with old Fontenelle,[8] which I should have liked, but am unfortunately engaged in another party. I am to dine with her on Tuesday to take my *bonne bouche* of Paris, for on Wednesday I propose to leave it, having seen almost all my sights, and had what I reckon full enough of it without I was to take a great deal more; for it's a thing to drink deep of or not taste; I don't call it tasting to live as we generally do here; it's only seeing in the literal sense; and though there are some things that deserve it very well, they are not, I believe, very many and don't last long.

Nothing has pleased me like the Palais Royal,[9] which seems to me a noble collection of pictures; I have already been there twice, and could visit it much oftener with pleasure. I want to know if the great collections in Italy are quite to eclipse this; to me at present I own it seems hard to conceive. I saw a private one today of a Monsieur Julien's,[10] which really has a good many valuable things.

6. Mary Lepell (1700–68), m. (1720) John Hervey, summoned to Parliament as Bn Hervey of Ickworth, 1733; later HW's friend and correspondent. She had been in France since Aug. 1750 and remained until Feb. 1752 (MORE 416, n. 10).

7. She had become a Jacobite (Augustus Hervey, *Journal*, ed. Erskine, 1953, p. 105).

8. Bernard Le Bovier de Fontenelle (1657–1757); Lady Hervey bequeathed HW a drawing of him, which was hung in the Breakfast Room at SH (MORE 137).

9. The pictures collected by the Regent.

10. Chevalier Jean de Jullienne or Julienne (1686–1766), director of the Gobelin factory and art collector. HW visited

I don't tell you of all the travelling English that are here; most of 'em you know nothing of, so that it would be but a list of names. Lord Stormont[11] is worth mentioning, though I question if you know him. I am not sure if Lord Burford[12] is, for he seems to have all the coldness and stiffness of his father.[13] I won't abuse him, because I know him not, but his air *ne me plaît pas*. Here's our poor old acquaintance, Lord Tilney,[14] wandering here with a Mr Wynn,[15] who have not two words of French between 'em. He made an escapade from his family, and left poor Lady Dorothy[16] in fits, I think, and quite inconsolable. However, he's vastly civil and good-natured, and I must say, has been particularly so to me since I came here, which I take the better, as I am not clear we did not leave him and his family off a little shamefully.[17]

I could scribble a great deal longer, but I believe you'll be satisfied at least with this, so conclude, dear Horry,

Most truly and affectionately yours,

H. S. C.

Direct for me *chez Monsieur Selwyn,*[18] *banquier à Paris.*

the collection 18 Dec. 1765 and in 1767 acquired two items at the auction of it (MANN vi. 523 and references cited in n. 6).

11. David Murray (1727–96), 7th Vct Stormont, 1748; 2d E. of Mansfield, 1793; diplomatist. Although DNB says he was an attaché at the British embassy in Paris in 1751, he seems rather to have been on the Grand Tour, since he was at Florence by late Nov. 1751 and accompanied Conway to Rome in Jan. 1752 (MANN iv. 285; *post* 23 Jan. 1752 NS).

12. George Beauclerk (1730–86), styled E. of Burford 1730–51, 3d D. of St Albans, 27 July 1751 OS.

13. Charles Beauclerk (1696 – 27 July 1751 OS), 2d D. of St Albans.

14. John Tylney (formerly Child) (1712–84), 2d E. Tylney of Castlemaine, 1750.

15. Not identified.

16. Presumably his sister, Lady Dorothy Child (d. 1786) (GM 1786, lvi pt i. 82). The only other reference found to this affair is in a letter from Smart Lethieul-

lier, an Essex neighbour, to Charles Lyttelton in the summer of 1751: 'Tylney you know is gone abroad, Lady Dorothy so ill (brooks the loss of her coach and six, etc.) that she is really gone out of her senses, and retired with Mr Child to the Lake House, where Dr Monroe attends her and God knows whether she will ever recover. Mr Harvey's behaviour in the late affair I have too much reason to resent, to hold any further correspondence with him and did you know all you would not think I should ever receive young Gascoine within my doors' (C. H. Iyan Chown, 'The Lethieullier Family of Aldersbrook House,' pt ii, *Essex Review*, 1927, xxxvi. 10).

17. The nature and date of this quarrel are unknown; it was obviously made up, since HW later visited Tylney at Wanstead (HW to Bentley 17 July 1755, CHUTE 238).

18. Charles Selwin (ca 1716–94) (GRAY i. 239, n. 12).

PS. I have heard by this evening's post of poor Selwyn's death,[19] which really gives me great concern; though it does not surprise me much as I have almost expected it every post. His poor father and mother will be inconsolable.

From CONWAY, Saturday 4 September 1751 NS

Printed from the MS now WSL, formerly Rutnam. First printed *Fraser's Maga- zine*, 1850, xlii. 337–8.

Memoranda (by HW):[1] Mr Fox
Miss Town[shend] } 21
Mr R[igby]—28
Mr Gr[ay]—

Mahon,[1a] September 4, NS, 1751.

Dear Horry,

IF I waited till I heard from you in all appearance I should never write to you again; I have now been near a month in this cursed island and out of England almost two and have not had a single line, not a word from you[2] or any of my friends, except one only; yet I don't mean to complain of you; but of my own stupidity or negligence that did not take my measures better; of my ill fortune, of roads, distances, seas, winds etc. 'Twould be but a little hyperbole to say your letters were afraid to come here; for yours, I am sure, they have wit and sense enough and the least hint of what Minorca is must frighten 'em from it. Imagine what is ugliest in nature, and dullest in human society and you'll perhaps have a better notion of this place than I can give you. The country is one entire heap of rock and sand; not a tree for shelter nor a brook for refreshment in the whole island. Where Cardinal Retz[3] got his ideas, who describes this

19. John Selwyn died 'of a polypus in the heart' 27 June 1751 OS (GM 1751, xxi. 284).

—

1. This is apparently a list of letters received or written. No letters to Henry Fox, the Hon. Mary Townshend, or Richard Rigby in 1751 have been recovered; but HW was visiting Rigby in August, for he writes to Mann 31 Aug. OS from Mistley, Rigby's seat in Essex (MANN iv.

271). HW apparently wrote Thomas Gray early in September, and sent him a parcel, which Gray answered 29 Sept. OS (GRAY ii. 51).

1a. Port Mahon, Minorca.

2. Conway received none of HW's letters until just before he left Florence in Jan. 1752 and then only one 'of a prodigious old date' (*post* 23 Jan. 1752 NS).

3. Jean-François-Paul de Gondi (1614–79), Cardinal de Retz.

as a paradise,[4] or what fortunate island he mistook for it I don't know. The inhabitants are in appearance fit inhabitants for such a place, ugly in form, poor, proud, mean, ignorant and superstitious; I believe really at an average I have seen two or three processions a day ever since I have been here. So you see they enjoy their own religion; they have their own laws, too, liberty enough, at least much more than they ever knew, no taxes for our government and a free trade and yet they say they are very discontent, and sigh for a Spanish government![5]

I had the pleasure and entertainment t'other day of seeing the great races of Mahon on the Festival of St John the Baptist's Decapitation,[6] which they celebrate with great mirth and festivity. The games themselves very noble really, and such as I believe exceed everything of the kind ancient or modern. There are four races, viz. of horses, of mules, of jackasses and a foot race. In the first the prize is a silver teaspoon, value three or four shillings; the victor in the second is rewarded with an halter, the third obtains a set of shoes for his ass and the fourth a pair for himself. At night there was a public ball in an open place of the town called Moor Fields where our regiments generally exercise; in one corner of it they light a kind of bonfire, not for warmth as you'll imagine, but to supply the place of wax lights, and the ball is regulated in this manner: a damsel is set up in a conspicuous place to auction, where the men bid for her in proportion to her beauty, merit and accomplishments; from a doubler,[7] or $\frac{1}{3}$ of a penny, as high as sixpence; the highest bidder is her partner, takes her out and dances three *reprises* of a sort of grave jig but with such decorum that he is not allowed to touch her hands; the women dance generally with castanets, a slow step and with very little variety but sometimes not without grace. There's a stupid description of a stupid ceremony for you.

Since that, I have seen a Jew's wedding which is odd enough but I'll spare you the description; we were all almost smothered, and having escaped that, for heat, as Mr Quin[8] said, I think may bid the

4. His praise of Minorca, particularly the setting of Port Mahon which he visited in 1654, is in his *Mémoires*, first published in 1717 (*Œuvres*, ed. Feillet *et al.*, 1870–1920, iv. 558–60, 571).

5. Minorca had been occupied by the English since its capture in 1708.

6. 29 August.

7. Dublero, a Spanish copper coin; 144 dubleros were equal to about three shillings sixpence (John Armstrong, *The History of the Island of Minorca*, 1752, pp. 114–15).

8. James Quin (1693–1766), actor and wit.

devil kiss our a——. Imagine in one of the hottest days of the hottest season that has been known in this hot climate, an hundred and fifty people from ten till twelve in the morning in a room little bigger than a closet, with a great lustre of candles' light and two immense flaming tapers; after this dancing minuets, and a narrow escape of country dances! These good people were married on Tuesday; he went into bed for half an hour to his lady but in presence of witnesses, so married as it were by proxy for himself; and is not to lie with his wife till eight or nine days are past. Tonight we finish the ceremony with another dance. For me I am a perfect salamander in these heats; they don't the least affect my health and have much to do to make me complain. *Triste avantage!* It puts in mind of what I was reading t'other day in St Anthony's speech to the fishes[9] where he congratulates 'em upon their happiness in not feeling or suffering by the deluge. *Poi che fra tutte le creature de l'universo, voi solo non sentiste il diluvio universale dell'acqua!* [10] However, it is an advantage when one is here and since it is one's fate to live in a furnace it's a comfort not to be scorched.

In the meantime I have a constant eye upon Italy and meditate my flight there with the very first occasion that offers; I am a little sorry that I did not get recommendations there from you, Lord Orford,[11] etc. for Florence and Rome; for since I have been out now I have found it a melancholy thing to go into a strange town without 'em; at Marseilles I was as if a Chinese had been there knowing not a soul nor conversing but with our table d'hôte; I have some hopes from Mr Mann but not knowing him shall wish I had had letters.[12] Adieu, dear Horry, this is a tedious scroll; but excuse it pray, you can't think the comfort there is in writing and complaining. I know no more of England at present than Grand Tartary! Not one line from thence yet, even from Lady A. since I have been here. Indeed, this is very melancholy. Pity me, do, and believe me

Very sincerely and affectionately yours,

H. S. C.

9. The sermon preached to the fishes on the banks of the Brenta near Padua by St Anthony (1195–1231) of Padua.

10. 'Then that among all the creatures of the universe, you alone should not feel the universal deluge of water.'

11. George, 3d E. of Orford, who had left on his Grand Tour in 1748 and was still abroad when his father died in March 1751 (R. W. Ketton-Cremer, *A Norfolk Gallery*, 1948, p. 166; MANN iii. 510–11).

12. HW had recommended Conway to Mann in a letter of 16 July OS and again on 31 Aug. OS (ibid. iv. 264–5, 272) under the impression that Conway was going to visit Italy while stationed at Minorca.

From CONWAY, Sunday 26 September 1751 NS

Printed from the MS now WSL, formerly Rutnam. First printed, *Fraser's Magazine*, 1850, xlii. 338–9. HW received this shortly before 14 Oct, 1751 OS (MANN iv. 280); see also HW's memoranda listed on Gray to HW 8 Oct. 1751 (GRAY ii. 52).

Mahon, Sept. 26 NS, 1751.

Dear Horry,

I CAN'T say how much disappointed I was on the arrival of the packet t'other day among a great bundle of English letters, after being absent almost eleven weeks and after having writ to you twice to find none from you; I don't care to think you have quite forgot or neglected me; and therefore choose to suppose either my letters to you or yours to me have been lost; for I can assure you there never was a worse place to be forgot in by one's friends than this! It's really a better place to be writ to in than to write in by much, though I write as you find without ceasing; but without it I could not expect to hear from my friends and without that this horrid place and life that nothing can reconcile would be quite intolerable; there's a relief in complaining, too, and for that purpose I own I write chiefly at present, to complain of you, to complain of everything here and to complain of the worst fortune in the world without which I might by this time have made my escape for some time at least; as to the first I shall say no more, though I could a great deal; on the second head of complaint I could talk forever; 'tis such a complication of ugliness, dullness and ennui; rocks, sands, mountains, bareness, brownness, barrenness, no mirth, no joy, no society, much ignorance, much poverty and superstition! 'Tis a horrid little spot indeed, an abominable one beyond all other abominations. Of my ill fortune, too, I could say a good deal but shall only tell you now how it has served me in regard to my voyage to Italy, which as I have told you my mind has been set upon from the moment I left England. There has been a man of war[1] expected here a good while from Portugal in her way to Italy; two days ago she was met at sea. They told us she'd come in immediately having money for the garrison and letters for the governor;[2] I asked his leave to go in her and was preparing every-

1. Probably the *Nightingale* (below, n. 4).

2. William Blakeney (1672–1761), cr. (1756) Bn Blakeney; Lt-Gen., 1747; Lt-Gov. of Minorca 1748–56 and in chief command there in the absence of the governor, Lord Tyrawley.

thing for my voyage. Now judge of my ill luck! Last night she comes in at twelve o'clock, knocks up the coffee-house man for lemons and greens,[3] I think, drops her money and letters, sets sail immediately and this morning was irrevocably gone before I knew she had been here. The silly captain,[4] it seems, was in an hurry to see his wife,[5] whom he had left in Italy. So there's an end of my Italian scheme for the present,[6] at least, though I am still bent upon pursuing it whenever an opportunity offers. And apropos to that if you ever write to Mr Mann as I suppose you do, 'twill be a vast comfort to me if you'll just mention me to him, as I am sure I shall run headlong into Italy, *sans aveu*, without any acquaintance or recommendation and appear like a vagabond.

I am just returned from the tour of the island, from seeing it all over and finding it all the same [as] I saw and thought it at first and in our neighbourhood. Our journey or at least our expedition was of six days for I should own I lay still three of 'em; and in the course of it presented us with nothing but two ordinary towns[7] and a village,[8] two mountains[9] and a cavern; at Ciudadella I stayed three days with Col. Lockart[10] and by way of [a] visit for it's a mean place enough though in the Spaniards' time the capital of the island; on one of our mountains[11] is a convent of Augustine friars who with all the air of austerity and retreat such a situation bears, live if the world belies 'em not *a ripaglia*[12] as the Italians say, and more like the herd of Epicurus than the flock of St Austin; however, the place is in great odour of sanctity and as full of lies and miracles as it can hold; they gave us a good breakfast and we a small tribute to

---

3. As a preventative for scurvy.

4. Marriot Arbuthnot (ca 1711–94), Capt., 1747; Rear-Adm., 1778; Vice-Adm., 1787; Adm., 1793. He was in command of the *Nightingale*, stationed in the Mediterranean, from the autumn of 1749 until after 27 Sept. 1750 (MANN iv. 284–5; *Barrington Papers*, ed. D. Bonner-Smith, Navy Records Society LXXVII, LXXXI, 1937–41, i. 54, 59, 61, 65; Augustus Hervey, *Journal*, ed. Erskine, 1953, pp. 94, 120).

5. She is probably the Mrs Arbuthnot who was at Florence in Aug. 1752 (MANN iv. 327).

6. Conway finally left Mahon for Italy about the middle of October (*post* 3 Dec. 1751 NS).

7. Ciudadela and Alayor, the two largest places on the island after Port Mahon.

8. Probably Mercadal, between Alayor and Ciudadela.

9. Monte Toro and Santa Águeda.

10. Probably Sir James Lockhart (after 1754, Ross Lockhart) (ca 1717–60), 4th Bt, 1758, at this time Lt-Col. of the 33d Foot which was stationed in Minorca; Col. of the 38th Foot, 1756; Maj-Gen., 1759 (*Court and City Register*, 1751, pp. 157, 160; Robert Beatson, *Political Index*, 1806, pp. 143, 234).

11. Monte Toro.

12. *Sic* in MS; presumably *alla paglia*, 'on the straw.'

their favourite image[13] with which both parties were equally content. Our other mountain[14] is curious for an ancient Moorish fortress
and our cavern,[15] by description like that vulgarly called the devil's
a[rse] in Derbyshire.[16] Adieu! dear Horry, these are foolish stories
but I know no better, so believe me ever

Very sincerely yours,

H. S. C.

Direct *recommandé à Mons[ieur] Selwyn, banquier à Paris.*

To LADY AILESBURY, ca Friday 1 November 1751 OS

Missing; answered *post* 3 Nov. 1751 OS.

---

13. It was presumably the 'rude sculp-
ture, representing a bull hewing out a
statue of the Virgin with its horns' considered the greatest treasure of the monastery at the beginning of the 19th century (Gaston Vuillier, *The Forgotten Isles,*
trans. Breton, New York, 1896, p. 86). A
contemporary description of the monastery and the friars is in John Armstrong,
History of the Island of Minorca, 1752,
pp. 51–2.

14. Santa Águeda or Mount Agatha.
The mountain and fortifications, now
destroyed, are described ibid. 54–6.

15. 'Our soldiers have given this hole
the name of *the Devil's Bellows*' (ibid. 73).

16. Probably Peak Cavern at Castleton.

From LADY AILESBURY, Sunday 3 November 1751 OS

Printed for the first time from the MS now WSL, formerly Rutnam.
Memoranda (by HW):　34—17—0
　　　　　　　　　　　15—15—0
　　　　　　　　　　123—16—6
　　　　　　　　　　　4—14—6
　　　　　　　　　　　1— 5—0
　　　　　　　　　　―――――――
　　　　　　　　　　180— 8—0

K. Henry
Williams
[illegible]

Latimers, November 3, 1751.

Dear Mr Walpole,

I AM vastly obliged to you for your goodness in thinking of me in my distress, which indeed is very great, from this disappointment[1] in regard to Mr Conway's coming home. I believe if circumstances don't alter pretty suddenly in our behalf, which at present I have no reason to expect, I shall be quite determined in a scheme I have formed of going to make him a visit, which I wrote to him some time ago for his approbation of;[2] I am in hopes from a letter[3] I have received from him today that he is by this time diverting himself with fine sights in Italy, which makes me much easier upon his account, as he will be released at least for a time from the

1. From Conway's letter to his brother, Hertford, Florence, 30 Dec. 1751 NS (MS now WSL; printed *Colburn's United Service Magazine*, 1880, lii pt iii. 406–8), replying to a missing one of 18 Nov. OS and a 'former of a much older date,' it is clear that this 'disappointment' related to a regiment for which Conway had asked, but which the D. of Cumberland had indicated he intended to give to Lord Ancram. The specific details are obscure: Conway actually received a regiment of dragoons (the 13th), on 21 Dec. 1751 OS, two months before Ancram succeeded his great-uncle Lord Mark Ker as Colonel of the 11th Dragoons on 15 Feb. 1752 OS. It is possible, however, that Conway had asked for the succession to the 11th Dragoons in the event of Lord Mark Ker's

death, was told that it would be given to Ancram, and then was given the 13th Dragoons when it became available on its colonel's death 12 Nov. 1751 OS (*London Gazette* Nos 9120, 9140, 17–21 Dec. 1751, 11–15 Feb. 1752 OS; GM 1751, xxi. 523; Robert Beatson, *Political Index*, 1806, ii. 193–5). The promotion would have enabled Conway to return to England.

2. This projected visit, which did not take place, is discussed in Conway to Hertford, 30 Dec. 1751 NS. Mann heard in late November NS 'that Lady Ailesbury was either at Mahon or to meet Mr Conway at Marseilles or some other place, to make the tour of Italy with him' (MANN iv. 285).

3. Missing.

terrible place of his banishment, which, I conclude, he has often described to you. I am going in a few days to Miss Townshend's[4] where I propose staying about a fortnight and then returning home, where if you have charity enough to come and see me you'll make me very happy, though it is what I can hardly expect after passing by my house[5] without calling upon me; I think it a little unjust I must own to make you this reproach after the kindness you have just shown me, for which I am very grateful.

I am your obedient and faithful servant,

C. AILESBURY

From CONWAY, Friday 3 December 1751 NS

Printed for the first time from the MS now WSL, formerly Rutnam. HW had received this letter by 12 Dec. OS (MANN iv. 291).

Memoranda (by HW possibly for his reply):

Lord Halif[ax][1]

Mirepo[i]x[2]

Florence,[3] December 3, NS, 1751.

Dear Horry,

IF I have no great right to trouble you after being so unfortunate as not to receive a line from you since I left England (an endless time!) I have still less to be silent were I inclined to it, after owing to you all the goodness, civility and *agrément* that I meet with here from your friend Mr Mann, which besides the immediate pleasure it gives me, secures me the additional satisfaction of knowing you have not quite forgot me and of flattering myself you have writ to me

4. Ewhurst, Hants (*ante* 29 Oct. 1750 OS, n. 9).

5. Presumably either on his visit to Ragley in mid-July or his visit to Woburn at the beginning of October (MONTAGU i. 117, 123), the routes to and from either of which might have taken him close to Latimers.

1. George Montagu (after 1741, Montagu Dunk (1716-71), 2d E. of Halifax. For his political conduct at this time, see *Mem. Geo. II* i. 220.

2. Probably Gaston-Charles-Pierre de Lévis de Lomagne (1699-1757), Marquis (Duc, 1751) de Mirepoix, French ambassador to England 1749-55 (MONTAGU i. 95, n. 36; Henri Jougla de Morenas, *Grand armorial de France*, 1934-49, iv. 456). HW gives an anecdote about him in his letter to Mann 22 Nov. 1751 OS (MANN iv. 289).

3. Mann describes Conway's arrival at Florence in a letter to HW 3 Dec. 1751 NS (ibid. iv. 290-1).

though by some ill luck or other I can't come at your letters for I am resolved to think that is the case; especially as by my calculations on my arrival here I find an interval of a whole month in my correspondence, *hiatus multum deflendus!*[4] I am but just come here as you may imagine or you should have heard from me before, having been tossed about at sea and land but the first particularly for a good six weeks now since I left Mahon: eighteen days at sea, with horrid winds and weather instead of four or five which is the common passage, and twelve more in quarantine[5] still on board. Judge if I was tired of my cage and if even my patience that I know you have a good opinion of was not *poussé à bout;* I longed to be at Florence where I had ordered my letters[6] to hear from my friends and know my fate, which I look upon as determined for the present in regard to my return[7] so that I have now settled myself to my Italian tour happy enough if at the end of it I can escape a second voyage to that dismal place[8] that you have heard a little of in my former letters. But to return to Mr Mann of whom I have not said half enough, nor can't, there's no expressing the extreme goodness and obliging civility with which he has insisted upon my being in his house,[9] the trouble I give him in it and out of it, in going about with me, presenting me, etc. The matter of it I may owe to you and it's a great deal, but the manner which in most people in the same situation and with a total stranger would be constrained, but in him is all ease and natural complaisance can proceed from nothing but his own good heart and disposition. I hear of you from all quarters, and see nothing but your friends and acquaintance; yet I have not yet seen either Madame Griffoni[10] or the Prince de Craon,[11] besides which most people, they

4. The usual form of this phrase is 'Hiatus valde deflendus' ('A gap much to be regretted').

5. Apparently at Genoa, from Conway's description of his travels further on in this letter.

6. A packet of letters for Conway had reached Florence shortly before 26 Nov. NS (ibid. iv. 285).

7. For the reasons for this, see *ante* 3 Nov. 1751 OS and n. 1.

8. Minorca.

9. 'Mr Conway lay one night at the English inn, where he was arrived before I knew he had left Mahon. . . . The next morning I brought him hither and lodged him in your apartment. I thought you had prepared him for it, but he made some resistance, nor yielded till I threatened to complain to you. Now, however, I have nothing to complain of or desire, for he is all goodness and complaisance, and exactly in every respect what I expected from your accounts and letters about him' (Mann to HW 3 Dec. 1751 NS, MANN iv. 290).

10. Elisabetta Capponi (1714–80), m. (1732) Cavaliere Pietro Grifoni; HW's cicisbea at Florence (ibid. i. 33, n. 7).

11. Conway was apparently unaware that Craon had left Florence permanently in May 1749 (ibid. iv. 45).

tell me, are out of town and I have been here but three days. You
may be sure I have but little farther to say of Florence yet; I have
seen the Gallery[12] and that's all; the country appears as agreeable as
you used to think it but I have had the disadvantage of bad weather
in the little I have seen of it. Of the few other places and things I
have seen I shall say little to you who know 'em much better; I
thought Genoa from the sea one of the finest and most uncommon
sights I have seen; that infinite range of buildings all along the coast
that lengthen the town to such an immense extent, those hills covered
with villas and villages, and mountains behind, some crowned with
castles, some with churches and some with snow, make a most pecu-
liar scene. Within, to me at least, it did not quite so well answer the
idea of the proud Genoa; the streets are so terribly narrow that the
best of 'em lose all their dignity as the houses do great part of theirs
for want of an area to show 'em and the painting of 'em I must
think a tawdry and false taste; within indeed the four or five that I
saw are very magnificent, particularly those of Durazzo[13] and Brig-
nole,[14] the former of which, by the by, is entirely in the French taste
and the latter in a good measure so. The country is rougher and
more barren than I could have imagined as the state is poorer and
weaker: a dependent sovereignty and a slavish republic for so they
are pleased to call themselves though a mere and pure aristocracy,
and a commercial state without a naval force! They have the poorest
and at the same time the richest nobility almost in the world. I saw
one myself of no less a name than Doria[15] living with his family in a
garret, literally, and they tell me there are no less than five hospitals
or charity houses full of decayed nobility, one of which is kept by the
Marquess Durazzo[16] close to his palace and has fourteen families in
it. There's no antiquity, I think, to be seen there but an old rostrum

12. The Uffizi; Mann told HW on the
same day: 'I have introduced Mr Conway
into the Gallery, and presented him to
old Bianchi in your name, preparatory to
the course [of medals] he is to go through
with him' (ibid. iv. 290).

13. The Palazzo Durazzo Pallavicini in
the Via Balbi, 'incontestably the finest
private building in the whole city, and its
furniture is answerable to its outward
magnificence' (J. G. Keyssler, Travels,
1756–7, i. 378). Further details of its ap-

pearance in the 18th century are in
[Thomas Martyn], Gentleman's Guide in
his Tour through Italy, 1787, pp. 61–2.

14. The Palazzo Rosso in the Via Gari-
baldi.

15. Not identified.

16. Perhaps Conte (or Marchese) Gia-
como Durazzo (1718–95), Genoese ambassador to Austria 1749–52, imperial ambassador to Venice 1764–?95 (MANN vii.
272, n. 18).

of a ship[17] which might as well be a piece of an old iron crow;[18] and
an abbé of Genoa told me they were curious of no other antiquities
but relics in which indeed they abound sufficiently and are curious
enough of. I saw a moderate quarto book[19] writ upon the emerald
dish in which our Saviour eat the paschal lamb, and the same which
the Queen of Sheba made a present of to Solomon. It's the whole
history of it from that day to this; and in the same is a list[20] of sacred
legs, arms, skulls, teeth etc. to the amount of some hundreds.

The country continues improving, I think, from Lerici where I
came in a felucca but which is in the Genoese state, to this place; the
Duke of Modena[21] is hard at work upon his new port at Lavenza[22]
in the Duchy of Massa and his road from thence to Modena, which
he is carrying on at great expense under the direction of French engineers. This makes a new door to Italy and a direct entrance into
the Duchy of Parma, etc., and 'tis imagined the French contribute
more than their engineers to it. I have not begun to see Florence yet
properly, so say nothing of that: I had said that before but in the
length of my letter forget what I do say; I wish you may too. The
cicisbeo and the *uomo nero*,[23] a personage I dare say you are well
acquainted with, both divert me much.

I hear Lady Pembroke[24] has married a Capt. Bernard. I want to
know if it's that melancholy creature, that *uomo nero*, that used to
walk tête-à-tête with the elder Dives?[25] Adieu: I am advised to say

17. That is, the beak-like projection on
a Roman ship. It hung over the entrance
to the arsenal in the Doge's palace; according to an inscription it was dug up
when the harbour was cleaned in 1597
(Keyssler, op. cit. i. 377).

18. Crow-bar.

19. *Il catino di smeraldo orientale
gemma consagrata da N.S. Gesu' Cristo
nell'ultima cena degli azimi, e custodita
con religiosa pieta' dalla Serenissima Re-
pubblica di Genova*, Genoa, 1726, in over
300 pages 4to, by Fra Gaetano da Santa
Teresa. See also the account of the dish,
still preserved in the cathedral of San
Lorenzo, in Fernand Cabrol *et al., Dictionnaire d'archéologie chrétienne*, 1907–
, vi pt i. 900–3.

20. On pp. 295–9 of Fra Gaetano's book
is a 'Catalogo delle reliquie insigni, che

si custodiscono, e venerano nella metro-
politana di San Lorenzo in Genova.'

21. Francis III (1698–1780), Duke of
Modena, 1737.

22. Avenza.

23. A servant out of livery. HW did not
know what the term meant and had to
ask Mann (MANN iv. 291, 298).

24. Hon. Mary Fitzwilliam (1707–69),
m. 1 (1733) Henry Herbert, 9th E. of
Pembroke (ca 1689–1750); m. 2 (4 Sept.
1751 OS) North Ludlow Bernard (d. 1766),
Maj. of Dragoons (ibid. iv. 281 and nn.
13–14). The match is ridiculed in Henry
Harris to Sir Charles Hanbury Williams
15 Oct. 1751 OS in Williams' MSS (now
WSL) liv. f. 76.

25. Perhaps Charlotte Dyve (ca 1712–
73), m. (1762) Samuel Masham, 2d Bn
Masham; or one of her sisters, Frances or
Dorothy (Coke, *Journals* ii. 185, n. 3).

little of my Italian voyage for fear it should be ill taken at Court, so the less my friends talk of it the better. For the Parliament there's an end of my returning; there's no want of anybody there as you tell Mr Mann[26] without they first pick an opposition, but I'm afraid they won't send for me even for that though last year I got an ill name and one unlucky day acted a mute in one very well[27] for which perhaps I now suffer among my other demerits. You once talked of a voyage to Italy.[28] We'd give something to have you here and talk of you now and then as you'll believe, but you're now such a mere *campagnard* I dare say you have taken root at Strawberry Hill as much as any of your dear plantations. I may laugh at you now; the grapes are sour with me; but as soon as ever I come back I hope to plant and root myself with the best of you.

Yours, dear Horry, most sincerely,

H. S. C.

I have heard but a very dark story of a vast deal of trouble you have had in regard to Lord O[rford]'s affair[29] and but just enough to know what injustice has been done you. 'Twas really too much that should be added to your disappointment on that occasion.

To CONWAY, Thursday 12 December 1751 OS

Missing; mentioned MANN iv. 291. It did not reach Florence until about 28 Jan. 1752 NS, about three weeks after Conway had left for Rome (ibid. iv. 296–7). From Conway's letter to HW 23 Jan. 1752 NS it appears that HW had also written Conway at least three previous letters, one 'of a prodigious old date' received at Florence about 7 Jan. 1752 NS and two earlier ones never received at all.

26. HW to Mann 14 Oct. 1751 OS (MANN iv. 280).

27. On 25 Jan. 1751 OS, when Conway had followed Pitt into the minority by voting against the reduction in the number of seamen proposed by the ministry (ibid. iv. 223 and n. 10; *Mem. Geo. II* i. 12–13).

28. The last time HW seems to have talked seriously of revisiting Florence was in the autumn of 1747 (MANN iii. 443, 447–8).

29. HW's unsuccessful attempt to marry Margaret Nicoll to Lord Orford; see HW's narrative and supplementary documents in GRAY ii. 193–233.

From CONWAY, Sunday 23 January 1752 NS

Printed in full for the first time from the MS now WSL, formerly Rutnam. First printed, with an omission, *Fraser's Magazine*, 1850, xlii. 339–40.

Rome, Jan. 23, 1752 NS.

Dear Horry,

I RECEIVED a letter from you just before I left Florence[1] of a prodigious old date, by which I assure you I had a very particular satisfaction in finding not only that you had not quite forgot me but had been very good in writing two letters before which I never received, and which I assure you I very heartily regret; you won't suspect me of complimenting you when I say such letters must always be very agreeable to an indifferent person, nor when I say their value is doubled to me by all my connections and regards for you; I don't put it in a style of compliment as you see and I assure you I could very sincerely say much more; it felt more awkward and more mortifying than I can express to seem neglected by you; our acquaintance and connection are almost as old as our relation, that is almost as old as ourselves, which by the by begins to grow very old, and I feel both vain and happy when I can flatter myself it is not a mere habitude on your side, finding it so very different from it on my own. Why they robbed me of your letters that as you tell me were neither treasonous nor scandalous I don't know, unless for a very natural reason that might easily escape you though it's pretty obvious to me —because they liked 'em and chose to keep 'em. You see by this my Lady Townshend's bon mot[2] did not find me at Minorca; I am sorry for those poor people who don't hear one in an age, but I certainly was very glad for myself; you'll see where it found me by my last, and though I said something in it of the very easy, polite and agreeable reception I met with there I never can say enough; I never saw a better heart[3] nor with more turn to oblige and to please; I have seen but little of him, or rather but for a little while, for he is one of those marked characters one can't but know immediately, especially in the situation I was in, where I had such constant ex-

---

1. Conway planned to leave Florence for Rome 8 Jan. NS (MANN iv. 295); the 'very old letter' to him from HW is mentioned ibid. iv. 296.

2. This has not been found.
3. Than Mann's.

perience of it; I left Florence with great regret I assure you, but after staying five weeks instead of five days found it absolutely necessary;[4] or to abandon all thoughts of Rome, which besides my curiosity for the *Gran' Città* that you know I have long entertained I thought 'twould really be too ridiculous after coming so far and so near it. I saw but little of the Griffoni at Florence and by the little I did see it's a shocking truth, but it must out some time or other, I can't think her handsome; as to agreeable, there are so many tastes, I shall say nothing; to say the truth it is not fair, I saw so little of her, but her sister Antinori[5] pleased me vastly; she's infinitely agreeable and sensible and for a beauty of that age very handsome. The loves and scandals and odd stories of Florence would fill a volume; there are of all sorts serious and comic; but much more of the latter; it's a scene of cicisbeship, of intrigue and lewdness beyond anything, in all kinds of people of all orders, ages, and conditions and in all ways.[6] There's a strange creature, a countryman of ours, one Harper,[7] brother-in-law to the Rutlands,[8] an ugly middle-aged man, who is desperately in love with Senator Pucci,[9] one of his own standing or older; they have such disputes and jealousies and *amantium ira* it's a farce; he has been leaving Florence this year or two but can't quit his dear Senator! The grand flame of Florence is a Madame Acciaiuoli,[10] Mr Pelham's[11] flame, a Mr Langley's[12] flame, now a young Floren-

4. Mann told HW 7 Jan. NS that Conway's 'last letters from England made him change the resolution he had taken to stay here some time longer' if he were to visit Rome at all (ibid. iv. 295); these were probably the letters Conway mentions below as flattering him 'with a regiment of dragoons and a sudden recall.'

5. Teresa Maria Capponi (1715–55), m. (1734) Senator Vincenzo Antinori (ibid. i. 33, n. 6).

6. Conway wrote to his brother shortly before leaving Florence: 'There are but two things at all thought of here—love and antiquities, of which the former predominates so greatly that I think it seems to make the whole history and the whole business of this place, and for a stander-by like me is really a comical scene enough' (30 Dec. 1751 NS, MS now WSL; printed *Colburn's United Service Magazine*, 1880, lii pt iii. 407–8).

7. Probably Edward Harpur (d. 1761), son of Sir John Harpur, 4th Bt (*London*

Magazine, 1761, xxx. 448; William Betham, *Baronetage*, 1801–5, i. 281, 282).

8. Harpur's eldest brother Sir Henry Harpur (?1708–48) 5th Bt, m. (1734) Lady Caroline Manners, half-sister of the 3d D. of Rutland.

9. Probably Lorenzo Orazio Pucci (1694–1764), senator, 1736; he seems to be the only Pucci who was a senator at this time (Pompeo Litta *et al.*, *Famiglie celebri italiane*, Milan, Turin, and Naples, 1819–1923, *sub* Pucci, table vii).

10. Marianna Acciaioli (b. 1725), m. (1742) Giacinto Emanuele Acciaioli (MANN i. 444, n. 11). Mann mentions her successive affairs at this time in his letter to HW 26 Nov. 1751 NS (ibid. iv. 284).

11. Thomas Pelham (1728–1805) of Stanmer, 2d Bn Pelham, 1768; cr. (1801) E. of Chichester; M.P. Rye 1749–54, Sussex 1754–68. For his affair with Mme Acciaioli between Feb. and Aug. 1750, see ibid. iv. 115–16, 129, 172–3.

12. Mann calls him 'Jacky Langlois'

tine's one Pecci's,[13] and soon they say to be another's, and what's particular, perhaps the homeliest young woman in Florence, and there really are many; of beauties I count but four.

I came hither with Lord Stormont, an acquaintance I just began at Paris[14] and improved at Florence and you'll believe I think myself lucky in it when I say he is one [of] the most agreeable young men I have known, both sensible and lively; we have lived together since we came here and shall, I suppose, till we go now; I mean till I go which I expect soon as all my letters flatter me of late with a regiment of dragoons and a sudden recall;[15] though whether I shall be able to obey it immediately I don't know; the weather is so very bad and such colds that I fancy the Alps must be impassable; with all that, you may imagine I shan't be very long in attempting it at least. In the meantime we live here in one perpetual hurry and *giro* enough to turn one's head, three hours every morning for the antiquities and two more for the palaces, pictures, etc.; late dinner, dressing after the opera and company. Here's your old friend the Venetian Ambassadress,[16] as silly and whimsical as ever; we have been at her balls and she insists upon having known me very well in England; she told us last night at the Princess Borghese's[17] that she had miscarried twice by country dances, and lost four children by it so they were both double. At her own t'other night she did not stir till it was just over and then danced forlanas,[18] dragged everybody about the room and made the fiddlers dance with her all round the house. Here's Lord Charlemont[19] here, and Lord Tilney driven hither from

when mentioning him as Pelham's successor with Mme Acciaioli; he was perhaps a younger brother of Christopher Langlois who was in trouble at Florence in 1747 (ibid. iii. 366 and n. 3, 374; iv. 284), and perhaps the John Langlois who died in Woodstock Street, Bond Street, in 1789 (GM 1789, lix pt i. 182).

13. Mann describes Mme Acciaioli's cicisbeo in Nov. 1751 as 'a young Marquis Pucci who succeeded Lord Rockingham with the Siristori' (MANN iv. 284). We guess there that this may have been Domenico Pucci, but it is more likely to have been Marchese Orazio Roberto Pucci (1730–1802), nephew of HW's friend Mme Pucci (Litta, op. cit., *sub* Pucci, table viii).

14. Conway had mentioned him *ante* 14 July 1751 NS.

15. This was true, although Conway had not yet learned of it officially; see *ante* 3 Nov. 1751 OS and n. 1, MANN iv. 297, 299, 304. Conway left Rome for England about 13 Feb. NS (ibid. iv. 304; *post* ca 15 Feb. 1752 OS).

16. Mme Capello (*ante* 27 June 1748 OS and n. 9).

17. Agnese Colonna (1702–80), m. (1723) Principe Camillo Borghese, a frequent hostess to visiting English at Rome (MANN i. 12, n. 51; SELWYN 5, n. 17).

18. Or furlanas, an Italian dance in 6–8 or 6–4 time, a favourite with the Venetian gondoliers (Sir George Grove, *Dictionary of Music and Musicians*, ed. Blom, 1954–61, iii. 429).

19. James Caulfeild (1728–99), 4th Vct Charlemont, cr. (1763) E. of Charlemont.

Calais by contrary winds in his way to England literally so; he was forced on shore at Ostend and set out immediately for Rome; with this he's really a good little creature. Adieu, dear Horry, believe me ever

Very sincerely yours,

H. S. C.

I'll talk of Rome at the end of Warwick Street.[20]

From Lady Ailesbury, ca Saturday 15 February 1752 OS

Printed for the first time from the MS now WSL, formerly Rutnam. Dated by the reference to the letter from Conway 6 Feb. NS from Rome, which could not have been received in England until about 15 Feb. OS at the earliest.

Address: To Mr Walpole.

Memoranda (by HW):[1]   40

$$\frac{28 = 7}{68 = 7}$$

145

Ly Catherine Pelham[2]	French Ambassador[5]
Ly Lincoln	Count Haslang[6]
Miss Pelhams[3]	Ly Yarmouth
Ld & Ly Hartington	Ld Winchelsea[7]
Ld & Ly Duncannon[4]	Mr Herbert[8]
Ld & Ly Holderness	D & Ds of Bedford

He had been abroad since 1746 and remained until 1754.

20. Charing Cross, where Conway lived in London (*Court and City Register,* 1751, p. 57).

---

1. This list of names may be a list of the guests at the 'immense assembly' given by Lord Chesterfield to show Chesterfield House in mid-February 1752 (MANN iv. 302).

2. Lady Catherine Manners (ca 1701–80), m. (1726) Henry Pelham.

3. Frances Pelham (1728–1804); Grace Pelham (ca 1731–77), m. (1752) Lewis Watson, cr. (1760) Bn Sondes; and Mary Pel-

ham (1739–94), the youngest daughter of Henry Pelham.

4. William Ponsonby (1704–93), styled Vct Duncannon 1739–58, 2d E. of Bessborough, 1758; m. (1739) Lady Caroline Cavendish (1719–60).

5. Mirepoix (*ante* 3 Dec. 1751 NS, n. 2).

6. Josef Frans Xaver (ca 1700–83), Freiherr (later Graf) von Haszlang, Bavarian minister to England 1741–83 (MONTAGU i. 185–6, n. 25).

7. Daniel Finch (1689–1769), 8th E. of Winchilsea and 3d E. of Nottingham.

8. Probably the Hon. Robert Sawyer Herbert (d. 1769), 2d son of the 8th E. of

Ly Ossory[9]
Ld Trentham[10]
Mr Leveson[11]
Ly Pembroke
Ld Harrington[12]
Mr Stanhope[13]
Mr Blair
Ld & Ly Chesterfield[14]
Ly Ch. Edwin[15]
Ly Townshend
Ly Ferrers[16]
Ly Albemarle
Ly Keppels[17]
Mr Keppel[18]
Ly Archibald[19]

Mr and Miss Hamilton
Ds of Norfolk
Miss Clifford[20]
Ly Bel Finch[21]
Mr Rigby[22]
Miss Sheperd[23]
Ld Hobart[24]
2 Miss Homes
Mr Seabright[25]
Ld & Ly Northum[berland][26]
Ld & Ly Hertford
Miss Conway[27]
Ly Mary Powis[28]
Ly Jane Scot[29]
Sir J. Bland[30]

Pembroke (Collins, *Peerage*, 1812, iii. 141–2).

9. Hon. Evelyn Leveson Gower (1725–63), m. 1 (1744) John Fitzpatrick, 2d Bn Gowran, cr. (1751) E. of Upper Ossory; m. 2 (1759) Richard Vernon (Sir Bernard Burke and A. P. Burke, *Peerage*, 1928, p. 2217).

10. Granville Leveson Gower (1721–1803), styled Vct Trentham 1746–54; 2d E. Gower, 1754; cr. (1786) M. of Stafford.

11. Either the Hon. Richard Leveson Gower (1726–53), 4th son of the 1st E. Gower, or one of his uncles, the Hon. William Leveson Gower (ca 1696–1756) and the Hon. Baptist **Leveson Gower** (?1703–82); all M.P.s.

12. William Stanhope (ca 1683–1756), cr. (1730) Bn and (1742) E. of Harrington.

13. Possibly Philip Stanhope (1732–68), natural son of Lord Chesterfield.

14. Petronille Melusine de Schulenburg (1693–1778), cr. (1722) Cts of Walsingham, s.j.; m. (1733) Philip Dormer Stanhope, 4th E. of Chesterfield.

15. Lady Charlotte Hamilton (ca 1703–77), m. (1736) Charles Edwin.

16. Lady Charlotte Compton (d. 1770), m. (1751) Hon. George Townshend, 4th Vct Townshend, 1764; Bns Ferrers, s.j., 1749; Bns Compton, s.j., 1754.

17. Lady Caroline Keppel (1737–69), m. (1759) Robert Adair; and Lady Elizabeth Keppel (1739–68), m. (1764) Francis Russell, styled M. of Tavistock.

18. Probably the Hon. Augustus Keppel

(1725–86), cr. (1782) Vct Keppel, Lady Albemarle's second son.

19. Lady Jane Hamilton (d. 1752), m. (1719) Lord Archibald Hamilton.

20. Probably Hon. Mary Clifford (1731–97), m. (1766) Sir Edward Smythe, 4th Bt.

21. Lady Isabella Finch (d. 1771), lady of the Bedchamber to Princess Amelia.

22. Richard Rigby (1722–88), politician.

23. Probably Frances Gibson Shepheard (1734–1807), illegitimate dau. and heiress of Samuel Shepherd of Exning, Suffolk; m. (1758) Charles Ingram, 9th Vct Irvine. Her eldest dau. eventually married Lord Hertford's eldest son (*post* 25, 30 Sept. 1775).

24. John Hobart (1723–93), styled Bn Hobart 1746–56, 2d E. of Buckinghamshire, 1756.

25. Probably Sir John Saunders Sebright (1725–94), 6th Bt, 1761 (BERRY i. 286).

26. Hugh Smithson (after 1750, Percy) (1714 *or* 1715–86), 4th Bt, 2d E. of Northumberland, 1750, cr. (1766) D. of Northumberland; m. (1740) Lady Elizabeth Seymour (1716–76).

27. Hon. Anne Seymour Conway.

28. Lady Mary Brudenell (b. ca 1717) m. 1 (1735) Richard Powys; m. 2 (1754) Thomas Bowlby (Sir Bernard Burke and A. P. Burke, *Peerage*, 1928, p. 79; Joan Wake, *The Brudenells of Deene*, 1954, pp. 222–3, 255; Namier and Brooke ii. 108; Sedgwick ii. 368).

29. (1723–79).

30. Sir John Bland (ca 1722–55), 6th Bt; M.P.

Ld & Ly Bath[31]	Ld & Mr Walgrave[36]
Ld & Ly Cobham	Ld March[37]
Ld Pulteney[32]	Ld Sussex[38]
Miss Banks[33]	Mr Brand[39]
Ld Eglington[34]	Ld & Ly Brooke[40]
Ld Cathcart	D. of Kingston
Col. Barrington[35]	Ld Tyrawley[41]

I'M afraid you'll think I plague you to death about my husband, but I must tell you that I have just received another letter from him of Feb. 6 NS.[42] in which he complains of not having had any letter from England in near a fortnight, and concludes I am either sick or dead, but as he has some hopes in the midst of all his fears, he is come to a resolution of waiting only one week longer at Rome, and then setting out for Paris to know his fate.[43] I desire to know your thoughts upon this subject, and that you will condole with me a little upon this occasion.

Yours,

C. AILESBURY

31. Anna Maria Gumley (ca 1694–1758), m. (1714) William Pulteney, cr. (1742) E. of Bath.

32. William Pulteney (ca 1731–63), styled Vct Pulteney 1742–63; M.P.

33. Margaret ('Peggy') Banks (d. 1793), m. (1757) Hon. Henry Grenville.

34. Alexander Montgomerie (1723–69), 10th E. of Eglintoun.

35. Hon. John Barrington (d. 1764), army officer (MONTAGU i. 127, n. 18).

36. James Waldegrave (1715–63), 2d E. Waldegrave; and his brother John Waldegrave (1718–84), 3d E. Waldegrave, 1763.

37. William Douglas (1725–1810), 3d E. of March; 4th D. of Queensberry, 1778.

38. George Augustus Yelverton (1727–58), 2d E. of Sussex.

39. Thomas Brand (ca 1717–70), HW's correspondent.

40. Francis Greville (1719–73), 8th Bn Brooke, cr. (1746) E. Brooke and (1759) E. of Warwick; m. (1742) Elizabeth Hamilton (ca 1721–1800), who married (2) Gen. Robert Clerk.

41. James O'Hara (ca 1682–1773), 2d Bn Tyrawley.

42. Missing. HW had previously written to Mann 2 Feb. 1752 OS that 'we are much surprised by two letters which my Lady Ailesbury has received from Mr Conway, to find that he had not yet heard of his new regiment' (MANN iv. 299).

43. Conway reached London about 10 March OS, a week earlier than he was expected (ibid. iv. 309).

From CONWAY, Tuesday ?March ?1752

Printed for the first time from the MS now WSL, formerly Rutnam. Dated tentatively on the assumption that it was written soon after Conway returned to England ca 10 March 1752 OS (MANN iv. 309). The inquiry after Mrs Leneve also suggests 1752, since it appears from *post* 2 May 1752 OS that she was then ill.

Address: To the Honourable Horatio Walpole Junior Arlington Street.

Tuesday evening.

I HAVE a little favour to beg of you, which is that you'll find out for me if you can who got a French *dessert*[1] of Lady Mary Churchill's out of the custom house yesterday and what duty was paid for it, because I sent my servant today to take out one of mine and they charged so monstrously for it that he was forced to leave it there; I know Lady Mary's is pretty much the same as my own which is the reason of my curiosity and a suspicion that they use me ill there for they told me at Paris I was to pay but 15 pence or some such thing in the pound *ad valorem* and they demand almost as much as the things cost me.

Yours, dear Horry, most faithfully,

H. S. C.

How does Mrs Leneve do?

---

1. Apparently a *desserte*, a name sometimes applied to a side-table or dumb-waiter; this usage is not listed in Littré, but is given in most French-English dictionaries as a meaning for the word. Henry Havard, *Dictionnaire de l'ameublement et de la décoration*, [1887–90], ii. 81–2, gives both *dessert* and *desserte*, but both of them seem to be types of fruit baskets and serving dishes.

From CONWAY, ca Thursday 30 April 1752 OS

Printed for the first time from the MS now WSL, formerly Rutnam. Dated tentatively from the contents which seem to have been written shortly before Conway and Lady Ailesbury left London ca 1 May OS to join his regiment in Ireland; on 5 May OS HW mentions that he has had Conway's daughter with him 'these four first days,' and on 2 May Conway apologizes for writing so soon after he had left (see *post* 2, 5 May 1752 OS).

Address: To Mr Walpole.

MY operator is Cuenotte:[1] but for the dimensions of the chimney pieces[2] and doors they are unknown; and for the doors we seem determined to have 'em plain so that there remains only the chimney piece and a frame for our glasses about which I question if it's worthwhile to trouble Mr Bentley,[3] as Cuenotte is to bring me a design today and seems to understand the affair. I wish you much health and as Lord Lovat said, much pleasure with your *young* wife.[4]

Yours,

H. S. C.

1. Rupert Gunnis, *Dictionary of British Sculptors 1660–1851*, [1953], p. 90, mentions a John Ceunot (b. ca 1740, d. before 1782), whom he describes as the son of a French sculptor John Ceunot, but no person of this name is mentioned in French dictionaries of artists, sculptors, or architects. There was a François Cuenot (ca 1610 – after 1683), woodcarver, whose son Pierre-François received the reversion of engineer, architect and sculptor to the Duke of Savoy (Stanislas Lami, *Dictionnaire des sculpteurs de l'école française sous la règne de Louis XIV*, 1906, p. 139); and a Cuenot, a wax modeller, exhibited at the Society of Artists in 1771 (Algernon Graves, *Society of Artists of Great Britain 1760–1791; The Free Society of Artists 1761–83*, 1907, p. 68). See also *post* 23 Aug. 1752 OS.

2. Presumably at Park Place, Berks, the estate which Conway had recently purchased and was redecorating (*post* 2 May 1752 OS). Cuenot's drawing for a chimney piece is mentioned ibid.

3. Richard Bentley (1708–82), HW's friend and correspondent, who designed the early rooms at SH.

4. Conway's daughter, who was staying with HW during her parents' absence (MANN iv. 317; *post* 2, 5 May 1752 OS).

From CONWAY, Saturday 2 May 1752 OS

Printed for the first time from the MS now WSL, formerly Rutnam.
Address: To the Honourable Horatio Walpole, Junior, in Arlington Street, London.
Postmark: 4 MA. LICHFIELD.

Welch Harp,[1] May 2d, 1752.

Dear Horry,

YOU'LL be surprised perhaps at my hurry in troubling you with this; but not so much at Lady Ailesbury's having something to say about Miss;[2] I say Lady Ailesbury though we are both parties in the affair, which is that having agreed the country air is proper for her after the smallpox[3] we shall beg the favour if it is equally convenient that you'll send for Missy to Strawberry instead of keeping her in town; but if it is not entirely so to desire you'll be so good as to let her go with Mathews, our servant, who will be still in town, to Park Place[4] till the time you go to Strawberry[5] when upon your summons she shall be immediately conveyed to you; where I don't doubt she'll be as happy and as much obliged to you for your goodness as we are for that you have already showed in desiring to be troubled with brats before your time. We are advanced about 120 miles of our long journey with very good success. Adieu, 'tis not a place or time for long letters, but I am glad of this little opportunity to assure you how much

I am yours,

H. S. C.

Lady A. and Nanny[6] beg their compliments. Mine to poor Mrs Leneve; I hope she's better. I gave you my direction (at William

1. Apparently an inn in or near Lichfield, from the postmark and Conway's statement that they were 'advanced about 120 miles of our long journey.' Conway was en route to Sligo to join his regiment (MANN iv. 316; *post* 22 May 1752 OS).
2. Their daughter, who had been left with HW (*ante* ca 30 April, *post* 5 May 1752 OS).
3. That is, after her inoculation for it.
4. Near Henley, which Conway had just

purchased from the Ps of Wales (MANN iv. 316–17). The estate had been owned by the Prince since about 1738 (Percy Noble, *Park Place,* 1905, p. 14).
5. HW wrote *post* 5 May 1752 OS that she was to go to SH in 'two or three days' and that he would follow her 'in less than a fortnight.' On 12 May he wrote to Montagu that he was going to SH 'in three days for the summer' (MONTAGU i. 130).
6. Conway's sister Anne.

THE HONBLE. HENRY SEYMOUR CONWAY, CAROLINE COUNTESS OF AILESBURY
(IN FANCY DRESS), AND THEIR CHILD ANNE SEYMOUR CONWAY.
By permission of Mrs. Campbell Johnston.

HON. HENRY SEYMOUR CONWAY,
LADY AILESBURY AND THE HON. ANNE SEYMOUR CONWAY,
BY JOHN GILES ECCARDT

Chaignau's,[7] Esq. in Lower Castleyard, Dublin) and hope to hear from you. Lady Ailesbury says she has promises from you, but I desire she mayn't engross you. I have taken the liberty of sending Bromich[8] to you with green papers; be so good as to choose one of a small pattern for me; and as you allowed me to do it I shall take the same about our India-room chimney etc., the drawing of which Mr Cuenot[9] shall show you. He lives in Warwick Street; not ours.[10]

7. William Chaigneau (1709–81), novelist and 'principal agent to most of the regiments on the Irish establishment' (DNB).

8. Thomas Bromwich (d. 1787), a fashionable decorator who kept a shop on Ludgate Hill (GM 1787, lvii pt ii. 646). He did a great deal of work at SH after 1754; see the references collected in *Strawberry Hill Accounts*, ed. Toynbee, Oxford, 1927, pp. 66–7.

9. See *ante* ca 30 April 1752 OS, n. 1.

10. Warwick Street, Golden Square, or Warwick Street, St Marylebone.

To Conway, Tuesday 5 May 1752 OS

Printed from the MS now WSL; first printed, Wright ii. 419–20. For the history of the MS, see *ante* 29 June 1744 OS.

Endorsed: Mr H. Walpole Junior.

Memoranda: [in an unidentified hand in pencil]

> Welde in Castle Street[1]
> Hat and Hatter in Temple Bar
> Buff belt
> Fusil and Sword

> [in Conway's hand, in ink, apparently a
> list of army officers and personnel
> with their addresses in Dublin]

> Cap. Fitzgerald   Dawson Street 5
> Lord J. Murray[2]   Damas Street 4
> Cap. Lushington[3]   Cuff Street 6
> Mr Crom. Price[4]
> Mr Stevenson[5]   Grafton Street 7
> Capt. Killigrew[6]   Caple Street. Up. End 1
> Mr Rob[ert] Maxwell   Primate's Hill:
>   or Henrietta Str. 2
> Col. La Devise[7]

1. A street in Dublin.

2. Lord John Murray (1711–87), Col. of the 42d Foot (Black Watch) 1745–87, at this time stationed in Ireland (*Court and City Register*, 1753, p. 155; *Scots Peerage* i. 485–6; Archibald Forbes, *The 'Black Watch,'* New York, 1897, p. 40).

3. Probably William Lushington (d. 1786), Capt., 1749, in the 9th Dragoons, at this time stationed in Ireland; later Maj., 1756, and Lt-Col., 1760, of the 8th Dragoons (*Army Lists*, 1756, p. 117, 1758, p. 32, 1765, p. 32; *Court and City Register*, 1753, p. 152; GM 1786, lvi pt i. 620).

4. Not identified, but probably a descendant of Cromwell's son-in-law, John Claypoole, through his daughter by his second wife Bridget (d. 1738), m. Charles Price, army officer (Mark Noble, *Memoirs of the Protectoral House of Cromwell*, 1787, ii. 385–6).

5. Perhaps St George Stevenson, Lt

since 1747 in the 5th Dragoons, which was stationed in Ireland at this time; Capt., 1758 (*Court and City Register*, 1753, p. 151; *Army Lists*, 1756, p. 115, 1759, p. 29).

6. Probably George Augustus Killigrew, Capt., 1752, in the 3d Regiment of Horse, which was stationed in Ireland at this time (ibid., 1756, p. 113; *Court and City Register*, 1753, p. 150). He is perhaps the 'Major Killigrew of the Reg. of carabineers on the Irish Establishment' who died in 1757 (GM 1757, xxvii. 386).

7. No Col. or Lt-Col. of this or a similar name has been found in the *Army Lists*. A John Ladeveze had become a cornet in the 13th Dragoons (now Conway's) in 1750; a Lt in 1756; Capt. 5th Dragoons, 1764 (GM 1750, xx. 92; Robert Beatson, *Political Index*, 1806, ii. 195; *Army Lists*, 1756, p. 119, 1765, p. 29). He does not appear in the *Army Lists* after 1766.

Major Leslie[8]   Grafton Street 8
Mr Clements   Primate's Hill 3
Mr Commissary Richardson   Batchelor's Walk 2

Arlington Street, May 5th, 1752.

I NOW entirely credit all that my Lord Leicester[9] and his family have said against Lady Mary Coke and her family, and am convinced that it is impossible to marry anything of the blood of Campbell, without having all her relations in arms to procure a separation immediately![10] Pray, what have I done? Have I come home drunk to my wife within these four first days?[11] Or have I sat up gaming all night and not come home at all to her, after her Lady Mother[12] had been persuaded that I was the soberest young nobleman in England, and had the greatest aversion to play?[13] Have I kept my bride awake all night with railing at her father,[14] when all the world had allowed him to be one of the bravest officers in Europe—in short, in short, I have a mind to take counsel, even of the wisest lawyer now living in matrimonial cases, my Lord Coke—or I think rather[15] . . . country, and not let her se . . . To show you at lea . . . if other Norfolk husbands, and must entertain the town with a formal parting, at least it shall be in my own way: my wife shall neither run to Italy

8. Probably the Hon. William Leslie (d. 1764), at this time aide-de-camp to his brother, the 9th E. of Rothes, Lt-Gen. of Ireland; later major commandant of invalids in Ireland (*Scots Peerage* vii. 305; *Court and City Register*, 1753, p. 149).

9. Thomas Coke (1697–1759), cr. (1728) Bn Lovel and (1744) E. of Leicester.

10. Lady Mary Coke, Lady Ailesbury and her daughter belonged to the Campbell family (*post* 18 July, 29 Dec. 1759). HW is answering Conway's request about his daughter (*ante* 2 May 1752 OS) in terms of Lady Mary's 'separation' from Lord Leicester's son after the quarrels mentioned *ante* 27 June 1748 OS; see Lady Louisa Stuart's account in Coke, *Journals* i. pp. lxiv–lxxi.

11. 'He [Coke] almost immediately resumed his former habits of gaming and drinking' (ibid. i. p. lxi). See also HW to Mann 12 Jan. 1748 OS (MANN iii. 456–7).

12. Lady Ailesbury. Lady Mary Coke's mother was the Dowager Duchess of Argyll.

13. The Ds of Argyll wrote to her daughter Lady Dalkeith: 'You must know that with conversing a good deal with him [Coke], I like him very much; he appears to me to have a very good understanding, and a great deal of knowledge, and I think a very sweet disposition. That of his play, to be sure, was entirely owing to his father, which he designs to lay quite aside' (Coke, op. cit. i. p. cxxiii). See also Lady Louisa Stuart's account in ibid. i. pp. lix–lx.

14. 'He [Coke] lost no opportunity of attacking her father's memory, ridiculing her mother, disparaging the name of Campbell, and slyly throwing out whatever else could irritate her the most' (ibid. i. p. lxi).

15. A piece has been cut off the bottom of the MS, leaving only the first four words of the last three lines on the first page, and the last few words of the concluding three lines of the letter on the second page.

after lovers and books,[16] nor keep a dormitory in her dressing room at Whitehall for Westminster schoolboys,[17] your *Frederick Campbells*[18] and such like, nor yet shall she reside at her mother's house;[19] but shall absolutely set out for Strawberry Hill in two or three days, as soon as her room can be well-aired, for to give her her due, I don't think her to blame, but flatter myself she is quite contented with the easy foot we live upon; separate beds, dining in her dressing room when she is out of humour, and a little toad-eater[20] that I had got for her, and whose pockets and bosom I have never examined to see if she brought any *billets-doux* from Tommy Lyttelton[21] or any of her fellows. I shall follow her myself in less than a fortnight, and if her family don't give me any more trouble—why, who knows but at your return you may find your daughter with qualms and in a sack? If you should happen to want to know any more particulars, she is quite well, has walked in the park every morning, or has the chariot as she chooses, and in short, one would think that I or she were much older than we really are, for I grow excessively fond of . . . and exactness; I am . . . after these orders, . . . and your sincerely

H. W.

16. Like Lady Orford, HW's sister-in-law.

17. Like Lady Townshend.

18. Later Lord Frederick Campbell (1729–1816), Lady Ailesbury's brother; lord clerk register of Scotland 1768–1816; M.P. Glasgow burghs 1761–80, Argyllshire 1780–99; HW's executor. For Lady Townshend's fondness for him see SELWYN 84 and a letter from his father to Lady Townshend, 30 Sept. 1746, in Hist. MSS Comm., 11th Report, App. pt iv, *Townshend MSS*, 1887, pp. 360–2.

19. The Leicesters had finally agreed that Lady Mary Coke might live at Sudbrook, her mother's house 'unmolested; upon condition that she should withdraw her suit [for divorce], pay its expenses herself, never set her foot in town, and have no separate maintenance but her pin-money' (Coke, op. cit. i. p. lxxi). Lady Mary was released from this confinement by her husband's death in 1753.

20. Perhaps her nurse, Mrs Elizabeth Jones (*post* 23 Sept. 1755).

21. Thomas Lyttelton (1744–79), 2d Bn Lyttelton, 1773, the 'wicked' Lord Lyttelton. His mother, who had died in 1747, had been a close friend of Lady Ailesbury (SELWYN 327, n. 16) as was his step-mother, a frequent visitor at Park Place; the children were presumably playmates. See also *post* 16 Nov. 1752.

To Lady Ailesbury, ca Monday 18 May 1752 OS

Missing; mentioned *post* 9 June 1752 OS as having been received in Dublin 'above a fortnight ago'; it would have taken the letter about a week to reach Ireland.

From Conway, Friday 22 May 1752 OS

Printed in full for the first time from the MS now wsl, formerly Rutnam. First printed in part, *Fraser's Magazine*, 1850, xlii. 340.

Memorandum (by HW): One may guess at what people would do if they had some passions, or if they had an opportunity of gratifying their passions, by their manner of correcting or indulging the passions they have or can gratify. Dorinna loves play, and games, for she is rich. She loves eating, and eats excessively, for she has a good cook. She loves drinking and drinks, for she generally sups alone. If she was not hideous, she would be common, for she does love her husband.

Belturbet,[1] May 22d 1752.

I SHOULD have thanked you before for your ready compliance with our parental injunctions but was in such a continual hurry during the few days I stayed in Dublin I had not a moment to command; and now that you have complied and as I have great ambition to see my daughter in a sack and to become a grandfather, I think I may promise you shall have no farther trouble from her parents, for to do you and her justice she has yet made no complaint at all of you either for what you have done or have not, which I don't doubt she would as all modest young ladies do, had there been the least room for it and all the old ladies in town would have whispered it about to their neighbours at church long ago, but on the contrary I now see you settled at Strawberry, you and her and the *boy*[2] in all sorts of matrimonial comfort and harmony of which I desire you'll wish her joy in my name. I am not vain enough to send you congratulations, though I really flatter myself sometimes she makes a tolerable wife; a little capricious I doubt and subject to humour now and then but agreeable enough in her gayer hours, and even engaging when she pleases. However, to show how disinterested I am in my encomiums, if you don't like her upon trial (what few parents would), on our

1. In co. Cavan on the river Erne.   2. See *ante* 5 May 1752 OS, n. 21.

return we'll take her off your hands again towards the month of August or so, by which time you'll have had as much proof almost as any Dutch lover. I am at present under the circumstances of reviewing with an head full of firelocks, pistols, swords, jack-boots and returns; tomorrow we perform before Gen. Bligh[3] and in about a week after march for our new quarters at Sligo; Lady Ailesbury whom I left in Dublin joins me here and we proceed immediately, there to stay a decent time, see the regiment settled and then to Park Place, where you may imagine we are rather impatient to be and where we expect you'll bring your wife to make us a visit or if you are resolved to resign her I desire at least you'll come yourself and do it in a decent manner. What shall I tell you of Belturbet? It's a strange, dirty, Irish country town, a market town, if you will, and a borough town[4] but yet as mean in appearance as most of our villages and dirtier almost than any; yet here our whole regiment is assembled, here we have had horse races since I came and here we had a ball two nights ago and what is strangest of all, out of these dirty holes like rabbit burrows they turn eight or ten good genteel girls, really well dressed and fit to appear at any Yorke or Chester assembly, and good dancers. Lady Ailesbury and Nanny in the meantime are feasting and gadding in Dublin at their Vauxhalls and I don't know what. They pretend it's very dull but I am afraid they'll find Sligo rather more so. Adieu, give my love to your spouse and believe me, dear Horry,

Most sincerely yours,

H. S. C.

---

3. Thomas Bligh *or* Blighe (1685–1775), Maj.-Gen., 1747; Lt-Gen., 1754; M.P. Athboy (in Ireland) 1715–75.

4. That is, it returned members to Parliament.

From Lady Ailesbury, Tuesday 9 June 1752 OS

Printed for the first time from the MS now wsl, formerly Rutnam.
Address: To the Honourable Horatio Walpole at his house in Arlington Street, London. Free H.S. Conway [in Conway's hand].
Postmark: 20 IV.
Memoranda (by HW, unexplained):

Lord Abergavenny[1]	Lord Vere[4]
Lady Townsh[end]	Mr Harding[5]
Lady Cardigan	Mr Carey[6]
Mrs Clive[2]	Lord Northumb[erland]
Lady Fanny Shirley[3]	Mrs Cavendish[7]

Other memoranda on this letter for HW to Conway 23 June 1752 OS are printed with that letter.

Sligoe, June 9, 1752.

I HEAR from all sides that there never was so indulgent a husband or so fond a wife as Mr and Mrs Walpole; I must after this own myself a wicked stepmother in never thanking you before for all this goodness, and a letter I received from you above a fortnight ago; if I was to tell you that I had not a minute to myself, and was in a continual hurry of engagements all the time I was in Dublin you will scarce believe me, as perhaps you will not that Sligoe is a very gay place, and furnishes out an assembly once a fortnight. We have been settled here about five days, and have had the good luck to get a tolerable house, and find everything better than we expected, being as they say here a very plentiful country, yet I must own between friends that our greatest comfort is the thoughts of leaving it much sooner than we first intended,[8] so that I now begin to indulge myself sometimes in thinking of my young woman and Park Place, which I used to endeavour to hurry out of my head

1. George Nevill (1727–85), 17th, 10th, or 5th Bn Abergavenny, cr. (1784) E. of Abergavenny.
2. Catherine Raftor (1711–85), m. (1732) George Clive; actress.
3. Lady Frances Shirley (ca 1706–78).
4. Lord Vere Beauclerk (1699–1781), cr. (1750) Bn Vere of Hanworth.
5. Probably Nicholas Hardinge (1699–1758), clerk of the House of Commons 1731–48, M.P. Eye 1748–58, joint secretary to the Treasury 1752–8.

6. Possibly Walter Carey (1685–1757), M.P. Helston 1722–7, Dartmouth 1727–57; or a Mr Cary listed on HW's letter to Mann 4 May 1753 (MANN iv. 375).
7. Probably Elizabeth Cavendish (d. 1779), dau. of Lord James Cavendish, 3d son of 1st D. of Devonshire; m. (1732) Richard Chandler, later Cavendish (SELWYN 270, n. 13).
8. Conway had told HW in his previous letter that they did not expect to be back in England until August.

whenever they came there. If you hear of Miss Anne's being disposed of to one of the dragoon officers don't be surprised for I think
she has a passion already for a handsome lieutenant. I was vastly
surprised at a piece of news that came last night from Mrs Harris[9] in
a letter to Miss Anne and that was of Lady Die Egerton's[10] match
being off; if this is true I beg you will entertain us in your next
with all the reasons that are given for it and what everybody says
upon it, for we love news at Sligoe, though we are not so lost yet to
good taste as not to prefer some people's news to other. I often see my
daughter in a wheelbarrow going about from one strawberry bed to
another for I suppose it now grows uneasy to her to walk much; I am
afraid it will appear very hard to her to come home to her father's
house after having been the mistress of a family so long. I wish I
had anything worth telling you. Mr Conway and Miss Conway beg
their compliments to you, and I am

Sincerely yours,

C. AILESBURY

9. Margaret Tuckfield (d. 1754), m. 1
(ca 1704) Samuel Rolle; m. 2 (after 1719)
John Harris (post 29 Dec. 1754).
10. Lady Diana Egerton (1732–58), m.
(1753) Frederick Calvert, 6th Bn Baltimore. She had just broken her engagement to Henry Seymour; see the following
letter.

To CONWAY, Tuesday 23 June 1752 OS

Printed from the MS now WSL; first printed, Wright ii. 427–9. For the history of the MS, see *ante* 29 June 1744 OS; it was marked by HW for inclusion in *Works,* but was not included.

Memoranda (for this letter, on the back of Lady Ailesbury to HW 9 June 1752 OS):

distress of France
K. of France Staghunting Basilowitz
Miss Pelh[am]. Mr Watson
Lady Di Egerton has her caprices
Lady Suffolk Lord Falkland. Lord R. Bertie[1]
Lord Gower
Lady Coventry 2 childr[en]
Lady Gower 2 Misses
Lady Hart[ington] Lady Rachel
Prss Emily[2] Hampt. Court

Strawberry Hill, June 23d 1752.

BY a letter that I received from my Lady Ailesbury two days ago, I flatter myself I shall not have occasion to write to you any more. Yet I shall certainly see you with less pleasure than ever, as our meeting is to be attended with a resignation of my little charge. She is vastly well, and I think you will find her grown fat. I am husband enough to mind her beauty no longer, and perhaps you will say, husband enough too, in pretending that my love is converted into friendship; but I shall tell you some stories at Park Place of her understanding, that will please you I trust as much as they have done me.

My Lady Ailesbury says, I must send her news, and the whole history of Mr Seymour[3] and Lady Di Egerton; and their quarrel, and

---

1. He alone of the persons mentioned in the memoranda does not appear in the text. The reference may be connected with the 'anniversary quarrel' of Lady Townshend and Lady Caroline Petersham, mentioned below, since a 'violent squabble' between Lady Caroline and Lord Robert is mentioned *ante* 19 March 1746 OS, as are 'fifty quarrels' between Lady Townshend and Lady Caroline *ante* 30 March 1746 OS.

2. Amelia Sophia Eleanora (1711–86), 2d dau. of George II.

3. Henry Seymour (1729–1807), M.P. Totnes 1763–8, Huntingdon borough 1768–74, Evesham 1774–80; half-brother of the 4th E. of Sandwich; later the lover of Mme du Barry (Bernard Falk, *The Naughty Seymours,* 1940, pp. 27–115 *passim,* esp. p. 37, which discusses this passage and confirms HW's implied opinion of the rejected suitor). The match would be of particular interest to Conway, since he and Seymour's father were first cousins; see *post* 14 July 1752 OS and n. 6.

all that is said on both sides. I can easily tell her, all that is said on one side, Mr Seymour's, who says, the only answer he has ever been able to get from the Duchess or Mr Lyttelton[4] was, *that Di has her caprices*.[5] The reasons she gives, and gave him, were, the badness of his temper, and imperiousness of his letters; that he scolded her for the overfondness of her epistles, and was even so unsentimental as to talk, *of desiring to make her happy, instead of being made so by her*. He is gone abroad, in despair, and with an additional circumstance which would be very uncomfortable to anything but a true lover, his father[6] refuses to resettle the estate on him, the entail of which was cut off by mutual consent to make way for the settlements on the marriage.

The Speaker[7] told me t'other day that he had received a letter from Lord Hyde, which confirms what Mr Churchill writes me,[8] the distress and poverty of France; and the greatness of their divisions.[9] Yet the King's expenses are incredible; Madame de Pompadour[10] is continually busied in finding out new journeys and diversions, to keep him from falling into the hands of the clergy; the last party of pleasure she made for him, was a stag-hunting; the stag was a man in a skin and horns, worried by twelve men dressed like bloodhounds! I have read of Basilowitz, a Czar of Muscovy, who improved on such a hunt, and had a man in a bearskin worried by real dogs;[11] a more kingly entertainment!

4. Lady Di's mother and step-father: Lady Rachel Russell (d. 1777), m. 1 (1722) Scroop Egerton, 1st D. of Bridgwater, m. 2 (1745) Richard Lyttelton (1718–70), K.B., 1753; army officer; M.P. Brackley 1747–54; Poole 1754–61.

5. 'All the news I have been able to learn is that the match between Lady Die Egerton and Mr Seymour is quite off, and not very honourably on the lady's side, for after the writings were all finished, she declared she would not have him, without giving any reason but that she had changed her mind. I fancy the noble Duke [of Bridgwater] is at the bottom of the affair, as perhaps not liking the alliance' (Cts of Westmorland to Cts of Denbigh, 12 June 1752 OS, Hist. MSS Comm., *Denbigh MSS*, 1911, pp. 278–9).

6. Francis Seymour (1697–1761), of Sherborne, Dorset; M.P. Great Bedwyn 1732–4, Marlborough 1734–41; he was usually on

bad terms with his son (Falk, op. cit. 24–35, esp. pp. 27–8).

7. Arthur Onslow.

8. This letter is missing, but HW mentions what may be more of its contents in MANN iv. 325. The Churchills had gone to Paris before 12 May and returned towards the end of July (MONTAGU i. 130; MANN iv. 324).

9. The Jansenist controversy had revived about 1750, with the King, under the influence of the *dévot* party at Court, taking the side of the clergy against the parliaments.

10. Jeanne-Antoinette Poisson (1721–64), Marquise de Pompadour; Louis XV's mistress.

11. HW's source has not been found; he may be thinking of some account of an incident in 1543 when Ivan IV (1530–84), the Terrible, usually called John Basilovich by English writers, first exerted his

I shall make out a sad journal of other news; yet I will be like any gazette, and scrape together all the births, deaths, and marriages in the parish. Lady Hartington and Lady Rachel Walpole[12] are brought to bed of sons;[13] Lord Burlington[14] and Lord Gower[15] have had new attacks of palsies; Lord Falkland[16] is to marry the Southwark Lady Suffolk,[17] and Mr Watson[18] Miss Grace Pelham. Lady Coventry[19] has miscarried of one or two children, and is going on with one or two more, and is gone to France today. Lady Townshend and Lady Caroline Petersham have had their anniversary quarrel; and the Duchess of Devonshire[20] has had her secular assembly, which she keeps once in fifty years: she was more delightfully vulgar at it than you can imagine; complained of the wet night, and how the men would dirty the rooms with their shoes; called out at supper to the Duke, 'Good God, my Lord, don't cut the ham, nobody will eat any!' and relating her private ménage to Mr Obrien,[21] she said, 'When there's only my Lord and I, besides a pudding, we have always a dish of roast.' I am ashamed to send you such nonsense, or to tell you how the good women at Hampton Court are scandalized at Princess Emily's coming to chapel last Sunday in riding clothes with a dog under her arm; but I am bid to send news: what can one do at such a dead time of year! I must conclude as my Lady Gower[22] did

power by having Prince Andrei Shuisky arrested, murdered, and apparently thrown to the dogs, although modern accounts conflict (Hans von Eckardt, *Ivan the Terrible*, trans. C. A. Phillips, New York, 1949, p. 45; Stephen Graham, *Ivan the Terrible*, New Haven, 1933, p. 27; K. Waliszewski, *Ivan the Terrible*, trans. Loyd, 1904, p. 122; Jules Koslow, *Ivan the Terrible*, 1961, p. 22).

12. Lady Rachel Cavendish (1727–1805), m. (1748) Horatio Walpole, 2d Bn Walpole of Wolterton, 1757, cr. (1806) E. of Orford, HW's cousin.

13. Lady Hartington's son was Lord Richard Cavendish (19 June 1752 – 1781), M.P. Lancaster borough 1773–80, Derbyshire 1780–1 (*Daily Adv.* 22 June OS; GM 1752, xxii. 288). Lady Rachel's son was Horatio Walpole (13 June 1752 – 1822), 2d E. of Orford, n.c., 1809.

14. Richard Boyle (1694–1753), 3d E. of Burlington.

15. John Leveson Gower (1694–1754), 2d Bn Gower, cr. (1746) E. Gower.

16. Lucius Charles Cary (ca 1707–85), 7th Vct of Falkland.

17. Sarah Inwen (1714–76), m. 1 (1735) Henry Howard, 10th E. of Suffolk; m. 2 (10 Oct. 1752) Lucius Charles Cary, 7th Vct of Falkland. HW calls her 'Southwark' because her father was of that place, and to distinguish her from her mother-in-law and HW's friend, Lady Suffolk, George II's ex-mistress. Falkland had been her first love; see Montagu i. 139–40 and n. 12.

18. Lewis Watson (before 1746, Monson) (1728–95), cr. (1760) Bn Sondes, m. (12 Oct. 1752) Grace Pelham.

19. Mary Gunning (1732–60), m. (5 March 1752) George William Coventry, 6th E. of Coventry.

20. Catherine Hoskins (d. 1777), m. (1718) William Cavendish, 3d D. of Devonshire.

21. Probably Percy Wyndham (after 1741 Wyndham O'Brien) (ca 1723–74), cr. (1756) E. of Thomond.

22. Lady Mary Tufton (1701–85), m. 1

very well t'other day in a letter into the country, 'Since the two
Misses[23] were hanged, and the two Misses[24] were married, there is
nothing at all talked of.' Adieu! my best compliments and my wife's
to your two ladies.

Yours ever,

H. W.

From CONWAY, Tuesday 14 July 1752 OS

Printed from the MS now WSL, formerly Rutnam. First printed, *Fraser's
Magazine*, 1850, xlii. 341.
    Address: To the Honourable Horatio Walpole, Junior, in Arlington Street,
London.
    Postmark: IY 14. DUBLIN.
    There are four pencil drawings, presumably by HW, of Strawberry Hill.

Leixslip,[1] July 14.

Dear Horry,

WE have been here these two or three days on our road home. I
am not sure you know where *here* is; it is the Primate's[2] house
seven miles from Dublin; so here we are as I said on our road home.
On Saturday next, this being Tuesday, we propose to embark for
Holyhead, from whence eight days brings us to town so that with a
fair wind and barring accidents we expect to be there on Monday
sennight.[3] I don't summon you to give up your charge, but to a
performance of your promise of bringing her to us to Park Place,
which I was very glad to have under your hand in your last letter;

(1718) Anthony Grey, styled E. of Harold
1706–23; m. 2 (1736) John Leveson Gower,
2d Bn Gower, cr. (1746) E. Gower.
    23. Miss Blandy and Miss Jefferies
(HW). Mary Blandy (ca 1717–52) had
been hanged 6 April for poisoning her
father at Henley-on-Thames in 1751.
Lady Ailesbury is said to have used her
influence in a vain attempt to obtain a
pardon for her (Percy Noble, *Park Place*,
1905, pp. 18–20). Elizabeth Jeffreys (ca
1717–52) was hanged 28 March as an accomplice in the murder of her uncle at
Walthamstow on 3 July 1751 OS (MON-

TAGU i. 142, n. 11). See also MANN iv. 312
and nn. 23, 24, and *post* 8 Nov. 1752.
    24. The Gunnings (HW). Lady Coventry
(above, n. 19) and her sister Elizabeth
(1733–90), m. 1 (14 Feb. 1752) James Hamilton, 6th D. of Hamilton, m. 2 (1759)
John Campbell, 5th D. of Argyll, 1770,
Lady Ailesbury's brother; cr. (1776) Bns
Hamilton, s.j.

———

    1. Leixlip.
    2. George Stone (ca 1708–64), Abp of
Armagh and Primate of Ireland 1747–64.
    3. 27 July.

now when I say bring her that shall be as you please; we come to town first where I fancy Lady Ailesbury will be glad to see her and save you the trouble of carrying her down, but not that of coming there which we absolutely look upon as our right[4] nor will Lady A. receive your report anywhere else though we shall be very glad to meet you in town.[5]

My cousin's[6] and Lady Die's is an excellent history; but really the farce of it has ended a little too tragically in his losing his estate or at least the settlement of it which seems to put it in no[7] small danger with a father capricious enough to object to Lady seriously, as I hear he did *because she was not the sort of beauty he liked*. You complain of your want of news and send us a volume; I could talk of nothing but ourselves and our own uninteresting history at quarters and have not time for that; it has been made duller than usual by very bad weather which is not much mended here: you see it's time to finish when one comes to the weather; so till we meet which, I assure you, I think of with impatience, I remain

Most sincerely yours,

H. S. C.

Lady A. and Nanny salute you; I hope poor Mrs Leneve is better. Pray make my compliments to her.

PS. We are not sure we shan't be in town on Sunday and I fancy Lady A. would be very sorry not to find Missy in waiting for her so will beg you to send her then to our house.

---

4. HW paid this visit sometime between ca 10 Aug. OS, when he returned from a tour of Kent and Sussex, and the 20th of August; details are in HW to Montagu 28 Aug. 1752 OS, MONTAGU i. 141–2.

5. HW apparently did go to London to meet them, since he wrote to Mann from Arlington Street on 27 July OS (MANN iv. 321).

6. Henry Seymour (*ante* 23 June 1752 OS, n. 3). His father and Conway were grandsons of Sir Edward Seymour (1633–1708), 4th Bt, by different wives (Collins, *Peerage*, 1812, i. 198–9).

7. 'So' in MS.

To CONWAY, ca Thursday 20 August 1752 OS

'Two notes' missing, mentioned *post* 23 Aug. 1752 OS. They were presumably written after HW returned from his visit to Park Place where he had gone after his return from a tour of Kent and Sussex ca 10 Aug. (MONTAGU i. 141; HW to Bentley 5–9 Aug. 1752 OS, CHUTE 131–46).

From CONWAY, Sunday 23 August 1752 OS

Printed for the first time from the MS now WSL, formerly Rutnam. Dated '1752' in another hand; confirmed by the references to the gifts of pigs also mentioned *post* 8 and 16 Nov. 1752.

Address: To the Honourable Horatio Walpole, Junior, in Arlington Street, London.

Postmark: 24 AV.

Memoranda (by HW):[1] Mr Conw[ay]
                    Lady M[ary Churchill] } 27
                    Sir G. Lytt[elton] }
                    G. M[ontagu] 28
                    Mr Gr[ay] 29

Park Place, Sunday, Aug. 23d.

I HAVE received your two notes, with your two dragons, and thank you for all your kind offers of pigs,[2] cows and bantams, and not only thank but in both our names most bounteously accept; about the pigs we have no scruple as I conceive they were returned upon your hands; we have some bantams so you need not be too generous of them and only send one or two of the overflowings of your stock, or none if not absolutely convenient to you. As to the Alderneys,[3] we certainly languish after 'em but dread introducing the distemper[4] into the county. If Mrs Leneve or anybody there could

---

1. Of the letters mentioned in this list, only that to Montagu 28 August OS (MONTAGU i. 141–4) has been recovered. The letter to Gray may have been the one to which Gray replies ca Aug. 1752 (GRAY ii. 60–1); for other possible topics of correspondence between HW and Gray at this time, see MONTAGU i. 143–4.

2. These were Chinese pigs; see *post* 8, 16 Nov. 1752.

3. 'The Alderney breed is only to be

met with about the seats of our nobility and gentry, upon account of their giving exceeding rich milk, to support the luxury of the tea-table' (George Culley, *Observations on Live-Stock*, 1807, p. 72). The name is now obsolete, the breed being considered the same as Guernseys.

4. It had been endemic among cattle in England since 1745 (*ante* 24 June 1748 NS, n. 11).

get us a perfect assurance of their health we should certainly be glad to treat for two or three and a bull and when they come they shall perform quarantine in our little retired rosary field.

I don't find out by your dates at all where you are; I should hope in town or that you will be there towards Tuesday night when we shall lie there in our way to Tunbridge, for which we received sentence today and are to lose no time in getting there. I go to settle Lady Ailesbury there, then have thoughts of returning to my business here and afterwards calling [for] her at Tunbridge towards the time when her waters are over or meeting her at Coombank[5] according as my affairs here permit; for my dragondom goes on poorly; I have indeed got, besides yours, a fine wooden one from Cuenot to breed out of, but my plasterer has left me almost in despair, and never got a step farther than that foolish tombstone face that you saw. Adieu. We shall depend upon meeting you at Coombank and as you say all times are equally convenient to you, Lady Ailesbury will let you know when her waters will let her come there.

Yours most sincerely,

H. S. C.

Tonight we go to the Cooperhood,[6] the wealth and greenth[6a] of whose garden, that we admired from our hill, together with the agreeable shelterdom and shadedom of the walks and pleasantdom of the situation on the river, we hope will take off a little the irksomth and tediousdom of a Sunday country visit. The hours of love[7] are the quintessence of modern poetry.

You say when and how shall the bantams come? I have a notion in a basket by the coach from London, but when and how will the Chinese boar and sow come? That I have no notion of; I'll inquire, or

5. Combe Bank, Coomb Bank, or Combebank, Sundridge, Kent, which had been purchased by Lady Ailesbury's father and was later the seat of her brother Frederick (Edward Hasted, *History . . . of Kent*, Canterbury, 1797–1801, iii. 140, 142).

6. Gislingham Cooper (ca 1688–1768), banker in the Strand and lord of the manor of Henley since 1724; m. (1721) Ann Whitelock (d. 1771). They lived at Phillis Court, demolished about 1788, on the Thames north of Henley (J. S. Burn, *History of Henley-on-Thames*, 1861, pp. 253, 267, 281, and genealogical table facing p. 248; MONTAGU i. 142 and n. 9).

6a. A favourite word with HW; Conway is presumably mocking him, as he is in the whole passage. See ibid. i. 155, 162 and *post* 9 June 1757.

7. Perhaps a reference to something HW had written; see GRAY ii. 61.

if you know, do send 'em. If we buy the cows they may come together. *Ecco vi un' rebus* that I made since I finished this.

> The thinnest of blades, I don't mean of the town,
> Who holds up his proud head while his betters keep down;
> With something that's nothing (it's not a mistake)
> That's not gen'rous to give, yet not handsome to take
> These two make together the name of a man
> That I need not to tell, you may guess if you can.

To CONWAY, Thursday 27 August 1752 OS

Missing; listed in the memoranda on the preceding letter.

From CONWAY, Wednesday 4 October 1752

Printed for the first time from the MS now wsl, formerly Rutnam. Dated by the references in the preceding letter to Tunbridge and Combe Bank and to the discussion of the Chinese pigs. The period between this and the previous letter is less than it appears because of the 11 days dropped from the calendar in Sept. 1752.

Address: To the Honourable Horatio Walpole, Junior, in Arlington Street, London.

Postmark: 5 OC. TUNBRIDGE.

Tunbridge Wells, Oct. 4, 1752.

OUR motions are now settled and I write by Lady Ailesbury's desire and my own inclination to summon you to Coombank on Tuesday next; we depart this place on Sunday but Lady A. has engaged herself and me to go to Lord Westmorland's[1] which we propose leaving on Tuesday, unless they should happen to leave it sooner, which we don't apprehend; I believe you know all this from General Campbell[2] who has had our plan but it's my duty to inform you nevertheless, and we have a mind to make you as secure as we can; we have just heard from him and he talks of having invited you

1. Mereworth Castle, near Hadlow, Kent, seat of John Fane (1686–1762), 7th E. of Westmorland. HW had visited it in August (HW to Bentley 5–9 Aug. 1752, CHUTE 143–4 and nn. 110–11).

2. Lady Ailesbury's father.

for Friday but I hope no such thing will happen, as I know there would be no hope of keeping you. There's little to be said of Tunbridge, and that little will keep till we meet. Lady Townshend and everything that's lively is gone; it's late in the autumn with us already and the few dry old leaves that remain are falling off every day. Adieu. You hate compliments or Lady A. has a quantity at your service. I hope my little sow is well after her lying in and has brought you a fine family; when you come next to Park Place you'll fancy yourself in the land of Liliput, as we are laying in all the diminutive beasts we can get at and I have begun a little plantation much fitter for such small deer than the beech groves.

To CONWAY, Wednesday 8 November 1752

Printed from the MS now WSL; first printed, Wright ii. 453–4. For the history of the MS see *ante* 29 June 1744 OS.
Endorsed: Mr H. Walpole.

Strawberry Hill, Nov. 8, 1752.

Dear Harry,

AFTER divers mistakes and neglects of my own servants and Mr Fox's,[1] the Chinese pair have at last set sail for Park Place: I don't call them boar and sow, because instead of being fit for his altar, I believe when you see them, you will think it is Ticchi Micchi himself, the Chinese god of good eating and drinking, and his wife. They were to have been with you last week, but the chairmen who were to drive them to the waterside, got drunk, and said, that the creatures were so wild and unruly, that they ran away and would not be managed. Do but think of their running! It puts one in mind of Mrs Nugent's[2] talking of just *jumping* out of a coach! I might with as much propriety talk of having all my clothes let out.[3] My coachman is vastly struck with the goodly paunch of the boar, and says, it would fetch three pounds in his country; but he does not

1. Henry Fox (1705–74), cr. (1763) Bn Holland; politician; M.P.; at this time one of HW's closest friends.

2. Probably Anna Craggs (ca 1697–1756), m. 1 (1712) John Newsham; m. 2 John Knight (d. 1733); m. 3 (1736) Robert

Nugent (Claud Nugent, *Memoir of Robert, Earl Nugent*, 1898, pp. 9–10). HW elsewhere calls her 'a great fool' (MONTAGU i. 65); she was very fat.

3. HW was very thin.

consider, that he is a boar with the true brown edge,[4] and has been fed with the old original wheatsheaf: I hope you will value him more highly: I dare say Mr Cutler[5] or Margas[6] would at least ask twenty guineas for him, and swear that Mrs Dunch[7] gave thirty for the fellow.

As you must of course write me a letter of thanks for my brawn, I beg you will take that opportunity of telling me very particularly how my Lady Aylesbury does, and if she is quite recovered, as I much hope. How does my sweet little wife do? are your dragons all finished? have the Coopers seen Miss Blandy's ghost,[8] or have they made Mr Cranston[9] poison a dozen or two more private gentlewomen![10] Do you plant without rain as I do, in order to have your trees die that you may have the pleasure of planting them over again with rain? have you any Mrs Clive[11] that pulls down barns that intercept your prospect; or have you any Lord Radnor[12] that plants trees to intercept his own prospect, that he may cut them down again to make an alteration—there, there are as many questions as if I were your schoolmaster or your godmother—good night!

Yours ever,

H. W.

4. HW is referring to decorations on china.

5. Wright calls him, like Margas, proprietor of a fashionable china-shop, but he does not appear in Sir Ambrose Heal's collection of tradesman's cards, and no other reference to him has been found.

6. Philip Margas (d. 1767), a tea and china importer and fashionable china dealer in Bucklersbury near Stocks Market (SELWYN 116, n. 21, where HW jokes about his Turkish sheep looking like a purchase from Margas's).

7. Elizabeth Godfrey (ca 1672–1761), dau. of Arabella Churchill, James II's mistress; m. (1702) Edmund Dunch of Little Wittenham, Berks (MONTAGU i. 104, n. 9; Miscellanea genealogica et heraldica, 1898, 3d ser. ii. 46). HW purchased an enamel of James II at her auction in 1761 and mentions that her 'fine china . . . sold for nothing' (MONTAGU i. 412).

8. For a few details concerning Miss Blandy's ghost see Percy Noble, Park Place, 1905, p. 20.

9. Hon. William Henry Cranstoun (1714 – 2 Dec. 1752), son of the 5th Bn

Cranstoun, had been Miss Blandy's suitor (although married), and an accomplice in the murder of her father, but had escaped punishment (Scots Peerage ii. 597–8).

10. Cooper, as lord of the manor of Henley, had received property belonging to both Miss Blandy and Miss Jeffreys in forfeiture at their executions (MONTAGU i. 142 and nn. 11, 12).

11. Catherine Raftor (1711–85), m. (1732) George Clive; actress. HW's earliest mention of Mrs Clive as settled at Little Strawberry Hill is in his letter to Richard Bentley of 3 Nov. 1754 (CHUTE 185); she had previously lived at Little Marble Hill and, reportedly, at Riverside (R. S. Cobbett, Memorials of Twickenham, 1872, pp. 245, 248; Strawberry Hill Accounts, ed. Toynbee, Oxford, 1927, pp. 85, 136).

12. John Robartes (1686–1757), 4th E. of Radnor. His house, which HW and Bentley called Mabland from its profusion of small houses and statues, was across the road from SH to the north (MONTAGU i. 53; HW to Bentley 18 May 1754, CHUTE 174).

From CONWAY, Thursday 16 November 1752

Printed for the first time from the MS now WSL, formerly Rutnam.
Memoranda (by HW): Vetusta monumenta[1] ⎫
                    Milles's Catalogue[2] ⎬ for Mr Fox
                    To Mr F. 18. ⎭
                    K. 17.
                    [Drawings of columns, in pencil].

Park Place, Nov. 16, 1752.

I DO thank you, my dear Horry, very heartily for your charming brindled couple; I waited to do it till I saw 'em safe arrived which did not happen till this morning; they have been eight days on their voyage and the poor Lady Ticchi-Micchi no doubt horribly seasick; notwithstanding which they are come in all the glory of their fat with their bellies sweeping the ground; so that Lady Lyttelton,[3] Lady Ailesbury and all our jury of matrons have absolutely determined the goddess far gone with child and reject entirely your history of her being brought to bed before her journey; if so, it increases her value perhaps tenfold, and fills us with the happiest prospect of seeing numerous branches spring up to support that royal family. Ticchi-Micchi himself is of a wildness and majesty not to be described; his high bristles on his neck and his low belly forming a most complete line of beauty; in short, they are all perfection and we all thanks.

I think you gave us hopes of a visit[4] sometime or other before our breaking up, which we don't intend till about the meeting of Parliament;[5] and whenever you can spare yourself a little from your business, your plantations, your charming neighbours or your pleasures, 'twill make us very happy; Sir George and Lady Lyttelton who talked of staying with us till towards Christmas, are going away on Tuesday next; Nanny comes to us on Sunday; that's the

1. A folio volume of prints put out by the Society of Antiquaries in 1747; HW's copy is Hazen, *Cat. of HW's Lib.*, No. 3658.

2. *The Catalogue of Honour*, London, 1610, by Thomas Milles (ca 1550–1627); Fox acknowledged his receipt of it in his letter to HW 23 Nov. 1752 (ibid., No. 605; SELWYN 119).

3. Elizabeth Rich (ca 1716–95), m. (1749) George Lyttelton, 5th Bt, 1751, cr. (1756) Bn Lyttelton. She and her sister Mary (*post* ca 25 March 1753, n. 1) were close friends of Lady Ailesbury.

4. There is no evidence that this visit was made.

5. On 31 Oct. 1752 Parliament had been further prorogued to 11 Jan. 1753 (*Journals of the House of Commons* xxvi. 518).

state of us and our visits. Miss Townshend[6] has talked of coming but I give her up; and notwithstanding other general promises scarce expect anybody else but Jack[7] or Fred Campbell very late; I tell you so much that you may know you won't be like to take up too much room and may come whenever you find it most convenient. I have planted through frosts and winds and drought and want you to see my plantings; I have hung up my prints in my dressing room and want you to approve of 'em if you please; I have finished my dragons with tolerable success; I have made my new passage and almost fitted up another bedchamber: these are all my doings. How could you so undervalue Park Place as to suppose anybody's trees intercept our prospect? Know you not how much we are above all our neighbours?[8] If you don't, come and try one of our westerly winds and you'll be convinced: the *highest* house in the neighbourhood we have been to see today and is an house of one story high. I intend Ticchi-Micchi should never set his little pig's eyes upon it for he'll certainly desert to it. Lady Ailesbury is a good deal better, so that I am now in great hopes, with her care of herself and constant exercise, she'll soon see an end of this tiresome disorder. I write in great haste to save the post. Adieu. I hope I have answered all your questions; if not, the rest when we meet and pray let it be soon,

Yours most faithfully,

H. S. C.

All the house desire their compliments. You have a dangerous rival here with your wife, Tommy Lyttleton, and must come soon to prevent too deep an impression. Long separations are perilous things.

6. The Hon. Mary Townshend.
7. John Campbell (1723–1806), styled M. of Lorn 1761–70; 5th D. of Argyll, 1770; Lady Ailesbury's brother.
8. Park Place is on top of a hill.

From Lady Ailesbury, December ?1752

An invitation card drawn and designed by Richard Bentley, printed for the first time from the original, now WSL, in *Drawings and Designs by Richard Bentley, Only Son of Dr Bentley, Master of Trinity College Cambridge*, p. 14; see illustration. The date is conjectural; the Monday, 1 Jan., could be in 1753 or 1759. For references to Lady Ailesbury's cards see her letter and Conway's letters of March 1758.

Lady Ailesbury's compliments to Mr Walpole and desires the favour of his company on Monday evening the 1st of January.

From Lady Ailesbury, Sunday ca 25 March 1753

Printed for the first time from the MS now WSL, formerly Rutnam. Dated by the references to 'Thisbe' and her praying 'that all wicked walls may be cast down' (see below, nn. 2, 3).
Address: To Mr Walpole.

Sunday morning.

MISS Rich[1] had asked more company; therefore can't comply with our desire of changing the party. Thisbe[2] bids me tell you that it is her earnest request that you should meet us at Miss Rich's; she is just gone to church to pray that all wicked walls may be cast down.[3]

Ever yours,

C. A.

1. Mary Rich (d. 1769), daughter of Field Marshal Sir Robert Rich; a close friend of the Conways and of HW (MONTAGU ii. 260, n. 11).
2. The Cts of Coventry. Lady Ailesbury humorously nicknames her 'Thisbe' presumably because of her mispronunciation of the name at a private ball recently held at George Pitt's (see HW to Mann 27 March 1753, MANN iv. 367).
3. Lady Ailesbury is alluding to an incident at the same ball; Lady Coventry, indignant at an allegedly impious remark made by Charles Churchill, HW's brother-in-law, declared that 'she wished the house would fall upon his head' (ibid.).

To Conway, Saturday 5 May 1753

Printed from *Works* v. 33–5. From Conway's reply *post* 19 May 1753, it is evident that passages about the death of Lord Hyde and John Spencer's projected marriage were omitted when the letter was first printed.

Strawberry Hill, May 5, 1753.

THOUGH my letter bears a country date, I am only a passenger here, just come to overlook my workmen,[1] and repose myself upon some shavings, after the fatigues of the season. You know balls and masquerades always abound as the weather begins to be too hot for them, and this has been quite a spring-tide of diversion.[2] Not that I am so abandoned as to have partaken of all; I neither made the Newmarket campaign under the Duke,[3] nor danced at any ball, nor *looked well* at any masquerade: I begin to submit to my years, and amuse myself—only just as much as I like. Indeed, when parties and politics are at an end, an Englishman may be allowed not to be always grave and out of humour. His Royal Highness has won as many hearts at Newmarket as he lost in Scotland; he played deep, and handsomely;[4] received everybody at his table[5] with the greatest good humour, and permitted the familiarities of the place with ease and sense.

There have been balls at the Duchess of Norfolk's, at Holland House,[6] and Lord Granville's,[7] and a subscription masquerade: the dresses were not very fine, not much invention, nor any very absurd. I find I am telling you extreme trifles; but you desired me to write,

1. For the transformation of SH into a 'castle' at this time, see MANN iv. 380–2 and notes.

2. 'Gaiety of all kinds reigns here at present. Balls, masquerades, and parties for plays and suppers abound so much, that not only each night furnishes one, but many nights produce two or three' (Lady Hervey to Rev. Edmund Morris 12 May 1753, Lady Hervey, *Letters*, ed. Croker, 1821, p. 197).

3. William Duke of Cumberland (HW).

4. 'Not less than an hundred thousand pounds have been carried thither [to Newmarket] for the hazard of this single week [22–29 April]' (MANN iv. 373).

5. 'We hear that his Royal Highness the Duke of Cumberland has ordered four tables to be kept open during his residence at Newmarket, for the entertainment of the nobility and gentry' (*Daily Adv.* 27 April).

6. 'On Tuesday night [1 May] the Right Hon. Henry Fox gave a ball and a grand entertainment, at Holland House, to his Grace the Duke of Richmond, and a great number of persons of quality and distinction' (ibid. 4 May).

7. Lady Hervey, loc. cit. mentions this ball.

and there literally happens nothing of greater moment. If I can fill out a sheet even in this way, I will; for at Sligo[8] perhaps I may appear a journalist of consequence.

There is a Madame de Mézières[9] arrived from Paris, who has said a thousand impertinent things to my Lady Albemarle, on my Lord's not letting her come to Paris.[10] I should not repeat this to you, only to introduce George Selwyn's account of this woman, who, he says, is mother to the Princess of Montauban,[11] grandmother to Madame de Brionne,[12] sister to General Oglethorpe,[13] and was laundress to the Duchess of Portsmouth.[14]

Sir Charles Williams, never very happy at panegyric, has made a distich on the Queen of Hungary,[15] which I send you for the curiosity, not the merit of it:

O regina orbis prima et pulcherrima, ridens
Est Venus, incedens Juno, Minerva loquens.[16]

8. Mr Conway was then with his regiment quartered at Sligo in Ireland (HW).

9. Eleanor Oglethorpe (1684–1775), m. (1707) Eugène-Marie de Béthisy, Marquis de Mézières; an active Jacobite (A. A. Ettinger, *James Edward Oglethorpe*, Oxford, 1936, pp. 19, 56, 305, *et passim*, which corrects and amplifies DU DEFFAND iv. 213, n. 1). For details of her visit to England, which began in Sept. 1752 and during which she was suspected by the government of involvement in the Elibank Jacobite plot, see Ettinger, op. cit. 281–2 and notes.

10. Lord Albemarle was then ambassador at Paris (HW).

11. Catherine-Éléonore-Eugénie de Béthisy de Mézières (1707–57), m. (1722) Charles de Rohan-Guémené, Prince de Montauban (Chevalier de Courcelles, *Histoire . . . des pairs de France*, 1822–3, i. sub Béthisy, p. 11; *Répertoire . . . de la Gazette de France*, ed. de Granges de Surgères, 1902–6, iv. 72).

12. Louise-Julie-Constance de Rohan-Montauban (1734–1815), m. (1748) Charles-Louis de Lorraine, Comte de Brionne; one of the great beauties of her time (DU DEFFAND ii. 25, n. 8; MORE 47–8).

13. James Edward Oglethorpe (1696–1785), general, philanthropist, and founder of Georgia.

14. Louise-Renée de Penancoët de Kéroualle (1649–1734), cr. (1673) Ds of Portsmouth; Charles II's mistress. Selwyn, whose account is accurate up to this point, has confused Mme de Mézières with her mother Eleanor (or Ellen) Wall (1662–1732), m. (1680) Theophilus Oglethorpe, Kt, 1685, who began her career as personal maid to the Ds of Portsmouth but became head laundress and 'sempstriss' to the King at £2000 per annum in 1680 (Ettinger, op. cit. 17–19, 26, 126, *et passim*).

15. Williams had been on a special, but unofficial mission to Vienna in the early spring of 1753 (SELWYN 321 and n. 117).

16. HW also quotes this in his account of Williams, ibid. 321. Mrs Toynbee thanks Professor Littledale for pointing out 'that the best part of this epigram is "conveyed" from one written in cent. xvi by Hieronymus Angerianus, who said of a certain lady:—

Caelia ridens
Est Venus, incedens Juno, Minerva
loquens'

(Toynbee iii. 155, n. 4).

That Williams was sincere in his praise of Maria Theresa appears evident from his praise of her in a letter to Fox 6 April 1753 and an official memorandum of 15

It is infinitely admired at Vienna, but Baron Munchausen[17] has received a translation of it into German in six verses,[18] which are still more applauded.

There is another volume published of Lord Bolinbroke's;[19] it contains his famous letter to Sir William Windham,[20] with an admirable description of the Pretender and his Court, and a very poor justification of his own treachery to that party; a flimsy unfinished state of the nation,[21] written at the end of his life, and the commonplace tautology of an old politician, who lives out of the world and writes from newspapers; and a superficial letter to Mr Pope, as an introduction to his *Essays,* which are printed, but not yet published.[22]

What shall I say to you more? You see how I am forced to tack paragraphs together, without any connection or consequence! Shall I tell you one more idle story, and will you just recollect that you once concerned yourself enough about the heroine of it, to excuse my repeating such a piece of tittle-tattle? This heroine is Lady Caroline Petersham,[23] the hero is—not entirely of royal blood; at least I have never heard that Lodomie[24] the toothdrawer was in any manner descended from the House of Bourbon. Don't be alarmed; this plebeian operator is not in the catalogue of your successors. How the lady was the aggressor is not known; 'tis only conjectured that French politeness and French interestedness could never have gone such lengths without mighty provocation. The first instance of the toothdrawer's ungentle behaviour was on hearing it said that Lady Car-

July 1753, both quoted in Lord Ilchester and Mrs Langford-Brooke, *Life of Sir Charles Hanbury-Williams,* 1929, pp. 265, 268–9.

17. Gerlach Adolph (1688–1770), Freiherr von Münchhausen; Hanoverian statesman and diplomatist (MANN iii. 99, n. 9), at this time Hanoverian minister resident in England.

18. HW is probably joking, although Conway did not think so (*post* 19 May 1753).

19. The three works described below were published in a single volume by Mallet on 1 May (*Daily Adv.* 1 May). Bolingbroke's *Letters on the Study and Use of History* and some other writings had been published by Mallet the previous year. HW apparently did not keep copies of

these separate volumes, since they cannot be found in the records of his library.

20. Written in 1717 but published for the first time in this volume.

21. 'Some Reflections on the Present State of the Nation, Principally with Regard to her Taxes and her Debts; and on the Causes and Consequences of Them,' written in 1749, occupies pp. 323–421 in the volume.

22. Bolingbroke's collected works in 5 vols quarto were published 6 March 1754 (MANN iv. 454, n. 11).

23. Her name is deleted in *Works;* that this is the person intended is clear from HW's reference to her old connection with Conway and Conway's reply *post* 19 May 1753.

24. Not further identified.

oline was to have her four girls[25] drawn by Liotard;[26] which was wondered at, as his price is so great—'Oh!' said Lodomie, *chacune paie pour la sienne.*' Soon after this insult, there was some dispute about payments, and tooth-powder, and divers messages passed. At last the lady wrote a card, to say she did not understand such impertinent answers being given to her chairman by an *arracheur de dents.* The angry little gentleman, with as much intrepidity as if he had drawn out all her teeth, tore the card in five slits, and returned it with this astonishing sentence, 'I return you your impertinent card, and desire you will pay me what you owe me.' All I know more is, that the toothdrawer still lives; and so do many lords and gentlemen, formerly thought the slaves of the offended fair one's will and passions, and among others, to his great shame,

Your sincere friend,

Hor. Walpole

From Conway, Tuesday 8 May 1753

Printed from the MS now WSL, formerly Rutnam. First printed, *Fraser's Magazine,* 1850, xlii. 341–2.

Sligo, May 8, 1753.

Dear Horry,

I TOLD you I'd write to you and now perform my promise according to rule by letting you know of my good journey and safe arrival; events so much of course that I have a notion you have no great curiosity about 'em; and much less to hear the detail of a dull, solitary journey of a dull person to a dull place; which is my history in three words. I lost my chaise, that is, broke it and left it three

25. Lady Caroline Stanhope (1747–67), m. (1765) Kenneth Mackenzie, styled Lord Fortrose 1761–6, cr. (1766) Vct Fortrose and (1771) E. of Seaforth; Lady Isabella Stanhope (1748–1819), m. (1768) Charles William Molyneux, 8th Vct Molyneux, cr. (1771) E. of Sefton; Lady Amelia (Emily) Stanhope (1749–80), m. (1767) Richard Barry, 6th E. of Barrymore; and Lady

Henrietta Stanhope (1750–81), m. (1776) Thomas Foley, 2d Bn Foley.

26. Jean-Étienne Liotard (1702–89), pastel and enamel painter. He had come to England about the beginning of March 1753, having raised his prices above the sixteen guineas apiece that he had been charging in Paris in 1752 (Mann iv. 325, 362; Thieme and Becker).

miles from Chester; and have not recovered it since. That's my only event and in consequence of it I have most unmercifully jumbled myself down here for four days successively upon these stony roads in an hackney coach that it's a mercy I have a whole bone in my skin. I stayed very little at Dublin and learnt no news in the world but the death of old Gen. Read[1] who is since come to life again, to the disappointment of half a dozen colonels that expected his regiment. Gen. Degrangue[2] was thought to be dying, too, when I came from Dublin; but in short, death, that is vulgarly reckoned the most certain, is, of all things, the most uncertain and there's no depending upon it. I have no interest in these deaths, observe, but we military men all make *cause commune* of it and take it seriously ill if an old general does not die when he should and are quite peevish. There's poor Lord Molesworth,[3] too, whom I saw in Dublin; if he lives long will give great cause of complaint. I never saw in anybody living a stronger appearance of decay and mortality and though I must not talk such language in the barracks here, to you I may own that I am heartily sorry for it as he will leave a young wife,[4] two young women by his first,[5] grown up, and five or six children by this,[6] all, I believe, without a penny.[7] One must be very military

1. George Read *or* Reade (d. 1756), entered the army in 1703; Brig.-Gen., 1739; Maj.-Gen., 1743; Lt-Gen., 1747; Col. 29th Foot, 1733; 9th Foot, 1739; 9th Dragoons, 1749 (GM 1756, xxvi. 206; Robert Beatson, *Political Index*, 1806, ii. 132, 192, 210, 228; Richard Cannon, *Historical Record of the Ninth . . . Foot*, 1848, p. 121).

2. Henry de Grangues (d. 1754), Brig.-Gen., 1745; Maj.-Gen., 1747; Lt-Gen., 1754; Col. 30th Foot, 1742; 9th Dragoons, 1743; 4th Horse (7th Dragoon Guards), 1749 (GM 1754, xxiv. 340; Beatson, op. cit. ii. 133, 192, 228; Richard Cannon, *Historical Record of the Seventh . . . Dragoon Guards*, 1837, p. 85). Conway succeeded to his regiment when he finally died.

3. Richard Molesworth (ca 1680–1758), 3d Vct Molesworth; Gen., 1746; field marshal, 1757; at this time Col. 5th Dragoons (John Lodge and Mervyn Archdall, *Peerage of Ireland*, 1789, v. 146).

4. Mary Jenney Usher (d. 1763), m. (1744) Richard Molesworth, 3d Vct Molesworth. She, two of her daughters, her brother, and several others were burned

to death in her house in 1763; see MANN vi. 138–41.

5. Jane Lucas (d. 1742); the date of their marriage is not known. At this time two of his three daughters by her were unmarried; Letitia (d. 1787), m. (Oct. 1753) Lt-Col. James Molesworth; and Amelia (d. 1758), who never married (Lodge and Archdall, loc. cit.). A third daughter Mary (d. *post* 1774) m. (1736) Robert Rochfort, cr. (1738) Bn and (1751) Vct Belfield and (1756) E. of Belvidere.

6. Molesworth had so far had seven children by his second marriage, six of whom were living: Richard Nassau (1748–93), 4th Vct Molesworth, 1758; Henrietta (1745–1813), m. (1774) Rt Hon. John Staples; Melesina (1746–63); Mary (1747–63); Louisa (1749–1824), m. 1 (1769) William Brabazon Ponsonby, cr. (1806) Bn Ponsonby; m. 2 (1823) William Wentworth Fitzwilliam, 4th E. Fitzwilliam; and Elizabeth (1751–1835), m. James Stewart (ibid. v. 146–7; MANN vi. 139–40, nn. 19, 21, 23).

7. This was partly rectified by George II's grant in 1755 of a pension of £500 a

indeed to be pleased with such an event! To think of entertaining you with anything from Sligo would be a folly. You know no thing nor creature here; it won't bear describing and I am bad at description, too, so shall make this short: let me hear the news of the town from you and particularly your own I desire, and believe me, dear cousin,

Most faithfully yours,

H. S. C.

From CONWAY, Saturday 19 May 1753

Printed from the MS now WSL, formerly Rutnam. First printed, *Fraser's Magazine*, 1850, xlii. 342–3.

Sligo, May 19th 1753.

I AM vastly obliged to you for thinking of me and writing to me at a time when by all the rules of correspondence it was my business to write first; and the more because it looks as if we were not to write by rule. What you call your tittle-tattle indeed wanted no apology. I need not tell anybody else but I find it's necessary to inform you that it's more agreeable, more entertaining and generally more interesting than greater and graver events as they are commonly told; not but that some of your paragraphs would figure in a gazette. The death of poor Lord Hyde[1] is indeed but too grave; I saw it in the newspaper but was in hopes it was not true. I am sorry as you seem to be for the disposition he has made of his estate, particularly on poor Lord Charles's[2] account, who, I believe, has a

year to Lady Molesworth and £70 a year to each of Molesworth's unmarried daughters to begin on the day of Molesworth's death (Lodge and Archdall, op. cit. v. 146, n.); after the fire in 1763 George III gave the three surviving daughters a pension of £390 a year during pleasure (*Calendar of Home Office Papers*, 1760–1765, ed. Joseph Redington, 1878, p. 375).

1. Who had died in Paris 26 April after a fall from his horse. The news reached London 30 April (*Daily Adv.* 2 May). From what follows, it appears that HW had discussed his death and will *ante* 5 May 1753 in a passage omitted when that letter was first printed.

2. Lord Charles Douglas (1726–56), 2d son of 3d D. of Queensberry, styled E. of Drumlanrig 1754–6; M.P. Dumfriesshire 1747–55. His mother was Lord Hyde's sister, but Hyde 'had no value for her' and left her nothing, apparently in the belief that she was actually the daughter of Lord Carleton (Lady Mary Wortley Montagu, *Letters and Works*, ed. Lord Wharncliffe and W. Moy Thomas, [?1861], ii. 238, 274).

great deal of merit and wants it much more, I fancy, than they where it's gone.[3] I don't understand how he came to have so much to dispose of;[4] or what power he has over anything that falls by Lord Clarendon's[5] death!

We live as dully as possible here, yet I neither envy nor regret your balls and masquerades, I submit a little to my age *as you do;* that is, to my disposition and situation; I think to be always in those whirlwinds of diversion without gallantry is childish and tiresome and insipid and to be gallant neither suits my present state nor inclination. I am not wiser nor better than other people, but you have always told me I was more indifferent; I believe that might be true to a degree, always, at least comparatively, and it's more so now; I don't mean that I am insensible either to the people or things that make me happy now; that can't be since I feel myself happy, I think positively so, and not by a mere absence of misfortunes or wants; but then it is not that turbulent happiness of the gay and gallant, that revelling and enthusiastic pleasure, with which people are carried in the air and in the clouds, looking down with pity and contempt upon such poor veterans as you and I that crawl peaceably upon the earth. I look up at 'em with wonder sometimes but not with envy; not even my Lady Northumberland nor my Lord Holdernesse, whom I regard as the two Lotharios of the age. Here am I daily fighting my squadrons and battalions and amusing myself, poor thing, as well as anyone can with their mere dry duty, with an head so full of firelocks, swords and bayonets, and so stuffed with buff accoutrements, slings and belts and pouches, and boots and spurs, bridles and saddles, I have scarce room for any other idea there; don't wonder, therefore, if I talk strangely and incoherently. It's much for me to talk at all out of my occupation, I assure you; nor does this metropolis afford a single event great or small, that could bear the telling

3. Lord Hyde left the bulk of his property to his niece, Lady Charlotte Capel (1721–90), m. (1752) Hon. Thomas Villiers, 2d son of 2d E. of Jersey, cr. (1756) Bn Hyde of Hindon and (1776) E. of Clarendon, and the heirs male of her body (GEC iii. 269). The Villiers family were apparently much richer than the Douglases. Some further details of Hyde's bequests of the family papers and pictures and the subsequent litigation concerning them are in V. J. Watney, *Cornbury and the*

Forest of Wychwood, 1910, pp. 191–2.
4. Conway apparently did not know that by family settlements in Nov. 1749 Lord Hyde had been 'put into possession of his father's estates, as if they had already devolved upon him by inheritance, an annuity of £2000 being reserved for Lord Clarendon' (ibid. 190), apparently because of Clarendon's business incompetence.
5. His father, Henry Hyde (1672 – 10 Dec. 1753), 4th E. of Clarendon.

even by yourself. I must therefore go back to yours: as to Mr Spencer's[6] match, knowing nothing of the parties, I can only guess at it by the opinion of others. Lord Granville,[7] you say, is for it, and Lady Cowper,[8] I hear, is in despair about it, which would rather make one think well of it but he is vastly young to marry; I hear but eighteen, so there's a dreadful time to cool and grow tired and at a season when I doubt one's most likely to be so. Your history of my ancient princess[9] is admirable; I don't think her quite incapable of giving provocations, but what provocation could move her antagonist to such an outrageous pitch of violence and impertinence I am curious to know; you civil people that bow to her don't quite lose your reputation, I think, but it's a mercy neither Col. V[ane][10] nor I are any longer her lovers; as to my Lord, I suppose he's out of the question.[11] It's a shocking violence to be sure; in France he'd be put in prison for it or worse, but here when you and all her friends have exclaimed, they'll get my Lady Yarmouth not to have her teeth drawn or cleaned by him and so it will end. I expected to hear a fracas of another kind about a person[12] I named, and am curious to know if her victorious and happy rival[13] has hazarded a conflict or retreated to her castle in Yorkshire.

6. John Spencer (1734–83), cr. (1761) Vct and (1765) E. Spencer; ultimately heir of Sarah, Ds of Marlborough. He had fallen in love with one of Sir Cecil Bisshopp's daughters at Lord Granville's ball mentioned *ante* 5 May 1753. 'Mr Spencer's family are happy that he is the Cymon of any Iphigenia that is a gentlewoman, and they say the match is agreed upon' (Lady Hervey to Rev. Edmund Morris 12 May 1753, Lady Hervey, *Letters*, ed. Croker, 1821, p. 197). The marriage, however, did not take place and Spencer married Margaret Georgiana Poyntz in 1755. HW's comments about the match in his letter of 5 May 1753 were omitted when that letter was published.

7. Spencer's grandfather.

8. Spencer's mother, Lady Georgiana Caroline Carteret (d. 1780), m. 1 (1734) Hon. John Spencer; m. 2 (1750) William Cowper (after 1762, Clavering Cowper), 2d E. Cowper (GM 1734, iv. 107).

9. Lady Caroline Petersham.

10. Hon. Henry Vane (1726–92), styled Vct Barnard 1754–8, 2d E. of Darlington, 1758; at this time Lt-Col. in the Coldstream Guards. His affair with Lady Caroline in 1750 is alluded to in MANN iv. 140 and MONTAGU i. 104, 107, where we have confused him with his father; this reference to 'Col. V.' makes it clear that it was the younger 'Harry' Vane who was involved with Lady Caroline; his father had succeeded to the peerage as 3d Bn Barnard in April 1753 and was never in the army.

11. Lady Caroline and her husband were usually on bad terms; see for example ibid. i. 107–8.

12. Perhaps Lady Caroline again, although the 'fracas' has not been explained.

13. Possibly the Hon. Isabella Byron (1721–95), m. 1 (1743) Henry Howard, 4th E. of Carlisle; m. 2 (1759) Sir William Musgrave, 6th Bt. Lord Carlisle's seat, Castle Howard, was in Yorkshire. In 1758 Lady Mary Wortley Montagu wrote about Lady Carlisle, 'I am sorry for Lord Carlisle. He was my friend as well as ac-

You are reading Lord Bolinbroke's last volume of letters, you say, and I have just taken up Lord Orrery's[14] in which I am an age behind all the world. They were read by everybody last year before I came home and I either did not hear or have forgot the opinions about 'em. But for myself except the character of Swift had raised people's curiosity I should wonder they were read at all, and are I think in as florid and flimsy a style as anything I have seen a great while.

I think Sir Charles's distich neither very new nor very ingenious, I must own. How the German language may have brightened it up I don't know. Monsieur Muchausen looks like a judge.

I wrote to you on my arrival here which I hope you have received; merely that you may know I did write which is all you can possibly learn from it but that I did arrive here. Early in the next month we shall move from hence.[15] I propose making a tour through my new quarters and soon after returning to England,[16] where I shall soon put you in mind of your promise to let us see you at Park Place; and remain most

Sincerely yours,

H. S. C.

You'll not be sorry to hear that by my accounts from Lady Ailesbury she grows better at Bath and is convinced the waters do her good.

---

quaintance, and a man of uncommon probity and good nature. I think he has showed it by the disposition of his will in the favour of a lady he had no reason to esteem. It is certainly the kindest thing he could do for her, to endeavour to save her from her own folly, which would have probably precipitately hurried her into a second marriage, which would most surely have revenged all her misdemeanours' (Lady Mary to Lady Bute 31 Oct. 1758, Lady Mary Wortley Montagu, op. cit. ii. 343).

14. John Boyle (1707–62), 5th E. of Orrery, 1731; 5th E. of Corke, 3 Dec. 1753. His *Remarks on the Life and Writings of Dr Jonathan Swift . . . in a Series of Letters . . . to his Son, the Honourable Hamilton Boyle* had been published in Nov. 1751 (GM 1751, xxi. 483–6, 527).

15. Probably to Athlone, whence Conway wrote to HW on his visit to his regiment the following year (*post* 15 May 1754).

16. Conway reached Park Place 22 June (*post* 24 June 1753).

To Conway, Thursday 24 May 1753

Printed from *Works* v. 35–7. This is probably the letter mentioned in HW's memoranda on Mann to HW 4 May 1753 (MANN iv. 375).

Strawberry Hill, May 24, 1753.

IT is well you are married! How would my Lady A. have liked to be asked in a parish church for three Sundays running?[1] I really believe she would have worn her weeds forever, rather than have passed through so impudent a ceremony! What do *you* think? —But you will want to know the interpretation of this preamble. Why, there is a new bill, which, under the notion of preventing clandestine marriages, has made such a general rummage and reform in the office of matrimony, that every Strephon and Chloe, every dowager and her Hussey,[2] will have as many impediments and formalities to undergo as a treaty of peace. Lord Bath invented this bill, but had drawn it so ill, that the Chancellor[3] was forced to draw a new one[4]—and then grew so fond of his own creature, that he has

1. Section one of the bill for preventing clandestine marriages (subsequently the Marriage Act, 26 Geo. II c. 33), now being debated in the House of Commons, provided that all banns of matrimony should be announced in an audible manner during divine service in a parish church for three Sundays preceding the marriage except under special licence from the Abp of Canterbury (provided for by section six) (Owen Ruffhead, *Statutes at Large*, 1763–1800, vii. 525–8; *Journals of the House of Commons* xxvi. 810, 820, 827, 830, 832–8).

2. Edward Hussey (after 1749, Hussey Montagu) (ca 1721–1802), cr. (1762) Bn and (1784) E. of Beaulieu, had secretly married Isabella, Dowager Ds of Montagu, in 1743, but the marriage was not revealed until 1746 (MONTAGU i. 36).

3. Philip Yorke Earl of Hardwicke (HW).

4. 'The bill had been originally moved by my Lord Bath, who, attending a Scotch cause, was struck with the hardship of a matrimonial case, in which a man, after a marriage of thirty years, was claimed by another woman on a pre-

contract. The Judges were ordered [31 Jan. 1753] to frame a bill that should remedy so cruel a retrospect. They did; but drew it so ill, and it was three times printed so inaccurately, that the Chancellor was obliged to give it ample correction. Whether from mere partiality to an ordinance thus become his own, or whether . . . new views of power opened . . . so it was, that the Chancellor gave all his attention to a statute into which he had breathed the very spirit of aristocracy and insolent nobility' (*Mem. Geo. II* i. 337). HW's account of the debates on the bill and its aftermath (ibid. i. 336–53) is the most complete contemporary report, but is strongly coloured by his own and his friends' opposition to the bill and by his animosity to Hardwicke; see *Hardwicke Corr.* ii. 58–68, 121–4. Subsequent historians have pointed out that the opposition, which became increasingly factious and personal, ignored all the real defects of the original bill and attempted amendments only in details (G. E. Howard, *A History of Matrimonial Institutions*, 1904, i. 449–50, 460–4; *Hardwicke Corr.* ii. 72–5; Lord Ilchester, *Henry*

crammed it down the throats of both Houses—though they gave many a gulp before they could swallow it. The Duke of Bedford attacked it first with great spirit and mastery, but had little support, though the Duke of Newcastle did not vote.[5] The lawyers were all ordered to nurse it through our House;[6] but, except the poor Attorney-General,[7] who is nurse indeed to all intents and purpose, and did amply gossip over it, not one of them said a word. Nugent[8] shone extremely in opposition to the bill, and, though every now and then on the precipice of absurdity, kept clear of it, with great humour and wit and argument, and was unanswered—Yet we were beat.[9] Last Monday[10] it came into the committee: Charles Townshend[11]

Fox, 1920, i. 185–6, 191–2; J. T. Hammick, *The Marriage Law of England*, 1887, pp. 10–14).

5. The bill had been introduced in the House of Lords 19 March, read a second time, debated and committed 29 March, debated in committee 5 and 9 April, reported with amendments 17 April, and finally passed on the third reading 4 May (*Journals of the House of Lords* xxviii. 54, 68, 78, 81–2, 98, 112–13). HW says elsewhere that the bill had passed through the Lords 'almost without notice . . . having been carried by an hundred Lords against the Duke of Bedford and eleven others' (*Mem. Geo. II* i. 336). Bedford's arguments 4 May, as recorded in Hardwicke's notes on the debate, are summarized in *Hardwicke Corr.* ii. 61, and a brief account of Bedford's speech on the amended bill 5 June appears in Cobbett, *Parl. Hist.* xv. 84n.

6. The bill was sent down from the Lords 7 May and received its first reading (apparently without opposition) 8 May (*Journals of the House of Commons* xxvi. 807, 810); debate began with the second reading 14 May when according to Henry Fox 'every lawyer in the House was sent down to vote for it' (Fox to Ilchester 15 May 1753, Ilchester, op. cit. i. 187).

7. Sir Dudley Rider (HW). Sir Dudley Ryder (1691–1756), Kt, 1740; attorney-general 1737–54; chief justice of the King's Bench 1754–6; M.P. St Germans 1733–4, Tiverton 1734–54. His speech opening the debate on the second reading is printed Cobbett, op. cit. xv. 1–12. According to Fox he 'gave up almost every

objection,' but this does not seem an accurate gloss to Ryder's granting 'that objections may be made to some parts of the bill. However, they are all such as, I think, we may easily remove by a few alterations or additions in the committee' (Ilchester, loc. cit.; Cobbett, op. cit. xv. 12).

8. Robert Nugent [1709–88], afterwards created [1767] Lord [Vct] Clare and [1776] Earl Nugent (HW); M.P. His speech on the second reading of the bill, 14 May, is printed ibid. xv. 12–24; see also *Mem. Geo. II* i. 340.

9. 116–55 (*Journals of the House of Commons* xxvi. 820; *Mem. Geo. II* loc. cit.). According to Fox the negative voice on the vote for commitment was so loud 'the Speaker gave it for the Noes, and the House seemed almost unanimous on our side till the division showed the contrary' (Ilchester, loc. cit., where Fox gives the division as 116–58). HW was one of the tellers for the Noes in the division (*Journals of the House of Commons*, loc. cit.).

10. 21 May.

11. Hon. Charles Townshend (1725–67), chancellor of the Exchequer 1766–7; M.P. Great Yarmouth 1747–56, Saltash 1756–61, Harwich 1761–7. This was his first major speech; the only accounts of it are in the present letter and *Mem. Geo. II* i. 340–1 where HW writes: 'He spoke long and with much wit, and drew a picture, with much humour at least, if not with much humility, of himself and of his own situation, as the younger son of a capricious father, who had already debarred

acted a very good speech with great cleverness, and drew a picture of his own story[12] and his father's[13] tyranny, with at least as much parts as modesty. Mr Fox[14] mumbled the Chancellor and his lawyers, and pinned the plan of the bill upon a pamphlet he had found of Dr Gally's,[15] where the doctor, recommending the French scheme of matrimony, says, *It was found that fathers were too apt to forgive.*[16] The gospel, I thought, said Mr Fox, enjoined forgiveness; but pious Dr Gally thinks fathers are too apt to forgive.[17] Mr Pelham, ex-

him from an advantageous match: "were new shackles to be forged to keep young men of abilities from mounting to a level with their elder brothers?" ' In the same passage HW draws a parallel between Townshend and Conway, both of whom then 'seemed marked by nature for leaders, perhaps for rivals in the government of their country.' For Townshend's speech on the third reading, 4 June, see Cobbett, op. cit. xv. 49–62.

12. The details of Charles Townshend's thwarted marriage plans have not been found, but a draft of a letter to him from his father 20 Jan. 1753, printed Hist. MSS Comm., 11th Report, App. pt iii, *Townshend MSS*, 1887, p. 381, indicates Lord Townshend's uncooperative attitude. He says in part: 'But give me leave to remind you that if your income in your present situation is so strait and severe as you represent what a melancholy situation must you and your lady be in if you marry with the additional income of only £700 per annum at the most. The reversionary expectations which as you say attend the lady's fortune are not as you truly observe objects to a person in your situation. . . . I am indeed very sorry to hear that you have entered upon such a scheme and project as this is, but it is your own and I will have nothing to do with it. I am equally surprised to find that you call on me to make up the fortune of this match. It is not in my power to advance anything on any such like occasion; nor were it in my power would it be in my disposition to make any advance upon a match which cannot be made suitable to your present circumstances. I desire therefore that I may hear no more of this, and am determined to give no further answer about it.'

13. Charles Townshend (1700–64), 3d Vct Townshend; Lord Townshend's uncompromising strictness in financial matters alienated his son Charles permanently (Sir Lewis Namier and John Brooke, *Charles Townshend*, 1964, pp. 34–6; see also pp. 20–8).

14. Henry Fox, afterwards created Lord Holland (HW). He was the leading opponent of the bill, partly out of opportunism and dislike of Hardwicke and lawyers in general, but as his letters to his brother show, partly from honest objections based on his own happy clandestine marriage (Ilchester, op. cit. i. 187–8, 195–7).

15. *Some Considerations upon Clandestine Marriages*, 1750, by Henry Gally (1696–1769), D.D., 1728; divine and classical scholar; rector of St Giles-in-the-Fields, 1732. Fox, in a letter of 15 May, urged his brother to read the book where he would 'see the bill with reasons' (ibid. i. 187).

16. This passage occurs in a sentence in Gally's introductory remarks (2d edn, 1750, p. 104) to the declaration of Louis XIII on marriage 29 Dec. 1639: 'And as it was found by experience, that parents were but too apt to forgive their children the offences, which they had committed against them by their clandestine marriages, this declaration took it out of their power to forgive them the offence of such transgressions against the laws of this country.'

17. HW in his other account of the debate merely says that Fox 'neither spared the bill nor the author of it, as wherever he laid his finger, it was not wont to be light' (*Mem. Geo. II* i. 342).

tremely in his opinion against the bill, and in his inclination too, was forced to rivet it,[18] and, without speaking one word for it,[19] taught the House how to vote for it; and it was carried against the chairman's leaving the chair by 165 to 84.[20]

This is all the news I know, or at least was all when I came out of town; for I left the tinkering of the bill,[21] and came hither last Tuesday to my workmen. I flatter myself I shall get into tolerable order to receive my Lady A. and you at your return from Sligo, from whence I have received your letter,[22] and where I hope you have had my first.[23] I say nothing of the exile of the Parliament of Paris,[24] for I know no more than you will see in the public papers; only, as we are going to choose a new Parliament, we could not do better than choose the exiles: we could scarce choose braver or honester men. I say as little of Mademoiselle Murphy,[25] for I conclude you hear nothing but her health drank in whisky. Don't all the naked Irish flatter themselves with preferment, and claim relation with her? Miss Chudleigh says there is some sense in belonging to a king who turns off an old mistress when he has got a new one.[26]

18. Fox told his brother 24 May that Pelham, 'drove by Lord Chancellor,' was 'driving against his own opinion the House into passing' the bill (Ilchester, op. cit. i. 188). HW elsewhere relates that 'at the very beginning, on the Duke of Newcastle's declining to vote in the bill, the Chancellor told Mr Pelham, "I will be supported in this, or I never will speak for you again"' (*Mem. Geo. II* i. 344). There is no substantial evidence that Pelham was driven to support the bill by Hardwicke's threat; rather he seems to have interpreted the opposition as an attack on his power and reacted accordingly. See also John W. Wilkes, *A Whig in Power*, Evanston, Ill., 1964, p. 185.

19. HW, however, in his account of the debate *Mem. Geo. II* i. 342 mentions Pelham as supporting the bill.

20. HW gives the same figures ibid. and in MONTAGU i. 147; the division, having occurred in committee, is not given in the Commons *Journals*.

21. In committee; from the present letter it is clear that HW's accounts of the debates there on the 23d, 25th and 28th

(*Mem. Geo. II* i. 342–3) were derived from someone else, quite probably Fox, since HW was at SH during the period.

22. *Ante* 8 May 1753; HW would not yet have received that of 19 May.

23. *Ante* 5 May 1753.

24. Louis XV exiled the parliament of Paris to Pontoise on 12 May; the news apparently did not reach London until the Paris *à-la-main* arrived 20 May (*Daily Adv.* 22 May). See n. 36 below.

25. An Irishwoman who was for a short time mistress to Louis XV (HW). Marie-Louise Morphy (ca 1738–1815), m. 1 (1755) Jacques de Beaufranchet d'Ayat; m. 2 (ca 1759) François-Nicolas Le Normant, cr. (1765) Comte de Flaghac; m. 3 (before 1798) Louis-Philippe Dumont (divorced, 1798); Louis XV's mistress 1753–5 (MANN iv. 542, n. 14).

26. Miss Chudleigh had engaged in a protracted flirtation with George II about 1750, but apparently was never his mistress. The expectation that the rise of Mme Morphy meant the decline of Mme de Pompadour proved false.

Arlington Street, May 29.

I am come to town for a day or two, and find that the Marriage Bill has not only lasted till now in the committee,[27] but has produced, or at least disclosed, extreme heats. Mr Fox and Mr Pelham have had very high words on every clause,[28] and the former has renewed his attacks on the Chancellor under the name of Dr Gally. Yesterday on the nullity clause[29] they sat till half an hour after three in the morning, having just then had a division on adjournment, which was rejected by the ministry by above 80 to 70.[30] The Speaker,[31] who had spoken well against the clause, was so misrepresented by the Attorney-General, that there was danger of a skimmington between the great wig and the coif, the former having given a flat lie to the latter.[32] Mr Fox, I am told, outdid himself for spirit, and severity on the Chancellor and the lawyers.[33] I say I am told; for I was content with having been beat twice, and did not attend. The heats between the two ministers[34] were far from cooling by the length of the debate. Adieu! You did little expect in these times, and at this season, to have heard such a Parliamentary history! The bill is not near finished;[35] Mr Fox has declared he will dispute every inch of ground. I hope he won't be banished to Pontoise.[36] I shall

27. See above, n. 21.

28. Fox wrote to his brother on the 26th: 'I was yesterday for the third time in the House till near 11 at night in the committee . . . and we got through three clauses only. I fight strongly, and give great offence, I believe, both to those who drive and are driven in this cursed affair' (Ilchester, op. cit. i. 188).

29. The 8th clause, annulling marriages contracted contrary to the inhibitions of the bill (Ruffhead, op. cit. vii. 526).

30. In *Mem. Geo. II* i. 343, HW gives the figures as 'above 80 to 40 odd'; the division, being in committee, is not in the Commons *Journals*.

31. Arthur Onslow (HW).

32. This altercation is not mentioned elsewhere; in *Mem. Geo. II* i. 342 HW merely comments that 'the Speaker argued with great weight against the clause.'

33. 'Mr Fox, at one in the morning, spoke against it for above an hour, and

laid open the chicanery and jargon of the lawyers, the pride of their Mufti [Hardwicke], and the arbitrary manner of enforcing the bill' (ibid. i. 343). He made an even more violent attack on Hardwicke on the 30th (ibid. i. 343–4), to which Hardwicke replied finally in the Lords on 6th June (ibid. i. 349).

34. Fox and Pelham.

35. It was debated again in committee on the 30th and 31st, reported on 1 June and passed on the 4th. HW gives accounts of these debates ibid. i. 343–6; that of the 4th is given in Cobbett, op. cit. xv. 33–84.

36. The parliament of Paris having espoused the cause of religious liberty, and apprehended several priests who by the authority of the Archbishop of Paris and other prelates had refused the sacraments to those who would not subscribe to the bull Unigenitus, were banished by the King, Louis XV, to Pontoise (HW). See *Hardwicke Corr.* ii. 69–71, 124.

write to you no more, so pray return. I hear most favourable accounts of my Lady A.

Yours ever,

Hor. Walpole

From Conway, Sunday 24 June 1753

Printed in full for the first time from the MS now wsl, formerly Rutnam. First printed, with omissions, *Fraser's Magazine*, 1850, xlii. 343–4.

Address: To the Honourable Horatio Walpole, Junior, in Arlington Street, London.

Postmark: 25 IV.

Memoranda (by HW): Answered 26.

R. 30.

There is a pencil drawing of trees and a tower.

Park Place, Sunday, June 24, 1753.

THE day before yesterday I returned from my travels in Ireland, which I notify to you that I may learn at the same time where you are, what becomes of you, and when one may hope to see you;[1] all that I know of myself worth remarking to you is that I think of coming to town towards Saturday next for two or three days, and that I am engaged to go to Stowe[2] and Hagley[3] I think in the beginning of August. I shall have some hopes of meeting you in town; I want to see Strawberry when you'll let me, and I want you to see Park Place, that is, I want to see you there very much. In all and every part of this you'll please to understand Lady Ailesbury and me as one, though I have so impertinently spoke in the first person; we go together, return together and think entirely so in what relates to you.

I received your letter with the history of the Marriage Bill, which diverts me a good deal and puzzles me a little; I think by yours and other accounts it seems more than the zeal for or against the scheme could naturally have produced, and yet the policy of ministers show-

1. For HW's visit to Park Place see *post* 26 July 1753 and n. 1.

2. Bucks, Lord Temple's seat; HW originally planned to join Conway there 28 July, but changed his plans and did not arrive until 2 August (Montagu i. 152; HW to Chute 4 Aug. 1753, Chute 75).

3. Worcs, Sir George Lyttelton's seat.

ing their teeth and snarling at one another when it is not time to bite I don't clearly understand; but I must own myself and very honestly do a miserable politician. Perhaps as the last general war of politics ended by the event of two years ago,[4] these skirmishes are only to keep our orators in breath till another breaks out; and it's so much the nature of Englishmen to divide and subdivide that if there were but two left in the world I believe they'd form two parties and if there was but one he'd quarrel with himself. I have actually heard of two living in a lighthouse off the coast of Cornwal, where they see no soul but themselves, who quarrelled and did not speak to one another for a twelvemonth, though as I have said they had no mortal to speak to and I believe could neither read nor write.

Adieu! I hope Strawberry has fared better than Park Place. We are choked with drought, all our ponds emptied, our trees dead and our turf burnt. If there is any news tell me and believe me

Most sincerely yours,

H. S. C.

To CONWAY, Tuesday 26 June 1753

Missing; mentioned in HW's memoranda on the previous letter.

From CONWAY, Thursday 28 June 1753

Printed for the first time from the MS now WSL, formerly Rutnam. HW's 'R. 30' on Conway's letter *ante* 24 June 1753 is probably the date he received this one.

Park Place, Thursday, June 28, 1753.

I AM very sorry not to accept your invitation which you are sensible how well we are disposed to, but part of my scheme for town which I thought I had mentioned was to go to Court on Sun-

4. The dismissal of the Bedford faction and the general ministerial rearrangement in June 1751 following the Regency Act disputes.

day and see the Duke[1] etc.; that, I am informed, is the best day and this is of consequence as a whole week depends upon it. Besides, we have Nanny with us and in this unsettled state of your house there's no running in a guest upon you you did not expect. I am glad your business falls in with ours so as to bring us together in town where we may plot our future meetings, journeyings and visitings.

I heartily wish you joy of the charming, plentiful rain that is falling at this minute; I have been watching it like a child half the morning and can now scarce keep my eyes off it. We wanted it at least as much as you could and a good many teacups of it; for besides our usual dryness and tawniness we have been new turfing and new planting just before our windows and new sowing with grass seed, and have been browner than any Finch,[2] till this good rain came. I now have a little hopes; already I think we begin to look of a sort of green-goose colour, something between green and yellow like a young Levison.[3] Adieu, my dear Horry, I am vastly happy in the prospect of seeing something of you I hope for more than a day and an half, being

Most sincerely yours,

H. S. C.

Missy came hopping down just as I had finished this. I asked her what I should say to you and she said, 'Give my duty to him and tell him I hope I shall see him soon.' There's a wife! Gives her duty to her husband and *hopes* to see him! Things unheard of almost in these days and you call her inconstant!

---

1. Of Cumberland.
2. The swarthiness of the Finch family is frequently alluded to in HW's letters; he wrote to Montagu 18 May 1749

OS that at Strawberry 'the turf is as brown as Lady Bell Finch' (MONTAGU i. 82).
3. I.e., Leveson Gower.

From CONWAY, Thursday 26 July 1753

Printed for the first time from the MS now wsl, formerly Rutnam.
Address: To the Honourable Horatio Walpole, Junior, in Arlington Street, London.
Postmark: 27 IY.
There are extensive pencil sketches of a building and grounds.

Park Place, July 26.

Dear Horry,

WE have been in constant expectation of hearing from you and hopes of seeing you: the time of our going to Stowe now draws so near that I have almost given up any but those of meeting you there, which as you flattered us with I now write to tell you that we think of going the first of next month which I think is Wednesday next. If you don't make us a comfortable visit,[1] stay till after that and let us in the meantime see you there. But if you do think of calling on us as you go we shall have nobody but Nanny with us and you know at all times how glad we are to see you. Lady Ailesbury and all here are much yours down to little Missy, as is most sincerely

Your aff[ectionate] friend and coz,

H. S. C.

To LADY AILESBURY, October 1753

Two letters missing, mentioned *post* 23 Oct. 1753; one of them had arrived 'last post,' and was possibly addressed to Conway rather than to Lady Ailesbury.

1. HW paid this visit in the next few days on his way to visit George Montagu at Greatworth; he gives a few details in his letter to Chute 4 Aug. 1753, from Stowe, where he spent two days after leaving Greatworth (CHUTE 69–78).

From CONWAY, Tuesday 23 October 1753

Printed for the first time from the MS now WSL, formerly Rutnam.

Memorandum (by HW):

Does any noble family exting[uish], one should grieve that such a succession of heroes, statesmen, patriots should fail if a little knowledge of mankind did not call forth the blemishes which these varnishers have slobbered over— Must ⟨vices⟩ avarice pass unmentioned, because he did not set fire to the City. Hatton.[1]

There is a smudged pencil drawing of an arched doorway.

Park Place, Oct. 23, 1753.

Dear Horry,

I AM vastly ashamed of the rusticity of my lady wife and have nothing to say in her defence but that I believe she waited to answer your letter for an event which by some fatality or negligence is not yet accomplished, which is the fitting up a certain little brick pond for the accommodation of the gold-fish;[2] I gave orders for it soon after your first letter to Lady A. and was confused at the receipt of your second last post to find those orders had not been punctually executed; which I shall look into myself without delay and as soon as the work is sufficiently advanced for their reception will send over a careful person if I can find one to bring 'em on horseback, which I shall think much the best way, as notwithstanding our past negligences we are too impatient to have 'em here to bear they should undergo a fortnight's or three weeks' voyage and run any hazard of being lost in the Thames and confounded with vulgar gudgeons. The seed came safe and is most of it sown. As to kindness, good humour, etc., I only wish you may receive this with as much as I write it and as much forgiveness as we feel contrition for our respective negligences. But as to being well at Park Place, I shall never think you thoroughly well there nor that you think yourself so, till you are a little more there.[3] But this only by the by and not by way of complaint but pure desire of seeing as much of you as possible. You tell me no news twenty-six miles nearer the fountain-

1. Perhaps Sir Christopher Hatton (1540–91), lord chancellor 1587–91; see OSSORY ii. 256, n. 5.

2. These were not finally delivered until the following July (*post* 3, 6, 7 July 1754).

3. In addition to his visit at the end of July, HW had dined at Park Place in early September on his way to Hagley and Matson (HW to Bentley Sept. 1753, CHUTE 147 and n. 7).

Lady Ailesbury's Comp.ts
to Mr. Walpole
and desires the Favour of
his Company on Monday
Evening the 1st of Jan:

LADY AILESBURY'S INVITATION CARD TO HORACE WALPOLE

head so expect none from me. Lady Ailesbury really intended to write from the moment she received yours but I have got the start of her. She sends many compliments and excuses. Nanny is much yours and I most exceedingly and faithfully so.

H. S. C.

I said I'd tell you no news but to show you I can, we are to have a *grandissime* New Interest cavalcade next Monday,[4] at which only imagine me parading with an embroidered furniture, with four or five monkeys at my heels in green and orange cockades[5]—then drinking bumpers with four hundred stinking freeholders; and pity me.

---

4. 'On Monday last [29 Oct.] Lord Parker and Sir Edward Turner [the 'New Interest' candidates for Oxfordshire] were met by their friends at the end of Fair Mile near Henly; from whence they went in procession to the town. They were preceded by a large band of music, playing *God bless great George our King*, after that came the flags, on one of which was inscribed, PARKER AND TURNER; and on the reverse of it, THE RIGHT AND PRIVILEGE OF VOTING RESTORED, 1753. On the other flag was painted LIBERTY AND LOYALTY, and on the reverse of it, THE PROTESTANT RELIGION AND SUCCESSION; then followed upwards of 800 real freeholders by three in a row, headed by the Duke of Marlborough riding between Lord Parker and Sir Edward Turner, by the Earl of Macclesfield, Earl Harcourt and Lord Cadogan, and by a great number of gentlemen and clergy. The rear was brought up by the equipages of the gentlemen present, and by an immense crowd of people. When they came to Henley, they were most nobly entertained at the Town Hall, and at several public houses; the same loyal healths were again drank [as] at Watlington [two days before]; the highest joy and unanimity were expressed on the occasion, which gave a melancholy forecast to the enemies of the future success of Lord Parker and Sir Edward Turner' (*Oxford Journal* 3 Nov. 1753, ostensibly quoted from a London source). The affair is ridiculed in the *Oxford Journal*, an organ of the 'Old Interest,' in the issues for 27 Oct., 3 Nov., and 10 Nov. The election campaign is fully treated in R. J. Robson. *The Oxfordshire Election of 1754*, Oxford, 1949; this incident is dated there 3 Nov. (pp. 57–8) although based on the sources cited above. The Henley gathering is also mentioned as 'a most grand entertainment' in the *Daily Adv.* 31 Oct.

5. The colours of the 'New Interest.'

From CONWAY, Tuesday 18 December 1753

Printed for the first time from the MS now WSL, formerly Rutnam.

Park Place, Dec. 18, '53.

Dear Horry,

I HAVE received a letter[1] from my brother today which I answer to you as the chief matter of it is your seeming to desire that I should come to town, which, though I am vastly ready to do if I can be of any use to you or our affairs, I venture now to defer till I hear from you, at least, because my brother mentions no new matter that makes me necessary—except the advertisement[2] and because I think that cannot possibly occasion any alteration in our proceedings till we see if any effect is produced by it, which for one, I own, I am not much apprehensive there will, and then it seems to me as if that advertisement itself would in a matter cut off all future difficulties, as nothing farther can be done by anybody, unless they advertise a reward for anyone who shall make a will for the late Capt. Erasmus Shorter; which I am now fully persuaded he has not done for himself and as I believe nobody but ourselves know exactly the state of his affairs and fortune I scarce think any but ourselves could make a will for him.

As for what has lately happened,[3] it surprises me very little. I did not imagine the matter would be suffered to sleep till all possible methods had been taken to produce the supposed will. I think they

1. Missing; Conway's letter to Hertford, 16 Dec. 1753, to which this was probably a reply, is now WSL, printed *Colburn's United Service Magazine*, 1881, liii pt i. 254–6; it throws a little light on the present letter.

2. 'If any gentleman has any knowledge of the will of the late Capt. Erasmus Shorter, of Park Place, St James's, he is hereby humbly desired to give what intelligence thereof he can to Mr A. B. at the White Hart Tavern in Holborn, over against Chancery Lane' (*Daily Adv.* 17 Dec.). From this letter and Conway's to Hertford 16 Dec., it appears that this advertisement may have been inserted by Sir Edward Walpole. HW's and Conway's uncle Erasmus Shorter had died 23 Nov.

without leaving a will, so that his fortune of £30,000 would be divided equally among his surviving niece and nephews: HW, Sir Edward Walpole, Conway, Hertford, and Hon. Anne Seymour Conway. There had been trouble with his servants, who were suspected of robbing their master, and one of them was even suspected of murdering him (HW to Bentley 19 Dec. 1753, CHUTE 158–9; MONTAGU i. 156–7; MANN iv. 403; GRAY i. 25; *Daily Adv.* 26 Nov.).

3. The advertisement; it had been preceded by a proposal, apparently by Sir Edward Walpole, to issue such an advertisement, which Hertford and HW had rejected on the part of the other heirs (Conway to Hertford, 16 Dec. 1753).

are taken now and though a little uncouth at present will soon, I am persuaded, even give us fuller satisfaction in the affair than we could properly have given ourselves. As to consulting, I am sure you know much better how to proceed than I can tell you; what you did in regard to the proposal was certainly right; in regard to this advertisement I think nothing can be done; if it could have a right effect we should none of us be against it; if it is to have a bad one we can none of us prevent it; so that I believe the taking no particular notice of it is the best thing we can do. I recommended to my brother great temper and coolness in all our dealings with yours,[4] as nothing is more disagreeable than family *éclats*, especially in money affairs; I take the same liberty with you;[5] and so, dear Horry, don't think me idle, much less neglectful. I don't think my presence worth a halfpenny to you; if it is let me know and I'll be with you in a moment. I should go a thousand miles, I assure you, with the same readiness I shall 34 to do you the smallest service and satisfaction, being most faithfully, your affectionate friend and coz,

H. S. C.

PS. I really think a few days hence when this advertisement has had its operation will be the time and not before to do anything we may have to do, but must repeat that I really come with the greatest pleasure if you do but think you want me.

---

4. 'I had that opinion of our friend in question, and of the bias his mind would take on this occasion, that something of the kind, though not exactly that, I really did expect. You can scarce doubt of my approving your answer; it was both reasonable and moderate, and of the kind that I think all negotiations with that person should be—I mean, sticking firm to what is sensible and right, without showing any suspicion of the motives from which such propositions must be supposed to proceed' (ibid.).

5. Conway alludes to HW in his letter to Hertford 16 Dec.: 'I shall only add, what I believe is unnecessary (to you at least) that in any future discussions upon this head, I hope we shall bestow a double portion of coolness and temper to allay the extreme heat and frequent wrongheadedness of a particular person.' HW and Sir Edward were on bad terms until some years later.

From CONWAY, Wednesday ?1754–8

Printed for the first time from the MS now WSL, formerly Rutnam.

The note is dated conjecturally from the references to 'Chiswick' and to 'Mr Southcoat's'. Chiswick was the seat of Conway's friend and political patron, the M. of Hartington, later (1755) 4th D. of Devonshire; Hartington had inherited it from his father-in-law, the 3d E. of Burlington, upon the Earl's death, 3 Dec. 1753. Philip Southcote (see below, n. 2), whose seat, Woburn Farm, was during his lifetime and afterwards the object of expeditions of people interested in the gardening, died 25 Sept. 1758 (GM 1758, xxviii. 453). Presumably the present note lies somewhere between these two dates, since Conway would probably no longer have referred to Woburn Farm as 'Mr Southcoat's' after Southcote's death.

Address: To the Honourable Horatio Walpole, Twickenham.

Wednesday.

Dear Horry,

I AM afraid you'll think us very troublesome and impertinent, but having an old engagement to go to Chiswick[1] which among the few days remaining to me I had some difficulty in finding one for, we have therefore determined if it's equally convenient to you to come to you from Chiswick on Saturday after dinner and dine with you on Sunday after our expedition to Mr Southcoat's.[2] If you have any objection to this little change in our scheme be so good as to let us know; if not, depend upon us at that time, till when, adieu.

H. C.

To CONWAY, April 1754

Missing; mentioned *post* 15 May 1754.

1. Chiswick House, Chiswick, Middlesex, seat of the M. of Hartington (see headnote).

2. Philip Southcote (d. 1758), whose seat, Woburn Farm, at Chertsey, Surrey, was 'one of the first places improved according to the principles of modern gardening, and laid the foundation of a taste which is admired by all true lovers of that science' (John Nichols, *Literary Anecdotes of the Eighteenth Century*, 1812–15, ix. 629). HW credits Southcote with inventing the '*ferme ornée*' ('On Modern Gardening,' *Works* ii. 541).

From CONWAY, Wednesday 15 May 1754

Printed for the first time from the MS now WSL, formerly Rutnam.

Athlone,[1] May 15, 1754.

IT'S scarce fair to answer a note with a letter, yet I reserved thanking you for yours from town and for the trouble I gave you there[2] till I had an opportunity or rather an excuse for writing one; to be sure it is not very necessary to tell you of my good voyage and safe arrival; as I am a man of consequence here[3] I know you may have seen it in the newspapers;[4] but the truth is I hate leaving off and I dread being left off by my old friends; I both want to hear from them and of them; and feel detached from the world and almost out of it when I am away from 'em without it: therefore don't think I pretend to entertain you. I should not have chose this dull time and place and if that was the only end of correspondence should write but little. I don't pay this as a duty neither, but take it as a right, which I think three or four hundred miles distance entitles me to; I say nothing of my time as I hope it won't be long enough to improve my title much; you'll just have enough to answer this if you have leisure and disposition and if you have not do it at Park Place and let me know when I shall hope to see you there or come with your answer when you hear I am come back. I shall go to town, Kensington, etc., when I do for a day or two and then it's just possible we may meet.

I found the Duke of Dorset on my arrival just upon the point of departing;[5] people had formed either hopes or apprehensions of ter-

---

1. Co. Westmeath, 78 miles west of Dublin, where Conway was visiting his regiment.

2. Unexplained.

3. As colonel of a regiment on the Irish establishment, brother of one of the greatest landowners in Ireland, and M.P. for co. Antrim, although he had never taken his seat. Conway is probably alluding, too, to the importance he would have had under the abortive plan of March–April 1754 to send his brother, Lord Hertford, to Ireland as lord deputy to compose the political disputes there. HW elsewhere asserts that this scheme had been defeated largely by Lord George Sackville's jealousy of the part Conway would play as his brother's assistant; but in fact the project was abandoned by the Cabinet Council as administratively unworkable, although the members and the Sackvilles otherwise approved of Hertford as the man for the post (*Mem. Geo. II* i. 390; Hist. MSS Comm., *Stopford-Sackville MSS*, 1904–10, i. 209; BM Add. MSS 32734, f. 283; 32735, ff. 62, 86; 32995, f. 209).

4. Not found.

5. Dorset, lord lieutenant of Ireland since 1751, left Dublin for England 10 May (see following note). His tenure had been accompanied by violent political quarrels since 1752; for the most recent developments see MANN iv. 409–10 and nn. 17–21, 425–6 and nn. 4–8; MORE 5 and n. 10.

rible things that were to happen on his going; how he was to be mobbed, insulted etc. I did not stay in Dublin to see the end of it but hear all parties were disappointed, that he went away with the usual state and quiet,[6] and that the mob themselves were in greatest danger of being mobbed by a superior mob that attended his Grace. Upon the whole I found and was vastly glad to find things much quieter here than I expected; the last changes,[7] if they made any alteration seem rather to have made 'em more so and as nothing is so unreasonable or so unsteady as party spirit, what seemed naturally calculated to set 'em in a flame seems rather to have damped that they have been in this six months. There's as much politics as you could reasonably expect; perhaps you knew it all before, but it was not for that I wrote as I told you; it was not to give you an account of Athlone, nor our reviews and exercisings; in short, if I had not told you so you'd easily have found out it was for writing sake and for nothing but the pleasure of telling you how sincerely I am, dear Horry,

Your affectionate friend and coz,

H. S. C.

If you write, direct to Athlone.

---

6. A correspondent wrote to Lord George Sackville, Dorset's son, 14 May, on the Duke's departure, '. . . among the prodigious number of people who assembled to see him pass there was no sign of ill humour, but all the decency and respect imaginable. . . . This behaviour of the people in general must have proceeded from good will, and it may certainly be concluded from it that the attempts to poison and enflame them have by no means had the desired effect' (*Stopford-Sackville MSS*, loc. cit.). Further details of Dorset's departure are in the *Whitehall Evening Post* 16–18 May.

7. The dismissal of Speaker Boyle, leader of the opposition to Dorset, from the chancellorship of the Exchequer 19 April, and the concurrent removal of several of his allies from their offices (MANN iv. 425–6 and nn. 4–5).

From CONWAY, Wednesday 3 July 1754

Printed for the first time from the MS now WSL, formerly Rutnam.

Park Place, July 3, 1754.

Dear Horry,

I HAVE given orders to Mr Chifang[1] to fit up the apartment for the Chinese fish;[2] and on Friday if it be convenient will send for them.—Tell me when we shall see you; I hope you'll come to their house-warming. Pray come while we're green; we shall never be able to keep fresh for you in this parching month of July, and I am at this moment so divided between my grass and my hay, my pleasure and my profit, I don't know what to do. In the meantime pray for fair weather and rain by turns. But I think the latter preponderates, till you come at least; as I'd give a ton of hay with pleasure to make Park Place a bit more agreeable to you, or our greenth a shade brighter in your eye, *non ita certandi cupidus quam propter amorem.*[3]

Accept all our compliments and believe me

Most sincerely yours,

H. S. C.

1. Another attempt at a Chinese name; see *ante* 8 Nov. 1752.

2. Conway's 'little basin with gold and silver fish' is referred to in a description of Park Place written in 1787; see Appendix 15.

3. Lucretius, *De Rerum Natura* iii. 5: 'Not so desirous of contending as on account of love.'

To Conway, Saturday 6 July 1754

Printed from *Works* v. 38. This is probably the letter referred to in HW's memoranda written on Mann's letter of 14 June 1754 (MANN iv. 436).

Strawberry Hill, Saturday, July 6, 1754.

YOUR letter certainly stopped to drink somewhere by the way, I suppose with the hearty hostess at the Windmill;[1] for, though written on Wednesday, it arrived here but this morning: it could not have travelled more deliberately in the Speaker's body-coach.[2] I am concerned, because, your fishmonger not being arrived, I fear you have stayed for my answer. The fish[3] are apprised that they are to *ride* over to Park Place, and are ready booted and spurred; and the moment their pad arrives, they shall set forth. I would accompany them on a pillion, if I were not waiting for Lady Mary,[4] who has desired to bring her poor little sick girl[5] here for a few days to try the air. You know how courteous a knight I am to distressed virgins of five years old, and that my castle gates are always open to them.[6] You will, I am sure, accept this excuse for some days; and as soon as ever my hospitality is completed, I will be ready to obey your summons, though you should send a water-pot for me. I am in no fear of not finding you in perfect verdure; for the sun, I believe, is gone a great way off to some races or other, where his horses are to run for a king's plate: we have not heard of him in this neighbourhood. Adieu!

Yours ever,

HOR. WALPOLE

1. Perhaps the Windmill Inn at Salt Hill, between Slough and Maidenhead on the main road from London or Twickenham to Park Place.

2. A vast, heavy, Jacobean coach, used as the Speaker's state coach (Ralph Straus, *Carriages and Coaches*, 1912, pp. 113–14; Edward Croft-Murray, 'Three Famous State Coaches,' *Country Life*, Coronation Number, 6 June 1953, pp. 79–82).

3. Gold fish (HW).

4. Lady Mary Churchill (HW).

5. Mary Churchill (b. 1750), m. (1777) Charles Sloane Cadogan, 3d Bn Cadogan, cr. (1800) E. Cadogan, by whom she was divorced in 1796.

6. Mr Conway's only daughter had been left with Mr Walpole at Strawberry Hill, when he and Lady Ailesbury went to Ireland with his regiment [in 1752] (HW).

From Conway, Sunday 7 July 1754

Printed for the first time from the MS now wsl, formerly Rutnam.
Memoranda (by HW):

[in ink]¹   Mr B[entley]   11
         R[igby]
         Shelv[ocke]² } 13

[in pencil]   Mrs Pigot³
         Sir Crisp Gascoyne⁴
         Ware
         jars—tuscan vase
         17–6
         5–5–0
         Biograph. 3d.

Park Place, July 7, '54.

I NEED not explain to you all the foolish confusions I made about dates and days, and scarce can; you'd have much more reason to think I had been tippling than my letter.—I shall only endeavour to be a little more exact now when I tell you I shall send for the fish on Tuesday and expect you and them that afternoon or any day afterwards with great pleasure. There are two houses preparing for 'em as I don't care to trust all my treasure on one bottom.

If Miss Churchill likes or wants a very wholesome air indeed there are many here would be vastly glad you'd bring her; I say nothing of Lady Mary for she has refused us already; we have no such *preux chevaliers,* nor such Gothic castles; but hills and groves and meads and purling streams in abundance and a little fairy of the mountain here that will come in the garden-pot to fetch her with all her heart. We are all most exceedingly

Yours.

---

1. Presumably a list of letters written in July; HW wrote Bentley 9 July.

2. He also appears in HW's list on Mann's letter of 14 June 1754 (MANN iv. 436).

3. See *post* 30 July 1754, n. 1.

4. (1700–61), lord mayor of London, 1752, who ordered a reprieve of the convicted kidnapper of Elizabeth Canning and an indictment against the latter for perjury (William Maitland, *The History and Survey of London,* 1756, i. 694–701). Gascoyne's address to the liverymen of London justifying his actions is summarized in *London Magazine* July 1754, xxiii. 317–20.

To CONWAY, ca Saturday 20 July 1754

Missing; mentioned *post* ?23 July 1754.

From CONWAY, ?Tuesday ?23 July 1754

Printed for the first time from the MS now WSL, formerly Rutnam. Although Conway has clearly dated this 'July 21,' it appears from his own references that he was not at Park Place on Sunday, and from the postmark that it was written a day or two later.

Address: To the Honourable Horatio Walpole, Esq., in Arlington Street, London.

Postmark: 24 IY.

Park Place, July 21 [?23], 1754.

I AM sorry I did not get your letter on Sunday which I missed by being gone to town to kiss hands;[1] I don't know whether I could say our house was not full at the time you proposed to come but it must be very full indeed if we could not or would not make room for you. Lord and Lady Temple, Miss Banks[2] and Mr Pitt,[3] have been here these three or four days and stay till Thursday or Friday, which is an handsome and friendly visit; and a thing of good example. We are very jolly and merry and should all be very glad you could enjoy and improve our mirth. After they are gone we shall be very empty, and have no immediate engagement at all but that I must go once more on Saturday evening or Sunday to kiss hands again and come back at latest Monday morning. Do take your measures on this as suits you best only with a little leaning to our impatience to see you.

Your fable[4] is charming and though you, very modestly indeed, said you could not show it me I have boldly shown it to the company here who are all delighted with it. That I am mercenary I own where

1. On his appointment as colonel of the 4th Horse (later 7th Dragoon Guards): his appointment is dated 8 July in the regimental lists, but is first mentioned in the newspapers in the *Whitehall Evening Post* 18–20 July.

2. Probably Margaret ('Peggy') Banks (d. 1793), who married Lord Temple's brother, the Hon. Henry Grenville, three years later. A 'Miss Banks' was living with

Lady Temple at this time (Pitt to Temple 23 May, ca Oct., 1 Nov., Temple to Wilkes 12 Oct., *Grenville Papers* i. 122, 125, 127, 131, MSS now WSL.).

3. Apparently William Pitt; he planned to visit Stowe in June (Pitt to Temple 23 May, ibid. i. 122, MS now WSL), but his exact movements are not known between May and August.

4. *The Entail,* written in July 1754,

such gain is to be made, yet, I assure you, shall set your farther absence at a furious price; so think of no more corruption at present for as well as I love your bribes I love your company better, being

Most sincerely yours,

H. S. C.

From CONWAY, Tuesday 30 July 1754

Printed for the first time from the MS now WSL, formerly Rutnam. The year is supplied by the references to the 'second course of kissing,' mentioned *ante* ?23 July 1754 as to take place around 28 July, and to the gold-fish, which HW had sent to Park Place at the beginning of the month (*ante* 3, 6, 7 July 1754).

Park Place, July 30.

I HAD certainly rather you had a good excuse than a bad one when you stay away from us, yet I assure you am very sorry for that you have now, which is indeed too just to leave any room for me either for hopes or endeavours to elude it. I am sorry for our very old acquaintance poor Mrs Pigot[1] and very sorry for Mrs Leneve who has too much low spirits and too much mortification already from her bad health; pray make my compliments to her.

Your fish thrive vastly and Lady Ailesbury says are grown; I am in great hopes my puddles agree with 'em in one of which I have made an island and a charming bed of rushes for 'em to lie in.

Adieu. Let us only hope we shall see you as soon as you can come; it can't be soon enough, and believe me

Sincerely yours,

H. S. C.

I have now finished my second course of kissing.[2]

'occasioned by the author being asked (after he had finished the little castle at Strawberry Hill and adorned it with the portraits and arms of his ancestors) if he did not design to entail it on his family' (*Works* i. 28; 'Short Notes,' GRAY i. 25). There is a copy in HW's *MS Poems*, pp. 222–4; another copy in HW's hand with drawings by Bentley is now WSL, reproduced in W. S. Lewis, *Bentley's Designs for Walpole's Fugitive Pieces*, 1936.

1. As Elizabeth Le Neve (*ante* 31 Oct. 1741, n. 18), the niece of 'Mrs' Isabella Le Neve, she had been a member of Sir Robert Walpole's household (SELWYN 37, 80; MONTAGU i. 69; MANN ii. 36). This letter suggests that her death, previously uncertain, may have occurred at this time.

2. See *ante* ?23 July 1754 and n. 1.

From CONWAY, Sunday 4 August 1754

Printed for the first time from the MS now WSL, formerly Rutnam.
Address: To the Honourable Horatio Walpole, Jun., in Arlington Street, London.
Postmark: ?5 AV. ?HENLEY.

Park Place, Aug. 4, 1754.

I HAVE been asked for a copy of your fable; may I give it? I would not without asking, though I am quite sure it cannot be seen or read or admired enough.—I want to know when you think of coming and must now beg you'll let us know when you do; as we are in danger of being for a few days quite full, even to the garrets. I shall be sorry if it delays your coming a single day after wishing for you so long.

I was yesterday at the Lodge[1] to see the Duke with whom I had like to have had on Thursday a most terrible accident at the review near Reading;[2] where my horse, being in a fright and closing towards his and I spurring and striving to get out of his way, my horse kicked and unluckily hit his leg; but yet luckily in an unfortunate accident so as to do him no farther harm than a slight bruise; you may imagine the concern and fright I was in; which I did not soon recover though he assured me he was not hurt and was as good-natured and took as much pains to make me easy as possible. Adieu! I am retired from a circle of *beau monde* so must seal in haste.

---

1. Cumberland Lodge in Windsor Great Park.
2. 'Thursday his Royal Highness the Duke of Cumberland reviewed Lord Robert Manners's regiment of Foot on Bullmarsh Heath, near Reading, which made a very fine appearance, and went through their exercise and firings very much to his Highness's satisfaction. During the review his Highness received a smart kick on his leg from Col. Conway's horse, but, having on a strong boot, received but little injury' (*Daily Adv.* 5 Aug.).

To Conway, Tuesday 6 August 1754

Printed from the MS now wsl; first printed Wright iii. 69–70. For the history of the MS, see *ante* 29 June 1744 OS; it was marked by HW for inclusion in *Works,* but was not included.

Endorsed: Mr H. Walpole Aug. 6 – 1754.

Strawberry Hill, Aug. 6, 1754.

FROM Sunday next, which is the eleventh, till the four- or five-and-twentieth, I am quite unengaged, and will wait upon you any of the inclusive days, when your house is at leisure, and you will summon me; therefore you have nothing to do but to let me know your own time. Or if this period does not suit you, I believe I shall be able to come to you any part of the first fortnight in September, for though I ought to go to Hagley,[1] it is incredible how I want resolution to tap such a journey.

I wish you joy of escaping such an accident as breaking the Duke's leg; I hope he and you will be known to posterity together by more dignified wounds than the kick of a horse; as I can never employ my time better than in being your biographer, I beg you will take care that I may have no such plebeian mishaps upon my hands; or if the Duke is to fall out of battle, he has such delicious lions and tigers,[2] which I saw the day before yesterday at Windsor, that he will be exceedingly to blame if he does not give some of them an exclusive patent for tearing him to pieces. There is a beautiful tiger at my neighbour Mr Crammond's[3] here, of which I am so fond, that my Lady Townshend says it is the only thing I ever wanted to kiss. As you know how strongly her Ladyship sympathizes with the Duke,[4] she contrived to break the tendon of her foot, the very day that his leg was in such danger. Adieu!

Yours ever,

H. W.

PS. You may certainly do what you please with the fable; it is neither worth giving or refusing.

1. There is no evidence that HW went there in 1754 or that he visited Park Place.

2. Details of the Duke's menagerie are collected in Evan Charteris, *William Augustus Duke of Cumberland and the Seven Years' War,* [1925], pp. 22–3.

3. Not identified; HW mentions a 'Mr Crammond' in his 'Paris Journals' in 1766 and 1767 (DU DEFFAND v. 309, 316).

4. Sarcasm: Lady Townshend had Jacobite sympathies (*ante* 16 April 1747 OS, n. 16).

From CONWAY, ?Friday 9 August ?1754

Printed for the first time from the MS now WSL, formerly Rutnam. The year of this letter is uncertain. Conway's brother had apparently leased the manor house of Taplow, Bucks, for seven years from Midsummer Day 1754 and resided there occasionally until 1759 at least (*post* 1 Sept. 1759); 1757, 1758, and 1759 can be eliminated, and 1755 and 1756 seem unlikely, from what we know of the movements of HW, Conway, and the Hertfords in each August. HW's repeated postponements of a visit to Park Place in July 1754 suggest that year, and the present letter can be read as a reply to HW's of 6 Aug. 1754.

Address: To the Honourable Horatio Walpole, Jun., at his house at Twickenham.

Postmark: 10 AV.

Taploe, August 9.

THIS will come very near you tomorrow but how or when it will reach you I don't know as it's committed to my brother who says he can't send his servant with it but I hope it will somehow or other reach you soon as it's to tell you that both our house and ourselves are in perfect readiness to receive you. I am only sorry we could not see you in the summer as the country is much pleasantest in that season and our cold place shows to much greater advantage. I say no more, being in company and hoping you'll let us see [you] very, very soon.

All Taploe and Park Place who are assembled here desire their compliments. Adieu.

TO HON. ANNE SEYMOUR CONWAY (LATER MRS HARRIS), September 1754

Missing; answered *post* 30 Sept. 1754.

From HON. ANNE SEYMOUR CONWAY (LATER MRS HARRIS), Monday 30 September 1754

Printed for the first time from the MS now wsl, formerly Rutnam. 1754 seems to be the only possible year; Hertford apparently did not lease the house at Taplow until 1754 (*post* 1 Sept. 1759), while the Hon. Anne Seymour Conway married John Harris 10 March 1755 (Collins, *Peerage*, 1812, ii. 563).

Endorsed (by HW): From Anne Seymour Conway sister of the Earl of Hertford, afterwards 2d wife of John Harris of Hayne, Devon.

Sept. 30th.

Dear Mr Walpole,

I RECEIVED your letter at Park Place, and have by this post sent orders to my servant in town that you may have Lady Hertford's picture whenever you call for it. I believe it will be difficult to take it down, but as you are so good as to say you will see it carefully done I have no fear about it, and you are extremely welcome to have it copied.[1] I came yesterday to Lady Hertford at Taplow; she desires her compliments to you. My brother[2] is gone to Newmarket. I left the family at Park Place very well; they all desire their best compliments to you.

I am your faithful humble servant,

A. S. CONWAY

From CONWAY, Sunday 20 October 1754

Printed for the first time from the MS now wsl, formerly Rutnam.

Park Place, Oct. 20, 1754.

Dear Horry,

AS you are good enough to flatter me you take some interest in what concerns me, and seemed to approve the view I told you t'other day I had in regard to the Bedchamber,[1] I will now tell you

1. This may have been the portrait of Lady Hertford by Vanloo, which HW had copied by Eccardt, and hung in the Library at SH ('Des. of SH,' *Works* ii. 444); it was bought SH xx. 17 by Lord Waldegrave.

2. Lord Hertford.

1. Conway wished to become a groom of the Bedchamber.

what steps I have taken in that and how far they have succeeded; my brother had intelligence that poor Col. H[erbert][2] had a relapse and was in great danger, on which by his advice I went to the Duke of N[ewcastle] and desired him to name me to his Majesty; my reception there was gracious and kind beyond what I could have imagined; the strongest professions towards me and the highest flattery of opinion, etc. He spoke of no engagement nor no difficulty and said he would mention it that very day, as I suppose he actually did for it was Wednesday I was at N[ewcastle] House and yesterday I had a gracious letter[3] from his Grace acquainting me he had spoke, that his M[ajesty] did not care to give absolute promises especially on such events which he hoped would not happen; but that upon the whole he hoped it would end as he wished,[4] and that if I would come to him on Wednesday next I should know all that had passed.—Thus far I think all looks pretty promising.

On Friday I went to the Lodge and acquainted the Duke what I had done, hoping it would have his R[oyal] H[ighness]'s approbation; he received it very kindly indeed, told me he approved it entirely and had before thought of it as a proper thing for me, but then added he was afraid it was probably engaged; for that he knew one who thought himself very sure of it but said his was not of authority but only second-hand intelligence. I said that as that person, who is Mr Brudenell's[5] application, must probably be known, if not moved by the Duke of N[ewcastle] and he had not mentioned it to me, I was in hopes it might be otherwise, on which he only smiled and said I must not *believe too implicitly, from certain quarters;* next morning Lord Bury told me it was he had told the Duke of Mr B[rudenell]'s expectations and I think that he had it from himself.

I shall go to town either tomorrow or Tuesday as my brother and Lady Hertford do too, shall see the Duke of N[ewcastle] Wednesday morning and perhaps know more. In the mean[time] beg you to keep all that relates to these negotiations secret. I should be happy but have little hopes to meet you in town, as you talked of distant expeditions.[6] Adieu.

2. Hon. William Herbert (ca 1696–1757), Col. in the army, 1745; Col. 2d Dragoon Guards, 1753; Maj.-Gen., 1755; groom of the Bedchamber 1740–57; M.P. Wilton 1734–57.

3. Missing.

4. Conway received the post when Herbert died in 1757 (MANN v. 75).

5. Hon. James Brudenell (1725–1811), cr. (1780) Bn Brudenell of Deene; 5th E. of Cardigan, 1790. He became deputy-cofferer of the Household in 1755.

6. HW and Chute visited Belhus, Thomas Barrett Lennard's seat, and Thorndon Hall, Lord Petre's seat; and HW took George Montagu and his

I answer for the compliments of Nanny and Lady Ailesbury and your little wife's love which is more and am, dear Horry, with great truth and affection,

Ever yours,

H. S. C.

I hear there have been sad to-do's in the house of Petersham.[7] The Duke[8] has just lost his girl[9] which affected him a good deal.

To CONWAY, Thursday 24 October 1754

Printed from the MS now WSL; first printed, Wright iii. 73–5. For the history of the MS, see *ante* 29 June 1744 OS; it was marked by HW for inclusion in *Works,* but was not included.
Endorsed: Mr Walpole 24 Oct. 1754.

Strawberry Hill, Oct. 24, 1754.

YOU have obliged me most extremely by telling me the progress you have made in your most desirable affair.[1] I call it progress; for notwithstanding the authority you have for supposing there may be a counter-promise, I cannot believe that the Duke of Newcastle would have affirmed the contrary so directly, if he had known of it: Mr Brudenel very likely has been promised my Lord Lincoln's interest, and then supposed he should have the Duke's: however, that is not your affair; if anybody has reason to apprehend a breach of promise, it is poor Mr Brudenel. He can never come into competition with you; and without saying anything to reflect on him, I don't know where you can ever have a competitor, and not have the world on your side.

Though the tenure is precarious, I cannot help liking the situation for you. Anything that sets you in new lights, must be for your advantage. You are naturally indolent, and humble, and are content with being perfect in whatever you happen to be. It is not flattering

brother to visit Chute at the Vyne (HW to Bentley 3 Nov. 1754, CHUTE 183–4; *post* 24 Oct. 1754).

7. HW confirms this report *post* 24 Oct. 1754, but does not elucidate it.

8. Of Cumberland.

9. Not identified, but probably one of the Duke's mistresses.

1. His application to become a groom of the Bedchamber; see *ante* 20 Oct. 1754.

you to say, nor can you deny it with all your modesty, that you have always made yourself master of whatever you have attempted; and have never made yourself master of anything, without shining extremely in it. If the King lives, you will have his favour; if he lives at all, the Prince must have a greater establishment,[2] and then you will have the King's partiality to countenance your being removed to some distinguished place about the Prince: if the King should fail, your situation in his family and your age, naturally recommend you to an equal place in the new household. I am the more desirous of seeing you at Court, because when I consider the improbability of our being in a situation to make war,[3] I am earnest to have you have other opportunities of being one of the first men in this country, besides by being a general. Don't think all I say on this subject compliment. I can have no view in flattering you; and you have a still better reason for believing me sincere, which is, that you know well, that I thought the same of you and professed the same to you, before I was of an age to have either views or flattery—indeed I believe you know me enough to be sure that I am as void of both now as when I was fourteen: and that I am so little apt to court anybody, that if you heard me say the same to anybody but yourself, you would easily think that I spoke what I thought.

George Montagu and his brother[4] are here,[5] and have kept me from meeting you in town; we go on Saturday to the Vine.[6]

I fear there is too much truth in what you have heard of your old mistress.[7] When husband, wife, lover and friend tell everything, can there but be a perpetual fracas? My dear Harry, how lucky you was in what you escaped and in what you have got! People do sometimes avoid, not always, what is most improper for them; but they do not afterwards always meet with what they most deserve. But how lucky you are in everything! and how ungrateful a man to Providence if you are not thankful for so many blessings as it has given you! I won't preach; though the dreadful history which I have just heard of

2. When he came of age in 1756.

3. Relations with France were deteriorating after clashes in America and India, but HW apparently thought that political turpitude at home would prevent serious resistance by England; see *Mem. Geo. II* i. 393–401.

4. Charles Montagu (d. 1777), K.B., 1771; army officer (MONTAGU i. 31, n. 14).

5. HW gives details of their visit and the subsequent expedition to the Vyne in his letter to Bentley 3 Nov. 1754, CHUTE 184–5; see also MONTAGU i. 165–6.

6. The Vyne, Hants, Chute's seat, to which he had succeeded on his brother's death in May 1754 (CHUTE 82).

7. Lady Caroline Petersham.

poor Lord Drumlanrig[8] is enough to send one to La Trape. My compliments to all yours and adieu!

Yours ever,

H. W.

From Conway, Sunday 29 December 1754

Printed for the first time from the MS now wsl, formerly Rutnam.

Park Place, Dec. 29, 1754.

Dear Horry,

I AM at this moment in so disagreeable a distress you'd pity me if you knew how I felt; though at the same time you must be very angry with me, as I deserve. I am afraid I have lost your paper with notes on the debate,[1] etc.; it is not likely you should have a copy of it and when I hear that certainly though I am very uneasy now I shall be ten times more so if possible; I have had my room searched in London and my bureau where I know I first locked it up; and took it according to my remembrance out when I came down here only to lock it up in a box I brought with me, with several other papers; I thought most carefully, as I am sure I meant to be of it. All I can say is I found it not in that box; and have been in vain search of it ever since. I do indeed remember the morning I set out, having been to do some business for my brother in the City, and being pretty late, Lady Ailesbury came and hurried me to set out in the midst of my preparations, but have no notion by what means I could lose or mislay your paper. If you feel angry as you must, do vent it all that I may expiate a little by that additional suffering; for though I don't know how, I must be somehow or other unpardonable except I find the paper.

I give over all hopes of seeing you, and am one degree less sorry now as I really should be ashamed to look upon you.

8. Henry Douglas (1722 - 19 Oct. 1754), styled E. of Drumlanrig 1722–54, had shot himself on his way to London with his parents and newly married wife. His death was reported as an accident in the Daily Adv. 23 Oct., which it probably was, although it was generally believed at the time to be a suicide; see the quotations collected in GEC x. 700, n. b.

1. Perhaps the debate on the Mutiny Bill 11 Dec., which HW summarizes in Mem. Geo. II i. 421–2.

I have not had an opportunity of telling you that old Jack[2] has actually made his proposals to Nanny,[3] has writ to my brother and is I suppose at this moment in treaty with him; he opened himself to me just before I came out of town, which only ended in general civilities and references to my sister's inclinations and my brother's return, to whom I was very glad to leave the weight of such a negotiation, which though very prudent and much to be wished if she likes it, I know my brother can manage much better than me and I had much rather he did. I think she has no dislike to the thing, and as he is I believe a man of good character and she very prudent, as I think she is, I do not see any objection. I should be sorry our family interfered in anything that might be of prejudice to Lord Orford,[4] but, am in reality so persuaded of Mr Harris's determination to marry[5] that I do honestly think him not at all affected by it; he told me himself that he had lived so long in a family way and was so happy in it that he could not bear to live in all his great houses alone. Adieu, dear Horry, do forgive me *as much* and as soon *as you can* and believe me your most contrite and affectionate cousin

H. S. C.

All the Campbelhood salute you with Christmas compliments.

To CONWAY, ca Wednesday 1 January 1755

Missing; implied *post* 9 Jan. 1755.

2. John Harris (?1690–1767), of Hayne, Devonshire; master of the Household 1741–67; M.P. Helston 1727–41, Ashburton 1741–67 (MANN i. 486, n. 18). His first wife had died the previous March (GM 1754, xxiv. 142).

3. Hon. Anne Seymour Conway; they were married 10 March 1755, and HW gave a dinner party in their honour 19 March (see HW to Bentley 27 March 1755, CHUTE 217).

4. Harris's late wife was Lord Orford's grandmother; she had, however, left 'everything' to her grandson after her husband's death (MANN iv. 418).

5. It was reported in mid-December that he was going to marry Mary Drax, second dau. of Henry Drax (Hist. MSS Comm., *Hastings MSS*, 1928–47, iii. 90; Burke, *Landed Gentry*, 1868, p. 389).

From CONWAY, Thursday 9 January 1755

Printed for the first time from the MS now wsl, formerly Rutnam.
Address: To the Honourable Horatio Walpole, Arlington Street.

Park Place, Jan. 9, 1755.

Dear Horry,

I WRITE but one word to thank you for your great goodness about the paper; and to tell you that poor Fred[1] whose illness you'll have heard of has continued in so disagreeable and doubtful a state and Lady Ailesbury in so much anxiety I could not leave 'em; though I know I had many reasons to think I should be in town and have had my chaise at the door these two or three last mornings: if anything very extraordinary has happened, or but to tell me I have done very wrong or right, you'll oblige me much by a single short line on the return of my servant tomorrow morning.

Fred is I hope recovering, but so slowly and with so many turns and alarms that we are far from easy about him. However his worst symptoms are certainly gone and what remains is I hope no more than the natural and almost constant effect of these tedious fevers. Excuse my great hurry and believe me most faithfully yours as are I'm sure all those you speak so kindly of.

1. Frederick Campbell, Lady Ailesbury's brother.

From CONWAY, Thursday 8 May 1755

Printed from the MS now WSL, formerly Rutnam; first printed, *Fraser's Magazine*, 1850, xli. 273–4. HW probably received this about 15 May, since Hartington's letter to Newcastle, written from Dublin on the same day as Conway's letter, was endorsed as received on 15 May (BM Add. MSS 32854, f. 425). See below, n. 1.

Dublin,[1] 8 May 1755.

Dear Horry,

I SHOULD have writ to you immediately on my arrival[2] but, besides being in as much hurry and puzzle as I could possibly, I had nothing but that to tell you which was no great news, and which such as it was I knew you'd hear from my brother and Lady A., to whom I had squeezed out two short letters.[3]

Journeys seldom afford anything worth relating, at least such journeys as these; it's all one uniform joggle in a post-chaise, or as uniform a trot through Wales. The news here tells us our voyage was very tempestuous which exceeds the truth, though the night was something rough[4]—I am sure you wish me at the end of it, and want to know how things go here. And as yet I can tell you but little of it. Here has been a great appearance of all sorts of people at the Castle;[5] great civilities, great expressions of satisfaction, etc.

1. Conway was now chief secretary to the M. of Hartington, the new lord lieutenant of Ireland. According to HW, Conway had received the post 'entirely unsought, uncanvassed,' for when Hartington was offered the lord-lieutenancy 'he refused to accept so uncommon an honour, unless Mr Conway, with whom he was scarce acquainted, would accompany him as secretary and minister. Mr Conway's friends would not let him hesitate' (*Mem. Geo. II* ii. 3).

2. 5 May; the Dublin newspaper *Pue's Occurrences* 3–6 May 1755, *sub* Dublin 6 May reports, 'Yesterday morning, about six o'clock, his Excellency the Marquis of Hartington, lord lieutenant of this kingdom, landed at Skerries from on board the Wyville Packet Boat from Hollyhead. His Excellency was received at the bounds of the city near Drumcondra by a great number of the nobility and gentry, the sheriffs of this city on horseback, attended by the proper officers, and a regiment of dragoons. . . . The following persons arrived with his Excellency the Lord Lieutenant on board the Wyville Packet Boat, viz. the Right Hon. Lord Frederick Cavendish, his Excellency's brother, and Col. Conway his secretary. . . .'

3. Both of these are missing; the one to Lady Ailesbury is mentioned *post* ca 9 May 1755.

4. 'We landed on Monday morning about twenty miles north of this place [Dublin] after a disagreeable and rough passage, though at the same time I believe not at all dangerous' (Hartington to Newcastle 8 May 1755, BM Add. MSS 32854, f. 422).

5. Dublin Castle, residence of the lord lieutenant. 'Tuesday last [6 May] the Right Hon. the Lord Mayor, aldermen, Recorder, sheriffs, and commons of this

But between ourselves not that general expansion of heart, nor those acclamations, bonfires, and illuminations that might have been expected on one hand, and from one sort of people I mean the lower, nor those unreserved declarations from the higher.[6] Patriot meetings and patriot healths have continued; patriot papers writ,[7] and in short the minds of people kept in a sort of suspense, as it seems, waiting for the event of things to see how well-satisfied they *are to be*. The great men have now all, or most, been at Court and seen Lord H[artington] in public and in private;[8] have all agreed in general expressions of satisfaction in his government, and of esteem for his person; yet something still remains behind—something of conditions not yet totally explained,[9] which it is impossible to say what degree of difficulty they may create; though in general I am in hopes it won't be great.[10]

city, waited upon the Lord Lieutenant at the Castle, to compliment his Excellency upon his safe arrival to the government of this kingdom. . . . Same day the fellows and scholars of Trinity College. . . . On Thursday the dissenting clergy in a body. . . .' (*Pue's Occurrences* 6–10 May, *sub* Dublin 10 May).

6. Hartington was equally guarded in describing his immediate reception in his letter to Newcastle on the same day: 'I can only say that in general my reception here was such as I think I have no reason to be displeased with, everybody very civil and expressing their desire of supporting the King's affairs, but I do not think that much stress is to be laid upon outward civilities or general professions. . . . I own I shall not flatter myself that things will go quietly, until I have some further proofs of their good intentions' (BM Add. MSS 32854, ff. 422, 424).

7. Conway wrote his brother 16 June 1755 of 'the *Universal Advertiser* as you may see going on in a kind of indirect, though sometimes pretty direct, abuse, under the auspices and direction of Sir Richard Cox [a patriot]' (MS now WSL, printed in *Colburn's United Service Magazine*, 1881, liii pt ii. 195).

8. There had been formal council meetings and levees since Hartington's arrival (*Dublin Journal* 10–13 May) but he told Newcastle on the 8th that the only people he had yet had conversations with were

the Primate (Stone), the Chancellor (Lord Newport), and the Speaker (Henry Boyle) (BM Add. MSS 32854, f. 422). Stone and Boyle were the leaders of the two opposing factions in Ireland.

9. Abp Stone had been completely submissive to Hartington, but Boyle in a longer conversation 'endeavoured to justify the Previous Consent [the constitutional issue raised by the factional struggle], complained that he had been very ill used [by being dismissed from his government post], that all the influence and favour of government had been thrown into a certain person's [Stone's] hands, which was a thing that neither he and his friends or the country would bear and concluded with asking me what I would do on that head.' Hartington then declared his intention of absolute impartiality (below, n. 11), to which 'the Speaker answered that that was as much as he desired and upon that condition he told me that they would not bring on the Previous Consent and hoped I would not, he also seemed to acquiesce in having no censures or any retrospect whatsoever' (Hartington to Newcastle 8 May 1755, BM Add. MSS 32854, ff. 423, 424). Hartington gives a similar, but rather more detailed account of his conversation with Boyle in a letter to Fox 17 May 1755 (*Letters to Henry Fox*, ed. E. of Ilchester, Roxburghe Club, 1915, p. 63).

10. As soon as the opening honeymoon

This is such a sketch as I can give you at present of the state of things. Lord H[artington] continues to hold one steady and uniform language of a single and settled view to do the King's business and the nation's by plain and direct ways, and by an equal and impartial government, favouring no party nor faction, nor setting up none.[11] And though he may meet with rubs in this road from the ambition of some and the warmth or weakness of others, I am persuaded such a behaviour and such intentions, well supported, will carry him through.

We have had no mail since our arrival, so begin to grow impatient for news; I desire you'll tell me a great deal and soon, for we don't intend to stay very long.[12] We have heard nothing of the French[13] nor seen nothing of them yet; so are a little inquisitive to know what's become of them.[14] Our military preparations go on; but we begin, I think, to believe we shan't have much occasion for 'em, after seeing the French fleet distinctly at almost every port for this fortnight.[15]

We have been hitherto in a course of great, troublesome dinners,[16]

was over, the opposition began to create difficulties over the appointment of lords justices; see *post* 18 June 1755.

11. Hartington told Boyle in their interview 'that neither he nor any man in Ireland should prescribe to me what I was to do or who I was to show favour to. That I had no view but to support the honour of the King's government and the interest of the country and that if he and his friends would concur with me in carrying on the King's affairs and endeavour to allay the heats and animosities that still subsist among them, that upon those conditions I would offer him my friendship and assure him that he and his friends should have that share of power and influence that was due to them, that I had, nor would have no attachments in public life to any of them, but would show favour and friendship impartially to them all as they deserved' (BM Add. MSS 32854, ff. 423–4). See also *Letters to Henry Fox*, loc. cit.).

12. Hartington had originally planned to leave 'in four or five weeks,' but the impossibility of appointing acceptable lords justices kept him in Ireland; Conway, however, left for England 9 July and was back in London by 14 July (Con-

way to Hartington 15 July 1755, Chatsworth MSS, 416/0; *Leinster Corr.* i. 19; HW to Bentley 17 July 1755, CHUTE 235; *post* 18 June 1755, n. 11).

13. A French descent on Ireland had been expected since mid-April (HW to Bentley 13 April 1755, CHUTE 218–19; MANN iv. 474; Thomas Adderley to Lord Charlemont 22 April 1755, Hist. MSS Comm., *Charlemont MSS*, 1891–4, i. 216–17).

14. The French fleet, which in fact did not sail until 3 May instead of in March or April as believed at that time, went to America, not to Ireland (Georges Lacour-Gayet, *La Marine militaire de la France sous le règne de Louis XV*, 1902, p. 238; MANN iv. 474, nn. 1, 5).

15. A typical example was the report current in Dublin 29 April that 'five sail of men-of-war, supposed to be French' had been seen off Dungarvan 21 April; this 'fleet' turned out to be a collection of fishing boats and two East-Indiamen (*Daily Adv.* 6, 10 May). Other reports circulating in Dublin at the same time were all contradicted on 2 May (*London Evening Post* 8–10 May, *sub* Dublin 3 May).

16. 'Tuesday last [6 May] his Excellency our Lord Lieutenant dined with his Grace

and so may continue some time. Indeed it's one constant feast in this country; it's the great business of life to stuff and be stuffed. Immoderate eating is among the prime social virtues, but immoderate drinking lifts you up to the skies.[17] One would think such furious politics would interrupt it; but it's quite the contrary, and more than half the warfare is carried on by bumpers of confusion to their enemies and success to their friends. Adieu! don't think I abuse the country. All this is right and only errs in a little excess. I am dreadfully encumbered with all sorts of encumbrance of the most disagreeable kind, and am amazed to find myself almost at the end of a long letter:—visits, dispatches, applications, attendance, politics, steams of meat, and fumes of wine, all conspiring to confound me.

Yours most faithfully,

H. S. C.

From LADY AILESBURY, ca Friday 9 May 1755

Printed for the first time from the MS now WSL, formerly Rutnam. The letter must have been written during the first week of May 1755, the only time that Conway would have been at Holyhead on his way to Ireland without Lady Ailesbury during Ricciarelli's operatic career in England (below, nn. 4, 7).

Address: To Mr Walpole.

[Warwick Street].

I AM always sorry not to wait upon you, but I think if you'll excuse me, it shall not be on Monday;[1] for I am but little acquainted with any of the company except Lord Stormont, and some of them have not much partiality for me. I shall be very glad to see you at

the Lord Primate; on Wednesday with the Right Hon. the Lord Chancellor; on Thursday with the Right Hon. the Earl of Bessborough; yesterday with his Grace the Lord Archbishop of Dublin; and we hear he is to dine this day with the Right Hon. the Lord Molesworth' (*Pue's Occurrences* 6–10 May, *sub* Dublin 10 May; see also *Leinster Corr.* i. 9).

17. Lord Kildare, in describing a dinner given by Hartington on the 12th at which Conway was present, says 'I don't think I ever drank so hard and fast in my life;

every one of the company complain today' (ibid. i. 16).

———

1. On Monday 12 May, HW gave a dinner for Lady Hervey and the Rochfords at SH (MONTAGU i. 168); Lord Stormont is not mentioned as a guest, but he was well acquainted with Lady Hervey, who the year before had called him 'one of the prettiest and most amiable kind of young men I ever was acquainted with' (D. M. Stuart, *Molly Lepell, Lady Hervey,* 1936, p. 248).

supper either tonight or tomorrow, or both. Tonight the Wests[2] and Miss Rich[3] will be here, tomorrow Lady Lyttelton and Ricciarelli;[4] he insists upon coming, so I am to be taken by surprise after the opera,[5] and it will be safe to have a relation near. I have just been at the Tower *pour voir les dogues et les ourses.*[6]

Yours,

C. A.

Mr Conway got well to Holyhead.[7] I have just had a letter from him.[8]

---

2. Probably some of the children of the 7th Bn (later 1st E.) De la Warr: Hon. John West (1729–77), styled Vct Cantelupe 1761–6, 2d E. De la Warr, 1766; Hon. George West (1733–76), later Conway's aide-de-camp; Hon. (later Lady) Henrietta Cecilia West (1727–1817), m. (1762) Col. (later Gen.) James Johnston, later a close friend of HW and the Conways (*post* 6 Feb. 1764, nn. 41, 44); and Hon. (later Lady) Diana West (1731–66), m. (1756) Gen. John Clavering.

3. Mary Rich, dau. of Sir Robert Rich, 4th Bt, and sister of Lady Lyttelton (*ante* ca 25 March 1753, n. 1). She later lived much of the time with Lady Ailesbury.

4. The 'first man' in the London opera 1754–7, 'a neat and pleasing performer, with a clear, flexible, and silver-toned voice, but so much inferior to Mingotti [the principal woman], both in singing and acting, that he was never in very high favour.' He later sang at Drury Lane 1757–8, and became travelling teacher to Adm. Sir Robert Harland's family, returning with them to England about 1760 as Miss Harland's singing teacher (Charles Burney, *General History of Music,* ed. Mercer, 1935, ii. 853, 856n.; *London Stage* Pt IV, ii. 608). He is probably the Giuseppe Ricciarelli, from Rome, who sang in operas at Venice 1747–9 (Taddeo Wiel,

I teatri musicali veneziani del settecento, Venice, 1897, pp. 165, 169, 172, 175). See also MANN iv. 557; HW to Bentley 19 Oct. 1755, CHUTE 256–7; and Hist. MSS Comm., *Hastings MSS,* 1928–47, iii. 90.

5. The only opera performed during the week in which this letter must have been written was *Ezio,* given at the King's Theatre on 6 and 10 May (*London Stage* Pt IV, i. 485–6).

6. In the menagerie there; for an account of the animals in the Tower see David Henry, *An Historical Description of the Tower of London,* 1778, pp. 12–27; see also OSSORY ii. 197, n. 17; MONTAGU i. 28, n. 17.

7. He was en route to Ireland. HW told Bentley 17 April that Conway and Hartington were going on the 24th (HW to Bentley 13–17 April 1755, CHUTE 220), but they left London the 29th, embarked at Holyhead at 7 A.M. on 4 May and arrived in Dublin on the 5th (*Daily Adv.* 1, 13 May; *London Evening Post* 10–13 May; *ante* 8 May 1755, n. 2). They probably reached Holyhead on the evening of 3 May; a letter from there would hardly have reached London before the 8th or 9th.

8. Missing; probably the 'short letter' mentioned by Conway *ante* 8 May 1755.

To CONWAY, May–June 1755

Missing; answered *post* 18 June 1755.

From CONWAY, Wednesday 18 June 1755

Printed in full for the first time from the MS now WSL, formerly Rutnam. First printed, with the omission of the last two paragraphs, *Fraser's Magazine*, 1850, xli. 274–5.

Memoranda (by HW):

Sir Edw. W.   3d

Mrs Drelincourt
Lady Dacre[1]
Mr Hay[2]   2-9-6
Mr Loyd[3]

hair cutter
Mr Dagge[4]
Mr [Henry] Fox
Sir Dudl. Diggs[5] Compleat Embassador
Mrs Metavyer [?Mestivyer, Mrs Clive's sister]
morter-cloth [mortcloth, a funeral pall]

Dublin Castle, 18 June 1755.

I DON'T understand your returning me so many thanks for my last letter; it seems strange it should, but it really displeases me, as it looks too like ceremony, and seems to make what I thought a step of course in our correspondence appear like something extraordinary; I would not on any account do less than you expected from me, but I would not have you expect too little as it seems like doing injustice to my friendship of which that was certainly but a slight and ordinary expression.—I am hurried and perplexed with business

1. Lady Anne Lennard (1684 – 26 June 1755), m. 1 (1716) Richard Barrett; m. 2 (1718) Henry Roper, 8th Bn Teynham; m. 3 Robert Moore; Bns Dacre of the South, s.j. (MONTAGU i. 170).

2. William Hay (1695 – 19 June 1755), M.P. Seaford 1734–55.

3. John Lloyd (?1717 – 3 June 1755), M.P. Cardiganshire 1747–55.

4. Possibly Henry Dagge (d. 1779), solicitor; see MANN v. 32, n. 1.

5. Sir Dudley Digges (1583–1639), diplomatist. HW's copy of his *Compleat Embassador*, 1655, is Hazen, *Cat. of HW's Lib.*, No. 1110; see also COLE i. 180–1.

beyond what I can express,[6] but that perplexity must go far indeed if it makes me neglect you; and I assure you the correspondence of my friends is my chief relief and refuge from it. I don't pretend that is quite a disinterested taste in me but to show you how much it is so in the present instance: you must know that I neither desire nor expect you to answer this.—Lord Hartington has in a manner determined not to go over to England; but at the same time that I should;[7] the difficulty in appointing the lords justices was between ourselves the chief or perhaps only reason of this resolution.[8] The dignity of government it seems allowed of no change in the Regency;[9] and the state and temper of the country by no means allowed of his leaving the same, which therefore could end only as it does; for

6. Conway wrote to his brother two days earlier: 'I live a dismal life of hurry and business, some of consequence, many trifles, but such a mass of it, civil and military, public and private, as sometimes almost turns my head and makes me often sigh for Park Place and a little of my beloved indolence. . . . What supports me and makes everything tolerable is the great ease, good nature and friendship of Lord Hartington which is beyond expression. Had I been under any other lord lieutenant in the world, I should either have deserted or died of it' (MS now WSL; printed *Colburn's United Service Magazine*, 1881, liii pt ii. 197).

7. 'At all events Col. Conway will go over to fetch Lady Ailesbury, which I approve of very much as he will be able to explain the state of our affairs more fully than I can do by letter' (Hartington to Newcastle 1 June 1755, BM Add. MSS 32855, f. 297).

8. Conway summarizes the grounds for Hartington's decision in his letter to his brother: 'I should have mentioned to you first that my Lord H. finding by representations from all quarters and the opinions of all he has consulted of all parties, and the best acquainted with the state and temper of this nation, that he could not leave the same lords justices here on his return without raising the greatest flame and risking the ease of his administration, has very prudently, I think, resolved to stay. This I find is looked upon as a condescension to the Speaker and his party by many in England, partic-

ularly the Dukes of N[ewcastle] and Grafton and my Lord Chancellor and it is therefore thought too much now to gratify the Speaker in the other point [by restoring him to the chancellorship of the Exchequer]; for my own part, I look upon this as a thing apart, not done at the request of that party particularly, but as I said, a step prudentially taken on the opinion of all those my Lord has conversed with of all parties and I do really think though much against my own private inclination, as wise and necessary a step as ever was taken.' Hartington had made his decision to remain by 23 May, when he communicated it to Newcastle and Fox, asking them not to mention it to anyone but Cumberland (*Letters to Henry Fox*, ed. Ilchester, Roxburghe Club, 1915, p. 66; Hartington to Newcastle 23 May 1755, BM Add. MSS 32855, ff. 156–8). Further details of Hartington's difficulties at this time are in his correspondence with Newcastle, BM Add. MSS 32854, ff. 521–3, and 32855, ff. 170–1, 297–8, 330–4, 534–5; in Newcastle's correspondence with Holdernesse, Hardwicke and Devonshire about Irish policy, ibid. 32855, ff. 56, 61, 86, 137–9, 284, 373–4; and in *Letters to Henry Fox*, pp. 68–9. For evidence that Fox was encouraging the Irish opposition and trying to influence Hartington towards concessions to Boyle, see *Leinster Corr.* i. 21–31 *passim*.

9. Which had consisted of Abp Stone, the Lord Chancellor, and the E. of Bessborough.

myself I own I thought the latter point much clearer than the former; however I don't know if, all considered, the present measure may not be better than either.

Your exhortations to me are very friendly and very well adapted to this time and place as possible; my temper as you say is tolerable and that of my principal is excellent, which is not amiss for us both.

I find much more temptation and trial in the way of that than my ambition, of which you'll easily believe I have but just leaven enough in my composition to carry me through a scene that we probably shall not soon clear of all its embarrassments; those ingredients of rage, nonsense and ambition, which to be sure have flourished not a little here being I am sure much beyond any state chemistry I know to convert into the qualities you mention. Yet am I not without hopes that the honesty, candour, sense and spirit of Lord H[artington] which he really possesses will at least make 'em subside, and when the first has lost its force, one may reckon the venom is in a manner taken out of the rest. They may still prick and tease a little, but won't do any of that violent mischief.—

We are a little off and on and don't quite know our own minds and sometimes we are disposed to bully a little and sometimes to be pacific; however as there is a right resolution taken by Lord H[artington] in regard to the most obnoxious things and *persons*,[10] who I hope will be allowed to pursue those resolutions properly, I have really on the whole good hopes of success.

You must be content with this dull political stuff, for I am conversant in no other ideas whatever; except what is more dull to you at least which is the military part of my amphibious province.—I will also spare you all the long history of our progress:[11] which you

10. That is, Stone and Boyle. Hartington had declared he would neither disgrace Stone nor make him minister (Conway to Hertford 16 June 1755), but insisted that some mark of favour should be shown to Boyle, at least before the opening of the Irish Parliament (Hartington to Newcastle 15 June 1755, BM Add. MSS 32855, ff. 534–5). When Conway was in London in July, Newcastle suggested 'that the Primate might be brought to make it his motion and desire to be left out of Government—but then that it should be somehow given to understand it was his request and that if that was done the

King would by no means consent to putting the Speaker in' (Conway to Hartington 16 July, Chatsworth MSS, 416 / 2). The plan evolved that the Primate should make application to be relieved of office and should not be appointed a lord justice, but that the Speaker should be restored to his place as chancellor of the Exchequer (Conway to Hartington 23, 27, 30 July, ibid. 416 / 4, 6, 7). See also MANN iv. 503, n. 28.

11. Through the province of Munster to Duncannon, Besborough, Fort Cork, and Limerick, which began 25 May and lasted until 11 June; the object was to re-

have had an hundred times in all the newspapers; our honours, speeches, freedoms, gold boxes for my Lord, silver ones for Mr Secretary,[12] etc.—We have seen some fine and some pretty things; we have danced with the ladies, and got drunk with the men; and all such proper and decorous things.

My Lord Lieutenant thinks of going soon to Castle Town, Mr Conolly's,[13] which is lent him about 8 miles from town; a moderate place but very good house,[14] in a week or ten days;[15] at which time I hope to be setting out:[16] just to peep at you to see how the weather is on your side the water and return to my ark, I hope with an olive branch;[17]—I shall insist upon seeing as much of you as my time and yours will allow. And shall let you hear of my motions for that purpose.

view troops and inspect fortifications (*Pue's Occurrences* 24–7 May, *sub* Dublin 27 May, gives the complete itinerary; see also *Letters to Henry Fox*, p. 65; Conway to Hertford 16 June 1755; *Daily Adv.* 3, 14 June, *sub* Dublin 27 May, 7 June; *London Evening Post* 19–21 June, *sub* Dublin 12 June).

12. In Dublin on 17 June 'the Right Hon. the Lord Mayor, aldermen, Recorder, sheriffs, and commons of this city, waited on his Excellency the Lord Lieutenant at the Castle, and presented him with his freedom in a gold box, when the Recorder addressed him a handsome speech, to which he was pleased to return a very obliging answer. At the same time they also presented the Right Hon. Col. Conway, his Excellency's secretary, with his freedom in a silver box' (*Pue's Occurrences* 17–21 June, *sub* Dublin 21 June). Conway was voted the freedom of Cork and a silver box 29 May, and the freedom of Kinsale 2 June (*Council Book of the Corporation of the City of Cork*, ed. Richard Caulfield, Guildford, Surrey, 1876, p. 686; *Council Book of the Corporation of Kinsale*, ed. Richard Caulfield, Guildford, Surrey, 1879, p. 262).

13. Thomas Conolly (?1737–1803), Irish politician; M.P. Malmesbury 1759–68, Chichester 1768–80. He had succeeded to Castletown on his father's death in 1754; his mother was a sister of HW's friend Lord Strafford. He was later married to Lady Louisa Lennox.

14. When built in the years immediately following 1722, it was the largest house in Ireland and the first house there to be built of stone in the classical style; details are in Brian Fitzgerald, *Lady Louisa Conolly*, 1950, pp. 19–20. The house was at this time uninhabited, since Conolly was a minor and living with his mother in England; he did not resume residence there until 1759 (ibid. 23, 39).

15. Hartington apparently went to Castletown about 24 June (*Daily Adv.* 7 July, *sub* Dublin 28 June).

16. Wednesday 9 July 'the Dorset yacht sailed for Hollyhead with . . . Col. Conway, secretary to his Excellency the Lord Lieutenant' (*Pue's Occurrences* 8–12 July, *sub* Dublin 12 July).

17. That is, permission from the English government to restore Boyle to the chancellorship of the Exchequer. Conway writes Hartington 23 July, 'On the head of the Speaker's being restored to his place I said I fancied you wished to have the power in your hands as soon as possible, which I think was not objected to and which I could wish you by all means to have' (Chatsworth MSS, 416 / 4). See Hartington to Fox 22 June 1755, *Letters to Henry Fox*, pp. 68–9, outlining his instructions to Conway; and Conway's letters to Hartington from 15 July to 27 Aug. 1755, which describe his conferences with Newcastle and Hardwicke in London (Chatsworth MSS, 416 / 0–14).

I must now say one word from myself and Lady A. and Jack[18] in return for your excessive kindness on a certain subject that you'll guess;[19] and inform you that it is a thing much to our inclination, and that if you find a proper method and opportunity of hinting anything of it, merely as from yourself, we shall be much obliged. Lady A. has already expressed her inclinations to us and I suppose to you.—My only fears are the two old men,[20] one of whom I much fear will do nothing and the other expect much. However if you think proper there's no harm in sounding and if the females were gained, the others are at worst not immortal and a little time might do great things.

Do you know that this very thing has been mentioned some time ago as a thought of a friend of Jack's for him; which was Lord Cathcart[21] who has also a connection there and might possibly be of use. Adieu; believe us all much obliged and that I am, dear Horry, most faithfully and sincerely

Yours,

H. S. C.

Jack's thought and thanks are included in this.

To HERTFORD, ca Friday 29 August 1755

Missing; answered *post* 1 Sept. 1755.

---

18. John Campbell, Lady Ailesbury's brother; he was in Ireland with Conway as one of Hartington's aides-de-camp (*Leinster Corr.* i. 16; *London Evening Post* 17–20 May, *sub* Dublin 13 May).

19. In the absence of HW's letter to Conway, this paragraph remains obscure; HW was evidently trying to help John Campbell to become an aide-de-camp to the King, which he did become in November (ibid. 18–20 Nov.).

20. Not identified.

21. Cathcart was a friend of the Duke of Cumberland who was a member of the Council of Regency at this time during the King's absence in Hanover. Military appointments were under the control of the Duke, to whom Cathcart had been aide-de-camp in 1745 and became lord of the Bedchamber in 1760 (*Hardwicke Corr.* i. 393, n. 5, 413, ii. 199).

From HERTFORD, Monday 1 September 1755

Printed for the first time from a photostat of BM Add. MSS 23218, f. 3. Sketches in pencil by ?HW seem to be a rough draft for additions made at Strawberry Hill in the early 1760s, showing the outline of the Round Tower, Gallery, and bay of the Blue Bedchamber.

Ragley, September 1st 1755.

Dear Horry,

YOU was very good to intend us a visit at Ragley.[1] We can only be sorry for the reason[2] that prevents you and wish it had less weight. At every place belonging to us you will be welcome;[3] at this we are particularly interested to see you, for your advice and opinion,[4] and when we are here again we hope you will give us leave to expect it.

I have heard nothing of Mr Clarck's[5] illness except from you; if he dies you may command me in favour of any friend of yours. I should not have a doubt but in relation to the borough[6] in case his

1. Hertford's principal seat, near Alcester in south Warwickshire, begun about 1680 by Edward, Earl of Conway, but not completed until Hertford's occupancy. The house is described and illustrated by H. Avray Tipping in *Country Life* 22, 29 March 1924, lv. 438–45, 476–82; see also *Vict. Co. Hist. Warwick*, 1904–69, iii. 27, 29, HW to Montagu 22 July 1751 (MONTAGU i. 120–1), which describes HW's first visit there when the house was barely habitable, and Christopher Hussey, *English Country Houses: Early Georgian 1715–1760*, 1955, p. 8 (a photograph of the great hall at Ragley, remodelled at this time).

2. Probably a prior engagement with Chute, whom HW visited in early September (HW to Bentley 18 Sept. 1755, CHUTE 249; *post* 23 Sept. 1755).

3. HW had just visited Sudbourne Hall, Hertford's house in Suffolk (HW to Bentley 28 Aug. 1755, CHUTE 247).

4. Concerning improvements and decoration at Ragley (above, n. 1); some further details are discussed *post* 19 July 1760.

5. Not identified, although apparently someone holding office in the borough of

Orford or on Hertford's Suffolk estates.

6. Of Orford, Suffolk. In 1753 Hertford had purchased the Suffolk estate of Price Devereux (1694–1748), 10th Vct Hereford, which included among others the manors of Orford and Sudbourne. By this purchase Hertford had hoped to gain immediate control of the rotten borough of Orford, whose members were then safely within the nomination of the Treasury; but his efforts in that direction were unavailing until 1766, when 'his Majesty's interest' in Orford was finally transferred to Hertford as a reward for his services in France and Ireland. From 1768 until 1832 its successive representatives were either members or close allies of the Seymour Conway family (Namier and Brooke i. 382; Sir Lewis Namier, *The Structure of Politics at the Accession of George III*, 2d edn, 1960, pp. 389–401; W. A. Copinger, *The Manors of Suffolk*, Manchester, 1905–11, v. 119–20, 134, 150, 178; see also T. H. B. Oldfield, *The Representative History of Great Britain and Ireland*, 1816, iv. 563–7, and Hertford's letter of 31 Aug. 1778 to George III concerning the town of Orford, in Geo. III's *Corr.*, ed. Fortescue, iv. 190–2).

son were to succeed him at Orford. That is a very distant object I fear to me and the case may not happen; if it should you may still command me. I do not propose being in town till the ninth, the Duke of Grafton having sent me notice that the King intended being at home between the 10th and 15th.[7] I shall be very glad to meet you there at that time, and am with Lady Hertford's best compliments, dear Horry,

Most truly and sincerely yours,

HERTFORD

From CONWAY, Tuesday 16 September 1755

Printed from the MS now WSL, formerly Rutnam. First printed, *Fraser's Magazine*, 1850, xli. 275.

Dublin Castle, 16 Sept. 1755.

Dear Horry,

YOU should have heard from me the very night of our arrival;[1] but merely to tell you of a long, dismal passage, and not tell you of our having, I hope, concluded our peace here,[2] *à quoi bon?* One

7. The King returned to London from Hanover on 16 Sept. (*Daily Adv.* 17 Sept.). Hertford, a lord of the Bedchamber (1751–64), would be expected to be in attendance upon the King's arrival. Grafton, as lord chamberlain, would give formal notice of the King's expected return; he was also Hertford's father-in-law.

1. Conway had been in England for consultations about Irish politics (see *ante* 18 June 1755); he had left for Ireland on or shortly after 31 Aug. and arrived in Dublin 13 Sept. (BM Add. MSS 32858, f. 370; 32859, ff. 120, 124; Conway to Hartington 27 Aug., 14 Sept. 1755, Chatsworth MSS, 416 / 14, 15). 'Saturday, Sept. 13 . . . Colonel Conway and his Lady . . . arrived here in the Leicester packet boat from Hollyhead' (*Pue's Occurrences* 13–16 Sept., *sub* Dublin 13 Sept.).

2. In a letter of 7 Aug. to Hartington,

Conway summarizes the plan he brought from London: 'It all turns on one single point . . . the only difficulty you had or apprehended was the supporting the Primate; and your Lordship thinks . . . that he should be removed but you think you ought not to declare that, now at least, without at the same time declaring that you mean to appoint a lord deputy; or to leave the Speaker out: Now, my Lord, if it be necessary to remove the Primate, as you think; is it not equally necessary to let your intentions on that head be known? . . . as it will probably secure you a quiet sessions; fix you in the hearts of the people and make you known to them; . . . But your Lordship is apprehensive, this will be too great a triumph given to the Speaker and his party, and that the Primate's people will abandon you and leave you at his mercy; . . . Upon the whole I do really think your Lordship should if possible agree to

single post makes the difference; and I can now tell you this very morning the agreement was finished by my Lord H[artington]³ with the Speaker,⁴ Mr Malone,⁵ and Mr Carter;⁶ on the footing of his promising, as far as depended on him, the Primate⁷ should not be left one of [the] lords justices;⁸ and on his seeing and allowing of certain heads to be put in the Address,⁹ to express in general terms their concern that any part of their behaviour should have occasioned the least suspicion of their duty to his Majesty, etc., or of any design to attempt the least encroachment on his prerogative, which they protest was the most distant thing from their thoughts, with many expressions of duty, loyalty, and unbounded affection. I think the whole may fairly be looked upon as an *excuse* to his Majesty for

leave out the P. without clogging your treaty with any circumstance that may defeat it' (Chatsworth MSS, 416 / 8).

3. Hartington's report is in his letter to Newcastle 17 Sept.: 'Upon the strength of your Grace's letter Mr Conway and I had a meeting on Monday [15 Sept.] with the Speaker, Carter and Malone and upon my assuring them, that I would use my endeavours to get his Majesty's consent to leave the Primate out of Government provided everything was quiet, they have closed with me and we have finally adjusted everything, the only point they have insisted upon was the inserting some words in the Address to endeavour to show they did not mean to attack the King's prerogative and to justify themselves. My answer was that it would depend entirely upon the wording. . . . We had yesterday a second meeting when they brought the heads of the Address which after some modelling we have settled and of which I send your Grace a copy' (BM Add. MSS 32859, ff. 112–13; duplicates of the letter, sent by various routes, are ibid. ff. 120–2, 124–6).

4. Henry Boyle (ca 1683–1764), cr. (1756) E. of Shannon; Speaker of the Irish House of Commons 1733–56; leader of the 'patriot' party at this time.

5. Anthony Malone (1700–76), Irish politician and lawyer; M.P. (Irish) Co. Westmeath 1727–60, 1769–76, Castlemartyr 1761–8; one of Boyle's principal allies.

6. Thomas Carter (1690–1763), Irish politician; Master of the Rolls in Ireland 1731–54; secretary of state in Ireland

1755–63 (F. E. Ball, *The Judges in Ireland, 1221–1921*, New York, 1927, ii. 202). His discontent at this time is discussed BM Add. MSS 32859, ff. 413–14, 416.

7. George Stone (ca 1708–64), Bp of Ferns and Leighlin, 1740; of Kildare, 1743; of Derry 1745; Abp of Armagh and Primate of Ireland 1747–64.

8. Stone had formally requested his exclusion, at the insistence of Newcastle, on 8 Sept. (BM Add. MSS 32859, f. 106).

9. To the King, at the opening of the Irish Parliament. Copies of the proposed Address, with the alterations made in England, are ibid. ff. 114–15, 116–17. Conway wrote Newcastle 20 Sept. at Hartington's request, backing up the arguments for the proposed Address, on the grounds that the Government should 'yield a little even of their strict dignity to the necessity of the times in order to recover it more surely hereafter'; this recovery he thought inevitable once the full extent of the Irish leaders' bargain was known, since there were already signs of dissension among their followers which could be exploited and 'shortly beget a sort of uneasiness and separation sufficient to weaken them; but not to distress Government' (ibid. ff. 164–5). For the success of these representations, see *post* 7 Oct. 1755 and nn. 4, 5; Conway's letter undoubtedly had considerable effect, since Newcastle had written to Hartington this same week that 'I entirely depend' upon Conway's 'good sense and integrity' (BM Add. MSS 32859, f. 158).

their behaviour, and am only anxious till I hear Lord H[artington]'s conduct in these very delicate affairs has his Majesty's approbation.

Well, I have told you all our news. I hope you think it a great deal. Poor Sir John Bland![10] I scarce knew him at all but am really affected with so miserable and unfortunate an end.

I have really no news but our long voyage as I told you, no less than 40 hours from Holyhead; Lady Ailesbury was very sick and is very well; poor little Missy was a little sick and is perfectly so.

I hear things don't go so smooth on your side the water as ours: nothing but non-acceptances and non-compliances,[11] which I own I did not expect. I see no end through it; and for me that am so little of a party man, 'tis terrible to hear there's scarce one of any party satisfied or like to be so.

Pray let me hear from you, and soon. I know I am an odious correspondent; 'tis a perfect dry scroll like any minister's and writ in as much haste and puzzle. Excuse me, write to me, and believe me most sincerely yours,

H. S. C.

To CONWAY, Tuesday 23 September 1755

Printed from *Works* v. 39–40.

Strawberry Hill, Sept. 23, 1755.

Dear Harry,

NEVER make me excuses for a letter that tells me so many agreeable things as your last; that you are got well to Dublin;[1] that you are all well, and that you have accommodated all your politics to your satisfaction—and I may be allowed to say, greatly to your credit.[2] What could you tell me that would please me so much?

10. Who had committed suicide in France ca 3 Sept. because of his gambling debts; see MONTAGU i. 172–3 and nn. 2–3.

11. Refusals to defend the subsidy treaties with Hesse and Russia in the House of Commons. HW elsewhere mentions approaches made to, and rejected by, Murray, Egmont, and Pitt (*Mem. Geo. II* ii. 40–1), before Newcastle approached Fox on 20 Sept. See also MANN iv. 501–2 and notes, and *post* 23 Sept. 1755.

1. Mr Conway was now secretary of state to the Marquis of Hartington, lord lieutenant of Ireland (HW).

2. HW expressed himself even more strongly to other correspondents. He wrote to Mann 29 Sept., 'Mr Conway . . . has with great prudence and skill pacified that kingdom [Ireland]; you may imagine that I am not a little happy at his acquiring renown' (MANN iv. 503); and to Bentley 30 Sept.: 'In Ireland, Mr Conway has

When I have indulged a little my joy for your success and honour, it is natural to consider the circumstances you have told me; and you will easily excuse me if I am not quite as much satisfied with the conduct of your late antagonists, as I am with yours. You have tranquillized a nation, have repaired your master's honour, and secured the peace of your administration;—but what shall one say to the Speaker, Mr Malone and the others? Don't they confess that they have gone the greatest lengths, and risked the safety of their country on a mere personal pique? If they did not contend for profit, like our patriots (and you don't tell me that they have made any lucrative stipulations),[3] yet it is plain that their ambition had been wounded, and that they resented their power being crossed. But I, who am Whig to the backbone, indeed in the strictest sense of the word, feel hurt in a tenderer point, and which you, who are a minister, must not allow me: I am offended at their agreeing to an address that avows such deference for prerogative, and that is to protest so deeply against having intended to attack it. However rebel this may sound at your Court, my Gothic spirit is hurt; I do not love such loyal expressions from a parliament. I do not so much consider myself writing to Dublin Castle, as from Strawberry Castle, where you know how I love to enjoy my liberty. I give myself the airs, in my nutshell, of an old baron, and am tempted almost to say with an old Earl of Norfolk,[4] who was a very free speaker at least, if he was not an excellent poet,

> When I am in my castle of Bungey,
> Situate upon the river Waveney,
> I ne care for the king of Cockney.[5]

pacified all things' (CHUTE 254). Conway's importance as trusted intermediary between Hartington and Newcastle is demonstrated by his letters to Hartington during July and August, especially 7 Aug. 1755 (Chatsworth MSS, 416 / 0–14).

3. They received lucrative rewards, however, which all but destroyed their reputations (post 6 March 1756), and these were already under discussion between Hartington and Newcastle (BM Add. MSS 32859, ff. 136–7), and were, indeed, the basis of Conway's argument to Newcastle on 20 Sept. that if the government now yielded to their demands, it would be

able subsequently to destroy their power (ibid. ff. 164–5; ante 16 Sept. 1755, n. 9).

4. One of the sources (Harrison) for the verses (see following note) attributes them to Hugh Bigot in about the fifth year (ca 1220) of the reign of Henry III; the other sources attribute them to Hugh Bigod (d. ca 1177), cr. (1140 or 1141) E. of Norfolk, a turbulent baron under Stephen and Henry II.

5. Versions of these verses, differing slightly from HW's, are in Harrison's *Description of England* II xiv. printed in Holinshed's *Chronicles*, 1807, i. 328: 'If I were in my castell of Bungeie

I have been roving about Hampshire,[6] have been at Winchester and Southampton and twenty places, and have been but one day in London—consequently know as little news as if I had been shut up in Bungey Castle. Rumours there are of great bickerings and uneasinesses,[7] but I don't believe there will be any bloodshed of places, except Legge's,[8] which nobody seems willing to take—I mean as a sinecure.[9] His Majesty of Cockney is returned exceedingly well, but grown a little out of humour at finding that we are not so much pleased with all the Russians and Hessians that he has hired[10] to recover the Ohio.[11] We are an ungrateful people!

Make a great many compliments for me to my Lady A. I own I am in pain about Missy.[12] As my Lady is a little coquette herself, and loves crowds and admiration and a court life, it will be very difficult for her to keep a strict eye upon Missy. The Irish are very forward and bold:—I say no more; but it would hurt you both extremely to have her marry herself idly; and I think my Lord Chancellor has not extended his matrimonial foresight to Ireland.[13] How-

Upon the water of Waueneie
I wold not set a button by the King of Cockneie;'
and in James Howell's *Proverbs*, 1659, *sub* 'English,' p. 21:
'Were I near my Castle of Bungey
Upon the river of Wavenley
I would ne care for the King of Cockeney.'
Bungay Castle, on the Suffolk-Norfolk border, was almost surrounded by the Waveney River.

6. HW describes this tour, from which he had returned by 18 Sept., in his letter to Bentley 18 Sept. 1755 (CHUTE 249–51).

7. HW did not yet know of the negotiations under way with Fox, nor apparently, of the earlier approaches to other politicians (*ante* 16 Sept. 1755, n. 11).

8. Henry Bilson Legge, second son of William Earl of Dartmouth; he was chancellor of the Exchequer (HW). Smarting under slights from Newcastle (see following note), Legge decided to oppose the subsidy treaties and according to HW 'refused peremptorily to sign' the Treasury warrants in July for the execution of the provisions of the Hessian treaty concluded in June (MANN iv. 493 and nn. 20 and 23, 501 and n. 11; *Mem. Geo. II* ii. 35–6). He was finally dismissed

20 Nov. (*post* 27 Nov. 1755 and n. 8).

9. For Newcastle's treatment of Legge as chancellor see *Mem. Geo. II* i. 391–2. For the negotiations during the summer to replace him by Sir George Lee, see MANN iv. 493 and n. 25.

10. The subsidy treaty with Hesse was signed 18 June (ibid. iv. 493, n. 20); that with Russia had originally been concluded 9 Aug. [OS?], but because of a blunder in protocol was cancelled and a new one concluded which was not signed until 30 Sept. (Lord Ilchester and Mrs Langford-Brooke, *Life of Sir Charles Hanbury-Williams*, 1929, pp. 319–22; *Journals of the House of Commons* xxvii. 310). The Hessian treaty provided for 8,000 troops; the Russian for 55,000 (ibid. xxvii. 309, 313).

11. HW is being ironical; the sole object of the treaties was the defence of Hanover and England (see MANN iv. 501); but the soldiers covered by the treaties would enable the King to send to the Ohio British troops otherwise necessary for the defence of Hanover and England.

12. Anne Seymour Conway, only child of Mr Conway and Lady Ailesbury, then an infant (HW).

13. The Marriage Act (*ante* 24 May 1753) was never extended to Ireland

ever, I have much confidence in Mrs Elizabeth Jones:[14] I am sure, when they were here, she would never let Missy whisper with a boy that was old enough to speak.[15]

Adieu! As the winter advances, and plots thicken, I will write you letters that shall have a little more in them than this. In the meantime I am going to the Bath,[16] not for my health, you know I never am ill, but for my amusement. I never was there, and at present there are several of my acquaintance. The French academy[17] have chosen my Lord Chesterfield, and he has written them a letter of thanks[18] that is the finest composition in the world:[19] indeed, I was told so by those who have not seen it; but they would have told me so if they had seen it, whether it was the finest or the worst; suffices it to be his!

Yours ever,

HOR. WALPOLE

To Conway, ca Tuesday 30 September 1755

Missing; Conway acknowledges *post* 7 Oct. 1755 two letters from HW, one of which was clearly *ante* 23 Sept. 1755; the other contained an 'account of a certain transaction' which was probably the negotiation with Fox.

(J. T. Hammick, *The Marriage Law of England*, 1887, p. 232, see also pp. 8–10, 12–15; G. E. Howard, *A History of Matrimonial Institutions*, 1904, i. 318, n. 2, 473, n. 2).

14. Miss Conway's nurse (HW).

15. HW jokes along these lines *ante* 5 May 1752.

16. HW also told Chute 29 Sept. that he had 'some thoughts of going to Bath for a week,' but he did not go (CHUTE 89 and n. 18). On 16 Oct. 'Gilly' Williams wrote to Selwyn from Bath: 'Try if you can't revive these intentions in Mr Walpole, say everything of this place it de-

serves, and give it ten thousand things which it wants' (SELWYN 125).

17. The Académie des Inscriptions et Belles-Lettres, of which Chesterfield had been elected an Académicien-Libre-Étranger in succession to Cardinal Quirini in June or July 1755 (Chesterfield, *Letters*, ed. Dobrée, 1932, v. 2144; *Histoire de l'Académie Royal des Inscriptions et Belles-Lettres*, 1717–1809, 1843, xxvii. 4).

18. Printed Chesterfield, op. cit. v. 2150–2; it was read to the Académie 8 Aug. 1755.

19. Chesterfield called his letter 'the poor offspring of a rape upon my reluctant mind' (ibid. v. 2162).

From CONWAY, Tuesday 7 October 1755

Printed from the MS now WSL, formerly Rutnam. First printed, *Fraser's Magazine*, 1850, xli. 276–7.

Memorandum (by HW):[1] Lord Kild[are] had been set ag[ainst] the Primate by men who meant their own power, therefore the moment the Eng[lish] government offered to sacrifice the Primate, Lord K[ildare] was content, which they who set him on, did not intend he should be so easily. It happened as ridiculously in England. The Duke of Devon[shire] had been unmeasurably set up by the ministry; he grew to have an opinion of his own, declared ag[ainst] the Treaties; they were forced to sacrifice the Stones and Ireland and the Dorsets to gain the Duke of D[evonshire] for the Treaties, by granting everything that would make Lord Hart[ington] easy.

Dublin Castle, 7 Oct. 1755.

Dear Horry,

I BEGIN with our own politics and you'll excuse their being uppermost in my thoughts when I tell you that yours are very high there. First after sweating for the answer from England this week past,[2] and debating schemes for prorogation and adjournment,[3] it arrived the night before last, and with such condescension and concession from his Majesty's part to every part of Lord H[artington]'s plan as went beyond our hopes. You know the heads of address I mentioned, which it was much suspected here would by no means be received or allowed; on the contrary sent back with such emendations as scarce amount to an alteration[4] and were at once agreed to

1. This is probably a note for a projected passage in the *Memoirs*, where HW discusses Kildare's satisfaction at the sacrifice of Primate Stone (*Mem. Geo. II* ii. 25–6), and describes the ministerial consent to Lord Hartington's measures as being given 'to soften' Devonshire's opposition to the Subsidy Treaties (ibid. ii. 39).

2. Contrary winds had delayed the packets from Ireland with Hartington's letter of 17 September (*ante* 16 Sept. 1755, n. 3); duplicates of the letter, sent by various routes, were received in London on 27 and 28 September. Newcastle after consultation with Hardwicke replied on the 30th (BM Add. MSS 32859, f. 279) and his letter reached Dublin on Sunday, 5 Oct. at 3 P.M. (ibid. f. 413).

3. The Irish parliament had been re-

peatedly adjourned and prorogued from 15 Jan. 1754 until 7 Oct. 1755 (*Journals of the House of Commons ... Ireland, 1753–71*, ix. 237–8); the government was discussing the possibility of further postponement until directions arrived from England.

4. The projected alterations, all suggested by Lord Hardwicke, are discussed in BM Add. MSS 32859, f. 261ff., 279ff. and 413ff. It was finally strongly recommended by the English government that the words 'Our concern at having been deprived of an opportunity' in the proposed heads for the Address be changed to 'Our concern at not having had an opportunity,' but Hartington was allowed to dispense with the change if necessary (ibid. ff. 279–80; see also ff. 138, 280, 281).

by the chiefs here.[5] Yet have we not been without alarms, of grand opposition from more parties than one, and many angry spirits in truth there were; some thought it too soft and some too hard and some talked of the dignity of Parliament and an address sent to England;[6] anonymous letters were writ and pamphlets published in the course of one single day;[7] however, with much parley and persuasion from the respective heads people were in general kept quiet and our address, that is, *heads* for a committee passed *nem. con.* in the votes:[8] in the House two insignificant speeches from as insignificant men were all the objection we heard: one[9] a warm patriot and Whig to the backbone like you said it was an *apology*. The other,[10] an old discontented courtier, made a medley of reflections pretty foreign to the matter but both mentioned the message to England.[11] But there it stopped and I believe will end.[12]

The pamphlets I mentioned abuse Lord Kildare, etc. and his face on several signs have, they say, already been blacked.[13] He does not seem to care and on the whole there appears a more cordial disposi-

5. Hartington wrote to Newcastle 7 Oct., 'I sent for the Speaker and proposed the alterations which were desired; he has consented to them so that there will be no difficulties' (ibid. f. 413).

6. 'We have been since [the agreement of the chiefs to the alterations to the Address] alarmed by several rumours of opposition from various quarters: particularly Sir R[ichard] Cox who had declaimed to a numerous audience in his bookseller's shop, on the unprecedented and unparliamentary manners of *sending over an Address* for the approbation of the *Ministry* . . . 'twas said many of the discontented in the Old Court party joined in this' (Conway to Hertford 7 Oct. 1755, MS WSL, printed *Colburn's United Service Magazine*, 1881, liii pt iii. 52–4).

7. Conway mentions 'one or two' pamphlets published on the 6th in his letter to his brother on the 7th (ibid.); they have not been identified.

8. On 7 Oct. (*Journals of the House of Commons . . . Ireland* ix. 254).

9. Robert French (d. 1767), M.P. Galway, 1753 (GM 1767, xxxvii. 144); Conway mentions him to his brother as 'a warm patriot . . . who called it an *apology*' (Conway to Hertford 7 Oct. 1755).

10. Apparently Nicholas Archdall (until 1728, Montgomery) (d. 1763), of Castle Archdall, co. Fermanagh; M.P. co. Fermanagh 1731–61 (Burke, *Landed Gentry of Ireland*, 1958, p. 27). Conway and Hartington call him 'Mr Arsdale' or 'Arsdal' (Conway to Hertford 7 Oct. 1755; BM Add. MSS 32859, f. 416).

11. Archdall 'said for the *apology* he liked it very well but had heard it was sent over to England to be approved and thought it ought to be inquired what men or set of men *dared advise so unconstitutional a thing*—and the other [French] said he heard it was penned in England' (Conway to Hertford 7 Oct. 1755).

12. Conway wrote to his brother the same day: 'Being thus begun I was afraid it would have gone much farther but luckily indeed here the parties were in general well disposed and well managed; though many seemed to have a bridle on 'em . . . 'twas easy enough to evade this attack. The heads of Address being only the private thoughts of particulars that move them till received by the House.'

13. Conway also mentions this in his letter to his brother as does HW in *Mem. Geo. II* ii. 40.

tion and resolution on their part and a more general satisfaction in the plan than one could have expected.[14]

As to your little politics on that side, I fancy they'll do very well to amuse you good part of the winter;—I am seriously and heartily happy in the accommodation with Mr Fox,[15] which all the Duke of Newcastle's letters say is as complete and cordial as possible.[16] I have seen nothing to the contrary elsewhere and therefore am willing to hope it will be firm and of long continuance.

I am vastly obliged to you for your two letters;[17] your excuses for them are quite idle and offensive, particularly as a bad symptom for the future; the news of the Castle of Bungey is as agreeable to me as that of the Castle of Cockney and the old news of Cockney is new again when you tell it.

And yet your account of a certain transaction[18] does not please me so well as others nor correspond with what we hear from others. Time will show. There's riddle for your riddle though I believe mine is not quite so inexplicable as yours which remains unintelligible to all the committee from the House of Riddles[19] in Berkshire.

You are such a traveller one never knows where to have you; you seem to live upon the road;[20] but by this new improvement of daily posts,[21] I shall hope to shoot you flying tolerably well. But as you are

---

14. Conway told his brother that 'our good friends [Boyle's party] . . . in truth seem now I think to have taken their part and resolved to carry it through . . . in general I think there is as much content and satisfaction in the present plan as could well be expected from any' (Conway to Hertford 7 Oct. 1755).

15. Which had been concluded 25 Sept., when Fox agreed to accept the Seals as secretary of state for the southern department with leadership of the House of Commons (MANN iv. 502 and nn. 17–20). Conway wrote to his brother, 'I am vastly happy in the present turn and only wish it much continuance and solidity' (Conway to Hertford 7 Oct. 1755).

16. Newcastle wrote to Hartington in his private letter of 30 Sept.: 'We [Fox and himself] are both perfectly satisfied with each other at present and I doubt not, but we shall continue to be so. It seems the resolution and intention of

both parties' (BM Add. MSS 32859, f. 282).

17. *Ante* 23 Sept. 1755 and a missing letter.

18. Probably Newcastle's alliance with Fox; HW suspected each of intending to ruin the other; see MANN iv. 502 and HW to Chute 29 Sept. 1755 (CHUTE 88–9).

19. Park Place.

20. Besides HW's tour of Hampshire in early September, mentioned in his last letter, and his projected trip to Bath, he had visited Rigby in Essex 'for a week or ten days' in late August (HW to Bentley 15, 28 Aug. 1755, CHUTE 242, 247; MANN iv. 490, n. 1).

21. An extensive addition to the number of places to which posts would be dispatched daily, instead of three times a week, from London had been made in September, to be effective on 10 Oct. (GM 1755, xxv. 425; Herbert Joyce, *History of the Post Office*, 1893, p. 170).

so fond of expeditions and changes are now making, I wish you would apply for a messenger's place[22] that one might sometimes have a chance of seeing you here, where I doubt nobody comes but for their duty though really your going to Bath is so excellent that one can despair of you nowhere after it.

Missy has many followers and pretenders as you may imagine; but as she does not know the merit of broad shoulders and strong legs, and is more taken with the charms of conversation, and is not quite reconciled to a story told with a brogue, I hope she may be tolerably safe for this session, especially as I think they seldom begin to ravish 'em under nine years old.

Adieu. I wish you much pleasure at Bath; I have not yet seen a list of the quality there, nor had an account of the players or musicians, which I scarce fancy are so good as ours in Dublin, nor can the assemblies be half so full; we sometimes reckon four hundred people at a Castle ball, and then we have Mr Arne[23] just come over, and I hear Mr Mossop[24] and Mrs Gregory;[25] I shall send you all the advertisements[26] as they come out; we talk of preparing another ball, to exceed the last; the floor is to be green velvet (and 'tis said the ladies will dance barefoot), the ceiling blue ditto, all the milliners in town are at work upon a large wood of green silk that it is reported will be at least ten foot square; the fountains and cascades all to be natural and performed by the nymphs of the town who will *make* orange flowers, water and *eau sans pareille;* it will in short be beyond anything of the kind even here and vastly worth your seeing.

22. A King's messenger, who carried official dispatches.

23. Thomas Augustine Arne (1710–78), composer; some details of his visit to Ireland in 1755–6 are in Hubert Langley, *Doctor Arne*, Cambridge, 1938, pp. 53–5. According to the *Dublin Journal* 4–7 Oct., 'Mr Arne, who is arrived in this kingdom with several vocal performers, having agreed with the managers of the Theatre Royal, proposes, by subscription, to entertain the **town ten nights, with** three operas in the English language (viz.) . . . *Eliza* . . . *Alfred* . . . *The Fairies* . . . The first performance will be in the beginning of November . . . Mr Arne will accompany the operas on the harpsichord.'

24. Henry Mossop (?1729–74), actor, who had begun his career at the Smock Alley Theatre, Dublin, revisited it 1755–6 (DNB, supplemented by C. B. Hogan, 'Eighteenth-Century Actors in the DNB: Additions and Corrections,' *Theatre Notebook*, Oct. 1951 – July 1952, vi. 90).

25. Mary Flannigan (d. 1790), m. 1 Capt. Gregory; m. 2 (ca 1757) ——Fitzhenry, a lawyer; an Irishwoman who made her debut in London in Jan. 1754, returned to Dublin by the beginning of 1755 and acted there throughout 1756 (DNB, supplemented by Hogan, op. cit. 69).

26. The *Dublin Journal* Nov.–Dec. 1755 contains many advertisements of plays in which Mossop and Mrs Gregory performed, and the paper for 13–16 Dec. prints a poem 'On seeing Mr Mossop perform.'

Once more good-bye. Tell me if I shall get a ticket for you and believe me

> Most sincerely yours,
>
> H. S. C.

Lady Ailesbury, whom I have taken no notice of, sends her compliments; she is better here and I think better reconciled to the place than I expected.

To Conway, Saturday 15 November 1755

Printed from *Works* v. 41–3. From Conway's reply it would appear that some remarks about riots at Drury Lane and some 'misfortunes' suffered by Conway's sister may have been omitted; see *post* 27 Nov. 1755, n. 13.

Arlington Street, Nov. 15, 1755.

I PROMISED you histories, and there are many people that take care I should have it in my power to keep my word. To begin in order, I should tell you, that there were 289 members at the Cockpit meeting,[1] the greatest number ever known there: but Mr Pitt, who is too great a general to regard numbers, especially when there was a probability of no great harmony between the commanders,[2] did not however postpone giving battle. The engagement was not more decisive than long:[3] we sat till within a quarter of five in the morning;[4] an uninterrupted serious debate from before two. Lord Hillsborough[5] moved the Address,[6] and very injudiciously supposed an Opposition. Martin,[7] Legge's secretary, moved to omit in the Address the indirect approbation of the treaties, and the direct assurances of

1. 12 Nov.; HW gives a brief account in *Mem. Geo. II* ii. 47.

2. Fox and Newcastle.

3. On 13–14 Nov., the day of the opening of Parliament (*Journals of the House of Commons* xxvii. 297).

4. HW told Mann they sat until five and Bentley, until past five (MANN iv. 510; CHUTE 260).

5. Wills Hill (1718–93), 2d Vct Hillsborough, cr. (1751) E. of Hillsborough and (1789) M. of Downshire, all in the Irish

peerage, had not yet received an English peerage and was M.P. for Warwick 1741–56, and an adherent of Fox in English politics (SELWYN 129, n. 1). His speech is described *Mem. Geo. II* ii. 49–50.

6. The Address as moved is printed *Journals of the House of Commons* xxvii. 298; the Address as actually presented, ibid. xxvii. 300–1.

7. Samuel Martin (1714–88), M.P. Camelford 1747–68, Hastings 1768–74; secretary of the Treasury 1756–7, 1758–63.

protection to Hanover.[8] These questions were at length divided; and against Pitt's inclination, the last, which was the least unpopular, was first decided by a majority of 311 against 105.[9] Many then went away; and on the next division the numbers were 290 to 89.[10] These are the general outlines. The detail of the speeches, which were very long, and some extremely fine, it would be impossible to give you in any compass.[11] On the side of the Opposition (which I must tell you by the way, though it set out decently, seems extremely resolved) the speakers (I name them in their order) were:[12] the third Colebrook,[13] Martin, Northey,[14] Sir Richard Lyttleton, Doddington, George Grenville,[15] Sir F. Dashwood, Beckford,[16] Sir G. Lee,[17] Legge, Potter,[18] Dr Hay,[19] Geo. Townshend, Lord Egmont,[20] Pitt, and Admiral Vernon: on the other side[21] were, Lord Hillsborough, Obrien,[22]

8. 'Martin . . . proposed to omit that part of the Address that engaged assistance to Hanover; but forgetting the paragraph relative to the treaties, and the Court party taking advantage of that slip, he corrected his motion' (*Mem. Geo. II* ii. 50). The motion as corrected is in *Journals of the House of Commons* xxvii. 298.

9. The division was on an amendment to Martin's amendment: the motion was to retain in the Address the promise of assistance to Hanover (*Mem. Geo. II* ii. 61; *Journals of the House of Commons* xxvii. 298).

10. The division was on retaining in the Address the rest of the words which Martin had proposed to omit because they implied approval of the subsidy treaties (ibid.). When the motion passed, it meant that the Address as a whole was approved unamended.

11. HW's account of the debate in the House of Commons, the most complete that survives, is in *Mem. Geo. II* ii. 49–62.

12. Another list of opposition speakers (BM Add. MSS 32960 f. 471) gives them in the same order as HW, but omits Adm. Vernon; a third list (ibid. f. 476), omits Egmont, Dodington, and Dashwood, but includes an explanation of their qualified opposition.

13. George Colebrooke (1729–1809), 2d Bt, 1761; M.P. Arundel 1754–74; 3d son of James Colebrooke, the banker (*ante* 7 May 1746, n. 11); merchant and banker and later (1767–71, 1772–3) director and

chairman of the East India Company.

14. William Northey (?1722–70), M.P. Calne 1747–61, Maidstone 1761–8, Great Bedwyn 1768–70; groom of the Bedchamber 1760–70; lord of Trade, 1770.

15. (1712–70), M.P. Buckingham borough 1741–70; first lord of the Treasury 1763–5.

16. William Beckford (1709–70), M.P. Shaftesbury 1747–54, London 1754–70; lord mayor of London 1762, 1769; one of Pitt's principal allies.

17. Sir George Lee (ca 1700–58), Kt, 1752; civil lawyer; M.P. Brackley 1733–42, Devizes 1742–7, Liskeard 1747–54, Launceston 1754–8; dean of arches and judge of the prerogative court of Canterbury 1751–8.

18. Thomas Potter (?1718–59), wit and politician; M.P. St Germans 1747–54, Aylesbury 1754–7, Okehampton 1757–9.

19. George Hay (1715–78), Kt, 1773; civil lawyer and politician; M.P. Stockbridge 1754–6, Calne 1757–61, Sandwich 1761–8, Newcastle-under-Lyme 1768–78. In his *Memoirs* HW ranks Hay as one of the twenty-eight outstanding speakers in the House of Commons (*Mem. Geo. II* ii. 144).

20. John Perceval (1711–70), 2d E. of Egmont.

21. The lists of speakers in the Newcastle Papers (above, n. 12) gives them in slightly different order: f. 471 reverses Stanhope and Hamilton, while f. 476 puts Nugent at the end.

22. Percy Wyndham O'Brien (*ante* 23 June 1752, n. 21).

young Stanhope,[23] Hamilton,[24] Alstone,[25] Ellis,[26] Lord Barrington,[27] Sir G. Lyttelton, Nugent, Murray, Sir T. Robinson,[28] my uncle, and Mr Fox. As short as I can, I will give you an account of them. Sir Richard,[29] Beckford, Potter,[30] G. Townshend,[31] the Admiral of course,[32] Martin, and Stanhope[33] were very bad: Doddington was well, but very *acceding:*[34] Dr Hay by no means answers his reputation; it was easy, but not striking.[35] Lord Egmont was doubling, absurd, and obscure.[36] Sir G. Lee and Lord Barrington were much disliked;[37] I don't think, so deservedly. Poor Alston was mad, and spoke ten times to order. Sir George,[38] our friend, was dull and timid.[39] Legge was the latter.[40] Nugent roared,[41] and Sir Thomas rumbled.[42] Mr Fox was extremely fatigued, and did little.[43] Geo. Grenville's was very fine and much beyond himself, and very pathetic.[44] The Attorney-General[45] in the same style, and very artful, was still finer. Then

23. Philip Stanhope (1732–68), diplomatist; Lord Chesterfield's natural son and the recipient of his letters; M.P. Liskeard 1754–61, St Germans 1761–5.

24. William Gerard Hamilton (1729–96), M.P. Petersfield 1754–61, Pontefract 1761–8, Old Sarum 1768–74, Wareham 1774–80, Wilton 1780–90, Haslemere 1790–6; lord of Trade 1756–61; chief secretary to the lord lieutenant of Ireland 1761–4; chancellor of the Irish Exchequer 1763–84.

25. Thomas Alston (ca 1724–74), 5th Bt, 1759; M.P. Bedfordshire 1747–61.

26. Welbore Ellis (1713–1802), cr. (1794) Bn Mendip; politician; M.P. Cricklade 1741–7, Weymouth and Melcombe Regis 1747–61, 1774–90, Aylesbury 1761–8, Petersfield 1768–74, 1791–4.

27. William Wildman Barrington Shute (1717–93), 2d Vct Barrington.

28. Sir Thomas Robinson (1695–1770), K.B., 1742, cr. (1761) Bn Grantham; diplomatist; M.P. Thirsk 1727–34, Christchurch 1748–61; at this time secretary of state for the southern department.

29. HW, in a sentence omitted from the printed *Memoirs*, comments that he 'sluiced that volubility, that continued so copious and fatiguing.'

30. HW describes him as speaking 'flimsily' (*Mem. Geo. II* ii. 54).

31. HW summarizes his speech, delivered 'poorly,' ibid.

32. HW writes in the *Memoirs:* 'The attention of the House was entirely put

an end to, as it generally was, by Admiral Vernon' (ibid. ii. 61).

33. It was his maiden (and only) speech; see Chesterfield, *Letters*, ed. Dobrée, 1932, iv. 2165–6.

34. HW summarizes his speech in *Mem. Geo. II* ii. 51–2, describing it as 'nibbling at the negotiations,' and betraying 'his willingness to turn defendant' (ibid. ii. 51). He opposed approving the treaties, but would pass the assurances to Hanover.

35. HW merely described him as speaking 'tritely,' ibid. ii. 54.

36. 'Lord Egmont assembled in one speech more defects than had been dispersed through all the others: he was capricious, obscure, contradictory, dubious, absurd; he declared for the negotiations, but would vote against the Address, as it seemed to appropriate the treaties, which he thought beneficial to England, to the service of the Electorate' (ibid. ii. 54–5).

37. HW describes Lee's speech briefly ibid. ii. 53, but does not mention Barrington's.

38. Sir George Lyttelton (HW).

39. HW summarizes his speech in *Mem. Geo. II* ii. 52.

40. His speech is ibid. ii. 54.

41. Ibid. ii. 52.

42. Ibid. ii. 53–4; he was a notoriously poor speaker.

43. Fox's speech is ibid. ii. 61.

44. HW also describes Grenville's speech as 'fine, pathetic' ibid. ii. 52.

45. William Murray, afterwards Lord

there was a young Mr Hamilton, who spoke for the first time, and was at once perfection:[46] his speech was set, and full of antithesis, but those antitheses were full of argument: indeed his speech was the most argumentative of the whole day; and he broke through the regularity of his own composition, answered other people, and fell into his own track again with the greatest ease. His figure is advantageous, his voice strong and clear, his manner spirited, and the whole with the ease of an established speaker. You will ask, what could be beyond this? Nothing, but what was beyond what ever was, and that was Pitt! He spoke at past one, for an hour and thirty-five minutes:[47] there was more humour, wit, vivacity, finer language, more boldness, in short, more astonishing perfections than even you, who are used to him, can conceive. He was not abusive, yet very attacking on all sides: he ridiculed my Lord Hillsborough, crushed poor Sir George, terrified the Attorney, lashed my Lord Granville, painted my Lord of Newcastle, attacked Mr Fox, and even hinted up to the Duke.[48] A few of the Scotch were in the minority, and most of the Princess's people, not all: all the Duke of Bedford's in the majority. He himself spoke in the other House for the Address (though professing uncertainty about the treaties[49] themselves), against my Lord Temple and Lord Halifax, without a division.[50] My Lord Talbot[51] was neuter; he and I were of a party: my opinion was strongly with the Opposition; I could not vote for the treaties; I would not vote against Mr Fox. It is ridiculous perhaps, at the end of such a debate, to give an account of my own silence; and as it is of very little consequence what I did, so it is very unlike me to justify myself. You know how much I hate *professions* of integrity; and my pride is generally too great to care what the generality of people say

Mansfield (HW). HW summarizes his speech *Mem. Geo. II* ii. 52–3, but says he eventually 'over-acted the pathetic, almost to lamentation.'

46. This was the speech that won him the nick-name 'Single-Speech,' although he made others (Namier and Brooke ii. 574). HW writes in the *Memoirs* 'his voice, manner, and language, were most advantageous; his arguments sound though pointed; and his command of himself easy and undaunted' (ibid. ii. 51).

47. HW gives a full report of Pitt's speech ibid. ii. 55–60, and in a letter to Bentley 16 Nov. 1755 (CHUTE 260).

48. The Duke of Cumberland (HW).

49. Treaties of subsidy with the Landgrave of Hesse and the Empress of Russia for the defence of Hanover (HW).

50. HW gives a brief account of the debate in the Lords in *Mem. Geo. II* ii. 48–9. An amendment was moved, but was rejected without a division; Temple, however, entered a formal protest (*Journals of the House of Lords* xxviii. 427).

51. William Talbot (1710–82), 2d Bn Talbot; cr. (1761) E. Talbot.

of me: but your heart is good enough to make me wish you should think well of mine.

You will want to know what is to be the fate of the ministry in opposition: but that I can't tell you. I don't believe they have determined what to do, more than oppose, nor that it is determined what to do with them. Though it is clear that it is very humiliating to leave them in place, you may conceive several reasons why it is not eligible to dismiss them. *You* know where you are, how easy it is to buy an opposition who have not places; but tell us what to do with an opposition that has places? If you say, turn them out; I answer, that is not the way to quiet any opposition, or a ministry so constituted as ours at present. Adieu!

Yours ever,

HOR. WALPOLE

From CONWAY, Thursday 27 November 1755

Printed from the MS now WSL, formerly Rutnam. First printed *Fraser's Magazine*, 1850, xli. 277–8.

Endorsed (by HW): Received Dec. 3d.

Memoranda (by HW, in pencil; names crossed out are marked by an asterisk; others in ink for HW's reply are printed under the heading for that missing letter):

2–4–6
1–11–6

Lady Anne Conolly[1]	Lady Bath
Mrs Hardinge[2]	Lady Harvey*
Lady Mary Bolby[3]	Duchess of Dorset*
Lord Bath*	Mr Fox
D. of Bedford*	Lady Stafford[6]
Dean of Exeter[4]	Lady Townshend
Lord Orford	Lady Mary Bolby
Lord Digby[5]	Lady Sophia Thomas

Dublin Castle, 27 Nov. 1755.

Dear Horry,

I AM more obliged to you than you can imagine for all your intelligence, which has fully gratified all the rage I had for English news; such as you may imagine it at such a critical time, and after a fast of five packets. I felt vast satisfaction in your very good account of what passed: a furious battle it was; and, as I fancied, could not end without what you call some *bloodshed of places,*[7] though the lists of the killed and wounded[8] did not come till this morning's post. Among the former, I most lament Legge whom I now conclude lost and given up to resentment; among the latter our friend Sir Geo[rge],[9] who will be the butt of as much censure as envy and

---

1. Lady Anne Wentworth (1713–97), m. (1733) William Conolly.

2. Probably Jane Pratt (d. 1807), m. (1738) Nicholas Hardinge (Collins, *Peerage*, 1812, v. 266; John Nichols, *Literary Anecdotes*, 1812–15, v. 346; GM 1807, lxxvii pt i. 480–1).

3. See *ante* ca 15 Feb. 1752, n. 28.

4. Hon. Charles Lyttelton.

5. Edward Digby (1730–57), 6th Bn Digby; nephew of Henry Fox.

6. Henrietta Cantillon (d. 1761), m. 1

(1743) William Matthias Stafford Howard, 3d E. of Stafford; m. 2 (1759) Robert Maxwell, 2d Bn Farnham, cr. (1760) Vct Farnham and (1763) E. of Farnham; an intimate friend of Lady Hervey (MORE 7, n. 10).

7. HW uses this phrase *ante* 23 Sept. 1755.

8. Pitt, Legge, and George Grenville had been dismissed 20 Nov. for their opposition (MANN iv. 512, n. 8).

9. Lyttelton became chancellor of the

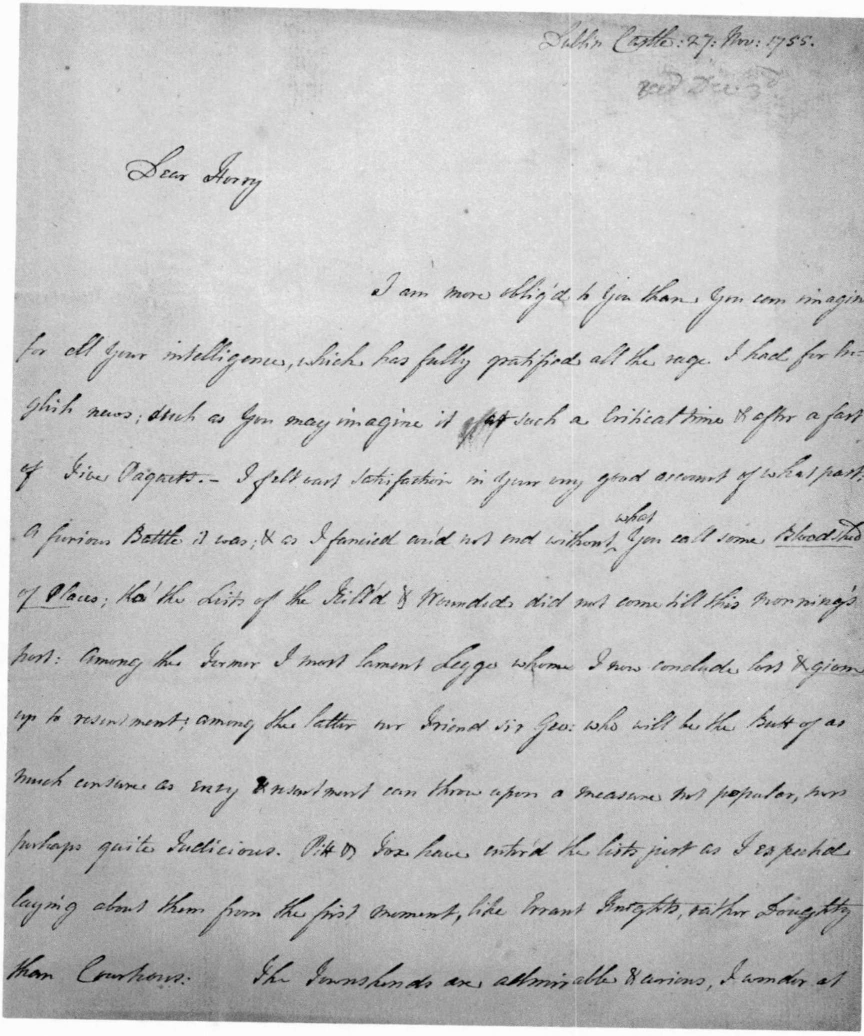
Dublin Castle: 27: Nov: 1755.

Recd Dec 3

Dear Harry

I am more oblig'd to You than You can imagine for all Your intelligence, which has fully gratified all the rage I had for English news; such as You may imagine it at such a Critical time & after a fast of Five Paquets.— I felt vast satisfaction in Your very good account of what past. A furious Battle it was; & as I fancied could not end without what You call some Bloodshed of Places; tho' the Lists of the Kill'd & Wounded did not come till this morning's post: Among the Former I most lament Legge whome I now conclude lost & given up to resentment; among the latter our Friend Sir Geo: who will be the Butt of as much censure as envy & resentment can throw upon a measure not popular, nor perhaps quite Judicious. Pitt & Fox have enter'd the lists just as I expected laying about them from the first moment, like Errant Knights, rather Doughty than Courteous: The Townshends are admirable & curious, I wonder at

LETTER FROM CONWAY TO WALPOLE 27 NOVEMBER 1755

resentment can throw upon a measure not popular nor perhaps quite judicious. Pitt and Fox have entered the lists just as I expected, laying about them from the first moment, like errant knights, rather doughty than courteous. The Townshends are admirable and curious, I wonder at Charles's silence the first day, but more at Geo[rge]'s speech and motion the second,[10] what says my Lady[11] for her old friend Mr Fox?

I am a little sorry for your qualm (excuse me), as such a thin member as you would have added but little to the bulk of such a majority, and perhaps your friend Mr Fox may be sorry you were not with him.

I hate not to be amongst you in these curious times. One feels tied to a stake here, in a miserable little circle; of pretty rich clover indeed but yet confined; and one had rather play about the barrenest fields. I don't really mean for ambition and to make a figure among these heroes, which in truth I could not expect; but for curiosity and amusement. We are plodding on in dull elections[12] which I don't attend or care about, or but little, and from some anxiety for their remote consequences.[12a] Yet are our Irish heads as full and as eager about them as any of you can be for your subsidies.

I don't know your Mr Hamilton, even by sight; but admire him much in your description; particularly in his happy gift of confidence, so remarkable on his first appearance.

You say less than I expected on the furious playhouse battles,[13] which I think beat the combats of St Stephen's. I thought you joked about Nanny,[14] till I saw a more *serious* account of her misfortunes

Exchequer; he had broken with Pitt and his Grenville cousins the previous year.

10. 21 Nov., in a debate provoked by G. Townshend over Fox's circular letter under 'pretence' of moving a call of the House; HW gives an account *Mem. Geo. II* ii. 64–7.

11. Lady Townshend.

12. The committee on privileges and elections was by this time considering election petitions concerning Wexford, Navan, Maryborough, Clonmell and Carrick (*Journals of the House of Commons . . . Ireland*, Dublin, 1753–71, ix. 307, 331, 369–70, 382–3, 387). Conway discusses the conclusion of the first two *post* 11 Dec. 1755; the last three were decided 17 Dec. 1755, 19 Jan. and 29 Jan. 1756 re-

spectively (*Journals . . . Ireland* ix. 586–7, 653–730, 737–8).

12a. That is, the way they were decided might indicate the drift of feeling towards the administration in the Irish parliament.

13. There were 'nightly riots' at Drury Lane against French dancers; see HW to Bentley 16 Nov. 1755 (CHUTE 260–1). Neither of the subjects mentioned in this paragraph appears in HW's letter, but it is not wholly clear whether the paragraphs relating to them were omitted when that letter was printed, or whether HW wrote a second (and missing) letter to Conway in mid-November.

14. Conway's sister Anne; nothing further is known about her 'misfortunes' at this time.

from herself. I have no notion how she outlived it; and think it one of the most tragical stories I ever heard.

Whose was the *World* about people of fashion?[15] We think it a good one. Do send me Voltaire's new history of the late war,[16] and his new play,[17] and the *Nuit et Moment*,[18] and any sharp pamphlet or other new thing you please; I do nothing but tease and trouble you; I wish you'd send for some Irish stuffs, or some kid gloves, or oilskin coats, or something of our Irish produce. News we have none; books fewer, so you must e'en be content, as I must be, to continue craving and running over head and ears in debt with you for everything that's clever, as indeed is apt to be the case. Adieu!

To CONWAY, Saturday 6 December 1755

Missing; answered *post* 11 Dec. 1755. Memoranda for it in ink, all crossed out, are printed here from *ante* 27 Nov. 1755:

Earthquake[1]
Prize Bill[2]
Army[3]
Mrs Hodges[4]
books anecd[ote] in Voltaire[5]
Townshends[6]
the *World* on fashion[7]

15. The *World*, No. 151, by Lord Chesterfield, dated 20 Nov. 1755.
16. *Histoire de la guerre de mil sept cent quarante et un*, written 1746–9, and pirated and published in Paris in the late summer of 1755 (Georges Bengesco, *Voltaire: Bibliographie de ses œuvres*, 1882–90, i. 363–5). An English edition is mentioned in Nov. 1755 (Voltaire, *Correspondence*, ed. Bestermann, Geneva, 1953–65, xxviii. 160), but is dated 1756 on the title-page; HW's copy is Hazen, *Cat. of HW's Lib.*, No. 1308.
17. *L'Orphelin de la Chine*, performed for the first time in Paris 20 Aug. 1755; the privilege to publish is dated 19 Sept. 1755 (Bengesco, op. cit. i. 52–3). An extensive summary in English is in the GM for Dec. 1755 (xxv. 545–9). HW's copies of the original and translation are Hazen, op. cit. Nos 1263, 1818:17:6.
18. By Claude-Prosper Jolyot de Crébillon (1707–77).

1. The Lisbon earthquake, 1 Nov. 1755; the first reports reached London via France 24 Nov. and further details in a letter from Keene at Madrid, 10 Nov., arrived on the 27th (MANN iv. 511–12 and nn. 1–7). A copy of Keene's letter in HW's hand is now WSL.
2. Which was debated and rejected by the House of Commons 2 Dec.; HW gives an account in *Mem. Geo. II* ii. 78–85.
3. The debate on the augmentation of the army, 5 Dec.; HW gives an account ibid. ii. 86–97.
4. She was robbed; see *post* 11 Dec. 1755.
5. Probably the 'lying anecdote of old Marlborough' which HW discusses in his letter to Bentley 17 Dec. 1755 (CHUTE 264).
6. See *post* 11 Dec. 1755, n. 2.
7. See *ante* 27 Nov. 1755, n. 15.

From CONWAY, Thursday 11 December 1755

Printed from the MS now WSL, formerly Rutnam. First printed, *Fraser's Magazine*, 1850, xli. 278–9.
Endorsed (by HW): Received 17th.
Memoranda in ink, probably for HW's missing letter to Lady Ailesbury ca 20 Dec. 1755, are printed under the heading for that letter.

Thursday night, 11 December 1755.

Dear Horry,

I SIT down for a moment just to thank you for your letter of the 6th, which I received this evening. What I told you before was most exactly true, that I was vastly pleased and obliged by what you call your scraps of politics.[1] Short as they are, they contain enough to give me ideas, and, as you contrive them, pretty strong and adequate ones of what passes. If they were ten times as long, I can't say but they would be ten times as agreeable, but I am not unreasonable enough to expect it, I that have scarce scraps to send, and scarce time to send them.

Our elections here are like the earthquake of Lisbon and take place even of that. I have, as a measure, attended none;[1a] by which I have at least avoided one species of plague, the worst of all parliamentary plagues, though there has remained enough at home to torment me sufficiently.

I am much obliged to you for the books you have sent and shall have some impatience for their arrival, particularly those of Voltaire. I have heard before a good character of the *Orphelin*, which has somehow or other got over here, which is strange, for the progress of new books hither is surprisingly slow; so that, to speak in the language of the country, all our new books are really old.

What you tell me of my Lady T.[2] is strange, but not a bit surprising. I fancy you are all very lively and clever this year, a little too quarrelsome and serious I suppose, yet do I terribly regret not being amongst you. You are so good as to wish for me, but alas! I see little

1. The accounts of the debates on the Prize Bill and the augmentation of the army, mentioned in HW's memoranda *ante* 6 Dec. 1755.

1a. In order to avoid the appearance of the Castle interfering in elections, es-

pecially since Hartington's relatives were involved (see below, n. 6).

2. Lady Townshend. This anecdote is not mentioned in any of HW's other surviving letters.

prospect of moving; our dull business goes on in the dullest and most sluggish way and is like to be very tedious I doubt.

Apropos to books I have been dabbling at an auction here, or rather more than dabbling, and bought a parcel towards my future library: two great books particularly that I think not dear, Rymer's *Fœdera*[3] for little more than £14 English (a Dutch edition) and Monfaucon's *Antiquities*,[4] for about 16 guineas, Paris edition and in very good order.

Never was so strange a disaster as our poor friend Mrs Hodges's;[5] I think our age has carried the arts of robbery and murder to their perfection. You don't say if anybody was with her in the coach; I suppose not; but can't help thinking the artist would have had some difficulty if he had found six or eight or ten legs to scramble through! His trusting to this tête-à-tête looks a little like intelligence in the family.

I told you my Lord Lieutenant did not interfere in elections here, from whence his friends and relations, the Ponsonbys,[6] have already lost the Wexford,[7] and will lose the Navan[8] today. But why do I talk of this stuff to you that don't know the county of Wexford from

3. *Fœdera*, by Thomas Rymer (1641–1713), first published in seventeen volumes 1704–17. The edition Conway purchased was in ten volumes, published by John Neaulme at The Hague 1737–45, 'of greatly superior typographical accuracy, and supplies some new documents' (DNB sub 'Rymer, Thomas').

4. *Antiquitas explanatione et schematibus illustrata, l'Antiquité expliquée et representée en figures*, 1719, in ten volumes folio, by Bernard de Montfaucon (1655–1741). A supplement in five volumes folio was published in 1724.

5. Rigby wrote Bedford 4 Dec. 1755, 'I must tell you of the most curious of all robberies that was committed last night. A Mrs Hodges of Hanover Square got into her coach at the playhouse, and from under the seat of the coach, as it was going along, up jumps a thief, and with a pistol in his hand demands her money and jewels, and orders her, upon pain of instant death, to stop her coach at a certain place and let him out and wish him good night, all which she complied with,

and he carried off a thousand pounds' worth of her jewels' (*Bedford Corr.* ii. 177–8). The robbery and jewels are described in the *London Evening Post* 4–6 Dec.

6. Two of Hartington's sisters had married the two sons of Brabazon Ponsonby (1679–1758), 2d Vct Duncannon, cr. (1739) E. of Bessborough: Lady Caroline Cavendish (1719–60), m. (1739) William Ponsonby (1704–93), styled Vct Duncannon 1739–58, 2d. E. of Bessborough, 1758; and Lady Elizabeth Cavendish (d. 1796), m. (1743) Rt Hon. John Ponsonby (1713–89), Speaker of the Irish House of Commons, 1756–71.

7. The report on the Wexford election, made 29 Nov., declared that Robert Leigh had not been duly elected, but that Andrew Ram was (*Journals of the House of Commons . . . Ireland*, Dublin, 1753–71, ix. 401–92).

8. The Navan election report was made 12 Dec.; John Preston was declared unduly elected and replaced by Richard Hamilton (ibid, ix. 504–74).

the town of Navan? Nor I warrant you don't care a halfpenny who is Speaker of the Irish House of Commons five year hence.

We are sending beef and butter in abundance to the Portuguese.[9] I heard last night an account from the City more favourable than yours,[10] which I hope may prove true.

Don't be discouraged from writing by the dullness and nothingness of my letters. You know how to account for both and you know well enough if I could anyhow make mine like yours I would. Perhaps things may mend; the minds of people are purely fermented with these elections, and may yet produce something more lively. Adieu!

PS. I don't mention the Duke of Devonshire.[11] You know enough of that melancholy story and enough of that family to know their distress is as great as can be on such an occasion. The Duke[12] goes with Lady Caroline and Lady Betty[13] into the country for a few days.

---

9. The *Dublin Journal* 2–6 Dec. reports, 'We hear that an express was dispatched yesterday to Corke, to send all sorts of provisions with the utmost expedition to Lisbon, for the relief of the miserable inhabitants who may be living'; and in the paper of 6–9 Dec., 'It is said that the beef that had been purchased in Ireland by the French, is converted into a more laudable channel; it being to be sent to the relief of the unhappy, destitute inhabitants of Lisbon. . . . We hear that the embargo is taken off the ships in this kingdom that were loaded with provisions, and that they are to sail forthwith to Lisbon; and that great quantities of pork, peas, bacon and meal will be sent thither by the Government for the relief of the distressed Portuguese.' See also *Public Advertiser* 3 Dec., and *London Evening Post* 4–6 Dec.

10. The account HW had sent to Conway was probably similar to that he sent to Mann on 4 Dec. (MANN iv. 511–12).

11. Who had died 5 Dec., according to HW, 'of a dropsy contracted by drinking' (*Mem. Geo. II* ii. 85–6, where the last three words are omitted, but they are in HW's MSS in the possession of Lord Waldegrave).

12. I.e., the former Lord Hartington, who was now D. of Devonshire. Conway wrote him 14 Dec., 'I know of no business that can hurry your Grace to town before Tuesday; as soon after that as is agreeable and convenient, I suppose you will see the Speaker and settle farther the remaining part of the public business particularly as to the Addresses . . .' (Chatsworth MSS, 416 / 19).

13. His sisters Lady Caroline Duncannon and Lady Elizabeth Ponsonby (above, n. 6).

To Lady Ailesbury, ca Saturday 20 December 1755

Missing; mentioned *post* 5 Jan. 1756. What are probably memoranda for it are on the MS of *ante* 11 Dec. 1755:

[smell] to Lisbon[1]
H[enry] V[ane] a paymaster[x2]
Lady F. fears wind
Go to Bath for reg. fit of earthq.
Pitt, you don't stay to kiss hands[x3]
Legge on H.W.[x]

1. The *Daily Adv.* 11 Dec. queries, 'Whether the late calamity, which hath happened at Lisbon by the dreadful earthquake, and which hath occasioned the death of so many thousands of people, may not also be the occasion of another as bad, when all the dead bodies, which have lain so long in heaps under the rubbish, come to be found, by the stench and bad smell which may come by their having lain there so long: I mean whether it may not occasion a sickness, or the plague. . . .'

2. A witticism by George Selwyn (HW to Bentley 17 Dec. 1755, Chute 263) on the appointment of Henry Vane (ca 1705–58), 3d Bn Barnard, 1753, cr. (1754) E. of Darlington, as joint paymaster-general of the forces. HW turned it into an epigram (Gray ii. 87–8; Selwyn 125).

3. A remark made to Pitt by HW; see HW to Bentley 17 Dec. 1755 (Chute loc. cit.).

From Conway, Monday 5 January 1756

Printed for the first time from the MS now wsl, formerly Rutnam.
Memoranda (by HW, for a missing letter):

> Mart. Folkes coins[1]
> Gen. Campbell[2]
> Anderson[3]
> ───────
> Mrs Rice[4]
> Lady H. Vernon
> Lady Ilchester[5]
> Lady B. Mckinsy[6]
> Ds of Portland[7]
> Lord Abergavenny[8]

Other memoranda, for *post* 22 Jan. 1756, are printed with that letter.

Dublin Castle, 5 January 1756.

Dear Horry,

I DON'T know any business I have to write to you as I find you have fairly or rather, most unfairly and unfaithfully, cast me off for my wife;[9] I was a true and faithful correspondent to you, and if I was a little dull it was no legal cause of divorce, nor am I so easily to be got rid of; I'll haunt you, and torment you and insist upon my dues and my rights; and punish you by being more disagreeable than ever, and add crossness and peevishness to all my other disagreements, by which it will be very hard if I don't regain you; if I don't I'll continue to torment you.

Your heroes are now breathing during the cessation,[10] but breath-

---

1. Martin Folkes (1690–1754), numismatist and antiquary; D.C.L.; P.R.S. 1741–52; President of the Society of Antiquaries 1749–54. HW's copy of his *Table of English Silver Coins from the Norman Conquest*, 1745, is Hazen, *Cat. of HW's Lib.*, No. 267. Folkes's coins and medals were sold at auction by Langford 27–31 Jan. 1756 (Frits Lugt, *Répertoire des Catalogues de ventes publiques*, The Hague, 1938–64, No. 904).

2. John Campbell, 4th D. of Argyll, 1761; Lady Ailesbury's father.

3. Not identified.

4. Probably Lucy Trevor (b. 1705), m. (1722) Edward Rice of Newton, Glamorganshire; George Montagu's double first cousin; or her unmarried daughter Lucy

(ca 1726–1818) (MONTAGU i. 12, n. 7).

5. Elizabeth Strangways Horner (1723–92), m. (1736) Stephen Fox, cr. (1741) Bn and (1756) E. of Ilchester.

6. Lady Elizabeth Campbell (ca 1722–99), m. (1749) Hon. James Stuart Mackenzie.

7. Lady Margaret Cavendish (1715–85), m. (1734) William Bentinck, 2d D. of Portland.

8. George Nevill (1727–85), 17th Bn Abergavenny, cr. (1784) E. of Abergavenny.

9. HW's previous letter (missing) had been to Lady Ailesbury.

10. Parliament had adjourned 23 Dec. until 13 Jan. (*Journals of the House of Commons* xxvii. 348).

ing fire and smoke, I suppose, against one another; and whetting
their weapons for new engagements. What are like to be the topics?
Militia and money schemes[11] or what? I want to have the war renewed that we may hear a little more of your spirit. I hope you'll
make your journals very ample[12] that at least I may see them when I
come back; as to details I have never had any yet; I saw a foolish
letter of Macklin the player's[13] which they have printed now in the
newspaper, with an account of the first debate.[14] It's the most particular I have seen but not clever.

I am angry with you for not telling me one of the cleverest things
of Mr Fox's that I ever heard which was his answer to Pitt on his en-
graving his sentiments on his tombstone.[15] I think there was as much
wit and smartness in it as I ever heard.

I grow to dislike our own dull scene more and more every day and
wish more to be amongst you; when it will be my fate God knows!
We don't reckon we have a vast deal of business to come but then
we don't quite know the bottom of it. We are jogging on through
your common dirty roads of bills, country jobs and city jobs, juries
and prisoners and insolvent debtors and turnpikes and such trash.[16]
Lord Limerick[17] has endeavoured to put a little life into the House
of Lords by taking the state of popery into consideration;[18] which has
produced some resolutions and some little debates;[19] his scheme is
to revive an old law of the second Queen Anne[20] to establish a certain number of registered secular priests and drive out all the rest;[21]

11. As they had been before Christmas.

12. One of the few indications that
Conway was aware that HW was writing
journals. See also *post* 6 July 1756.

13. Charles Macklin (?1697–1797), actor. His letter has not been found.

14. On the King's speech, 13–14 Nov.
(*ante* 15 Nov. 1755).

15. HW denies knowing anything about
this supposed witticism *post* 22 Jan.
1756; Conway gives details *post* 20 Feb.
1756.

16. The Irish House of Lords began
consideration of the heads of a bill for
regulating juries on 5 Jan.; the House of
Commons was considering heads of a bill
to discharge acquitted persons without
fees on 11 Dec., heads of a bill for the relief of insolvent debtors on 3 Dec., and
turnpike bills for Clonmell and Mallow
on 14–15 Nov. and 24 Dec. respectively.

All were eventually passed and received
the royal assent 8 May (*Journals of the
House of Lords . . . [Ireland]*, Dublin,
1779–1800, iv. 37; *Journals of the House
of Commons . . . Ireland*, Dublin, 1753–
71, ix. 394–5, 495, 501, 609, 922–4).

17. James Hamilton (d. 1758), cr. (1719)
Vct Limerick and (24 Nov. 1756) E. of
Clanbrassill, formerly one of the leaders
of the opposition to Sir Robert Walpole
in the British House of Commons.

18. The Irish House of Lords resolved
on 22 Dec. to 'take into consideration the
present state of popery in this kingdom'
(*Journals of the House of Lords . . . [Ire-
land]*, iv. 35).

19. On 2 and 5 Jan. (ibid. iv. 36–7).

20. 2 Anne c. 7 (*Statutes at Large . . .
Ireland*, Dublin, 1765, iv. 31–3).

21. On 5 Jan. the Lords resolved 'that
the allowing a competent number of

amounting, they say, to ten or twelve thousand.[22] I believe under proper restrictions a very good law, in quiet times, but not very expedient at the present critical juncture. Another part is to make it felony to any French officer, a native here, who comes without permission into this kingdom.[23] I think a good regulation, too, if so thought by the Government and that we have no managements with France.

I am glad to hear the Mingotti[24] is in such good humour; though I can't hope it will last to my return, but perhaps she may be out and in again. As to her singing and acting, that's of course and one hears nothing of it. I see in the papers that Giziello[25] is coming back from Portugal; if so perhaps he might be had; I wish you'd tell Lord Hobart[26] or some of the opera ministers; if they can't afford to pay him it is but making it up by a pension on Ireland.

Adieu. Pray for my return, say a mass a day for me, for I lead a wearisome life; I seldom stir from this room but to the House and my meals and a little cribbage, and have stirred from this place but two

popish secular priests to exercise their functions, under proper rules and restrictions, with due execution of the laws against regulars, and persons exercising ecclesiastical jurisdiction, would tend to deliver this Kingdom from the great number of monks and friars that at present infest it.' On the 6th Limerick presented the heads of a bill for 'a register of popish priests,' which were read a first time; further consideration in the present session was postponed after a debate and close division on 29 Jan. The bill was revived in the next session (in Nov.–Dec. 1757) and passed after two debates and divisions, but thrown out by the English Privy Council (*Journals of the House of Lords . . . [Ireland]*, iv. 37, 39, 46, 95–6, 98; W. E. H. Lecky, *History of England in the Eighteenth Century*, New York, 1883, ii. 305–6, 475).

22. A gross exaggeration: there were probably not as many as nine hundred Roman Catholic clergy in Ireland.

23. The Lords had resolved on 2 Jan. 'that to prohibit the return into the Kingdom of such of his Majesty's subjects as now are, or at any time hereafter shall be, in the service of the French King, would greatly tend to prevent others of his Maj-

esty's subjects from being seduced into that service.' The heads of a bill for this purpose were presented 25 Feb., went through the usual stages, and were passed by the Lords 5 March. They went through the House of Commons 5–29 March and received the royal assent 8 May (*Journals of the House of Lords . . . [Ireland]*, iv. 36, 50–2; *Journals of the House of Commons . . . Ireland*, ix. 815, 822, 866–7, 869, 922).

24. Regina Valentini (1722–1808), m. (1747) Pietro Mingotti; opera singer. She was notoriously temperamental, and as Conway predicted, was out of humour again by March 1756 (MANN iv. 557 and n. 5; *post* 16 April 1756; *Enciclopedia dello spettacolo*, Rome, 1954–62, vii. 615). Lady Ailesbury later had difficulties with her about an opera box (*post* 21 Oct. 1756).

25. Gioacchino Conti (1714–61), called Gizziello, castrato opera singer (MANN i. 56, n. 15; *Enciclopedia dello spettacolo* iii. 1346–7), had sung in England 1736–7, but did not return at this time; instead he retired home to Naples.

26. John Hobart (1723–93), styled Bn Hobart 1746–56, 2d E. of Buckinghamshire 22 Sept. 1756; an opera enthusiast.

days since the Parliament met; which was to Cartown,[27] Lord Kildare's, where I could have had great pleasure in staying longer. Their house is very agreeable; my Lord is civil and polite and Lady Kildare as sensible and agreeable a woman as ever I saw. I forgot if she is one of your favourites but I think she must.[28]

Lady Ailesbury and Missy send their compliments and duties, especially the latter who begs to know if she is your wife still, being strongly solicited here and in a dangerous disposition, I assure you. Here's a sturdy little fellow kisses and plays with her from morning to night and swears he'll marry her. Judge if he's a dangerous rival; and if it is not time to interpose.

Yours ever,

H. S. C.

To CONWAY, Thursday 22 January 1756

Printed from the MS now WSL. First printed in part Wright iii. 187–9 and in full Toynbee iii. 385–7. For the history of the MS see *ante* 29 June 1744 OS; it was marked by HW for inclusion in *Works* but was not included.

Endorsed: Mr H. Walpole 20 Jan. 1756.

Memoranda (on *ante* 5 Jan. 1756 for this letter):

> D. sore leg
> Prussia
> France
> Colebrook[1]
> Christening
> Lady Cov[entry] best
> Sir H. Erskine
> No masquerade

Arlington Street, Jan. 22d 1756.

AS my Lady Aylesbury is so taken up with turnpike bills, Popish recusants, and Irish politics, and you are the only idle person in the family (for Missy I find is engaged too) I must return to corre-

---

27. Carton, co. Kildare, a seventeenth-century house much altered and enlarged after 1739 by Richard Castle at a cost of nearly £21,000 (Brian Fitzgerald, *Emily, Duchess of Leinster*, 1950, pp. 22–3).

28. She was; HW included her in 'The Beauties,' written in 1746 (*Horace Wal-*

pole's Fugitive Verses, ed. W. S. Lewis, 1931, p. 25; SELWYN 99–106, 324–9). See also the following letter.

---

1. Not mentioned in the letter. Possibly George Colebrooke (*ante* 15 Nov. 1755, n. 13).

spond with you. But my letters will not be quite so lively as they have been: the Opposition like school-boys don't know how to settle to their books again after the holidays. We have not had a division, nay, not a debate. Those that like it, are amusing themselves with the Applebee election:[2] now and then we draggle on a little militia.[3] The recess has not produced even a pamphlet. In short there are none but great outlines of politics: a memorial in French billings-gate has been transmitted hither, which has been answered very laconically.[4] More agreeable is the guarantee signed with Prussia:[5] Monsieur Mechell[6] is as fashionable as ever General Wall[7] was. The Duke[8] has kept his bed with a sore leg, but is better—oh! I forgot, Sir Harry Erskine[9] is dismissed from the army, and if you will suffer so low a pun as upon his face, is a rubric martyr for his country: bad as it is, this is the best bon mot I have to send you; Ireland, which one did not suspect, is become the staple of wit, and I find coins bons mots for our greatest men: I might well not send you Mr Fox's repartee, for I never heard it, nor has anybody here: as you have, pray send it me. Charles Townshend t'other night hearing somebody say, that my Lady Falmouth,[10] who had a great many diamonds on, had a very fine stomach, replied, by God my Lord[11] has a better. You will be entertained with the riot Charles makes in the sober house of

2. Hearings on the petitions arising from the contested election at Appleby, Westmoreland, were held before the House of Commons on 20 and 22 Jan., but the case was not determined until 10 Feb. (*Journals of the House of Commons* xxvii. 391, 397, 443–4).

3. The House discussed the militia in committee on 21 Jan., when leave was given 'to bring in a bill for the better ordering of the militia force in . . . England' (ibid. xxvii. 395). HW mentions the debate in *Mem. Geo. II* ii. 152.

4. The French *mémoire*, 21 Dec. 1755, and Fox's reply, 13 Jan., are described in MANN iv. 524 and n. 7.

5. The Treaty of Westminster, signed 16 Jan., in which England and Prussia agreed to oppose the entry of any foreign troops into Germany (ibid. iv. 523, n. 5).

6. Abraham or Andreas Ludwig Michell (ca 1712–82), Prussian chargé d'affaires in London 1747–64 (*Repertorium der diplomatischen Vertreter aller Länder*, Vol. II, ed. F. Hausmann, Zurich, 1950, p. 297;

Allgemeine Deutsche Biographie, Berlin, 1967–70, xxi. 694–5).

7. Richard Wall (1694–1778), Maj.-Gen.; Spanish minister to England 1747–51 and ambassador 1751–4; Spanish secretary of state 1754–64 (MANN iii. 504, n. 10). For his popularity see ibid. iv. 51 and n. 40; HW to Chute 30 April 1754 (CHUTE 79).

8. Of Cumberland. 'Yesterday his Royal Highness the Duke of Cumberland was so well recovered as to go out in his post-chaise' (*Daily Adv.* 22 Jan.).

9. Sir Henry (or Harry) Erskine (?1710–1765), 5th Bt; M.P. Ayr burghs 1749–54, Anstruther Easter burghs 1754–65; Capt. in the 1st Foot 1743, and Lt-Col. in the army, 1746. He was dismissed for opposing the subsidy treaties in November; see *Mem. Geo. II* ii. 150.

10. Hannah Catherine Maria Smith (ca 1707–86), m. 1 Richard Russel; m. 2 (1736) Hugh Boscawen (1707–82), 2d Vct Falmouth.

11. Falmouth.

Argyle:[12] t'other night on the Duchess's bawling to my Lady Suffolk,[13] he, in the very same tone, cried out, *large stewing oysters!*[14] When he takes such liberties with his new parent, you may judge how little decency he observes with his wife:[15] last week at dinner at Lord Strafford's, on my Lady Dalkeith's mentioning some dish that she loved, he replied before all the servants, yes, my Lady Dalkeith, you love it better than anything but one!—I thread gossiping stories, for want of something better to tell you: my Lady Coventry has been at Woburn; after dinner, the Duchess,[16] my Lady Gower[17] and six-and-twenty people at table, the Duke asked my Lady Coventry for her toast—she gave, *The Best.* Rigby said, who says we can't drink my Lady Coventry's health before her face?

We were to have had a masquerade tonight, but the bishops, who you know have always persisted in God's hating dominoes, have made an earthquake point[18] of it, and postponed it till after the fast.[19]

Your brother has got a sixth infanta;[20] at the christening t'other night, Mr Trail[21] had got through two prayers, before anybody found out that the child was not brought downstairs.—You see by my *pauvreté* how little I have to say; do accept the enclosed *World*[22] in part of payment for the remainder of a letter. I must conclude this with telling you, that though I know her but little, I admire my Lady Kildare as much as you do. She has writ volumes to Lady Caroline Fox in praise of you and your Countess: you are a good soul

12. Into which he had married 18 Sept. 1755 (below, n. 15).

13. Henrietta Hobart (ca 1688–1767), m. 1 (1706) Charles Howard, 9th E. of Suffolk; m. 2 (1735) Hon. George Berkeley; HW's friend and correspondent. She was deaf.

14. A street cry.

15. Lady Caroline Campbell (1717–94), cr. (1767) Bns Greenwich, s.j., m. 1 (1742) Francis Scott, styled E. of Dalkeith; m. 2 (1755) Hon. Charles Townshend.

16. Of Bedford.

17. Lady Louisa Egerton (1723–61), m. (1748) Granville Leveson Gower, 2d E. Gower, cr. (1786) M. of Stafford; the Ds of Bedford's sister-in-law.

18. The clergy said that the earthquakes of 1750 were owing to gaming, lewdness, etc.; see MANN iv. 130–1, 133–5, 137.

19. The King's proclamation for a general fast on Friday, 6 Feb., to avert the danger of an earthquake, was published in the *London Gazette* No. 9538, 16–20 Dec. 1755. See also the *London Evening Post* 18–20, 20–3 Dec. 1755, 3–5 Feb. 1756; *Public Advertiser* 22 Dec. 1755.

20. Lady Isabella Rachel Seymour-Conway (25 Dec. 1755–1825), m. (1785) George Hatton (Collins, *Peerage*, 1812, ii. 565; GM 1825, xcv pt i. 476).

21. James Trail (1725–83), D.D. 1760; Hertford's chaplain; Bp of Down and Connor 1765 (Burke, *Landed Gentry of Ireland*, 1904, p. 601). Further biographical details are in a letter from Lady Hertford to unknown, [ca 12 March 1762]; he appears in Patch's conversation piece of Beauchamp at Florence (illustration ii. 219).

22. No. 160, 22 Jan. 1756, by HW; reprinted *Works* i. 179–84. See *post* 31 Jan., 12, 20 Feb. 1756.

—I can't say so much for Lady Ailesbury—as to Missy, I am afraid I must resign my claim: I never was very proper to contest with an Hibernian hero, and I don't know how, but I think my merit does not improve.

Adieu! Yours ever,

H. W.

To Conway, Saturday 24 January 1756

Printed from *Works* v. 43–4.

Arlington Street, January 24, 1756.

OH! Sir, I shall take care how I ever ask favours of you again! It was with great reluctance that I brought myself to ask this:[1] you took no notice of my request; and I flattered myself that I was punished for having applied to you so much against my inclination. Just as I grew confirmed in the pride of being mortified, I hear that you have outgone my application, and in the kindest manner in the world have given the young man a pair of colours.[2] It would have been unpleasant enough to be refused; but to obtain more than one asked is the most provoking thing in the world! I was prepared to be very grateful if you had done just what I desired; but I declare I have no thanks ready for a work of supererogation. If there ever was a saint that went to heaven for mere gratitude, which I am persuaded is a much more uncommon qualification than martyrdom, I must draw upon his hoard of merit to acquit myself. You will at least get thus much by this charming manner of obliging me: I look upon myself as doubly obliged: and when it cost me so much to ask one favour, and I find myself in debt for two, I shall scarce run in tick for a third.

What adds to my vexation is, that I wrote to you but the night

1. From Conway's reply, *post* 20 Feb. 1756, it appears that HW had asked his assistance for Charles Baldwyn or Baldwin (d. after 1775), who became an ensign in the 2d Foot (then stationed in Ireland) on 10 Dec. 1755. He became Lt in the same regiment 22 Nov. 1756; Capt.-Lt, 1770; Capt. 1772; and retired in 1775 (*Army Lists*, 1756, p. 123; 1757, p. 130; 1772, p. 56; 1773, p. 56; MS notation in Yale University Library copy of ibid., 1775, p. 56; *Court and City Register*, 1756, p. 163).

2. I.e., his ensign's commission (OED *sub* 'colour,' II. 7. c).

before last. Unless I could return your kindness with equal grace it would not be very decent to imitate you by beginning to take no notice of it; and therefore you must away with this letter upon the back of the former.

We had yesterday some history in the House: Beckford produced an accusation in form against Admiral Knowles[3] on his way to an impeachment. Governor Verres[4] was a puny culprit in comparison! Jamaica indeed has not quite so many costly temples and ivory statues, etc. as Sicily had: but what Knowles could not or had not a propensity to commit in rapine and petty larceny, he has made up in tyranny. The papers are granted,[5] and we are all going to turn jurymen.[6] The rest of the day was spent in a kind of avoirdupois war. Our friend Sir George Lyttelton opened the budget;[7] well enough in general, but was strangely bewildered in the figures; he stumbled over millions, and dwelt pompously upon farthings.[8] Pitt attacked him pretty warmly on mortgaging the sinking fund:[9] Sir George kept up his spirit, and returned the attack on eloquence.[10] It was entertaining enough, but ended in high compliments; and the division was 231 to 56.

Your friend Lady Caroline Petersham, not to let the town quite

3. Sir Charles Knowles (ca 1704–77), cr. (1765) Bt; Rear-Adm., 1747; Vice-Adm., 1755; Adm., 1760; governor of Jamaica 1752–6; M.P. Gatton 1749–52. HW gives a brief account of the debate on this occasion in *Mem. Geo. II* ii. 152–3, commenting that Beckford 'abused' Knowles 'immeasurably.' Knowles had offended the inhabitants of Jamaica by insisting on the supreme jurisdiction of Parliament, and by moving the capital from Spanish Town to Kingston.

4. Gaius (or Caius) Verres (d. 43 B.C.), governor of Sicily, denounced by Cicero for plundering his province.

5. A list of the papers requested in the Address to the King on the 23d is in the *Journals of the House of Commons* xxvii. 399–400, but the formal consent to this presentation was not given until 26 Jan. (ibid. xxvii. 404). Further papers were requested on the 27th and granted on the 28th (ibid. xxvii. 407, 414).

6. The papers relating to Knowles were presented on 18 and 24 Feb. and 17 March, but no further action was taken

until Feb. 1757, when they were referred to a Committee of the Whole House, which finally reported 23 May 1757 and by implication completely exonerated Knowles of the charges of arbitrary proceedings (ibid. xxvii. 457, 468, 530, 674, 910–11).

7. In the Committee on Ways and Means.

8. HW makes similar comments in *Mem. Geo. II* ii. 153, and adds in a passage crossed out in the MS: 'A monkey in a banker's shop would mimic the gravity of an arithmetician with more address.'

9. Part of the supplies for the ensuing year was to be raised by annuities charged on the sinking fund (*Journals of the House of Commons* xxvii. 401).

10. In his account of the debate HW says that Lyttelton 'told Pitt that truth was a better answer than eloquence' and that at the end of the debate Pitt had said 'with regard to the imputation of eloquence . . . he found there were certain ways of answering certain men' (*Mem. Geo. II* ii. 153).

lapse into politics, has entertained it with a new scene. She was t'other night at the play with her court; viz. Miss Ashe,[11] Lord Barnard,[12] Monsieur St Simon,[13] and her favourite footman Richard, whom, under pretence of keeping places, she always keeps in her box the whole time to see the play at his ease. Mr Stanley,[14] Colonel Vernon,[15] and Mr Vaughan[16] arrived at the very end of the farce, and could find no room, but a row and half in Lady Caroline's box. Richard denied them entrance very impertinently. Mr Stanley took him by the hair of his head, dragged him into the passage, and thrashed him. The heroine was outrageous—the heroes not at all so. She sent Richard to Fielding[17] for a warrant—he would not grant it—and so it ended—and so must I, for here is company. Adieu!

Yours ever,

Hor. Walpole

My letter would have been *much cleverer,* but George Montague has been chattering by me the whole time, and insists on my making you his compliments.

From Lady Ailesbury, Saturday 31 January 1756

Printed from the MS now wsl, formerly Rutnam. First printed, *Fraser's Magazine,* 1850, xli. 279.

Dublin, January 31, 1756.

INDEED, Sir, I can't forgive your sending sheer politics to me[1] and sheer wit to my husband;[2] but as I flatter myself you are sufficiently punished by my total neglect of you so long, I will now vouch-

11. Elizabeth Ashe, m. 1 (1751, secretly) Edward Wortley Montagu; m. 2 (1761) Robert Faulknor (Montagu i. 106, n. 13). See also Mann iv. 140.

12. See *ante* 19 May 1753, n. 10.

13. Probably Maximilien-Henri, Marquis de Saint Simon (1720–99), whom HW met in July 1755, and who consulted him about a translation of Swift's *Tale of a Tub* (HW to Bentley 17 July, 4 Aug. 1755, Chute 238–9, 241).

14. Hans Stanley (*ante* 18 July 1744 NS, n. 8).

15. Charles Vernon (1719–1810), Lt-Col. 1753; Maj.-Gen., 1762; Lt-Gen., 1773; Gen., 1783; lieutenant of the Tower of London 1763–1810; M.P. Tamworth 1768–74 (More 95, n. 1).

16. Probably Hon. Wilmot Vaughan (ca 1730–1800), 4th Vct Lisburne, 1766; cr. (1776) E. of Lisburne.

17. Sir John Fielding (1721–80), Kt, 1761, the magistrate.

———

1. HW's missing letter of ca 20 Dec. 1755.

2. *Ante* 22 Jan. 1756.

safe to bestow a line upon you still in your own method, though, of reversing the order of things, by answering the letter wrote to Mr Conway. Judge how I must be taken with the beauties of the *World*,[3] when I own to one who has not blushed to make his readers blush, that it is the prettiest performance of the kind I ever read. Lady Kildare and I read it together, and said so many pretty things about it and its author, that I believe, if he could have heard them, they would have effected what his own words could not.

Mr Conway is fuller than ever of business, so that he is forced to neglect cribbage, and all his intimate friends here, Mr Licehead, Mr Stoppart, Colonel Plucknet of Cold-blow-Lane, and the Bishop of Clonfert.[4] The sudden departure of the two poor regiments ordered for America[5] has employed him every moment for some days past. I am quite out of spirits for the Highland regiment,[6] and have no comfort in but its having lost its lieutenant-colonel.[7] Captain Cunningham[8] too I am much concerned for; his family[9] are in the utmost distress. But I'll turn from this melancholy subject, and inform you

---

3. The *World*, No. 160, by HW. He sent it with his letter of 22 Jan.

4. The first three of these names are apparently facetious, but there was a Bp of Clonfert who may have been an acquaintance of Conway: Hon. William Carmichael (1702–65), Bp of Clonfert, 1753; Ferns, 1758; Meath, 1758; Abp of Dublin, 1765 (*Scots Peerage* iv. 593–4). He was the brother-in-law of Charles O'Hara, an Irish politician who was a friend of Conway; see Edmund Burke, *Correspondence*, Vol. I, ed. T. W. Copeland, Cambridge, 1958, pp. 211, 214, 219.

5. Orders were received in Dublin on 29 Jan. for the second battalion of Lt-Gen. Otway's regiment (the 35th Foot) and the Royal Highland Regiment (the 42d Foot) to embark for America (*Daily Adv.* 9 Feb., *sub* Dublin 31 Jan.); they finally sailed in March (A. Forbes, *The 'Black Watch,'* New York, 1897, p. 44).

6. The 42d Foot; there were 13 Campbells among its officers.

7. Lady Ailesbury's brother John had been Lt-Col. of the Highland regiment since 1749, but had been commissioned Col. of a new regiment to be raised (the 56th, later the 54th Foot) on 23 Dec. 1755 (*Army Lists*, 1756, p. 76; GM 1755, xxv. 572).

8. Probably Robert Cuninghame (ca 1728–1801), cr. (1796) Bn Rossmore, at this time a Capt. in the 35th Foot, one of the regiments ordered to America. He was a close connection of Lord George Sackville, and was almost immediately made Adjutant-Gen., presumably to prevent his going to America, by the joint intercession of Devonshire, Abp Stone, and Newcastle (Newcastle to Devonshire 16 Feb., Newcastle to Abp Stone 16 Feb., Abp Stone to Newcastle 24 Feb., BM Add. MSS 32863, ff. 5, 6, 79–80; Abp Stone to Lord George Sackville 17 May, Hist. MSS Comm., *Stopford-Sackville MSS*, 1904–10, i. 238; MANN iv. 315–16). His younger brother, James Cuninghame (ca 1731–88), was commissioned a Capt. in the 45th Foot, stationed in Nova Scotia, on 1 Oct. 1755, and did go to America. He was later patronized by Conway's brother (SELWYN 199 and n. 1; Namier and Brooke ii. 283–4; *Army Lists*, 1756, p. 66; *Court and City Register*, 1755, p. 157).

9. Robert Cuninghame m. (1754) Elizabeth Murray, 'a Scots-Irish heiress with influential family and parliamentary connexions' (Namier and Brooke ii. 284). James Cuninghame was unmarried.

that we hope soon to get our dismission, the bills being to go, as they say, in about ten days,[10] so that in about six weeks I think we may be released.[11] I must tell you that I lately passed an evening with a grand-daughter of Madame Jenings;[12] her name is Hussey.[13] They say she has more wit than anybody, but I could not be a good judge of it, as we played at pharaoh the whole evening, and I did not perceive she made a sept-et-le-va[14] with more wit than other people. Mr Conway has told you how much I admire Lady Kildare, so I will only say I always knew her to be very good and very handsome, but never that she was excessively clever till now: she has lent me several books I never read before, one that I am much charmed with, though I should be ashamed of owning it if you had not set me the example of saying everything. It is *Le Triomphe du Sentiment*,[15] but to be sure you have read it, for now I recollect it is pretty old, though it never happened to fall my way before. Missy is sitting by throwing all the ink and sand about, and tormenting me to death to read fairy tales to her, so that I don't know what to say, and may as well leave off. Adieu! I am,

Dear Mr Walpole, faithfully yours,

C. A.

---

10. The heads of bills passed by the Irish Parliament had to be sent to England for approval by the Privy Council before they could be finally enacted.

11. The Irish Parliament was not prorogued until 8 May (*Journals of the House of Commons . . . Ireland*, Dublin, 1753–71, ix. 926; *post* 29 April 1756).

12. Frances Jennings (ca 1649–1731), m. 1 (ca 1666) Sir George Hamilton, Count Hamilton in France; m. 2 (1681) Richard Talbot, cr. (1685) E. and (1689) D. of Tyrconnell; 'la belle Jennings' of Gramont's *Mémoires* (MASON i. 387–8 and n. 8; BERRY i. 93–4 and nn. 17–18).

13. Hon. Catherine Parsons (d. 1766), m. (1705) James Hussey, of Westown, co. Dublin, and Courtown, co. Kildare. She was the daughter of Elizabeth Hamilton (d. 1724), eldest dau. of 'la belle Jennings'

by her first husband, who had m. (1685) Sir Richard Parsons, 3d Bt, cr. (1681) Vct Rosse (GEC xi. 167; Sir Bernard Burke, *A Genealogical History of the Dormant . . . Peerages of the British Empire*, 1866, pp. 294, 419). Lady Kildare mentions playing cards at her house in 1762 (*Leinster Corr.* i. 156, 157).

14. A move in pharaoh where the player, having gained a parolet (three times his stake), risks the whole again and tries to win seven times his stake (*Hoyle's Games Improved*, New York, 1829, p. 120; OED *sub* 'septleva').

15. Jean Galli de Bibiena, *Le Triomphe du sentiment*, La Haye, 1750 (Bibl. Nat. Cat.). L'Abbé Raynal praises the idea of the novel as 'neuve et assez belle' (Grimm, *Correspondance*, ed. Tourneux, 1877–82, i. 419).

To Conway, Thursday 12 February 1756

Printed from *Works* v. 45–7. From Conway's reply *post* 6 March 1756, it would appear that a witticism of Charles Townshend has been omitted.

Arlington Street, Feb. 12, 1756.

I WILL not write to my Lady A. tonight, nor pretend to answer the prettiest letter in the world, when I am out of spirits. I am very unhappy about poor Mr Mann,[1] who I fear is in a deep consumption: the doctors do not give him over, and the symptoms are certainly a little mended this week; but you know how fallacious that distemper is, and how unwise it would be to trust to it! As he is at Richmond, I pass a great deal of my time out of town to be near him,[2] and so may have missed some news; but I will tell you all I know.

The House of Commons is dwindled into a very dialogue between Pitt and Fox—one even begins to want Admiral Vernon again for variety. Sometimes it is a little piquant; in which though Pitt has attacked, Fox has generally had the better.[3] These three or four last days we have been solely upon the Pennsylvanian regiment,[4] bickering, and but once dividing 165 to 57.[5] We are got but past the first reading yet.[6] We want the French to put a little vivacity into us. The Duke of Newcastle has expected them every hour:[7] he was terribly alarmed t'other night; on his table he found a mysterious card with only these words, *Charles is very well, and is expected in England every day.* It was plainly some secret friend that advertised him of

1. Galfridus Mann, twin brother to Sir Horace Mann, the envoy at Florence: he died the end of this year (HW). He had been ill since October (MANN iv. 520, 522–3, 525–6).

2. HW told Horace Mann on 5 Feb. that he had just spent a week at SH to be near Galfridus (ibid. iv. 525).

3. Accounts of the debate of 28 Jan. are printed in Lord Ilchester, *Henry Fox,* 1920, i. 312–13.

4. HW gives an account of the debates on commissioning foreign Protestants to serve in American regiments in *Mem. Geo. II* ii. 156–75, saying that eventually 'seven [correctly, six] tedious days were

wasted' on the subject in the House of Commons. See also *post* 4 March 1756, n. 2 and MANN iv. 531 and nn. 7–8.

5. 10 Feb. (*Journals of the House of Commons* xxvii. 443; *Mem. Geo. II* ii. 162).

6. Which took place that day (*Journals of the House of Commons* xxvii. 447; *Mem. Geo. II* ii. 162).

7. HW repeats the fear of a French invasion in MANN iv. 526, 531, 535. Newcastle wrote Col. Yorke on 10 Feb. that he thought the French 'will make an attempt, and most probably more than one, upon parts of our coast' (BM Add. MSS 32862, ff. 430–1).

the Pretender's approaching arrival. He called up all the servants, ransacked the whole house to know who had been in his dressing-room:—at last it came out to be an answer from the Duchess of Queensberry to the Duchess of Newcastle[8] about Lord Charles Douglas.[9] Don't it put you in mind of my Lord Treasurer Portland[10] in Clarendon, *Remember Cæsar!*[11]

The French have promised letters of *noblesse* to whoever fits out even a little privateer.[12] I could not help a melancholy smile when my Lady A. talked of coming over soon. I fear Major-General *you*[13] will scarce be permitted to return to your plough at Park Place, when we grudge every man that is left at the plough. Between the French and the earthquakes,[14] you have no notion how good we are grown; nobody makes a suit of clothes now but of sackcloth turned up with ashes. The fast was kept so devoutly,[15] that Dick Edgecumbe,[16] finding a very lean hazard at White's, said with a sigh, 'Lord, how the times are degenerated! Formerly a fast would have brought every-

8. Lady Henrietta Godolphin (d. 1776), m. (1717) Thomas Pelham Holles, 1st D. of Newcastle.

9. (1726 – 24 Oct. 1756), styled E. of Drumlanrig 1754–6, the Ds of Queensberry's younger son. He had been travelling for his health and had been at Lisbon at the time of the earthquake. A letter from the Duke to George Selwyn 11 Dec. 1755, says that 'late last night [he] received a letter from his son wrote by himself. Safe and well and on board a ship the letter dated the 5 of November. This paper is sent and to be left at Arthurs that any of his friends may partake the intelligence, and contact who may happen frequent that place' (MS now WSL).

10. Richard Weston (1577–1635), cr. (1628) Bn Weston and (1633) E. of Portland; lord high treasurer 1628–35.

11. The anecdote is in Clarendon's *History of the Rebellion*, Oxford, 1704; HW's copy of the Oxford 1707–17 edn is Hazen, *Cat. of HW's Lib.*, No. 41; see W. D. Macray's edn, Oxford, 1888, i. 64–7. The E. of Tullibardine had given Portland a memorandum reading 'Remember Cæsar' to remind the Lord Treasurer of some business of Sir Julius Cæsar (1558–1636), master of the rolls. Portland forgot the purpose and on coming across the note,

interpreted it as an assassination threat.

12. The *Mercure historique,* Feb. 1756 (cxl. 174–6) quotes a 'lettre circulaire . . . aux négociants de toutes nos villes maritimes' which offers a premium for every gun and every man taken aboard a privateer, and 'des gratifications particulières et des marques de distinction aux capitaines et aux officiers qui se seront signalés dans les combats. Sa Majesté pourra même les admettre à son service. . . . Sa Majesté promet aussi des marques de distinction aux armateurs en course.' See also *Daily Adv.* 12 Jan., and 11 Feb., *sub* Brussels 6 Feb., and *London Gazette* No. 9553, 7–10 Feb., *sub* Brussels 6 Feb.

13. Conway's commission as Major-General is dated 30 Jan. (*Army Lists,* 1756, p. 3); it was reported in the *Daily Adv.* 6, 9 Feb.

14. The dreadful earthquake which had taken place at Lisbon towards the end of the preceding year (HW).

15. On 6 Feb. (*ante* 22 Jan. 1756, n. 19). 'There were the greatest crowds at most of the churches, both in London and Westminster, ever known on any occasion' (*Daily Adv.* 7 Feb.).

16. Richard Edgecumbe second Lord Edgecumbe (HW).

body hither; now it keeps everybody away!' A few nights before, two men walking up the Strand, one said to t'other, 'Look how red the sky is! Well, thank God! there is to be no masquerade!'

My Lord Ashburnham[17] does not keep a fast; he is going to marry one of the plump Crowleys:[18]—they call him the noble lord upon the woolsack.

The Duchess of Norfolk has opened her new house:[19] all the earth was there last Tuesday. You would have thought there had been a comet, everybody was gaping in the air and treading on one another's toes. In short, you never saw such a scene of magnificence and taste. The tapestry, the embroidered bed, the illumination, the glasses, the lightness and novelty of the ornaments, and the ceilings, are delightful. She gives three Tuesdays, would you could be at one! Somebody asked my Lord Rockingham[20] afterwards at White's, what was there? He said, 'Oh! there was all the company afraid of the Duchess, and the Duke[21] afraid of all the company.'—It was not a bad picture.

My Lady A. flatters me extremely about my *World*, but it has brought me into a peck of troubles. In short, the good-natured town have been pleased to lend me a meaning, and call my Lord Bute, *Sir Eustace*.[22] I need not say how ill the story tallies to what they apply it;[23] but I do vow to you, that so far from once entering into my im-

17. John Ashburnham (1724–1812), 2d E. of Ashburnham.

18. Elizabeth Crowley (ca 1728–81), m. (28 June 1756) John Ashburnham, 2d E. of Ashburnham. She reportedly had a fortune of £200,000 (GEC).

19. In St James's Square. It had just been remodelled by Matthew Brettingham, who had combined two houses, the original Norfolk House and the one next door which Norfolk acquired in 1743 (Hugh Phillips, *Mid-Georgian London*, 1964, p. 65; Royal Commission on Historical Monuments, *London, Vol. II. West London*, 1925, p. 135). It was demolished in 1938.

20. Charles Watson Wentworth (1730–82), 2d M. of Rockingham.

21. Edward Howard (1686–1777), 9th D. of Norfolk.

22. Sir Eustace Drawbridgecourt. See *World*, No. 160, 5th Vol. (HW). Most of HW's *World* was devoted to an account of the penances imposed on Elizabeth (d. 1411), dau. of the Margrave of Juliers, and widow (m. 1348) of John Plantagenet (1330–52), Earl of Kent, grandson of Edward I. She took a vow of chastity after her husband's death, but broke it in 1360 to marry Sir Eustace d'Aubrécicourt (d. 1372). HW's source was William Dugdale, *Baronage of England*, 1675–6, ii. 94–5; his copy is Hazen, *Cat. of HW's Lib.*, No. 590. HW had commented that the Countess was 'smitten (as tradition says she affirmed) by his extreme resemblance to her late lord; though, as other creditable writers affirm, he was considerably younger' (*Works* i. 181–2).

23. To Lord Bute's supposed affair with the Princess Dowager of Wales. It had apparently begun to be talked about in the autumn of 1755 (*Hardwicke Corr.* ii. 250–1); HW says in the *Memoirs* under 4 June 1756 that 'it had already been whispered' previously (*Mem. Geo. II* ii. 204–5; the passage has been much edited, but the omitted sentences and phrases merely dilate on the evidence of her fondness for Bute).

agination, my only apprehension was, that I should be suspected of flattery for the compliment to the Princess in the former part.[24] It is the more cruel, because you know it is just the thing in the world on which one must not defend one's self. If I might, I can prove that the paper was writ last Easter, long before this history was ever mentioned, and flung by, because I did not like it: I mentioned it one night to my Lady Hervey, which was the occasion of its being printed.

I beg you will tell my Lady A. that I am sorry she could not discover any *wit* in Mrs Hussey's making a septleva. I know I never was so vain of any wit in my life as in winning a thousand leva and two five hundred levas.[25]

You would laugh if you saw in the midst of what trumpery I am writing. Two porters have just brought home my purchases from Mrs Kennon the midwife's sale.[26] Brobdignag combs, old broken pots, pans, and pipkins, a lanthorn of scraped oyster-shells, scimitars, Turkish pipes, Chinese baskets,[27] etc. etc. My servants think my

24. HW, after relating some details about the will of Joan, Princess Dowager of Wales, the mother of Richard II, remarks that they were 'an instance of simplicity and moderation in so great and illustrious a princess, which I fear I should in vain recommend to my cotemporaries, and which is only likely to be imitated, as all her other virtues are, by the true representative of her fortune and excellence' ('The World,' *Works* i. 180). A note on the passage in *Works* reads, 'The present princess dowager of Wales,' i.e., Augusta (1719–72) of Saxe-Gotha, m. (1736) Frederick Louis, P. of Wales (d. 1751).

25. HW had won the milleleva and received 1023 sixpences for one in the winter of 1748 (MANN iii. 494). He also mentions it to Bentley 27 March 1755 (CHUTE 217) and to Mary Berry in 1790 (BERRY i. 147). He had won one of the five hundred levas and received £25. 11s. in March 1755, and the other at an earlier time (CHUTE loc. cit.).

26. Sidney Kennon (d. 1754), midwife (MANN iv. 122, n. 24). The most recent auction of her collections began 11 Feb. by Langford and consisted of her 'genuine, large and valuable collection of shells, fossils, ores, minerals, and natural curiosities' (*Daily Adv.* 11 Feb.; earlier sales of

her collection are recorded in Frits Lugt, *Répertoire des catalogues de ventes publiques*, The Hague, 1938–64, Nos 863, 901). The bill for HW's purchases, paid in full 26 Feb. 1756, to his agent at the sale, John Bastin, is BM Add. MSS 35335:

1 day [lot]	
19 two large clumps [clam shells] with mahogany stands	1. 1.–
59 an India bow, 8 arrows, a dagger, etc.	2. 3.–
65 an antique can, an ivory cup, and an antique incense pot	3. 4.–
67 two water-pots and covers, 2 dishes, and a scalloped bowl	1.15.–
68 seven curious antique pieces of earthenware	1. 5.–
78 a Chinese lanthorn and an India basket	1.10.–
2 day	
53 a basso relievo in ivory and a large comb	–.17.–
5 day	
46 a large and curious crucifix	4. 4.–

27. The 'Des. of SH' also mentions an 'earthen bottle' in the China Room, 'a red velvet coffer . . . containing six dram-bottles of the old Venetian glass' in

head is turned; I hope not: it is all to be called the personal estate and moveables of my great-great-grandmother, and to be reposited at Strawberry. I believe you think my letter as strange a miscellany as my purchases.

Yours ever,

Hor. Walpole

PS. I forgot, that I was outbid for Oliver Cromwell's nightcap.[28]

From Conway, Friday 20 February 1756

Printed from the MS now WSL, formerly Rutnam. First printed, *Fraser's Magazine,* 1850, xli. 279–81.

There are memoranda in pencil by HW for his answer printed *post* 4 March 1756.

Dublin Castle, 20 Feb. 1756.

Dear Horry,

I HAVE many thanks to return you: first, for two kind and agreeable letters,[1] next, for a charming *World,* a *World* we all admired much and admired impartially before we guessed, otherwise than by the style, whose it might be. Lady Ailesbury knew it immediately, and liked it so much she exposed herself inconsiderately in its praise, forgetting how indecent your ancient couple are.[2]

I must next thank you for your thanks to me on Mr Baldwyn's account,[3] which are so genteel and so abundant, I have no reply to make but to wish for an opportunity of being so thanked again. As to the poor man, he must be vastly disappointed, coming over in

the Green Closet, and 'an amber standing cup and cover' in the Great North Bedchamber, all from the collection of the 'virtuosa midwife' (*Works* ii. 408, 434, 499).

28. It would have joined, at SH, Cardinal Wolsey's hat, a spur worn by William III at the Boyne, and a pair of gloves worn by James I (ibid. ii. 455, 499, 502).

_____

1. *Ante* 22 and 24 Jan. 1756. Conway apparently had not yet received HW's let-

ter of 12 Feb.; he says below that six mails were due.

2. HW had made a great point of one of the penances imposed upon them: 'the next day after any repetition of their transgression had passed between them, they should competently relieve six poor people, and both of them that day to abstain from some dish of flesh or fish, whereof they did most desire to eat' (*Works* i. 183). He goes on to apply this penance to contemporary life.

3. *Ante* 24 Jan. 1756.

quest of 100,000 pounds[4] and picking up a miserable pair of colours.

I hear poor Mr Mann[5] has been very ill, which gives me great concern. I say, has; though indeed 'tis only from my desire to hope it's over, not having heard of him since; for there are now no less than six mails due;[6] that's amongst the uncomfortable things in our present situation; and this winter the packets have been more irregular than ever. You may imagine our impatience at such a juncture, and the strange expectations we form of fights at sea and at land; wars and invasions and God knows what. We have no particular reason to think the French are not at London by this time, which they might have been, and back again. 'Tis recorded, I think, that Richard II, being on an expedition here, was greatly surprised to hear, after a delay of seventeen packets, that another had taken possession of his kingdom;[7] but I have great dependence on your care in framing the militia bill; on that noble plan of Mr Pitt's,[8] which you seemed to admire so much,[9] but which has not yet reached us.

You say you never heard of Mr Fox's repartee,[10] and that it is the invention of Ireland. I am glad we are so ingenious; but, as you ask for it, the story is this: that Mr Pitt, in one of his enthusiasms, said on some occasion, I have forgot what, that he wished the sentiments he ex[pressed] that day might be writ on his tomb; and that Mr Fox replied, it was a laudable ambition—that the actions of many great men had been commemorated in that manner; of which many instances, ancient and modern occurred, but none that struck him

---

4. I.e., in search of a rich heiress; though it is possible that Baldwyn had such an intention, it is more likely that Conway is joking.

5. Galfridus Mann; see *ante* 12 Feb. 1756.

6. These all arrived on the 22d (Devonshire to Newcastle 24 Feb., BM Add. MSS 32863, f. 77).

7. Conway may have read in Holinshed's *Chronicles* of Richard II's lack of news while in Ireland: 'The seas were so troubled by tempests, and the winds blew so contrarie for anie passage, to come over foorth of England to the king, remaining still in Ireland, that for the space of six weeks, he received no advertisements from thence' (*Holinshed's Chronicles, Richard II 1398–1400 and Henry V*, ed. R. S. Wallace and A. Hansen, Oxford, 1917, pp. 21–2).

8. Which he had proposed in a long speech on 8 Dec. 1755, in a committee to consider previous laws on the subject (*Mem. Geo. II* ii. 98–102; *Journals of the House of Commons* xxvii. 331). Another committee had been scheduled for 18 Dec. but was postponed, and nothing further was done until leave to bring in a bill was granted 21 Jan. and more members added to the committee for it on the 22d. It was not discussed again until the first reading on 12 March (ibid. xxvii. 345, 395, 396, 523; *ante* 22 Jan. 1756, n. 3; *post* 4, 25 March 1756).

9. Not in any letter that has been seen. HW questions the feasibility of any militia scheme in *Mem. Geo. II* ii. 98.

10. *Ante* 22 Jan. 1756.

more than that of the famous fiddler, Signor Corelli,[11] who had not only commemorated the invention of his favourite jig, but put the jig itself on his tombstone.[12] I repeat it ill, but in these parts it passes for an excellent Parliamentary repartee; perhaps it's nothing amongst you.

I am sensible I am a miserable correspondent, having neither time to write, nor matter to write upon, nor wit to invent, as you may imagine when I am reduced to retail your own wit back to you, which I believe does not improve, like Madeira, by the voyage.

Our life here continues dull and uniform; mine is the whole morning *dans mon cabinet,* like the King of France, *à travailler,* and to receive the impertinent and troublesome visits of all that come. If I had the taste or the pride of a minister about me, I think I might find something like enjoyment in this, but with me it is quite otherwise. It turns my head and my stomach, and almost my temper. If I don't grow quite cross, it is something very like it. You may guess how bad it is when the regular journey to our most dull Parliament House is an actual relief to me. My dinners are as it happens; my afternoons divided between *mon cabinet* again and cribbage. The chief comfort at the last stage of the day is supper, which sometimes falls in tolerable parties, and makes what the workmen call a good *finish.*

I admire your account of Charles Townshend,[13] but don't wonder a bit. Apropos to diamond stomachers: we have one here that you may remember, a Lady Athronree,[14] that used to flourish at the Duchess of Dorset's with a brilliant nosegay. She gave us a supper t'other night of three courses and dessert. In the first were four soups; and in the last an house, landscape, and pack of hounds in blancmange, enclosed in hartshorn jelly that looked like amber; the whole dessert-service, plates and all, of Bohemian glass, cut, with gilt edges. 'Twas curious to see, but, perhaps, not worth describing.

'Tis odd to wonder at anything about Lady Coventry, but really her toasting the *best*[15] almost staggers my belief; Rigby's reply was good. 'Tis as odd to wonder at Lady Caroline, but I, that long

11. Arcangelo Corelli (1653–1713), violinist and composer.

12. The epitaph on Corelli's tomb in the Pantheon does not mention the 'jig', nor is there any music on it (Marc Pincherle, *Corelli,* trans. H. E. M. Russell, New York, 1956, pp. 41–2).

13. See *ante* 22 Jan. 1756.

14. Probably Ellis Agar (ca 1709–89), m. 1 (1726) Theobald Bourke, 7th Viscount Mayo; m. 2 (1745) Francis Bermingham, 14th Baron Athenry; cr. (1758), Countess of Brandon, s.j.

15. *Ante* 22 Jan. 1756.

admired her, can't cease to admire at her, and your last story[16] is certainly a masterpiece. How her heroes answered the suffering those indignities to her man, unless they were jealous of him, I can't conceive. 'Twas, upon the whole, a tragical catastrophe. I wonder whom she quarrelled with most—those that did the outrage, or they that suffered it.

We are dismal dull here, as I told you; neither an intrigue, nor a duel, not even a marriage nor a division in Parliament[17] to amuse you with. We don't yet see the end of the session, but go groping and grovelling on, and covering ourselves with a heap of dirty business,[18] that we shall never find our way out of.

Adieu. Lady A. and Missy desire their proper compliments.

Yours ever,

H. S. C.

To CONWAY, Thursday 4 March 1756

Printed from *Works* v. 47–9.
Memoranda (by HW, for this letter, written in pencil on *ante* 20 Feb. 1756):
   Ch[arles] T[ownshend] performing wife
   [see *ante* 22 Jan. 1756]
   ⟨Nugent and⟩ Ld Irwin
   Hamilton
   ⟨Edgecumbe⟩
   Ld ⟨Gow⟩er
   ⟨Richmond⟩
   All gamester's day Twelfth Day [6 Jan.]

Arlington Street, March 4, 1756.

Dear Harry,

I HAVE received so kind and so long a letter from you, and so kind too because so long, that I feel I shall remain much in your debt, at least for length. I won't allow that I am in your debt for warmth of friendship. I have nothing worth telling you: we are

16. *Ante* 24 Jan. 1756.
17. There had been no division in the Irish House of Commons since the one on 7 Feb. over the heads of a bill for the encouragement of tillage (*Journals of the House of Commons . . . Ireland*, Dublin, 1753–71, ix. 748–9).
18. Bribing the opposition leaders; see *post* 6 March 1756.

hitherto conquered only in threat: for my part, I have so little expectation of an invasion, that I have not buried a single enamel, nor bought a pane of painted glass the less: of the two panics in fashion, the French and the earthquake, I have not even made my option yet. The Opposition get ground as little as either: Mr Pitt talks by Shrewsbury clock,[1] and is grown almost as little heard as that is at Westminster. We have had full eight days on the Pennsylvanian regiment.[2] The young Hamilton has spoken and shone again;[3] but nothing is luminous compared with Charles Townshend:—he drops down dead in a fit, has a resurrection, thunders in the capitol, confounds the Treasury Bench,[4] laughs at his own party, is laid up the next day, and overwhelms the Duchess[5] and the good women that go to nurse him! His brother's[6] militia bill does not come on till next week:[7] in the meantime he adorns the shutters, walls, and napkins of every tavern in Pall Mall with caricatures of the Duke[8] and Sir George Lyttelton, the Duke of Newcastle and Mr Fox.[9] Your friend Legge has distinguished himself exceedingly on the supplies and taxes,[10] and retains all the dignity of chancellor of the Exchequer.

1. 'Fought a long hour by Shrewsbury clock' (*1 Henry IV*, V. iv).

2. Since HW's previous letter (*ante* 12 Feb. 1756) the bill had been debated on the second reading and committed after a division of 215–63 on 18 Feb.; debated in committee on the 20th after a division of 213–82; on the report of the committee on the 23d with divisions of 177–60, 158–52, and 151–46; and finally on the third reading on the 26th when it passed after a division of 198–64 (*Journals of the House of Commons* xxvii. 458, 463, 466–7, 481). HW made one of his rare Parliamentary speeches in the debate on the 18th (*Mem. Geo. II* ii. 163–9). George Bubb Dodington commented that the bill throughout had been 'opposed with insufferable length, and obstinacy, by Mr Pitt and his friends' (*The Political Journal of George Bubb Dodington*, ed. J. Carswell and L. A. Dralle, Oxford, 1965, p. 338).

3. William Gerard Hamilton. He spoke on 18 Feb.; HW gives a brief account of his speech in *Mem. Geo. II* ii. 170. His maiden speech on 13 Nov. 1755 had made a sensation (*ante* 15 Nov. 1755).

4. HW is apparently alluding specifically to his speeches on 20 and 26 Feb., described in *Mem. Geo. II* ii. 172–3, 174. The latter is misdated in the *Memoirs*; see Sir Lewis Namier and John Brooke, *Charles Townshend*, 1964, p. 45, n. 1.

5. Of Argyll, his mother-in-law.

6. Hon. George Townshend.

7. The bill was presented by Townshend and read for the first time on 12 March (*Journals of the House of Commons* xxvii. 523).

8. The Duke of Cumberland (HW).

9. One of his caricatures of this group is reproduced in SELWYN, facing p. 123; another, 'The Recruiting Serjeant,' published in April 1757 is in MANN v. facing p. 77. He began to publish them in the summer of 1756 (*Mem. Geo. II* ii. 228–9; MONTAGU i. 195; *post* 2 Sept. 1756). A collection of his sketches is in the possession of the National Trust at Felbrigg Hall; others are at Raynham and Farmington. See CHUTE 280, n. 19.

10. HW praises speeches by him on 25 Feb. in the committee on ways and means and on 3 March on the report of the committee (*Mem. Geo. II* ii. 177–80). Further brief accounts of the latter speech are in letters from James West to New-

I think I never heard so complete a scene of ignorance as yesterday on the new duties![11] Except Legge, you would not have thought there was a man in the House had learned troy weight: Murray quibbled—at Hume Campbell the House groaned! Pitt and Fox were lamentable;[12] poor Sir George never knew prices from duties, nor drawbacks from premiums! The three taxes proposed were on plate, on bricks and tiles, on cards and dice.[13] The earthquake has made us so good, that the ministry might have burned the latter in Smithfield[13a] if they had pleased. The bricks they were forced to give up,[14] and consented graciously to accept £70,000 on ale-houses,[15] instead of £30,000 on bricks. They had nearly been forced to extend the duty on plate beyond £10 carrying the restriction by a majority of only two.[16]

castle [3 March], BM Add. MSS 32863, f. 180 and Charles Jenkinson to Sanderson Miller, March 1756, in *An Eighteenth-Century Correspondence*, ed. Lilian Dickins and Mary Stanton, New York, 1910, p. 323.

11. On the report from the committee of ways and means; in his account in *Mem. Geo. II* ii. 179–80, HW also calls it 'a day of total ignorance.'

12. HW comments ibid. ii. 179: 'Fox, Hume Campbell, and Pitt all showed how little they understood the subject. The shrewdness of the first, the assertions of the second, the diction of the latter, were ridiculously employed on a topic that required only common sense, and a little knowledge of business.'

13. Of the sixteen resolutions reported from the committee, the first eight concerned a new tax on silver plate, the next five a tax on bricks and tiles, and the following two a doubling of the tax on cards and dice; the last one proposed that receipts from all these duties be added to the Sinking Fund (*Journals of the House of Commons* xxvii. 494). See also *Mem. Geo. II* ii. 176–7.

13a. As heretics had been burned under Mary Tudor.

14. The five resolutions dealing with the tax on bricks and tiles were recommitted without a division (*Journals of the House of Commons* xxvii. 495). Lyttelton had previously recommended to Newcastle that they be abandoned after talk-

ing to 'some persons of the highest distinction and hearty friends to your Grace, who say that they find wherever they go a universal dislike to the brick tax, and a desire that your Grace would consent to give it up' (letter of Monday [1 March], BM Add. MSS 32863, f. 150).

15. The committee on ways and means reported new resolutions on 4 March imposing a 20s. tax on all licences for ale-houses, and an attempt to amend it to a 10s. tax was defeated 90–30 (*Journals of the House of Commons* xxvii. 496–7). Charles Jenkinson commented: 'Every public house is taxed a guinea in its [the brick tax's] stead and as a number of these is thought to be 70,000 it is imagined that it may destroy 20,000 of them (a very good thing) and that the remainder may produce £50,000 per annum to the Government' (Dickins and Stanton, loc. cit.).

16. A motion to recommit the eighth resolution, providing that 'every person or body corporate, having two thousand ounces or upwards' should pay a tax of £10 p.a., was defeated 158–156, but the immediately subsequent motion to agree with the resolution carried 203–107. An earlier attempt to recommit all the resolutions dealing with the plate tax had failed 203–123 (*Journals of the House of Commons* xxvii. 494–5). Charles Jenkinson wrote: 'When the Opposition could not carry their point against the tax entirely they then moved that persons who had

An embargo is laid on the shipping,[17] to get sailors. The young Court lords were going to raise troops of light horse,[18] but my Lord Gower[19] (I suppose by direction of the Duke)[20] proposed to the King, that they should rather employ their personal interest to recruit the army; which scheme takes place,[21] and, as _____[22] said in the House, they are all turning recruiting sergeants. But notwithstanding we so much expect a storm from France, I am told that in France they think much more of their own internal storms than of us. Madame Pompadour wears devotion, whether forced or artful is not certain:[23] the disputes between the King and the Parliament run very high,[24] and the Duke of Orléans[25] and the Prince of Conti[26] have set themselves at the head of the latter.[27] Old N.[28] came fuddled to the opera last week, and jostled an ancient Lord Irwin,[29] and then called him fool for being in his way: they were going to fight; but

above 2000 oz. might be taxed in proportion to what they had; but the Administration carried by two votes only that above that number of ounces should not be subject to the tax; and one of the two votes was Lord Pulteney who had always voted in the Opposition before, and who was on this occasion prevailed on by his father to change sides on principle of economy' (Dickins and Stanton, loc. cit.).

17. 'On Wednesday evening [3 March] expresses were dispatched to our several ports; and we are informed, an embargo has been laid upon all shipping for six weeks, in the River. It's supposed the contents of the aforementioned expresses were to the same purpose' (*Daily Adv.* 5 March).

18. 'The Marquis of Rockingham, Lord Northumberland, Lord Downe and others, had offered to raise troops of light horse, which had been accepted' (*Mem. Geo. II* ii. 202). The *Daily Adv.* 26 Feb. reported that Rockingham had set out for Yorkshire for this purpose.

19. *Ante* ca 15 Feb. 1752 OS, n. 10.

20. Of Cumberland.

21. The decision had been made by 26 Feb. when Newcastle mentioned that 'the lords lieutenant, noblemen and gentlemen of distinction' were going to assist in raising troops (BM Add. MSS 32863, f. 109). The *Daily Adv.* 6 March reported that Rockingham was offering a special bounty of a guinea to every Yorkshire

man who enlisted in Gen. Napier's regular regiment. HW mentions some of the other successes in the scheme in *Mem. Geo. II* ii. 202–3.

22. This was expanded by Wright to George Townshend; subsequent editors have followed him, but no confirmation has been found. Townshend's caricature 'The Recruiting Serjeant' (above, n. 9) relates to the ministerial crisis of April 1757.

23. HW makes a similar comment and describes these rumours in detail in his letter to Mann of 23 Feb. (MANN iv. 530 and nn. 1–6).

24. A report that the Parliament of Paris had presented a remonstrance to the King appeared in the *Daily Adv.* 4 March.

25. Louis-Philippe de Bourbon (1725–85), Duc d'Orléans.

26. Louis-François de Bourbon (1717–76), Prince de Conti.

27. The *Daily Adv.* 4 March reported that Orléans had presented a petition of the dukes and peers of France to the King about privileges, especially their privilege of assembly.

28. This was expanded by Wright to Nugent; the other editors have followed him. None of the anecdotes has been confirmed, but none of them is improbable if ascribed to Robert Nugent.

29. Henry Ingram (1691–1761), 7th Vct Irvine.

my Lord Talbot, professing that he did not care if they were both hanged, advised them to go back and not expose themselves. You will stare perhaps at my calling N. *old:* it is not merely to distinguish him from his son;[30] but he is such a champion and such a lover, that it is impossible not to laugh at him as if he was a Methuselah! He is *en affaire réglée* with Lady _____:[31] at a supper there a few nights ago of two-and-twenty people, they were talking of his going to————[32] to direct some alterations: Mrs N.[33] in the softest infantine voice called out, 'My Lady _____, don't let him do anything out of doors; but you will find him delightful within!'

I think I have nothing else to tell you but a bon mot or two; with that sort of news I think I take care to supply you duly. I send you constantly the best that London affords. Dick Edgecumbe has said that his last child[34] was born on *All-Gamester's-Day;* Twelfth-Night.

This chapter shall conclude with an epigram; the thought was George Selwyn's, who you know serves all the epigram-makers in town with wit. It is on Miss Chudleigh crying in the Drawing-Room on the death of her mother:[35]

> What filial piety! what mournful grace,
> For a lost parent, sits on Chudleigh's face!
> Fair virgin, weep no more, your anguish smother!
> You in this town can never want a mother.[36]

I have told poor Mr Mann how kind you are to him: indeed I have been exceedingly frightened and troubled for him, and thought him in immediate danger. He is certainly much mended,[37] though I

---

30. If the subject of these anecdotes is Nugent, this would be Edmund Nugent (1731–71), later an army officer; M.P. Liskeard 1754–9, St Mawes 1761–70.

31. This was altered by Wright (followed by later editors) to 'the young Lady Essex.' Frances Hanbury Williams (1735–59) m. (1754) William Anne Holles Capel, 4th E. of Essex (MANN v. 53–4 and n. 31). No other reference to a liaison with Nugent has been found; in January 1757 her name was linked with Prince Edward (ibid.; MONTAGU i. 207). The *affaire réglée* might refer to the Dowager Lady Berkeley (*ante* 29 Aug. 1748 OS, n. 15), whom Nugent married on 2 Jan. 1757, after his second wife died on 22 Nov. 1756.

32. Filled in by Wright and later editors as Cassiobury, Essex's seat near Watford, Herts.

33. Perhaps Mrs Nugent (*ante* 8 Nov. 1752, n. 2).

34. Edgcumbe had two daughters by his mistress Ann Franks, alias Nancy Day (GRAY i. 36, n. 242). It was the custom to play hazard at Court on Twelfth Night; see *post* 18 Oct. 1766.

35. Harriet Chudleigh (d. 18 Jan. 1756), m. Col. Thomas Chudleigh (MANN iv. 213, n. 12; *Daily Adv.* 21 Jan.).

36. Included by WSL in *Horace Walpole's Fugitive Verses,* 1931, p. 122. Although the epigram sounds like him, no proof that he wrote it has been found.

37. HW reported improvement to Horace Mann on 23 Feb. and 18 March (MANN iv. 529, 537).

still fear a consumption for him: he has not been able to move from Richmond this whole winter: I never fail to visit him twice or thrice a week. I heartily pity the fatigue and dullness of your life; nor can I flatter you with pretending to believe it will end soon: I hope you will not be forced to gain as much reputation in the camp as you have in the cabinet!—You see I must finish.

Yours ever,

Hor. Walpole

From CONWAY, Saturday 6 March 1756

Printed from the MS now WSL, formerly Rutnam. First printed, *Fraser's Magazine*, 1850, xli. 281–2.

Dublin Castle, 6 March, 1756.

IF I thought you cared sixpence for our Irish politics I would have writ to you last post, to give you the cream and flower of our wonderful revolutions.[1] By this time you have heard them. They have put this little world here in such a flutter and agitation as never was. The old patriots are all in confusion;[2] the town is in

1. The final stage in Devonshire's 'pacification' of Ireland had been the arranging of the uncontested succession of John Ponsonby to the Speakership and the settling of the lords justices for his departure. This had entailed further concessions to Henry Boyle, the old Speaker, and his principal allies, which Devonshire had been secretly negotiating with Boyle throughout the winter. The English government approved the proposals during late January and early February (Fox to Devonshire 28 Jan., Lord Ilchester, *Henry Fox*, 1920, ii. 79–80; Newcastle to Devonshire 16 Feb., BM Add. MSS 32863, ff. 3–4); Devonshire closed with Boyle on the 27th (Devonshire to Newcastle 27 Feb., ibid. f. 116); and the new arrangements, discussed below, were common knowledge in Dublin by 2 March (Devonshire to Newcastle 2 March, ibid. f. 169; *Dublin Journal* 28 Feb.–2 March). Conway wrote his brother 3 March, 'Our work is now complete . . . . the thing is

now quite public and makes as much noise as might be expected from such an explosion and such a sudden revolution' (MS now WSL); he told Fox on the 2d that the government seemed to set out on a new footing and be once more vested in the hands of the lord lieutenant (Ilchester, op. cit. ii. 81).

2. Boyle had communicated the projected arrangements with Devonshire to no one but Malone (J. L. McCracken, 'The Conflict between the Irish Administration and Parliament, 1753–6,' *Irish Historical Studies*, 1942, iii. 177); the announcement that he had accepted a peerage and a pension and would support Ponsonby, his old rival, for the Speakership, had taken his followers entirely by surprise, particularly Sir Arthur Gore, his previous candidate for the succession. Devonshire wrote to Newcastle on 2 March that 'it was matter of great surprise to all his party, many of them are prodigiously angry particularly Sir Arthur Gore, and

amaze, and are pleased or angry, or scold or laugh, just as their humour is. The Speaker has been burnt in effigy;[3] Malone[4] mobbed at his door; and the *Patriots* by that name groaned at the playhouse.[5] Malone, who was to have had a place, can stand it no longer and declines.[6] The angry part try to rally under his banner, but he has not yet erected it, and says he is in the same disposition to Government.[7] Sir Arthur Gore[8] does not accept a peerage for the present but disclaims opposition.[9] Forty-six of the party met last night but hatched nothing; and on the whole I flatter myself will not be able

abuse him prodigiously. It has had the desired effect and entirely put an end to all parties. . . . Many of the most considerable persons that have been in opposition come to me and declare that they will never enter into party connections again, but will attach themselves to Government for the future' (BM Add. MSS 32863, ff. 169–70). Similar details are in Conway's letter to Lord Hertford 3 March.

3. By a mob of 1000 (McCracken, loc. cit.).

4. Anthony Malone (*ante* 16 Sept. 1755, n. 5).

5. On 5 March (Devonshire to Newcastle 6 March, BM Add. MSS 32863, f. 205).

6. Devonshire wrote to Newcastle on 2 March that Malone was 'very desirous of being chancellor of the Exchequer at the same time hopes there may be an addition of £600 a year, his business being now £4000 and the salary of the chancellor but £600 and that really he shall not be able to live without it. My answer was that I would endeavour to get it for him but that I was not sure of success. . . . It certainly is of great consequence to have him in good humour for he is the only man now that can raise any disturbance in the country' (ibid. ff. 169–70). But Malone came to Devonshire again on the 5th 'and begged of me not to recommend him to his Majesty for chancellor of the Exchequer, that if he took it just at present he should be undone in his character, and should be of no service and that he had no other way of convincing his friends that he was not in the secret but by refusing to take this employment at present' (Devonshire to New-

castle 6 March, ibid. f. 205). HW incorporates some of Conway's account in *Mem. Geo. II* ii. 183.

7. Malone had told Devonshire 'most solemnly that he was not out of humour and that he would support me and Government the same as if he had accepted it, and in short gave me reason to think that if it is kept open a little while he will accept it' (Devonshire to Newcastle 6 March, loc. cit.). Malone did so in 1757.

8. (1703–73), 3d Bt; cr. (1758) Vct Sudley and (1762) E. of Arran; M.P. (Ireland) Donegal borough 1727–58.

9. Gore had told Devonshire by 2 March that, angry as he was at Boyle, 'as this affair had been managed he had no chance of carrying the Chair and therefore he would give no trouble, that he would enter into no more engagements with any party, but should always be ready to support Government and serve me. . . . He hesitates at being a baron and wishes to be a viscount. I told him that the King loved honours should go in their proper stages and that I could not promise, so he has taken time to consider of it' (Devonshire to Newcastle 2 March, ibid. f. 169). Gore soon called on Devonshire again and asked him not to apply for the peerage 'as it would ruin him with all his friends, if he was to accept of anything at present,' but promised to support Government nevertheless (Devonshire to Newcastle 4 March, ibid. f. 186). Both Devonshire and Conway mention elsewhere Gore's civility to Ponsonby and his promises of support, as well as his anger at Boyle (Devonshire to Newcastle 2 March, ibid. f. 170; Conway to Hertford 3 March).

to stir up anything formidable, being broke and at present without heads to guide or strength to support 'em.

What I dread most from their efforts is a prolongation of this endless session, which has almost exhausted even my stock of patience, that you allow to be pretty good. I do long for my plough and my cabbages more than can be expressed, with respect to my major-generalship[10] be it said, and am not without hopes of enjoying them for part of the summer at least; for I think, notwithstanding the Duke of Newcastle's card and his fidgets, and all your fidgets, we may escape an invasion. I would prepare for it as if I thought it would come tomorrow; but still doubt our being so much in their thoughts as is imagined. Besides, I am no major-general here,[11] but a mere secretary. So that till it is serious enough to keep my Lord Lieutenant as general here I shall probably be at liberty.

The Lord upon the woolsack was excellent; our friend Charles rather coarse.[12] We have much Irish wit stirring at present, but none that will repeat. I think they say there's a ballad that is tolerable. I don't very highly esteem Lord Marchmont's[13] pamphlet;[14] nor *The Opposition*[15] that's cried up.

Yours most sincerely,

H. S. C.

10. See *ante* 12 Feb. 1756 and n. 13.

11. That is, his appointment was on the English, not the separate Irish, military establishment.

12. If HW had quoted him in the letter to which Conway is replying (*ante* 12 Feb. 1756), the passage was omitted when the letter was printed.

13. Hugh Hume Campbell (1708–94), 3d E. of Marchmont.

14. Probably *Reflections upon the present state of affairs. . . . In a letter from a* *Member of Parliament*, 1755. HW dated it on the title-page of his copy 'Novr.' and added 'Supposed, by Lord Marchmont' (Hazen *Cat. of HW's Lib.*, No. 1608:80:5). It was a defence of the subsidy treaties.

15. Probably *The Opposition. To be published occasionally*, 1755. HW dated it on the title-page of both his copies 'Dec. 1755,' and on one copy wrote 'Supposed to be by W. Gerard Hamilton' (ibid. Nos 1608:80:6, 81:1).

To CONWAY, Thursday 25 March 1756

Printed from the MS now WSL; first printed Wright iii. 206–8. For the history of the MS see *ante* 29 June 1744 OS.
Endorsed: Mr H. Walpole 25th Mar. 1756.

Arlington Street, March 25th, 1756.

INSTEAD of being sorry as I certainly ought to be, when your letters are short, I feel quite glad, I rejoice that I am not much in your debt, when I have not wherewithal to pay. Nothing happens worth telling you; we have had some long days in the House, but unentertaining; Mr Pitt has got the gout in his oratory, I mean in his head, and does not come out.[1] We are sunk quite into argument— but you know when anything is as it should be, it is not worth talking of. The plate tax has made some noise; the ministry carried one question on it but by nine.[2] The Duke of Newcastle, who reserves all his heroism for the war, grew frightened, and would have given up the tax, but Mr Fox bolstered up his courage, and mustered their forces, and by that and softening the tax till it was scarce worth retaining,[3] they carried the next question by an hundred.[4]

1. Pitt described himself on the 21st as suffering from 'the pain in my face and ear' and as 'at present muffled up with flannel' (*Grenville Papers* i. 156); his absence from the debate on 22 March because of a 'cold and swelled face' is mentioned by Lyttelton and Charles Jenkinson (Robert Phillimore, *Memorials and Correspondence of George, Lord Lyttelton*, 1845, ii. 508; *An Eighteenth-Century Correspondence*, ed. Lilian Dickins and Mary Stanton, New York, 1910, p. 327). He reappeared on the 29th, to oppose the address for Hanoverian troops, 'with blisters behind his ears, and flannel over his cheeks,' but in April a friend reported that he 'has left off his flannel which only served to keep warm one of his cheeks which had been attacked with a cold aguish complaint' (Phillimore, op. cit. ii. 507; Dickins and Stanton, loc. cit.).

2. After the first reading of the bill on 17 March, a motion for setting the day for the second reading was carried by only 129–120 (*Journals of the House of Commons* xxvii. 530). Lyttelton relates, somewhat confusedly, that 'Mr Legge, having declared that he would not oppose it at

the first reading, our friends did not attend, and some of his having divided the House on the question, we carried it but by two votes [*sic*]' (Phillimore, op. cit. ii. 508).

3. 'They have altered the plan of the Bill to make it go down, for the lowest that is now taxed is 100 ounces, and they pay five shillings, and so it increases five shillings to every hundred ounces up to 4,000, which now pays £10 and the tax goes no higher' (Charles Jenkinson to Sanderson Miller 23 March, Dickins and Stanton, loc. cit.; see also Phillimore, loc. cit.). These changes, although probably announced in the debate on the second reading, 22 March, were apparently not formally added until the 24th when several amendments were made to the bill in committee (*Journals of the House of Commons* xxvii. 545). HW says that the bill was at first estimated to produce £30,000, but as altered it produced only £18,000 (*Mem. Geo. II* ii. 176–7, 182). For Fox's part in the bill see Lord Ilchester, *Henry Fox*, 1920, i. 309–10.

4. On the second reading, 245–142 (*Journals of the House of Commons* xxvii.

The day before yesterday the King notified the invasion to both Houses, and his having sent for Hessians.[5] There were some dislikes expressed to the latter, but in general fear preponderated so much, that the cry was for Hanoverians too.[6] Lord George Sackville in a very artful speech a little maliciously even proposed them[7] and noblemen's regiments[8] which the Duke had rejected; Lord Ravensworth[9] in the other House moved in form for Hanoverians:[10] the Duke of Newcastle desired a few days to consider it, and they are to go upon it in the Lords tomorrow.[11] The militia which had been dropped for next year, is sprouted up again out of all this, and comes on today.[12] But we should not be English, if we were not still more intent on a very trifle: we are. A new road through Paddington has been proposed to avoid the stones:[13] the Duke of Bedford

538). HW gives an account of the debate in *Mem. Geo. II* ii. 180–2. A few further details are in Phillimore, loc. cit. and in Dickins and Stanton, op. cit. 326–7. The bill was considered in committee and amended on the 24th, reported on the 25th, and passed on the 29th after a motion to adjourn was defeated 187–88 (*Journals of the House of Commons* xxvii. 544, 545, 550).

5. The King's message of 23 March is ibid. xxvii. 539; *Journals of the House of Lords* xxviii. 537. The Hessians had been reported to have been sent for in early February, and arrived 15 May (MANN iv. 526 and n. 5, 550 and n. 6).

6. Henry Fox writes of the debate: 'Our addresses [in reply to the King's message] passed unanimously, but that in our House occasioned talk that has lasted till now, 7 o'clock. Hanover troops were mentioned, spoke against by the Opposition, and called for by our friends' (to Devonshire 23 March, Ilchester, op. cit. i. 306). HW says that the address 'was received with some murmurs, but not opposed' (*Mem. Geo. II* ii. 184).

7. HW gives a brief account of this speech (ibid.) saying that he did it 'either to throw difficulties on the Duke of Newcastle, with whom he was angry on Irish accounts, or to pay court to the Throne.' On 29 March, Sackville presented a formal address to the Crown for Hanoverian

troops and carried it after a motion for the order of the day was defeated 259–92 (*Journals of the House of Commons* 549–50; *Mem. Geo. II* ii. 185–6 where HW gives the incorrect month 'April'). According to Henry Fox, Sackville was not asked to make the address, but his proposal had the full support of the Ministry (Ilchester, op. cit. i. 307).

8. The projected troops of light horse (*ante* 4 March 1756).

9. Henry Liddell (1708–84), cr. (1747) Bn Ravensworth.

10. He had made a similar motion on 4 Feb., but had not been seconded (MANN iv. 526). There is no mention of Ravensworth's motion in the Lords *Journals*.

11. They apparently did not, but on 30 March the Lords concurred with the Commons' address for Hanoverians (*Journals of the House of Lords* xxviii. 547–8; *Mem. Geo. II* ii. 186; Phillimore, op. cit. ii. 507).

12. Although leave had been given to bring in the Militia Bill on 21 Jan., it had not received its first reading until 12 March (*ante* 22 Jan., n. 3, 20 Feb., n. 8, 4 March, n. 7). It was read a second time and committed on 19 March and discussed in committee on the 25th (*Journals of the House of Commons* xxvii. 535, 546). For its subsequent history, see *post* 16 April 1756.

13. A petition for this road had been

who is never in town in summer, objects to the dust it will make behind Bedford House, and to some buildings proposed, though if he was in town, he is too shortsighted to see the prospect. The Duke of Grafton heads the other side[14]—you may imagine how high this is carried![15] *You* can imagine it—*you* could compose the difference! *you* grand corruptor, you who can bribe pomp and patriotism, virtue and a *Speaker,* you that have pursued uprightness even to the last foot of land on the globe, and have disarmed Whiggism almost on the banks of its own Boyne[16]—don't you return hither, we shall have you attempt to debauch even Mr Onslow, who has preserved his chastity,[17] while all the band of chosen youths, while every Pultney, Pitt and Lyttelton have fallen around him[18]—I could not help laughing at the picture of Malone, bribed out of his virtue, and mobbed into it again!

Now I am in a serious strain, I will finish my letter, with the only other serious history I know. My Lady Lincoln has given a prodigious assembly to show the Exchequer House:[19] she sent to the por-

presented 18 Dec.; a petition against it by Bedford was presented 4 Feb.; the committee on it had reported 25 Feb. and was given leave to bring in a bill. This was presented 5 March and read a second time and committed on the 9th; the committee reported on the 16th, but further instructions were given to it. Another report was ordered on the 23d, which was presented on the 26th, when two attempts to amend it were defeated 135–83 and 139–85. The bill was finally passed by the Commons on the 30th after amendments (*Journals of the House of Commons* xxvii. 344, 428–9, 472–7, 498, 503–4, 527–8, 540, 546–7, 552). For its subsequent history see *post* 16 April 1756.

14. The road would pass through estates of his 'which, by future buildings likely to accompany such an improvement, would be greatly increased' (*Mem. Geo. II* ii. 186). According to HW, Grafton, 'old and indolent,' was initially indifferent about it, but was pushed into insistence upon it by the Duke of Argyll and others who wished to thwart Bedford (ibid. ii. 187).

15. HW interpreted it as eventually a contest of power between Fox, supporting

Bedford, and Newcastle, supporting Grafton (ibid. and *post* 16 April 1756).

16. Where William III had defeated James II in 1690. HW comments in the *Memoirs* that 'tranquillity was at last restored [in Ireland] by the prudence of Mr Conway, and by the venality of the patriots. Mr Conway was armed with all the powers and all the qualities that could compose the animosities of a factious people, inflamed by mercenary chiefs; for he had authority to satisfy their demands, his virtue gave no hold to abuse, his temper kept *him* impartial, and his good sense kept the Duke of Devonshire so' (*Mem. Geo. II* ii. 183). From the Newcastle-Devonshire correspondence it would appear that HW overestimates Conway's part in the last stages of the 'pacification.'

17. HW frequently ridicules Speaker Onslow's boasts of his impartiality; see especially Selwyn 292, n. 25, 301, n. 41.

18. Pulteney accepted a peerage and cabinet membership in 1742; Pitt first took office as vice-treasurer of Ireland in 1746; Lyttelton became a lord of the Treasury in 1744.

19. The official residence of the auditor

ter to send cards to all she visited—he replied he could easily do that, for his Lady visited nobody but Lady Jane Scot. As she has really neglected everybody, many refusals were returned; the Duchess of Bedford was not invited, and made a little Opposition supper,[20] which was foolish enough. As the latter had refused to return my Lady Falmouth's visit, my Lady Lincoln singled her out, and visited and invited her. The dignity of the assembly was great: Westminster Hall was illuminated for chairs:[21] the passage from it hung with green baize and lamps and matted. The cloister was the prettiest sight in the world, lighted with lamps and Volterra vases.[22] The great apartment is magnificent.[23] Sir Thomas Robinson the Long, who you know is always propriety itself, told me how much the House was improved since it was my brother's![24] The Duchess of Norfolk gives a great ball next week to the Duke[25]—so you see that she does not expect the Pretender at least this fortnight.[26] Last night at my Lady Hervey's, Mrs Dives[27] was expressing great panic about the French: my Lady Rochford[28] looking down on her fan,

of the Exchequer (MANN i. 299, n. 39). Lord Lincoln had held the sinecure since 1751. Lady Lincoln's assembly was on 16 March; its object was reportedly 'to out-shine' the Duchess of Norfolk's party on 10 Feb. (Mary Granville, Mrs Delany, *Autobiography and Correspondence*, ed. Lady Llanover, 1861–2, iii. 416; *ante* 12 Feb. 1756).

20. Lord Lincoln was nephew of the D. of Newcastle; the D. of Bedford was at this time in partial opposition.

21. The Exchequer House adjoined Westminster Hall on the west. 'All the coaches went the street way and the chairs through Westminster Hall, so that there was not the least confusion; the entrance was through a long passage matted and hung with bays, lighted with lamps and warmed by stoves' (Mrs Delany, loc. cit.).

22. 'From thence [the passage] into a fine gallery with an arched Gothic roof, with niches answering every window for statues. At each end a white alabaster vase, lighted on the inside with lamps, which had a mighty pretty effect, besides other lights very well placed' (ibid.).

23. 'The great apartment crimson damask and *very fine tapestry*' (ibid.).

24. HW's brother Robert lived there while auditor of the Exchequer 1739–51.

25. Of Cumberland. Her ball was on 31 March; Mrs Delany described it: 'The Duke of Norfolk's ball and supper which he gave the Duke was magnificent; our Whitehall friends danced till four in the morning. The suppers and the dessert were the prettiest that had ever been seen; the dessert, besides the candles on the table, was lighted by lamps in fine green cut glasses' (ibid. iii. 420). The Princess Dowager of Wales and 'the rest of the royal family' were the guests of honour (*Daily Adv.* 2 April).

26. The Norfolks were Roman Catholics, and so suspected of Jacobite sympathies.

27. Probably Charlotte Dyve (*ante* 3 Dec. 1751 NS, n. 25).

28. Lucy Young (ca 1723–73), m. (1740) William Henry Nassau de Zuylestein, 4th E. of Rochford. She was notorious for her affairs; see MONTAGU i. 42, nn. 18, 19; MANN iv. 58.

said with great softness, 'I don't know, I don't think the French are a sort of people that women need be afraid of.' Adieu!

Yours ever,

H. W.

From Conway, Monday 5 April 1756

Printed from the MS now wsl, formerly Rutnam. First printed, *Fraser's Magazine,* 1850, xli. 282.

Dublin Castle, 5th April, 1756.

Dear Horry,

I AM afraid to recollect when I wrote to you last.[1] Luckily for my own conscience I don't know, for I doubt it is a vast while. I hoped the recess[2] and the end of our Parliamentary business would have brought me some leisure, but hitherto am as much embroiled as ever. The augmentations[3] and the rest of our military business have succeeded to the civil, and made me just as uncomfortable to myself and friends.[4] Everybody's holidays are come but mine. Even my Lord Lieutenant is gone out of town, and with him *mia sposa.*

1. *Ante* 6 March 1756.

2. The Irish Parliament adjourned on 31 March until 26 April (*Journals of the House of Commons . . . Ireland,* Dublin, 1753–71, ix. 880).

3. Of the regiments in Ireland. Newcastle originally suggested that, in return for England's taking on the expenses of the regiments in Ireland sent to America (*ante* 31 Jan. 1756, n. 5), the Irish Parliament should contribute to the general expenses of the war, possibly by an application of the surplus revenue. Devonshire proposed instead that it vote funds for augmenting the regiments already in Ireland, as less likely to cause controversy. This was agreed to and proposed to the Irish House of Commons, which granted the augmentation on 31 March (Newcastle to Devonshire 16 Feb., Devonshire to Newcastle 27 Feb., Newcastle to Devonshire 7 March, BM Add. MSS 32863, ff.

4, 117, 214; *Journals . . . Ireland,* ix. 878). Some further correspondence about the plan is printed in Lord Ilchester, *Henry Fox,* 1920, i. 316–18.

4. Conway wrote to his brother the same day: 'I thought our business over when the recess came, but have hitherto found the contrary; the recruiting and augmenting the troops and other military affairs now take me up just at present as much as ever the civil did. It is holiday with every[one] almost but myself, even my Lord Lt is gone into the country and Lady Ailesbury. I hope to make up my ends of business and follow them on Wednesday or Thursday; they are now at Mr Ponsonby's at Bishop's Court; but adjourn from thence to Carton, where we are to pass part of the holidays' (MS now wsl). See also Conway's letters to Devonshire ?17, ?22, 27 April 1756, Chatsworth MSS, 416 / 22, 23, 24.

I am gathering up all my ends of business to follow them, and hope for it in a day or two when I am to meet them at Carton, Lord Kildare's.

I talk of my business quite to a pitch of affectation; the only difference is it is not affection, for in truth I have more of various kinds than my poor little head is made for. If I had three such heads and better, I have good employment for them in my triple capacity of civil and military and civi-military, by which I seem all at once to resemble the man's black horses, and white horses, and black-and-white horses; being civil as a secretary, military as general, and civi-military as secretary-at-war, a wonderful as well as tiresome combination, and now more so than ever it was known, I believe, by the untowardness of both our civil and military circumstances.

However, for the present I seem comfortably abridged in my threefold existence by having my civil part in a manner lopped off by the recess which I am ever in hopes will not sprout out again like a polypus after the recess, or like your militia that has long been thought dead and gone.[5] We have at least a better prospect of quiet at present, and I think less apparent marks of heat and ill humour on the Speaker's subject and downfall of patriotism than could so soon have been expected.[6] The Parliament ended quietly and temperately, and even nobly by their unanimous vote on the augmentation. We don't expect any contest for the chair,[7] to which everybody seems to have settled their mind now pretty quietly.

Your turnpike divisions both amaze, divert and shock one, as they torment and expose us.[8] I have some comfort for our honour in thinking the French, who take us for a wise nation, will not believe us in earnest now any more than they did on the same occasion, for

5. See *ante* 25 March 1756 and n. 12.

6. Conway wrote to Hertford the same day: 'Things seem to grow quieter and cooler in regard to the Speaker, who continues still in town; the Parliament broke up, I mean for the recess without any ill humour shown to him; and the general temper both of town and country seems to promise tolerable domestic peace to which among other things the free distribution of money in our supposed or real improvements, bounties, etc. has I believe not a little contributed; which indeed nothing else could make justifiable in our present situation.'

7. Since Henry Boyle was created E. of Shannon on 17 April, a new Speaker had to be elected as soon as Parliament reassembled. John Ponsonby was chosen without opposition (*ante* 6 March, *post* 29 April 1756).

8. 'I am heartily concerned for the home divisions talked of particularly that in which the D. of Grafton is concerned; which I doubt is serious though on a ridiculous subject' (Conway to Hertford 5 April).

just such another there was, in the same situation last war, when they heard of our furious divisions about a *barrière,* and said, '*Apparemment il y a quelque mystère là-dedans!*'9

Adieu! I write short and uncomfortably to myself and you; but yet must write as I even now fancy I feel the effects of my silence and dread feeling them more.10 But you must forgive me and show it by writing. If you know what pleasure I have in hearing from you and are not very angry, you will, for you are too wise and too happy to be busy.

I hope Mr Mann is better.11 Pray give my compliments to him.

I have only time to add that the post waits and that I am ever yours,

H. S. C.

To CONWAY, Friday 16 April 1756

Printed from *Works* v. 50–1.

Strawberry Hill, April 16, 1756.

YOU wrong me very much in thinking I omit writing because I don't hear from you as often as you have a mind I should: you are kinder to me in that respect than I have reason, considering your numerous occupations, to expect: the real and whole truth is, that I have had nothing to tell you; for I could not tire either you or myself with all the details relating to this foolish Road Bill,1 which has engrossed the whole attention of everybody lately.2 I have en-

9. Conway relates the same anecdote to Hertford: 'This is the second dire debate on a *barrière* that has occupied our senate and amazed the French in the midst of our grand apprehensions. You know on the last they could not believe it was really a turnpike that divided the British nation and employed their thoughts when *they* were going to invade them. . .' (ibid.).

10. That is, not hearing from HW.

11. HW reported on 18 April that Galfridus Mann was still improving, although slowly (MANN iv. 549).

———

1. The Paddington or New Road,

which the Duke of Bedford opposed as making a dust behind Bedford House, and from some intended buildings being likely to interrupt his prospect. The Duke of Grafton warmly espoused the other side of the question (HW).

2. After passing the House of Commons on 30 March (*ante* 25 March 1756, n. 13), the Paddington Road Bill was read for the first time in the Lords on 31 March, a second time and committed on 6 April, and discussed in committee 12 and 13 April, when further consideration was postponed until after the recess (*Journals of the House of Lords* xxviii. 549, 558, 569, 573). There had been very full houses on the three last days of discussion. After

tered into it less than anybody.[3] What will you say when you are told that proxies have been sent for to Scotland?[4] that my Lord Harrington has been dragged into the House of Lords from his coffin,[5] and Lord Arran[6] carried thither to take the oaths, who I believe has not appeared there since the Revolution? In short, it has become quite a trial for power; and though the Dukes of Grafton and Bedford have lent their names and their vehemence, you will guess what has been the engine behind the curtain.[7]

The French are so obliging as to wait till we have done with these important squabbles: the House of Commons takes care too not to draw off the attention of the nation. The Militia Bill has passed through that solitude,[8] but I hear will be stopped in the House of Lords.[9] I have lived lately in a round of great disagreeable suppers, which you know are always called, for my Lady Yarmouth,[10] as if the poor woman loved nothing but cramming: I suppose it will so much become the etiquette, that in the next reign there will be nothing but suppers for my Lord Bute.[11] I am now come hither to

the recess it was again discussed in committee 28 April, then read the third time and passed on the 30th (ibid. xxviii. 585–6, 588).

3. HW had apparently taken some part in assisting Grafton because of family connections (*post* ?April ?1756); since his political connections were still with Fox (SELWYN 337), he was forced into virtual neutrality.

4. No other account of this has been found.

5. Harrington died 8 Dec. He was listed as present on 6 April (*Journals of the House of Lords* xxviii. 556), but not on any of the other days that the bill was debated.

6. Charles Butler (1671–1758), cr. (1693) E. of Arran; chancellor of Oxford 1715–58. He was also cr. (1722) D. of Arran in the Jacobite peerage and was *de jure* 3d D. of Ormonde, but was not an active Jacobite. Although his earldom was in the Irish peerage, he was entitled to sit in the English House of Lords by virtue of his English barony of Butler of Weston, cr. 1694. The Lords *Journals* does not mention his taking the oaths at this time, nor does he seem to have been present at any of the debates on the bill.

7. Fox's rivalry with Newcastle (*ante* 25 March 1756, n. 15).

8. Since HW's previous letter (see ibid., n. 12) it had been twice discussed in committee on 30 March, reported but recommitted 31 March, further discussed in committee 5, 8, and 9 April, and reported on the 9th (*Journals of the House of Commons* xxvii. 553, 555, 565, 573, 577). It was further debated and amended 5 May and finally passed 10 May (ibid. xxvii. 595, 600).

9. It was stopped on the third reading, 24 May (*Journals of the House of Lords* xxviii. 612; *Mem. Geo. II* ii. 201–2; see also Cobbett, *Parl. Hist.* xv. 706–69; *Hardwicke Corr.* ii. 262–6; Elliot to Grenville 25 May, *Grenville Papers* i. 160–1, MS now WSL). 'Old' Horace Walpole wrote Hardwicke 4 April that it would be stopped in the Lords (Cobbett, op. cit. xv. 705–6, n.).

10. Lady Essex mentions giving a dinner for Lady Yarmouth on 3 April and of supping with her at Lady Hertford's shortly afterwards (Lady Essex to Sir Charles Hanbury Williams 28 March, [April], MS now WSL, lxi. ff. 23–6).

11. Another allusion to his alleged affair with the Princess Dowager of Wales

keep *my* Newmarket,[12] but the weather is cold and damp: it is uncertain whether the Duke makes that campaign,[13] or against the French. As the Road Bill extinguished the violence about the two operas of next year,[14] and they made the invasion forgot, and the invasion the earthquake, I foresee—and I go almost upon as sure grounds as prophets that take care to let the event precede the prediction—I foresee that the Hanoverians will swallow up all:[15] they have already a general named,[16] who ranks before any one of ours; and there are to be two Hanoverian aide-de-camps!

You will hear by this post of the death of Sir William Lowther,[17] whose vast succession falls to Sir James,[18] and makes him Crœsus:[19] he may hire the Dukes of Bedford and Marlborough for led-captains.[20] I am sorry for this young man, though I did not know him; but it is hard to be cut off so young and so rich: old rich men seldom deserve to live, but he did a thousand generous acts.[21] You will be diverted with a speech of Lord S.[22] one of those second-rate

(*ante* 12 Feb. 1756 and n. 23). Lady Yarmouth was the King's mistress.

12. His regular Easter house party for Edgcumbe, Selwyn, and 'Gilly' Williams; see MONTAGU i. 186. Newmarket races began 19 April (ibid. i. 183, n. 1).

13. Cumberland had been a major patron of Newmarket races since 1753 (Evan Charteris, *William Augustus Duke of Cumberland and the Seven Years' War*, [1925], chapt. xx). Mrs Grenville reported on 20 April that he had gone to Newmarket 'but is to stay but two days' (*Grenville Papers* i. 158).

14. HW mentions these quarrels between the manager of the opera Vanneschi and the singers Mingotti and Ricciarelli, which resulted in Mingotti's decision in March to set up her own opera (patronized by Cumberland) for the season of 1756–7, in a letter to Mann of 27 May (MANN iv. 557 and n. 5). See also *post* 21, 28 Oct. 1756.

15. The Hanoverian troops were expected very shortly, as were the Hessians, but the former did not begin to arrive until 20 May (MANN iv. 550 and nn. 6–7). As HW predicted, there were violent debates on the subject of the estimates for their charges in the House of Commons (*Mem. Geo. II* ii. 187–90; Cobbett, op. cit. xv. 703–4).

16. Christian Ludwig Isenburg, Lt-Gen., 'Knight of the Teutonic Order,' brother of Prince Isenburg (MANN iv. 563 and n. 25).

17. (ca 1727 – 15 April 1756), 3d Bt of Marske, M.P.

18. Sir James Lowther (1736–1802), 5th Bt of Lowther; cr. (1784) E. of Lonsdale.

19. Sir William and Sir James had been co-heirs of their cousin Sir James Lowther (ca 1673–1755), 4th Bt of Whitehaven. According to HW, Sir William was 'master of above twenty thousand pounds a year; sixteen of which comes to young Sir James, who was equally rich' (ibid. iv. 550 and n. 9). He elsewhere estimated Sir James's fortune by this death to be 'of one or two and forty thousand pounds a year' (MONTAGU i. 185).

20. HW told Montagu that by this unity of fortunes, the D. of Bedford 'is fallen to be not above the fourth rich man in the island' (ibid.). HW elsewhere comments on the D. of Bedford's wealth (MANN vii. 274 and n. 4); on the death of the 2d D. of Marlborough in 1758, HW estimated his estate at £45,000 a year (ibid. v. 259).

21. HW praises his will for its generosity (MONTAGU i. 184).

22. Presumably John Petty (until 1751, Fitzmaurice) (1706–61), cr. (1751) Vct Fitz-

fortunes, who have not above five-and-thirty thousand pounds a year.[23] He says, everybody may attain some one point if they give all their attention to it; for his part, he knows he has no great capacity, he could not make a figure by his parts; he shall content himself with being one of the richest men in England! I literally saw him t'other day buying pictures[24] for two-and-twenty shillings, that I would not hang in my garret; while I, who certainly have not made riches my sole point of view, was throwing away guineas, and piquing myself for old tombstones against your father-in-law the General.[25] I hope Lady A. will forgive my zeal for Strawberry against Coombank![26] Are you ever to see your Strawberry Hill again? Lord Duncannon[27] flatters us that we shall see you in May.[28] If I did not hope it, I would send you the only two new fashionable pieces; a comic elegy by C.[29] and a wonderful book by a more wonderful author, Greville.[30] It is called *Maxims and Characters:*[31] several of the former are pretty: all the latter so absurd, that one in particular,

maurice and (1753) E. of Shelburne.

23. He had inherited through his mother the Petty estates in Ireland, Wilts, and Bucks, and improved all of them; see John Norris, *Shelburne and Reform,* 1963, pp. 1–3.

24. Perhaps at Langford's sale of the pictures of Christopher Batt on 14–15 April (*Daily Adv.* 14 April; Frits Lugt, *Répertoire des catalogues de ventes publiques,* The Hague, 1938–64, No. 919). HW did not include Batt's among the 'Collections from which were purchased many of the curiosities at Strawberry Hill' (MS bound in his copy of the 1774 *Des. of SH*); Martin Folkes and Mrs Kennon do appear in it (see *ante* 5 Jan. 1756, n. 1; 12 Feb. 1756, n. 26).

25. General John Campbell, who upon the death of Archibald Duke of Argyll succeeded to that title (HW). HW, who advised on the preparation of Shelburne's collections for auction after his death describes him as having 'bought everything' (HW to Mann 22 March 1771, MANN vii. 286).

26. Campbell's seat in Kent (*ante* 23 Aug. 1752 OS, n. 5).

27. William, the D. of Devonshire's brother-in-law (*ante* ca 15 Feb. 1752 OS, n. 4).

28. They did (*post* 29 April 1756, n. 2).

29. *An Elegy written in an Empty Assembly Room* by Richard Owen Cambridge (1717–1802), HW's contemporary at Eton and neighbour at Twickenham. It was advertised as 'this day published' in the *Daily Adv.* 10 April; see also Ralph Straus, *Robert Dodsley,* 1910, p. 359. There seems to have been no copy of it in HW's library. Lady Essex mentions that it was supposed to have been written by a discontented person not invited to the ball at Norfolk House (*ante* 25 March 1756, n. 25) and that it was thought Garrick had a hand in it (Lady Essex to Sir Charles Hanbury Williams [April 1756], MS now WSL, lxi. f. 25).

30. Fulke Greville, Esq. (HW) (1717–ca 1805), of Wilbury, Wilts; M.P. Monmouth 1747–54; envoy to Bavaria 1764–70. He had married Frances Macartney whom HW had celebrated in 'The Beauties' (1746) (SELWYN 328), and who wrote much of his book. He was a considerable eccentric.

31. *Maxims, Characters, and Reflections, Critical, Satyrical and Moral.* It was advertised as 'this day published' in the *Daily Adv.* 12 April, but it is mentioned in the GM for March (xxvi. 143). HW's copy is Hazen, *Cat. of HW's Lib.,* No. 2009.

which at the beginning you take for the character of a man, turns out to be the character of a post-chaise.

You never tell me now any of Missy's bons mots. I hope she has not resided in Ireland till they are degenerated into bulls! Adieu!

Yours ever,

Hor. Walpole

From Conway, Thursday 29 April 1756

Printed from the MS now wsl, formerly Rutnam. First printed, *Fraser's Magazine*, 1850, xli. 282–3.

Dublin Castle, 29 April, 1756.

I HAVE little news to tell you, but it's so good I can't help telling it at the expense of my business and my time, which now thank God runs very short; and that is the whole news I have to tell you. We flatter ourselves we may get away the very beginning of the week after next. To save you the trouble of going to your almanac, or computing, I now write on this instant, Thursday, 29th April; so that Monday or Tuesday sennight will be more likely than any other, by my computation, to be the day of our deliverance. My Lord Lieutenant will be with you in three or four days from that;[1] but I who must travel, like the patriarchs, with my wife, and family, and servants, and cattle, and all my *attirail,* through Wales, shall be an age upon the road.[2]

I have not yet heard the fate of your famous Road Bill, which you talk so much of—I mean in the House of Lords;[3] nor of the Militia Bill.[4] I am glad to hear the French are so complaisant as to defer their invasions till those great points are settled—especially the former, which will undoubtedly put us in an excellent posture of

1. Devonshire returned to England 10 May (David Garrick, *Letters,* ed. Little and Kahrl, Cambridge, Mass., 1963, i. 240, n. 3).

2. Conway reached London 17 May (*Daily Adv.* 19 May).

3. The Road Bill was finally passed by the Lords on 30 April (*ante* 16 April 1756, n. 2).

4. Which was finally thrown out by the Lords 24 May (ibid., n. 9).

defence. I wish they had the same *politesse* in regard to Minorca,[5] which I doubt they will have been rude enough to take before our gentle admiral arrives,[6] and question much if they'll have the civility to restore it. I saw an extract of a letter from Paris, which says Richelieu[7] sailed the 12th with eighteen ships of the line and eight frigates, transporting sixteen thousand men.[8] I hope that's an exaggerated, Gascon account; but yet I always a little suspect our English intelligence and our calculations of force, as well as our estimations of our own bravery and excellent conduct of our commanders, all which are subject to frequent miscomputation.

Our political works here go on very well: we have seated our new Speaker very quietly in the chair.[9] Our late Speaker, dwindled into just such an earl as my Lord Bath,[10] still keeps his ground, has taken his seat,[11] and stood all his spattering and clamour with infinite spirit. The Opposition in Parliament, which it was expected would have much increased on these events, is, I think, just where it was. All the considerable people in the House are with us—even Sir

5. A French attempt on Minorca had been expected since mid-March, and it was reported in London by 20 April that they had sailed for the invasion, as they had indeed done on the 10th. News that they had landed there on the 18th did not reach London until 5 May (MANN iv. 538 and n. 1, 540–1 and nn. 2, 3, 545 and n. 6, 549–50 and nn. 4, 5; MONTAGU i. 183; *Political Journal of George Bubb Dodington*, ed. J. Carswell and L. A. Dralle, Oxford, 1965, p. 340).

6. Admiral John Byng (1704–57) sailed for the reinforcement of Minorca on 5 April, arriving at Gibraltar 2 May (MANN iv. 538, n. 2, 553, n. 10); he did not leave Gibraltar until 8 May and retired after an inconclusive naval engagement off Minorca on the 20th.

7. Louis-François-Armand Vignerot du Plessis (1696–1788), Maréchal-Duc de Richelieu, was commanding the French expedition against Minorca.

8. This same account is summarized in a letter of 28 April from Sir George Lyttelton to William Henry Lyttelton (Robert Phillimore, *Memoirs and Correspondence of George, Lord Lyttelton*, 1845, ii. 504); a similar report arrived in London on the 20th (*Grenville Papers* i. 158). These figures were essentially correct; the French fleet, consisting of 12 ships of the line and five frigates, escorting 166 transports carrying about 12,000 men, sailed from Toulon on 10 April (G. Lacour-Gayet, *La Marine militaire de la France sous le règne de Louis XV*, 1902, pp. 259–60).

9. John Ponsonby (1713–89) had been elected Speaker on 26 April (*Journals of the House of Commons . . . Ireland*, Dublin, 1753–71, ix. 880).

10. William Pulteney lost most of his political influence when he accepted the earldom of Bath in 1742. The comparison was originally Henry Fox's, who had written to Devonshire on 9 March, 'I own I always saw that when the Speaker had sold himself publicly, he would be in Lord Bath's situation, not only incapable himself of giving trouble, but a mark to deter others from setting up a man to give trouble, in order, like him, to be paid for leaving it off' (Lord Ilchester, *Henry Fox*, 1920, ii. 80).

11. In the Irish House of Lords as E. of Shannon on 26 April (GEC xi. 657).

Arthur and the Gores,[12] who have behaved very handsomely.[13] We had a little division yesterday[14] that mustered only twenty-nine, and not one considerable man amongst them.[15] The Primate[16] is, I hear, out of all temper, is come to town, but has not been at the Castle, and speaks with equal warmth on Mr Pons[onby]'s behaviour as that of the Castle, and very great in both;[17] so that with all the requisites to make a man happy and easy, and a good riddance from as much perplexity, odium, and trouble as man ever underwent, his passion for power will, I fancy, render him uneasy to himself and others.

Adieu, dear Horry. I can't feel my happiness, nor quite believe it, till I am on board; but yet have a presentiment that is very pleasant. I have made a sort of a letter out in much haste, and, I suppose, confusion. Missy grows almost too old for bons mots and cleverness; she'll soon be quite stupid. Lady A. begs her compliments.

Yours ever sincerely,

H. S. C.

12. 'It is worthy of remark, that *nine* of this family were in the Parliament which met 8 October 1751. . . . The unanimity of the nine Gores, long continued proverbial, consequently their influence in the senate, may be more easily imagined than described' (John Lodge and Mervyn Archdall, *The Peerage of Ireland*, 1789, iii. 285–6n). Sir Arthur, 3d Bt (*ante* 6 March 1756, n. 8); Sir Ralph (1725–1802), 6th Bt, 1746, cr. (1772) E. of Ross; Frederick (d. 1761), son of William, Dean of Down; Paul Annesley, of Cotlestown, brother of Sir Arthur, 3d Bt; William of Woodfort; Ralph, of Barrowmount; Arthur (d. ca 1757), of Tenelick; John (1718–84), cr. (1766) Bn Annaly of Tenelick; Henry, of Tenelick (ibid. iii. 112–16, 283–6; *Journals . . . Ireland* viii [1782]. 154–7).

13. Sir Arthur had hoped for the Speakership himself; see *ante* 6 March 1756, n. 9.

14. On a motion that an account of the pensions granted since the beginning of the session be laid before the House; it was defeated 93–29 (*Journals . . . Ireland*, ix. 886).

15. One of the tellers for the minority was Edmond Sexten Pery, later one of the principal Irish politicians and already an important figure.

16. George Stone, Abp of Armagh.

17. A long letter from Stone to Lord George Sackville, 17 May, detailing his complaints against his exclusion from power and his treatment by Ponsonby and his friends is summarized and quoted in Hist. MSS Comm., *Stopford-Sackville MSS*, 1904–10, i. 238–9. See also *Mem. Geo. II* ii. 183–4; Devonshire to Newcastle 15 April 1756 and Stone to Newcastle 8 May 1756, BM Add. MSS 32864, ff. 275, 494–6.

To HERTFORD, ?April ?1756

Missing; answered Wednesday, ?April ?1756.

From HERTFORD, Wednesday ?April ?1756

Printed for the first time from a photostat of BM Add. MSS 23219, f. 159.
Tentatively dated by the probability that the subject under discussion is a
prospective division in the House of Lords during the passage of the Paddington
Road Bill in April 1756, of which Grafton was the chief promoter and bene-
ficiary (*ante* 25 March 1756 and n. 14). It was the only Parliamentary business in
which Hertford was especially concerned at this time. The major crises in the
passage were during the committee stage in the middle of April, on the
report of the committee, 28 April, and on the third reading, 30 April, when
Bedford and his friends made unsuccessful attempts first to delay consideration
of the bill and then to defeat it (*ante* 16 April 1756, n. 2; *Journals of the House
of Lords* xxviii. 588). The handwriting is similar to that of Hertford's other letters of the mid-1750s.
Address: To Mr Walpole in Arlington Street

Wednesday morn.

Dear Horry,

I THANK you for your note and have communicated the contents of it to the Duke of Grafton. Our list[1] is improved since
we talked together, and I hear from good authority that the other
side despair of being able to carry it. The Bishops stand well.[2] I fear
nothing but quirks and law quibbles which I told his Grace some
time ago, but he was not then of opinion that any more of those
tricks would be employed against him. I remain

Always yours very sincerely,

HERTFORD

1. The peers supporting Grafton.
2. When the Bishop of London withdrew his objections to the new road about

20 April, it was generally assumed that
Bedford would be defeated (*Grenville
Papers* i. 157).

From Lady Ailesbury, Tuesday 15 June 1756

Printed for the first time from the MS now WSL, formerly Rutnam.
Memoranda (by HW, the first four lines crossed out):

> Wrote on Thursd. [?17 June 1756]
> D. of B[edford]
> Murray [Lord Mansfield]
> Ld Fred Cavendish [see *post* 11 Aug. 1757, n. 5]

> [Henry Bilson] Legge and Ch[arles] Townsh[end]

> 75
> Mr Muntz[1]
> Prestage [see below, n. 5]
> Paper   Dodsley[2]

> Squawking
> *C'est si bien decrotté*

> Ly Ailesb[ury]
> Mrs [John] Harris
> [Thomas] Brand [see *post* 6 July 1756 and n. 10]

> [Pencil drawings]

Park Place, June 15, 1756.

I SEE in the *Advertiser*[3] that there is going to be an auction of Mr Pestre's[4] furniture, which, if it really is his, as Mr Prestage[5] assures us, I imagine there must be some good things amongst it; what I am in great want of is a sideboard table, something pretty near six foot long; as it is for Park Place nothing very fine is required. As you sometimes go to auctions, if you should happen to go to this and see anything of this kind, I should be vastly obliged to

1. Johann Heinrich Müntz (1727–98), painter, at this time living with HW (MANN iv. 554; MONTAGU i. 190–2).

2. Robert Dodsley (1703–64), bookseller, whom HW may have asked about wallpaper (see *post* 2 Sept. 1756, n. 12).

3. The *Daily Advertiser*, which since 8 June had been carrying an advertisement 'To be sold at auction by Mr Prestage, on Wednesday the 23d instant, and the following days, the genuine and rich

household furniture, sideboard of plate, and wardrobe of linen, of John de Pesters, Esq.' followed by a description of some of the items.

4. John de Pesters, a cousin of the Cts of Denbigh. Lady Bolingbroke referred to his house in Hanover Square as a 'petit palais' in 1744 (Hist. MSS Comm., *Denbigh MSS*, 1911, pp. 139, 344).

5. (d. 1767), auctioneer (GM 1767, xxxvii. 430).

you to bid for me. If you had not shown so much goodness to me upon all occasions, I should be ashamed to write to you as I would to an upholsterer, but I am so hurried having company in the house to entertain, that I had not time to begin my letter properly.

I give you a thousand thanks for the beautiful snake; and your magnificence really puts me in mind of Aboulcaum in the Persian Tales,[6] who used to send his friends the next morning whatever they took a fancy to in his house; when everything is found out (as I have heard you say it will),[7] I believe you will invent a Gothic cart big enough to transport Strawberry upon to the first of your friends that takes a fancy to it. For my part I am satisfied since it is possible to find a post-chaise ready invented *big enough* to transport you to Park Place, where you are much wished for by Mr Conway[8] and I.

I am, dear Mr Walpole, your most faithful servant,

C. AILESBURY

If there should be any chair frames at the auction that you think good enough to put *my work* upon,[9] I should be very glad of them.

To CONWAY, before Tuesday 29 June 1756

Missing; implied *post* 29 June 1756.

6. The tale of Aboulcasem Basry in *The Persian and the Turkish Tales Compleat,* 1714, i. 5–15, translated by François Pétis de la Croix (1653–1713). HW had two sets of the 1729 edn (Hazen, *Cat. of HW's Lib.,* No. 2742).

7. See HW to Richard Bentley 18 May 1754 (CHUTE 175).

8. Who had returned from Ireland 17 May (MANN iv. 555).

9. Lady Ailesbury was an expert needlewoman; see *post* 16 Sept. 1757, 1 Sept. 1764, 3 Oct. 1773, n. 4.

From CONWAY, Tuesday 29 June 1756

Printed for the first time from the MS now WSL, formerly Rutnam.

Memoranda (by HW, apparently a list of engagements):

Ld Edgcumbe   Sat. and Sund.
Ly B[etty] Germ[ain] Ly Suff[olk] Monday˟
Garrick   Tuesd.
Ld Hilsb[orough] and Fox   Wedn.
H[?enry] T[?ownshend] Thursd.
˟Ly Northum[berland]

Park Place, 29 June, 1756.

I HAVE never thanked you for your anecdotes of the jerebo family,[1] for which, I assure you I retain a proper gratitude; yet is not that the sole motive of my writing. I acquainted the Duke of Devonshire with the great treasure he possessed and he seemed desirous if possible to be informed on what medal it is, for as his collection is large he might otherwise be a-jerebo hunting in it for a great while.[2] I presume so accurate a gentleman as Mr Hayms will not have failed to be as distinct as possible in a matter of such consequence and therefore conclude he has mentioned the medal on which this curiosity is to be found.

The doctor's etymology of the word from the Arabic *al jarbo* is, I dare say, very ingenious, if one knew the language and his learning in tracing it through so many nations, authors and languages equally admirable.[3] His or your *physical* observations seem very well chose[4] and upon the whole I am exceedingly desirous from your sample of reading the whole history.

1. Conway gave Lady Ailesbury a jerboa in 1752 (MONTAGU i. 142–3).

2. The medal of the jerboa in Devonshire's collection is described (in English p. 35 and Italian pp. 124–5) and illustrated (facing p. 124) in the second volume (dedicated to the 2d D. of Devonshire) of *Del Tesoro Britannico. Parte prima*, London, 1719–20, by Nicola Francesco Haym (ca 1679–1729) (*Enciclopedia dello spettacolo*, Rome, 1954–62, vi. 230); HW's copy is Hazen, *Cat. of HW's Lib.*, No. 269. The description in English, p. 35, reads, under Cyrene, Medal III, 'A man on horseback . . . The Silphium, under which is the little animal, which is engraved on the plate to its full bigness, in

three several postures. This medal is fine gold, and weighs 66 English grains. It's well preserved, and the workmanship good.'

3. Haym says that the jerboa 'plainly appeared to be the same with the *Musdipus* of Herodotus, with the *Saphan* of the Jews . . . and with the *Arctomos* of St Jerom . . . Teixeira, a Portuguese, calls it *Ratones Delmata* . . . it may be the same that was called *Aljarbuo*, which Bochart proves to be the same with the *Dipus*' (English text, p. 36; see also Italian text, pp. 125–6).

4. 'The creature one while put its four feet to the ground, and at other times it stood only upon its hind feet, and always

Your appendix on the subject of Little Mary[5] is natural and just what we expected; I wish those who know her figure mayn't take it for a continuation of the history of the jerebo, which considering your familiarity with her does not sound well for you;[6] she certainly is like in many parts; whether she has a long tail and but one hole for evacuation you know best.[7]

I come now to the grand view of this letter beyond Mary and the jerebo, Dr Haym, Dr Bentley and all, which is to know when we may hope to have the sight of you at Park Place,[8] how much you are wanted and wished for is of course; I shall say nothing, but it is most unfair of you to come so late when we visited Strawberry in the spring;[9] I verily believe you meant to stay till we were parched and burnt to a coal but Providence has hitherto preserved us from that calamity and if you mean us well you must still come while we are a little green.

I wish you could have sent a secret for saving Minorca;[10] or if

walked upon them. It would jump very high when frightened, and run very fast, and as it were, straight forward; it hopped like a bird as it ran on the ground; its eyes were in a manner black, and stood far out, and they had that liveliness in them which I never observed in any other animal; its coat was very fine, and exceeded that of the beaver; the ears were very thin, and the fore paws, or claws, very short, having as it were, human fingers in them, which were likewise five in number; it had two long teeth in the under, and as many in the upper jaw, which the creature opened and shut at pleasure, and its whiskers were extraordinary long and black; the hair upon the back had a mixture of yellow with some dark, and as it were black spots, somewhat like to that of a hare . . .' (English text, pp. 36–7).

5. Probably Mary Rich, Lady Ailesbury's friend, who visited SH with Conway and Lady Ailesbury for two days during the first week of June (CHUTE 275).

6. HW's 'familiarity' with Miss Rich is described by HW to Strafford 6 June: 'We were returning from Mrs Clive's through the long field, and had got over the high stile that comes into the road, that is, three of us [Conway, Lady Ailes-

bury, and HW]. It had rained, and the stile was wet. I could not let Miss Rich straddle across so damp a palfrey, but took her in my arms to lift her over. At that instant I saw a coach and six come thundering down the hill from my house; and hurrying to set down my charge, and stepping backwards, I missed the first step, came down headlong with the nymph in my arms: but turning quite round as we rushed to the ground, the first thing that touched the earth was Miss Rich's head. You must guess in how improper a situation we fell. . . .' (ibid. 275–6).

7. A reference to Haym's description of the jerboa: 'It had only one hole for evacuation like a bird, thro' which alone he eased nature; . . . the tail was all of one colour inclining to yellow, and the hair upon it very short; but there grew at the end of it, as it were, a white plume with a black list, which divided it in the middle . . .' (English text, p. 37).

8. HW finally went to Park Place on 13 July (MONTAGU i. 192).

9. They had been at SH for two days the first week of June (above, n. 5).

10. The fate of Minorca was still in doubt. Reports from France that Byng had failed to relieve it were current since 2 June and his own dispatches, received

that was too late as I doubt, something to prevent the abominable *lying* of admirals[11] and a preservative against councils of war.[12]

Yorke[13] sends word from The Hague that Monsieur d'Affry[14] said the French were beat.[15] How do you and Dr Haym account for that? You promised me politics but have sent me none.

I must tell you so far of my own history as that I go to town on Saturday for some few days: perhaps may see you there, if not let me hear of you.

Yours most sincerely,

H. S. C.

To Conway, ca Saturday 3 July 1756

Missing; answered *post* 6 July 1756.

on the 23d, confirmed his failure, though they were couched in more optimistic terms (Mann iv. 560–2 and nn. 9–13; *The Political Journal of George Bubb Dodington*, ed. J. Carswell and L. A. Dralle, Oxford, 1965, pp. 344–5).

11. Byng represented his encounter with the French fleet on 20 May as at worst a draw, and hinted that it might even have been a victory. Other reports, received just before the dispatches, described it as a victory. The French reports, however, described it accurately as an unqualified withdrawal of the British fleet (references cited in the previous note; *An Eighteenth-Century Correspondence*, ed. Lilian Dickins and Mary Stanton, New York, 1910, pp. 338–9; *Grenville Papers* i. 169).

12. Another allusion to Byng's dispatches which arrived on the 23d, saying that since on the advice of a council of war he would not relieve Port Mahon he was going back to Gibraltar to refit and wait for reinforcements (Carswell and Dralle, op. cit. 345). Conway is probably also thinking of the council of war at

Gibraltar on 4 May which had refused reinforcements to Byng (Mann iv. 560 and n. 2).

13. Hon. Joseph Yorke (1724–92), K.B., 1761; cr. (1788) Bn Dover; M.P. East Grinstead 1751–61, Dover 1761–74, Grampound 1774–80; Gen., 1777; minister to Holland 1751–61; ambassador 1761–80.

14. Louis-Auguste-Augustin (1713–93), Comte d'Affry; French minister to Holland 1755–6, 1756–8; ambassador 1758–62 (Mann v. 298, n. 5).

15. Yorke wrote Newcastle from The Hague 18 June, 'D'Affri told one of his friends in confidence, when the news first came, who said the account was a blind one, "Que voulez-vous—la vérité est que nous avons été bien frottés."—In short people here insist I should believe it, and in many places of this town Admiral Byng's health has been heartily drank, and my house has been full 'till now, past 12 o'clock, with people who forced my door to tell me this and to congratulate me' (extract in BM Add. MSS 32865, ff. 354–5).

From CONWAY, Tuesday 6 July 1756

Printed for the first time from the MS now WSL, formerly Rutnam. Dated by HW's projected visit to Park Place, the news from Minorca, and the history of the 'jerebo medal' requested in the previous letter; also, Conway was in London, where he said he would be by 3 July in the previous letter.

There are pencil drawing of the façade of Strawberry Hill.

Little Warwick Street, Tuesday evening.

Dear Horry,

I THANK you for your history of the jerebo medal; much more for your Parliamentary history[1] which has given me great delight and amusement. I will now own what I durst not before, that I had locked it up so carefully, when I went down to Park Place, that I left it behind me; when I found it out I was in a rage with myself, but durst not send my keys and was quite helpless, till I returned to town, which I did with great impatience upon that account, and it has fully answered though I could certainly wish you had been a little more diffuse. I fancy I should have liked your language at least as well as theirs.

I envy those who heard the best of those speeches, Pitt's particularly, and can imagine from the sketch what the complete pictures were. Fine ones indeed, some both portrait and history and now [and] then a little landscape. I fancy a storm daubed by Sir Thomas,[2] a Dutch piece by your uncle,[3] a fine battle by Mr Fox and a still life by our cousin Sir John.[4]

We shall be vastly glad to see you on Tuesday. I answer for myself and all my family, and I believe I shall come to Taplow where you dine and fetch you.

There's no news but that the last and best accounts pretend the French make but slow progress, have discontinued their sap,[5] etc.;

1. Of the debates in the preceding Parliamentary session; probably a draft for one of HW's accounts in the *Memoirs*.

2. Sir Thomas Robinson. HW mentions his 'pompous rumbling' in one debate (*Mem. Geo. II* ii. 93).

3. Horatio Walpole.

4. Sir John Philipps (?1701–64) 6th Bt, of Picton Castle; M.P. Carmarthen 1741–7, Petersfield 1754–61, Pembrokeshire

1761–4; first cousin of HW's and Conway's mothers. HW does not mention him as speaking during that session in the *Memoirs*.

5. That is, their drive: Fort St Philip had already capitulated on 29 June, but the news did not reach London until 15 July (MANN iv. 570, n. 2). Reports similar to these, from 'letters of the 15th June from Mahon' are in Joseph Yorke to Lord

from thence some glimmering of Hawke's[6] being got in time. The last letters from thence the 15th,[7] the last from Gibraltar the 10 or 11th—neither Byng[8] nor Brodrick[9] arrived. I hear Brand[10] is with you. Ask why he should not meet you with us on Tuesday?

Yours ever,

H. S. C.

To CONWAY, ca Thursday 22 July 1756

Missing; implied *post* 25 July 1756.

Royston, The Hague, 2 July, printed in part *Hardwicke Papers* ii. 303.

6. Sir Edward Hawke (1710–81), K.B., 1747; cr. (1776) Bn Hawke; Adm., 1757. He had been appointed to supersede Byng on 3 June and sailed for the Mediterranean on 16 June. He did not reach Gibraltar until 2 July, sailed on the 10th, and was not off Minorca until 19 July, three weeks too late (MANN iv. 561–2 and nn. 13, 15; 573, n. 10). Conway wrote Devonshire 29 July, 'The cargo of broken admirals and generals is arrived from the Mediterranean. . . . So Hawke is now in possession of the fleet but unfortunately at a time when Byng might as well command it for by the dates there is not the

least chance of his intercepting a single ship' (Chatsworth MSS, 416 / 30).

7. See above, n. 5.

8. Byng did not reach Gibraltar until 20 June (*Augustus Hervey's Journal*, ed. David Erskine, 1953, p. 215).

9. Thomas Brodrick (d. 1769), Rear-Adm., 1756; Vice-Adm., 1759. He reached Gibraltar with a reinforcement of five ships of the line on 15 June (MANN iv. 573, nn. 8, 9).

10. Thomas Brand (ca 1717–70), of The Hoo, Herts; M.P. New Shoreham 1741–7, Tavistock 1747–54, Gatton 1754–68, Okehampton 1768–70; HW's 'old school fellow' and occasional correspondent (GRAY i. 166, n. 37).

From CONWAY, Sunday 25 July 1756

Printed for the first time from the MS now WSL, formerly Rutnam. The year has been supplied by the references in the last paragraph.

Memoranda (by HW, in pencil): Watch

Hallet[1]

Bedford—milit. estim.

T⟨albot⟩

T[illegible]ler

Lady ⟨Ma⟩ry

Park Place, 25 July.

Dear Horry,

I AM vastly obliged to you for your care of my affairs: pray tell me how I can get more intelligence about my gardener; for being of such consequence to me I can't think even of seeing him till I hear a vast deal of his life and conversation; he is my first minister.

We cannot fix our day precisely yet but I believe the 4th, 5th or 6th if nothing intervenes.[2] You shall know more positively.

Did you think of my estimates? I actually am ashamed to think how I trouble you.

I had a letter from Stormont[3] who is scarce entered into German

1. Presumably William Hallett (1707–81), cabinet-maker (MONTAGU ii. 77, n. 2; Percy Maquoid and Ralph Edwards, *Dictionary of English Furniture*, 2d edn, 1954, ii. 252–3).

2. Conway and Lady Ailesbury planned to join HW on his visit to Lord and Lady Strafford at Wentworth Castle, Yorkshire; Conway wrote Devonshire 15 July, 'Hor. Walpole goes about the 2d of next month to Wentworth C. and stays he says but a week at most so we shall hope to meet your Grace there' (Chatsworth MSS, 416 / 27; see also ibid. 416 / 29). Conway was delayed by conferences with the D. of Cumberland on military business, explained in letters to Devonshire 29 and 31 July (ibid. 416 / 30, 31); but he wrote on 4 Aug., 'I set out this afternoon or tomorrow morning, to join Lady A. on the road. Shall I believe be at Nottingham on Thursday night and at Lord Strafford's on Saturday' (ibid. 416 / 33). On 7 Aug. he wrote

from Wentworth Castle, 'I say little to your Grace on our dispositions here as I know Lord Strafford writes fully on the subject: I most heartily wish to see your Grace here and think I may hope it as I fancy a week is the extent of W.'s stay' (ibid. 416 / 36).

3. Lord Stormont (*ante* 14 July 1751 NS, n. 11) had been appointed envoy extraordinary to Saxony-Poland in April 1756; he arrived at Dresden 9 June (D. B. Horn, *British Diplomatic Representatives 1689–1789*, 1932, p. 93 [Camden Society, 3d ser., Vol. XLVI]). His letter to Conway is missing. The two had been close friends since their travels together in Italy in 1752 (*ante* 23 Jan. 1752 NS). In Nov. 1757 Stormont wrote to the E. of Huntington: 'It is a great pleasure to me [to] find that our friend Conway has contrived to get much honour even from this fruitless expedition [to Rochefort], and has upon this as all former occasions distinguished

politics, but deep in German feasting at Count Bruhl's.[4] I have also had one from Jack[5] (—all well at Gibraltar and in whole skins: Byng and Brodrick and all).[6]

Yours most faithfully and hastily,

H. S. C.

To CONWAY, Thursday 2 September 1756

Printed from a photostat of the MS in the Pierpont Morgan Library. First printed (with omissions and misdated 1757), Wright iii. 314; first printed in full, correctly placed but undated, Toynbee iii. 451–2. For the history of the MS, see *ante* 31 Oct. 1741 OS; it was marked by HW for inclusion in *Works,* but was not included.

Endorsed: H. W. 2 Sep.—1756

Strawberry Hill, Thursday, Sept. 2d.

NOT being in town, there may be several more new productions, as the *Grubbæa frutex* blossoms every day; but I send you all I had gathered for myself while I was there.[1] I found the pamphlet[2] much in vogue, and indeed it is written smartly. My Lady Townshend sends all her messages on the backs of these political cards, the only good one of which, the two heads facing one

himself extremely, and appeared, what I have long thought him, one of the first men of his time' (Hist. MSS Comm., *Hastings MSS,* 1928–47, iii. 133). The friendship endured (MANN vii. 18).

4. Heinrich von Brühl (1700–63), Graf von Brühl, prime minister of Saxony-Poland (ibid. v. 2, n. 8).

5. His brother-in-law John Campbell. The letter is missing; a number of letters from Gibraltar up to 23 June had arrived in London by 24 July (Lord Ilchester, *Henry Fox,* 1920, i. 334–5; *London Gazette* No. 9602, 20–24 July).

6. This intelligence was received in London on 23 July and published ibid.; on the 24th HW wrote to Mann that it was believed Byng had sailed from

Gibraltar before his successor arrived (MANN iv. 578, 583). Byng himself, however, arrived a prisoner at Spithead on the 26th (Brian Tunstall, *Admiral Byng and the Loss of Minorca,* 1928, p. 171).

1. HW had in his library 'a bundle of tracts relative to the case of Admiral Byng' (Hazen, *Cat. of HW's Lib.,* No. 3403), and other pamphlets dated 1756 (ibid. No. 1608:81). See also MANN iv. 585–6.

2. Probably one of the pamphlets in the Byng controversy. Mrs Toynbee identifies it as *The Art of Political Lying,* an attack on George Townshend's caricatures, but this was not published until 19 April 1757 (ibid. v. 78 and n. 11).

another, is her son George's.[3] Charles met d'Abreu[4] t'other day, and told him he intended to make a great many good speeches next winter; the first, said he, shall be to address the King, not to send for any more foreign troops, but to send for some foreign ministers.

Mr Fox had a very bad sore throat, but never was in any danger.[5] You have heard I suppose what an abominable will Lord Fitzwilliams[6] left; did not mention his wife[7] or younger children[8] in it, but leaves all to his eldest son;[9] though she is one of the most deserving women in the world, and the younger son and five daughters will have but £2500 apiece![9a]

My Lord Chesterfield is relapsed:[10] he sent Lord Bath word lately that he was grown very lean and very deaf: the other replied, that he could lend him some fat, and should be very glad at any time to lend him an ear.

3. 'The Pillars of the State,' which shows Newcastle and Fox facing each other (British Museum, Catalogue of Prints . . . Political and Personal Satires, 1870–1954, iii pt ii. 997–8 [No. 3371]). See illustration. It was reproduced in A Political and Satirical History of the Years 1756 and 1757, [?1758], Plate I. HW also sent a copy of the card to Montagu 28 Aug. (Montagu i. 195). For Townshend's other caricatures see ante 4 March 1756.

4. Felix de Abreu y Bertodano, Spanish chargé d'affaires at London 1754–5, envoy 1754–60 (Mann iv. 561, n. 8).

5. As was reported in some of the papers (Lord Ilchester, Henry Fox, 1920, i. 351).

6. The 3d E. Fitzwilliam (ante 31 Oct. 1741, n. 40), died 10 Aug. His will, dated 29 June 1751, was probated 13 Nov. 1756.

7. Ibid., n. 14. She was probably omitted because she had a jointure of £1500 p.a. (Wentworth-Woodhouse MSS F 128 / 26).

8. He had a son, George, born posthumously, who d. 1786, and five surviving daughters: Lady Anne (b. 1744); Lady Charlotte (1746–1833), m. (1764) Thomas Dundas, cr. (1794) Bn Dundas; Lady Frances Henrietta (1750–1835); Lady Henrietta (b. 1752); and Lady Dorothy (1754–1809) (Collins, Peerage, 1812, iv. 398–9; Sir Bernard Burke and A. P. Burke, Peerage, 1928, p. 947).

9. William Fitzwilliam (after 1807 Wentworth-Fitzwilliam) (1748–1833), 4th E. Fitzwilliam.

9a. One of the reasons for these austere provisions was that Fitzwilliam was in rather straitened circumstances. His landed estate produced about £6000 p.a., but there was a debt of £45,000 charged on it, in addition to the jointure to his widow (above, n. 7), leaving a clear income of less than £3500. The debt included £15,000 settled on his sisters, and £15,000 settled on his 'younger children'; the sums HW mentions were apparently additional legacies (Wentworth-Woodhouse MSS F 128 / 26, 27, 36, 37).

10. He had been ill since the previous winter; on 16 Sept. he wrote to a friend, 'I have not wrote at all, I have spoke little, and I have thought less, for these last three months. The frequency of the attacks in my head and stomach gave me no time to recover from the weakness, languor, and dispiritedness, which they always leave behind them; and I am at this moment little stronger than I was sixty-one years ago—that is, at one year old. All these complicated ills, however, have not, I thank God, given me one moment's melancholy; and though in a manner they deprive me of existence, they do not deprive me of my natural tranquillity of temper, nor of my acquired philosophy' (Chesterfield, Letters, ed. Dobrée, 1932, v. 2199). If the message to Bath was in the form of a letter, it has not been found.

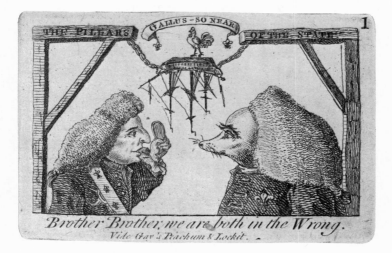

THE PILLARS · GALLUS—SO NEAR · OF THE STATE · 1

Brother Brother, we are both in the Wrong.
Vide Gay's Peachum & Lockit.

I shall go to London on Monday,[11] and if I find anything else new, I will pack it up with a flower picture for Lady Ailesbury, which I shall leave in Warwick Street, with orders to be sent to you.

Adieu! Yours ever,

H. W.

PS. The person I employed could meet with no such thing as Bowen's paper;[12] but the enclosed paper has all the supplies.[13] If this will not do, give me farther directions.

From CONWAY, Sunday 12 September 1756

Printed for the first time from the MS now WSL, formerly Rutnam.

Park Place, 12 Sept. 1756.

I HAVE been impatient for the post day to thank you for your present[1] so very pretty, so agreeable and so agreeably given; we agree that nobody does those things so cleverly as you and are full of praises and thankfulness. The likeness is perfect bating that you are a little too fat; the room is admirably drawn, the prospect the neatest and delicatest little prospect that ever was seen, and the whole *tout à fait* charming; Lady A. and I have almost quarrelled where it should hang. She wants to engross it for a little hole of a dressing room that she has just niched herself in and I for the great, public room, now fitting up with a bow window and everything that is magnificent.[2]

---

11. Conway was also in London, and wrote Devonshire from Little Warwick Street on Tuesday 7 Sept., 'I lost but a single day at Park Place and came immediately to town in quest of any business that might occur of which I found a good deal. . . .' He had conferred with the D. of Cumberland and with Fox (Chatsworth MSS, 416 / 38).

12. Possibly paper made from 'the stalk of flax or hemp after the fibre has been removed' (OED *sub* 'boon sb2,' 'bun sb1,' 'boun'). There is no mention of it in Al-

fred H. Shorter, *Paper Mills and Paper Makers in England, 1495–1800*, Hilversum, Holland, 1957.

13. Apparently 'specifications,' though that use of the word does not appear in the OED.

---

1. Müntz's pen and wash drawing of HW seated in the Library at SH; see C. Kingsley Adams and W. S. Lewis, 'The Portraits of Horace Walpole,' *Walpole Society*, 1970, xlii. 14.

2. The description of Park Place in

We parted so lately and I have seen so little since, and the country is so barren of topics you can expect nothing from hence.

The worst news (and it's the fashion to have none but the worst) is that our gold-fish[3] grow silver and the great big-bellied one has certainly got a tympany;[4] we have had the advice of physicians upon her case. Our partridge are devoured by vermin and our fruit blighted. Adieu: if you can come to such a place it longs much to see you. If this finds you with Lady Mary and Mr Churchill, pray make our compliments.

Yours ever,

H. S. C.

From LADY AILESBURY, Thursday 21 October 1756

Printed for the first time from the MS now WSL, formerly Rutnam.

Park Place, October 21, 1756.

I THINK myself vastly unlucky not to meet you in town, and I was very sorry not to be able to perform my promise of coming to Strawberry, but I had no time, and Mr Conway's fit of seeing camps was then very strong;[1] if it should suit you to be there after the Birthday,[2] and Mr Conway should have an intermission, we will wait upon you then if you'll accept us; though I say this without having consulted him, for he is gone to shoot off his gun with Mr Freeman[3] this morning.

I cannot prevail upon the Mingotti to give me an answer about the box,[4] though I have sent messages and notes without end, all in choice Italian, not penned by myself, for then she might have been supposed not to have understood them, but by Miss Rich; all she says is that the people who took them last year have not determined

the *World* 23 Oct. 1787 (Appendix 15) mentions 'the bow-window room, the best in the house.'

3. Conway's gold-fish were a present from HW (*ante* 23 Oct. 1753; 3, 6, 7 July 1754).

4. 'Sometimes used vaguely for a morbid swelling or tumour of any kind. Common from 16th to 18th c.' (OED).

———

1. Camps were established at Maidstone, Winchester, Blandford, Canterbury and Chatham during the spring and summer of 1756 (Rex Whitworth, *Field Marshal Lord Ligonier*, Oxford, 1958, p. 210).

2. The King's Birthday, 10 November (MANN v. 6, n. 19).

3. Sambrooke Freeman (ca 1721–82), of Fawley Court, Henley-on-Thames, Berks; M.P. Pontefract 1754–61, Bridport 1768–74; Conway's neighbour.

4. At the Opera.

whether they will take them for this or not, but this I know, that neither Lady Lyttelton nor Lady Mary Churchill intend to subscribe, so one of their boxes, I think, I might insist upon, if insisting would do, especially as she absolutely promised Mr Freeman that I should have one in case of any change. I believe you are heartily weary of all this and wish I would float upon my plank alone, but I can't help offering the case to your consideration, hoping you will have some good thought, and wanting to know what you think the best method of proceeding; it must not be by force, I believe, without we could pare her nails and pull out her teeth.

We are all charmed with the Memoirs of Gervase Hollis;[5] I only regret I did not read them before I went to Welbeck;[6] what a black story that is of Lord Leicester[7] and Lady Sheffield![8] I am very curious to know what Mr Stanhope[9] assaulted Sir William Cavendish for.[10] I must end abruptly, being in a great hurry. I am, dear Mr Walpole,

Your faithful servant,

C. Ailesbury

Lady Mary Churchill says she will positively not subscribe to the Opera but will not send her answer to the Mingotti in order to keep

5. *Memorials of the Holles Family* by Gervase Holles (1607–75), two manuscripts of which, both in Holles's own hand, were at Welbeck Abbey in 1756; one manuscript was taken in 1759 to Longleat. Lady Ailesbury presumably read the adaptation in Arthur Collins's *Historical Collections of the Noble Families of Cavendishe, Holles, Vere, Harley, and Ogle*, 1752 (see A. C. Wood, 'The Holles Family,' *Transactions of the Royal Historical Society*, 4th ser., 1936, xix. 146–7). Holles's *Memorials* were first printed in full, ed. A. C. Wood, Camden Society, 3d ser., Vol. LV, 1937; for the provenance of the manuscripts see Wood's introduction, pp. xi–xiii. HW's copy of Collins's *Collections*, with his notes, is in the British Museum (Hazen, *Cat. of HW's Lib.*, No. 565).

6. Conway and Lady Ailesbury probably accompanied HW when he visited Welbeck in August on an excursion from Wentworth Castle (HW to Bentley Aug. 1756, CHUTE 270; *ante* 25 July 1756, n. 2).

7. Robert Dudley (1532 *or* 1533–88), cr. (1564) E. of Leicester.

8. Douglas Howard (ca 1545–1608), m.

1 (ca 1562) John Sheffield, 2d Bn Sheffield; m. 2 (1579) Sir Edward Stafford. Holles says that she conspired with Leicester, her lover, to poison her husband in 1568 (quoted in Collins, op. cit. 77–8; A. C. Wood's edn, pp. 70–1). The story that both of them, or Leicester alone, poisoned Lord Sheffield is now generally rejected, although Leicester secretly (and irregularly) married Lady Sheffield in 1573. But when doubts were cast on the marriage's legality, both remarried others. See GEC *sub* Leicester.

9. John Stanhope (d. 1621), cr. (1605) Bn Stanhope of Harrington, although he was already a knight at the time of the incident to which Lady Ailesbury is referring. See next note.

10. A slip for Sir Charles Cavendish (1553–1617), Kt, 1582. Lady Ailesbury is referring to a document printed in Collins, op. cit. 21, entitled 'A Declaration of the Foul Outrage, by John Stanhope, against the Person of Sir Charles Cavendish, Knight,' describing an assault by Stanhope on Cavendish on 18 June 1599.

her in suspense; I think a good measure could be to persuade her
to send an answer, and you the proper person to do it.[11]

To HERTFORD, ca Friday 15 – Wednesday 20
October 1756

Two notes, missing; referred to *post* 24 October 1756.

From CONWAY, Sunday 24 October 1756

Printed for the first time from the MS now WSL, formerly Rutnam.
Address: To the Honourable Horatio Walpole in Arlington Street, London.
Postmark: 25 OC. HEN⟨LE⟩Y.
Memoranda (by HW): Iona[1]
　　　　　　　　Sharpe[2]

Park Place, 24 Oct. 1756.

YOU have been in town witness to all these extraordinary rum-
bles in the ministry[3] and have not let me hear a word. I saw, or
heard, rather, of two notes of yours to my brother but then nothing
seemed settled: now I hear, but indistinctly and uncertainly, that
the Duke of N[ewcastle] is going to retire.[4] These are rather curious
events; one can't but have a little impatience to know and actually
I am the most miserably served in intelligence in the world.

Yours, etc.,

H. S. C.

11. HW wrote to Lady Mary as requested (*post* 28 Oct. 1756).

1. Not explained.
2. Probably John Sharpe (?1700 – 22
Oct. 1756), M.P. for Lady Orford's borough of Callington 1754–6; his brother
Joshua Sharpe (d. 1788), Lady Orford's
lawyer (MANN iv. 547, n. 5); or his son
Fane William Sharpe (?1729–71), M.P.
Callington 1756–71, whom Lady Orford
'most earnestly recommended' to succeed
his father (Namier and Brooke iii. 427–8).

3. Fox had requested permission to resign on 13 October; negotiations with Pitt
had been under way since, but as yet
nothing had been settled (MANN v. 6 and
nn. 20–24, 11 and n. 2).
4. Newcastle told the King on the 15th
that he would be forced to resign if Pitt
refused to serve with him, but he did not
do so until 26 Oct. (ibid. v. 6, n. 24, 11, n.
3; SELWYN 128, n. 7). Conway also mentions this in his letter to Devonshire 24
Oct. (Chatsworth MSS, 416 / 40).

From CONWAY, Thursday 28 October 1756

Printed for the first time from the MS now WSL, formerly Rutnam. Year supplied by the endorsement and the contents.

Memoranda (by HW):[1] Pr. Edw.

Mr Cadogan.[2] Pr. Purse

Mr R. Brudenel[3] ⎫
Mr Moyston[4]   ⎬ grooms
                  ⎭

Mr G. West[5] ⎫
Mr Morrison[6] ⎬ equerries

K. Chan. Duke
Lord An[son] gravelled. Pitt stop clamour
how Duke
Wht Answer Pitt

Park Place, 28 Oct.

Dear Horry,

I AM much obliged to you for offering to meet me in town.[7] I am to be there on Monday and shall stay probably some few days, two or three at least, and shall be vastly glad to see you and the sooner the better; that's no great compliment as the town is. Since I wrote to you I have heard more of our confusions which I own I dread as they must, I doubt, affect the public which wants all the ability, steadiness and harmony an administration can have. I wish I saw a prospect of its being anyway properly settled.

1. The five names following 'Pr. Edw.' are his household. They were appointed at the same time as the household of the Prince of Wales, which was completed by 5 Nov. (MANN v. 6, n. 19). The last four lines relate to the current political crisis.

2. Hon. Charles Sloane Cadogan (1728–1807), M.P. Cambridge 1749–54, 1755–76; 3d Bn Cadogan, 1776; cr. (1800) E. Cadogan; m. 2 (1777) Mary Churchill, HW's niece. He remained privy purse until the Prince's death in 1767.

3. Hon. Robert Brudenell (1726–68), army officer; Lt-Gov. of Windsor Castle, 1752; M.P. Great Bedwyn 1756–61, Marlborough 1761–8. He is not mentioned in the list of Prince Edward's household in the *Court and City Register* for 1757, pp.

99–100, but appears as an equerry there for 1758, p. 99, and 1759, p. 99, and as a groom of his Bedchamber from 1760, p. 100, the first year in which grooms of the Bedchamber are mentioned.

4. Not identified. No member of the Mostyn family appears in the lists of Prince Edward's household in the *Court and City Register*.

5. Hon. George West (1733–76) (*ante* ca 9 May 1755, n. 2).

6. Capt. George Morrison (ca 1704–99); Col., 1772; Maj.-Gen., 1777; Gen., 1796 (MONTAGU i. 269, n. 12).

7. HW mentions dining with Conway at Lord Hertford's on 2 Nov. (*Mem. Geo. II* ii. 268–70).

The King of Pr[ussia] has made a pretty *coup de filet*.[8] I wish him well.

Lady A. is much obliged to you for writing to Lady Mary[9] as I find she has her box at heart.

Adieu,

H. S. C.

Poor Miss Audrey![10] How it could be worth her while to run away with any one man that might have stayed, been respected and had twenty.[11]

From HERTFORD, Monday 15 November 1756

Printed from the MS now wsl; previously printed Toynbee, *Supp.* ii. 96. The MS was sold Sotheby's 5 Dec. 1921 (Waller Sale, Lot 143) to Wells for 2s.; it then passed into the possession of Thomas Conolly, from whom wsl acquired it in 1937.

London, November 15th 1756.

Dear Horry,

I DO not know when you come to town,[1] so I take this as the earliest method to acquaint you that the King has today declared to the Duke of Grafton his intention of giving away the four vacant Garters[2] on Thursday next[3] to the Duke of Devonshire, Lord Carlisle,[4] Lord Northumberland and myself, and I am most sincerely obliged to you for the friendly part you take in whatever

---

8. Apparently a reference to Frederick's victory at Lobositz, 1 Oct., full details of which reached London on 16 Oct. (MANN v. 4 and n. 6).

9. HW's letter is missing.

10. The Hon. Audrey Townshend (d. 1781) had eloped with Capt. Robert Orme (MONTAGU i. 188, n. 8).

11. HW had reported in May that she would 'certainly get' Lord George Lennox (ibid. i. 188).

---

1. HW wrote from Arlington Street on 13 Nov. and again on the 25th (MANN v. 17; MONTAGU i. 203).

2. The number of knights of the Gar-

ter was limited to twenty-six, including the King, until 1786 when provision for supernumerary knights of royal blood was made. Devonshire took the place of Lord Burlington (d. 1753), Carlisle that of the Duke of Bolton (d. 1754), Northumberland that of Lord Albemarle (d. 1754), and Hertford that of William, 3d D. of Devonshire (d. 1755) (W. A. Shaw, *The Knights of England*, 1906, Vol. I, Introduction pp. ii–iii, 42–5).

3. 18 Nov., when the four peers were invested (ibid. i. 45).

4. Henry Howard (1694–1758), 4th E. of Carlisle.

Vol 2 Nov
96

Dear Horry   London Nov.ʳ 15.ᵗʰ 1756.

I do not know when you come to town, so I take
this as the earliest method to acquaint you that the
King has to day declared to the Duke of Grafton
his intention of giving away the four vacant
Garters on thursday next to the Duke of Devonshire
Lord Carlisle Lord Northumberland and myself,
and I am most sincerely obliged to you for the
friendly part you take in whatever concerns me
for I should be unapt to confine it to this or any
other particular instance.

Lord Temple and the Lords of the Admiralty kissed
the King's hand to day and were coldly received,
my friend Legge went into the Closet for the
Seals, Lord Boteman and Dick Edgecombe have
got two white sticks, Lord Hillsborough and S.ʳ George
Lyttleton kissed the King's hand for their Peerages.

I hope to see you soon in town and am with
great truth and affection Dear Horry

most sincerely yours
Hertford

**LETTER FROM LORD HERTFORD
TO WALPOLE 15 NOVEMBER 1756**

concerns me, for I should be unjust to confine it to this or any other particular instance.

Lord Temple[5] and the Lords of the Admiralty kissed the King's hand today and were coldly received,[6] my friend Legge[7] went into the Closet for the Seals, Lord Bateman[8] and Dick Edgecombe[9] have got the two white sticks,[10] Lord Hillsbro'[11] and Sir George Lyttleton[12] kissed the King's hand for their peerages.

I hope to see you soon in town, and am with great truth and affection, dear Horry,

Most sincerely yours,

HERTFORD

5. Who was first lord of the Admiralty in the new administration. The other lords were Admiral Temple West, Admiral Edward Boscawen, Dr George Hay, John Pitt, Gilbert Elliot, and Thomas Orby Hunter (GM 1756, xxvi. 548).

6. Lord Holdernesse told Newcastle 15 Nov. that most of the new officers 'were received in the least gracious manner possible' (BM Add. MSS 32869, f. 49). Lord Temple was particularly distasteful to the King.

7. According to HW, Legge, hoping to dominate the political scene himself, had proposed Hertford as first lord of the Treasury during the efforts to form a

government in the previous month (*Mem. Geo. II* ii. 265). He was chancellor of the Exchequer in the new administration.

8. John Bateman (1721–1802), 2d Vct Bateman (Ireland), just appointed treasurer of the Household.

9. Who had just been made comptroller of the Household, an office he retained until his death.

10. Symbols of their new Household offices.

11. Lord Hillsborough, an Irish peer, had just been granted an English peerage as Bn Harwich.

12. Lyttelton had been created Bn Lyttelton of Frankley.

From LADY HERTFORD, Monday ?7 ?March 1757

Printed for the first time from a photostat of BM Add. MSS 23218, f. 4. Dated 'April ?1757' in pencil (probably by J. W. Croker) but (as the letter is dated Monday) probably 7 March 1757, since Grafton's doctors reported a considerable improvement in his condition during the preceding weekend (Dr Shaw to Newcastle 5 March 1757, Dr Hawkins to Dss of Newcastle 6 March 1757, John South to Newcastle, n.d., BM Add. MSS 32870, ff. 243, 245, 247).

Address: To the Honourable Mr Walpole.

Monday, 12 o'clock.

Sir,

MY Lord called upon you just now to let you know that my father is today a great deal better.[1] We are fearful of flattering ourselves too far, but still the change is so great in his favour that the physicians[2] have no scruples of declaring it, and the wound is better today than it has been at all. You are always so good to us that it encourages me to give you this trouble, and this is so essential a point to our happiness that I am sure it will give you pleasure to be informed of it. I am

Your faithful humble servant,

I. HERTFORD

To CONWAY, ca Thursday 26 May 1757

Missing; answered *post* 29 May 1757.

---

1. Grafton had fallen from his horse, 17 Feb., severely injuring his face and leg; the cuts, particularly one in the leg, had become infected. This rally in early March continued until he was able to take the air on the 26th, but he soon relapsed and died of his injuries on 6 May (*London Chronicle* 19–22 Feb., 26–29 March, i. 178, 297; Dr Peter Shaw to Newcastle 5 March, BM Add. MSS 32870, f. 243).

2. Grafton was attended by Dr Peter Shaw (*ante* 29 Aug. 1748, n. 10), and Dr Caesar Hawkins (1711–86), cr. (1778) Bt; surgeon to George II and George III.

From CONWAY, Sunday 29 May 1757

Printed for the first time from the MS now WSL, formerly Rutnam.

Goodwood,[1] 29 May, 1757.

Dear Horry,

I WRITE just to thank you for your letter and to let you hear a little of our motions, which are first from hence to Park Place on Monday;[2] I think that was so settled after a scuffle this morning; when I talk of our motions you'll find the history of them very short for they end there at present; my next, except a little trip of business to town,[3] will be to camp and not till the end of next month.[4] Our expectations of company are Lord and Lady Strafford on Friday next,[5] and I believe the Duke of Devonshire on Saturday who all depart on Monday following;[6] I tell you the whole of this history as I know there are circumstances you like extremely in it and others not so well.[7] Soon after that we hope to have Lady Kildare and, I fancy, Lady Caroline and Mr Fox but the day not fixed.[8] The Duchess of Richmond will also either go with us or follow us immediately and stay, I believe, most of our time or good part:[9] but in any part of it we shall always have room and an equal welcome for you so you shall choose the time you like best and the company, but remember the sooner the better and very late is the only crime you can commit.

Our family here is as full as we expected and increased this morning by Lord Ilchester,[10] Mr Fox and my sister from Chi-

---

1. Sussex, seat of the D. of Richmond, who had married Lady Ailesbury's daughter by her first marriage, Lady Mary Bruce (1740–96), on 1 April (MONTAGU i. 234, n. 18). Lady Kildare also describes this visit (*Leinster Corr.* i. 38).

2. 30 May.

3. Conway and Lady Ailesbury planned to come to London for two parties on 21 June (*post* 16 June 1757).

4. Conway had arrived at the encampment at Bradford near Dorchester by 28 June (*post* 5 July 1757).

5. 3 June. Lady Strafford was Lady Ailesbury's cousin.

6. 6 June. See *post* 9 June 1757, n. 13.

7. HW would presumably have been less glad to see the D. of Devonshire than he would the Straffords.

8. Lady Kildare, whose party included her three sons and two sisters, came 11 June, and Fox apparently 12 June (*post* 9 June 1757 and *Leinster Corr.* i. 37, 43, 46).

9. Lady Kildare wrote from Park Place 12 June, 'the Duchess of Richmond is at Goodwood, and returns here tomorrow' (ibid. i. 46).

10. Stephen Fox (after 1758 Fox Strangways) (1704–76), cr. (1741) Bn and (1756) E. of Ilchester.

chester.[11] Never was such a collection of roots and branches.[12] You were accused this morning at the public breakfast of dreading our number; I knew how truly and could only say that as I knew you liked all the family or families and persons separately you should naturally like them collectively; the reasoning and conclusion were false and Lady Caroline Fox intends to tell you so.

I think you'd make a very good figure amongst us *boys and girls*. You love romping and all the *aimables folies* just as one should love 'em as long as one lives, and are one of those pleasant creatures *whose follies please*,[13] as well as their wit.

Adieu, I have no time nor humour for politics, and feel just now as if I did not care an halfpenny who won or lost, battles or ministries. I must not say so to everybody here.[14] Let me know when we shall see you.

Yours ever,

H. S. C.

From LADY AILESBURY, Friday 3 June 1757

Printed for the first time from the MS now WSL, formerly Rutnam. Dated by the reference to the eggs, also mentioned *post* 9 and 16 June 1757; the mention of 'the rains' indicates that it was written on Friday 3 June rather than Friday 10 June, since this temporary break in the drought is also mentioned in Montagu to HW ca 29 May and HW to Montagu 2 June (MONTAGU i. 209, 210).

Address: To the Honourable Horatio Walpole at his house in Arlington Street, London.

Park Place, Friday morn.

I AM vastly obliged to you, and Lord Orford, for the eggs[1] and beg you will send them to my porter, who will take care to convey them safe to me. We wish much to see you here, and if you could

11. Hon. Henrietta Seymour Conway, Conway's half-sister (*ante* 29 Aug. 1746 OS, n. 3).

12. Henry Fox wrote to Lord George Lennox on the 27th: 'I am within this hour setting out for Goodwood, which is fully furnished now, for there are Lady Albemarle and her daughters, all your sisters and their children, Mr Conway and Lady Ailsbury, and will be tomorrow morning my brother and myself' (Hist. MSS Comm., *Bathurst MSS*, 1923, p. 679).

13. 'Whom folly pleases, and whose follies please,' the concluding line (327) of Pope's *Second Epistle of the Second Book of Horace Imitated*.

14. Especially to Henry Fox, who was at this time deeply involved in the attempts to form a new ministry (MANN v. 91–3; Lord Ilchester, *Henry Fox*, 1920, ii. 50–2).

1. Presumably plovers' eggs; see MANN ix. 143.

persuade the Churchills to come with you it would be so much the better. Adieu. I wish you joy of the rains.

Faithfully yours,

C. AILESBURY

To CONWAY, ca Tuesday 7 June 1757

Missing; answered *post* 9 June 1757.

From CONWAY, Thursday 9 June 1757

Printed for the first time from the MS now WSL, formerly Rutnam.

Park Place, 9 June, 1757.

IT would be noble in me to be so much obliged to you as I am for pimping for my wife,[1] if I did not think to be the better for it myself, which I doubt leaves me upon the level with many husbands in like circumstances. I should be sorry if our eggs were like to be as much addled as the Ministry is by yours and all the accounts I have heard,[2] which is hard too after Sir John Rushout[3] and Mrs Gibbon[4] have *sat upon* it day after day[5] as I hear they have as constantly [as] any old hens in the parish. If our friend[6] undertakes it, as I doubt is too likely, he will not sit and addle it like them, but stand upon it and break it at once, at least I fear so; and

1. Presumably by asking Lord Orford for the eggs mentioned *ante* 3 and *post* 16 June 1757.

2. Newcastle had told the King on 7 June that he would not act with Fox nor accept the Treasury without Pitt (MANN v. 97 and n. 2).

3. (1685–1775), 4th Bt; M.P. Malmesbury 1713–22, Evesham 1722–68.

4. Phillips Gybbon (1678–1762), M.P. Rye 1707–62. HW frequently ridicules his old-maidishness (MANN i. 332, n. 22).

5. Both Rushout and Gybbon had been prominent opponents of Sir Robert Walpole, but by this time they were both supporters of Newcastle (Namier and Brooke ii. 563, iii. 384). They do not appear to be

otherwise mentioned in connection with this political crisis.

6. Henry Fox; he promised the King to undertake the formation of a ministry on 8 June (MANN v. 97 and n. 3, 99 and n. 1). Conway wrote Devonshire 15 June, 'I am sorry for the news your Grace tells me as I doubt Mr F.'s ambition and his sanguine disposition to believe what he wishes will make him undertake, much at his own risk and not a little I am afraid at that of a good deal of confusion to the public affairs; he should see that this last negotiation has brought the D. of N. and Mr P. closer together and that in this situation he is absolutely in their power; he calculates upon the

in truth I am sorry because I think it hard upon the poor old King to be so dictated to and from such a quarter on one hand[7] and so deserted on the other[8] as it's probable he will.

I see no comfort but in the *greenth*[9] of our lawns and the growth of our shrubs. Everything else seems blighted and out of order; after this boast I am almost afraid to invite you here but yet my wishes get so much the better of my fears that I shall venture. *Our parties* are much in the wane, and besides you love a little reasonable society. Lady Kildare, I believe, comes tomorrow[10] with her two sisters (the young ones).[11] I don't much expect Lady C[aroline] Fox and Mr Fox not at all.[12] So you see to what we are reduced, and you know nobody is so easy and so agreeable as Lady Kildare. The Duke of Dev[onshire] may possibly come for one day.[13] So do come soon; I have told you the whole truth; you see we have room and if you stay till the ministry or the nation are settled we mayn't see you till the French are in possession.

Yours ever,

H. S. C.

To CONWAY, ca Saturday 11 June 1757

Missing; implied *post* 12 June 1757.

vanity of mankind and the effect of his M[ajesty]'s favour and power; which might be just in most cases, but I think false in this; where the cry of the people, the general turn of the Parliament, and the influence of Leicester House are against him—or if upon their generosity, more so' (Chatsworth MSS, 416 / 42).

7. Leicester House, whose interest Pitt at this time represented. Newcastle had 'told the King that he could not take the Treasury unless terms were agreed upon to satisfy Leicester House' (Henry Digby to Sir Charles Hanbury Williams 12 June, Williams's MSS, now WSL, lxiii. f. 54).

8. By Newcastle's followers, who began resigning on the 10th and 11th (MANN v. 98 and n. 6, 99–100 and n. 4).

9. One of HW's favourite words to describe SH in the spring; see *ante* 23 Aug. 1752 OS, n. 6a.

10. She arrived Saturday 11 June (*Leinster Corr.* i. 45–6).

11. Lady Louisa Augusta Lennox (1743–1821), m. (1758) Rt Hon. Thomas Conolly; and Lady Sarah Lennox (1745–1826) m. 1 (1762) Sir Thomas Charles Bunbury, 6th Bt; m. 2 (1781) Hon. George Napier. Lady Kildare wrote ca 7 June of her visit to Park Place, 'The boys and girls are all to go with me; they [the Conways] insisted upon it I should bring them' (ibid. i. 43; see also ibid. i. 47).

12. Because of the ministerial negotiations (above, n. 6). However, Lady Kildare wrote 12 June from Park Place, 'We expect him [Fox] here this evening' (*Leinster Corr.* i. 46).

13. He arrived 12 June (ibid.; Conway to Devonshire, 15 June, loc. cit.).

From CONWAY, Sunday 12 June 1757

Printed for the first time from the MS now WSL, formerly Rutnam. The year is supplied by the allusion in the third paragraph.

Address: To the Honourable Horatio Walpole in Arlington Street, London.

Postmark: 13 IV.

Park Place, 16 June.

I THANK you for your pictures and list[1] which are safe arrived, the former much liked, but soon discovered as the makers of such presents are not numerous with folks of our note.

I am prepared to hear of a vast deal of good of your doing,[2] and not a little curious for it as you may guess; you say nothing about your coming here so for that we must trust to Providence and the way you are in of doing good works, and really besides our inclinations we actually want you to consult and advise, not about settling nations and ministries, but a little of our garden jobs, so do come before our beauty goes, and while our fine weather lasts.

I am not sorry affairs have taken this last turn[3] as it is much the least of two evils, public and private.

Adieu! Our company goes on Tuesday, so don't live in dread of our parties.

Yours ever,

H. S. C.

Lady A. will thank you *here*.

---

1. Missing and unexplained.

2. HW had proposed to Lord George Sackville, with Fox's consent, a scheme whereby 'the King should send *carte blanche* to Pitt, to place the Duke of Dorset at the head of the Treasury, with Lord George for secretary at war, and, by dissolving the Parliament, dissipate at once Newcastle's influence. . . . Lord George Sackville owned he should have liked the plan, but was now too far engaged. . . . Thus this plan failed' (*Mem. Geo. II* iii. 28–9).

3. On 11 June the King had accepted Fox's representation of the improbability

of his forming a ministry, and had authorized Lord Mansfield to tell Newcastle and Pitt 'to make what ministry they can' subject to certain conditions (MANN v. 99 and n. 3). Conway wrote Devonshire 15 June, 'I can form but little judgment how prudent or necessary it is for his M[ajesty] to accept them [Pitt's terms] or reject them, but think very clearly that nothing less than necessity should make him do the latter, as in the temper his Grace of N. seems to be in I own I look upon Mr F.'s attempt as a most desperate one' (Chatsworth MSS, 416 / 42).

From CONWAY, Thursday 16 June 1757

Printed from the MS now WSL, formerly Rutnam. Previously printed *Fraser's Magazine*, 1850, xli. 423. The year is supplied by the contents.

Memoranda (by HW):

> Why not Seals last Saturday [illegible]
> if Ld Winchelsea's message[1]
> D. of Bedf[ord]
> K. of Prussia's demands[2]
> What K. blamed him for if
> made overtures to Leicester H[ouse]
> What letter in contest today

> > Prosp[ero] Lambertini[3]
> >   Bishop of Rome
> > by the name of Ben[edict XIV]
> > Who tho' an absolute Prince
> >   reigned as harmlessly
> >   as a Doge of Venise
> > He restored the lustre of the Tiara
> >   by those arts alone,
> > by which alone He obtained it,
> >   his Virtues
> >   Adored by Papists
> > Esteemed by Protestants
> >   A Priest
> > Without insolence or interest
> >   A Prince
> > Without favourites
> >   A Pope
> > Without nepotism
> >   An Author
> > Without vanity
> >   In short
> >   A Man
> > Whom neither Wit nor Power
> >   could spoil

> Mr Conway
> Mr Montagu

1. References to the changes in the ministry discussed in *Mem. Geo. II* iii. 29–34; MANN v. 99, 103–5; see also HW's list in MONTAGU i. 211. Winchelsea acted 'with honour and noble spirit . . . he refused a pension, disdaining to accept any emolument, when his associates were excluded' (*Mem. Geo. II*, iii. 32).

2. See MANN v. 102; *Mem. Geo. II* iii. 36.

3. This inscription, written by HW behind a bas-relief in wax of Benedict XIV, is printed in MANN v. 105 and illustrated in COLE ii facing p. 79.

Mr Bentley
Mr Murray[?]

Park Place, 16 June.

Dear Horry,

I HEAR you are gone back to Strawberry,[4] but talk of coming here towards the end of the week;[5] I wish at once almost that you would and would not; the latter can only be for one reason which is that we shall have too little of your company which is always the case with us to a mortifying degree; however, we go to town only on Tuesday[6] for a party at Vauxhall and a party at Court and come back on Wednesday, so if you won't give us more of your company after that than you can before do come as soon as this can bring you, or if it is after Wednesday it must indeed be immediately after as my encampment follows dreadfully near it.

I am anxious to know something of the Duke[7] who I hear has probably been engaged by this time and with a much superior force,[8] so bring or send me all your news. I can't say I feel so much anxiety for the Ministry, be they who they will.[9]

Lady Ailesbury returns you ten thousand thanks for every one of the ten charming eggs you sent and desires they may be remitted to Lord Orford, who has been very good. They were set immediately and she has now a month of great anxiety to pass for their delivery. I hate to be importunate or should repeat how much we want and wish for you, being

Most truly yours,

H. S. C.

---

4. HW was still in London on 14 June, but he told Montagu on the 18th that he had come to town from SH the previous evening (MANN v. 99; MONTAGU i. 212).

5. HW apparently did not do so.

6. 21 June. Conway wrote Devonshire 19 June, 'I am very sorry we cannot have the honour of dining with your Grace as we have engaged ourselves if we stay in town as I don't believe we shall. I shall endeavour to see you in the morning, if you give me leave. Lady A. thinks your going to Vaux Hall would be a right and clever thing. We meet at Holland House and dine there at Vaux Hall if fine' (Chatsworth MSS, 416 / 44).

7. Of Cumberland, commanding the 'Army of Observation' in Germany.

8. News had reached London on the morning of the 15th that the French were within fifteen miles of Cumberland (Daily Adv. 16 June). No battle took place because the Duke retreated (MANN v. 109, n. 7).

9. The negotiations with Pitt for the formation of a new ministry, begun on the 11th (ante 12 June 1757, n. 3) were not completed until the 17th (MANN v. 103, nn. 1–3).

From CONWAY, Tuesday 5 July 1757

Printed from the MS now WSL, formerly Rutnam. Previously printed *Fraser's Magazine*, 1850, xli. 423–4.
Memoranda (by HW):

Ly A. ⎫
Mr C ⎬ 9th
£20 and 20 adv^d

Bradford,[1] near Dorchester 5 July 1757.

Dear Horry,

I HAVE now been a week at camp here and was beginning to think it was hard I should be so long without hearing from you, especially as that short period has been filled with the greatest events, foreign and domestic, but I have recollected that if I have been a week here without hearing from you I have also been no less without writing to you and that I should have let you know of my good journey and safe arrival: events which though they don't count with the settlement of ministries, and the decision of battles, I own I was wanting and neglectful not to inform you of; as well as of my direction which is explained in the date of this.

Amidst the terrible dilemma this last news must throw us into I was glad to hear some settlement was *made* in the Ministry,[2] though I much doubt there is more disjointure to our affairs in the King of Prussia's defeat[3] than any coalition of our ministers can retrieve, who whether they will or can do much towards it are

1. Bradford Peverell, about 3 miles from Dorchester. Conway also wrote Devonshire from Bradford on 4 July, 'I am now a little settled to my camp life, and, for myself, with as much convenience as fully satisfies me; how Lady A. will find it when she comes I don't know, tho' to do her justice she's a good soldier's wife and pretty easy about these things' (Chatsworth MSS, 416 / 41).

2. The settlement of the Ministry began on 18 June but was not completed until 29 June, when the new Ministry kissed hands (MANN v. 103, n. 3).

3. Frederick the Great had been defeated at the battle of Kolin on 18 June; the news reached London on 1 July, not

on 24 June as is generally stated (ibid. v. 95, n. 1, 109 and n. 4). Conway wrote Devonshire 4 July, 'The K. of Prussia was everything to us on the Continent, we scarce hold to it but by him, and that hold I look upon as in a manner lopped off by this disaster; for he was over-matched, his power was fictitious, and just so constituted as to be in a manner destroyed by the final check: this opinion I always had of it both before and since his late success, and I doubt shall now see too well confirmed by the conse-quences of this single action, tho' his troops were not half engaged and the mere loss in numbers may perhaps not be very considerable' (loc. cit.).

points I am little able to discuss. As to the old branches[4] I say nothing; as to the new ones[5] I know little of their abilities as statesmen and a great deal too much of all their shameful factions, jealousies and ambition.[6]

I hear Lady Ailesbury is to make you a visit at Strawberry,[7] which I congratulate her upon; I wish you would return it here, and really, as I have often told you, a camp is a sight well worth a journey, but if the love of novelty does not tempt you, perhaps the love of antiquity may and if you don't like English camps, here are Roman ones in abundance and Saxon and Danish,[8] and causeys and amphitheatres[9] and tumuli, barrows[10] and I don't know what fine things all older than each other: you may dig up coins and bones and old pavements by the cart-load;[11] here's an old house where a French king was lodged;[12] I don't know who he was but it's the oldest thing in the world except its master Mr Trenchard,[13] whom perhaps you remember, and his family who have been settled here since the Deluge.[14]

Our camp is now just formed and I am fairly set into my military

4. The followers of Newcastle and Fox.

5. Pitt's followers and the Leicester House representation.

6. Conway expressed this opinion to Devonshire 4 July: 'A thorough exertion of our force by sea and against the French settlements is now the only thing that humanly speaking can possibly restore our desperate game, and how well or how successfully our new coalition will play it time only can show; what their ability as ministers and statesmen is few know, but the shameful factions and jealousies amongst 'em we are all too well acquainted with.'

7. See the following letter.

8. The British (or Roman) camp of Poundbury is at Dorchester, which was the important Roman town of Durnovaria. Maiden Castle, one of the finest prehistoric forts in England, is two miles south.

9. The so-called Maumbury Rings at Dorchester, of prehistoric origin, were converted into one of the finest Roman amphitheatres in England (L. V. Grinsell, *The Archæology of Wessex,* 1958, pp. 76, 191–2, 306–7).

10. The numerous barrows in the parish

of Bradford Peverell are described in Royal Commission on Historical Monuments, *An Inventory of the Historical Monuments in Dorset,* 1952– , i. 35–6.

11. An account of some of the Roman remains in Dorchester is in Grinsell, op. cit. 187–92.

12. Wolfeton House at Charminster, 2 miles NW of Dorchester, built by John, father of Sir Thomas Trenchard in the reign of Henry VII. The king who had stayed there was not King of France, but Philip of Burgundy (1478–1506), King of Castile, who was forced to land in England by a storm in early 1506 and lived for a time at Wolfeton. There is an account of the house in *Memorials of Old Dorset,* ed. Thomas Perkins and Herbert Pentin, 1907, pp. 264–72.

13. George Trenchard (ca 1684–1758), M.P. Poole 1713–41, 1747–54 (John Hutchins, *History and Antiquities of the County of Dorset,* 3d edn, ed. W. Shipp and J. W. Hodson, Westminster, 1861–70, iii. 327).

14. The genealogy of the family in Hutchins, op. cit. iii. 326–7, traces them back to the reign of Henry I.

life. I won't tell you what sort of one it is for fear you should not like it.

Adieu. I can't help thinking when we are clubbing and shouldering here how little we shall probably contribute to support the Duke,[15] or the King of Prussia, or save poor Hanover! Pray let me have a word from you sometimes; you will when you know the pleasure it gives

Your aff[ectionate] friend and coz,

H. S. C.

From LADY AILESBURY, Thursday 7 July 1757

Printed for the first time from the MS now WSL, formerly Rutnam. Misdated by Lady Ailesbury: Thursday was 7, not 6, July in 1757.

Essendon,[1] Thursday, July 6 [7], '57.

I SHALL have in my power to visit you at Strawberry any day you please after Wednesday with my small companions, Miss Rich and Missy, so you have only to name the day.[2] I thought it best to give this early notice that I might not interfere with any other engagement of yours. The lawn's face at Park Place is now just the colour of my face,[3] and I hope when I have the pleasure of coming into the neighbourhood of Twickenham, to see but *one face* that is not of the same complexion. I shall not go home till Monday, so that if you have any commands for me before that time, pray send them to Essendon, near Hatfield. I am, dear Mr Walpole,

Faithfully yours,

C. AILESBURY

15. Conway wrote Devonshire 4 July that 'the news of this day has . . . given me more melancholy sensations both for his M[ajesty] and his R[oyal] H[ighness] than I have yet felt; I know nothing more to be pitied than they are. The Duke's situation was always bad but now it really appears desperate; to support himself till the K. of Prussia could assist him was I believe as much as his most sanguine friends could hope or expect from him, but now in truth I doubt the best can only be a protraction of some disagreeable I won't say fatal event.'

1. Herts, 3 miles east of Hatfield (*Vict. Co. Hist. Herts* iii. 458–61).

2. HW told Chute 12 July that he expected Lady Ailesbury on Thursday, the 14th (CHUTE 98).

3. HW makes similar comments about the drought in his letter to Strafford 4 July 1757 (ibid. 282).

From Conway, Thursday 4 August 1757

Printed for the first time from the MS now wsl, formerly Rutnam.
Endorsed (by HW): Aug. 4, 1757.

L[ittle] War[wick] Street, Thursday morning.

Dear Horry,

As I fancy we shall not be gone till Sunday or Monday[1] I could not help taking this chance of seeing you again by letting you know it though I would not have you hurry up any more without you are disengaged and quite choose it.[2]

I am heartily sorry to tell you the shocking news of the Duke's having lost a battle;[3] it does not seem to have been general.[4] I think only 12 or 14 battalions engaged, and the loss is said to be not very considerable;[5] yet there is retreat[6] and loss of spirits before a much superior army,[7] which are bad circumstances. The Duke and all his family[8] are said to be safe though he exposed himself very

1. Conway wrote Devonshire from London 19 July: 'I was hurried up from our camp on Wednesday last [13 July] with Sir J. Mordaunt by a sudden order, and found, as we imagined, that his M[ajesty] had some commands for us on another duty, which is to embark with some troops that are soon to be sent out, it is not said where, but intimated, to relieve the D. [of Cumberland]' (Chatsworth MSS, 416 / 45). Conway was appointed second in command of the land forces in a projected secret expedition to Rochefort, the general plan of which had been arranged at a Cabinet Council on 15 July (MANN v. 117–18 and nn. 6–8; *Grenville Papers* i. 200). According to HW, Conway had at first been designed to command alone, 'but the King said he was too young, and insisted on joining Mordaunt with him' (*Mem. Geo. II* iii. 46).

2. HW came to London on the evening of the 5th (HW to Lord George Sackville 6 Aug. 1757).

3. The battle of Hastenbeck 24–6 July; early reports through Hanover had reached London on 2 Aug. and were communicated to the King and ministers on the morning of the 3d, but full details were not received until the 9th (MANN

v. 119 and nn. 1–3; Newcastle to Hardwicke 3 Aug., BM Add. MSS 32872, f. 426). HW summarizes this account from Conway in his letter to Mann of 4 Aug. (MANN v. 119).

4. The early reports stated that only Cumberland's left wing had been engaged (Newcastle to Hardwicke 3 Aug., loc. cit.; Newcastle to Ashburnham 4 Aug., ibid. f. 443; *London Chronicle* 2–4 Aug., ii. 119–20).

5. 'The loss (that is our loss) is inconsiderable, not above 600 men' (Newcastle to Hardwicke 3 Aug., loc. cit.). The total casualties on the Hanoverian side, including wounded and missing, were in fact about 1500; the French lost about 2300 (Evan Charteris, *William Augustus, Duke of Cumberland and the Seven Years' War*, [1925], p. 280).

6. Cumberland retreated to Stade (MANN v. 119, n. 3).

7. Cumberland estimated the French forces to be 80,000 effectives (other estimates run from 65,000 to 100,000); he had a force of between 30,000 and 40,000 (Charteris, op. cit. 274).

8. His English staff, the only English with him; a list of them is in MANN v. 78.

much, which is the more extraordinary as the attack in some measure lasted three days. The first two were I suppose only cannonades and attack of posts.[9] On the third the French passed the Weser, which was on the Duke's right, with a fresh corps of 20,000 men,[10] the river being then exceeding low with the great dryness of the season. On the whole I think it throws Hanover into the hands of the French,[11] I mean the country, and will end the German War— which will put us again upon our defence and bring the whole weight of the French force against us.

Adieu. I don't mean this for my last; but if it is so most sincerely wish you health, spirits and better news till our return, being, dear Horry,

Most affectionately yours,

H. S. C.

They are to have, I believe, a final council on our affairs today[12] and the Dukes of B[edford] and D[evonshire] *invited to it*.[13]

---

9. This was correct.

10. This reinforcement, mentioned in the first reports of the battle, does not seem to have taken place. The main French army had crossed the Weser on 16 July (Newcastle to Hardwicke 3 Aug., loc. cit.; Newcastle to Campion 4 Aug., ibid. f. 445; Hardwicke to Newcastle 4 Aug., ibid. f. 441; Charteris, op. cit. 263, 266).

11. It effectively did so; Cumberland retreated to Stade and signed the Convention of Klosterzeven with the French, neutralizing Hanover, on 8 Sept. (MANN v. 136 and n. 1; SELWYN 142, n. 7).

12. Conway attended this meeting, at which it was recommended that the expedition 'be forthwith undertaken' and which 'unanimously approved' the instructions for the commanders drawn up by Pitt (Minutes, BM Add. MSS 32997, f. 241). The instructions themselves are dated the 5th. Both the naval and military officers, including Conway, had initially opposed the expedition as impracticable

(*post* 11 Aug. 1757, n. 6), but at a meeting on 2 Aug. a French pilot and Capt. Clerk (*post* 28 Sept. 1758, n. 4) were examined and gave 'entire satisfaction, both to the admirals and generals'; this change of opinion was 'fully confirmed' by Conway to Newcastle on the morning of the 3d (Newcastle to Hardwicke 3 Aug., BM Add. MSS 32872, f. 429; Holdernesse to Newcastle 2 Aug., ibid. f. 413; *Report of the General Officers, appointed . . . to inquire into the Causes of the Failure of the Late Expedition to the Coasts of France*, 1758, pp. 68–81).

13. On 24 July Newcastle had been asking whether Bedford 'should not be acquainted with . . . the expedition,' and on the 3d reported that Bedford and Devonshire had been added to the meeting on the 4th 'by the King's order.' They both attended ('Considerations for the Meeting on Tuesday,' 24 July, BM Add. MSS 32997, f. 233; Minutes, 4 Aug. ibid. f. 241; Newcastle to Hardwicke 3 Aug., loc. cit.).

From CONWAY, Thursday 11 August 1757

Printed from the MS now WSL, formerly Rutnam. Previously printed *Fraser's Magazine*, 1850, xli. 424.

Newport[1] in the Isle of Wight, 11 August 1757.

Dear Horry,

THIS is now the third day since my arrival here, and I find our situation just the same as when I came; that is, in an hourly expectation of the transports;[2] being constantly told the wind was fair and good, though, by the bye, it has been all round the compass. I saw the admirals[3] yesterday, and find, by their accounts, the men-of-war will be ready in a few days,[4] so that probably our stay may not be long.

I had this morning a long account from Lord Frederick[5] of the Hanoverian affairs, particularly the action of the 26th, etc., which confirms all that had been said of the small loss of troops, the safety of the Duke and his family, the retreat of the army, etc. I want much to hear of the ulterior operations; for though Hanover is, I think, destined to be lost, the time and manner are material.

Of certain other affairs I think much as I did;[6] though not quite

1. Where the troops for the expedition were being assembled. Conway also wrote Devonshire from Newport 14 Aug., giving similar news (Chatsworth MSS, 416 / 46).

2. 'On Thursday [11 Aug.] upwards of 50 large transports for the fleet at Portsmouth were seen in the Swin under sail, the wind at NNE' (*London Chronicle* 11–13 Aug., ii. 151). They were held in the Downs by contrary winds until 4 Sept. (*post* 7 Sept. 1757). A list of them is in the *Report of the General Officers, appointed . . . to inquire into the Causes of the Failure of the Late Expedition to the Coasts of France*, 1758, p. 85.

3. Sir Edward Hawke, the commander-in-chief; Vice-Adm. Knowles; and Rear-Adm. Brodrick (MANN v. 118, n. 6).

4. 'The Admirals have made a general muster of the men on board the fleet, and a survey of the ships, and have determined that the *Royal Anne* and *Royal Sovereign* are not fit to go; but all the rest of the men-of-war now at Spithead

are ordered. The greatest dispatch and vigilance are made use of by the Admirals; and if the transports would but make their appearance, a few days would send this great armament to sea' ('Letter from Portsmouth, dated August 9th,' quoted *Daily Adv.* 11 Aug.). The fleet was reported 'all completed for sea' in another letter from Portsmouth of 15 Aug. (ibid. 17 Aug.). A list of the ships ordered for the expedition is in *Report of the General Officers*, pp. 83–4.

5. Lord Frederick Cavendish (1729–1803), army officer; M.P. Derbyshire 1751–4, Derby 1754–80; one of Cumberland's lords of the Bedchamber, who was with him in Germany (MANN v. 78 and n. 13). His letter to Conway is missing; it presumably came on the 9th with the full accounts of the battle of Hastenbeck (ibid. v. 119, n. 3).

6. Despite his final approval of the expedition (*ante* 4 Aug. 1757, n. 12), Conway had grave reservations about it. HW

so neither, as more imprudences and mismanagements which I cannot specify⁷ have, I doubt, added to the hopelessness of it. I hate there should be a subject on which I cannot write freely to you; but so the present must be.

I desire you'll write a line, as I shall probably have it before I go, and if not will take care of it. I must now finish hastily, being to send this by a gentleman who calls for it.

This island is a most delightful spot and might rank with most part of our little continent. Adieu! dear Horry. You may perhaps hear from me again. If not, believe that I remain most affectionately and sincerely yours,

H. S. C.

To CONWAY, Sunday 14 August 1757

Printed from *Works* v. 52–3.

Strawberry Hill, August 14, 1757.

YOU are too kind to me, and, if it were possible, would make me feel still more for your approaching departure.¹ I can only thank you ten thousand times; for I must not expatiate, both from the nature of the subject, and from the uncertainty of this letter reaching you. I was told yesterday, that you had hanged a French spy in the Isle of Wight;² I don't mean you, but your government.

says that both he and Mordaunt 'had ill conceit of the service in question' and gives a brief account of Conway's initial criticisms of the plans before the Cabinet Council in *Mem. Geo. II* iii. 46–7. Newcastle describes him and Mordaunt as 'full of apprehensions' in a letter of 21 July; he mentions 'the doubts of the generals' and 'Sir John Ligonier's paper in answer to them' in memoranda of the 24th; and further describes their opposition in another letter of the 25th (Newcastle to Hardwicke 21, 25 July, BM Add. MSS 32872, ff. 286, 320; 'Considerations for the meeting on Tuesday,' 24 July, BM Add. MSS 32997, f. 234; Rex Whitworth, *Field Marshal Lord Ligonier*, Oxford,1958, pp. 220–2).

7. Some of these undoubtedly concerned the failure to give adequate instructions about court martials and about what to do if the fleet were unable to get into harbour after sighting the French coast, and above all, the failure to provide adequate transport space for the expedition, all subjects of much correspondence between the commanders and the authorities in London during August (*Report of the General Officers*, pp. 86–94; J. S. Corbett, *England in the Seven Years' War*, 1907, i. 205).

1. On the expedition to Rochfort (HW).
2. Conway denies this report *post* 29 Aug. 1757. No other mention of it has been found.

Though I wish no life taken away, it was some satisfaction to think that the French were at this hour wanting information.[3]

Mr Fox breakfasted here t'other day. He confirmed what you tell me of Lord Frederick Cavendish's account: it is universally said that the Duke[4] failed merely by inferiority, the French soldiers behaving in general most scandalously. They had fourscore pieces of cannon, but very ill served. Marshal d'Estrées[5] was recalled before the battle, but did not know it.[6] He is said to have made some great mistakes in the action.[7] I cannot speak to the truth of it, but the French are reported to have demanded two millions sterling of Hanover.[8]

My whole letter will consist of hearsays; for, even at so little distance from town, one gets no better news than hawkers and pedlars retail about the country. From such I hear that George Haldane[9] is made Governor of Jamaica, and that a Mr Campbell,[10]

---

3. The exact destination was kept a secret, although the preparations were causing general consternation all along the French coast (J. S. Corbett, *England in the Seven Years' War*, 1907, i. 194–6).

4. The Duke of Cumberland, in the affair at Hastenbeck (HW).

5. Louis-Charles-César le Tellier de Louvois (1695–1771), Comte (later, 1763, Duc) d'Estrées; Maréchal de France, 1757 (MANN vi. 47, n. 10).

6. He had been informed of his supersession by Richelieu in a letter from Louis XV of 30 July and although not recalled, resigned his command. The news apparently reached London with the full account of Hastenbeck about 9 Aug. (*Grenville Papers* i. 204–5); further details are in the *London Chronicle* 11–13 Aug., ii. 150. Louis XV's letter is quoted ibid. 18–20 Aug., ii. 175.

7. He had begun to order a retreat at the very time that Cumberland had decided to retire (Evan Charteris, *William Augustus, Duke of Cumberland, and the Seven Years' War*, [1925], pp. 279–80).

8. 'Some private letters by the last Dutch mail say, that the French have offered to evacuate the territories of Hanover, in consideration of two millions sterling, if they could find anybody in England foolish enough to give them such a sum; that is to say, they want

money to carry their point against Great Britain; being sensible that, in the long run, they will miscarry in Germany' (*London Chronicle* 9–11 Aug., ii. 138).

9. (1722–59), Lt-Col., 1749; Col. 1758; M.P. Stirling burghs 1747–58. The *London Chronicle* 18–20 Aug., ii. 170, prints the same report, but he was not appointed governor of Jamaica until 27 Jan. 1758. At this time he had apparently just been refused the governorship of New York (Namier and Brooke ii. 564). His appointment to Jamaica was a return for his services in obtaining the freedom of the guild merchants of Stirling for Pitt earlier in 1757 (Paul Langford, 'William Pitt and Public Opinion, 1757,' *English Historical Review*, 1973, lxxxviii. 61). See also Sir J. H. L. Haldane, *The Haldanes of Gleneagle*, Edinburgh, 1929, pp. 163–9.

10. Robert Campbell, Lt, 3d Foot Guards, 1745; Capt.-Lt, 1756; Capt., 1759; Lt-Col. in the army, 1756; Col., 1762; apparently retired, 1767 (*Army Lists*, 1756, p. 3[1]; 1757, pp. 9, 30; 1758, p. 44; 1759, p. 45; 1763, p. 7). His credentials as minister resident to Sweden were dated 12 Aug. and his instructions, 27 Aug. He left for Sweden 19 Aug. and was at Stockholm from 8 Sept. until about 22 Dec., but his mission was unsuccessful (D. B. Horn, *British Diplomatic Representatives*

whose father¹¹ lives in Sweden, is going thither to make an alliance with that country, and hire 12,000 men. If one of my acquaintance, as an antiquary, were alive, Sir Anthony Shirley,¹² I suppose we should send him to Persia again for troops; I fear we shall get none nearer!

Adieu, my dearest Harry! Next to wishing your expedition stillborn, my most constant thought is, how to be of any service to poor Lady A.,¹³ whose reasonable concern makes even that of the strongest friendship seem trifling.

Yours most entirely,

HOR. WALPOLE

1689–1789, 1932, p. 143 [Camden Society, 3d ser., Vol. XLVI]; *London Chronicle* 20–3 Aug., ii. 177). According to the newspapers he was 'bred' in Sweden 'and speaks most of the northern languages' (ibid. 18–20 Aug., ii. 170).

11. Robert Campbell (d. 1758), who had been in business in Stockholm since at least 1707 (*Svenskt Biografiskt Lexikon*, Stockholm, 1918– , vii. 263).

12. Sir Thomas [1564–ca 1630], Sir Anthony [1565–?1635], and Sir Robert Shirley [or Sherley] [ca 1581–1628] were three brothers, all great travellers, and all distinguished by extraordinary adventures in the reigns of Queen Elizabeth and James I (HW). Much confusion has ensued in their history from their adventures being confounded together. Lord Orford, it would seem, had intended to clear up these mistakes, as among his papers are many notes on this subject, and references to all the books which mention any part of their history. Sir Anthony Shirley, after sixteen years' travels, went into Persia, was in high favour with the Sophi, married a relation of his and was sent by him ambassador to James I in 1611. See Baker's *History of James I*, p. 132, who by mistake calls him Sir

Robert instead of Sir Anthony (Mary Berry). Sir Anthony had gone to Persia in 1599 on a commercial and political mission under instructions from the E. of Essex: he published a *Relation of his Travels into Persia*, 1613. At this time HW was familiar with it through the reprint in Green's *New General Collection of Voyages*, 1745–7 (Hazen, *Cat. of HW's Lib.*, No. 542; 3d vol. now wsl), as he noted in his MS 'Book of Materials,' 1759. He also refers to it in a long MS note in his copy of Vertue's *Catalogue and Description of King Charles I's Capital Collection*, 1757, p. 163 (Hazen, op. cit., No. 2478, now wsl). HW was subsequently given a copy of the original edition by Michael Lort in 1778 (CHATTERTON 173; Hazen, op. cit. No. 3827).

13. Conway wrote 19 July to Devonshire, 'Your Grace may imagine this causes some alarm in our little domestic system, which I must struggle with as well as I can; and in truth tho' Lady A. is as reasonable as anyone in her situation can well be, it would rather be affectation and injustice to her, than modesty in myself not to say that her uneasiness on this occasion is a great distress to me' (Chatsworth MSS, 416 / 45).

From CONWAY, Monday 29 August 1757

Printed from the MS now wSL, formerly Rutnam. Previously printed *Fraser's Magazine*, 1850, xli. 425.

Newport, 29 Aug. 1757.

Dear Horry,

YOU'LL be a good deal surprised that I am still writing to you from this place, and with so little news of *any kind* to tell you. I could make some reflections upon that if I might; whenever I do, I have a notion you and I shall not disagree in opinion on many things that pass.

As to our situation, it is just as it was; the transports still in the Downs, and the wind still at west, from which it has blown very hard of late, so that it has even been a doubt with some of our seafaring men whether the transports could ride it out there.

Your reflection upon the French spy was very just and very comfortable, but like many excellent reasonings, wanted the foundation of fact. We have hanged no French spies here; it is not the way with us; for, among the crowds of them that frequent us, from lords down to barbers, I don't remember an instance of such a cruelty exercised.

You have heard of Lady Die Spencer's match with Lord Bolingbroke,[1] which should break three or four hearts of our acquaintance; on his part, the beautiful Countess's[2] at least; and on hers, my poor aide-de-camp's[3] and George West's,[4] at least the latter, for Hamilton's, indeed, stood its trial when she changed to him.[5] It was ridiculous enough that, the morning before we heard this news, he and Fitzroy[6] were talking it over with me, and that Hamilton said

1. Lady Diana Spencer (1734–1808), m. 1 (8 Sept. 1757) Frederick St John (1734–87), 2d Vct Bolingbroke (divorced, 1768); m. 2 (1768) Topham Beauclerk.

2. Lady Coventry; HW mentions her 'passion' for Bolingbroke in MONTAGU i. 185, 203, 280 and CHUTE 163.

3. William Hamilton (1730–1803), Ensign 3d Foot Guards 1747, Lt 1753, ret. 1758; M.P. Midhurst 1761–4; envoy to Naples 1764–1800; K. B. 1772; HW's correspondent.

4. Hon. George West (*ante* ca 9 May 1755, n. 2).

5. HW, in announcing the approaching marriage in a letter to Selwyn 6 Sept., calls her 'Lady Diana Hamilton West' (SELWYN 137).

6. Charles Fitzroy (1737–97), cr. (1780) Bn Southampton; younger brother of the D. of Grafton; at this time a captain in the 1st Foot Guards (Namier and Brooke ii. 435).

he was sure that she would soon forget George West, and that he would lay a wager she married within an year from *inclination,* which I believe is quite the case.[7]

We have had a good many people here. Among the rest the Duke and Duchess of Richmond for one day from Goodwood, where they had leave from camp for a week.[8] Lord Huntington[9] remains, and is a great help to our society; to mine particularly, as I admire his life and good humour excessively.

When you have any news, if any reaches you at that great distance from town, do let me hear it, or, if you have none, I shall still hope to hear from you; for God knows how long I may stay. You are very good about Lady Ailesbury. I know she is good enough to want comfort; and the best you can give her is to go and see her, if you have time.[10]

You don't tell me a word of your great work[11] but as you seem so settled at Strawberry, I conclude it goes on fast.

Our Swedish envoy will, I hope, be more successful than our other ministers have been. I don't wonder we send there, nor should much if we did to Persia, as it seems quite our business to beat up for allies all over the world.

7. Mrs Delany wrote of the engagement 4 Sept. that it was 'not against the lady's consent as was reported. They were together on a party at Vauxhall, with the Duke and Duchess of Bedford; the company were teasing Lord Bolingbroke to marry, and he turned quick about to Lady Diana and said, "Will you have me?" "Yes, to be sure," she replied. It passed off that night as a joke, but with consideration on his side of the lady's merit . . . and the persuasion of his friends, he made a serious affair of it and was accepted' (Mary Granville, Mrs Delany, *Autobiography and Correspondence,* ed. Lady Llanover, 1861–2, iii. 465).

8. Richmond wrote to his brother Lord George Lennox on 9 Sept from Barham Downs camp: 'I got leave of absence from hence for a week and went to Goodwood and from thence to see them in the Isle of Wight. They were encamped between Niewport and Cowes. Then waiting for the transports, which were kept by contrary winds in the Downs' (Hist. MSS Comm., *Bathurst MSS,* 1923, pp. 680–1). Conway mentions this visit in a letter to Devonshire of 24 Aug. (Chatsworth MSS, 416 / 47).

9. Francis Hastings (1729–89), 10th E. of Huntingdon. For his friendship with Conway, see *ante* 25 July 1756, n. 3. Conway wrote Devonshire 24 Aug., 'We have had many visitors here among the rest my Lord Huntingdon who has been here a week and more and has made a red frock and is as military as any of us; we have plays and balls and horse races not of the first order you'll imagine but very good camp amusements.'

10. HW apparently did so in late September (*post* 16 Sept. 1757).

11. Printing at the SH Press. It had begun operation on 16 July; Gray's *Odes* were completed 8 Aug. and on the same day HW began to print Hentzner's *Journey into England,* which however was not finished until Oct. (Hazen, *SH Bibl.* 23, 31).

Adieu, and believe me, dear Horry, most faithfully yours,

H. S. C.

To Conway, ca Wednesday 31 August 1757

Missing; answered *post* 3 Sept. 1757. Since Conway says there that HW had not received his of the 29th when he wrote last, HW's letter must have been written at least a day or two after Conway's letter.

From Conway, Saturday 3 September 1757

Printed from the MS now WSL, formerly Rutnam. Previously printed *Fraser's Magazine*, 1850, xli. 425–6. The year is supplied by the contents.

Newport, 3d September.

IF you have received my letter, you'll know by this time that I have not lost yours,[1] though, as you had not when you wrote last, I begin to think you may not. It's only material that you should know I did not neglect you, for which purpose I now write.

I am grown a mere weathercock, and, as you say, can only tell you news about the wind. However, that news is news at present, as it has changed this very day,[2] and will now do very well for the transports if it continues. Other news, indeed, know I none; least of all relating to ourselves, who, as far as we know, are the last thing thought of, having had no communication with any of the great for some time.[3]

You'll have heard of all the American news;[4] the disappointment

1. *Ante* 14 Aug. 1757.
2. HW also mentions on the 3d that the wind, after having blown from the west for nearly three weeks, had just changed to the east (MANN v. 130).
3. The ministers were in fact discussing whether the expedition should be abandoned because of the lateness of the season and the accumulation of evidence of French preparations to meet it, or be diverted to Stade to assist Cumberland.

Any diversion or abandonment was vigorously opposed by Pitt, whose views prevailed (Newcastle's 'Memoranda' 29 Aug., 'Business' 29 Aug., 'Business with Lord Mansfield' 7 Sept., BM Add. MSS 32997, ff. 248, 251, 257; J. S. Corbett, *England in the Seven Years' War*, 1907, i. 198–200).
4. Which had arrived at Portsmouth by the *Baltimore* from Halifax on 29 Aug. and in London on the 30th (*Daily Adv.*

of Lord Loudon's expedition,[5] the state of the fleets,[6] the disagreeable apprehensions for New York;[7] with Col. Perry's[8] killing himself; Lord Charles Hay's[9] being in arrest, etc. They are all of them, like most of what we hear, very uncomfortable. But you'll doubtless have heard at the same time what we hear from all quarters, that the great hopes from our expedition keeps up the spirits of people, and makes 'em balance the real misfortunes we daily suffer by the expected, and, as yet, imaginary advantages of our undertaking. Some say it has had its effect already; I don't know what it is: except that of setting the French to think of their weaknesses, where there are any, and amending them. What orders they may have sent to the West Indies, or Minorca,[10] I can't tell; but, by several intelligences we pick up here, they are much alarmed, or, at least, much in motion on their coasts to prepare against us, by making reviews, marching troops, etc., even to unpaving the streets of towns, St Maloes particularly, from whence some prisoners just returned bring this account.[11] I suppose our ministry, who are in the secret, laugh in their sleeves, either in seeing how wrong a scent they are

31 Aug., 1 Sept.; *London Chronicle* 30 Aug. – 1 Sept., ii. 215). HW summarizes much of it in his letter to Mann 3 Sept. (MANN v. 130–1).

5. The Earl of Loudoun (*ante* 7 Feb. 1746), commander-in-chief in North America, had been ordered to attack Louisbourg in letters from Pitt of 4 and 17 March, the last not reaching him until 9 July (*Military Affairs in North America, 1748–1765*, ed. S. M. Pargellis, New York, 1936, p. 393). He had immediately begun preparations and had actually embarked his troops at Halifax at the beginning of August when intelligence arrived that the French were stronger than he expected, thus deciding him against the attack on 4 Aug. (MANN v. 130 and n. 20).

6. Adm. Holburne had reported, correctly, that his fleet was outnumbered by the French (ibid. v. 130–1 and n. 23).

7. The rumours of a French invasion of New York from Canada were magnified until the newspapers reported that 'some letters from New York advise that Mons. de Montcalm . . . was advancing towards Albany at the head of 9000 men' (*Daily Adv.* 5 Sept.).

8. George Perry (d. 1757), army officer; Col. of the 55th Foot; for him and his suicide see SELWYN 137, n. 5.

9. (ca 1700–60), Major-Gen. 1757; he had been placed under arrest for reflections on Loudoun's dilatoriness, and was believed insane (Loudoun to Cumberland 6 Aug., Pargellis, op. cit. 391–3).

10. Orders were sent to Toulon to prepare for the defence of Minorca (MANN v. 134, n. 4; *Mercure historique* 1757, cxliii. 31–2, 161–2, 255–7; *London Chronicle* 3–6 Sept., ii. 225).

11. 'Portsmouth, August 23. Yesterday arrived and came into the harbour the *Triton* cartel ship from St Maloes, with English prisoners' (*Daily Adv.* 25 Aug.). 'By private accounts from Brest and St Malo, we find they are apprehensive that the embarkation making in England is against them, and therefore they have taken up the pavement in those towns, for fear of a bombardment' (*London Chronicle* 27–30 Aug., ii. 207). Intelligence, grossly exaggerated, had reached Newcastle by 29 Aug. that the French had assembled 30,000 men on the coasts (BM Add. MSS 32997, ff. 248, 251).

upon, or having laid the bottom of their schemes so broad that it can't be defeated!

Among our visitors, the Duke of Kingston, Miss Chudleigh,[12] Colonel Prideaux[13] and his lady,[14] are just come here. Mr Hamilton, who has been employed in finding a lodging for them, has been at great difficulty in finding rooms and beds enough.

Adieu. If this wind continues, you'll not hear much of me yet. I remain, my dear Horry,

Most affectionately yours,

H. S. C.

From CONWAY, Wednesday 7 September 1757

Printed from the MS now wsl, formerly Rutnam. Previously printed *Fraser's Magazine*, 1850, xli. 426.

Portsmouth, 7 Sept. 1757.

Dear Horry,

I WRITE one hasty word, just in the article of our departure, to let you know that the transports came up to Cowes on Sunday night. Monday and yesterday everything was embarked.[1]

The fleet is now unmooring, and, as the wind is tolerably fair, with moderate weather, we expect to sail today or tomorrow.[2]

This surprises you; but know that, instead of countermands, as *you* might expect,[3] we had a *quickening* messenger:[4] for fear, I

12. She had been Kingston's mistress since before 1750 (*Trial of the Duchess of Kingston*, ed. Lewis Melville, 1927, p. 8).

13. John Prideaux (1718–59); Lt-Col. in the 3d Foot Guards, 1748; Col. of the 55th Foot, 1758.

14. Elizabeth Rolt, dau. of Edward Rolt of Sacombe, Herts, and sister of Sir Edward Bayntun Rolt of Spye Park, Wilts, cr. (1762) Bt (GEC, *Baronetage*, i. 201, v. 123).

1. Hawke reported to Pitt on the morning of the 6th that 'one brigade was embarked yesterday, as the other will be by noon today; so that the whole time taken up in the embarkation, from the arrival of the transports to this day at noon, will not exceed twenty-four hours' (*Report of the General Officers*, appointed . . . to inquire into the Causes of the Failure of the Late Expedition to the Coasts of France, 1758, p. 96).

2. Conway wrote the same news to Devonshire 7 Sept. (Chatsworth MSS, 416/48). The fleet finally got under way on the 8th (Hawke to Pitt 8 Sept., *Report of the General Officers*, pp. 97–8; MANN v. 137, n. 9).

3. HW may have mentioned in his missing letter of ca 31 Aug. some of the reports that the expedition might be abandoned (*ante* 3 Sept. 1757, n. 3).

4. Bearing a letter from Pitt to Mor-

suppose, that we should spoil the project by wilful delays:[5] I believe it made Sir John,[6] who had half embarked the troops with very particular dispatch, a little peevish, *comme de raison.*[7] I heartily wish you and I, for I find we think alike, may be much disappointed; and remain, my dear Horry,

Most affectionately yours.

To LADY AILESBURY, ca Wednesday 14 September 1757

Missing; implied *post* 16 Sept. 1757.

From LADY AILESBURY, Friday 16 September 1757

Printed for the first time from the MS now WSL, formerly Rutnam. The year has been added by HW.

Park Place. September 16, '57.

Dear Mr Walpole

I CAN never think you either troublesome, or neglectful of me. If I could I should be the most ungrateful creature in the world! I shall be very glad to see you here, since you are so good as to offer to come,[1] for besides the pleasure I always have in seeing you,

daunt and Hawke, dated 4 P.M. 5 Sept. and received very early the following morning, saying 'that his Majesty expects, with impatience, to hear that the troops are embarked; but if, by any delay, the embarkation should not be completed, when this letter reaches you, I am to signify to you the King's pleasure, that the most particular diligence be employed in getting the troops on board, and proceeding without the loss of a moment to the execution of your orders and instructions. . . . The King expects to hear by the return of this messenger that the fleet . . . with the troops on board have proceeded to sea' (*Report of the General Officers*, pp. 94–5).

5. Pitt was already suspicious of the land officers, and according to Newcastle, of the sea officers, too ('Business with

Lord Mansfield' 7 Sept., BM Add. MSS 32997, f. 257).

6. Sir John Mordaunt (1697–1780); K.B., 1749; Lt-Gen., 1754; Gen. 1770; M.P. Pontefract 1730–4, Whitchurch 1735–41, Cockermouth 1741–68; commander-in-chief of the land-forces on the expedition.

7. Mordaunt's reply 6 Sept. to Pitt's letter, somewhat sharp in tone, is in *Report of the General Officers*, p. 97; it reaffirms the embarkation of half of the troops on the 5th (above, n. 1).

1. HW apparently visited Lady Ailesbury about this time; he mentions being with her in Conway's absence to Mann on 20 Nov. and relates an anecdote he learned there about Conway's departure (MANN v. 155).

I shall like to have one that I can speak more freely to upon some occasions, than I can to anybody else. You will find complaints here, both of mind and body, for poor Miss Rich is so very ill with a cold, that I am quite frightened for her.

If I had had spirits I should have wrote to you long ago, to thank you for all those pretty verses,[2] which I am in great admiration of. I have been working a screen for Straberry[3] ever since I came into the country.

I am particularly miserable today, at having heard no news, as I thought we might have expected some; if it is possible that you should hear anything to make [me] glad, I should be vastly obliged to you to send me word of it, if you can't bring it yourself, which would make it still more pleasing.

I am dear Mr Walpole

Your faithful servant

C. AILESBURY

2. Probably, among others, the 'Vers sur cette expression ordinaire,' 'The Press Speaks, to Lady Townshend,' and 'The Press Speaks, to Lady Rochford,' all by HW and all printed at the SH Press 18–19 Aug. (Hazen, *SH Bibl.* 151–60).

3. There were at least two fire-screens worked by Lady Ailesbury at SH, one in the Refectory described as 'a fire-screen of admirable needle-work, representing a vase of flowers . . . it is mounted in mahogany, carved, and inlaid with ivory' ('Des. of SH,' *Works* ii. 404; sold SH xvi. 34 with the furnishings of the Great North Bedchamber); the other, in the Round Drawing Room, described as 'a screen worked in chenille, to suit with the chimney' ('Des. of SH,' *Works* ii. 468; sold SH xxiii. 45).

From CONWAY, Monday 26 September 1757

Printed from the MS now WSL, formerly Rutnam. Previously printed *Fraser's Magazine*, 1850, xli. 426.

On board the *Neptune* in the road of Aix,[1] 26 Sept. 1757.

Dear Horry,

I SNATCH a moment at the departure of an express[2] just to tell you that we came into this place on Thursday night,[3] and attacked and took the isle and fort of Aix[4] next morning: which was performed by two ships; viz. the *Magnanime*, Capt. Howe,[5] and *Barfleur*, Capt. Greaves:[6] I might almost say, the former alone, as the French fired hardly ten shot after he began, which he did with the greatest coolness and bravery, not firing a shot till he was within his ship's length of the walls.[7] This I was spectator of, being ordered up to land and sustain with three battalions,[8] if necessary; but, as you may judge, was not called upon.

I doubt our operations are like to end here; though I am grieved to go back without doing some little matter to talk of.[9] I can't positively say, though as for the grand object of Rochefort, I

1. More commonly known as the Rade des Basques, between the Île de Ré and the Île d'Oleron.

2. No express left the fleet until 30 Sept., when the *Viper* sloop, which had arrived with dispatches on the 22d, was sent home just ahead of the main fleet with preliminary accounts of the expedition. This intelligence reached London 6 Oct., but the private letters were detained (*Report of the General Officers appointed . . . to inquire into the Causes of the Failure of the Late Expedition to the Coasts of France*, 1758, pp. 100–1; James Wolfe to his father 30 Sept., Beckles Willson, *Life and Letters of James Wolfe*, 1909, p. 333; SELWYN 139, n. 1; *post* 8 Oct. 1757).

3. 22 Sept.

4. A small island which guarded the mouth of the Charente river and the approaches to Rochefort.

5. Richard Howe (1726–99), 4th Vct Howe, 1758; cr. (1788) E. Howe.

6. Samuel Graves (1713–87), Capt., 1744; Vice-Adm., 1770; Adm., 1778.

7. 'Notwithstanding the enemy kept a constant fire from several batteries for thirty minutes, he never returned a shot 'till such time he anchored his ship within fifty yards of the fort, and then kept so terrible and continual a fire for thirty-five minutes as drove them from their batteries, and obliged them to submit before the other ships of the squadron could get into their stations' (Capt. Rodney to Grenville, 23 Sept., *Grenville Papers* i. 208). See also Willson, op. cit. 330; *Report of the General Officers*, p. 100; *Daily Adv.* 8 Oct., where the taking of the fort is misdated 21 Sept.

8. The Buffs, Bentinck's, and the King's regiments. All Conway had to do was land and take possession of the citadel (*Report of the General Officers*, p. 109; *Grenville Papers* i. 208; Willson, loc. cit.). HW tells an anecdote of the occasion to Mann 20 Nov. (MANN v. 155).

9. For Conway's attempts to obtain further action from the expedition, see below, n. 12, and *post* 30 Sept., n. 7, 10 Oct., n. 5.

think it is determined to be what I always suspected it would (as we were equipped),[10] impracticable.[11]

Don't prepare abuse for us when we come back, and believe me, my dear Horry, ever most truly yours,

H. S. C.

PS. 28th. We are still to attempt, after much deliberation:[12] I can tell you much on that head one day or other. I expect to be on French ground tonight.

From CONWAY, Friday 30 September 1757

Printed from the MS now WSL, formerly Rutnam. Previously printed *Fraser's Magazine*, 1850, xli. 427.

On board the *Neptune,* road of Aix, 30 of Sept. 1757.

My dear Horry,

IN my last I told you we were just going to land;[1] you'll be surprised this should be to tell you we are just coming back to England.[2] We were, two nights ago, actually on board our boats for

10. They lacked the artillery and other equipment necessary for an attack on a fortified town that was prepared to resist.

11. This was decided at a council of war on the 25th, which, after examining witnesses, was 'unanimously of opinion that such an attempt [on Rochefort] is neither advisable nor practicable.' The minutes of the council are printed *Report of the General Officers*, pp. 104–6; HW describes the deliberation in *Mem. Geo. II* iii. 51–3. According to Wolfe the council 'sat from morning until late at night' (Willson, op. cit. 336); another report says it 'sat no less than sixteen hours' (*Grenville Papers* i. 216).

12. Another council of war on 28 Sept. had unanimously resolved 'to land the troops . . . with all possible dispatch' for an attack on the forts at the mouth of the Charente (*Report of the General Officers*, p. 107; a much larger minute, unofficial, is ibid. 111–13 and discussed, pp. 9–10). Conway had persistently urged this attack, especially on the fort of

Fouras (*post* 30 Sept., 10 Oct. 1757; *Grenville Papers* i. 216).

———

1. On the night of the 28th, for an assault on the forts at the mouth of the Charente River.

2. This decision was made on the evening of the 29th, after Hawke had written to Mordaunt, telling him if the land officers had no further operation to propose, he intended to return to England at once. Mordaunt consulted Conway, and offered him '(if it was his opinion) still to go on; but he replied, it was too delicate a matter for him to take upon himself, unless it was also Sir John's own opinion; that whatever might be his private sentiments, he should acquiesce in the general opinion, which he did accordingly.' Mordaunt then informed Hawke that the land officers 'all agree in returning directly to England' (*Report of the General Officers appointed . . . to inquire into the Causes of the Failure of the Late Expedition to the Coasts of*

the descent, and should have been now on the French shore; but so strangely are great events governed by trifles, that an easterly wind blowing a little fresh has saved us or the French, probably, from pretty serious accidents.[3] There's no telling, I cannot, nor must not, all the strange steps of these strange proceedings, and you'd scarce believe me if I did.[4] I gave my opinion against an undertaking I thought impracticable, *as then proposed*.[5] I have ever since been labouring to prevent the disgrace of coming away so poorly as I think we shall[6] and once succeeded so far as I have told:[7] but in

France, 1758, pp. 27–8, 39, 108, 110). HW gives an account of the deliberation about return and Conway's opposition to it but refusal to take the responsibility upon himself in *Mem. Geo. II* iii. 55–6. The fleet sailed 1 Oct. and arrived at Portsmouth on the evening of the 6th (*Report*, p. 114).

3. The abandonment of the attempt at landing on the night of the 28th–29th subsequently caused debate at the inquiry into the expedition, the land officers insisting that it was abandoned on the advice of the naval officers, and the naval officers arguing that the land officers wanted to wait for daylight. But all agreed that the adverse wind was a major factor (ibid. 22–4, 108, 109–10).

4. Conway wrote to his brother Hertford the same day: 'The steps and measures and motives of all these strange resolutions and irresolutions are endless and impossible and improper to relate' (MS now WSL).

5. The direct attack on Rochefort, which Conway had agreed in opposing in the council of war on the 25th (*ante* 26 Sept. 1757, n. 11).

6. Conway wrote to Hertford the same day: 'I am sorry to say that I think on the whole we make a pitiful figure in not attempting anything . . . I expect my share of blame, and for the only time of my life dread to come back to England, one among the number who have lain 9 or 10 days in a French harbour without a single attempt in any shape.' As early as the council of war on the 25th, he had opposed an immediate return to England 'as it was not in that view I gave my assent to the former question [abandoning an attack on Rochefort]; and thought

we should by all means see, what farther could be done to annoy the enemy' (*Report of the General Officers*, p. 37).

7. The decision to attempt a landing and attack on the fort of Fouras had been made largely at Conway's insistence. He had first proposed it on the 24th, and after the council of war on the 25th decided against an attack on Rochefort, revived his suggestion on the 26th and 27th, as well as proposing an attack on the Île d'Oleron. On the 27th 'there was some difference of opinion in regard to an attempt upon it, but we came to no final resolution 'till the afternoon, when a proposal was made to land at Chatelaillon, and make a sudden attack upon Fouras.' This was accepted at the council of war on the 28th, apparently after a good deal of further debate and examination of witnesses, and after 'Major-General Conway declared for the attempt, merely from his own opinion, without regard to the evidences.' After the attempt to land on the night of 28–29 Sept. was given up, Conway again returned to his project, and after a reconnoitring trip along the coast, urged another attempt at landing. 'On my [Conway's] report, Sir John Mordaunt called the land officers of the council of war together, to know their opinions, whether it was now proper to renew the attempt for the landing—I did declare it to be mine, but the other gentlemen being all of a contrary opinion, I acquiesced.' The decision was then made to return to England (ibid. 14–15, 18, 37–9 [Conway's own account of his conduct submitted to the commission of inquiry], 111–13). HW's account of Conway's insistence on an attack on Fouras in *Mem. Geo. II* iii. 53–6 closely parallels the

truth that, very oddly, pray let this be for yourself. When I see you,
I'll tell you the whole, by which you'll see how tender one must be
in speaking, as it's almost impossible not to hurt those I esteem
very much, and who have acted though not exactly as I should I
dare say, as prudently and as conscientiously.[8]

Yours, my dear Horry, most truly,

H. S. C.

From LADY AILESBURY, Sunday 2 October 1757

Printed for the first time from the MS now WSL, formerly Rutnam.

Park Place, October 2, 1757.

I AM very well pleased with my extravagant steward's proceedings,[1] and am in constant expectation of the blue-coat boys[2] coming post to give me notice of a great prize. I intend to be very
generous upon the occasion, and have settled the sum I shall give
them.

The post is again come in without a letter from Mr Conway,[3] or
a word of news, which surprises and frights me excessively. I beg to
know what you imagine can be the reason of this? This is the fourth
day that the wind has been to the northwest,[4] which increases my
fears.

one that can be constructed from the
records. However, according to Hawke,
Conway had initially joined with Mordaunt, while the fleet was still at sea, in
urging that no attempt of any sort be
made (to Pitt, 21 Oct., quoted J. S. Corbett, *England in the Seven Years' War*,
1907, i. 209–10).

8. Conway wrote to Hertford in very
similar terms at the same time: 'I have
taken much pains to prevent it [the re-
turn] and had once prevailed so far as
you have heard, but even that so heavily
and in such disagreeable way as you'll
scarce believe when you hear it. You must
be tender what you say, for I dread hurting anybody, especially those I have very
great regard for and who have acted I am

sure as conscientiously as I could, tho'
not in the same manner.'

1. Apparently HW had arranged to
send a special messenger to Park Place
with any news of the expedition, as he
later did (*post* 7 Oct. 1757).

2. Although 'blue-coat boy' means commonly a scholar of Christ's Hospital in
London, here blue-jackets are doubtless
what are meant, since Conway's rank
would entitle him to this special attention. HW refers to 'blue-coat boys' in a
letter to Lincoln (SELWYN 26).

3. Conway's letters were probably held
up by the Post Office (*post* 8 Oct. 1757, n.
6).

4. Which would hamper the return of
the fleet.

Miss Rich desires her compliments to you and is much better.

I am, dear Mr Walpole, sincerely yours,

C. AILESBURY

To LADY AILESBURY, ca Wednesday 5 October 1757

Missing; answered *post* 6 Oct. 1757.

From LADY AILESBURY, Thursday 6 October 1757

Printed for the first time from the MS now WSL, formerly Rutnam. The year is supplied by the references to the Rochefort expedition.

Park Place, October the 6th.

Dear Mr Walpole,

I CANNOT express the strong sense I have of your kindness to me and Mr Conway; hearing from you is really a great comfort to me, and though the news in your last filled me with many fears,[1] I might perhaps have had more of my own making; it appears very strange to me, that if the island of Aix was taken on the 20th or even on the 23d we should not have had news of their further progress, or retreat, as I should imagine they could not spend much time in deliberation, without they had changed their first resolution of surprising the place. What I dread is, that the ministry may

1. HW had presumably reported the first, indirect, accounts of the expedition to reach London. The earliest, in 'letters from Dunkirk by the Flanders mail,' which may have arrived on the 4th, said that the fleet had anchored off the Île de Ré on the 21st and that the troops had landed on the 'Isle of Dain' on the 23d (*Daily Adv.* 5 Oct.). Further information arrived from Holland on the 5th. Col. Yorke sent letters from France saying that the troops 'were put in shore three leagues below Rochefort' and containing enough other information to enable Pitt to write on the afternoon of the 5th of 'the promising aspect of our expedition to the coast of France' (Holdernesse to Newcastle 5 Oct., Pitt to Newcastle, Wednesday [5 Oct.], BM Add. MSS 32874, ff. 452, 454). Still other information indicated that the troops had landed on the Île d'Aix, had met with no opposition, and had successfully moved on to the mainland (*Grenville Papers* i. 210–11). Direct reports from the expedition were not received in London until the 6th; although these told the whole history down to the decision to return to England, at first nothing more was generally known than that the Île d'Aix had been taken, and a false report that Rochefort itself had been captured (SELWYN 139; *Daily Adv.* 7 Oct.).

have received news they choose to conceal. I hope to have a letter from you tomorrow; there is no mortal in town that I can expect to hear from except yourself, as Lord Hertford and the Duke of Devonshire are both at Newmarket; by sending a letter to my porter I can receive it the next day, between the post and the stage coach.

I am most faithfully yours,

C. Ailesbury

Be so good as to find out if there is any way of conveying a letter to the fleet.

To Lady Ailesbury, Friday 7 October 1757

Missing; answered in the following letter. It was sent by a servant.

From Lady Ailesbury, Friday 7 October 1757

Printed for the first time from the MS now wsl, formerly Rutnam. Dated on the assumption that it refers to Conway's return.
Address: To the Honourable Horatio Walpole.

Friday, 3 o'clock.

Dear Mr Walpole,

I GIVE you a thousand thanks for the most agreeable of all news,[1] which to me was quite unexpected, as you may easily perceive by my last letter. I am thoroughly satisfied, and don't even covet any of the nasty French money.[2] I say no more because I won't keep your servant. I am more obliged to you than I can express.

Ever yours,

C. A.

1. Accounts of the return of the expedition to Portsmouth on the evening of the 6th reached London on the 7th (*Daily Adv.* 8 Oct.).

2. That is, a French prize. For the King's proclamation on the distribution of prizes captured, see Robert Beatson, *Naval and Military Memoirs of Great Britain,* 1804, iii. 104–6.

To CONWAY, ca Friday 7 October 1757

Missing. Conway acknowledges two letters *post* 10 Oct.; one of them was certainly *post* 8 Oct.; HW probably had also written immediately on learning of Conway's return on the 7th.

From CONWAY, Friday 7 October 1757

Printed from the MS now WSL, formerly Rutnam. Previously printed *Fraser's Magazine*, 1850, xli. 427.

Portsmouth, 7 Oct. 1757.

Dear Horry,

I WRITE a single word on the departure of the post, just to let you know we are arrived all safe and well. I hope you won't think too much so. You'll have received a letter from me by the last express,[1] which has given you an hint of our affairs but a very imperfect one.

I have not writ in form for orders but if you are in town, and can hear what I am to do,[2] let me know; I shall probably have my commands in a day or two, and let me hear a word of any news that is stirring, particularly relating to the Duke and his arrival,[3] and, more particularly still, relating to ourselves. Adieu! I long much to see you.

H. S. C.

---

1. Conway's letters of 26 and 30 Sept. had both presumably been sent by the *Viper* sloop, whose mails reached London on the 6th (*ante* 26 Sept. 1757, n. 2). The private letters, however, were detained for a time (*post* 8 Oct. 1757, n. 6).

2. Conway stayed in Hampshire until 13 Oct. to supervise the debarkation of the troops at Portsmouth (*post* 10, 13 Oct. 1757; SELWYN 141–2; *Daily Adv.* 11 Oct.).

3. The D. of Cumberland reached London from Stade on 11 Oct. and immediately resigned all his offices (SELWYN 145, n. 1; MANN V. 145, nn. 1–8).

To Conway, Saturday 8 October 1757

Printed from the MS now wsl; first printed Wright iii. 324–5. Dated by the endorsement and contents. For the history of the MS, see *ante* 29 June 1744 OS.
Endorsed: Mr. H. W. 8 Oct. 1757.
Memorandum (by HW, in pencil, erased): About the expedition to Rochefort.

Arlington Street, Saturday.

My dearest Harry,

BUT one person in the world[1] may pretend to be as much over-joyed as I am at your return. I came hither today on purpose to learn about you—but how can you ask me such a question, as do I think you are come too safe? Is this a time of day to question your spirit? I know but two things on earth I esteem more, your good-ness and your sense. *You* cannot come into dispute, but by what I have picked up at my Lady T[ownshend]'s I find there is a scheme of distinguishing between the land and the sea.[2] The King has been told that Sir E[dward] H[awke] had written that after waiting two days, he asked the officers how long it would be before they took a resolution; that if they would not attack, he should carry the fleet home.[3] I should not entirely credit this report, if Mr Keith,[4] who was present, had not dropped in a dry way, that he supposed some distinction would be shown to Capt. Howe and Capt. Greaves.[5] What confirms my opinion is, that I have never received the letter you say you sent me by the last express—I suppose it is detained,[6]

1. Lady Ailesbury.
2. I.e., of blaming the failure exclu-sively upon the land officers. The naval officers vigorously attacked the indecision of the military officers and Pitt and the other ministers blamed them alone. The eventual inquiry was into the conduct of the land officers alone despite Mordaunt's request that it be general (Newcastle to Hardwicke 8 Oct., printed *Hardwicke Corr.* iii. 186–7; Newcastle to Hardwicke 15 Oct., Hardwicke to Newcastle 16 Oct., Newcastle to Ashburton 20 Oct., New-castle to Hardwicke 23 Oct., Hardwicke to Newcastle 24 Oct., BM Add. MSS 32875, ff. 124, 144, 198, 228, 254; *Grenville Papers* i. 213–29; *Bedford Corr.* ii. 280).
3. This is essentially what happened on 29 Sept. (*ante* 30 Sept. 1757, n. 2).

4. Probably Robert Keith (d. 1774), dip-lomatist, who had recently returned from Vienna where he had been minister plenipotentiary; and not his son Robert Murray Keith, a friend of Conway, and at this time a captain in the army (BM Add. MSS 32854, f. 143; D. B. Horn, *Brit-ish Diplomatic Representatives 1689–1789*, 1932, p. 37).
5. Who had distinguished themselves in the capture of the Île d'Aix (*ante* 26 Sept. 1757).
6. Capt. Rodney wrote to Grenville on 13 Oct. that he had discovered that 'the Post Office has thought proper to detain the letters that were sent from the offi-cers of the fleet employed on the late expedition'; the D. of Devonshire wrote the D. of Bedford on the 15th that 'all the

till proper emissaries have made proper impressions: but we will not let it pass so. If you had not bid me, I should have given you this intelligence, for your character is too sacred to be trifled with, and as you are invulnerable by any slanders, it is proper you should know immediately even what may be meditated.

The Duke is expected every hour[7]—as he *must* not defend himself,[8] his case will be harder than yours.

I was to go to Bath on Monday,[9] but will certainly not go without seeing you; let me know your motions and I will meet you anywhere. As I know your scrupulousness about saying anything I say to you privately, I think it necessary to tell you, that I don't mean to preclude you from communicating any part of this letter to those with whom it may be proper for you to consult—only don't let more weight be given to my intelligence than it deserves.

I have told you exactly where and what I heard—it may not prove so, but there is no harm in being prepared.

Yours most faithfully,

H. W.

From CONWAY, Monday 10 October 1757

Printed from the MS now WSL, formerly Rutnam. Previously printed *Fraser's Magazine*, 1850, xli. 427–8.

Bevismount,[1] 10th Oct. 1757.

My dear Horry,

I HAVE received this moment your two letters, and am more obliged to you than I can express for your excessive friendship and goodness on this as upon all other occasions. What you tell me

letters have been stopped—two from Mr Conway to me have never come to hand' (*Grenville Papers* i. 214; *Bedford Corr.* ii. 283).

7. He arrived on the 11th (*ante* 7 Oct. 1757, n. 3).

8. HW believed with some justice that Cumberland had acted under express instructions of the King in signing the Convention of Klosterzeven, although the King determined to punish him for doing so (SELWYN 142, nn. 8, 10; *Bedford Corr.* ii. 276–9).

9. He had also planned to visit George Selwyn at Matson (SELWYN 139).

1. Bevois Mount, Gen. Mordaunt's seat near Southampton, about 28 miles NE of Portsmouth.

gives me great pain, both on my own account and that of my friends; for though I feel and know that I was not only barely willing, but very earnest, to have attempted what I still think might have been undertaken with good prospect of success,[2] from one untoward circumstance or other my sentiments could not prevail; and as I took no proper pains to state and have things appear as I might have done,[3] it may now turn upon explanations difficult and delicate to make, which may be classed as selfish disputes between people *all in the wrong* to save themselves: I hate such disputes, and even the appearance of them; and I am heartily grieved by such a variety of odd circumstances as have brought it or to be brought upon any kind of defence, in an affair where I wished and strove not to stop at a bare defensive praise. We shall talk it all over soon. I can only say now, that after thinking, and therefore saying, I thought *one thing*[4] both extravagant and impracticable in one particular way, I set several other plans on foot,[5] all of which I thought, and must still think, were preferable to the doing nothing. It went so far on one of them, that we were actually in our boats once for the French shore;[6] but my opinion for pushing that operation was so little that of others, that it easily fell to the ground.[7]

I have never been easy since it was determined to come home with so little grace as I knew we must; for it's horrid to be anyhow a part of what is blamed in our way;[8] and besides that, I hate such

2. The attack on Fouras (*ante* 30 Sept. 1757, n. 7).

3. For example, after signing the minutes of the council of war against an attack on Rochefort, Conway had not officially spelled out his desire to attempt something else (*Report of the General Officers appointed . . . to inquire into the Causes of the Failure of the Late Expedition to the Coasts of France*, 1758, p. 38); nor had he made clear his opposition to returning to England without another attempt at landing (*ante* 30 Sept. 1757, n. 7).

4. A direct attack on Rochefort (*ante* 26 Sept. 1757, n. 11).

5. Conway had supported an attack on the Île d'Oleron as well as the attack on Fouras (*Report of the General Officers*, pp. 18, 37–8; *Mem. Geo. II* iii. 54).

6. On 28 Sept. to attack Fouras (*ante* 26, 30 Sept. 1757).

7. On 29 Sept. when Conway renewed his proposal, but no one would support him (*ante* 30 Sept. 1757, n. 7; *Mem. Geo. II* iii. 55–6).

8. Conway wrote Devonshire the same day 'that the suspicions which I mentioned in my last from Portsmouth are I hear confirmed and that great clamour and ill humour are brewing against the leaders of this unlucky expedition; I foresaw and forewarned it would be the case; . . . I know how difficult and delicate defences are that the world may call selfish debates of individuals to get out of a common scrape. I hate such debates; can't tell how to enter into them; and therefore as circumstances have fallen out, must I doubt submit to some share of blame, in an affair where I had both hoped and strove too we might have done something more than not be *blamed*' (Chatsworth MSS, 416 / 49).

defences: mine lies in distinctions that I have been either too thoughtless or too delicate to make; but of all these things, more when we meet.

At present, I shall conclude with an account of my motions. I came here yesterday a sort of volunteer, to attend the debarkation of five regiments—just half our army, to which no general officer was ordered.[9]

Lady Ailesbury came here today, and as we are very comfortably lodged, will stay as long as I do; which will be, I reckon, five days more. If you hear anything material that can reach me in that time, direct it here. If not, I'll let you know the very day I shall be on my return at Park Place, where, if it happens to be tolerably convenient, I should be happy to see you. If not, I hope on my arrival in town, which must follow a day or two after,[10] and am in the meantime dear Horry,

Most truly and affectionately yours,

H. S. C.

To CONWAY, Tuesday 11 October 1757

Missing; mentioned *post* 13 Oct. 1757.

To CONWAY, Thursday 13 October 1757

Printed from *Works* v. 53–4.

Strawberry Hill, October 13, 1757.

IF you have received mine of Tuesday, which I directed to Portsmouth, you will perceive how much I agree with you. I am charmed with your sensible modesty. When I talked to you of defence, it was from concluding that you had all agreed that the at-

9. Pitt, when giving Mordaunt permission to come to London on 7 Oct., ordered him to leave one of the major-generals at Portsmouth to superintend the debarkation (*Report of the General Officers*, pp. 115–16; see also Conway to Devonshire 10 Oct.).

10. Conway came to London on 16 Oct. (*Grenville Papers* i. 216).

tempt[1] was impracticable, nay impossible; and from thence I judged that the ministry intended to cast the blame of a wild project upon the officers. That they may be a little willing to do that, I still think —but I have the joy to find that it cannot be thrown on you. As your friend, and fearing, if I talked for you first, it would look like doubt of your behaviour, at least that you had bid me defend you at the expense of your friends, I said not a word, trusting that your innocence would break out and make its way. I have the satisfaction to find it has already done so. It comes from all quarters but your own, which makes it more honourable. My Lady Suffolk told me last night, that she heard all the *seamen* said they wished the general[2] had been as ready as Mr Conway.[3] But this is not all: I left a positive commission in town to have the truth of the general report sent me without the least disguise; in consequence of which I am solemnly assured that your name is never mentioned but with honour;[4] that all the violence, and that extreme, is against Sir John Mordaunt and Mr Cornwallis.[5] I am particularly sorry for the latter, as I firmly believe him as brave as possible.[6]

This situation of things makes me advise, what I know and find I

1. On Rochfort (HW).

2. Mordaunt.

3. HW passed this report on to Selwyn the same day (SELWYN 143).

4. This seems to have been the case at first: a correspondent informed Mrs Montagu shortly after 11 Oct. that 'Colonel Conway, I hear, showed the most spirit' (E. J. Climenson, *Elizabeth Montagu*, 1906, ii. 120). The outcry, however, was eventually directed at Conway as well, although less violently than against Mordaunt and Cornwallis. Jenkinson told Grenville on 22 Oct. that 'General Conway also by no means answered the idea that had been entertained of him, though he was better than the other two' and that when Conway was presented at Court 'the King spoke to him, but he did not to Cornwallis' (*Grenville Papers* i. 225, 226). After the inquiry into the expedition, Lady Elizabeth Waldegrave wrote to the D. of Bedford that 'Conway has not made the defence that was expected from so able a man' (*Bedford Corr.* ii. 305); and on 24 Dec. the King insulted Conway in the presence of Lords Bucking-ham, Waldegrave, and Ashburnham, the Hon. Edward Finch, and John Offley (*post* Conway to HW 13 Oct. 1757, n. 3). In Jan. 1758 Lord Lyttelton described 'the popular outcry' against the generals and complained of the injustice with respect to Conway (Robert Phillimore, *Memoirs and Correspondence of George, Lord Lyttelton*, 1845, ii. 602).

5. The Hon. Edward Cornwallis (*ante* 1 July 1744 NS, n. 16), third in command of the land forces on the expedition. He was apparently condemned particularly for having voted against the attempt to land on the 28th, 'but afterwards acquiesced with the majority,' according to the unofficial minutes of the council of war (*Report of the General Officers appointed . . . to inquire into the Causes of the Failure of the Late Expedition to the Coasts of France*, 1758, p. 113; *Mem. Geo. II* iii. 53-4, where HW seems to misconstrue the effects of his vote).

6. He had once been a close friend of HW, but they had drifted apart (see *ante* 1 July 1744 NS, n. 16).

need not advise, your saying as little as possible in your own defence, nay, as much as you can with any decency for the others. I am neither acquainted with, nor care a straw about, Sir John Mordaunt; but as it is known that you differed with him, it will do you the greatest honour to vindicate him, instead of disculpating yourself.[7] My most earnest desire always is, to have your character continue as amiable and respectable as possible. There is no doubt but the whole will come out,[8] and therefore your justification not coming from yourself will set it in a ten times better light. I shall go to town today to meet your brother; and as I know his affection for you will make him warm in clearing you,[9] I shall endeavour to restrain that ardour, of which you know I have enough on the least glimmering of a necessity: but I am sure you will agree with me, that, on the representation I have here made to you, it is not proper for your friends to appear solicitous about you.

The City talk very treason, and, connecting the suspension at Stade[10] with this disappointment, cry out, that the General had posi-

7. Conway followed this advice; Lord Lyttelton wrote to Mrs Montagu 28 Oct., on his way to visit Conway, 'I find there has been some difference of opinion between him and Sir J. Mordaunt as to the practicability and expediency of attempting something; but he speaks very modestly and diffidently of his own judgment' (quoted by Percy Noble, *Park Place*, 1905, p. 85).

8. The ministry were perplexed at the moment as to how to have the officers investigated so as to forestall a Parliamentary inquiry (references cited *ante* 8 Oct. 1757, n. 2). Mordaunt forced them to a decision by demanding an inquiry by a board of general officers. The D. of Marlborough, Lord George Sackville, and Gen. Waldegrave were appointed to hold it on 1 Nov. and it met 12–17 Nov. (MANN v. 145, 155, n. 18; *post* 24 Nov. 1757). Conway wrote Devonshire 31 Oct. of this board of inquiry, 'Your Grace sees by this that tho' they have no powers to condemn or inflict punishment those they have are in effect very great as they can direct their inquiry to what persons and things they please and give what opinion they please thereon; I believe nothing wrong can be appre-

hended from a board so constituted as to persons, as to powers I own I think it of a dangerous precedent; as the characters of those concerned at least seem too arbitrarily in their disposition. I don't yet know how or to what degree we inferiors can be made the objects of this; if I have my wishes for it from the feel and consciousness of good intentions on one hand I have also some little ground for fears on the other: in short even the being put on defence in its best shape is so odious, that I can in no way reconcile myself to my situation' (Chatsworth MSS, 416 / 50).

9. The only evidence of Hertford's intervention is a letter to Newcastle 30 Oct. on the warrant for the inquiry, requesting 'that the examination upon which anything is to be published to satisfy the world may be very particular; if my brother's conduct deserves censure, he must be content to bear it, if he does not let him be acquitted to the world . . . if he does not deserve reproach, the veil which at present in some measure hangs over his character should in justice be thrown off' (BM Add. MSS 32875, ff. 334–5).

10. The Convention of Klosterzeven.

tive orders to do nothing, in order to obtain gentler treatment of Hanover.[11] They intend in a violent manner to demand redress, and are too enraged to let any part of this affair remain a mystery.

I think, by your directions, this will reach you before you leave Bevismount: I would gladly meet you at Park Place, if I was not sure of seeing you in town a day or two afterwards at farthest; which I will certainly do, if you let me know. Adieu!

Yours ever,

HOR. WALPOLE

From CONWAY, Thursday 13 October 1757

Printed from the MS now WSL, formerly Rutnam. Previously printed *Fraser's Magazine*, 1850, xli. 428.

Southampton, Thursday 13 Oct. 1757.

Dear Horry,

I WRITE this single line just to tell you I shall set out from hence today and barring accidents certainly be at Park Place tomorrow morning, where if possible I should wish very much to see you on Saturday; the more as I hear from Sir John Mordaunt that our affairs are very serious and that the King has not sent for him in to talk with him.[1] For me, I feel as unpleasant as possible, and dread coming into that angry town or near the Court as much almost as if

11. HW makes similar comments to Selwyn the same day (SELWYN 143). The Duke of Newcastle, describing to Hardwicke on the 15th the uproar caused by the failure of the expedition, stated that the greater and most effective part of the criticism was based on the supposition 'that the fleet, etc. were recalled, to prevent the French from committing further violences upon the Electoral dominions, and this is connected with the late Convention. But . . . that is without the least foundation' (BM Add. MSS 32875, f. 124). Similar reports are mentioned in Newcastle to Ashburnham 20 Oct., ibid. f. 198; *Chatham Corr.* i. 277; *London Chronicle* 13–15 Oct., ii. 365. These ru-

mours were quashed by the publication in the *London Gazette* No. 9730, 11–15 Oct., of Pitt's orders to Hawke and Mordaunt of 15 Sept. that they should not be bound by their original instructions to be back in England by the end of Sept. but should complete their operation.

————

1. George II had virtually ignored Mordaunt when the latter appeared at Court on the 10th (SELWYN 142, n. 9; MANN v. 143–4). A correspondent of Mrs Montagu's informed her that Mordaunt was 'taken no notice of, 'tis said he stooped to kiss the royal hand, but it was pulled back from him' (E. J. Climenson, *Elizabeth Montagu*, 1906, ii. 120).

I had run away; to be rumped[2] at Court,[3] and looked awry at all over the town; and though I think I have much to say for myself, I don't know how to say it. I partly foresaw these things when we went as very likely, and strongly foretold them in all our deliberations there as certain. Adieu! Don't say much even *for me* till we meet.

Yours ever,

H. S. C.

From CONWAY, Thursday 24 November 1757

Printed from the MS now WSL, formerly Rutnam. Previously printed *Fraser's Magazine*, 1850, xli. 428. The year is supplied by the contents. On this letter there is a rough draft by HW in pencil of his verses to Conway, 'conceived and executed between Hammersmith and Hyde Park Corner,' given in full *post* ca 25 Nov.; the variations in text are there noted.

Address: To the Honourable Horatio Walpole at Twickenham.

Postmark: 24 NO.

London, 24 Nov.

Dear Horry,

I WANT to know when you come to town. I have forgot what day you said. You'll be glad to hear that Lady Ailesbury wants nothing but strength to be quite recovered.

For me, my spirits increase; I hear many are shocked with the

---

2. 'To turn one's back upon (a person), esp. as a mode of snubbing' (OED).

3. Conway wrote Devonshire 24 Dec., 'I write this full of as much indignation as it's well possible to feel for the extraordinary and unexpected ill usage which I met with today; you know I have been in waiting this week past, during which I have not had a word said to me; . . . but lest I should think myself too well used He [the King] this day for *bonne bouche* gave, before me, such a pointed lecture upon generals who misbehaved, as it was impossible not to know and feel the tendency of; it was apropos to the Prussian generals who had *executed their orders* so well; but *some had misbehaved,* he *believed their heads were cut off by this time.* It did not stop here he went on and rung the charges upon this agreeable and good-natured subject a great while longer. At last for fear I should mistake his meaning he said something . . . of generals *who went to the Grand Object;* and *did not propose Little Attempts that had small Danger and small Utility . . .* I had given him his hat or I own should have been vastly tempted to lay it down and walk away . . . in truth one might call it brutal usage and scarce manly to insult anyone so outrageously who was not in a situation to answer for himself' (Chatsworth MSS, 416/51).

late merciless report[1] and the ministry puzzled with it.[2] Nobody knows what will be done. I feel now much more angry than hurt and am prepared to fight it out, where I think it may probably come,[3] to the stumps. Adieu! One of the Prussian messengers is come,[4] but I have not heard his news.

1. The report of the inquiry into the failure of the Rochefort expedition, made to the King on 21 Nov. (MANN v. 155 and n. 19, 157). It was still not public (*Bedford Corr.* ii. 305), but was eventually published as *The Report of the General Officers appointed by his Majesty's Warrant of the first of November 1757 to inquire into the Causes of the Failure of the Late Expedition to the Coasts of France,* on 31 Dec. 1757 (*Daily Adv.* 31 Dec.), dated 1758. It passed a general censure on the conduct of the land officers, particularly in the council of war of 25 Sept., saying: 'It does not appear to us, that there were then, or at any time afterwards, either a body of troops or batteries on the shore, sufficient to have prevented the attempting a descent. . . . Neither does it appear to us, that there were any sufficient reasons to induce the council of war to believe, that Rochefort was so far changed in respect of its strength, or posture of defence, since the expedition was first resolved on in England, as to prevent all attempts of an attack on the place. . . . We cannot but look upon the expedition as having failed, from the time the great object of it was laid aside in the council of war of the 25th' (pp. 61–2).

2. Pitt, at least, was enraged at what he considered a whitewash of the land officers and wanted all of them court-martialled (Newcastle's 'Memoranda for my Lord Hardwicke' 28 Nov., BM Add. MSS

32997, f. 297). The naval officers were offended by a mild censure passed on them in one passage of the report (*Bedford Corr.* ii. 306). In the end only Mordaunt was tried by court martial and unanimously acquitted, which outraged the King and Pitt (MANN v. 164–5 and nn. 1–4).

3. Either in Parliament or in a court martial. Conway wrote Devonshire 24 Dec., 'I hear the persecution is to be removed from the Cabinet to the Parliament where at least one shall be at liberty to speak for oneself, and that I think is the only one left me: for with all the innocence I feel I am not now blind enough to be ignorant of the various modes by which my character is attacked and will very likely be crushed. I wanted but one favour which was to be employed and I doubt it's now too late for that. Amidst these misfortunes I assure your Grace I don't feel my spirits sink, but rather rise; for when injury and injustice go to a certain pitch they raise a kind of indignation that keeps 'em up. So that if I am to fall, I hope to do like a man' (Chatsworth MSS, 416 / 51).

4. One of the messengers bringing details of Frederick's victory at Rossbach 5 Nov. The first imperfect details reached London on 15 Nov., but six messengers on their way were separated and arrived at various dates between 21 and 28 Nov. (MANN v. 153 and nn. 4–7).

To CONWAY, ca Friday 25 November 1757

Printed from a photostat of the MS in the Pierpont Morgan Library. Previously printed, misdated 'February 1758' in *Extracts from the Journals and Correspondence of Miss Berry*, ed. Lady Theresa Lewis, 1865, ii. 63; reprinted, correctly placed in Nov. 1757, Toynbee iv. 113. For the previous history of the MS, see *ante* 31 Oct. 1741 OS.

Despite the endorsement, this was written between the receipt of the previous letter, and 26 Nov. when HW sent the verses to Grosvenor Bedford (HW to Bedford 26 Nov. 1757) for publication in the *Public Advertiser,* where they appeared on Monday 28 Nov. There are slight variations in the text of the version sent to Bedford. The version here was printed from Toynbee in HW's *Fugitive Verses,* ed. W. S. Lewis, 1931, pp. 124–5.

Endorsed: Mr H. Walpole February 1758
          with copy of verses

I AM this minute arrived and going to dine at Brand's[1]—I will come to you afterwards, before I go to North[umberland] House. In the meantime I send you a most hasty performance, literally conceived and executed between Hammersmith and Hyde Park Corner —the Lord knows if it is not sad stuff—I wish for the sake of the subject it were better!

To Mr Conway

When Fontenoy's impurpled plain
    Shall vanish from th'historic page,
Thy youthful valour shall in vain
    Have taught the Gaul to shun thy rage.

When hostile squadrons round thee stood
    On Laffelt's unsuccessful field,[2]
Thy captive sabre[3] drench'd in blood
    The vaunting Victor's triumph seal'd.

Forgot be these!—let Scotland too
    Culloden from her annals tear,
Lest Envy and her factious Crew
    Should sigh to meet thy laurels there.

1. Thomas Brand (*ante* 6 July 1756, n. 10) lived in St James's Square (*Court and City Register,* 1757, p. 56).

2. After this line there is the following line crossed out, 'Didst thou in vain op-pose thy heart,' in the draft written on *ante* 24 Nov.

3. 'Sabre' written above 'cuirass' crossed out; 'cuirass' in the draft written on *ante* 24 Nov.

When each fair deed is thus defac'd,
A thousand Virtues too disguis'd,
Thy *grateful* Country's voice shall haste
To censure Worth so little priz'd.

Thou, patient, hear the thunder roll;
Pity the Blind you cannot hate;
Nor, blest with Aristides' soul,
Repine at Aristides' fate.[4]

From Conway, Thursday ?16 or ?23 ?March 1758

Printed for the first time from the MS now WSL, formerly Rutnam. Dated tentatively by what seems to be a reference to a pamphlet by Conway (see below, n. 1). The reference to HW's *Royal and Noble Authors* at first suggests a date after 15 April, when the printing was completed, but the details mentioned occur in the first volume, the printing of which was finished, except for the dedication, preface, and index, on 27 Jan. (Hazen, *SH Bibl.* 33–5).

Address: To the Honourable Horatio Walpole.

London, Thursday evening.

LADY Ailesbury wishes to have the copper plate for her cards which if you order to be sent to our house we can leave directions to have filled up with proper compliments. My book[1] is not

---

4. This stanza is not in the draft written *ante* 24 Nov.

---

1. Two pamphlets published in the winter of 1758 in the controversy over the Rochefort expedition, were tentatively ascribed to Conway by the DNB. The attribution has not been confirmed, although HW in *Mem. Geo. II* iii. 79, and Sir Richard Lyttelton in a letter to W. H. Lyttelton, March 1758 (Maud Wyndham, *Chronicles of the Eighteenth Century*, 1924, ii. 257), mention a pamphlet war that winter between Conway and Thomas Potter. No pamphlets in the entire controversy are listed in HW's library. The two ascribed to Conway are *The Military Arguments, in the Letter to a Right Honourable Author, fully considered, by an Officer*, published by J. Robinson, 18 or 20 Feb. (*Daily Adv.* 15, 20 Feb.); and *The Officer's Answer to the Country Gentleman's Reply*, J. Robinson, 25 March (ibid. 25 March). The first pamphlet replied to *The Expedition against Rochefort fully stated and considered. In a letter to the Right Honourable the Author of the Candid Reflections on the Report of the General Officers, etc. By a Country Gentleman*, which had been published 17 Jan., with a second edn 25 Jan. (*Daily Adv.* 16, 17, 25 Jan.) and is ascribed to Potter. Conway's alleged second pamphlet replies to Potter's response to his first, *The Reply of the Country Gentleman to the answer of his Military Arguments, by the Officer*, published 4 March (ibid. 4 March). The controversy began with *Candid Reflections on the Report (as published by Authority) of the General Officers appointed . . . to enquire into the causes of the failure of the late expedition to the coast of France*, 6 Jan. which had a 2d edn 26 Jan. and a 3d, 7 Feb. (ibid. 6, 26

come home yet. I have stayed in town on purpose for it today; I have not yet read it and if I have it not tonight, I believe the thought of staying another day will cast the *balance* in my mind against the publication. Yours[2] we have almost finished; it improves much at Lord Essex,[3] your two Lord Brookes,[4] with the episode *in praise* of Sir Philip Sidney,[5] etc. If I had no idea of him but from your account I should think by that time Sir H. Erskine[6] has writ a long pedantic pastoral romance and some English hexameters he might be the Sir Philip of our times and perhaps may find a Lord Brooke to subscribe himself his friend on his tomb.[7] We shall leave your book as you desire.

Yours ever,

H. S. C.

Jan., 7 Feb.), and which, though attributed to Henry Fox in Halkett and Laing, is not mentioned in Lord Ilchester's *Henry Fox;* a MS note in a copy at Yale suggests Arthur Murphy as a possible author. Other pamphlets in the controversy are mentioned in the *Daily Adv.* 31 Jan., 2 Feb., 28 March.

2. *The Royal and Noble Authors.*

3. HW's account of Robert Devereux, 2d E. of Essex (*ante* 29 Oct. 1750 OS, n. 18) is in 'Royal and Noble Authors,' *Works* i. 314–28 (in the SH edn i. 111–41).

4. Sir Fulke Greville (1554–1628), cr. (1621) Bn Brooke; and his cousin Robert Greville (1607–43), 2d Bn Brooke. HW's accounts are in 'Royal and Noble Authors,' *Works* i. 342–5, 356–9 (in the SH edn i. 163–9, 182–7).

5. Much of HW's account of Sir Fulke Greville was a severe criticism of Sir Philip Sidney (1554–86), soldier, statesman, and poet. 'No man seems to me so astonishing an object of temporary admiration as the celebrated friend of the Lord Brooke, the famous Sir Philip Sidney. . . . In full of all other talents we

have a tedious, lamentable, pedantic, pastoral romance [the *Arcadia*], which the patience of a young virgin in love cannot now wade through; and some absurd attempts to fetter English verse in Roman chains; a proof that this applauded author understood little of the genius of his own language' (*Works* i. 342). As early as 1746 HW had called the *Arcadia* 'dolorous' (MONTAGU i. 26).

6. Sir Henry Erskine, who was dismissed from the army for supporting Pitt in 1755–6 (*ante* 22 Jan. 1756), had been much praised at the time for his military valour (*Mem. Geo. II* ii. 159), the only quality HW had found to praise in Sidney. More recently as a close ally of Bute, he had turned poet and written a 'patriot prologue' to John Home's *Agis*, first performed 21 Feb. 1758 and much patronized by Leicester House (*Mem. Geo. II* iii. 99; *London Stage* Pt IV, ii. 647–8).

7. HW had written that Lord Brooke 'piqued himself most, and it was his chief merit, on being, as he styled himself on his tomb, THE FRIEND OF SIR PHILIP SIDNEY' ('Royal and Noble Authors,' *Works* i. 343).

From LADY AILESBURY, Friday ?24 or ?31 ?March ?1758

Printed for the first time from the MS now WSL, formerly Rutnam. Dated by the reference to the copper plate, also mentioned in the previous letter, apparently of March 1758; this letter was presumably written either the first or second Friday before the dates mentioned in it, which fit Wednesday 5 April and Friday 7 April 1758, but no other month in the winter or spring of that year.
Address: To Mr Walpole.

Friday morning.

Dear Mr Walpole,

I HAVE sent to your house a card of invitation for Wednesday the 5th and Friday the 7th, which card I am afraid you will not receive,[1] therefore trouble you with this. On Wednesday if you do not dislike it, as I am to have a very small party, I shall ask the favour of you to deal a little at pharaoh to the Duchess of Grafton,[2] and sup here of course. Pray send me my copper plate for I intend to have it printed. Adieu! I am this moment going to Park Place, which would be still more agreeable, could I hope to see you there.

Yours,

C. AILESBURY

If you will give orders to have the copper plate left out, my servant shall call for it.

---

1. Presumably because he was at SH; he wrote to Charles Lyttelton from there on 23 March.

2. Hon. Anne Liddell (ca 1738–1804), m.

1 (1756) Augustus Henry Fitzroy, styled E. of Euston, 3d D. of Grafton, 1757 (divorced 1769); m. 2 (1769) John Fitzpatrick, 2d E. of Upper Ossory; HW's correspondent.

To ?CONWAY, ca Wednesday 10 May 1758

Missing; it is possible that the following otherwise unexplained memoranda on the back of Mann to HW 15 April 1758 are for a letter to Conway. Other memoranda on the same letter were for HW's reply to Mann 10 May (MANN v. 191, 198).

> Lord Tyrawley wigs from Paris
> Soldier, you only French I shall see
> Prawns 2 eyes to one tail
> Lady T. deaf—if deaf dumb as deaf I not know
> Don't pretend to be clever—in right not
> talent is an affectation
> Your Goatti and Wine Gotti

To CONWAY, ca Friday 26 May 1758

Missing; answered *post* 28 May 1758. It mentioned the disagreements of the judges in their testimony on 25 and 26 May (ibid. n. 3).

From CONWAY, Sunday 28 May 1758

Printed in full for the first time from the MS now WSL, formerly Rutnam. The first two paragraphs were previously printed in *Fraser's Magazine*, 1850, xli. 428–9.

The year is supplied by the contents.

Park Place, 28th May.

Dear Horry,

I THINK I had a narrow escape in not coming to town to hear the judges and attend the Habeas Corpus;[1] I dare say they were very ingenious in their way and very edifying to those who have any interest in this bill; otherwise to be sure rather tedious, nor

1. A bill for the extension of the writ of *habeas corpus*, which had passed the House of Commons on 24 April, had been referred by the House of Lords to certain judges for their opinion on ten questions after the second reading, 9 May (MANN v. 182 and nn. 7–8, 205 and nn. 16–21; *Journals of the House of Lords* xxix. 331). The judges presented their opinion before the Lords on 25, 26, and 30 May (ibid. xxix. 337–8, 339–41, 344–7; reprinted in Cobbett, *Parl. Hist.* xv. 903–20). HW gives an account in *Mem. Geo. II* iii. 118–20.

do I at all envy any of you who have patience and constitution to hear twelve judges talk law by the two hours 'in an hothouse for days together, so that I believe I shall quite give up the pleadings and content myself with the reports of the case, though if I knew certainly the very day of the actual debate[2] and had nothing else to do I am not quite sure I should not come. What you tell me in your last of the disagreement of the judges[3] will, I think, put the ministers in a fine ferment; I don't wonder the Duke of N[ewcastle] counts the hours he remains upon the rack where I dare say he will be as long as this bill lasts.[4]

I wish you *could* have told me where the expedition is going;[5] I am very curious to know and have scarce a guess at the place; if it is one of the few worth attempting with such force and parade, I doubt it will be found, if Lord Anson[6] cannot have a *miscarriage,*[7] as C[harles] Townshend says, *qu'il peut rater;* as to the rest of the coast, though it might do very well to destroy a fishing town or burn half a dozen privateers, under the conduct of a commodore[8] I think so many flags and truncheons[9] would be rather disgraced by successes so little worthy of their preparations; except the voice of Party be ready as I don't doubt it will to puff them up to the skies, especially as a contrast to our failings.[10]

We have had Mr and Mrs Hamilton[11] here for some days and did expect Jack and Fred[12] yesterday, but have heard nothing of them;

2. The bill was rejected on a motion to commit, 2 June, when the principal debate took place (*post* 4 June 1758).

3. HW writes in the *Memoirs:* 'When the judges came, they were to talk, to talk on law, and to *explain* that law by *jargon.* The field was so spacious and so inviting, that they ran into all the subtleties, distinctions, chicaneries, and absurdities of their profession. They contradicted one another, and no two of them but differed on some particular case' (*Mem. Geo. II* iii. 118). The Lords *Journals* merely give their formal opinions on each question, but not the reasons by which they explained them. HW's account of their degree of difference is apparently exaggerated (*Hardwicke Corr.* iii. 17–18 and n. 4).

4. The ministry were split on the bill, Pitt and his supporters favouring it, while Newcastle and his friends and Fox

opposed it (MANN v. 205 and nn. 18, 19).

5. An expedition had been preparing in the Isle of Wight since early April; it sailed for the Breton coast on 1 June (ibid. v. 190, 198, 204 and n. 10, 210–11 and nn. 1–9; *post* 4, 11, 16 June 1758).

6. Who was commanding the fleet.

7. An allusion to his supposed impotence; see also *post* 16 June 1758 and n. 6.

8. Commodore Howe, who was in immediate command of the transports, had originally been intended for sole command, but Lord Anson and Hawke, both admirals, had taken the chief command (MANN v. 210; *Mem. Geo. II* iii. 124).

9. I.e., admirals and general officers.

10. At Rochefort.

11. Catherine Barlow (d. 1782), m. (25 Jan. 1758) William Hamilton, K.B., 1772.

12. Conway's brothers-in-law, John and Frederick Campbell.

the wind has not disappointed what you prophesied of it; we have had delightful rains; our grass grows, our shrubs improve and our new plantations live. When shall we see you? I don't mean to be a dun, but can't help asking a little what our chance is and when; I know of no engagements of ours that will prevent it whenever you can think it agreeable to yourself. We shall have the Duchess[13] here, I believe, immediately and perhaps some visitor or other that may drop in but nothing particular, I think, either to tempt or deter you.

Our double flowering syringa has blown, but *very single,* by which Lady Ailesbury is disappointed of a triumph she intended over you and your climate.[14]

The weather is to be sure much better than it has been, but not half so pleasant.

Yours ever,

H. S. C.

To CONWAY, Sunday 4 June 1758

Printed from *Works* v. 55–6, except for the last two sentences of the first paragraph, which were added by Wright iii. 357, who presumably saw the MS, now missing.

Arlington Street, June 4, 1758.

THE Habeas Corpus is finished,[1] but only for this year. Lord Temple threatened to renew it the next; on which Lord Hardwicke took the party of proposing to order the judges to prepare a bill for extending the power of granting the writ in vacation to all the judges.[2] This prevented a division; though Lord Temple, who

13. Of Richmond; the Duke had gone on the expedition (*post* 16 June 1758, n. 16).

14. HW frequently mentions the syringa at SH (e.g., MONTAGU i. 149, 162, ii. 156).

1. On 2 June, when after a 'long debate,' a motion to commit the bill was rejected, thus throwing it out (*Journals of the House of Lords* xxix. 352).

2. 'Ordered, that the judges do prepare a bill to extend the power of granting writs of *habeas corpus ad subjiciendum*

in vacation time, in cases not within the statute 31 Ch. II, ch. 2 to all the judges of his Majesty's courts at Westminster, and to provide for the issuing of process in vacation time, to compel obedience to such writs; and that, in preparing such bill, the judges do take into consideration, whether, in any and what cases, it may be proper to make provision, that the truth of the facts contained in the return to a writ of *habeas corpus* may be controverted by affidavits or traverse, and, so far as it shall appear to be proper,

protested alone t'other day,[3] had a flaming protest ready, which was to have been signed by near thirty.[4] They sat last night[5] till past nine. Lord Mansfield spoke admirably for two hours and twenty-five minutes.[6] Except Lord Ravensworth and the Duke of Newcastle, whose meaning the first never knows himself, and the latter's nobody else, all who spoke, spoke well: they were Lord Temple, Lord Talbot, Lord Bruce,[7] and Lord Stanhope,[8] for; Lord Morton,[9] Lord Hardwicke, and Lord Mansfield, against the bill. T'other day in our House, we had Lady Ferrers'[10] affair:[11] her sister[12] was heard, and Lord Westmoreland,[13] who had a seat within the bar. Mr Fox opposed the settlement;[14] but it passed.

that clauses be inserted for that purpose; and that the judges do lay such a bill before the House in the beginning of the next session of Parliament' (ibid. xxix. 353). No such bill was brought in until 1816 (56 Geo. III, c. 100).

3. On 30 May, after his attempt to have another question referred to the judges was defeated. His protest is in *Journals of the House of Lords* xxix. 347.

4. His protest, signed by himself alone, is ibid. xxix. 352-3.

5. I.e., on the 2d.

6. HW wrote in his *Memoirs:* 'He spoke for two hours and half: his voice and manner, composed of harmonious solemnity, were the least graces of his speech. I am not averse to own that I never heard so much argument, so much sense, so much oratory united. . . . Perhaps it was the only speech that, in my time at least, had real effect; that is, convinced many persons. . . . I took as many notes of it as I possibly could; and prolix as they would be, I would give them to the reader, if it would not be injustice to Lord Mansfield to curtail and mangle, as I should by the want of connexion, so beautiful a thread of argumentation' (*Mem. Geo. II* iii. 120).

7. Thomas Bruce Bruce Brudenell (after 1767, Brudenell Bruce) (1729–1814), 2d Bn Bruce, cr. (1776) E. of Ailesbury, n.c.

8. Philip Stanhope (1714–86), 2d E. Stanhope, Pitt's first cousin.

9. James Douglas (1702 *or* 1703–68), 14th E. of Morton.

10. Mary Meredith (ca 1738–1807), m. 1 (1752) Laurence Shirley, 4th E. Ferrers;

m. 2 (1769) Lord Frederick Campbell.

11. HW is referring to the committee of the whole House on the private bill 'for separating Lawrence Earl Ferrers from Mary Countess Ferrers his wife, for the cruelty of the said Earl; and for settling a maintenance for the said Countess out of the estate of the said Earl,' held on 1 June. The bill, which had already passed the Lords, was read a first time 10 May and a second time and committed, 23 May. The committee on 1 June reported 'That they had heard counsel and examined witnesses for the said Countess Ferrers; and that no counsel or witnesses appeared on behalf of the said Earl Ferrers; and that the committee had gone through the bill, and made several amendments thereunto.' The bill, with amendments, was reported 2 June, and read a third time and passed 6 June. The Lords' agreement to the amendments on the 7th was reported to the Commons on the 9th; the bill received the royal assent 20 June as Private Act 31 Geo. II, c. 39 (*Journals of the House of Commons* xxviii. 241, 248, 263–4, 265, 268, 289, 315; MANN v. 183–4 and nn. 17–22).

12. She had four sisters: Elizabeth, m. William Bankes of Winstanley Hall, Lancashire; Martha; Henrietta, m. (15 June 1758) Hon. Frederick Vane; and Anne, m. (1770) Barlow Trecothick (Burke, *Extinct and Dormant Baronetcies*, 1844, p. 632; Namier and Brooke iii. 557, 572).

13. John Fane (1686–1762), 7th E. of Westmorland.

14. He was at some time a creditor of 'Lord Ferrers' (Lord Ilchester, *Henry Fox,*

The Duke of Grafton[15] has resigned. Norborne Berkeley[16] has converted a party of pleasure into a campaign, and is gone with the expedition,[17] without a shirt but what he had on, and what is lent him.[18] The night he sailed he had invited women to supper. Besides him, and those you know,[19] is a Mr Sylvester Smith.[20] Everybody was asking, 'But who is Sylvester Smith?' Harry Townshend[21] replied, 'Why, he is the son of Delaval,[22] who was the son of Lowther,[23] who was the son of Armitage,[24] who was the son of Downe.'[25]

The fleet sailed on Thursday morning.[26] I don't know why, but the persuasion is that they will land on this side Ushant,[27] and that we shall hear some events by Tuesday or Wednesday.[28] Some be-

1920, ii. 357n), although it is not clear whether it was this one or his successor.

15. Augustus Henry Fitzroy (1735–1811), 3d D. of Grafton, had resigned as a lord of the Bedchamber to the Prince of Wales. He wrote in his autobiography (mistakenly implying that it occurred in 1757): 'I retained . . . my place about the Prince, with great kindness from himself, until, from the absence of some of my colleagues and from the illness of others, the duty was become so irksome and constant that I was really compelled to ask leave to resign the post, Lord Bute not being able to give me any expectation of further relief' (Grafton, *Autobiography*, ed. Anson, 1898, p. 11).

16. (?1717–70), 4th Bn Botetourt, 1764; M.P. Gloucestershire 1741–63.

17. Against St Maloes (HW).

18. HW wrote to Chute on 29 June of Berkeley's precipitate departure 'to conquer France in a dirty shirt and a frock' (CHUTE 102). His going on the expedition was generally deplored; Lord Lyttelton wrote to Sanderson Miller ca 9 June: 'Norborne Berkeley's knight errantry in going with the young fellows upon this expedition is much blamed by the world and by all his best friends. Twenty years ago it might have done him some honour; but at his age and in his situation, with the whole Beaufort family left to his care, it is so very improper that one can only account for it by supposing that the military enthusiasm like the religious is catching in men of warm blood when they come within the sphere of its activity' (*An Eighteenth-Century Correspon-*

dence, ed. Dickins and Stanton, New York, 1910, p. 391).

19. Those mentioned in Harry Townshend's witticism below, and in *London Chronicle* 27–30 May, iii. 505, MANN v. 204, CHUTE 287–8, and *Mem. Geo. II* iii. 124.

20. Possibly John Silvester Smith (1734–89) of Newland Park, Yorks, cr. (1784) Bt (GEC, *Baronetage* v. 239).

21. Henry Townshend (1736–62), 3d son of Hon. Thomas Townshend; ensign 2d Foot Guards, 1755; Capt. 5th Foot, 1758; Capt.-Lt 1st Foot Guards and Lt-Col., 1762; M.P. Eye 1758–60, 1761–2.

22. Francis Blake Delaval (1727–71), K.B., 1761; M.P. Hindon 1751–4, Andover 1754–68. HW told Mann on 31 May that he was 'so ridiculous a character, that it [his volunteering] has put a stop to the mode which was spreading' (MANN v. 204).

23. Sir James Lowther (*ante* 16 April 1756, n. 18).

24. Sir John Armytage (1732–58), 2d Bt; M.P. York City 1754–8. He was mortally wounded at St-Cast in Sept. (*post* 19 Sept. 1758).

25. Henry Pleydell Dawnay (1727–60), 3d Vct Downe; M.P. Yorkshire 1750–60. The joke seems to lie in the order of their volunteering; they had all gone with the 10th Dragoons (R. S. Liddell, *Memoirs of the Tenth Royal Hussars*, 1891, p. 37).

26. 1 June.

27. At the tip of the Breton peninsula; the expedition landed at Cancale Bay, near St-Malo (*post* 11 June 1758).

28. The news of their successful land-

NINON de L'ENCLOS
from an Original Picture.
given by herself
to the Countess of Sandwich
and by the present Earl
of Sandwich
to Mr Walpole 1757

lieve that Lord Anson and Howe have different destinations.[29] Rochfort, where there are 20,000 men,[30] is said positively not to be the place. The King says there are 80,000 men and three marshals in Normandy and Bretagne.[31] George Selwyn asked General Campbell,[32] if the ministry had yet told the King the object?

Mademoiselle de l'Enclos[33] is arrived, to my supreme felicity—I cannot say very handsome or agreeable; but I had been prepared on the article of her charms. I don't say, like Harry VIII, of Anne of Cleves,[34] that she is a Flanders mare,[35] though to be sure she is rather large: on the contrary, I bear it as well as ever prince did who was married by proxy—and she does not find me *fricassé dans de la neige*.[36] Adieu.

Yours ever,

HOR. WALPOLE

PS. I forgot to tell you of another *galanterie* I have had, a portrait of Queen Elizabeth[37] left here while I was out of town. The servant said it was a present, but he had orders not to say from whom.

---

ing arrived on the night of 8–9 June (MANN v. 210 and n. 4).

29. Anson, with the battle fleet, was to lie off Brest, considerably west of the intended debarkation point of the expedition (J. S. Corbett, *England in the Seven Years' War*, 1907, i. 273–5).

30. It was reported that in April there were 12,000 men stationed near Rochefort and that this force was to be increased to 20,000 (Charles-Philippe d'Albert, Duc de Luynes, *Mémoires . . . sur la cour de Louis XV*, 1860–5, xvi. 405).

31. According to British intelligence from Paris, an army of 80,000 was to be assembled in four camps: between Calais and Dunkirk; at Havre; in Brittany near St-Malo, L'Orient, and Brest; and near Rochefort and La Rochelle (Corbett, op. cit. i. 254–5). HW describes the King as opposed to the expedition and as saying, 'I never had any opinion of it; we shall brag of having burnt their ships, and they, of having driven us away' (*Mem. Geo. II* iii. 125, n. 1).

32. Lady Ailesbury's father.

33. The portrait of Ninon de l'Enclos,

now at Strawberry Hill, given to Mr Walpole by the old Countess of Sandwich, daughter to the famous Lord Rochester. She died at Paris in the year 1755 (HW). For HW's portrait of Ninon de Lenclos (1620–1705), see illustration and MORE 6, n. 2.

34. (1515–57), m. (1540) Henry VIII.

35. The phrase is attributed to Henry VIII by Gilbert Burnet, *History of the Reformation of the Church of England*, ed. Pocock, Oxford, 1865, i. 434. No contemporary authority has been found; see A. F. Pollard, *Henry VIII*, 1951, p. 309 and n. 1.

36. Madame de Sévigné, in her letters to her daughter, reports that Ninon thus expressed herself relative to her son the Marquis de Sévigné, who was one of her lovers (HW). The passage is in Mme de Sévigné, *Lettres*, ed. Monmerqué, 1862–6, ii. 176.

37. Possibly the portrait by Zucchero of 'Queen Elizabeth, when a girl' in the Holbein Chamber at SH ('Des. of SH,' *Works* ii. 456); it was sold SH xx. 34 to J. Tollemache for 13 guineas.

To CONWAY, ca Wednesday 7 June 1758

Missing. Conway says *post* 11 June that he had three unanswered letters from HW; one of these was *ante* 4 June; the second (this one) may have been sent on the arrival of unfounded reports that the expedition had landed at Morlaix, about 25 miles from Brest, which reached London on the 6th and were published in the newspapers on the 7th (*ante* 4 June 1758, nn. 27–8).

To CONWAY, ca Friday 9 June 1758

Missing; from what Conway says *post* 11 June, HW had sent him an account of the first news of the landing of the troops at Cancale Bay, which had reached London during the night of 8–9 June (MANN v. 210 and n. 4).

From CONWAY, Sunday 11 June 1758

Printed in full for the first time from the MS now WSL, formerly Rutnam. The last four paragraphs were printed in *Fraser's Magazine*, 1850, xli. 429–30.

Park Place, 11 June 1758.

I DON'T know whether I should say I am ashamed to have three of your letters now before me unanswered; if I am ashamed on one hand I am very proud of it on the other, and so happy with them, that you come as near as possible to puzzling me with the option between your letters and your company, though not so near as to make me quite in peace with you for the paragraph in your last where you say if it is left to you your party here with the Churchills *will never be fixed;*[1] you say it's honest but certainly it is not *honnête* to tell one so; there is nothing so disagreeable as some kinds of honesty, and though you are so good in other respects I can't scold you, I must say you are very mortifying with your honesty, and that nothing can make it up to us but your repenting of it and forming the party soon, so pray tell Churchill and bestow some of your honesty in that, that we won't be fobbed off so; they have

1. The party was finally fixed for 21 June (*post* 16 June; see also CHUTE 289; HW to Lord Lyttelton 25 June).

promised and therefore their honesty won't shine if [you] don't perform and though you say the summer is long and all before us I don't agree with you at all; I think it short and past, probably the best part gone already. You never go to Vauxhall; Ranalagh is worn out, the secret of the expedition is over[2] and so will the exploits of it probably be soon; in short if your patience about those events and your impatience for our meeting were half as great as mine, you'd see all these things in a different light. I won't plague you any more with invitations but certainly the weather is too good to be thrown away on gazettes and expresses, or sauntered away at White's and Betty's.[3]

Our successes are indeed delightful as you say; it is the finest season of events I ever knew, but as Mr Pitt waters them and prunes them and keeps 'em growing one under another there will be no end of waiting for them all. I really hear them with great pleasure and find no fault with them but that I have not my mite embarked with 'em.[4] It's mortifying to anyone that has tasted a little though but ever so little of that sound: *carmine gratioris;* to be set down and finish with the bitter relish of reproach; and only concerned in a thing blamed and unsuccessful;[5] I own I feel that enough to dread a peace in our present circumstances and to feel some regret even in our successes as the probable forerunners of it.

I don't agree with you in thinking that we shall continue hussaring upon the coast; I fancy by the account you give we shall succeed at St Maloes whatever the business is and return. I suppose they'll take the town and destroy as much of the works as they can; but that the principal view is on the stores, docks, and shipping; of what nature and value they are I don't know; it is a very considerable

2. With the arrival of the news during the night of 8–9 June of the landing at Cancale Bay on the night of the 5th (*ante* 4 June 1758, nn. 27–8).

3. Elizabeth Munro (or Neale) (ca 1730–97), apple-seller, noted for her newsmongering (MONTAGU i. 109; MASON i. 81; SELWYN 148, 156).

4. Conway had pressed to go with the expedition '*in any capacity*' but had not been allowed to do so (MANN v. 198). His friend Lord Lyttelton had written on 5 May 'if Mr Conway was employed under his Grace [the D. of Marlborough, in command of the land forces], as he wished and desired to be, I should think nothing would be wanting in that command, but the same reasons that made Mr Pitt and his faction refuse him in America [see *post* 4 July, n. 15, 15 OCT., n. 4], have also prevailed to exclude him from any employment in Europe, which I fear will be, *magno reipublicæ detrimento.* God knows we have not more good generals than we want, and none better than he' (to W. H. Lyttelton, in Robert Phillimore, *Memoirs and Correspondence of George, Lord Lyttelton,* 1845, ii. 606).

5. The Rochefort expedition.

place for trade and a very famous one for privateers as everyone knows; the King, I believe, has neither docks nor stores there.[6] What the strength of the town is I don't know but one battalion if that be true can certainly not defend it;[7] especially if as you say there are no troops at hand.[8] I fancy it will be a very popular conquest if not a very valuable one as being such a nest of privateers: I think we have twice or thrice attempted to bombard it[9] with little success.

Adieu. Dear Horry, thank you a thousand times for your letters, your news, your bons mots, your verses,[10] which are all excellent but as Mr Cadwalladar[11] says: 'Damn your honesty.'

Yours ever,

H. S. C.

We have nobody here but the Duchess[12] nor expect immediately. I only mention this, I invite no more.

6. Although St-Malo was not a royal arsenal, it was an important harbour for the merchant marine, and the contiguous harbour of St-Servan had a large dockyard and extensive naval storehouses (R. Beatson, *Naval and Military Memoirs of Great Britain*, 1804, ii. 169–70, iii. 192; *post* 16 June 1758, n. 8).

7. The early reports were that there were not more than 700 men in St-Malo (Newcastle to Devonshire 9 June, BM Add. MSS 32880, f. 377). This was a considerable underestimate; although the town was inadequately garrisoned, there were about 2000 men there (G. Lacour-Gayet, *La Marine militaire de la France sous le règne de Louis XV*, 1902, pp. 312–13).

8. Marlborough reported on the 6th that it was said that troops were collecting 'but as yet we hear of no considerable body being collected' (Marlborough to Pitt 6 June, BM Add. MSS 32880, ff. 335–6). HW told Mann on the 11th that there were no troops within twenty leagues (MANN v. 210). Marshal de Belle-Isle wrote 9 June that the Duc d'Aiguil-

lon was near Dinan with 16 battalions and a regiment of dragoons (C. Hippeau, *Le Gouvernement de Normandie au xviime et au xviiime siècle*, Caen, 1863–9, Pt I, i. 177).

9. The most famous bombardment by the English was in 1693, followed by another in 1695 (E. Durtelle de Saint-Sauveur, *Histoire de Bretagne des origines à nos jours*, 1935, ii. 120–1; Société des Bibliophile Bretons et de l'histoire de Bretagne, *Le bombardement et la machine infernale des anglais contre Saint-Malo en 1693*, ed. Arthur de la Borderie, Nantes, 1885; Lacour-Gayet, op. cit. 10). In the early 18th century the English did not attack St-Malo (Saint-Sauveur, op. cit. ii. 137–8).

10. Not identified.

11. A character in *The Author* by Samuel Foote (1720–77), first performed 5 Feb. 1757 when Foote played Cadwallader; the exact phrase quoted does not appear in the printed versions, but there are numerous similar ones in his speeches.

12. Of Richmond.

To Conway, Friday 16 June 1758

Printed from *Works* v. 56–7.

June 16, 1758, 2 o'clock noon.

WELL, my dear Harry! you are not the only man in England who have not conquered France![1] Even Dukes of Marlborough[2] have been there without doing the business.[3] I don't doubt but your good heart has even been hoping, in spite of your understanding, that our heroes have not only taken St Maloes, but taken a trip cross the country to burn Rochfort, only to show how easy it was. We have waited with astonishment at not hearing that the French Court was removed in a panic to Lyons,[4] and that the Mesdames[5] had gone off in their shifts with only a provision of rouge for a week. Nay, for my part, I expected to be deafened with encomiums on my Lord Anson's continence,[6] who, after being allotted Madame Pompadour as his share of the spoils, had again imitated Scipio, and, in spite of the violence of his *temperament,* had restored her unsullied to the King of France.—Alack! we have restored nothing but a quarter of a mile of coast to the right owners.

1. Alluding to the expedition against Rochefort, the year before, on which Mr Conway was second in command (HW). As HW relates below, news that the expedition had re-embarked on 11–12 June after burning ships at St-Servan near St-Malo, had reached London during the night of 15 June in a letter from the D. of Marlborough of 12 June (MANN v. 212, n. 1; J. Grenville to G. Grenville [16 June], MS now WSL).

2. The Duke of Marlborough commanded the troops on this expedition against St Maloes (HW).

3. The allusion is to the 'Great' Duke of Marlborough in the War of the Spanish Succession. HW also alludes to the power of his 'very name' to Mann 11 June (MANN v. 211), to Strafford 16 June (CHUTE 287), and in *Mem. Geo. II* iii. 125.

4. 'We are informed by dispatches from Paris, that the arrival there of a courier from St Maloes, with an account of the landing of the English, had thrown the whole Court and city into the utmost confusion. The consternation amongst the people was so great, that all business was at a stand. On this occasion an extraordinary council was immediately held, and orders were dispatched for all the militia in that part of the kingdom to assemble forthwith. The regular troops, for above sixty miles round St Maloes, had likewise orders to march, who being joined by the militia, and several companies drawn out of the garrisons, formed in about four days, a body of between 20 and 30,000 men. They had all orders to join in the neighbourhood of Aurenches, about ten leagues from St Maloes' (*London Chronicle* 22–4 June, iii. 596, *sub* Hague 14 June).

5. The daughters of Louis XV.

6. An allusion to an incident related in Richard Walter's edition of Anson's *Voyage Round the World,* 1748, pp. 249–50, telling how he had allowed a Spanish lady and her two beautiful daughters to keep their quarters on a captured vessel without even seeing them. See the general index for the many references to his alleged impotence.

A messenger[7] arrived in the middle of the night with an account that we have burned two frigates and an hundred and twenty small fry;[8] that it was found impossible to bring up the cannon against the town;[9] and that, the French army approaching the coast, Commodore Howe, with the expedition of Harlequin as well as the taciturnity, re-embarked our whole force in seven hours,[10] volunteers and all, with the loss only of one man,[11] and they are all gone to seek their fortune somewhere else.[12] Well! in half a dozen more wars we shall know something of the coast of France. Last war we discovered a fine bay near Port l'Orient:[13] we have now found out that we knew nothing of St Maloes. As they are popular persons, I hope the City of London will send some more gold boxes to these discoverers.[14] If they send a patch box to Lord George Sackville, it will hold all his laurels.[15] As our young nobility cannot at present travel through

7. Joseph Fraine (fl. 1745–88), Lt, 1745; Post Capt., 1759; commander of the *Speedwell* sloop, 1758, which brought the news (John Charnock, *Biographia Navalis*, 1794–8, vi. 364; *London Gazette* No. 9800, 13–17 June). He died before 1804 (GM 1804, lxxiv pt ii. 695).

8. Marlborough's letter reported that they had burned 'one man of war of 50 guns, one of 36, all the privateers, some of 30, several of 20 and 18 guns, and in the whole, upwards of 100 ships' (*London Gazette* loc. cit.). For other contemporary estimates see MANN v. 214, n. 10. Other figures from later accounts are a 50-gun ship, two frigates under construction, some twenty privateers, and some sixty merchant ships (G. Lacour-Gayet, *La Marine militaire de la France sous le règne de Louis XV*, 1902, p. 313); 'at St-Servan four King's ships of from fifty to eighteen guns on the stocks and sixty-two merchantmen; and at Solidore hard by, eight fine privateers ready for sea and twelve other vessels, besides small craft' (J. S. Corbett, *England in the Seven Years' War*, 1907, i. 277); and L. H. Gipson, *British Empire before the American Revolution*, 1936–70, vii. 133, gives 166. HW's figure of 120 has not been found elsewhere, and he modifies it to 'about a hundred' to Mann 18 June (MANN v. 214).

9. Marlborough's letter merely said that they found it 'impracticable to attack that place' (*London Gazette* loc. cit.). It had

been found impossible to bring the siege train directly overland from Cancale Bay, and an attempt to land it from the sea at St-Servan failed (Corbett, op. cit. i. 278).

10. 'Commodore Howe had made so good a disposition of the boats and transports, that four brigades, and ten companies of grenadiers, were re-embarked in less than seven hours, the enemy not having attempted to attack them' (*London Gazette* loc. cit.).

11. 'One man only was shot by the enemy, two by our own people, for marauding' (James Grenville to George Grenville [16 June], loc. cit.; see also MANN v. 214 and n. 9).

12. Marlborough reported that on the 12th 'all the troops were on board, waiting to take advantage of the first wind, to pursue the farther objects of his Majesty's instructions' (*London Gazette* loc. cit.).

13. Quiberon Bay, the object of an unsuccessful expedition in 1746. HW makes a similar comment in the *Memoirs*, saying that the commander seemed 'dispatched . . . to *discover* the coast of France, rather than to master it' (*Mem. Geo. II* iii. 124–5).

14. As London and other cities had to Pitt in the spring of 1757 (ibid. iii. 5).

15. HW says ibid. iii. 125 that Marlborough 'and his troops remarked that Lord George Sackville was not among the first to court danger,' but the allusion

France, I suppose this is a method for finishing their studies. George Selwyn says he supposes the French ladies will have scaffolds erected on the shore to see the English go by.—But I won't detain the messenger any longer; I am impatient to make the Duchess[16] happy, who I hope will soon see the Duke returned from his coasting voyage.

The Churchills will be with you next Wednesday, and I believe I too; but I can take my own word so little, that I will not give it you. I know I must be back at Strawberry on Friday night; for Lady Hervey and Lady Stafford[17] are to be there with me for a few days from tomorrow sennight. Adieu!

Yours ever,

HOR. WALPOLE

To HERTFORD, Friday 16 June 1758

Missing; from *post* 16 June 1758 it is clear that HW had written to Hertford in similar terms as he had to Conway.

here is more likely to his current favour with Pitt, his outranking Conway, and HW's belief that he was the effective commander of the expedition (MANN v. 198; *Mem. Geo. II* iii. 107–8).

16. Lady Mary Bruce, Duchess of Richmond, only child of the Countess of Ailesbury by her first marriage. She was at Park Place with her mother during the Duke of Richmond's absence, who was a volunteer upon this expedition (HW). Richmond was not a volunteer, but Col. of the newly constituted 72d Foot (cre-

ated from the 2d Battalion of the 33d Foot, of which he had been Lt-Col., 9 May 1758, and disbanded in 1763); the regiment was on both the expeditions to the coast of France in 1758 (J. W. Fortescue, *History of the British Army*, 1910–30, ii. 346, n. 1, 348, n. 1; Richard Cannon, *Historical Record of the Seventy-Second Regiment*, 1848, p. xxxiv; *Army Lists* 1759, p. 124).

17. See *ante* 27 Nov. 1755, n. 6; she was an intimate friend of Lady Hervey (MORE 7, n. 10).

From CONWAY, Friday 16 June 1758

Printed from the MS now WSL, formerly Rutnam. Previously printed *Fraser's Magazine*, 1850, xli. 430. The year is supplied by the reference to the expedition to St-Malo.

Address: To the Honourable Horatio Walpole.

Taploe, 16 June.

Dear Horry,

YOUR letters found us at Taploe together and have made us all easy, and some happy: I will not be so affected between us, as to say I have not my share. I should have been happy in any considerable success our arms had and sorry for any misfortune we suffered; but as I had no great idea of a St Maloes expedition, I can't be very sorry our heroes, nor our ministers, nor our volunteers, have been disappointed in their views of killing and being killed. This will, I fancy, convince 'em all towns are not of course to be taken by a *coup de main;* that cannon is a little necessary to take fortified towns,[1] that it is not to be carried across a country in a portmanteau, and perhaps that the possession of a navigable river is not amiss on such an occasion.

We shall be glad to see the Churchills next week, and, pray let me say, you. I write for my brother and myself in the midst of his company, among whom is Lady Pembroke,[2] who wonders you can joke upon Lord Anson's misfortunes.

In earnest expectation of seeing you,

Yours ever,

H. S. C.

1. The absence of proper siege equipment was one of the factors in the decision not to attack Rochefort in Sept. 1757; though the St-Malo expedition was better prepared, it was impossible to bring up the cannon (*ante* HW to Conway 16 June). See HW's comments on the subject to Mann 18 June (MANN v. 213).

2. Probably Hon. Mary Fitzwilliam (1707–69), m. 1 (1733) Henry Herbert, 9th E. of Pembroke; m. 2 (1751) Maj. North Ludlow Bernard; and not her daughter-in-law Lady Elizabeth Spencer (1737–1831), m. (1756) Henry Herbert, 10th E. of Pembroke.

To CONWAY, ca Saturday 1 July 1758

Missing; answered *post* 4 July 1758. It included a draft (missing) of HW's proposed dedication to Conway of his *Fugitive Pieces.*

From CONWAY, Tuesday 4 July 1758

Printed from the MS now WSL, formerly Rutnam; probably a draft. The version printed in *Fraser's Magazine*, 1850, xli. 430–1 differs in many particulars, some of which seem closer to the text to which HW is replying *post* 8 July 1758 than does this one. See Appendix 5 and n. 5 below
Endorsed: To H. W. 4th July 1758 on his dedication.

Park Place, 4 July 1758.

YOU'LL be surprised you have not heard from me before; at least you have a good right to be so; you don't expect a regular answer, you tell me, to all the packets I have from you, but your last was certainly such an one as did deserve a little more than ordinary notice; the truth was I had a little feverish feel and was blooded by way of prevention rather than cure which disabled me. Nothing less than inability should have prevented it for you can't imagine how much in haste I was to let you know how very kindly I take your intention of dedicating to me[1] as well as the manner in which you do it; I can't help thinking how most authors would think a dedication thrown away upon so little a personage as myself,[2] and being still the more obliged to you and esteeming it just as much above common dedications as disinterested friendship is superior to mercenary adulation.

But having done this justice to you I am afraid I am going to betray myself by showing that you have not guessed at all right at the kind of objections I have to your dedication and that for *modest reasons,* which you seem to expect, I doubt you must read *vain ones.* First, then, I must own I do rather apprehend that *the censure*

1. HW was planning to dedicate his *Fugitive Pieces,* now being printed at the SH Press, to Conway. Printing had begun 24 April and was completed 13 July (HW,

Journal of the Printing Office at Strawberry Hill, ed. Toynbee, 1923, p. 7).
2. The printed version reads 'an insignificant cousin like myself.'

of a world governed by prejudice[3] does convey an idea that it is the censure of the *whole world* or greatest part of it I lie under, which though ever so true (and I hope it is not quite so), I should not like to see transmitted to posterity with your works, for though you call it a world governed by prejudice I should doubt if that expression from *a friend* would countervail the establishing the fact of *general censure* upon such authority. And as you say *your esteem is not to be shaken by that censure,* I own it does seem to me to imply that there was something in the nature of that censure which might *shake friendships* and that it required a sort of effort of yours not to be shaken. All this lies in the compass of one single line the alteration of which would, I think, leave it unexceptionable to any but *modest objections* which at present I feel very well disposed to waive:[4] I leave it, however, to your own much better judgment to do in regard to it as you think best, thinking myself safer in your hands than my own. I have also a mind especially if you leave it out in the first part to throw malice or prejudice in where I have put the cross;[5] this also I submit to you; excuse my tampering at all with a work I am perhaps only capable of spoiling and my vanity that is not content with more praise than I deserve.

I will say no more upon the subject but that I shall bethink myself happy and let me say honoured, too, in this public and, I dare say, permanent mark of your friendship.

The Duchess[6] had an express from the Duke yesterday morning[7]

3. This and the following clause quoted by Conway were from the original opening of the dedication. HW altered them as Conway requested to the version he quotes *post* 8 July, which was the one printed in the dedication.

4. Conway is probably alluding to the sentence 'If your virtues and your talents can be forgot, if your actions at Fontenoy and at Laffelt, in Flanders and in Scotland can fade away, shall such writings as mine endure?'

5. HW declined to make this change (*post* 8 July 1758); it was probably in the last sentence of the first paragraph, after 'scale against you': 'Nay, if Rochfort, which you alone (romantic as the attempt was) proposed to attack, can be thrown into the scale against you, my panegyric might be perverted to satire

too, for when real merit is obnoxious to blame, empty praise can hardly be incorruptible.' HW did make one other change in this sentence, suggested by Conway in the printed version of this letter: 'I forgot to say that I think *"proposed to attack"* is less exceptionable than *"would have undertaken to attack,"* as they did all consent in one council of war, etc.'

6. Of Richmond.

7. The expedition had returned to Spithead on 1 July (MANN v. 221, n. 3). Richmond went directly to Goodwood, as this sentence in the printed version makes clear: 'The Duchess of Richmond left us yesterday morning to go to Goodwood, where the Duke was just arrived when his express came away.' He summoned the Foxes on the 5th, and when Lady Caroline arrived on the 7th with

from Goodwood whither she posted soon after as you may conclude. You'll probably have heard all that relates to the expedition by this time. Lord Down, I hear, was in town on Sunday,[8] so that I am surprised I do not even see the expedition mentioned in yesterday's paper which is come.[9]

They have not even drunk tea under the cannon of Cherbourg[10] and having, as I hear, contented themselves with peeping at that and Havre,[11] are returned half starved and sickly[12] having twice threatened to land, but found that greater heroes than us might be prevented by high winds and open bays.

Our intelligence says none were allowed to come ashore and that

news of regiments (but not his) being ordered to Germany, he immediately decided to go to London 'to advise with Mr Conway whether he should not go immediately to the King to say how hard he thought it to continue going in this cruising about expedition all summer, that since some regiments went to Germany he begged his might be one. He was very warm about [it], said he gave up a great deal to be in the army. Learning his business was his point, and he had rather go quite out than continue this summer going about on this silly, useless, unhealthy, and unpleasant service. . . . I think Colonel Conway will advise him to take no step rashly about it' (Lady Caroline Fox to Lady Kildare 10 July, *Leinster Corr.* i. 169). Richmond got to London on the 8th or 9th, and was refused permission to go to Germany by the King, apparently before he consulted Conway. Lady Caroline reported on the 11th, 'he is much vexed about it, and I believe has thoughts of resigning. . . . However, he will consult the Duke, Lord Albemarle, General Conway and Mr Fox before he does take any step' (ibid. i. 171; *Daily Adv.* 10 July). He did not resign and was on the Cherbourg-St Cast expedition.

8. 'The Volunteers got to town on Sunday' (Elliot to Grenville 4 July, *Grenville Papers* i. 246–7, MS now WSL; *Daily Adv.* 3 July). They had apparently arrived almost as soon as news of the return of the expedition itself, which also reached London on the 2d (Pitt to Newcastle 2 July, BM Add. MSS 32881, f. 141). Conway

wrote in the printed version: 'Lord Downe, who was expeditious in his return as Mr Delaval was in his descent. . . .'

9. The return of the expedition is mentioned in the *Daily Adv.* 3 July. The printed version of this letter is much more full here: 'Their return was not even mentioned in the newspapers of yesterday, where there are only some *natural* accounts from Paris of their having destroyed to the amount of many millions at St Maloes, landed somewhere else—I don't know where, kept all their troops employed in continual marches, and harassed them to death; whereas my intelligence says they have landed nowhere.'

10. This was originally HW's suggestion, as the printed version makes clear by the insertion of 'as you suppose'; see also *post* 20 July 1758.

11. The fleet had made feints at Havre, Caen, Harfleur, and Cherbourg (MANN v. 214, n. 12). It had actually been reported that they had landed near Cherbourg (HW to Chute 29 June 1758, CHUTE 101–2), but the attempt, planned for the 29th, had been abandoned because of bad weather (Howe to Clevland 30 June, BM Add. MSS 32881, f. 145).

12. 'On the 7th [July] the troops disembarked and encamped, the foot in the Isle of Wight, and the horse on South-Sea Common, at Portsmouth. They had 1200 sick, occasioned by the inclemency of the weather' (*London Magazine* 1758, xxvii. 369; *post* 21 July 1758).

they expected to go out again.[13] I scarce think it will be to the coast of France, though they pretend the army for Flanders is all named.[14]

I wrote to Lord Ligonier[15] desiring to be sent there, but had for answer[16] that all the generals were named *by the King*, but that he [Ligonier] thought we remained weak at home and that if in case of any accident I cared to share my fate with him he should desire *no better second*. In short, by this, as well [as] other steps I have taken,[17] I think I seem condemned to home service for the present at least; my thoughts on that subject you know.

13. The newspapers reported that 'in about three days they think of sailing again' (*Daily Adv.* 4 July). Pitt had called a Cabinet meeting for the 5th 'to consider of the future destination of the troops'; the result was that 'our expedition is to go out again immediately. . . . It is to go, first, to Cherbourg, then, to Morlaix; and, if neither succeeds, there is *talk* of sending 4000 men only into the Bay of Biscay' (Newcastle to Anson 7 July, BM Add. MSS 32881, f. 190; Holdernesse to Newcastle 3 July, ibid. f. 149). Further accounts of the Cabinet meeting are in *Political Journal of George Bubb Dodington*, ed. J. Carswell and L. A. Dralle, Oxford, 1965, p. 372. The expedition did not sail again until 31 July (*London Magazine* 1758, xxvii. 424) because of delays in finding a commander (J. W. Fortescue, *History of the British Army*, 1910–30, ii. 348).

14. The decision to send troops, originally to Flanders but later changed to Germany, to reinforce Prince Ferdinand had been taken by 23 June (Pitt to Bute 23, 26 June, Romney Sedgwick, 'Letters from William Pitt to Lord Bute: 1755–1758,' in *Essays Presented to Sir Lewis Namier*, ed. Pares and Taylor, 1956, pp. 153–5). To those already selected were to be added three regiments of foot from the expedition; 'the whole reinforcement will be six regiments of horse and dragoons and six regiments of foot, amounting in all to upwards of 8000 men' (Newcastle to Legge 6 July, BM Add. MSS 32881, f. 178; see also Carswell and Dralle, op. cit. 372–3; Fortescue, op. cit. 347).

15. Conway summarizes this letter in writing to Devonshire 7 July; 'As soon as I had the answer you sent me in relation to my being employed in Germany, I wrote to Lord Ligonier on the same subject, saying that I had heard of no gen[eral] officer named but Lord Granby who I did presume would not be the only one sent; that I did not desire or expect any particular command but only to serve in my rank as major general: which I was very earnest in desiring' (Chatsworth MSS, 416 / 53).

16. Conway quotes Ligonier's answer as in this paragraph and then comments to Devonshire 7 July, 'This answer I think looks like a civil refusal to speak to the King for me to be employed and a sort of condemnation to home service; which I own in my present disposition I cannot patiently bear the thoughts of' (ibid.). When Ligonier had submitted the proposed staff for 1758, the King had 'struck off with his own hand Mordaunt, Conway and Cornwalis' (Ligonier to Lord George Sackville 12 Jan. 1758, Hist. MSS Comm., *Stopford-Sackville MSS*, 1904–10, i. 53). According to HW, when Ligonier then urged Conway's eagerness for employment and that he had at least tried to do something on the Rochefort expedition, the King replied, 'Yes, . . . *après dîner la moutarde*,' but said he would think of Conway, but not then (*Mem. Geo. II* iii. 91).

17. Conway wrote Devonshire 28 June 1758, 'I am extremely obliged to your Grace for the trouble you have had in speaking to Lady Yarmouth; tho' I must own a good deal mortified at the ill success of it: as to his M[ajesty]'s favour who perhaps with some pains (more than I shall ever think again of giving your Grace or any friend of mine) be brought to honour me with half a sentence a

Adieu, I have nothing new to tell you from hence. Lady Louisa[18] is still here; we are vastly glad of her company as nothing is more lively and good-natured. Lady An[19] has been this fortnight fetching her away, but I fancy waits for the return of the expedition when she may want her more at Charlton[20] than she does at Woburne.

Yours ever.

To CONWAY, Saturday 8 July 1758

Printed from the MS now WSL; first printed Wright iii. 368–70. For the history of the MS see *ante* 29 June 1744 OS.

Endorsed: Mr H. W. 8 July 1758.

Arlington Street, July 8th 1758.

YOU have made me laugh: do you think I found much difficulty to persist in thinking as well of you as I used to do, though you have neither been as great a Poliorcetes as Almanzor,[1] who could take a town alone, nor have executed the commands of another Almanzor,[2] who thought he could command the walls of a city to tumble down as easily as those of Jericho did to the march of Joshua's first regiment of guards?[3] Am I so apt to be swayed by popular clamour—but I will say no more on that head—as to the wording of the sentence, I approve your objection,[4] and as I have at least so little of the author in me as to be very corrigible, I will, if you think proper, word the beginning thus;

twelvemonth hence, but thinks too ill of me to let me be employed in my profession, the only favour I care about, I should think much more meanly of myself if I was solicitous about it. The end I proposed from favour is it seems not attainable and the favour itself without it is in my present disposition the least of my ambition. My comfort is that if I am ill at one Court I am worse at the other, so that if I fail of employment in the probably short period of his M[ajesty]'s life and of this war, still less likely to last, it may possibly be forever' (Chatsworth MSS, 416 / 52).

18. Lady Louisa Ker (1739–1830), eldest dau. of Lady Ancram, m. (1759) Lord George Henry Lennox (MORE 116–17, n. 1).

19. Countess of Ancram.

20. Charlton House, Kent, seat of the Earls of Egmont; it was 'rented for a short time by the Marquis of Lothian [i.e., Lord Ancram]' (Daniel Lysons, *Environs of London*, 1792–6, iv. 328–9). Ancram had not returned yet, for the *London Chronicle* reports (8–11 July, iv. 30), 'Lord Ancram continues very ill at Portsmouth, labouring under a stone in the bladder.'

1. The hero of Dryden's *Almanzor and Almahide: or, The Conquest of Granada.*

2. Pitt.

3. Joshua vi. 20.

4. See *ante* 4 July 1758.

'In dedicating a few trifles to you, I have nothing new to tell the world. My esteem still accompanies your merit, on which it was founded, and to which, with such abilities as mine, I can only bear testimony; I must not pretend to vindicate it. If your virtues etc.'

It shall not be said that I allowed prejudice and clamour[5] to be the voice of the world against you. I approve too the change of *proposed* for *would have undertaken:* but I cannot like putting in *prejudice and malice.* When one accuses others of malice, one is a little apt to feel it; and could I flatter myself that such a thing as a dedication would have weight, or that anything of mine would last, I would have it look as dispassionate as possible. When after some interval I assert coolly that you was most wrongfully blamed, I shall be believed—if I seem angry, it will look like a Party quarrel still existing.

Instead of resenting your not being employed in the present follies, I think you might write a letter of thanks to my Lord Legonier, or to Mr Pitt, or even to the *Person* who is *appointed* to *appoint* generals himself,[6] to thank them for not exposing you a second year. All the puffs in the newspapers cannot long stifle the ridicule which the French will of course propagate through all Europe on the foolish figure we have made.[7] You shall judge by one sample; the Duc d'Aiguillon[8] has literally sent a vessel with a flag of truce to the Duke of Marlborough, with some teaspoons which in his hurry he left behind him.[9] I know the person[10] who saw the packet before it was delivered to Blenheimcino.[11] But what will you say to this wise commander[12] himself? I am going to tell you no secret, but what he uttered publicly at the levee.[13] The King asked him if he had raised great contributions? *'Contributions! Sir, we saw nothing but old women.'*—What becomes of the thirty thousand men that made them retire *with such expedition* to their transports?[14]

5. See ibid. n. 3.

6. The King.

7. The French took the expedition rather more seriously than HW allows; see the references cited in MANN v. 213, n. 2.

8. Emmanuel-Armand Vignerot du Plessis-Richelieu (1720–88), Duc d'Aiguillon; governor of Brittany (ibid. v. 221, n. 4).

9. HW relates this anecdote to Mann the same day (ibid. v. 221) and in *Mem. Geo. II* iii. 126.

10. Not identified.

11. I.e., Little Blenheim, this Duke of Marlborough being 'little' compared to the great Duke who defeated the French at Blenheim.

12. Marlborough.

13. Marlborough had arrived in London on the evening of 4 July (Elliot to Grenville [4 July], *Grenville Papers* i. 247, MS now WSL; *Daily Adv.* 6 July).

14. According to HW the original explanation of the decision to re-embark at

My Lord Downe, as decently as he can, makes the greatest joke of their enterprise, and has said at Arthur's, that five hundred men posted with a grain of common sense would have cut them all to pieces. I was not less pleased at what Monsieur de Monbazon,[15] the young prisoner, told Charles Townshend t'other day at Stanley's: he was actually in Rochfort when you landed, where he says they had six thousand men, most impatient for your approach, and so posted that not one of you would ever have returned.[16] This is not an evidence to be forgot.

Howe and Lord George are upon the worst terms,[17] as the latter is with the military too. I can tell you some very curious anecdotes when I see you, but what I do not choose, for particular reasons, to write.[18] What is still more curious, when Lord

St-Malo had been the approach of 10,000 French troops, which number had been magnified in London the next day (17 June) to 30,000 (MANN v. 213). The figure 30,000 is given in the *Daily Adv.* 17 June and the *London Chronicle* 15–17 June, iii. 574. The original 10,000 is mentioned in J. Grenville to G. Grenville [16 June], *Grenville Papers* i. 238, MS now WSL; in *A Genuine and Particular Account of the Late Enterprise on the Coast of France, 1758. By an Officer*, p. 36, quoted *London Magazine* 1758, xxvii. 350; and in *Political Journal of George Bubb Dodington*, ed. J. Carswell and L. A. Dralle, Oxford, 1965, p. 371.

15. Louis-Armand-Constantin (1731–94), Chevalier de Rohan, Prince de Montbazon (DU DEFFAND ii. 259, n. 22). He was captain of the *Raisonnable* which had been captured by the *Dorsetshire* 29 April, and was a prisoner in England until the end of July when he was allowed to return to France (G. Lacour-Gayet, *La Marine militaire de la France sous le règne de Louis XV*, 1902, pp. 311, 498, 506; *Daily Adv.* 5 Aug.).

16. A very similar account by Montbazon is also mentioned by George Bubb Dodington, who says he learned it from Henry Fox, who in turn heard it from Lords Waldegrave and Gower, who separately heard it from Montbazon's captor. Their version was that Montbazon 'was, at that time, in Rochefort—or La Rochelle (the Lords in comparing notes had

no other doubt in their narrative); that they had 7 or 8,000 men there at least; that there was 3,500 men behind the sand banks, and a masked battery at each end; that if we had landed when we first appeared, we should have embarrassed them. But they thought themselves betrayed, when they found we did not land at the time we attempted it' (Carswell and Dralle, op. cit. 368). This report of French preparedness was apparently grossly exaggerated; Lacour-Gayet, op. cit. 307–8, asserts that despite reinforcement of the Rochefort garrison after the arrival of the English, it could easily have been taken by the expedition.

17. HW says in the *Memoirs* that 'Howe, who never made friendship but at the mouth of a cannon, had conceived and expressed a strong aversion to him' and relates an anecdote illustrating his dislike (*Mem. Geo. II* iii. 125 and n.).

18. HW mentions ibid. iii. 125 that on the expedition Marlborough 'and his troops remarked that Lord George Sackville was not among the first to court danger,' but this may represent hindsight since the *Memoirs* for 1758 were written between 17 Aug. and 27 Oct. 1759, after the battle of Minden (GRAY i. 34 and n. 229). In this letter HW is more likely referring to Lord George's discontentment over Bligh's appointment to command the army going to Germany; on 3 July Lord George wrote to Pitt from Portsmouth, 'I was in hopes, should any troops

George kissed hands at Kensington, not a word was said to him.[19]

How is your fever? Tell me, when you have a mind to write, but don't think it necessary to answer my gazettes; indeed I don't expect it.

Yours ever,

H. W.

From Conway, Thursday 20 July 1758

Printed from the MS now WSL, formerly Rutnam. Previously printed *Fraser's Magazine*, 1850, xli. 431–2.

Park Place, 20 July, 1758.

YOU tell me I may write when I have a mind; and, by the time I have took, it looks as if I had very little mind. Without meaning to make excuses, I actually feel ashamed when I look over your letter. I was to tell you how my fever did, which was gone before I wrote last, if ever it could be said to be come, and as to the work, you are so accommodating that you actually leave me to dedicate to myself. I would not have *the world* know that I have been so called into council on my own praises, to which in the present shape I don't pretend to object. Your thinking I could seriously suspect you of giving me up on account of the expedition, and mean my correction for *you* and not for that *vile world* we have talked of, is at least as good as my suspicion would have been if it had been real. I have no sort of partiality for that *prejudice and malice* which I slipped in, and agree entirely to the force of your argument against it. The time of prejudice is certainly not the time to conquer it. If it is to be done, I am clear it is in the way you mention; for there is a contradicting spirit in the mind of men that

be destined for Germany, that I might have had the command of them,' and requested 'after this mark of his Majesty's disapprobation, to be struck off the staff' (*Chatham Corr.* i. 326–7). Conway wrote Devonshire 7 July that 'the D. of Marlborough *must have Lord George with him;* they are *both* too much for the Ger-man command; and Lord George will go no more expeditioning if he can help it' (Chatsworth MSS, 416 / 53).

19. This has not been confirmed; Lord George had arrived in London on the 4th (Elliot to Grenville [4 July], *Grenville Papers* i. 247, MS now WSL).

would make them much more likely to keep up their *prejudice* and exert their *malice* for being accused of it.

Having thus settled the preliminaries, pray let me ask when one is to see your work,[1] which I feel rather impatient for. I shall like the old again and like to see them collected; but I hope for some new too.[2]

I agree with you in everything but the point of serving, and had better agree in that too, as I find my efforts quite vain for the purpose; in the meantime, am got so far as to be much easier, and, as far as the last expedition went, quite easy. If they want me, they may have me; and when they have worn out all their Hospital Generals, and tired all their Lords of Expeditions, perhaps I may be thought of.

Your story of the teaspoons[2a] is excellent and corresponds extremely well with your own idea of drinking tea on the French coast.[3] They drank tea and left their teaspoons behind.

You tell me you have anecdotes for me when we meet. When will that be? I shall be here till Sunday sennight.[4] Our desire to see you here is constant, and, of course, it's one of the evergreens of Park Place. On Sunday sennight I come into waiting,[5] when I may possibly catch a glimpse of you. After that we go our northern circuit.[6]

I hear Lord Ancram[7] is not trusted with the expedition alone; and that Blighe,[8] who was appointed for Germany, is turned over

1. HW promised one to Conway 'very soon,' even though he did not intend to distribute the rest until the next spring (*post* 21 July 1758, *sub* 22 July).

2. Nine of HW's pieces were first printed in the *Fugitive Pieces* (Hazen, *Bibl. of HW* 42–3).

2a. See MANN v. 221.

3. HW had suggested this in a missing letter; see *ante* 4 July 1758, n. 10.

4. 30 July.

5. Conway had been made a groom of the Bedchamber to the King in April 1757 (MANN v. 75). On 7 July he wrote to Devonshire, 'I am still in suspense about our waitings till I see what becomes of the expeditioners. If they go out again [I] shall probably take my own and have it over before the time of waiting on you' (Chatsworth MSS, 416 / 53).

6. To visit the Straffords at Wentworth

Castle, the Devonshires at Chatsworth, and others (*post* 27 Aug., 17 Sept. 1758).

7. The Earl of Ancram (*ante* 31 Oct. 1741). On the 15th Holdernesse had written to Newcastle, 'Lord Ancram has sent word to my Lord Ligonier that as his physician is now of opinion his complaint is not the stone, and having had a good night and some prospect of improvement, if it is thought proper to entrust him in his precarious state of health his services are at his Majesty's devotion' (BM Add. MSS 32881, f. 322). The newspapers also reported on the 17th that he and Lord George Sackville were to command the expedition (*Daily Adv.* 17 July), but neither of them did so.

8. Lt-Gen. Thomas Bligh (*ante* 22 May 1752). He was originally appointed to command all the troops going to Germany, and then, after Marlborough's ap-

to that. I don't think this will please the Earl[9] if it's true.

You see my letters are but a poor comment on yours, yet I like to write as long as you can bear them. It's a poor venture I send, but it brings me an excellent return. *Que faire?* We ride and walk and bowl and see our neighbours; and, ambition apart, live, I assure you, a comfortable trifling life as can be. We have had a good many of our friends at times, and *some have visited us twice:* Lady Louisa[10] is still here, as jolly and good-natured as ever. We are much obliged to her for her company, and by trying to amuse her, I think we amuse ourselves rather more than usual. This is our history—the sum and substance of it. You see what matter it furnishes for relation. Adieu! Continue your gazettes, though they should have no more in them that *the Gazette.* They are charming and refresh us infinitely in these barren climes.

Yours most sincerely,

H. S. C.

To CONWAY, Friday 21 July 1758

Printed from *Works* v. 58–9.

Strawberry Hill, July 21, 1758.

YOUR gazette, I know, has been a little idle; but we volunteer gazettes, like other volunteers,[1] are not easily tied down to regularity and rules. We think we have so much merit, that we think we have a right to some demerit too; and those who depend upon us, I mean us gazettes, are often disappointed. A common foot newspaper may want our vivacity, but is ten times more useful. Besides, I am not in town, and ten miles out of it is an hundred miles out of it for all the purposes of news. You know of course that Lord

pointment to the chief command, the horse only. He had, in fact, already been appointed sole commander-in-chief of the expedition, reportedly at two days' notice (Romney Sedgwick, 'Letters from William Pitt to Lord Bute: 1755–1758,' in *Essays Presented to Sir Lewis Namier,* ed. Pares and Taylor, 1956, p. 159; Rex Whitworth, *Field Marshal Lord Ligonier,* Oxford,

1958, p. 257; Sir R. Lyttelton to Grenville [22 July], *Grenville Papers* i. 250, MS now WSL).

9. Ancram.

10. *Ante* 4 July 1758, n. 18.

1. Such as those in the recent expedition.

George Sackville refused to go *a-buccaneering* again, as he called it;[2] that *my friend* Lord A.[3] who loves a dram of anything, from glory to brandy, is *out of order;* that just as Lord Panmure[4] was going to take the command, he missed an eye;[5] and that at last they have routed out an old General Blighe from the horse armoury in Ireland,[6] who is to undertake the codicil to the expedition. Moreover, you know that Prince Edward is bound 'prentice to Mr Howe.[7] All this you have heard; yet, like my cousin the *Chronicle,*[8] I repeat what has been printed in every newspaper of the week, and then finish with one paragraph of *spick and span.*[9] Alack! my postscript is not very fortunate: a convoy of 12,000 men, etc. was going to the King of Prussia, was attacked unexpectedly by 5000 Austrians, and cut entirely to pieces;[10] provisions, ammunition, etc. all taken. The King instantly raised the siege,[11] and retreated with so much precipitation, that he was forced to nail up 60 pieces of cannon.[12] I con-

2. His use of the phrase at this time is also mentioned in the *Political Journal of George Bubb Dodington,* ed. J. Carswell and L. A. Dralle, Oxford, 1965, p. 373. Immediately after his return he first threatened to resign and then demanded to be sent to Germany; the King at first refused, but finally was forced to consent (*ante* 8 July 1758, n. 18; Newcastle to Legge 6 July, BM Add. MSS 32881, f. 178; Carswell and Dralle, loc. cit.; *Mem. Geo. II* iii. 126n).

3. Presumably Ancram, who had been considered for the command, even though he was ill (*ante* 20 July 1758 and n. 7).

4. William Maule (1700–82), cr. (1743) E. of Panmure.

5. Pitt wrote to Bute 11 July saying that Panmure had written Ligonier 'a second letter, whereby he accepts the command of the expedition,' but on the 14th reported that 'Lord Panmure cannot go' (Romney Sedgwick, 'Letters from William Pitt to Lord Bute: 1755–1758,' in *Essays Presented to Sir Lewis Namier,* ed. Pares and Taylor, 1956, p. 157).

6. He was previously a cavalry commander, and had been colonel of the 2d Irish Horse since 1747.

7. The King had given him permission to go before the end of June (Bute to Pitt 27 June, *Chatham Corr.* i. 319–20). His appointment is further discussed in

letters from Pitt to Bute 5–18 July, printed Sedgwick, op. cit. 155–9. HW mentions him in connection with the expedition in MANN v. 228, 232, 245; *Mem. Geo. II* iii. 126, 133; *post* 19 Sept. 1758.

8. The *London Chronicle,* which had begun publication 1 Jan. 1757.

9. The *London Chronicle,* which was tri-weekly, usually reprinted articles and items from the dailies, but its last page contained the most recent news at the time of publication.

10. A Prussian supply train under Gen. von Zieten had been attacked at Domstadtl by the Austrian generals Siskovics and Loudon on 30 June; of the 4000 wagons (940 with munitions) 3000 were destroyed (MANN v. 224, n. 4). The first reports had reached England through Austrian sources from Brussels on 2 July, and were generally disbelieved, but they were confirmed by Dutch mails arriving on the 21st (*Daily Adv.* 21, 22 July; Wallace to Newcastle 20 July, BM Add. MSS 32881, ff. 417–18; Jenkinson to Grenville 22 July, *Grenville Papers* i. 251, MS now WSL; Sedgwick, op. cit. 160).

11. Of Olmütz. The news of the disaster reached Frederick on 1 July and he raised the siege the same day (MANN, loc cit.).

12. The source of this information has not been found; a report from the Austrian army headquarters printed in the

clude the next we hear of him will be a great victory:[13] if he sets overnight in a defeat, he always rises next morning in a triumph— at least, we that have nothing to do but expect and admire, shall be extremely disappointed if he does not. Besides, he is three months debtor to fame.[14]

The only private history of any freshness is, my Lady Dalkeith's christening;[15] the child had *three* godfathers: and I will tell you why: they had thought of the Duke of Newcastle, my Lord[16] and George Townshend; but of two Townshends and his Grace, God could not take the word of any two of them, so all three were forced to be bound.[17]

I draw this comfort from the King of Prussia's defeat, that it may prevent the folly of another expedition: I don't know how or why, but no reason is a very good one against a thing that has no reason in it. Eleven hundred men are ill from the last enterprise.[18] Perhaps Don William Quixote[19] and Admiral Amadis[20] may determine to send them to the Danube; for, as no information ever precedes their resolutions, and no impossibilities ever deter them, I don't see why the only thing worthy their consideration should not be, how glorious and advantageous an exploit it would be, if it could be performed. Why did Bishop Wilkins[21] try to fly? Not that he thought it practicable, but because it would be very convenient. As he did not happen to be a particular favourite of the City of London, he was laughed at; they prepossessed in his favour, and he

Daily Adv. 24 July reported the Prussians as having abandoned five mortars and three pieces of battering cannon.

13. It was; see *post* 2 Sept. 1758. Virtually nothing was heard from him in the interval (MANN v. 234).

14. Frederick's only triumph in his present campaign had been the capture of Schweidnitz on 16 April, news of which had reached England on the 27th (ibid. v. 198 and n. 1).

15. Of her son Thomas Charles Townshend (22 or 25 June 1758–82), later Capt. 45th Foot (Collins, *Peerage*, 1812, ii. 476; *London Magazine* 1758, xxvii. 313). The christening took place on 18 July; see Sir Lewis Namier and John Brooke, *Charles Townshend*, 1964, p. 56.

16. Lord Townshend (*ante* 24 May 1753), the child's grandfather.

17. Charles Townshend's letter to Newcastle 19 July, thanking him for standing sponsor, is BM Add. MSS 32881, f. 394.

18. When the troops disembarked 7 July, it was reported that 1200 were sick (*ante* 4 July 1758, n. 12).

19. William Pitt, afterwards Earl of Chatham, then secretary of state (HW).

20. Lord Anson, then first lord of the Admiralty (HW).

21. John Wilkins (1614–72), Bp of Chester, 1668–72, a founder of the Royal Society. An appendix to the 1640 edn of his *Discovery of a World in the Moone* had proposed a 'flying chariot' to reach it (p. 238); there is no evidence that he tried to fly himself (DALRYMPLE 168).

would have received twenty gold boxes,[22] though twenty people had broken their necks off St Paul's with trying the experiment.

I have heard a whisper, that you do not go into Yorkshire this summer.[23] Is it true? It is fixed that I go to Ragley[24] on the 13th of next month; I trust you do so too. Have you had such deluges for three weeks well counted, as we have? If I had not cut one of my perroquet's wings, and there were an olive tree in the country, I would send to know where there is a foot of dry land.

You have heard, I suppose, if not, be it known to you, that Mr Keppel,[25] the canon of Windsor, espouses my niece Laura; yes, Laura.[26] I rejoice much so I receive your compliments upon it, lest you should, as it sometimes happens, forget to make them. Adieu!

Yours ever,

Hor. Walpole

July 22.

For the pleasure of my conscience I had written all the above last night, expecting Lord Lyttelton, the Dean,[27] and other company, today. This morning I receive yours; and having already told you all I know, I have only a few paragraphs to answer.

I am pleased that you are pleased about my book:[28] *you* shall see it very soon; though there will scarce be a new page: nobody else shall see it till spring.[29] In the first place, the prints will not be

22. As Pitt had in the spring of 1757 (*Mem. Geo. II* iii. 5).

23. Conway had already told HW they were going in his letter of 20 July, but HW had not yet received it; see the postscript below.

24. The seat of the Earl of Hertford (HW). HW describes this visit to Montagu 20 Aug. (Montagu i. 223–5).

25. Hon. Frederick Keppel (1729–77), canon of Windsor, 1754; Dean, 1765; Bp of Exeter, 1762.

26. Eldest daughter of Sir Edward Walpole (HW). Laura Walpole (ca 1734–1813), m. (10 Sept. 1758) Hon. Frederick Keppel. HW had been informed of the approaching engagement in a letter from Sir Edward 6 July (Family 34–5). Keppel had been courting her since at least 1753

(Laura Walpole to Edward Walpole 6 Aug. 1755, Maria Walpole to Edward Walpole [ca June–July 1755], MSS now wsl).

27. Charles Lyttelton (*ante* ca 8 March 1737 OS, n. 5), Lord Lyttelton's brother, had been Dean of Exeter since 1748.

28. *The Anecdotes of Painting* (HW). This is a mistake; it was his *Fugitive Pieces.* HW did not purchase George Vertue's MSS, on which the *Anecdotes* were based, until 22 Aug. 1758, nor begin writing the *Anecdotes* until 1 Jan. 1760 ('Short Notes,' Gray i. 33, n. 226, 34).

29. According to the 'Short Notes' HW did not begin to distribute copies until 17 March 1759, although he had given away some earlier in that month (ibid. i. 31; Selwyn 151–2).

finished:[30] in the next, I intend that two or three other things shall appear before it from my press, of other authors;[31] for I will not surfeit people with my writings, nor have them think that I propose to find employment alone for a whole press—so far from it, I intend to employ it no more about myself.[32]

I will certainly try to see you during your waiting.[33] Adieu!

From CONWAY, Thursday 27 July 1758

Printed for the first time from the MS now WSL, formerly Rutnam.

Park Place, 27 July 1758.

I AM by Lady Ailesbury's commands to write one word just to tell you that *we* both of us are to be in town on Saturday evening[1] and to invite you to meet us; it will give us very great pleasure. It's a short journey for you; we shall have just time for a little chapter upon the events of the day and settle many things on the subject of journeys, visits, etc., which I am not now allowed to discuss, being ordered to the bowling-green. I have many thanks to return you for your last and though *à regret* receive all your excuses about the most interesting of discussions[2] and am in charity with you. I *do* go to Ragley towards the 13th or 14 of next month and should be particularly proud to attend you if it suited you.[3] I can either rise or lie abed, make long or short stages, be quite silent, read, or talk a little; these things we'll talk over; you'll wonder what becomes of Lady A.; why she is going in quest of something as

30. 'Mr Müntz took off the copper plates, which (being the frontispiece, fleuron and coin of Q. Eliz.) were engraved by Grignion' (*Journal of the Printing-Office at Strawberry Hill*, ed. Toynbee, 1923, pp. 6–7, *sub* 11 April 1758).

31. Before he began to distribute the *Fugitive Pieces*, HW had published Whitworth's *Account of Russia* (printing completed by 29 Sept.) and Spence's *Parallel* (printing completed 11 Nov.; published 2 Feb. 1759) (ibid. 7, 8).

32. HW's next work to be published at the SH Press was the *Anecdotes of Paint-*

ing, which he began to print 24 Nov. 1760 but did not publish until 15 Feb. 1762 (ibid. 9–10).

33. As groom of the Bedchamber to the King (HW).

1. The day before Conway was to come into waiting (*ante* 20 July 1758 and n. 5).

2. Presumably about the appointment of a commander for the expedition (*ante* 21 July 1758).

3. HW did go with Conway (MANN v. 228).

nauseous as a Kensington waiting, and for that purpose sets out for Harrowgate, a source of stinking waters and bad company in Yorkshire.[4]

Adieu. I honour your account of the triple sponsorship though I own the nature of the satisfaction rather passes *human* understanding, for though the multiplication of negatives make out affirmation I never heard that a multiplication of dishonesty made fair dealing.

I am glad of the family match as I think it is good for the whole branch and will cause some excessive happiness.

The Russians, Prussians and buccaneers I leave to our meeting; the attack of Hanover[5] I have long thought probable, and rather more likely to succeed than our offensive war in Flanders,[6] so wisely laid down to the satisfaction of our stupid Tories.

Yours ever,

H.S.C.

From CONWAY, Tuesday 1 August 1758

Printed for the first time from the MS now WSL, formerly Rutnam. The year is supplied by the contents.

Kensington, 1st August.

Dear Horry,

THOUGH I am far from positive this will find you, I owe you so much on the head of gazette that my conscience obliges me to take the first opportunity of attempting to discharge part of my debt

4. Lady Caroline Fox describes to Lady Kildare (*Leinster Corr.* i. 181–2) a letter Lady Ailesbury wrote from thence to the Duchess of Richmond, 'the only one she has received from her in six weeks. It's a pretty letter, with an account of Harrogate, which is a strange place, but not the least like the letter of a mother to a daughter, a coldness and form in it that astonishes me. Dear siss, how could you ever take to anybody that has such a cold, reserved disposition. . . . Such a want of frankness and openness. . . . I can't conceive how Conway and she ever could produce a child with such icy dispositions, but to speak seriously, I do think there is in mother and daughter as much insensibility and want of that sort of cordial unreserved affection in their nature which I can't describe . . . than ever I saw in any people.'

5. It was believed that the Prince de Soubise was about to invade Hanover, but he did not do so (MANN v. 226–7 and nn. 12, 13; *post* 1 Aug. 1758).

6. It was beginning to be rumoured that Prince Ferdinand was going to invade Flanders (ibid. and n. 15).

though it be but a penny in the pound. It's true my news is bad which might have made me in less hurry to tell it, but as I know you for one of those indifferent mortals that love bad news almost as well as good and one of those ingenious ones that can extract something good out of the worst, that makes little difference.

The mails came in last night, and they prudently made haste to inform the King just before he was going to bed that his country was once more at the mercy if not in the hands of the French.[1]

Count Isemberg[2] who was posted in the Landgravate of Hesse somewhere not far from Cassel[3] to defend that country and what's worse, Hanover too with 5,000 men[4] against the Prince de Soubize[5] who marched thither with 18,000, has to the great astonishment of many generals and ministers been beat;[6] the poor Landgrave,[7] Princess,[8] etc. are gone to Bremen;[9] the Hanover ministry have already taken their flight to Stadt[10] and all is in the confusion and terrors of last year;[11] you who are neither general nor minister may think that rather a natural event that 18,000 men should beat 5,000; but so extraordinary has it appeared in the eyes of Prince Ferdinand[12] that as I hear he has changed his whole plan of opera-

1. As a result of the battle of Sandershausen, 23 July, described in the next paragraph. The first reports had arrived in the mails from Holland on the 31st (J. Yorke to Newcastle, The Hague, 28 July, Newcastle to J. Yorke 1 Aug., BM Add. MSS 32882, f. 84, 180), but details were not published in the papers until the 5th (*Daily Adv.* 5, 7 Aug.; see also MANN v. 227, n. 14).

2. The commander of the Hessian army was Prince, not Count, Isenburg: Johann Casimir (1715–59), Prinz von Isenburg, Hessian Lt-Gen., April 1758 (*Genealog. hist. Nachrichten* 1760–1, 2d ser. xi. 112–16).

3. Sandershausen is slightly east of Cassel.

4. Isenburg had 6000 men (MANN, loc. cit.).

5. Charles de Rohan (1715–87), Prince de Soubise; Maréchal de France 19 Oct. 1758.

6. The battle was fought not by Soubise's entire army, which numbered some 30,000, but by his vanguard of 8,500,

commanded by the Duc de Broglie (MANN v. 226–7, nn. 12, 14).

7. Wilhelm VIII (1682–1760), Landgraf of Hesse-Cassel 1730–60 (ibid. i. 345, n. 17).

8. Princess Mary (*ante* 14 May 1740 OS), daughter of George II, who had married the Prince of Hesse in 1740.

9. They had fled from Cassel to Rintelen on the 21st; Joseph Yorke's letter to Newcastle of the 28th, received on the 31st, mentioned that the 'Landgrave is gone from Rintelen to Bremen' (BM Add. MSS 32882, f. 84; *Daily Adv.* 2 Aug.).

10. This was not mentioned in Yorke's letter, but Newcastle in his reply, 1 Aug. mentioned that the Hanoverian minister had gone there (BM Add. MSS 32882, f. 180).

11. In August 1757 after the battle of Hastenbeck (*ante* 4 Aug. 1757).

12. (1721–92), of Brunswick-Wolfenbüttel, Duke of Brunswick and Lüneburg; Prussian field marshal; had replaced Cumberland as commander of the allied forces in Germany 16 Nov. 1757 (MANN v. 167, n. 15).

tions upon it:[13] in what manner I don't know distinctly, but by his position which is at Ruremonde on the Maeze while M. de Contades[14] is at Cologne on the Rhine[15] and by some hints I have heard it seems to me as if he was abandoning the Rhine in order to make an offensive war in Flanders[16] in which he so much outflies all the *flying* system, if it be so, that I can scarce believe it. A little time will clear it up as his plan must be immediately formed one way or t'other.

Our troops[17] which are just arrived[18] (all, I think, but Nappier's regiment and the Greys)[19] must in this case, I suppose, join Count Isemberg's remnant of a remnant and what else they can collect to make a stand against Monsieur de Soubize. They can never see Prince Ferdinand,[20] who, I suppose, has appointed Gen. Blighe a rendezvous at Paris.

The Prussian victory is quite vanished,[21] or has subsided into

13. Prince Ferdinand was at this time west of the Rhine contemplating a march into Flanders (below, n. 15), but on the 10th he recrossed the Rhine (MANN v. 227, n. 15; see also ibid. v. 223, n. 2).

14. Louis-Georges-Erasmé (1704–93), Marquis de Contades; Maréchal de France, 24 Aug. 1758; commander of the French army on the Rhine (ibid. v. 227, n. 15).

15. This account had come in Joseph Yorke's letter from The Hague 28 July: 'Prince Ferdinand was on the 25th at Wassemberg upon the Roer about two leagues from Roermonde; he marched from his camp at Bedbendyck on the 24th at 10 at night, without the French perceiving it, and his march was 14 leagues; he had sent before a large body to seize upon Roermonde; we believe he is marching straight to Brussels, with a view of bringing the French back from Lower Saxony. . . It's said the French marched the same day to Cologne, which would be curious enough' (BM Add. MSS 32882, f. 84).

16. As Yorke had reported on the 28th (see the previous note).

17. The expeditionary force being sent to Germany (*ante* 4 July 1758, n. 14).

18. 'Admiralty Office, August 1. By letters received of the 26th and 28th past from Capt. Wheeler, of his Majesty's ship the *Isis,* off Embden, there is advice of the arrival, in the River Embs, of the first

embarkation of the troops under his convoy, consisting of the troops under the command of the Marquis of Granby; also of the arrival of those, which went under convoy of the *Dolphin,* under the command of Major-General Waldegrave; and of the invalids from Shields, under convoy of the *Deptford;* and likewise of another convoy being in sight, which it was concluded were the transports with the troops under the command of the Duke of Marlborough' (*London Gazette* No. 9813, 29 July – 1 Aug.). Similar details are in a letter from Cleveland to Newcastle 1 Aug., which also mentions that Marlborough had arrived on 28 July (BM Add. MSS 32882, f. 178).

19. The 12th Foot, whose Colonel was Major-Gen. Robert Napier (d. 1766), and the 2d Dragoons (*Army Lists* 1758, p. 62; GM 1766, xxxvi. 551). These were with Marlborough and had also arrived (see the previous note).

20. They did in fact join him on 21 Aug. at Coesfeldt, since he recrossed the Rhine instead of marching into Flanders (MANN v. 228, n. 22; above, n. 13).

21. The first rumours of this 'victory' arrived 26 July, and further accounts in the Dutch mails on the 28th reported that in an action on the 12th 'the victory was as complete in favour of his Prussian Majesty, as that of Lissa. It is added, that the Austrians are obliged to fly on

something little more than a skirmish, with some advantage, denied by the Austrians.

The ministers, I hear, say the Russians are retired to Poland; the newspapers say they advance; you may believe which you will.[22] I don't know what the King of Prussia's present plan is, but I hear the Austrians are strong and not so likely to be beat as one would wish.

So stands the Continent; no news from America,[23] where as I believe it's best our chief hopes are fixed. A French squadron disappointed there is said to be sailed to the West Indies[24] where they may do some mischief.

I shall hear of you and, I hope, see you on your return,[25] and have the greatest comfort in thinking our party is fixed for Warwickshire. It's so pleasant I doubt it almost makes me wish my present party over.

The great men (both of them)[26] look as cold as ever, but I grow every day more callous; 'tis a provision nature has made for the unfortunate, or one should die of such mortifications.

Your friend Lady Mary[27] called here at Lady B[etty] Walgrave's[28] yesterday and stayed one whole quarter of an hour in the same

all sides, had set fire to eleven villages in order to cover their precipitate retreat' (*Daily Adv.* 27, 29 July; Sir R. Lyttelton to Grenville [28 July], *Grenville Papers* i. 252, MS now WSL; *London Gazette* No. 9812, 25–29 July; *London Magazine* 1758, xxvii. 375). Favourable accounts continued to arrive until the 30th, but the mails from Holland on the 31st reported that it was at best uncertain what had happened, and even included some suggestion of an Austrian victory (*Daily Adv.* 31 July, 1 Aug.; Yorke to Newcastle, The Hague, 28 July, BM Add. MSS 32882, f. 84; Pitt to Bute 1 Aug., Romney Sedgwick, 'Letters from William Pitt to Lord Bute: 1755–1758,' in *Essays Presented to Sir Lewis Namier*, ed. Pares and Taylor, 1956, p. 161).

22. Both reports were appearing in the *Daily Advertiser*, often on the same day (see especially 27, 31 July, 28 Aug., 1 Sept.); the *London Gazette* loc. cit. reported: 'The Russians, who had made a motion towards Frankfort upon the Oder, are retired towards Poland.'

23. From Louisbourg; news of its fall did not arrive until 18 Aug. (MANN v. 226, n. 10; *post* 27 Aug. 1758, n. 8).

24. A squadron of six ships under the Comte du Chaffault de Besné, arriving too late at Louisbourg, had gone on to Quebec, not to the West Indies (G. Lacour-Gayet, *La Marine militaire de la France sous le règne de Louis XV*, 1902, pp. 361, 511).

25. HW was apparently visiting Chute at the Vyne in Hampshire; he mentions having been there in a letter to Montagu 20 Aug. (MONTAGU i. 222). Gray writes 22 July that he will accompany HW there (GRAY ii. 102).

26. Presumably the King and Pitt.

27. Lady Mary Coke.

28. Lady Elizabeth Leveson Gower (1724–84), m. (1751) Col. John Waldegrave, 3d E. Waldegrave, 1763; lady of the Bedchamber to the Princesses Amelia and Caroline 1749–57, to the Princess Amelia 1757–63 (OSSORY i. 275, n. 1; *Court and City Register* 1750, p. 101, 1758, p. 102, 1763, p. 108, 1764, p. 103).

place; I saw her green chaise flash by me but had not time for half a bow; I hear she has *not yet refused Lord M[arch]*; is it true?[29] She was at Vauxhall this year with Miss Pelham,[30] Charles Townshend of the party, where after they had sighed at the moon, and admired the *charming moon* by turns half a dozen times, he said, *'come, prithee don't both fall in love with the moon, too.'*[31]

This is a long scrawl as we are to meet so soon, and you'll think perhaps it might have kept very well to our meeting, but there's a way not to be tired which is not to read. Adieu.

From CONWAY, Friday 11 August 1758

Printed for the first time from the MS now WSL, formerly Rutnam.

Kensington, 11 Aug. 1758.

I SUPPOSE I just hit the proper time of telling you our news when it is no longer so. Do you know that the troops are once more safely landed on the coast of France?[1] Do you know that it was on the 6th of this month,[2] six miles from Cherbourg, that some

---

29. March's 'courtship' of Lady Mary Coke, which was manœuvred entirely by her, is described in Lady Louisa Stuart, 'Some Account of John Duke of Argyll and his Family,' in Coke, *Journals* i. pp. lxxiii–lxxviii. He had openly denounced her at White's for announcing his intention of marrying her, vaunted his mistress before her, and finally 'paid her a morning visit; what passed never fully transpired; but he got what he wanted, an outrageous box o'the ear, and a command never to approach her doors again. Overjoyed, he drove straight to Queensberry House with a cheek still tingling; put on a doleful face, and was mortified beyond expression at having unwittingly incurred Lady Mary's displeasure. . . . Though quite unconscious of any offence, he had tendered the humblest apologies; but she would listen to none; and since everybody knew the noble firmness of her determinations, he feared (alas!) he must look upon his rejection as final' (p. lxxviii). That this had happened

recently is clear from a letter to Lady Mary from her sister, Lady Betty Mackenzie 17 Aug., quoted ibid. i. p. cxxix.

30. Frances Pelham (*ante* ca 15 Feb. 1752 OS, n. 3).

31. Miss Pelham had wanted to marry Lord March, but her father forbade the match (MONTAGU i. 53, n. 7).

---

1. The information below was all contained in letters of 7 and 8 August from Bligh and Howe which had reached London on the afternoon of the 10th (MANN v. 225, n. 1; *Daily Adv.* 11 Aug.). They are summarized in ibid. and more fully printed in the *London Gazette* No. 9816, 8–12 Aug., *Daily Adv.* 12 Aug., and *London Chronicle* 10–12 Aug., iv. 142.

2. A slip for the 7th, according to all the versions of Howe's despatch. The fleet had anchored in Cherbourg Road on the evening of the 6th. 'The next day, at seven in the morning, the fleet got underway, and at nine anchored in a sandy bay, two leagues to the westward

troops appeared but retired on the firing of the ships which covered the landing;[3] that Gen. Dury[4] with the Guards[5] marched towards the said troops who again made a show of defence; that they again retired, and that our loss on the whole was supposed not to exceed 18 or 20 men?[6] Moreover, that a fort[7] was attacked by our ships and a magazine blew up?[8] If you do, you know all I can tell you. Do you know that they will take Cherbourg,[9] or find any more ships mislaid on the beach?[10] If you do you know more than I or, I believe, our ministers can tell.

I shall breakfast with you on Sunday morning[11] and if you please dine at Park Place. How happy was I to see the face of my successor[12] this morning! He's the best friend I have at Court.

Adieu.

of Cherburg. . . . At two the boats landed the Guards and Grenadiers' (*Daily Adv.* 12 Aug.).

3. 'At half past one, all the frigates, sloops, bombs, and armed cutters began to fire on the French troops behind the banks of sand, computed to be 3000 horse and foot' (ibid.). Another item in ibid. 11 Aug. says, 'Their landing was opposed by 2500 of the militia, who, at their first firing on them, all laid down their arms and ran away.' See also Jenkinson to Grenville 10 Aug., *Grenville Papers* i. 253, MS now WSL.

4. Alexander Dury (d. 11 Sept. 1758), Maj.-Gen., 1757 (SELWYN 146, n. 2).

5. A brigade composed of the first battalion each of the Grenadier, Coldstream, and Scots Guards (1st, 2d, and 3d Regiments of Foot Guards) (MANN v. 226, n. 5).

6. 'At three General Drury [*sic*] marched them [the Guards and Grenadiers], and received three fires before he began his attack, which was executed with such spirit and vigour, that they immediately ran for shelter behind hedges and woods, but were pursued, and driven from their skulking places before night. We had about twenty men killed and

wounded, but amongst the enemy there was great slaughter, and our people took two pieces of brass cannon, which were brought down to oppose their landing' (*Daily Adv.* 12 Aug.).

7. Querqueville Fort (MANN v. 226, n. 4).

8. 'On Tuesday [8 Aug.] our horse and artillery were landed without opposition, and at noon the army marched for Cherburg, having taken two pairs of colours. At four the troops had possession of the West Fort, and blew up the magazine' (*Daily Adv.* 12 Aug.). HW virtually transcribed Conway's letter to this point in his letter to Selwyn of 12 Aug. (SELWYN 146); it also served as the basis of his account to Mann on the same day (MANN v. 226).

9. They did, the evening of the 8th; see the next letter.

10. As had been the case at St-Malo in June, when they burned ships but did not attempt to take the town (*ante* 16 June 1758).

11. HW told Mann on Sunday morning that 'Mr Conway . . . is just come in to carry me away' (MANN v. 228).

12. As groom of the Bedchamber.

From CONWAY, Friday 11 August 1758 *bis*

Printed for the first time from the MS now WSL, formerly Rutnam. Dated by the contents.
Address: To the Honourable Horatio Walpole at Strawberry Hill, Twickenham.
Postmark: 11 AV. SR.

Friday, 5 o'clock.

CHERBOURG is taken—still without loss.[1]

From CONWAY, Sunday 27 August 1758

Printed for the first time from the MS now WSL, formerly Rutnam.

Wentworth Castle, 27th August 1758.

IT looks a little Irish to say I put off answering your letter till I could execute your commission about Mr Zouch[1] and not be able to give you any answer on his subject; it may seem more unnecessary that I should mention Mr Zouch now as I hope to do it by and by more to the purpose, but first I had a mind to let you know the reason why I did not write sooner was that I could tell you nothing about Mr Zouch, and the reason why I write now is that I expect to hear of Mr Zouch from my Lord's parson[2] who dines here today, but must get as forward as I can in my letter before dinner as I shall not be allowed to write after. Your other commission, to Lord Strafford, I have executed; he thanked you much for your intelligence about the picture, said he would write to you himself and begs[3] that you will secure it for him. The person whom he takes to be second wife[4] to the great Lord Strafford's son[5] belonged to a

1. On the evening of 8 Aug.; the news had been brought by 'Howe's first lieutenant' who arrived in London the afternoon of the 11th (MANN v. 225, n. 1, 226, n. 6).

———

1. Rev. Henry Zouch (ca 1725–95), antiquary. He had written to HW ca 31 July (missing) with criticisms of the *Royal and Noble Authors;* HW replied 3 August; Zouch wrote again about the 9th

(missing) and HW replied on the 12th (CHATTERTON 3–10). HW had apparently asked Conway to find out more about him in Yorkshire.

2. Not identified.

3. Substituted in the MS for 'intends to,' which is crossed out.

4. Henrietta de la Rochefoucauld (d. 1732), m. (1694) William Wentworth, 2d E. of Strafford.

5. William Wentworth (1626–95), 2d E.

branch, which his is not obliged to;[6] however, he seems to think that no objection to making furniture of their heads, in which I entirely agree with him as it is the name more than the person that one has to do with in these cases.

P.M. I have now got all the intelligence I can have at present touching your friend Mr Zouch which is not very much, as it came from a modest, speechless chaplain of my Lord's, who answered as if he was examined before the Inquisition; all I could draw from him is that he has only a small living of about £80[7] but a fortune of 300 a year; his patron is Lord Rockingham; he has a good character and may be very learned for aught our deponent knew; he said he never heard the contrary and therefore concluded he was. I don't think his conclusion quite logical but if I see Lord Rockingham I'll ask him, or shall find means to be better informed.

I am glad your Oxford landlord had not reason to be quite so much pleased with the news as you apprehended;[8] that of Louisbourg is really great,[9] but the *Gazette Extraordinary* upon our repulses at Ticonderoga[10] is an extraordinary gazette indeed; 'tis the first time our ministry have been so prodigal of their ill news, nor do I yet comprehend their treating it with that distinction which has hitherto been kept sacred to glad tidings.

You ask what improvements are making here? The first is a bridge over the Serpentine River,[11] where the road came up; a bridge of stone and of one arch 20 foot high;[12] the two ends of the

---

of Strafford; only surviving son of Thomas Wentworth (1593–1641), cr. (1628) Vct Wentworth and (1640) E. of Strafford.

6. The Wentworths of Wentworth Castle were descended from a brother of the great E. of Strafford; nearly all of the Strafford estates, however, had passed to the Watson family (on the death of Strafford's son) through the marriage of Strafford's eldest daughter Anne to Edward Watson, 2d Bn Rockingham (Joseph Foster, *Pedigrees of Yorkshire Families,* 1874, *sub* Wentworth). This had led to great ill-feeling between the two branches of the family.

7. Henry Zouch was vicar of Sandal Magna 1754–89.

8. HW had learned of the fall of Louis-

bourg at Oxford on his way back to SH from Ragley (SELWYN 149). The allusion is to the supposed Jacobitism of Oxford.

9. Boscawen had taken Louisbourg on 26 July; accounts of its fall reached London 18 Aug. (*London Gazette Extraordinary* 18 Aug.).

10. News that the English had been repulsed in an attack on Fort Ticonderoga was published nearly in full in a *Gazette Extraordinary* on the 22d (SELWYN 148, n. 4; MANN v. 233 and nn. 6–8).

11. This was an artificial river (CHUTE 267).

12. HW mentions *post* 23 Aug. 1760 'two bridges built besides' at Wentworth Castle. This is probably the one illustrated in *Country Life,* 1924, lvi. 641.

water that you now pass between to be joined there. It will not be seen from the house which I don't think the worse as you see so much there, but will have a very good effect in many other places. The other work is the turning a farm into an abbey,[13] not much advanced yet; I believe it will be very good of the kind but not conspicuously placed. As to the rest this nor no other place was ever in greater beauty; how much that is improved by the good and agreeable company of the owners you can tell. We are at present confined to our *parti carré,*[14] Missy goes for nothing, and clever as this is you can't imagine how much we agree in wishing for you to spoil it.

We shall stay here to the end of this week, and then go to Chatsworth[15] taking Worksop[16] in our way for a day, for thither we must go, or be quite ruined at that court; we have had so many polite invitations.

Lady Mary[17] left us on Thursday and, to my great astonishment, to go to Ragley,[18] from which nothing could divert her; she has made a sudden intimacy with Lady Hertford and according to rule gives all due preference to the last new friend. We found her full of Louisbourg and Cherbourg[19] up to the brim, but luckily rather more in earnest about ninepins. She had a great mind to be of our party to Chatsworth but besides her inviolable engagement to Ragley and one, she says, she has made with herself to be in town on a certain day, I believe *il y entrait un peu de pique,* on account of the Chatsworth party being a little deferred in favour of the Duchess of Grafton, etc.

If you are disposed to marry I can give you the earliest intelligence of the youngest, handsomest and wittiest widow in England, even the Countess of Carlisle:[20] this morning came an account that the Earl[21] was left speechless at York, probably within a few hours

---

13. HW notes in 1760 among Lord Strafford's improvements, 'He is ornamenting a farm like the ruins of an abbey' (*Country Seats* 28).

14. That is, the Straffords, Lady Ailesbury, and himself.

15. To visit the D. of Devonshire.

16. Worksop Manor, near Worksop, Notts, seat of the D. of Norfolk.

17. Lady Mary Coke; she was Lady Strafford's sister.

18. Her arrival there is described *post* 2, 17 Sept. 1758.

19. She had apparently arrived at Wentworth Castle shortly after the news of the fall of Louisbourg had arrived on 18 Aug. (above, n. 9).

20. Hon. Isabella Byron (1721–95), m. 1 (1743) Henry Howard, 4th E. of Carlisle; m. 2 (1759) Sir William Musgrave, 6th Bt. For accounts of her, see Lady Louisa Stuart, *Notes on George Selwyn . . . by . . . Jesse,* ed. W. S. Lewis, New York, 1928, pp. 47–9, and OSSORY iii. 89 and n. 4.

21. The Earl of Carlisle (*ante* 15 Nov.

of his end. Adieu. I had much more to say to you from this house, but have said too much to have room for it.

To CONWAY, Saturday 2 September 1758

Printed from *Works* v. 60–1.

Strawberry Hill, September 2, 1758.

IT is well I have got something to pay you for the best letter that ever was! A vast victory, I own, does not entertain me so much as a good letter; but you are bound to like anything military better than your own wit, and therefore I hope you will think a defeat of the Russians a better bon mot than any you sent me. Should you think it clever if the King of Prussia has beaten them?[1] How much cleverer, if he has taken three lieutenant-generals and an hundred pieces of cannon?[2] How much cleverer still, if he has left fifteen thousand Muscovites dead on the spot?[3] Does the loss of *only* three thousand of his own men,[4] take off from or sharpen the sting of this

1756) d. 3 Sept. 'The . . . Earl of Carlisle was taken ill at York Races and died in that city on Saturday last' (*Daily Adv.* 8 Sept.).

———

1. The first news of Frederick's victory over the Russians at Zorndorf on 25 Aug. reached London on 2 Sept. at 8 A.M. by an express from The Hague (MANN v. 237, n. 2; Jenkinson to Grenville 2 Sept., *Grenville Papers* i. 263–4, MS now WSL), and was published in the *London Gazette* No. 9822, 29 Aug. – 2 Sept. Confirmation of the victory and further details arrived on the 6th (*Daily Adv.* 7 Sept.; *London Gazette Extraordinary* 8 Sept.; Jenkinson to Grenville 7 Sept., *Grenville Papers* i. 264–6, MS now WSL).

2. 'Their military chest, all their artillery, and three lieutenant-generals, had been taken' (*London Gazette* No. 9822, 29 Aug. – 2 Sept.). The account arriving on the 6th mentioned as prisoners 'several general officers, namely, Generals de Soltikoff, de Chernichew, Manteuffel,

Tieremhausen, Chivers, etc.'; and said that 73 pieces of cannon had been taken (*London Gazette Extraordinary* 8 Sept.). A letter from a Prussian officer, 27 Aug., printed in the *London Magazine* for 1758 gives the captured artillery as '104 pieces of cannon, 12 mortars' (xxvii. 488). Dodington records '100 cannon taken' in his *Political Journal*, ed. J. Carswell and L. A. Dralle, Oxford, 1965, p. 377.

3. The defeat of the Russians at Zornsdorff (HW). 'Fifteen thousand Russians had been left on the field of battle' (*London Gazette* No. 9822, 29 Aug. – 2 Sept.).

4. 'The Prussians had lost about three thousand, killed and wounded' (ibid.). The fuller account which arrived on the 6th gave the Prussian losses 'at about six hundred killed, and not eleven hundred wounded' (*London Gazette Extraordinary* 8 Sept.). The account in the Prussian officer's letter in the *London Magazine*, loc. cit., gives '30 officers killed, and 87 wounded, 768 soldiers killed, 1372 wounded and 358 missing.'

joke? In short, all this is fact, as a courier arrived at Sion Hills[5] this morning affirms. The City, I suppose, expect that his Majesty will now be at leisure to step to Ticonderoga, and repair our mishap[6] But I shall talk no more of politics: if this finds you at Chatsworth, as I suppose it will, you will be better informed than from me.

Lady Mary Coke arrived at Ragley between two and three in the morning—how unlucky that I was not there to offer her part of an aired bed! But how could you think of the proposal you have made me? Am not I already in love with *the youngest, handsomest and wittiest widow in England?*[7] As *Herculean a labourer* as I am, as Tom Hervey says,[8] I don't choose another. I am still in the height of my impatience for the chest of old papers from Ragley,[9] which, either by the fault of their servants or of the wagoner, is not yet arrived. I shall go to London again on Monday in quest of it; and in truth think so much of it, that, when I first heard of the victory this morning, I rejoiced, as we were likely now *to recover the Palatinate.*[10] Good night.

Yours ever,

HOR. WALPOLE

5. At Isleworth, seat of the Earl of Holdernesse, one of the secretaries of state.

6. The repulse of General Abercrombie at Ticonderoga (HW). See *ante* 27 Aug. 1758, n. 10.

7. Lady Mary Coke.

8. Hon. Thomas Hervey (1699–1775), eccentric pamphleteer; M.P. Bury St Edmunds 1733–47. He makes this remark in *A Letter . . . to Sir Thomas Hanmer,* [1741], p. 51. HW also quotes the phrase to Fox 19 July 1746 (SELWYN 101).

9. The Conway papers in the reign of James I (HW). HW had found them during his visit to Ragley in August; he describes the discovery to Montagu 20 Aug. (MONTAGU i. 223–4), and more briefly to Chute 22 Aug. (CHUTE 104), and to Zouch 5 Oct. (CHATTERTON 17). HW was planning to publish the 'most curious' at this time, but did not do so (CHATTERTON 17 and n. 30). The originals are now in the BM and Public Record Office (DAL-RYMPLE 73, n. 3, 339).

10. One of the objects of English policy during the reign of James I. The Spanish had overrun it in 1620 after James's son-in-law, the Elector Palatine, who had accepted the crown of Bohemia, had been defeated at the Battle of the White Mountain.

From CONWAY, Sunday 17 September 1758

Printed for the first time from the MS now WSL, formerly Rutnam.

Park Place, 17 Sept. 1758.

I DON'T quite know why I have not writ to you sooner; I thought I had several very good reasons when I was at Chatsworth,[1] but on review of them find them very moderate ones to my own satisfaction and quite insufficient to excuse to myself the pleasure I may have lost in not hearing from you. As to want of time when one's sauntering and doing mere idlenesses all day long, I can't accept that; my having little to say and no news to tell won't go down as you are so indulgent to the nothings I write; my best is the fear of disturbing a man of so much business and that's serious; I think I can excuse myself to you with that; not quite to myself as I am very selfish about the article of our correspondence and had rather disturb you a little than not hear from you.

I beg your pardon for attempting your constancy with the charms and perfections of the *new widow*,[2] while your own dainty *widow*[3] remains so fair and faithful as I don't doubt she is; I am afraid I had forgot just then that she had *refused* my Lord M.[4]—Don't you honour the spirit of your widow and love her ten times more for it, I mean her noble perseverance in coming to Ragley *that night* because she had said she would.[5] What resolution and love of truth! At Henley Harding they told her it was *impossible;* she said that did *not signify.* It was then pitch dark, raining dogs and cats, the road the most execrable in the world. She knew nothing of the way, she had no key for my brother's fields and the lanes are impassable. On she goes; pretty soon stuck fast; called up a farmer to know if she could get, or how she could get to Ragley? He said it was *impossible,* unless she went round by Stratford-upon-Avon; here I

---

1. Conway wrote Devonshire 19 Sept., 'We performed our journey back with great success and ease; the weather was good and the roads so excellent we could have no objection to them but their carrying us from Chatsworth' (Chatsworth MSS, 416/54).

2. Lady Carlisle (*ante* 27 Aug. 1758).

3. Lady Mary Coke.

4. Lord March (*ante* 1 Aug. 1758, n. 29).

5. Conway wrote a similar account to Devonshire 19 Sept., loc. cit., beginning, 'At Henley Harding we picked up a little news of Lady Mary's expedition, as it was from thence she took her horses for Ragley. . . .'

think she fell off a little and seemed almost to own there was such a thing as impossible. She took the farmer's advice and went by Stratford, a circuit of nine miles, that she might prove she could get to Ragley *that night* by coming there next morning.—But Lady Hertford, as I told you, is her new *female* passion; it's very violent and the commonest things should in such cases be done in the most uncommon way. A visit is an ordinary thing and therefore good for little, but a visit through dark nights, bad roads, and bad weather, executed at two or three in the morning has all the graces of novelty and impatience.

On any other subject I should beg your pardon for dwelling so long but apropos to dainty *widow,* I must tell you an accident I hear happened to Lady C[aroline] Russel[6] singing the song of which that is the burthen;[7] she inadvertently went a little too far and sung a stanza which Lord Newbattle[8] had added, not quite so *dainty,* and which she was not supposed to know, in much company.

And apropos to mistakes I must tell you a most ridiculous one that happened at Worksop in that style, where at a great card table of twelve or thirteen *outlaws*[9] and all sorts a certain Sir Harry Hunlock[10] who had been betting with Lady Ailesbury, after he was out at commerce[11] and all seemed to be over, and after engaging the attention of the company by calling out pretty earnestly to Lady Ailesbury, said, 'Madam, I'll lay with you tomorrow night.' Lady A. said she was very sorry she could not as she was to go away next morning, though in truth she could scarce speak, she was so thunderstruck by the strange sound of that public proposal.

Worksop, you know,[12] is fine from its magnificent size,[13] its grand

6. Lady Caroline Russell (1743–1811), dau. of John Russell, 4th D. of Bedford, m. (1762) George Spencer, 3d D. of Marlborough.

7. Not identified.

8. William John Ker (1737–1815), styled E. of Ancram 1767–75; 5th M. of Lothian, 1775. While his father was styled E. of Ancram, he was known by this courtesy title; see *Life and Letters of Lady Sarah Lennox,* ed. Countess of Ilchester and Lord Stavordale, 1902, i. 28–30. He was said to be in love with Lady Caroline Russell (ibid.).

9. Worksop Manor is in Sherwood Forest.

10. Sir Henry Hunloke (1724–1804), 4th Bt, of Wingerworth, Derbyshire.

11. A card game in which exchange or barter of cards is the principal part.

12. HW had been there for two days in 1756 (CHUTE 270).

13. The building was begun by George Talbot, 6th E. of Shrewsbury, and finished by his wife 'Bess of Hardwick' in the late 16th century. 'This magnificent structure contained nearly five hundred apartments, which, together with a fine library, an extensive and curious collection of paintings, the famous Arundelian marbles, . . . nearly the whole of the splendid furniture, and many invaluable

plantations,[14] etc. They are going to improve it vastly by flowing part of that great bushy flat[15] that lies between the house and the great plantations. The Duke does not positively know whether he shall do it or not, but the Duchess does and says, 'My Lord Duke intends to do it very soon.' I fancy she is in the right. They are building a great Gothic farm[16] on the same plain which will be a fine object, though not chaste enough in the building to suit your delicacy.

Lady Hillesborough[17] who was there has been in the *sanctum sanctorum,* even his Grace's conjuring room,[18] but was afraid to say so as anger might come on her friends who carried her there; I envied her on my own account a good deal, still more, I think, on yours.[19]

I thank you for your great Prussian news[20] which by the ingenuity of the postmaster at Chesterfield reached me there as we were dining in our way from Worksop, at the very time the ribbons and

articles of virtu, in almost every department of nature and art, were either totally or partially destroyed' by fire on 20 Oct. 1761 (Thomas Bailey, *Annals of Nottinghamshire, History of the County of Nottingham*, [?1853–1855], iii. 1255–6). There is a detailed description in Robert White, *The Dukery Records*, [Nottingham], 1904, pp. 328–9, and an illustration from a drawing by S. Buck in John Summerson, *Architecture in Britain 1530 to 1830*, 1953, p. xi, plate 17a.

14. HW mentions the 'evergreen plantations' in his description to Bentley in Aug. 1756 (CHUTE loc. cit.); in 1777 he calls it 'an artificial ugly forest of evergreens' (OSSORY i. 375). 'The Park is extensive, being eight miles in circumference, and containing within its limits the greatest diversity of scene, and a range of hills sufficiently high to bound the view from the house on one side, and richly covered with woods. Near one thousand acres of wood in the vicinity were planted, at various periods, by the late Duke and his father' (J. P. Neale, *Views of the Seats of Noblemen and Gentlemen, in England, Wales, Scotland, and Ireland,* 1818–29, iii. ser. i, *sub* 'Worksop Manor, Nottinghamshire').

15. The descriptions of the Manor Park speak of an extensive open plain and also of 'the Menagerie, with its sheet of water' (Robert White, *The Visitors' Handbook to Worksop and its Neighbourhood,* Worksop, 1853, p. 33; idem, *Worksop, 'The Dukery,' and Sherwood Forest,* Worksop, 1875, p. 76). 'A view of the Menagerie as designed by the late Duchess, painted by P. Sanby, R.A. was exhibited at Spring Gardens in 1764' (John Throsby, *Thoroton's History of Nottinghamshire,* 1797, iii. 398).

16. 'Within a short distance of the house, there is a beautiful sweep of woodland scenery studding the "Manor Hills" on the left, at the foot of which the Castle Farm, with its gothic and embattled parapet, forms an object at once striking and picturesque' (Robert White, *Worksop, 'The Dukery,' and Sherwood Forest,* p. 75).

17. Lady Margaretta Fitzgerald (1729–66), m. (1748) Wills Hill, 1st E. of Hillsborough.

18. Two secret rooms at Worksop are described in a deposition among the State Papers relating to the rebellion of 1745; perhaps one of these is being referred to, or the Duke's Catholic chapel. See idem, *The Dukery Records,* p. 331.

19. HW says *post* 19 Sept. 1758 that he had been in it too.

20. Of the victory at Zorndorf (*ante* 2 Sept. 1758).

streamers were flying for it in the postilions' hats. The ministry must have vast milliners' bills for this new manner of announcing victories; for us, we travelled that day with all these fools' colours like a pair of new married citizens or election candidates.

The loyalty of our parts had some very ridiculous effects. One man,[21] a sort of steward of the Duke of Dev[onshire]'s got drunk and tumbled off his horse 40 times in going twelve miles, for joy. If Lady Mary had known this she could not in decency have been overturned less than twenty times for her dear King.[22]—But I admire most two of the Chesterfield Corporation, who, having a dismal quarrel on their politics, stripped, as they imagined to fight stark to their buff, but instead of fighting tumbled down and fell asleep, in which condition they were found next morning; never were enmity and friendship so near allied nor war and peace so much alike.

I hear all our trophies are encamped in Hyde Park;[24] our ministers have one quality of great generals about them, that they really know how to make the most of their victories. The Louisbourg colours paraded through the City like my Lord Mayor to go to church at St Paul's,[25] and parade back to Westminster Abbey,[26] where, I suppose, they'll hear the new form of prayer for their taking. I am ashamed to find my nonsense creeping from one sheet of paper to another, but I must tell you that being condemned as *inutile lignum* by Mr Pitt and the King I have the honour to find more grace in the eyes of the Duke of St Alban's[27] from whom I yesterday received a commission of deputy lieutenant for the militia of our county,[28] so that I may be of use to my country

21. Not identified.

22. Lady Mary Coke was a great admirer of royalty; Lady Louisa Stuart's 'Some Account of John Duke of Argyll and his Family' abounds with her infatuations for royal persons and her rebuffs by them (Coke, *Journals* i. *passim*).

24. The cannon captured at Cherbourg had been placed in Hyde Park on 8 Sept. (*Daily Adv.* 9 Sept.; *London Chronicle* 7–9 Sept., iv. 239).

25. The colours captured at Louisbourg had been carried in procession from Kensington Palace to St Paul's on 6 Sept. (*Daily Adv.* 7 Sept.; MANN v. 238, nn. 3, 5). An elaborate description is in *Daily Adv.* 11 Sept.

26. They were to remain at St Paul's (ibid.), although the *London Chronicle* (7–9 Sept., iv. 234) had reported, 'It is said that the French colours carried on Wednesday to St Paul's, will be . . . after a certain time, carried to Westminster.'

27. Lord lieutenant of Berkshire 1751–60, 1771–86.

28. 'His Majesty does very well approve of the lords and persons following to be deputy lieutenants of the county of Berks . . . Hon[oura]ble Major General Henry Conway . . . And his Grace George Duke of St Albans, lord lieutenant of the said county of Berks, is to issue out their deputations accordingly. Given at Whitehall the twenty-second day

still; I intend to send to George Townshend for instructions.[29]

I did intend to finish here but cannot help inserting an excellent country churchyard epitaph which I heard lately, and as genuine.

> Under this stone lies a very wise head.
> Once he was living but now he is dead.
> Now he stinketh who once was very wholesome.
> The wisest man in all our parish: my Uncle Thomson.

If the Duke of N[ewcastle] dies I think one would make a present of it to Lord L[incoln]. Adieu. Lady A. desires something may be said for her but I have neither time nor room nor confidence to say any more than that I am

Most sincerely yours,

H.S.C.

To CONWAY, Tuesday 19 September 1758

Printed from the MS now WSL; first printed Wright iii. 393–5. For the history of the MS see *ante* 29 June 1744 OS.

Endorsed: Mr H. W. 19 Sept. 1758.

Arlington Street, Sept. 19, 1758.

I HAVE all my life laughed at ministers in my letters; but at least with the decency of obliging them to break open the seal. You have more noble frankness, and send your satires to the post with not so much as a wafer, as my Lord Bath did sometimes in my father's administration. I scarce laughed more at the inside of your letter than at the cover—not a single button to the waistband of its breeches, but all its nakedness fairly laid open!—What was worse, all Lady Mary's nakedness was laid open at the same time. Is this your way of treating a *dainty widow?* nay, and your own wife! Every clerk in the post office knows that a gentleman before your face desired *to lay with her?* What will Mr Pitt think of all this?

of September 1758' (S.P. 44/190, ff. 394, 399). Conway found that he was not legally qualified to serve (*post* 28 Sept. 1758).

29. Townshend had been actively pro-

moting the militia since Dec. 1755 (Namier and Brooke iii. 549–50). In Jan. 1757 Conway had offered, as a counter-proposal, a militia bill framed on a different plan from his (*Mem. Geo. II* ii. 302–3).

Will he be pleased with your suffering such proposals to your wife, or begin to believe that you have some spirit, when, with no fear of Dr Shebbear's[1] example before your eyes, you speak your mind so freely without any modification? As Mr Pitt may be cooled a little to his senses, perhaps he may *now* find out that a grain of prudence is no bad ingredient in a mass of courage—in short, he and the mob are at last undeceived, and have found by sad experience that all the cannon of France has *not* been brought into Hyde Park.[2] An account, which you will see in the *Gazette*[3] (though a little better disguised than your letters), is come, that after our troops had been set on shore,[4] and left there, till my Lord Howe[5] went somewhere else[6] and cried, hoop![6a] having nothing else to do for four days to amuse themselves, nor knowing whether there was a town within an hundred miles, went staring about the country to see whether there were any Frenchmen left in France, which Mr Pitt in very fine words had assured them there was not, and which my Lord Howe in very fine silence[7] had confirmed.[8] However, somehow or other (Mr Deputy Hodges[9] says they were not French but

1. John Shebbeare (1709–88), self-styled M.D. and political writer, had been tried for treasonable expressions in his *Sixth Letter to the People of England*. He was sentenced 28 Nov. and stood in the pillory 5 Dec. (*Mem. Geo. II* iii. 152–4).

2. Full details of the failure of a second attempt to take St-Malo and of an attack on the rear-guard of the re-embarking troops had reached England late at night on the 16th (MANN v. 243, n. 1; *London Gazette Extraordinary* 18 Sept.). The fleet itself returned to Spithead on the 18th (*Daily Adv.* 20 Sept.).

3. The *London Gazette Extraordinary* 18 Sept. printed Howe's letter of the 12th and Bligh's of the 13th with details of the failure of the expedition. Conway comments on this account to Devonshire 19 Sept. (Chatsworth MSS, 416/54).

4. The troops had landed 4 Sept. at Dinard in St-Lunaire Bay (MANN v. 243, nn. 3, 4). This news had reached England on 13 Sept. (*Daily Adv.* 15 Sept.; MANN v. 243, n. 1).

5. Howe had succeeded his brother George as 4th Vct Howe when the latter was killed at Ticonderoga 6 July.

6. On the 6th Howe had informed the land officers that it was impossible to re-embark the troops in St-Lunaire Bay and that they would have to march to St-Cast (*London Magazine* 1758, xxvii. 517). The reason for this, adverse winds, was not made apparent in the first accounts.

6a. I.e., played hoop and hide (hide-and-seek); see *post* 28 Sept. 1758 and n. 1.

7. HW frequently comments on Howe's taciturnity (MANN v. 244 and n. 9; OSSORY i. 321; *Mem. Geo. II* iii. 50).

8. The general confusion and uncertainty as to what had happened is also reflected in Newcastle's letter to Joseph Yorke 19 Sept.: 'But what seems the most extraordinary is, the landing at one place, the having no object immediately upon their landing; their waiting six days doing nothing; their re-embarking afterwards at a considerable distance from the place where they landed, their not knowing the forces of the enemy, that were coming upon them; and (if they were no more than 12 battalions, as is reported) their not keeping their whole force, near double that number, to oppose them' (BM Add. MSS 32884, f. 61).

9. James Hodges (d. 1774), Kt, 1759, town clerk of London (GM 1774, xliv. 542; W. A. Shaw, *The Knights of England*, 1906, ii. 289).

Papists sent from Vienna to assist the King of France), twelve battalions fell upon our rear-guard,[10] and, which General Blighe says is *very common* (I suppose he means that rashness and folly should run itself into a scrape) were all cut to pieces or taken.[11] The town says Prince Edward ran hard to save himself, I don't mean too fast, but scarcely fast enough;[12] and the General says that Lord Frederick[13] your friend is safe;[14] the thing he seems to have thought of most, except a little vain parade of his own self-denial on his nephew.[15] I shall not be at all surprised, if to show he was not in the wrong, Mr Pitt should get ready another expedition by the depth of winter[16] and send it in search of the cannon and colours of

10. On 11 Sept.; news of the enemy's approach was received on the 10th, and the English troops were re-embarking on the 11th when the French attacked the rear-guard (MANN v. 243 and nn. 6, 7).

11. 'In about an hour after we began to embark, we saw the enemy begin to appear on the heights above, and soon after they began to fire on us with their cannon, but did not attempt marching down, till almost all the troops were re-embarked except the Grenadiers, which made the rear-guard of the whole, who marched up to oppose their advancing, and behaved with great bravery and resolution, till, overpowered by numbers, they were at last obliged to give way, and retire to the water-side, till the boats could come in to take them, where they suffered much by the enemy's fire. We have lost some officers and men, which must always be the consequence when there is an enemy to oppose our landing or our re-embarking' (Bligh's letter of the 13th in *London Gazette Extraordinary* 18 Sept.). An eyewitness account in a letter from Sir John Irwin to Lord George Sackville 21 Sept., Hist. MSS Comm., *Stopford-Sackville MSS*, 1904–10, i. 296–301, places the losses much higher and criticizes the published accounts.

12. An account mentioned in the *London Magazine* for 1758 reported that he 'continued on shore, till commanded by Lord Howe to return to his ship' (xxvii. 518n). HW told Mann on the 22d that he had 'behaved with much spirit' (MANN v. 245).

13. Lord Frederick Cavendish (1729–

1803), army officer; M.P. Derbyshire 1751–4, Derby 1754–80; at this time a captain in the 1st Foot Guards and colonel in the army (*Army Lists* 1759, p. 40). Conway wrote Devonshire 19 Sept. (Chatsworth MSS, 416 / 54), 'As I was concerned for Lord Frederick's disagreeable accident in being taken prisoner so I assure you it was with the greatest pleasure and satisfaction I heard at the same time that he was safe and well, as there is nobody for whom I have a sincerer or can have a more deserved regard' (see also ibid. 416/ 55).

14. 'Lord Frederick Cavendish is among the prisoners, and well' (Bligh's letter, *London Gazette Extraordinary* 18 Sept.). He was the only one of the prisoners mentioned in the letter. He had received a contusion the previous day in crossing a river against opposition (Sir John Irwin to Lord George Sackville 21 Sept., *Stopford-Sackville MSS*, i. 299). He was back in England by 24 Oct. (MANN v. 251).

15. 'I shall do justice to every regiment in the filling up the commission, and shall not prefer my nephew, Lieutenant St George, to hurt any regiment' (Bligh's letter, *London Gazette Extraordinary* 18 Sept.). The nephew was George St George (d. *post* 1769), Lt 20th Foot, 1756; Capt.-Lt, 1759; Capt., 1761; he was one of the three sons of Bligh's sister Elizabeth, who had married George St George, of Woodsgift, co. Kilkenny (*Army Lists* 1757, p. 53; 1760, p. 71; 1762, p. 73; Sir Bernard Burke and A. P. Burke, *Peerage*, 1928, p. 2025).

16. The expedition to the West Indies

these twelve battalions[17]—pray Heaven, your letter don't put it in his head to give you the command. It is *not* true, that he made the King ride upon one of the cannons to the Tower.[18]

I was really touched with my Lady Howe's[19] advertisement, though I own at first it made me laugh, for seeing an address to the voters for Nottingham signed *Charlotte Howe*, I concluded (they are so manly a family) that Mrs Howe,[20] who rides a fox chase and dines at the *table d'hôte* at Grantham, intended to stand for member of Parliament.

Sir John Armitage died on board a ship before the landing;[21] Lady Hardwicke's[22] nephew Mr Cocks,[23] scarce recovered of his Cherbourg wound,[24] is killed—he had £7000 a year, and was a volunteer[25]—I don't believe his uncle and aunt advised his venturing so much money.

My Lady Burlington[26] is very ill—and the distemper shows it-

(*post* 15, 17 Oct. 1758) was already being prepared (Newcastle's memoranda for the King, 18, 19 Sept., BM Add. MSS 32884, ff. 46, 63).

17. Which had attacked the rear-guard.

18. The cannon from Cherbourg which were placed in Hyde Park on 8 Sept. (*ante* 17 Sept. 1758, n. 24) were taken to the Tower in a procession on 16 Sept. (*Daily Adv.* 18 Sept.).

19. Mary Sophia Charlotte von Kielmansegge (1695–1782), m. (1719) Emanuel Scrope Howe, 2d Vct Howe. Her advertisement, asking for the votes and interest of the 'gentlemen, clergy, freeholders, and burgesses of the town and county . . . of Nottingham' for her son Lt-Col. William Howe, dated 14 Sept., had appeared in the *Daily Adv.* 15 and 16 Sept.; it was reprinted *Annual Register* 1758, p. 73. She concluded, 'Permit me therefore to implore the protection of every one of you, as the mother of him [the 3d Vct] whose life has been lost in the service of his country.' Her son was elected without a contest.

20. Hon. Caroline Howe (ca 1721–1814), m. (1742) John Howe of Hanslope, Bucks (MANN i. 209, n. 3). Sister of Capt. (later Adm.) Richard, Lord Howe and Col. (later Gen.) William Howe, she took a leading part in the negotiations of Benjamin Franklin in 1774–5 for a peaceful

settlement of the dispute between Great Britain and the colonies; see Franklin, *Writings*, ed. Smyth, New York, 1905–7, vi. 324–94 *passim*.

21. Other reports say that he was killed on the spot at St-Cast, that he was 'shot as he sat upon a rock, to which he had swum for safety', and that he died on board ship before the fleet landed at Portsmouth (*London Magazine* 1758, xxvii. 518 and n; *Daily Adv.* 21 Sept.; *London Chronicle* 19–21 Sept., iv. 278).

22. Margaret Cocks (d. 1761), m. 1 John Lygon; m. 2 (1719) Philip Yorke, cr. (1733) Bn and (1754) E. of Hardwicke.

23. James Cocks, d. 11 Sept. 1758. HW gives similar details about his fortune to Mann on the 22d (MANN v. 245).

24. He had been wounded in the shoulder 'but not dangerous' at Cherbourg (Jenkinson to Grenville 14 Aug., *Grenville Papers* i. 257, MS now WSL; Lady Caroline Fox to Lady Kildare 12 Aug., *Leinster Corr.* i. 175).

25. He had in fact been an ensign in the 1st Foot Guards since 11 Nov. 1757 (MANN v. 245, n. 13), and was there with the Guards.

26. Lady Dorothy Savile (1699 – 21 Sept. 1758), m. (1721) Richard Boyle, 3d E. of Burlington. Details of her last illness in a letter from Garrick to the D. of Devonshire, her son-in-law, 14 Sept. (Garrick,

self oddly—she breaks out all over in—curses and blasphemies. Her maids are afraid of catching them, and will hardly venture into her room.

On reading over your letter again, I begin to think that the connection between Mr Pitt and *my dainty widow* is stronger than I imagined—one of them must have caught of the other that noble contempt which makes a thing's being *impossible not signify*.—It sounds very well in *sensible* mouths, but how terrible to be the chambermaid or the army of such people! I really am in a panic, and having some mortal impossibilities about me which a dainty widow might not allow to signify, I will balance a little between her and my Lady Carlisle, who I believe knows that impossibilities *do signify*. These were some of my reflections on reading your letter again; another was, that I am now convinced you sent your letter open to the post on purpose; you knew it was so good a letter that everybody ought to see it—and yet you would pass for a modest man!

I am glad I am not in favour enough to be consulted by *my Lord Duchess*[27] on the Gothic farm; she would have given me so many fine and unintelligible reasons why it should not be as it should be, that I should have lost a little of my patience. You don't tell me if the goose-board in hornbeam is quite finished; and have you forgot that I actually was in t'other goose-board, the conjuring room?[28]

I wish you joy on your preferment in the militia,[28a] though I do not think it quite so safe an employment as it used to be. If George Townshend's *disinterested* virtue should grow impatient for a *regiment*,[29] he will persuade Mr Pitt that the militia are the only troops in the world for taking Rochfort. Such a scheme would answer all his purposes; would advance his own interest, contradict

Letters, ed. Little and Kahrl, Cambridge, Mass., 1963, i. 287–8) confirm HW's account; see also Montagu i. 226 and n. 5.

27. The Duchess of Norfolk. She had planted a game of the goose in hornbeam, at Worksop (Mary Berry). 'A game played with counters on a board divided into compartments, in some of which a goose was depicted' (OED).

28. When he was at Worksop in Aug. 1756. See *ante* 17 Sept. 1758, n. 18.

28a. I.e., his appointment as deputy-lieutenant of Berkshire, one of whose special duties was the militia.

29. Townshend, who had resigned from the army in 1750, had been reinstated by Pitt as a colonel in May 1758; he received a regiment, the 64th Foot, in June 1759 (Namier and Brooke iii. 549–51). Most recently (27 Aug.) he had applied to go on the expedition to St-Malo (*Chatham Corr.* i. 346–7).

the Duke's[30] opinion who holds militias cheap, and by the ridiculousness of the attempt would furnish very good subjects to his talent of buffoonery in black lead.[31]

The King of Prussia you may believe is in Petersburg, but he happens to be in Dresden.[32] Good night. Mine and Sir Harry Hemlock's services to my Lady Ailesbury.

Yours ever,

H.W.

From CONWAY, Thursday 28 September 1758

Printed for the first time from the MS now WSL, formerly Rutnam. There are two pencil drawings of buildings.

Park Place, 28 Sept. 1758.

YOU lay an heavier charge of indiscretion and vanity upon me than I deserve; I neither left my letter open to brave Mr P[itt], nor imagining to show my wit; you are quite out in your guesses and by this I am glad to find that I am a deeper politician than you.—I left my letter open that it might *not* be read, for the last letters read by clerks or carried to ministers I dare say are those which come open. If I had sealed it with five seals and half an ounce of wafers there could not have been any doubt of its being read.

As to our expeditioners I think they were playing at blind-man's-buff as well as *hoop-hide*[1] or they never would have stumbled upon an enemy whom, as it seems they had it so much in their power as well as inclination to avoid. For besides their having so little previous intelligence, and their stealing away from before the enemy

30. Of Cumberland. He and Townshend hated each other (Namier and Brooke iii. 549).

31. His caricatures.

32. News had arrived on the 17th that he 'was within eight German miles of Dresden, and had secured the junction with his brother, and with Margrave

Charles from Silesia' (Wallace to Newcastle [17 Sept.], BM Add. MSS 32884, f. 25). Further accounts of his approach to Dresden are in the *Daily Adv.* 20 Sept.

———

1. 'Hoop and hide: the game hide-and-seek' (OED *sub* 'hoop,' v. 2, 1b).

by *beat of drum* in a dark night as I hear they did,[2] Lord Howe had found them a snug island[3] where they might have hid very cleverly and had horse-room and cart-room to run away. But Col. Clerke[4] had told the General he would now make good what he had always maintained, *that with three companies of grenadiers he would march through France.* I suppose he meant *prisoners,* which might have been verified if he had stayed with Gen. Dury to march

2. Conway had apparently heard reports similar to that which Sir John Irwin, a member of the expedition, had sent to Lord George Sackville on 21 Sept. He related that on the night of the 10th–11th 'our advanced posts were frequently attacked, we heard the enemy's drums, yet we beat ours (I mean the general and assemblée) though it was dark night before we marched' (Hist. MSS Comm., *Stopford-Sackville MSS*, 1904–10, i. 300).

3. According to Irwin, on the 6th or 7th, 'The Commodore [Howe] proposed our marching to an island near us, which we could get to at low water, where we could be safe from the whole force of France, and from whence we could embark with the greatest safety to the ships and the troops. This we all understood was to be executed, but to our great astonishment when we began to march we found ourselves going from the coast into the country' (ibid. i. 298).

4. Robert Clerk (also spelled in contemporary sources Clerke, Clark and Clarke) (d. 1797), military engineer; a Scots protégé of Lord Bute's. His account of the defenceless state of Rochefort (whose fortifications he had inspected in 1754) had been communicated to Ligonier and Pitt in July 1757 and had served as the foundation for the expedition of 1757. At that time he was a sub-engineer with the rank of Lt of Foot, but was breveted Lt-Col. 8 Aug. 1757 to accompany the expedition; Conway wrote Devonshire 14 Aug. 1757, 'Our friend Clarke has the most extraordinary instance of favour done him; being made a lieutenant Col. in the army; from a quondam *lieutenant,* for he had no commission now. This is really paying handsomely beforehand' (Chatsworth MSS, 416 / 46).

He was subsequently Col. 1762, Maj.-Gen. 1772, Lt-Gen. 1777, Gen. 1793. In the second phase of the expedition of 1758 he had been made quartermaster-general under Bligh, and apparently in collusion with Bligh, Howe, and Leicester House, but without the knowledge of Pitt or any other ministers, had been primarily responsible for the decision to make a second attempt on St-Malo. He was accused of gross mismanagement of his responsibilities as quartermaster, and, according to HW, was also court-martialled by his superior officer 'for some misdemeanour' after the return of the expedition, but escaped. Pitt's refusal to insist, as Bute asked him to do, that Clerk be made a colonel of marines or at least be breveted as colonel in the army, was one of the elements in Pitt's break with Bute and Leicester House in the autumn of 1758. According to HW, Conway while in Ireland as chief secretary had also had difficulties with Clerk in addition to the more serious grievances against him in connexion with the Rochefort expedition. See *Army Lists* 1756, p. 136, 1757, p. 152, and 1758–97 *passim* under the list of general officers at the beginning of each number; GM 1797, lxvii pt i. 447; *Mem. Geo. II* iii. 43–4, 51, 77, 137; DU DEFFAND v. 357; *Letters from George III to Lord Bute 1756–1766,* ed. Sedgwick, 1939, pp. 15–16, 117–18; Romney Sedgwick, 'Letters from William Pitt to Lord Bute: 1755–1758,' in *Essays Presented to Sir Lewis Namier,* ed. Pares and Taylor, 1956, pp. 164–5; Rex Whitworth, *Field Marshal Lord Ligonier,* Oxford, 1958, pp. 219–20, 223, 239–40, 260, 263–7; and the various MS sources cited by Sedgwick and Whitworth.

over the dike that enviously put itself between the 12 battalions our whole army was flying from, and his 12 companies of grenadiers.[5]

I am only sorry poor Lord Fredrick is marching *through France* with the grenadiers instead of Mr Clerke.

That there is another expedition going on, I believe is certain,[6] but your fears about my commanding it are excellent, especially as the effect of my last letter had it not been sent with all the caution it was.

No, notwithstanding the Duke of D[evonshire]'s idea of my *favour with his Majesty* and my brother's sanguine notions;[7] I am now almost convinced that's a point *determined,* and so destined am I not to have any military employment that even the militia escapes me: for on looking over the Act I find I am not qualified.[8] You'll believe my mortification on this head is not quite so great, and since I cannot hope to make the figure our generals have of late made in the field, or that of George Townshend and Lord Shaftsbury[9] in the militia, you can't think how much I console myself in my little domestic amusements, savoured with a little spice of philosophy, which helps me sometimes to look with the utmost indifference at the great nobodies and the great nothings that keep this foolish world in a fluster.

I don't know whether I do much to improve my philosophy. I

5. Dury had commanded the rear-guard of 12 companies of grenadiers and four of the 1st Guards at St-Cast and had been killed (MANN v. 244, n. 8).

6. This was the expedition to the West Indies which sailed 12 November (*ante* 19 Sept. 1758, n. 16; *post* 15, 17 Oct. 1758; MANN v. 251, n. 13; J. S. Corbett, *England in the Seven Years' War,* 1907, i. 374). The newspapers had recently reported: 'It's said that Lord Howe is going out again on a new expedition, with a much greater force than before'; and 'The officers are all ordered to be in readiness, to repair to Portsmouth, on another expedition of great importance which is going forwards' (*Daily Adv.* 22, 23 Sept.). Pitt had at first thought of sending out the fleet again in a feint against Bordeaux, but had abandoned the idea by 19 Sept. (Corbett, op. cit. i. 303–4).

7. For the possible grounds of these at this time, see *post* 15 Oct. 1758, n. 2.

8. Conway had received a commission of deputy lieutenant for the county of Berkshire from the D. of St Albans (*ante* 17 Sept. 1758). According to the militia act passed in 1757, 30 Geo. II c. 25, the qualification for a deputy lieutenant was to have an estate of £400 per annum or to be heir to £800 per annum, 'one moiety of which said estates, required as qualifications . . . shall be situate or arising within such respective county or riding in which he shall be so appointed to serve' (*Statutes at Large,* ed. Owen Ruffhead, 1763–1800, viii. 80–1; see also 31 Geo. II c. 26 in ibid. viii. 246–7).

9. Anthony Ashley Cooper (1711–71), 4th E. of Shaftesbury, had been very active in organizing the Dorset militia.

neither read Aristotle nor Plato, nor Doctor Young[10] nor Doctor
Hill[11] but I read Tull upon husbandry,[12] and grow a prodigious
farmer. I visit my farm almost every day. I have seen my hops
picked and dried and bagged; I have visited my barns and my fields.
The only fault is I don't grow rich; on that head I really am ashamed
of myself. I talked of buying estates, building rooms, etc., and find
I have no money; so much richer at least I am grown as to have
acquired that knowledge, for I actually did not know it before. And
as the philosopher studied to find he knew nothing, so have I
calculated only to discover I have *nothing*. However, nothing for
nothing; my little nothings may perhaps be as good as the great
nothings I mentioned above, if they amuse me. There's a woman at
Somerset House who has spent some years of her life in attempting
to split hairs. It's true she is a little starving, but she amuses herself,
and her life is not unlike that of many great divines and philosophers who pass their time in the same occupation. Adieu.

What becomes of the Conway letters?[13] Are they arrived?

From CONWAY, Sunday 15 October 1758

Printed for the first time from the MS now wsl, formerly Rutnam.

Park Place, 15 Oct. 1758.

Dear Horry,

I HAVE just had a letter from Lord Milton[1] wherein are these
words. *They are very sorry to have carried matters to so great
extremity as they did last winter. You are now wanted and it has*

10. Presumably Edward Young (1683–
1765), D.C.L., 1719, poet; author of *Night
Thoughts,* whose 'philosophy' was enor-
mously popular at this time.

11. Presumably 'Dr' John Hill (?1716–
75), miscellaneous writer and medical
quack. He published 11 pamphlets in
1758 alone (see the list of his writings in
DNB), but Conway is probably thinking of
such things as his *Thoughts Concerning
God and Nature,* 1755.

12. *The Horse-hoing Husbandry,* first
published in 1731 by Jethro Tull (1674–
1741), agricultural reformer. A third edition had appeared in 1751 (BM Cat.).

13. See *ante* 2 Sept. 1758, n. 9.

1. Joseph Damer (*ante* 6 March 1746
OS, n. 1) had been created Bn Milton in
1753.

been much wished that you had offered yourself to command the intended expedition.[2] He speaks from some authority.[3] Nothing could surprise me more than this did, nor seem more inconsistent with all that has passed this twelvemonth last, and with all the repeated applications I have made[4] through all sorts of persons and channels *to serve* so that as I have told him there cannot be a single person from his Majesty down to the fag end of everything pretending to be ministerial who does not know my earnest desire to serve, and now to hear it wished I should ask for a particular command, probably a difficult one, neither the nature nor destination of which I know and to be as it were asked to ask (though I don't know that Lord M[ilton]'s commission was such) is a little surprising.—To

2. Conway had been considered for the command of the expedition to the West Indies after Gen. Elliot, the original commander, had to give it up because of illness. Newcastle wrote to Hardwicke, 5 Oct., 'Conway, Albemarle, Mostyn, Hobson [Hopson] and Cornwallis, will be laid before the King by my Lord Legonier to choose a general from.' Hardwicke replied the following day: 'Conway won't go down with Mr Pitt. Though if my Lord Ligonier should propose him to the King, I shall change this last opinion. For my own part, I wish General Conway were employed; for I think it is going too far to discard the services of a man, who had a very good reputation, for one error, where he had not the chief command and must have been a volunteer in taking risk upon himself' (Mostyn to Newcastle 4 Oct., Newcastle to Hardwicke 5 Oct., Hardwicke to Newcastle 7 Oct., BM Add. MSS 32884, ff. 248, 262, 266, 290–1). This was, however, the first step in Conway's return to employment. On 26 Oct. Conway wrote Devonshire from Kensington, 'I now come to a grand piece of news which I can't omit informing you of and which may possibly surprise your Grace as it did me, but yesterday morning as it seems a sort of overture was made by the Great Man [Pitt] to my brother; he accosted him very politely, said the subject was a little delicate, but that he was desirous it should be known that he neither was

nor would be any impediment to my being employed; that on the contrary he thought nobody fitter for it, that he should be unhappy if he thought I was not to be employed, and that on a late, the very last occasion, my name was one of five for the command, and was carried to the Closet where it seems he noways objecting, he did not pretend he had proposed.—The manner was polite and manly, he could not but think as he did on the subject of R[ochefor]d, that was opinion, but he also thought as he had done of me etc.— Your Grace will form your own judgment of this and for the present be so good as not to talk much of it, as I would not seem to brag of favours of this sort, the extent of which I don't quite know. But what became of me in the Closet where it seems I went? That's still a mystery: Lord Albemarle, who was one of the five, I hear was offered; Mostyn, another, pressed by his M. himself; where do I stick?' (Chatsworth MSS, 416 / 56). This incident is described more fully by HW in *Mem. Geo. II* iii. 154–5.

3. Lord Milton was a brother-in-law of Lord George Sackville.

4. He had asked to serve on the first expedition to St-Malo and with the forces being sent to Germany (*ante* 11 June 1758 and n. 4; 4 July and n. 15). Conway's letter of 17 Oct. to Devonshire expresses the same sentiments (Chatsworth MSS, 416/55).

trust myself in the hands of those, who it's pretty plain have little management or regard for me, in *accepting* such a command might by some of my friends be thought too much and my own diffidence gives me no little check upon it, but to ask is doubling the risk, and after so much asking it really requires a good deal of Christian philosophy to continue the suppliant style. I have not much pride but really I have a little and as I am quite sure there is not one man in the verge of the ministry unacquainted with my earnest desire to be employed I don't think it very safe or very honourable to make this application, though in truth I feel some inclination. Tell me what I shall do? You know how I rely both upon your friendship and judgment and though the present matter is probably or will be decided I should be very glad of your opinion and also if you could find out what the nature of this thing is.—For, all modesty apart, I really think I should rather serve to learn than to teach. You know how they have been hawking about their commands and employments[5] and even now don't condescend to offer me, knowing how I am inclined. I scarce know how to understand this if it be true.

I have read your Lord Whitworth[6] with great pleasure; it's a plain, sensible thing and an useful one, such as it's pity the world should have lost. Your Press shines much in paper and letter; some little inaccuracies however I observed in the printing which you have not taken notice of;[7] if you think of a new edition I would tell you 'em, though they are such as almost tell themselves and probably won't have escaped your second perusal.

You are very ingenious about not putting your letter in a cover, but though the joke might be good, the practice is very bad and I desire you'll not let 'em go naked anymore in this cold season.

I have had a letter from Lord Strafford[8] who does not talk of stirring; very busy at his bridge[9] which goes on as he says prosperously, and I hope grows a little humbler; when I was there a fly could not crawl up it. He was to have made his third visit at my

5. This had been particularly true of the expedition to Cherbourg (*ante* 20, 21 July 1758).

6. *An Account of Russia as it was in the Year 1710*, by Charles Whitworth (1675–1725), cr. (1721) Bn Whitworth, envoy and ambassador to Russia 1704–12. HW had completed the printing at the SH Press 29 Sept. (Hazen, *SH Bibl.* 42; 'Short Notes,' GRAY i. 29 and n. 196). None of Conway's copies of the SH Press publications has reappeared.

7. There was already an errata leaf.

8. Missing.

9. For the new bridge at Wentworth Castle, see *ante* 27 Aug. 1758.

Lord *Duchess's*[10] but being put off by the Duke of Devonshire's call to town,[11] he now says he thinks there would be *more variety* in not going again. Your ideas of the reasonings of her Grace on the farm are so ridiculously the thing I was obliged to hear that one would swear you had overheard them. Twenty reasons why the farmer's kitchen was turned to the north and his passage was four feet and one half wide and his scullery had a window such a way, all to persuade me it was right there should be a strange unnatural projection in the front.—

I am sorry the Conway papers give you so much trouble though I long to see the effect of it and think it vastly *convenient to Lord Castlecomer*.[12]

Adieu! Is it possible one should ever see you? If you meant to answer no, pray don't that one may live in some little expectation.

Yours,

H.S.C.

To Conway, Tuesday 17 October 1758

Printed from the MS now WSL; printed for the first time Wright iii. 404–7. For the history of the MS, see *post* 9 Aug. 1767.

Endorsed: Mr H. W.—17 Oct. 1758.

Arlington Street, Oct. 17, 1758.

I HAVE read your letter, as you may believe, with the strictest attention, and will tell you my thoughts as sincerely as you do and have a right to expect them.

In the first place, I think you far from being under any obligation for this notice. If Mr Pitt is sensible that he has used you

10. To the Ds of Norfolk at Worksop; HW had referred to her by this title *ante* 19 Sept. 1758.

11. Probably in connection with the death of Lady Burlington (his mother-in-law) and the capture of Lord Frederick Cavendish (his brother). He seems to have been expected shortly after 5 Oct. (David Garrick, *Letters*, ed. Little and Kahrl, Cambridge, Mass., 1963, i. 289).

12. This 'Strawberry proverb' concerning Christopher Wandesford (1717–36), 3d Vct Castlecomer, is explained by HW to Mary Berry in 1789; he told her then that 'this saying was adopted forty years ago into the phraseology of Strawberry' (BERRY i. 55–6). HW's earliest use of it himself in a letter seems to be to Montagu 1 July 1770 (MONTAGU ii. 311).

very ill, is it the part of an honest man to require new submissions, new supplications from the person he has injured? If he thinks you proper to command, as one must suppose by this information, is it patriotism that forbids him to employ an able officer, unless that officer sues to be employed! Does patriotism bid him send out a man that has had a stroke of a palsy,[1] preferably to a young man of vigour and capacity, only because the latter has made no application within these two months?—but as easily as I am inclined to believe that your merit makes its way even through the cloud of Mr Pitt's proud prejudices, yet I own in the present case I question it. I can see two reasons why he should wish to entice you to this application; the first is, the clamour against his giving all commands to young or improper officers is extreme: Holmes,[2] appointed Admiral of the Blue but six weeks ago, has writ a warm letter[3] on the chapter of subaltern commanders: the second, and possibly, connected in his mind with the former, may be this; he would like to refuse you, and then say, you had asked when it was too late; and at the same time, would have to say, that he would have employed you, if you had asked sooner. This leads me to the point of time— Hobson is not only appointed, but Haldane, though going governor to Jamaica, is made a brigadier and joined to him[4]—Colonel Barrington[5] set out to Portsmouth last night. All these reasons, I think, make it very improper for you to ask this command *now*. You have done more than enough to satisfy your honour, and will certainly have opportunities again of repeating offers of your service. But though it may be right to ask in general to serve, I ques-

1. The commander of the projected expedition to the West Indies, Maj.-Gen. Peregrine Thomas Hopson (d. 1759), who had accepted it after others refused, had had a stroke (MANN v. 252 and n. 14).

2. Charles Holmes (1711–61), Rear-Adm. of the Blue, 1758; Rear-Adm. of the White, 1759; M.P. Newport (I. of W.) 1758–61 (R. Beatson, *Naval and Military Memoirs of Great Britain*, 1804, ii. 92, 201; Namier and Brooke ii. 631).

3. Not found.

4. George Haldane (*ante* 14 Aug. 1757) was appointed governor of Jamaica 27 Jan. He had been promoted colonel at the same time, but was now made a brigadier-general and attached to the ex-

pedition with instructions to proceed to Jamaica only afterwards. A contemporary commented, 'The new expedition and general staff are all extraordinary and . . . Lt-Col. Haldane (now Brig.-Gen.) not the least. I do not despair if I live a few years to see an excellent new farce acted on the stage by that name' (Allan Whitefoord to Loudoun, Oct. 1758, quoted Namier and Brooke ii. 564).

5. Hon. John Barrington (d. 1764), Col. 1756, in command of the expedition during its later stages (MONTAGU i. 127, n. 18). Gen. Hopson himself set out for Portsmouth on the 20th (MANN v. 252, n. 14).

tion much if it is advisable to petition for particulars, any failure
in which would be charged entirely on you. I should wish to have
you vindicated by the rashness of Mr Pitt and the miscarriages of
others, as I think they hurry to make you be; but while he bestows
only impracticable commands, knowing, that, if there is blood
enough shed, the City of London will be content even with disap-
pointments, I hope you will not be sacrificed either to the mob or
the minister. And this leads me to the article of the expedition itself. Martinico is the general notion;[6] a place, the strongest in the
world, with a garrison of 10,000 men.[7] Others now talk of Guarda-
loupe, almost as strong and of much less consequence.[8] Of both,
everybody that knows, despairs. It is almost impossible for *me* to
find out the real destination. I avoid every one of the three factions[9]
—and though I might possibly learn the secret from the chief of one
of them,[10] if he knows it, yet I own I do not care to try; I don't
think it fair to thrust myself into secrets with a man of whose ambition and views I do not think well, and whose purposes (in those
lights) I have declined and will decline to serve. Besides, I have
reason just now to think that he and his court are meditating some
attempt which may throw us again into confusion;[11] and I had rather not be told what I am sure I shall not approve—besides I cannot ask secrets of this nature without hearing more with which I
would not be trusted, and which if divulged, would be imputed to
me. I know you will excuse me for these reasons, especially as you
know how much I would do to serve you, and would even in this
case, if I was not convinced that it is too late for you to apply; and

6. This was correct; the Cabinet Council had considered it in detail at the beginning of October (ibid. v. 252, n. 13).

7. Beatson estimates the French force
as 'at least ten thousand men' and the
British army as 'no more than four thousand four hundred and forty-four men'
(op. cit. ii. 230–1). There was an opinion
current in London that Martinique was
too strong to be captured except by a
very large expedition (L. H. Gipson, *The
British Empire before the American Revolution*, New York, 1936–70, viii. 93, n. 30).
The attempt to take it at this time failed.

8. After the failure at Martinique, a
landing was made on Guadeloupe, which
succeeded (*post* 17 June 1759).

9. Newcastle's, Pitt's, and Fox's. HW describes his attitude towards politics and
all the major politicians at this time in
Mem. Geo. II iii. 158–63 (written in Oct.
1759), and to Montagu 24 Oct. (MONTAGU
i. 227–9).

10. Henry Fox.

11. HW may be referring to the beginnings of the attempts to establish a
connection between the Bedfords and
Cumberland on the one hand and Newcastle on the other against Pitt, to which
he alludes in the spring of 1759 as having
been arranged partly by Fox (*Mem. Geo.
II* iii. 181; MONTAGU i. 232–3; Lord Ilchester, *Henry Fox*, 1920, ii. 109–10).

being too late they would be glad to say you had asked too late. Besides, if any information could be got from the channel at which I have hinted, the Duke of R[ichmond] could get it better than I;[12] and the Duke of D[evonshire] could give it you without.[13]

I can have no opinion of the expedition itself, which certainly started from the disappointment at St Cas,[14] if it can be called a disappointment where there was no object. I have still more doubts on Lord Milton's authority; Clarke was talked to by the Princess yesterday much more than anybody in the room[15]—Cunningham[16] is made quartermaster-general to this equipment; these things don't look as if *your interest* was increased—as Lord George has sent over his commands for Cunningham, might not his art at the same time have suggested some application to you—tell me, do you think he would ask this command himself? I who am not of so honest and sincere a nature as you are, suspect that this hint is sent to you with some bad view—I don't mean on Lord Milton's part, who I dare say is deceived by his readiness to serve you: and since you do me the honour of letting me at all judge for you, which in one only light I think I am fit to do, I mean, as your spirit naturally makes you over-look everything to get employed, I would wish you to answer to Lord Milton, 'that you should desire of all things to have had this command, but that having been discouraged from asking what you could not flatter yourself would be granted, it would look, you think, a vain offer, to sue for what is now given away, and would not be consistent with your honour to ask when it is too late.'[17] I hint

12. Richmond was Henry Fox's brother-in-law.

13. As lord chamberlain, and as one of the principal political figures, he would be likely to know the inner secrets of the government.

14. This is not correct; the expedition to the West Indies was being planned by the first week of September, two weeks before the disaster at St-Cast was known (J. S. Corbett, *England in the Seven Years' War*, 1907, i. 373–4; *ante* 19 Sept. 1758, n. 16).

15. Clerk was the favourite of Bute and the whole Leicester House clique; according to HW he was being court-martialled at this time, but 'the Princess unwisely countenanced the latter, who had made himself odious to the army,

and who escaped' (*Mem. Geo. II* iii. 137; see also *ante* 28 Sept. 1758, n. 4).

16. James Cuninghame (*ante* 31 Jan. 1756, n. 8), Capt. 45th Foot. Beatson lists Cuninghame as quartermaster-general on Gen. Hopson's staff (op. cit. iii. 210); the *London Chronicle* 19–21 Oct. (iv. 390) announces the appointment, 'Capt. Cuningham, aide-de-camp to General Abercrombie, is appointed quartermaster-general . . . of the forces to be employed in General Hopson's expedition; and . . . to rank as lieutenant-colonel.'

17. According to HW in *Mem. Geo. II* (iii. 155), 'On these overtures Conway visited Pitt, neglecting nothing that might procure him to be sent on action,' which resulted in the commission discussed *post* 10 Dec. Also Conway wrote Devonshire

this, as such an answer would turn their arts on themselves, if, as I believe, they mean to refuse you, and to reproach you with asking too late.

If the time is come for Mr Pitt to want you, you will not long be unemployed; if it is not, then you would get nothing by asking. Consider too how much more graceful a reparation of your honour it will be, to have them forced to recall you, than to force yourself on desperate service, as if you yourself, not they, had injured your reputation.

I can say nothing now on any other chapter, this has so much engrossed all my thoughts. I see no one reason upon earth for your asking *now*. If you ever should *ask* again, you will not want opportunities; and the next time you ask, will have just the same merit that this could have, and by asking in time, would be liable to none of the objections of that sort which I have mentioned. Adieu! *Timeo* Lord George *et dona*.[18]

Yours ever,

H.W.

From CONWAY, Sunday 10 December 1758

Printed from the MS now WSL, formerly Rutnam. Previously printed *Fraser's Magazine*, 1850, xli. 432–3.

Park Place, 10 December 1758.

Dear Horry,

AS I have just received notice of a commission that will, I suppose, immediately hurry me up to town, I write this hasty note to acquaint you with it in hopes of seeing you soon, and talking over this and other matters, as I love to communicate with you, and begin to grumble in my mind that in these last two comings out of town I have not had a word of news or conversation from you.

2 Nov. after Marlborough's death that 'as Lord George will I imagine probably have the command for I don't know who else they can send (Lord Tyrawley they will not), I had a mind you should know that I have no objection to being under his Lordship or any other general his M[ajesty] has, if I was so lucky as to be thought of' (Chatsworth MSS, 416/57).

18. 'Timeo Danaos et dona ferentis' (*Æneid* ii. 49): 'I fear the Danaans, though they bear gifts.'

I am appointed commissary to treat with the French about a cartel at Sluys;[1] the commission is honourable, and, though not just of the kind I wanted, is a *distinction*. Lord Albermarle treated it last war with the Duke de Chaulnes.[2] It brings me on the staff, as I go on the foot of a military officer, and, in that light, as Lord Ligonier, from whom I had my notice,[3] hints to me, leads to other employment.

Adieu. Yours in haste most sincerely,

H.S.C.

My servant returns tomorrow morning early.

1. The cartel for the exchange of prisoners, executed at Sluys 6 Feb. 1759 and signed by Conway and the Marquis du Barail, is in the Public Record Office, W.O. 1/863, ff. 545–76; it is summarized (misdated 9 Feb.) in Sir Reginald A. Savory, *His Britannic Majesty's Army in Germany during the Seven Years' War*, Oxford, 1966, pp. 462–4. The *Daily Adv.* reported 22 Dec. that 'Colonel Conway is gone to the Court of France, with a commission to settle a cartel for the ex-change of prisoners,' but he did not set out until 13 Jan. (*post* 21 Jan. 1759). For the part played by the Conway Cartel in relation to the exchange of prisoners during the American Revolution, see Washington's *Writings*, ed. Fitzpatrick, Washington, 1931–44, vii. 190 and xvi. 325.

2. Michel-Ferdinand d'Albert d'Ailly (1714–69), Duc de Pecquigny, 1731; Duc de Chaulnes, 1744.

3. Missing.